THE LOEB CLASSICAL LIBRARY

FOUNDED BY JAMES LOEB 1911

EDITED BY

JEFFREY HENDERSON

CLEMENT OF ALEXANDRIA

LCL 92

CLEMENT
OF ALEXANDRIA

EXHORTATION TO THE GREEKS
THE RICH MAN'S SALVATION
TO THE NEWLY BAPTIZED

WITH AN ENGLISH TRANSLATION BY

G. W. BUTTERWORTH

HARVARD UNIVERSITY PRESS
CAMBRIDGE, MASSACHUSETTS
LONDON, ENGLAND

First published 1919
Reprinted 1939, 1953, 1960, 1968, 1979,
1982, 1999, 2003

ISBN 0-674-99103-6

*Printed and bound by Edwards Brothers, Ann Arbor, Michigan
on acid-free paper made by Glatfelter, Spring Grove, Pennsylvania*

CONTENTS

THE EXHORTATION TO THE GREEKS

CONTENTS

CONTENTS

CONTENTS

Poetry is entirely concerned with fiction, yet it cannot
help bearing some witness to truth. Examples
from Aratus, Hesiod, Sophocles, Orpheus. Even
comic poets know the truth, for instance, Menander. Homer, too, and many others speak ill
of the gods ; but especially Euripides.

The sacred writings are simple in style, but of great
power. A prelude from the Sibyl. Many quotations to show the majesty of the one true God
and His love for man ; from Jeremiah, Isaiah,
Moses, Hosea, Solomon, David. But Christ the
Word speaks with even greater authority. He
invites us into His kingdom, to be sons of God.
Punishment awaits unbelievers. We must then
obey God " to-day." The meaning of " to-day."
We must choose between God's grace and His
displeasure. Salvation is beyond price ; yet it
can be bought for faith and love. God is our
teacher, through the scriptures. All may become
His children.

Ought men to abandon their traditional ways ? Yes,
just as children abandon childish ways. Custom
is the real obstacle to godliness. It refuses
all guidance. The sight of filthy and degraded
priests ought to bring men to God, who is a
loving Father. Yet some men are like worms

CONTENTS

and swine, loving what is foul. God has a splendid inheritance for His children; heaven and earth are theirs without cost. An innate faith in goodness is possessed by all, and is worthy of trust. Custom is stupid; it deifies mere human beings, and sets up stones for worship. God's Word is His true image; and man's mind is an image of the Word. Custom is rooted in ignorance. But ignorance is only an excuse for him who has never heard God's message. Custom destroys men. It is utterly absurd. Those who follow it are like drugged men; they also become like stones when they worship stones. Men are the really sacred things, not animals or stones. Unbelievers are deaf and blind in heart; or like serpents, wriggling on the earth. Life is the reward for finding God. Divine wisdom helps man to do life's duties well. God's children follow God's laws, which are severe, but health-giving. The Word has brought untold blessings to men.

Man was created innocent and free; but he fell through pleasure. The Word became incarnate, and died on the Cross to save him. So man gains more than he lost. The Word is now man's teacher. He brings light and reveals God. The night of earth gives place to the day of God. The Word is also an amulet that can save from sin. This is ever God's purpose—to save men. It is proclaimed to men by Christ's bloodless army. Those who obey God become His delight as well as His handiwork, and they inherit a kingdom.

CONTENTS

Custom must be shunned as a deadly peril. It is like
Circe's island. Follow Odysseus' example, and
be bound to the Cross. Be warned by the madness of Pentheus. The Word's mysteries are
sober ; performed by pure maidens and righteous
men. These mysteries alone give a vision of
God. Christ is the true hierophant. He offers
rest and immortality. It is sheer madness to remain in ignorance when truth is within reach.
Man can become a friend and son of God, but
only by following Christ. Finally, the reader is
exhorted to make for himself the great choice
between life and destruction.

INTRODUCTION

FEW facts are known to us concerning the life of Clement of Alexandria. His title comes from the city which was the scene of all his important work; but an early tradition spoke of him as being an Athenian by birth, and this may be correct. The date of his birth can be fixed roughly at 150 A.D. We are told nothing of his parentage or early training. It seems clear, however, that he was not a Christian to begin with. He is so well acquainted with the mystery cults that there is a strong probability that he had been initiated into some of them. We have it on his own authority that he wandered through many lands and heard many teachers. Six of these he singles out for mention, though not by name; they were "blessed and memorable men," who spoke "plain and living words." Doubtless all of them were Christians. The last of the six, who was "first in power," and whom he found in Egypt, is almost certainly Pantaenus, then head of the Catechetical School at Alexandria. Here Clement's wanderings ceased. He became a presbyter of the Church, and taught in Alexandria for more than twenty years, succeeding Pantaenus as head of the School. On the outbreak of persecution under Severus in 202 A.D. he left Alexandria, never to return. We get one more glimpse of him; in 211 A.D. he was the bearer of a letter from Alexander, afterwards bishop of Jerusalem, to the Church at Antioch. In this letter he is described as " Clement the blessed presbyter, a virtuous and esteemed man . . . who upheld and extended the Church of the Lord." Alexander was one of Clement's old pupils, and a fellow-pupil with the great Origen. Clement must have died not long after this letter was written; for the same Alexander, writing to Origen a few years later, speaks of him together with Pantaenus as " those blessed men who have trodden the road before us."

The extant works of Clement are as follows :— the *Exhortation to the Greeks*; the *Pedagogue* or *Tutor*; eight books of *Stromateis* or *Miscellanies*; a short treatise entitled, *Who is the rich man that shall be saved?* together with some fragments called *Selections from the Prophets*, being comments upon portions of the Scriptures. There are also a number of short extracts from the writings of a certain Theodotus with comments thereon. Of the lost works the most important is the *Hypotyposes*, or *Outlines*, a commentary upon the Scriptures. Possibly the *Selections from the Prophets* formed part of this work.

INTRODUCTION

The writings of Clement are considerable in extent, and remarkable in character. Hardly a page can be found without some quotation from the Old or New Testaments. Besides this, Clement makes constant references to the Greek poets, dramatists, philosophers and historians. He can illustrate his argument by a passage from Plato, or by lines from Homer or Euripides. He can strengthen his attack by quoting Heracleitus or Democritus. Items of information about curious, absurd or immoral Greek customs he can glean from a crowd of minor authors whose works have now perished. It is said that he mentions by name more than three hundred such authors, of whom otherwise we know nothing. Some of these may have been known to him only through books of extracts; but there can be no question as to his thorough reading of Plato and Homer. For Plato he has a sincere admiration, and Platonic expressions and ideas, to say nothing of direct quotations, are everywhere to be met with in his writings. Generally speaking he betrays no interest in his authorities except in so far as they are useful to establish some point. But this wide reading is evidence of a large and generous mind, that welcomed the true and the good wherever they might be found, confident that every ray of light proceeds from the same sun.

This fearless acceptance of truth from every available source makes Clement not only important for his own times, but also interesting for the world of to-day. He was faced by a problem that ever recurs, the problem of blending old truth with new. In the second century Christianity had become a power. No longer was the Church weak, poor and neglected. Educated men inquired about its faith, and asked admittance within its fold; but they would bring with them an inheritance of thought and culture, unknown to the simple Christians of an earlier age. The question was bound to arise, What relation has this to the Christian faith? Is it to be set aside as superfluous, or injurious? Or is all the good in it to be accepted and welcomed, a proof that God's revelation extends in a measure to all men, to Greeks as well as Jews? Clement himself had come to Christianity with a mind steeped in Greek learning, and he answered this question with clearness and confidence. Greek learning was not to be rejected. Philosophy at its best had stood to the Greeks in the same relation as prophecy to the Jews; it had been, he held, a preparation for Christ. It abounded in glimmerings and foreshadowings of the divine teaching, and could not have come from the devil, as timid Christians maintained. It was therefore a proper object of study, and the exercise of human reason which it pre-supposed could do no harm to the Christian faith. Thus Clement, taking his stand upon the oneness of truth, laid down the lines upon which Christian theology could safely proceed.

But while Clement asserted that a real revelation had been made to the higher minds of Greece, he knew well how slight was its effect on the popular morality and religion. Hence the fierce attack which is the subject of his first work, the *Exhortation to the Greeks*. With bitter scorn he describes the mysteries, seizing upon any disgraceful legend or piece of childish ceremonial which seems to stamp them as worthless and debasing. As for the gods, with their human needs and passions, they are subjects for ridicule, to which Clement adds a burning indignation when he thinks of the low standard of morality attributed to them in the current mythology. The worship of images, too, is stupid; the true God cannot be represented in material form. Yet Clement can prove by quotations that philosophers, Plato especially, and even poets, had clearly taught the unity, supremacy, and goodness of God. But the greatest witnesses of all were the Hebrew prophets, through whom God gave His promises to men. The Greeks are prevented from accepting the truth by Custom, that dead weight of inherited tradition, which must be abandoned. Christianity offers man the true mysteries, culminating in the vision of God.

Thus the Greek religion which Clement attacks is a thing far removed from the lofty conceptions of Plato or Aeschylus. It is the religion of the multitude in the Greek-speaking world. Five hundred years before this, Plato censured the immoralities of the gods in terms hardly less severe than those of Clement, but Plato's words were ineffective to change what he himself was heartily ashamed of. The Christian Church, however, under the leadership of men like Clement, was slowly gathering the common people into a society which upheld a higher view of the divine character, and demanded a correspondingly higher standard of human conduct. No doubt the evil of the popular religion is exaggerated; certainly Clement omits all reference to its good. Yet there must have been enough of the evil before men's eyes to make Christian life and teaching stand out in noble contrast. In the house, in the street, in the market-place, at feasts, assemblies and religious processions, Christian converts were exposed to sights and sounds from which they had learnt instinctively to shrink. It is such things, and all that was bound up with them, that Clement denounces. To-day we may admire Greek art without paying much attention to the mythology which was then inseparable from it; we may probe mystery religions in search of those elements of good which made them for centuries the chief spiritual food of the common people. Such discrimination is not to be looked for in the second century. Clement claimed a place for philosophy in the Church; later on a home was found for art too, and even the fundamental ideas of the mysteries were not refused

xviii

admission. Time was necessary to show what could be assimilated and what could not. In Clement's day Christianity was still struggling for existence, and popular religion was its deadliest enemy. This fact should serve as an excuse for the over-elaboration of his attack and for one or two passages which are unpleasant to a modern reader.

In preparing the present translation I have had the great advantage of being able to work from the text of Stählin, published in 1905. All students of Clement must be grateful, not only for this clear and accurate text, but also for the references collected by Stählin, which throw light on many a difficult passage. The text printed here is substantially that of Stählin's edition, though I have occasionally preferred the conjectures of other scholars or retained the manuscript reading where Stählin departs from it. All deviations of any importance from the MSS. are noted at the foot of each page. So far as concerns the *Exhortation*, the chief extant MS. is the Parisian, referred to by Stählin as P. A description of this MS. is to be found in the introduction to Stählin's text (vol. i. pp. xvi–xxiii). Depending on P is the Codex Mutinensis, known as M.

This translation was first drafted several years ago as part of a complete edition of the *Exhortation to the Greeks*; and I am still working towards the accomplishment of this larger plan. A grateful acknowledgment is due to the committee of the Bodington Memorial Fund, in connexion with the University of Leeds, for grants which have materially assisted the progress of my work. I desire also to record my deep indebtedness to the late Dr. Joseph B. Mayor, who in the closing years of his life gave me most generous and patient help both in the details of the translation and in my general study of Clement. Most of all, I thank Professor W. Rhys Roberts, of the University of Leeds, at whose suggestion I first began to read Clement, and to whose kindly encouragement and ungrudging help is largely due my perseverance hitherto in so difficult an undertaking.

BIBLIOGRAPHY

The chief editors of Clement of Alexandria are as follows :—

    JOHN POTTER, Archbishop of Canterbury. His edition in two vols. was issued at Oxford in 1715, and is reprinted in Migne, *P.G.* vols. viii. and ix.

    WILLIAM DINDORF. 4 vols. Issued at Oxford in 1869.

    OTTO STÄHLIN. 3 vols. Issued at Leipzig 1905–1909. This supersedes all previous editions.

Out of the very large literature that has grown up around Clement's works the following books in English may be mentioned :—

    BISHOP KAYE. *Some Account of the Writings and Opinions of Clement of Alexandria.* London, 1835.

    BIGG. *The Christian Platonists of Alexandria.* Oxford, 1886.

    HORT. *Six Lectures on the Ante-Nicene Fathers.* London, 1895.

    HITCHCOCK. *Clement of Alexandria* (Fathers for English Readers series, S.P.C.K. 1899).

    TOLLINTON. *Clement of Alexandria: a Study in Christian Liberalism.* 2 vols. 1914.

    PATRICK. *Clement of Alexandria* (The Croall Lecture for 1899–1900). 1914.

BIBLIOGRAPHY

The whole of Clement's extant works (with the exception of the *Extracts from Theodotus* and the newly-discovered *Exhortation to Endurance*) are translated into English in *The Ante-Nicene Christian Library* by the Rev. W. Wilson. The vols. marked Clement of Alexandria, I. and II., contain the *Exhortation to the Greeks*, the *Pedagogue or Tutor* and the *Stromateis*. The *Rich Man's Salvation* is to be found at the end of the volume marked Lactantius II., and the *Selections from the Prophets* and various Fragments are at the end of a small volume entitled *Early Liturgies: Fragments.*

The Seventh Book of the *Stromateis* is translated by the Rev. J. B. Mayor in Hort and Mayor's edition of that book. Cambridge, 1902.

The *Rich Man's Salvation* has been translated by P. M. Barnard (*Who is the Rich Man that is being saved?* Early Church Classics series. S.P.C.K. 1901).

The Fragment entitled *Exhortation to Endurance, or, To the Newly Baptized* has been translated by J. Patrick in his book *Clement of Alexandria*, pp. 183–185.

CLEMENT
OF ALEXANDRIA

ΚΛΗΜΕΝΤΟΣ ΑΛΕΞΑΝΔΡΕΩΣ

ΠΡΟΤΡΕΠΤΙΚΟΣ ΠΡΟΣ ΕΛΛΗΝΑΣ

I

Ἀμφίων ὁ Θηβαῖος καὶ Ἀρίων ὁ Μηθυμναῖος
ἄμφω μὲν ἤστην ᾠδικώ, μῦθος δὲ ἄμφω· καὶ τὸ
ᾆσμα εἰσέτι τοῦτο Ἑλλήνων ᾄδεται | χορῷ, τέχνῃ

2 P. τῇ μουσικῇ ὁ μὲν ἰχθὺν δελεάσας, ὁ δὲ Θήβας
τειχίσας. Θράκιος δὲ ἄλλος σοφιστὴς (ἄλλος οὗτος
μῦθος Ἑλληνικός) ἐτιθάσευε τὰ θηρία γυμνῇ τῇ
ᾠδῇ καὶ δὴ τὰ δένδρα, τὰς φηγούς, μετεφύτευε τῇ
μουσικῇ. ἔχοιμ' ἄν σοι καὶ ἄλλον τούτοις ἀδελφὸν
διηγήσασθαι μῦθον καὶ ᾠδόν, Εὔνομον τὸν Λοκρὸν
καὶ τέττιγα τὸν Πυθικόν. πανήγυρις Ἑλληνικὴ
ἐπὶ νεκρῷ δράκοντι συνεκροτεῖτο Πυθοῖ, ἐπιτάφιον
ἑρπετοῦ ᾄδοντος Εὐνόμου· ὕμνος ἢ θρῆνος ὄφεως

---

[a] Arion was returning from Sicily to Greece laden with
prizes and presents. The sailors thought to kill him for his
wealth, but after playing his lyre he jumped into the sea.
Dolphins, charmed by the music, gathered round him, and
one of them took the bard on its back to Corinth.

[b] The stones were said to have moved into their proper
places at the sound of Amphion's music.

CLEMENT OF ALEXANDRIA

THE EXHORTATION TO THE GREEKS

I.

AMPHION of Thebes and Arion of Methymna were both minstrels. Both are celebrated in legend, and to this day the story is sung by a chorus of Greeks how their musical skill enabled the one to lure a fish [a] and the other to build the walls of Thebes.[b] There was also a Thracian wizard,[c]—so runs another Greek legend,—who used to tame wild beasts simply by his song, yes, and to transplant trees, oaks, by music. I can also tell you of another legend and another minstrel akin to these, namely, Eunomus the Locrian and the Pythian grasshopper.[d] A solemn assembly of Greeks, held in honour of a dead serpent, was gathering at Pytho,[e] and Eunomus sang a funeral ode for the reptile. Whether his song was a hymn

Minstrels of legend and their wonderful deeds:
Arion
Amphion
Orpheus

Eunomus and the Pythian grasshopper

[c] *i.e.*, Orpheus. Cp. Euripides, *Rhesus* 924, δεινῷ σοφιστῇ Θρῃκί.

[d] Strictly cicala, here and elsewhere.

[e] *i.e.*, Delphi. According to the Greek legend the serpent was the ancient guardian of the Delphic shrine, and was slain by Apollo.

3

CAP.
I

ἦν ἡ ᾠδή, οὐκ ἔχω λέγειν· ἀγὼν δὲ ἦν καὶ ἐκιθά-
ριζεν ὥρᾳ καύματος Εὔνομος, ὁπηνίκα οἱ τέττιγες
ὑπὸ τοῖς πετάλοις ᾖδον ἀνὰ τὰ ὄρη θερόμενοι ἡλίῳ.
ᾖδον δὲ ἄρα οὐ τῷ δράκοντι τῷ νεκρῷ, τῷ Πυ-
θικῷ, ἀλλὰ τῷ θεῷ τῷ πανσόφῳ αὐτόνομον ᾠδήν,
τῶν Εὐνόμου βελτίονα νόμων· ῥήγνυται χορδὴ τῷ
Λοκρῷ· ἐφίπταται ὁ τέττιξ τῷ ζυγῷ· ἐτερέτιζεν ὡς
ἐπὶ κλάδῳ τῷ ὀργάνῳ· καὶ τοῦ τέττιγος τῷ ἄσματι
ἁρμοσάμενος ὁ ᾠδὸς τὴν λείπουσαν ἀνεπλήρωσε
χορδήν. οὔκουν ᾠδῇ τῇ Εὐνόμου ἄγεται ὁ τέττιξ,
ὡς ὁ μῦθος βούλεται, χαλκοῦν ἀναστήσας Πυθοῖ
τὸν Εὔνομον αὐτῇ τῇ κιθάρᾳ καὶ τὸν συναγωνιστὴν
τοῦ Λοκροῦ· ὁ δὲ ἑκὼν ἐφίπταται καὶ ᾄδει ἑκών,
Ἕλλησι δὲ ἐδόκει[1] ὑποκριτὴς γεγονέναι μουσικῆς.

Πῇ δὴ οὖν μύθοις κενοῖς πεπιστεύκατε, θέλγεσθαι
μουσικῇ τὰ ζῷα ὑπολαμβάνοντες; ἀληθείας δὲ
ὑμῖν τὸ πρόσωπον τὸ φαιδρὸν μόνον, ὡς ἔοικεν,
ἐπίπλαστον εἶναι δοκεῖ καὶ τοῖς ἀπιστίας ὑποπέ-
πτωκεν ὀφθαλμοῖς. Κιθαιρὼν δὲ ἄρα καὶ Ἑλικὼν
καὶ τὰ Ὀδρυσῶν ὄρη καὶ Θρακῶν, τελεστήρια τῆς
πλάνης, διὰ τὰ μυστήρια[2] τεθείασται καὶ καθύμνηται.
ἐγὼ μέν, εἰ καὶ μῦθός εἰσι, δυσανασχετῶ τοσαύταις
ἐκτραγῳδουμέναις συμφοραῖς· ὑμῖν δὲ καὶ τῶν
3 P. κακῶν αἱ ἀναγραφαὶ | γεγόνασι δράματα καὶ τῶν
δραμάτων οἱ ὑποκριταὶ θυμηδίας θεάματα. ἀλλὰ

---

[1] δοκεῖ Wilamowitz.
[2] τελεστήρια τῆς πλάνης, διὰ τὰ μυστήρια Schwartz. τελεστήρια, τῆς πλάνης τὰ μυστήρια MSS.

---

[a] Mt. Cithaeron was sacred to Zeus; Mt. Helicon to the
Muses; and the Thracian mountains were the home of
Dionysus-worship. For the meaning of these mountain-
cults in Greek religion see A. B. Cook, *Zeus*, i. pp. 100–163.

in praise of the snake, or a lamentation over it, CHAP.
I cannot say; but there was a competition, and I
Eunomus was playing the lyre in the heat of the
day, at the time when the grasshoppers, warmed by
the sun, were singing under the leaves along the
hills. They were singing, you see, not to the dead
serpent of Pytho, but to the all-wise God, a spontane-
ous natural song, better than the measured strains of
Eunomus. A string breaks in the Locrian's hands;
the grasshopper settles upon the neck of the lyre
and begins to twitter there as if upon a branch:
whereupon the minstrel, by adapting his music to the
grasshopper's lay, supplied the place of the missing
string. So it was not Eunomus that drew the grasshopper by his song, as the legend would have it,
when it set up the bronze figure at Pytho, showing
Eunomus with his lyre, and his ally in the contest.
No, the grasshopper flew of its own accord, and sang
of its own accord, although the Greeks thought it to
have been responsive to music.

How in the world is it that you have given *Why believe*
credence to worthless legends, imagining brute *such legends*
beasts to be enchanted by music, while the bright *and yet*
face of truth seems alone to strike you as deceptive, *the truth?*
and is regarded with unbelieving eyes? Cithaeron, *Mountains*
and Helicon, and the mountains of Odrysians and *are held*
Thracians,[a] temples of initiation into error, are held *sacred*
sacred on account of the attendant mysteries, and
are celebrated in hymns. For my own part, mere *Dramas are*
legend though they are, I cannot bear the thought *made from*
of all the calamities that are worked up into tragedy; *stories of*
yet in your hands the records of these evils have *and wicked-*
become dramas, and the actors of the dramas are *ness*
a sight that gladdens your heart. But as for the

5

CAP.
I

γὰρ τὰ μὲν δράματα καὶ τοὺς ληναΐζοντας ποιητάς,
τέλεον ἤδη παροινοῦντας, κιττῷ που ἀναδήσαντες,
ἀφραίνοντας ἐκτόπως τελετῇ βακχικῇ, αὐτοῖς
σατύροις καὶ θιάσῳ μαινόλῃ, σὺν καὶ τῷ ἄλλῳ
δαιμόνων χορῷ, ⟨ἐν⟩[1] Ἑλικῶνι καὶ Κιθαιρῶνι κατα-
κλείσωμεν γεγηρακόσιν, κατάγωμεν δὲ ἄνωθεν ἐξ
οὐρανῶν ἀλήθειαν ἅμα φανοτάτῃ φρονήσει εἰς ὄρος
ἅγιον θεοῦ καὶ χορὸν τὸν ἅγιον τὸν προφητικόν.
ἡ δὲ ὡς ὅτι μάλιστα τηλαυγὲς ἀποστίλβουσα φῶς
καταυγαζέτω πάντῃ τοὺς ἐν σκότει κυλινδουμένους
καὶ τῆς πλάνης τοὺς ἀνθρώπους ἀπαλλαττέτω, τὴν
ὑπερτάτην ὀρέγουσα δεξιάν, τὴν σύνεσιν, εἰς σωτηρίαν. οἱ δὲ ἀνανεύσαντες καὶ ἀνακύψαντες Ἑλι-
κῶνα μὲν καὶ Κιθαιρῶνα καταλειπόντων, οἰκούντων
δὲ Σιών· '' ἐκ γὰρ Σιὼν ἐξελεύσεται νόμος, καὶ
λόγος κυρίου ἐξ Ἱερουσαλήμ,'' λόγος οὐράνιος, ὁ
γνήσιος ἀγωνιστὴς ἐπὶ τῷ παντὸς κόσμου θεάτρῳ
στεφανούμενος. ᾄδει δέ γε ὁ Εὔνομος ὁ ἐμὸς οὐ
τὸν Τερπάνδρου νόμον οὐδὲ τὸν Καπίωνος, οὐδὲ μὴν
Φρύγιον ἢ Λύδιον ἢ Δώριον, ἀλλὰ τῆς καινῆς
ἁρμονίας τὸν ἀίδιον νόμον, τὸν φερώνυμον τοῦ θεοῦ,
τὸ ᾆσμα τὸ καινόν, τὸ Λευιτικόν, '' νηπενθές τ' ἄ-
χολόν τε, κακῶν ἐπίληθες ἁπάντων.'' γλυκύ τι καὶ
ἀληθινὸν φάρμακον πειθοῦς[2] ἐγκέκραται τῷ ᾄσματι.

---

[1] ⟨ἐν⟩ inserted by Mayor. [2] πένθους Reinkens and Stählin.

[a] Clement is not referring to the works of the great
dramatists, but to the contests at the Lenaea, a festival
held annually at Athens in honour of Dionysus. In
Clement's day the competitors would be for the most part
poets of a very minor order. [b] Isaiah ii. 3.

[c] The modes (ἁρμονίαι, see p. 12, n. a) were the scales in
which Greek music was written. Phrygian, Lydian and
Dorian were the chief modes, others being, it would seem,
formed from them by modification or combination. The

dramas and the Lenaean poets, who are altogether CHAP. like drunken men,[a] let us wreathe them, if you like, I with ivy, while they are performing the mad revels Confine of the Bacchic rite, and shut them up, satyrs and dramas and frenzied rout and all,—yes, and the rest of the com- their sacred pany of daemons too,—in Helicon and Cithaeron mountains now grown old; and let us bring down truth, with wisdom in all her brightness, from heaven above, to But bring the holy mountain of God and the holy company truth to God's holy of the prophets. Let truth, sending forth her rays mountain, of light into the farthest distance, shine every- Sion where upon those who are wallowing in darkness, and deliver men from their error, stretching out her supreme right hand, even understanding, to point them to salvation. And when they have raised their heads and looked up let them forsake Helicon and Cithaeron to dwell in Sion; "for out of Sion shall Whence go forth the law, and the Word of the Lord from comes the Word, the Jerusalem,"[b] that is, the heavenly Word, the true true champion, who is being crowned upon the stage of champion the whole world. Aye, and this Eunomus of mine sings not the strain of Terpander or of Capio, nor yet in Phrygian or Lydian or Dorian mode[c]; but the Who sings new music, with its eternal strain that bears the song name of God. This is the new song, the song of Moses,

Soother of grief and wrath, that bids all ills be forgotten.[d]

There is a sweet and genuine medicine of persuasion[e] blended with this song.

Dorian mode was of a solemn character, answering to our minor scale; the Phrygian and Lydian were brighter.
   [d] Homer, *Odyssey* iv. 221.
   [e] A slight change in the Greek, suggested by Reinkens, would give the meaning "remedy against grief."

7

CLEMENT OF ALEXANDRIA

4 P.

Ἐμοὶ μὲν οὖν δοκοῦσιν ὁ Θρᾴκιος ἐκεῖνος Ὀρφεὺς[1]
καὶ ὁ Θηβαῖος καὶ ὁ Μηθυμναῖος, ἄνδρες τινὲς οὐκ
ἄνδρες, ἀπα|τηλοὶ γεγονέναι, προσχήματί ⟨τε⟩[2]
μουσικῆς λυμηνάμενοι τὸν βίον, ἐντέχνῳ τινὶ γοητείᾳ δαιμονῶντες εἰς διαφθοράς, ὕβρεις ὀργιάζοντες,
πένθη ἐκθειάζοντες, τοὺς ἀνθρώπους ἐπὶ τὰ εἴδωλα
χειραγωγῆσαι πρῶτοι, ναὶ μὴν λίθοις καὶ ξύλοις,
τουτέστιν ἀγάλμασι καὶ σκιαγραφίαις, ἀνοικοδο-
μῆσαι τὴν σκαιότητα τοῦ ἔθους, τὴν καλὴν ὄντως
ἐκείνην ἐλευθερίαν τῶν ὑπ᾽ οὐρανὸν πεπολιτευμένων
ᾠδαῖς καὶ ἐπῳδαῖς ἐσχάτῃ δουλείᾳ καταζεύξαντες.

Ἀλλ᾽ οὐ τοιόσδε ὁ ᾠδὸς ὁ ἐμὸς οὐδ᾽ εἰς μακρὰν
καταλύσων ἀφῖκται τὴν δουλείαν τὴν πικρὰν τῶν
τυραννούντων δαιμόνων, ὡς δὲ τὸν πρᾶον καὶ
φιλάνθρωπον τῆς θεοσεβείας μετάγων ἡμᾶς ζυγὸν
αὖθις εἰς οὐρανοὺς ἀνακαλεῖται τοὺς εἰς γῆν ἐρριμ-
μένους. μόνος γοῦν τῶν πώποτε τὰ ἀργαλεώτατα
θηρία, τοὺς ἀνθρώπους, ἐτιθάσευεν, πτηνὰ μὲν τοὺς
κούφους αὐτῶν, ἑρπετὰ δὲ τοὺς ἀπατεῶνας, καὶ
λέοντας μὲν τοὺς θυμικούς, σύας δὲ τοὺς ἡδονικούς,
λύκους δὲ τοὺς ἁρπακτικούς. λίθοι δὲ καὶ ξύλα οἱ
ἄφρονες· πρὸς δὲ καὶ λίθων ἀναισθητότερος ἄνθρωπος ἀγνοίᾳ βεβαπτισμένος. μάρτυς ἡμῖν προφητικὴ
παρίτω φωνή, συνῳδὸς ἀληθείας, τοὺς ἐν ἀγνοίᾳ
καὶ ἀνοίᾳ κατατετριμμένους οἰκτείρουσα· " δυνατὸς
γὰρ ὁ θεὸς ἐκ τῶν λίθων τούτων ἐγεῖραι τέκνα τῷ
Ἀβραάμ." ὃς κατελεήσας τὴν ἀμαθίαν τὴν πολλὴν

---

[1] [Ὀρφεὺς] Wilamowitz.
[2] ⟨τε⟩ inserted by Wilamowitz.

---

[a] For examples see pp. 35–43.
[b] St. Matthew iii. 9 ; St. Luke iii. 8.

In my opinion, therefore, our Thracian, Orpheus, and the Theban and the Methymnian too, are not worthy of the name of man, since they were deceivers. Under cover of music they have outraged human life, being influenced by daemons, through some artful sorcery, to compass man's ruin. By commemorating deeds of violence in their religious rites, and by bringing stories of sorrow into worship,[a] they were the first to lead men by the hand to idolatry; yes, and with stocks and stones, that is to say, statues and pictures, to build up the stupidity of custom. By their chants and enchantments they have held captive in the lowest slavery that truly noble freedom which belongs to those who are citizens under heaven.

But far different is my minstrel, for He has come to bring to a speedy end the bitter slavery of the daemons that lord it over us; and by leading us back to the mild and kindly yoke of piety He calls once again to heaven those who have been cast down to earth. He at least is the only one who ever tamed the most intractable of all wild beasts— man: for he tamed birds, that is, flighty men; reptiles, that is, crafty men; lions, that is, passionate men; swine, that is, pleasure-loving men; wolves, that is, rapacious men. Men without understanding are stocks and stones; indeed a man steeped in ignorance is even more senseless than stones. As our witness let the prophetic voice, which shares in the song of truth, come forward, speaking words of pity for those who waste away their lives in ignorance and folly,—"for God is able of these stones to raise up children unto Abraham." [b]   And God, in compassion for the great dulness and the hardness of those

CHAP.
I

Orpheus,
Amphion
and Arion
were
deceivers

And
originators
of idolatry

The
heavenly
minstrel

He tames
savage men

He changes
stones, *i.e.*
men without
understanding, into
virtuous
men

9

CAP.
I

καὶ τὴν σκληροκαρδίαν τῶν εἰς τὴν ἀλήθειαν λελι-
θωμένων ἤγειρεν θεοσεβείας σπέρμα ἀρετῆς αἰσθό-
μενον ἐκ λίθων ἐκείνων, τῶν λίθοις πεπιστευκότων
ἐθνῶν. αὖθις οὖν ἰοβόλους τινὰς καὶ παλιμβόλους
ὑποκριτὰς ἐφοδεύοντας δικαιοσύνῃ " γεννήματα
ἐχιδνῶν " κέκληκέ που· ἀλλὰ καὶ τούτων εἴ τις
τῶν ὄφεων μετανοῆσαι ἑκών, ἑπόμενος δὴ τῷ λόγῳ
" ἄνθρωπος " γίνεται " θεοῦ." " λύκους " δὲ ἄλλους
ἀλληγορεῖ προβάτων κωδίοις ἠμφιεσμένους, τοὺς
ἐν ἀνθρώπων μορφαῖς ἁρπακτικοὺς αἰνιττόμενος.
καὶ πάντα ἄρα ταῦτα τὰ ἀγριώτατα θηρία καὶ τοὺς
τοιούτους λίθους ἡ οὐράνιος ᾠδὴ αὐτὴ μετεμόρ-
φωσεν εἰς ἀνθρώπους ἡμέρους. " ἦμεν γάρ, ἦμέν
ποτε καὶ ἡμεῖς ἀνόητοι, ἀπειθεῖς, πλανώμενοι,
δουλεύοντες ἡδοναῖς καὶ ἐπιθυμίαις ποικίλαις, ἐν
κακίᾳ καὶ φθόνῳ διάγοντες, στυγητοί, μισοῦντες
5 P. ἀλλήλους," ᾗ φησιν ἡ ἀποστολικὴ γραφή·|" ὅτε
δὲ ἡ χρηστότης καὶ ἡ φιλανθρωπία ἐπεφάνη τοῦ
σωτῆρος ἡμῶν θεοῦ, οὐκ ἐξ ἔργων τῶν ἐν δικαιοσύνῃ,
ἃ ἐποιήσαμεν ἡμεῖς, ἀλλὰ κατὰ τὸ αὐτοῦ ἔλεος
ἔσωσεν ἡμᾶς."

Ὅρα τὸ ᾆσμα τὸ καινὸν ὅσον ἴσχυσεν· ἀνθρώπους
ἐκ λίθων καὶ ἀνθρώπους ἐκ θηρίων πεποίηκεν. οἱ
δὲ τῇ ἄλλως νεκροί, οἱ τῆς ὄντως οὔσης ἀμέτοχοι
ζωῆς, ἀκροαταὶ μόνον γενόμενοι τοῦ ᾄσματος ἀν-
εβίωσαν. τοῦτό τοι καὶ τὸ πᾶν ἐκόσμησεν ἐμμελῶς καὶ τῶν στοιχείων τὴν διαφωνίαν εἰς τάξιν
ἐνέτεινε συμφωνίας, ἵνα δὴ ὅλος ὁ κόσμος αὐτῷ
ἁρμονία γένηται· καὶ θάλατταν μὲν ἀνῆκεν λε-
λυμένην, γῆς δὲ ἐπιβαίνειν κεκώλυκεν αὐτήν, γῆν
δ' ἔμπαλιν ἐστερέωσεν φερομένην καὶ ὅρον αὐτὴν[1]

---

[1] αὐτήν Stählin.   αὐτῇ MSS.

10

whose hearts are petrified against the truth, did raise up out of those stones, that is, the Gentiles who trust in stones, a seed of piety sensitive to virtue. Again, in one place the words "offspring of vipers" [a] are applied to certain venomous and deceitful hypocrites, who lie in wait against righteousness; yet if any even of these snakes chooses to repent, let him but follow the Word and he becomes a "man of God." [b] Others are figuratively called "wolves" [c] clothed in sheepskins, by which is meant rapacious creatures in the forms of men. And all these most savage beasts, and all such stones, the heavenly song of itself transformed into men of gentleness. "For we, yea we also were aforetime foolish, disobedient, deceived, serving divers lusts and pleasures, living in malice and envy, hateful, hating one another," as the apostolic writing says; "but when the kindness of God our Saviour, and His love toward man, appeared, not by works done in righteousness, which we did ourselves, but according to His mercy He saved us." [d]

See how mighty is the new song! It has made men out of stones and men out of wild beasts. They who were otherwise dead, who had no share in the real and true life, revived when they but heard the song. Furthermore, it is this which composed the entire creation into melodious order, and tuned into concert the discord of the elements, that the whole universe might be in harmony with it. The ocean it left flowing, yet has prevented it from encroaching upon the land; whereas the land, which was being carried away, it made firm, and fixed as a

The New Song also gave order and harmony to the universe

---

[a] St. Matthew iii. 7 ; St. Luke iii. 7.   [b] 1 Tim. vi. 11.
[c] St. Matthew vii. 15.   [d] Titus iii. 3–5.

CAP.
I

ἔπηξεν θαλάττης· ναὶ μὴν καὶ πυρὸς ὁρμὴν ἐμάλαξεν ἀέρι, οἱονεὶ Δώριον ἁρμονίαν κεράσας Λυδίῳ· καὶ τὴν ἀέρος ἀπηνῆ ψυχρότητα τῇ παραπλοκῇ τοῦ πυρὸς ἐτιθάσευεν, τοὺς νεάτους τῶν ὅλων φθόγγους τούτους κιρνὰς ἐμμελῶς. καὶ δὴ τὸ ᾆσμα τὸ ἀκήρατον, ἔρεισμα τῶν ὅλων καὶ ἁρμονία τῶν πάντων, ἀπὸ τῶν μέσων ἐπὶ τὰ πέρατα καὶ ἀπὸ τῶν ἄκρων ἐπὶ τὰ μέσα διαταθέν, ἡρμόσατο τόδε τὸ πᾶν, οὐ κατὰ τὴν Θρᾴκιον μουσικήν, τὴν παραπλήσιον Ἰουβάλ, κατὰ δὲ τὴν πάτριον τοῦ θεοῦ βούλησιν, ἣν ἐζήλωσε Δαυίδ. ὁ δὲ ἐκ Δαυὶδ καὶ πρὸ αὐτοῦ, ὁ τοῦ θεοῦ λόγος, λύραν μὲν καὶ κιθάραν, τὰ ἄψυχα ὄργανα, ὑπεριδών, κόσμον δὲ τόνδε καὶ δὴ καὶ τὸν σμικρὸν κόσμον, τὸν ἄνθρωπον, ψυχήν τε καὶ σῶμα αὐτοῦ, ἁγίῳ πνεύματι ἁρμοσάμενος, ψάλλει τῷ θεῷ διὰ τοῦ πολυφώνου ὀργάνου καὶ προσᾴδει τῷ ὀργάνῳ τῷ ἀνθρώπῳ. " σὺ γὰρ εἶ κιθάρα καὶ αὐλὸς καὶ ναὸς ἐμοί "· κιθάρα διὰ τὴν ἁρμονίαν, αὐλὸς διὰ τὸ πνεῦμα, ναὸς διὰ τὸν λόγον, ἵν' ἡ μὲν κρέκῃ, τὸ δὲ ἐμπνέῃ, ὁ δὲ χωρήσῃ τὸν κύριον. ναὶ μὴν ὁ Δαυὶδ ὁ βασιλεύς, ὁ κιθαριστής, οὗ μικρῷ

6 P. πρόσθεν ἐμνή|σθημεν, προύτρεπεν ὡς τὴν ἀλήθειαν, ἀπέτρεπε δὲ εἰδώλων, πολλοῦ γε ἔδει ὑμνεῖν αὐτὸν τοὺς δαίμονας ἀληθεῖ πρὸς αὐτοῦ διωκομένους μουσικῇ, ἧ τοῦ Σαοὺλ ἐνεργουμένου [1] ἐκεῖνος [2] ᾄδων μόνον αὐτὸν ἰάσατο. καλὸν ὁ κύριος ὄργανον ἔμ-

---

[1] τοῦ Σαοὺλ ἐνεργουμένου Mayor. τῷ Σαοὺλ ἐνεργουμένῳ M. τῳ ἔναυλος ὁ ἐνεργούμενος P.
[2] ἐκείνοις Stählin.

---

[a] See p. 6, n. c.   [b] See Genesis iv. 21.
[c] The source of this quotation is unknown. It may be a fragment of an early Christian hymn, the metaphors being

12

boundary to the sea. Aye, and it softened the rage of fire by air, as one might blend the Dorian mode with the Lydian [a]; and the biting coldness of air it tempered by the intermixture of fire, thus melodiously mingling these extreme notes of the universe. What is more, this pure song, the stay of the universe and the harmony of all things, stretching from the centre to the circumference and from the extremities to the centre, reduced this whole to harmony, not in accordance with Thracian music, which resembles that of Jubal,[b] but in accordance with the fatherly purpose of God, which David earnestly sought. He who sprang from David and yet was before him, the Word of God, scorned those lifeless instruments of lyre and harp. By the power of the Holy Spirit He arranged in harmonious order this great world, yes, and the little world of man too, body and soul together ; and on this many-voiced instrument of the universe He makes music to God, and sings to the human instrument. " For thou art my harp and my pipe and my temple " [c]—my harp by reason of the music, my pipe by reason of the breath of the Spirit, my temple by reason of the Word—God's purpose being that the music should resound, the Spirit inspire, and the temple receive its Lord. Moreover, King David the harpist, whom we mentioned just above, urged us toward the truth and away from idols. So far was he from singing the praises of daemons that they were put to flight by him with the true music ; and when Saul was possessed, David healed him merely by playing the harp.[d] The Lord fashioned man a beautiful,

CHAP.
1

The New Song is the Word of God

Who makes music to God through the universe and through man

suggested by such passages as Psalm lvii. 8 ; 1 Corinthians vi. 19.

[d] See 1 Samuel xvi. 23.

13

CLEMENT OF ALEXANDRIA

CAP.
I

πνουν τὸν ἄνθρωπον ἐξειργάσατο κατ' εἰκόνα τὴν
ἑαυτοῦ· ἀμέλει καὶ αὐτὸς ὄργανόν ἐστι τοῦ θεοῦ
παναρμόνιον, ἐμμελὲς καὶ ἅγιον, σοφία ὑπερκόσμιος,
οὐράνιος λόγος.

Τί δὴ οὖν τὸ ὄργανον, ὁ τοῦ θεοῦ λόγος, ὁ κύριος,
καὶ τὸ ᾆσμα τὸ καινὸν βούλεται; ὀφθαλμοὺς
ἀναπετάσαι τυφλῶν καὶ ὦτα ἀνοῖξαι κωφῶν καὶ
σκάζοντας τὼ πόδε ἢ πλανωμένους εἰς δικαιοσύνην
χειραγωγῆσαι, θεὸν ἀνθρώποις ἀφραίνουσιν ἐπιδεῖξαι, παῦσαι φθοράν, νικῆσαι θάνατον, υἱοὺς
ἀπειθεῖς διαλλάξαι πατρί. φιλάνθρωπον τὸ ὄργανον
τοῦ θεοῦ· ὁ κύριος ἐλεεῖ, παιδεύει, προτρέπει,
νουθετεῖ, σῴζει, φυλάττει καὶ μισθὸν ἡμῖν τῆς
μαθήσεως ἐκ περιουσίας βασιλείαν οὐρανῶν ἐπαγγέλλεται, τοῦτο μόνον ἀπολαύων ἡμῶν, ὃ σῳζό-
μεθα. κακία μὲν γὰρ τὴν ἀνθρώπων ἐπιβόσκεται
φθοράν, ἡ δὲ ἀλήθεια ὥσπερ ἡ μέλιττα, λυμαινομένη
τῶν ὄντων οὐδέν, ἐπὶ μόνης τῆς ἀνθρώπων ἀγάλ-
λεται σωτηρίας. ἔχεις οὖν τὴν ἐπαγγελίαν, ἔχεις
τὴν φιλανθρωπίαν· τῆς χάριτος μεταλάμβανε.

Καί μου τὸ ᾆσμα τὸ σωτήριον μὴ καινὸν οὕτως
ὑπολάβῃς ὡς σκεῦος ἢ ὡς οἰκίαν· "πρὸ ἑωσφό-
ρου" γὰρ ἦν, καὶ "ἐν ἀρχῇ ἦν ὁ λόγος καὶ ὁ λόγος
ἦν πρὸς τὸν θεὸν καὶ θεὸς ἦν ὁ λόγος"· παλαιὰ δὲ
ἡ πλάνη, καινὸν δὲ ἡ ἀλήθεια φαίνεται. εἶτ' οὖν
ἀρχαίους τοὺς Φρύγας διδάσκουσιν αἶγες μυθικαί,
εἴτε αὖ τοὺς Ἀρκάδας οἱ προσελήνους ἀναγράφοντες

---

a Psalm cix. 3 (Septuagint).
b St. John i. 1.
c See the story in Herodotus ii. 2. Psammetichus, king
of Egypt, being desirous of discovering which was the most
ancient people, put two children in charge of a herdsman.

14

breathing instrument, after His own image; and CHAP.
assuredly He Himself is an all-harmonious instrument I
of God, melodious and holy, the wisdom that is above
this world, the heavenly Word.

What then is the purpose of this instrument, the The Word's
Word of God, the Lord, and the New Song? To beneficent
open the eyes of the blind, to unstop the ears of the toward men
deaf, and to lead the halt and erring into the way of
righteousness; to reveal God to foolish men, to make
an end of corruption, to vanquish death, to reconcile
disobedient sons to the Father. The instrument of
God is loving to men. The Lord pities, chastens,
exhorts, admonishes, saves and guards us; and, over
and above this, promises the kingdom of heaven as
reward for our discipleship, while the only joy He
has of us is that we are saved. For wickedness feeds
upon the corruption of men; but truth, like the bee,
does no harm to anything in the world, but takes
delight only in the salvation of men. You have then
God's promise; you have His love to man: partake
of His grace.

And do not suppose that my song of salvation is The Word is
new in the same sense as an implement or a house. called a
For it was "before the morning star"[a]; and, "in New Song;
the beginning was the Word, and the Word was with "in the
God, and the Word was God."[b] But error is old, beginning
and truth appears to be a new thing. Whether then
the Phrygians are really proved to be ancient by the
goats in the story[c]; or the Arcadians by the poets

Goats were to be brought to them for giving milk, but no
human speech was to be uttered in their presence. The first
articulate sound they made was taken to be the Phrygian
word for bread; hence the king assumed that Phrygians
were the primitive race.

CAP.
1
ποιηταί, εἴτε μὴν αὖ τοὺς Αἰγυπτίους οἱ καὶ πρώτην ταύτην ἀναφῆναι τὴν γῆν θεούς τε καὶ ἀνθρώπους ὀνειρώσσοντες· ἀλλ᾿ οὐ πρό γε τοῦ κόσμου
τοῦδε τούτων οὐδὲ εἷς, πρὸ δὲ τῆς τοῦ κόσμου
καταβολῆς ἡμεῖς, οἱ τῷ δεῖν ἔσεσθαι ἐν αὐτῷ
πρότερον γεγεννημένοι τῷ θεῷ, τοῦ θεοῦ λόγου τὰ
λογικὰ πλάσματα ἡμεῖς, δι᾿ ὃν ἀρχαΐζομεν, ὅτι " ἐν
ἀρχῇ ὁ λόγος ἦν." ἀλλ᾿ ὅτι μὲν ἦν ὁ λόγος ἄνωθεν,
ἀρχὴ θεία τῶν πάντων ἦν τε καὶ ἔστιν· ὅτι δὲ νῦν
ὄνομα ἔλαβεν τὸ πάλαι καθωσιωμένον, δυνάμεως
ἄξιον, ὁ Χριστός, καινόν ᾆσμά μοι κέκληται.

7 Ρ.   Αἴτιος [1] γοῦν ὁ λόγος, | ὁ Χριστός, καὶ τοῦ εἶναι
πάλαι ἡμᾶς (ἦν γὰρ ἐν θεῷ), καὶ τοῦ εὖ εἶναι· νῦν
δὴ ἐπεφάνη ἀνθρώποις αὐτὸς οὗτος ὁ λόγος, ὁ
μόνος ἄμφω, θεός τε καὶ ἄνθρωπος, ἁπάντων ἡμῖν
αἴτιος ἀγαθῶν· παρ᾿ οὗ τὸ εὖ ζῆν ἐκδιδασκόμενοι
εἰς ἀΐδιον ζωὴν παραπεμπόμεθα. κατὰ γὰρ τὸν
θεσπέσιον ἐκεῖνον τοῦ κυρίου ἀπόστολον " ἡ χάρις
ἡ τοῦ θεοῦ σωτήριος πᾶσιν ἀνθρώποις ἐπεφάνη, παι-
δεύουσα ἡμᾶς, ἵνα ἀρνησάμενοι τὴν ἀσέβειαν καὶ
τὰς κοσμικὰς ἐπιθυμίας σωφρόνως καὶ δικαίως καὶ
εὐσεβῶς ζήσωμεν ἐν τῷ νῦν αἰῶνι, προσδεχόμενοι
τὴν μακαρίαν ἐλπίδα καὶ ἐπιφάνειαν τῆς δόξης τοῦ
μεγάλου θεοῦ καὶ σωτῆρος ἡμῶν Ἰησοῦ Χριστοῦ."
τοῦτό ἐστι τὸ ᾆσμα τὸ καινόν, ἡ ἐπιφάνεια ἡ νῦν
ἐκλάμψασα ἐν ἡμῖν τοῦ ἐν ἀρχῇ ὄντος καὶ προόντος
λόγου· ἐπεφάνη δὲ ἔναγχος ὁ προὼν σωτήρ, ἐπεφάνη ὁ ἐν τῷ ὄντι ὤν, ὅτι " ὁ λόγος [2] ἦν πρὸς

---

[1] αἴτιος Stählin. οὗτος MSS.   [2] λόγος ὃς MSS.

---

[a] St. John i. 1.   [b] Titus ii. 11–13.
[c] Literally, " He who exists in Him who exists."

16

who describe them as older than the moon; or, again,
the Egyptians by those who dream that this land
first brought to light both gods and men; still, not
one of these nations existed before this world. But
we were before the foundation of the world, we who,
because we were destined to be in Him, were begotten
beforehand by God. We are the rational images
formed by God's Word, or Reason, and we date from
the beginning on account of our connexion with
Him, because "the Word was in the beginning." [a]
Well, because the Word was from the first, He was
and is the divine beginning of all things; but because
He lately took a name,—the name consecrated of old
and worthy of power, the Christ,—I have called Him
a New Song.

The Word, then, that is the Christ, is the cause
both of our being long ago (for He was in God) and
of our well-being. This Word, who alone is both
God and man, the cause of all our good, appeared
but lately in His own person to men; from whom
learning how to live rightly on earth, we are brought
on our way to eternal life. For, in the words of
that inspired apostle of the Lord, "the grace of
God that bringeth salvation hath appeared to all men,
instructing us, to the intent that, denying ungodli-
ness and worldly lusts, we should live soberly and
righteously and godly in this present world, looking
for the blessed hope and appearing of the glory
of the great God and our Saviour Jesus Christ." [b]
This is the New Song, namely, the manifestation
which has but now shined forth among us, of Him
who was in the beginning, the pre-existent Word.
Not long ago the pre-existent Saviour appeared on
earth; He who exists in God [c] (because "the Word

17

CAP. τὸν θεόν," διδάσκαλος, ἐπεφάνη ᾧ τὰ πάντα
I δεδημιούργηται λόγος, καὶ τὸ ζῆν ἐν ἀρχῇ μετὰ
τοῦ πλάσαι παρασχὼν ὡς δημιουργός, τὸ εὖ ζῆν
ἐδίδαξεν ἐπιφανεὶς ὡς διδάσκαλος, ἵνα τὸ ἀεὶ ζῆν
ὕστερον ὡς θεὸς χορηγήσῃ.

Ὁ δὲ οὐ νῦν γε πρῶτον ᾤκτειρεν ἡμᾶς τῆς
πλάνης, ἀλλ᾿ ἄνωθεν ἀρχῆθεν, νῦν δὲ ἤδη ἀπολ-
λυμένους ἐπιφανεὶς περισέσωκεν. τὸ γὰρ πονηρὸν
καὶ ἑρπηστικὸν θηρίον γοητεῦον καταδουλοῦται καὶ
αἰκίζεται εἰσέτι νῦν τοὺς ἀνθρώπους, ἐμοὶ δοκεῖν,
βαρβαρικῶς τιμωρούμενον, οἳ νεκροῖς τοὺς αἰχμα-
λώτους συνδεῖν λέγονται σώμασιν, ἔστ᾿ ἂν αὐτοῖς
καὶ συσσαπῶσιν. ὁ γοῦν πονηρὸς οὗτοσὶ τύραννος
καὶ δράκων, οὓς ἂν οἷός τε ᾖ[1] ἐκ γενετῆς σφετε-
ρίσασθαι, λίθοις καὶ ξύλοις καὶ ἀγάλμασιν καὶ
τοιούτοις τισὶν εἰδώλοις προσσφίγξας τῷ δεισιδαιμονίας ἀθλίῳ δεσμῷ, τοῦτο δὴ τὸ λεγόμενον,
ζῶντας ἐπιφέρων συνέθαψεν αὐτούς, ἔστ᾿ ἂν καὶ
συμφθαρῶσιν. οὗ δὴ χάριν (εἷς γὰρ ὁ ἀπατεὼν
ἄνωθεν μὲν τὴν Εὔαν, νῦν δὲ ἤδη καὶ τοὺς ἄλλους
ἀνθρώπους εἰς θάνατον ὑποφέρων) εἷς καὶ αὐτὸς < ὁ >[2]
ἐπίκουρος καὶ βοηθὸς ἡμῖν ὁ κύριος, προμηνύων
ἀρχῆθεν προφητικῶς, νῦν δὲ ἤδη καὶ ἐναργῶς εἰς
σωτηρίαν παρακαλῶν.

Φύγωμεν οὖν ἀποστολικῇ πειθόμενοι παραγγελίᾳ
" τὸν ἄρχοντα τῆς ἐξουσίας τοῦ ἀέρος, τοῦ πνεύματος τοῦ νῦν ἐνεργοῦντος ἐν τοῖς υἱοῖς τῆς ἀπει-
θείας," καὶ τῷ σωτῆρι τῷ κυρίῳ προσδράμωμεν,
ὃς καὶ νῦν καὶ ἀεὶ προύτρεπεν εἰς σωτηρίαν, διὰ

---

[1] ᾖ Mayor.   εἴη MSS.   [2] < ὁ > inserted by Mayor.

---

[a] St. John i. 1.   [b] Ephesians ii. 2.

was with God "[a]) appeared as our teacher; the
Word appeared by whom all things have been created.
He who gave us life in the beginning when as
creator He formed us, taught us how to live
rightly by appearing as our teacher, in order that
hereafter as God He might supply us with life
everlasting.

This was not the first time that He pitied us for He has
our error. He did that from heaven from the rescued us when,
beginning. But now by His appearing He has through
rescued us, when we were on the point of perishing. the serpent's wiles, we
For the wicked, crawling wild beast makes slaves of were about
men by his magical arts, and torments them even to perish
until now, exacting vengeance, as it seems to me,
after the manner of barbarians, who are said to bind
their captives to corpses until both rot together.
Certain it is that wherever this wicked tyrant and
serpent succeeds in making men his own from their
birth, he rivets them to stocks, stones, statues and
suchlike idols, by the miserable chain of daemon-
worship; then he takes and buries them alive, as
the saying goes, until they also, men and idols
together, suffer corruption. On this account (for
it is one and the same deceiver who in the
beginning carried off Eve to death, and now does
the like to the rest of mankind) our rescuer and
helper is one also, namely, the Lord, who from the
beginning revealed Himself through prophecy, but
now invites us plainly to salvation.

Let us then, in obedience to the apostolic precept,
flee from " the prince of the power of the air, the
spirit that now worketh in the sons of disobedience." [b]
And let us take refuge with the Saviour, the Lord,
who even now exhorts men to salvation, as He ever

CLEMENT OF ALEXANDRIA

τεράτων καὶ σημείων ἐν Αἰγύπτῳ, ἐν ἐρήμῳ ⟨ δὲ ⟩[1] διὰ
τε τῆς βάτου καὶ τῆς ἀκολουθούσης χάριτι φιλανθρωπίας θεραπαίνης δίκην Ἑβραίοις νεφέλης. τούτων μὲν δὴ τῷ φόβῳ τοὺς σκληροκαρδίους πρού-
τρεπεν· ἤδη δὲ καὶ διὰ Μωσέως τοῦ πανσόφου
καὶ τοῦ φιλαλήθους Ἡσαΐα καὶ παντὸς τοῦ προφητικοῦ χοροῦ λογικώτερον ἐπὶ τὸν λόγον[a] ἐπιστρέφει τοὺς ὦτα[2] κεκτημένους· καὶ ἔσθ' ὅπῃ μὲν
λοιδορεῖται, ἔστιν δ' οὗ καὶ ἀπειλεῖ· τοὺς δὲ καὶ
θρηνεῖ τῶν ἀνθρώπων· ᾄδει δὲ ἄλλοις, καθάπερ
ἰατρὸς ἀγαθὸς τῶν νοσούντων σωμάτων τὰ μὲν
καταπλάττων, τὰ δὲ καταλεαίνων, τὰ δὲ καταντλῶν,
τὰ δὲ καὶ σιδήρῳ διαιρῶν, ἐπικαίων δὲ ἄλλα, ἔστι
δ' οὗ καὶ ἀποπρίων, εἴ πως οἷόν τε κἂν παρὰ μέρος
ἢ μέλος τὸν ἄνθρωπον ὑγιᾶναι. πολύφωνός γε ὁ
σωτὴρ καὶ πολύτροπος εἰς ἀνθρώπων σωτηρίαν·
ἀπειλῶν νουθετεῖ, λοιδορούμενος ἐπιστρέφει, θρηνῶν
ἐλεεῖ, ψάλλων παρακαλεῖ, διὰ βάτου λαλεῖ (σημείων
ἐκεῖνοι καὶ τεράτων ἔχρῃζον) καὶ τῷ πυρὶ δεδίττεται
τοὺς ἀνθρώπους, ἀνάπτων ἐκ κίονος τὴν φλόγα,
δεῖγμα ὁμοῦ χάριτος καὶ φόβου· ἐὰν ὑπακούσῃς, τὸ
φῶς, ἐὰν παρακούσῃς, τὸ πῦρ. ἐπειδὴ δὲ καὶ
κίονος καὶ βάτου ἡ σὰρξ τιμιωτέρα, προφῆται
μετ' ἐκεῖνα φθέγγονται, αὐτὸς ἐν Ἡσαΐα ὁ κύριος
λαλῶν, αὐτὸς ἐν Ἠλίᾳ, ἐν στόματι προφητῶν
αὐτός· σὺ δὲ ἀλλ' εἰ προφήταις μὴ πιστεύεις,
μῦθον δ' ὑπολαμβάνεις καὶ τοὺς ἄνδρας καὶ τὸ

---

[1] ⟨δὲ⟩ inserted by Stählin.
[2] τοὺς ὦτα Mayor. τοὺς τὰ ὦτα MSS.

---

[a] Or, "to reason." The Greek *Logos* means either
"Word" (personal), or "rational word," "reason" (im-
personal). All through his writings Clement plays upon

did, by wonders and signs in Egypt, and in the desert by the burning bush and the cloud that, through favour of His love, followed the Hebrews like a handmaid. By the fear that these wonders inspired He exhorted the hard-hearted; but afterwards, through all-wise Moses and truth-loving Isaiah and the whole company of the prophets, He converts to the Word [a] by more rational means those who have ears to hear. In some places He rebukes; in others He even threatens; some men He laments; for others He sings: just as a good doctor, in dealing with diseased bodies, uses poulticing for some, rubbing for others, and bathing for others; some he cuts with a knife, others he cauterizes, and in some cases he even amputates, if by any means he can restore the patient to health by removing some part or limb. So the Saviour uses many tones and many devices in working for the salvation of men. His threats are for warning; His rebukes for converting; His lamentation to show pity; His song to encourage. He speaks through a burning bush (for the men of old had need of signs and portents), and He strikes terror into men by fire, kindling the flame out of a cloudy pillar, as a token at the same time of grace and fear,—to the obedient light, to the disobedient fire. But since flesh is of more honour than a pillar or a bush, after those signs prophets utter their voice, the Lord Himself speaking in Isaiah, the Lord Himself in Elijah, the Lord Himself in the mouth of the prophets. As for you, however, if you do not trust the prophets, and if you suppose both the fire and the men who saw it to be a legend, the Lord Himself

this double meaning of *Logos*. Other instances occur on pp. 27, 275, 277.

21

CAP.
I

πῦρ, αὐτός σοι λαλήσει ὁ κύριος, "ὃς ἐν μορφῇ
θεοῦ ὑπάρχων οὐχ ἁρπαγμὸν ἡγήσατο τὸ εἶναι ἴσα
θεῷ· ἐκένωσεν δὲ ἑαυτόν" ὁ φιλοικτίρμων θεός,
σῶσαι τὸν ἄνθρωπον γλιχόμενος· καὶ αὐτὸς ἤδη
σοι ἐναργῶς ὁ λόγος λαλεῖ, δυσωπῶν τὴν ἀπιστίαν,
ναί φημι, ὁ λόγος ὁ τοῦ θεοῦ ἄνθρωπος γενόμενος,
ἵνα δὴ καὶ σὺ παρὰ ἀνθρώπου μάθῃς, πῇ ποτε ἄρα
ἄνθρωπος γένηται θεός.

Εἶτ' οὐκ ἄτοπον, ὦ φίλοι, τὸν μὲν θεὸν ἀεὶ
προτρέπειν ἡμᾶς ἐπ' ἀρετήν, ἡμᾶς δὲ ἀναδύεσθαι
τὴν ὠφέλειαν καὶ ἀναβάλλεσθαι τὴν σωτηρίαν; ἢ
γὰρ οὐχὶ καὶ Ἰωάννης ἐπὶ σωτηρίαν παρακαλεῖ καὶ
τὸ πᾶν γίνεται φωνὴ προτρεπτική; πυθώμεθα
τοίνυν αὐτοῦ· "τίς πόθεν εἰς ἀνδρῶν;" Ἡλίας
μὲν οὐκ ἐρεῖ, Χριστὸς δὲ εἶναι ἀρνήσεται· φωνὴ
δὲ ὁμολογήσει ἐν ἐρήμῳ βοῶσα. τίς οὖν ἔστιν
Ἰωάννης; ὡς τύπῳ λαβεῖν, ἐξέστω εἰπεῖν, φωνὴ
τοῦ λόγου προτρεπτικὴ ἐν ἐρήμῳ βοῶσα. τί βοᾷς,
ὦ φωνή; "εἰπὲ καὶ ἡμῖν." "εὐθείας ποιεῖτε τὰς
ὁδοὺς κυρίου." πρόδρομος Ἰωάννης καὶ ἡ φωνὴ
πρόδρομος τοῦ λόγου, φωνὴ παρακλητική, προ-
ετοιμάζουσα εἰς σωτηρίαν, φωνὴ προτρέπουσα εἰς
κληρονομίαν οὐρανῶν· δι' ἣν ἡ στεῖρα καὶ ἔρημος

9 P. | ἄγονος οὐκέτι.

Ταύτην μοι τὴν κυοφορίαν προεθέσπισεν ἀγγέλου
φωνή· πρόδρομος ἦν κἀκείνη τοῦ κυρίου, στεῖραν
εὐαγγελιζομένη γυναῖκα, ὡς Ἰωάννης τὴν ἔρημον.
διὰ ταύτην τοίνυν τοῦ λόγου τὴν φωνὴν ἡ στεῖρα

---

[a] Philippians ii. 6–7.   [b] Homer, *Odyssey* i. 170, etc.
[c] See St. John i. 20–23.   [d] *Odyssey* i. 10.
[e] Isaiah xl. 3, quoted in St. Matthew iii. 3; St. Mark
i. 3; St. Luke iii. 4; St. John i. 23.
[f] *i.e.*, Elizabeth; St. Luke i. 7–13.

shall speak to you, He "who being in the form of ^{CHAP.} God did not count His equality with God as an ^I opportunity for gain, but emptied Himself," *a* the God of compassion who is eager to save man. And the Word Himself now speaks to you plainly, putting to shame your unbelief, yes, I say, the Word of God speaks, having become man, in order that such as you may learn from man how it is even possible for man to become a god.

Then is it not monstrous, my friends, that, while God is ever exhorting us to virtue, we on our part shrink from accepting the benefit and put off our salvation? Do you not know that John also invites us to salvation and becomes wholly a voice of exhortation? Let us then inquire of him. "Who and whence art thou?" *b* He will say he is not Elijah; he will deny that he is Christ; but he will confess, "a voice crying in the desert." *c* Who then is John? Allow us to say, in a figure, that he is a voice of the Word, raising his cry of exhortation in the desert. What dost thou cry, O voice? "Tell us also." *d* "Make straight the ways of the Lord." *e* John is a forerunner, and the voice is a forerunner of the Word. It is a voice of encouragement that makes ready for the coming salvation, a voice that exhorts to a heavenly inheritance; and by reason of this voice, the barren and desolate is fruitless no longer.

It was this fruitfulness, I think, which the angel's voice foretold. That voice was also a forerunner of the Lord, inasmuch as it brought good tidings to a barren woman, *f* as John did to the desert. This voice of the Word is therefore the cause of the barren woman being blest with child and of the

John also exhorts to salvation

John's voice and the angel's voice are two forerunners of the Word

CAP.
I
εὐτεκνεῖ καὶ ἡ ἔρημος καρποφορεῖ. αἱ πρόδρομοι
τοῦ κυρίου φωναὶ δύο, ἀγγέλου καὶ Ἰωάννου,
αἰνίσσονταί μοι τὴν ἐναποκειμένην σωτηρίαν, ὡς
ἐπιφανέντος τοῦ λόγου τοῦδε εὐτεκνίας ἡμᾶς καρπὸν
ἀπενέγκασθαι, ζωὴν ἀΐδιον. ἄμφω γοῦν ἐς ταὐτὸν
ἀγαγοῦσα τὰ φωνὰ ἡ γραφὴ σαφηνίζει τὸ πᾶν·
" ἀκουσάτω ἡ οὐ τίκτουσα· ῥηξάτω φωνὴν ἡ οὐκ
ὠδίνουσα, ὅτι πλείονα τὰ τέκνα τῆς ἐρήμου μᾶλλον
ἢ τῆς ἐχούσης τὸν ἄνδρα." ἡμῖν εὐηγγελίζετο
ἄγγελος, ἡμᾶς προὔτρεπεν Ἰωάννης νοῆσαι τὸν
γεωργόν, ζητῆσαι τὸν ἄνδρα. εἷς γὰρ καὶ ὁ αὐτὸς
οὗτος, ὁ τῆς στείρας ἀνήρ, ὁ τῆς ἐρήμου γεωργός,
ὁ τῆς θείας ἐμπλήσας δυνάμεως καὶ τὴν στεῖραν καὶ
τὴν ἔρημον. ἐπεὶ γὰρ πολλὰ τὰ τέκνα τῆς εὐγενοῦς,
ἄπαις δὲ ἦν διὰ ἀπείθειαν ἡ πολύπαις ἀνέκαθεν
Ἑβραία γυνή, ἡ στεῖρα τὸν ἄνδρα λαμβάνει καὶ ἡ
ἔρημος τὸν γεωργόν· εἶτα ἡ μὲν καρπῶν, ἡ δὲ
πιστῶν, ἄμφω δὲ μητέρες διὰ τὸν λόγον· ἀπίστοις
δὲ εἰσέτι νῦν καὶ στεῖρα καὶ ἔρημος περιλείπεται.

Ὁ μὲν Ἰωάννης, ὁ κῆρυξ τοῦ λόγου, ταύτῃ πῃ
παρεκάλει ἑτοίμους γίνεσθαι εἰς θεοῦ, τοῦ Χριστοῦ,
παρουσίαν, καὶ τοῦτο ἦν ὃ ᾐνίσσετο ἡ Ζαχαρίου
σιωπή, ἀναμένουσα τὸν πρόδρομον τοῦ Χριστοῦ
καρπόν, ἵνα τῆς ἀληθείας τὸ φῶς, ὁ λόγος, τῶν
προφητικῶν αἰνιγμάτων τὴν μυστικὴν ἀπολύσηται
σιωπήν, εὐαγγέλιον γενόμενος· σὺ δὲ εἰ ποθεῖς

---

a Isaiah liv. 1. When Clement says that Scripture brings
together the two voices, he is interpreting the first clause of
this quotation as referring to the desert, and the second as
referring to the woman.

b i.e., the Gentiles ; cp. Stromateis ii. 29. 1.

c See St. Luke i. 20, 64.

desert bearing fruit. The two forerunning voices of
the Lord, that of the angel and that of John, seem
to me to speak darkly of the salvation laid up in
store for us, namely that, after the manifestation of
this Word, we should reap the fruit of productiveness,
which is eternal life. Certainly the Scripture makes
the whole matter plain by bringing together the two
voices. For it says, " Let her hear that brings not
forth ; let her that is not in travail utter her voice ;
for more are the children of the desolate than of her
that hath an husband." [a] We are they to whom the
angel brought the good tidings ; we are they whom
John exhorted to recognize the husbandman and to
seek the husband. For He is one and the same, the
husband of the barren woman and the husbandman
of the desert, He who has filled both the barren
woman and the desert with divine power. For since
the woman of noble birth had many children, but
was afterwards childless through unbelief,—that is,
the Hebrew woman who had many children to begin
with,—the barren woman [b] receives her husband and
the desert its husbandman. So then by reason of
the Word both become mothers, the desert of fruits
and the woman of believing children ; yet even now
the words " barren " and " desert " remain for unbelievers.

In some such way as this John, the herald of the
Word, summoned men to prepare for the presence
of God, that is, of the Christ. And this was the
hidden meaning of the dumbness of Zacharias, which
lasted until the coming of the fruit which was forerunner of the Christ,[c]—that the light of truth, the
Word, should break the mystic silence of the dark
prophetic sayings, by becoming good tidings. But

25

CAP. ἰδεῖν ὡς ἀληθῶς τὸν θεόν, καθαρσίων μεταλάμβανε
I θεοπρεπῶν, οὐ δάφνης πετάλων καὶ ταινιῶν τινων
ἐρίῳ καὶ πορφύρᾳ πεποικιλμένων, δικαιοσύνην δὲ
ἀναδησάμενος καὶ τῆς ἐγκρατείας τὰ πέταλα περι-
θέμενος πολυπραγμόνει Χριστόν· " ἐγὼ γάρ εἰμι ἡ
θύρα," φησί που· ἣν ἐκμαθεῖν δεῖ νοῆσαι θελήσασι
τὸν θεόν, ὅπως ἡμῖν ἀθρόας τῶν οὐρανῶν ἀνα-
πετάσῃ τὰς πύλας· λογικαὶ γὰρ αἱ τοῦ λόγου πύλαι,
10 P. πίστεως | ἀνοιγνύμεναι κλειδί· " θεὸν οὐδεὶς ἔγνω,
εἰ μὴ ὁ υἱὸς καὶ ᾧ ἂν ὁ υἱὸς ἀποκαλύψῃ." θύραν
δὲ εὖ οἶδ᾽ ὅτι τὴν ἀποκεκλεισμένην τέως ὁ ἀνοιγνὺς
ὕστερον ἀποκαλύπτει τἄνδον καὶ δείκνυσιν ἃ μηδὲ
γνῶναι οἷόν τε ἦν πρότερον, εἰ μὴ διὰ Χριστοῦ
πεπορευμένοις, δι᾽ οὗ μόνου θεὸς ἐποπτεύεται.

II

Ἄδυτα τοίνυν ἄθεα μὴ πολυπραγμονεῖτε μηδὲ
βαράθρων στόματα τερατείας ἔμπλεα ἢ λέβη-
τα Θεσπρώτιον ἢ τρίποδα Κιρραῖον ἢ Δωδω-
ναῖον χαλκεῖον· γεράνδρυον δὲ ψάμμοις ἐρήμαις
τετιμημένον καὶ τὸ αὐτόθι μαντεῖον αὐτῇ δρυΐ
μεμαρασμένον μύθοις γεγηρακόσι καταλείψατε.
σεσίγηται γοῦν ἡ Κασταλίας πηγὴ καὶ Κολοφῶνος
ἄλλη πηγή, καὶ τὰ ἄλλα ὁμοίως τέθνηκε νάματα

---

[a] St. John x. 9. [b] See p. 20, n. a.
[c] St. Matthew xi. 27.
[d] e.g., the cave of Trophonius at Lebadeia in Boeotia.
[e] Clement refers to the Libyan oracle of Zeus Ammon.
There was a close connexion between this and the oracle of
Zeus at Dodona. For the existence of a sacred oak in

as for you, if you long to see God truly, take part CHAP. in purifications meet for Him, not of laurel leaves I and fillets embellished with wool and purple, but Purifi- crown yourself with righteousness, let your wreath necessary be woven from the leaves of self-control, and seek for the diligently after Christ. "For I am the door," [a] He of God says somewhere; which we who wish to perceive God must search out, in order that He may throw open wide for us the gates of heaven. For the gates of the Word are gates of reason,[b] opened by the key of faith. "No man knoweth God, save the Son, and him to whom the Son revealeth Him." [c] And I know well that He who opens this door, hitherto shut, afterwards unveils what is within, and shows what could not have been discerned before, except we had entered through Christ, through whom alone comes the vision of God.

II.

Do not therefore seek diligently after godless Sanctuaries, sanctuaries, nor after mouths of caverns full of oracles, sacred trees jugglery,[d] nor the Thesprotian caldron, nor the Cir- and springs rhaean tripod, nor the Dodonian copper. As for the of date old stump honoured by the desert sands,[e] and the oracular shrine there gone to decay with the oak itself, abandon them both to the region of legends now grown old. The Castalian spring, at least, is all silent. So is the spring of Colophon; and the rest of the prophetic streams are likewise dead.

Libya see A. B. Cook, *Zeus*, vol. i. pp. 361–366. Strabo (54 B.C.–A.D. 24) says that in his day the oracle was " almost entirely deserted " (Strabo 813).

CAP. μαντικὰ καὶ δὴ τοῦ τύφου κενὰ ὀψὲ μέν, ὅμως
II δ' οὖν διελήλεγκται τοῖς ἰδίοις συνεκρεύσαντα
μύθοις. διήγησαι ἡμῖν καὶ τῆς ἄλλης μαντικῆς,
μᾶλλον δὲ μανικῆς, τὰ ἄχρηστα χρηστήρια, τὸν
Κλάριον, τὸν Πύθιον, τὸν Διδυμέα, τὸν Ἀμφιάρεω,
τὸν † Ἀπόλλω,[1] τὸν Ἀμφίλοχον, εἰ δὲ βούλει, καὶ
τερατοσκόπους καὶ οἰωνοσκόπους καὶ τοὺς ὀνείρων
κριτὰς ἀνίερου σὺν αὐτοῖς· στῆσον δὲ ὁμοῦ παρὰ
11 p. τὸν Πύθιον τοὺς ἀλευρομάντεις ἄγων | καὶ κριθο-
μάντεις καὶ τοὺς εἰσέτι παρὰ τοῖς πολλοῖς τετιμη-
μένους ἐγγαστριμύθους· ναὶ μὴν ἄδυτα Αἰγυπτίων
καὶ Τυρρηνῶν νεκρομαντεῖαι σκότῳ παραδιδόσθων.
μανικὰ ταῦτα ὡς ἀληθῶς ἀνθρώπων ἀπίστων
σοφιστήρια καὶ πλάνης ἀκράτου κυβευτήρια· συν-
έμποροι τῆσδε τῆς γοητείας αἶγες αἱ ἐπὶ μαντικὴν ἠσκημέναι καὶ κόρακες ἀνθρώποις χρᾶν ὑπὸ
ἀνθρώπων διδασκόμενοι.

Τί δ' εἴ σοι καταλέγοιμι τὰ μυστήρια; οὐκ
ἐξορχήσομαι μέν, ὥσπερ Ἀλκιβιάδην λέγουσιν,
ἀπογυμνώσω δὲ εὖ μάλα ἀνὰ τὸν τῆς ἀληθείας λόγον
τὴν γοητείαν τὴν ἐγκεκρυμμένην αὐτοῖς καὶ αὐτούς
γε τοὺς καλουμένους ὑμῶν θεούς, ὧν αἱ τελεταὶ
⟨αἱ⟩[2] μυστικαί, οἷον ἐπὶ σκηνῆς τοῦ βίου τοῖς

_____

[1] τὸν †Ἀπόλλω is probably corrupt. τὸν Τροφώνιον (Cobet)
and τὸν Μόψον (Wilamowitz) have been suggested. Markland puts τὸν Ἀπόλλω before τὸν Κλάριον, a re-arrangement
which has been followed in the translation.

[2] ⟨αἱ⟩ inserted by Mayor.

_____

[a] An attempt has been made here to reproduce the
striking word-play which is a constant feature of Clement's
writing. For other examples see pp. 37, 191 (n. *b*), 199 (n. *a*),
255 (n. *d*), 299 (n. **a**).

Stripped of their absurd pretensions, though none CHAP.
too soon, they are at last thoroughly exposed; the II
waters have run dry together with the legends
attached to them.   Relate to me the utterly vain
utterances ^a of that other form of divination,—I should
rather say hallucination,^a—the oracles of Apollo,
Clarian, Pythian and Didymean, and those of Amphi-
araus and Amphilochus; and, if you will, devote to
destruction along with them the soothsayers, augurs
and interpreters of dreams.   At the same time, take
and place by the side of Pythian Apollo those who
divine by flour, and by barley,^b and the ventriloquists^c
still held in honour among the multitude.   Yes, and
let the sanctuaries of Egypt and the Tuscan oracles
of the dead be delivered over to darkness.   Homes
of hallucination in very truth they are, these schools
of sophistry for unbelieving men, these gambling-
dens of sheer delusion.   Partners in this business of
trickery are goats, trained for divination; and ravens,
taught by men to give oracular responses to men.

But what if I were to recount the mysteries for The gods
you?   I will not burlesque them, as Alcibiades is of the mysteries
said to have done, but will thoroughly lay bare, in
accordance with the principle of truth, the trickery
they conceal; and as for your so-called gods themselves, to whom the mystic rites belong, I will display
them on the stage of life, as it were, for the spectators

^b Flour and barley were used in the sacrifices, and
omens were obtained by watching the movements of the
flames.

^c The Greek word is used in the Septuagint to denote
those who have " familiar spirits," such as the witch of Endor
(1 Samuel xxviii. 7).   Their ventriloquism was employed to
simulate the voices of the spirits ; see Isaiah viii. 19 (" that
chirp and that mutter ").   Also Leviticus xix. 31, etc.

CAP.
II τῆς ἀληθείας ἐκκυκλήσω θεαταῖς. Διόνυσον μαι-
νόλην ὀργιάζουσι Βάκχοι ὠμοφαγίᾳ τὴν ἱερομανίαν
ἄγοντες καὶ τελίσκουσι τὰς κρεονομίας τῶν φόνων
ἀνεστεμμένοι τοῖς ὄφεσιν, ἐπολολύζοντες Εὐάν,
Εὐὰν ἐκείνην, δι' ἣν ἡ πλάνη παρηκολούθησεν· καὶ
σημεῖον ὀργίων βακχικῶν ὄφις ἐστὶ τετελεσμένος.
αὐτίκα γοῦν κατὰ τὴν ἀκριβῆ τῶν Ἑβραίων φωνὴν
τὸ ὄνομα τὸ Ἔυια δασυνόμενον ἑρμηνεύεται ὄφις
12 P. ἡ | θήλεια· Δηὼ δὲ καὶ Κόρη δρᾶμα ἤδη ἐγενέσθην
μυστικόν, καὶ τὴν πλάνην καὶ τὴν ἁρπαγὴν καὶ τὸ
πένθος αὐταῖν Ἐλευσὶς δᾳδουχεῖ.

Καί μοι δοκεῖ τὰ ὄργια καὶ τὰ μυστήρια δεῖν
ἐτυμολογεῖν, τὰ μὲν ἀπὸ τῆς ὀργῆς τῆς Δηοῦς τῆς
πρὸς Δία γεγενημένης, τὰ δὲ ἀπὸ τοῦ μύσους
τοῦ συμβεβηκότος περὶ τὸν Διόνυσον· εἰ δὲ καὶ
ἀπὸ Μυοῦντός τινος Ἀττικοῦ, ὃν ἐν κυνηγίᾳ δια-
φθαρῆναι Ἀπολλόδωρος λέγει, οὐ φθόνος· ὑμῶν
δεδόξασται τὰ μυστήρια ἐπιτυμβίῳ τιμῇ. πάρεστι
δὲ καὶ ἄλλως μυθήριά σοι νοεῖν ἀντιστοιχούντων
τῶν γραμμάτων τὰ μυστήρια· θηρεύουσι γὰρ εἰ
καὶ ἄλλοι τινές, ἀτὰρ δὴ καὶ οἱ μῦθοι οἱ τοιοίδε
Θρᾳκῶν τοὺς βαρβαρικωτάτους, Φρυγῶν τοὺς
ἀνοητοτάτους, Ἑλλήνων τοὺς δεισιδαίμονας. ὄλοιτο
οὖν ὁ τῆσδε ἄρξας τῆς ἀπάτης ἀνθρώποις, εἴτε ὁ
Δάρδανος, ὁ Μητρὸς θεῶν καταδείξας τὰ μυστήρια,
εἴτε Ἠετίων, ὁ τὰ Σαμοθρᾴκων ὄργια καὶ τελετὰς

---

[a] "Eva" (εὖα, εὐάν) is one form of the cry "evoe" or
"evae" (εὐοῖ, εὐαί) uttered by worshippers in the orgiastic
rites of Dionysus.

[b] Clement catches at a slight verbal resemblance as
affording some support for his idea that there is a connexion
between Eve and the Bacchic serpent. Elsewhere (*Stroma-*

of truth. The raving Dionysus is worshipped by CHAP.
Bacchants with orgies, in which they celebrate their II
sacred frenzy by a feast of raw flesh. Wreathed with Dionysus
snakes, they perform the distribution of portions of
their victims, shouting the name of Eva,[a] that Eva
through whom error entered into the world; and
a consecrated snake is the emblem of the Bacchic
orgies. At any rate, according to the correct
Hebrew speech, the word "hevia" with an aspirate
means the female snake.[b] Demeter and Persephone Demeter
have come to be the subject of a mystic drama, and and Per-
Eleusis celebrates with torches the rape of the sephone
daughter and the sorrowful wandering of the mother.

Now it seems to me that the terms "orgy" and Derivation
"mystery" must be derived, the former from the of terms
wrath (*orgē*) of Demeter against Zeus,[c] and the "mystery"
latter from the pollution (*mysos*) that took place in
connexion with Dionysus.[d] But even if they are
named after a certain Myus of Attica, who according
to Apollodorus was killed in hunting, I make no
objection. Your mysteries have received the glory
of funeral honours! You may also, in another way,
suppose them to be hunting-stories (*mytheria*), since
the letters correspond; for as surely as there are
men who hunt wild beasts, so do legends like these
hunt the rudest among Thracians, the silliest among
Phrygians, and the daemon-fearers among Greeks. A
curse then upon the man who started this deception The alleged
for mankind, whether it be Dardanus, who introduced originators
the mysteries of the Mother of the Gods; or Eëtion, of mysteries
who founded the Samothracian orgies and rites; or

teis iii. 80. 2) he gives the Hebrew derivation, Eve = Life (see
Genesis iii. 20).
    [c] See p. 35.   [d] See p. 73.

31

ὑποστησάμενος, εἴτε ὁ Φρὺξ ἐκεῖνος ὁ Μίδας, ὁ παρὰ τοῦ Ὀδρύσου μαθών, ἔπειτα διαδοὺς τοῖς ὑποτεταγμένοις ἔντεχνον ἀπάτην. οὐ γάρ με ὁ Κύπριος ὁ νησιώτης Κινύρας παραπείσαι ποτ᾽ ἄν, τὰ περὶ τὴν Ἀφροδίτην μαχλῶντα ὄργια ἐκ νυκτὸς ἡμέρα παραδοῦναι τολμήσας, φιλοτιμούμενος θειάσαι πόρνην πολίτιδα. Μελάμποδα δὲ τὸν Ἀμυθάονος ἄλλοι φασὶν ἐξ Αἰγύπτου μετακομίσαι τῇ Ἑλλάδι
13 P. τὰς Δηοῦς ἑορτάς, πένθος ὑμνούμενον. τούτους ἔγωγ᾽ ἂν ἀρχεκάκους φήσαιμι μύθων ἀθέων καὶ δεισιδαιμονίας ὀλεθρίου πατέρας, σπέρμα κακίας καὶ φθορᾶς ἐγκαταφυτεύσαντας τῷ βίῳ τὰ μυστήρια.

Ἤδη δέ, καὶ γὰρ καιρός, αὐτὰ ὑμῶν τὰ ὄργια ἐξελέγξω ἀπάτης καὶ τερατείας ἔμπλεα. καὶ εἰ μεμύησθε, ἐπιγελάσεσθε μᾶλλον τοῖς μύθοις ὑμῶν τούτοις τοῖς τιμωμένοις. ἀγορεύσω δὲ ἀναφανδὸν τὰ κεκρυμμένα, οὐκ αἰδούμενος λέγειν ἃ προσκυνεῖν οὐκ αἰσχύνεσθε. ἡ μὲν οὖν " ἀφρογενής " τε καὶ " κυπρογενής," ἡ Κινύρα φίλη (τὴν Ἀφροδίτην λέγω, τὴν " φιλομηδέα, ὅτι μηδέων ἐξεφαάνθη," μηδέων ἐκείνων τῶν ἀποκεκομμένων Οὐρανοῦ, τῶν λάγνων, τῶν μετὰ τὴν τομὴν τὸ κῦμα βεβιασμένων), ὡς ἀσελγῶν ὑμῖν μορίων ἄξιος [Ἀφροδίτη][1] γίνεται καρπός, ἐν ταῖς τελεταῖς ταύτης τῆς πελαγίας ἡδονῆς τεκμήριον τῆς γονῆς ἁλῶν χόνδρος καὶ φαλλὸς τοῖς μυουμένοις τὴν τέχνην τὴν μοιχικὴν ἐπιδίδοται· νόμισμα δὲ εἰσφέρουσιν αὐτῇ οἱ μυούμενοι, ὡς ἑταίρᾳ ἐρασταί.

---

[1] [Ἀφροδίτη] Schwartz.

---

[a] This phrase is quoted from Hesiod, *Theogony* 200. See also Liddell and Scott under (1) φιλομμηδής and (2) φιλομμειδής.

that Phrygian Midas, who learnt the artful deceit
from Odrysus and then passed it on to his subjects.
For I could never be beguiled by the claims of the
islander Cinyras, of Cyprus, who had the audacity to
transfer the lascivious orgies of Aphrodite from night
to day, in his ambition to deify a harlot of his own
country. Others say that it was Melampus the
son of Amythaon who brought into Greece from
Egypt the festivals of Demeter, that is, the story of
her grief celebrated in hymns. These men I for my
part would call originators of mischief, parents of
godless legends and deadly daemon-worship, seeing
that they implanted the mysteries in human life to
be a seed of evil and corruption.

But now, (and high time too,) I will convict your
orgies themselves of being full of deception and
jugglery, and if you have been initiated you will
smile the more at these legends you are wont to
honour. I will tell openly the secret things, and
will not shrink from speaking of what you are not
ashamed to worship. There is, then, the "foam-
born" "Cyprus-born" goddess, the darling of
Cinyras. I mean Aphrodite, who received the
name Philomēdes because she was born from the
mēdea,ᵃ those lustful members that were cut off
from Uranus and after the separation did violence to
the wave. See how lewd are the members from
which so worthy an offspring is born! And in the
rites which celebrate this pleasure of the sea, as a
symbol of her birth, the gift of a cake of salt and a
phallos is made to those who are initiated in the
art of fornication; and the initiated bring their
tribute of a coin to the goddess, as lovers do to a
mistress.

33

CAP.
II

Δηοῦς δὲ μυστήρια αἱ[1] Διὸς πρὸς μητέρα
Δήμητρα ἀφροδίσιοι συμπλοκαὶ καὶ μῆνις (οὐκ
οἶδ᾽ ὅ τι φῶ λοιπόν, μητρὸς ἢ γυναικός) τῆς Δηοῦς,
ἧς δὴ χάριν Βριμὼ προσαγορευθῆναι λέγεται, <καὶ>[2]
ἱκετηρίαι Διὸς καὶ πόμα χολῆς καὶ καρδιουλκίαι καὶ
ἀρρητουργίαι· ταῦτά οἱ Φρύγες τελίσκουσιν Ἄττιδι
καὶ Κυβέλῃ καὶ Κορύβασιν· τεθρυλήκασιν δὲ ὡς
ἄρα ἀποσπάσας ὁ Ζεὺς τοῦ κριοῦ τοὺς διδύμους
φέρων ἐν μέσοις ἔρριψε τοῖς κόλποις τῆς Δηοῦς,
τιμωρίαν ψευδῆ τῆς βιαίας συμπλοκῆς ἐκτιννύων,
ὡς ἑαυτὸν δῆθεν ἐκτεμών. τὰ σύμβολα τῆς μυή-
σεως ταύτης ἐκ περιουσίας παρατεθέντα οἶδ᾽ ὅτι
κινήσει γέλωτα καὶ μὴ γελασείουσιν ὑμῖν διὰ

14 P. τοὺς | ἐλέγχους· " ἐκ τυμπάνου ἔφαγον· ἐκ κυμ-
βάλου ἔπιον· ἐκερνοφόρησα· ὑπὸ τὸν παστὸν
ὑπέδυν." ταῦτα οὐχ ὕβρις τὰ σύμβολα; οὐ χλεύη
τὰ μυστήρια; τί δ᾽ εἰ καὶ τὰ ἐπίλοιπα προσθείην;
κυεῖ μὲν ἡ Δημήτηρ, ἀνατρέφεται δὲ ἡ Κόρη,
μίγνυται δ᾽ αὖθις ὁ γεννήσας οὑτοσὶ Ζεὺς τῇ
Φερεφάττῃ, τῇ ἰδίᾳ θυγατρί, μετὰ τὴν μητέρα τὴν
Δηώ, ἐκλαθόμενος τοῦ προτέρου μύσους (πατὴρ
καὶ φθορεὺς κόρης ὁ Ζεύς[3]) καὶ μίγνυται δράκων
γενόμενος, ὃς ἦν, ἐλεγχθείς. Σαβαζίων γοῦν
μυστηρίων σύμβολον τοῖς μυουμένοις ὁ διὰ
κόλπου θεός· δράκων δέ ἐστιν οὗτος, διελκόμενος
τοῦ κόλπου τῶν τελουμένων, ἔλεγχος ἀκρασίας

---

[1] αἱ Lobeck. καὶ MSS.   [2] <καὶ> inserted by Schwartz.
[3] πατὴρ . . . Ζεύς. These words are not found in Eusebius (Praep. Ev. ii. 3), and are rejected as a gloss by Stählin.

[a] i.e. the Grim or Terrible One.
[b] Compare this formula of the Phrygian with that of
the Eleusinian mysteries, quoted on p. 43. See also the
Appendix on the Mysteries, p. 388.

EXHORTATION TO THE GREEKS

The mysteries of Demeter commemorate the amorous embraces of Zeus with his mother Demeter, and the wrath of Demeter (I do not know what to call her for the future, mother or wife) on account of which she is said to have received the name Brimo[a]; also the supplications of Zeus, the drink of bile, the tearing out the heart of the victims, and unspeakable obscenities. The same rites are performed in honour of Attis and Cybele and the Corybantes by the Phrygians, who have spread it abroad how that Zeus tore off the testicles of a ram, and then brought and flung them into the midst of Demeter's lap, thus paying a sham penalty for his violent embrace by pretending that he had mutilated himself. If I go on further to quote the symbols of initiation into this mystery they will, I know, move you to laughter, even though you are in no laughing humour when your rites are being exposed. " I ate from the drum; I drank from the cymbal; I carried the sacred dish; I stole into the bridal chamber."[b] Are not these symbols an outrage? Are not the mysteries a mockery? But what if I were to add the rest of the story? Demeter becomes pregnant; the Maiden grows up; and this Zeus who begat her has further intercourse, this time with Persephone herself, his own daughter, after his union with her mother Demeter. Totally forgetful of his former pollution Zeus becomes the ravisher as well as father of the maiden, meeting her under the form of a serpent, his true nature being thus revealed. At any rate, in the Sabazian mysteries the sign given to those who are initiated is " the god over the breast "; this is a serpent drawn over the breast of the votaries, a proof of the licentiousness of Zeus. Persephone

Marginal notes: CHAP. II (ii.) of Demeter; (iii.) of Attis, Cybele and the Corybantes; which are the same as those of Demeter; The story of Persephone

35

CAP. Διός. κυεῖ καὶ ἡ Φερέφαττα παῖδα ταυρόμορφον·
II ἀμέλει, φησί τις ποιητὴς εἰδωλικός,

> ταῦρος δράκοντος καὶ πατὴρ ταύρου δράκων,
> ἐν ὄρει τὸ κρύφιον, βουκόλος, τὸ κεντρίον,[1]

βουκολικόν, οἶμαι,[2] κέντρον τὸν νάρθηκα ἐπικαλῶν,
ὃν δὴ ἀναστέφουσιν οἱ βάκχοι. βούλει καὶ τὰ
Φερεφάττης ἀνθολόγια διηγήσωμαί[3] σοι καὶ τὸν
κάλαθον καὶ τὴν ἁρπαγὴν τὴν ὑπὸ Ἀιδωνέως καὶ
τὸ χάσμα[4] τῆς γῆς καὶ τὰς ὗς τὰς Εὐβουλέως
τὰς συγκαταποθείσας ταῖν θεαῖν,[5] δι᾽ ἣν αἰτίαν ἐν
τοῖς Θεσμοφορίοις μεγαρίζοντες χοίρους ἐμβάλ-
λουσιν; ταύτην τὴν μυθολογίαν αἱ γυναῖκες ποι-
κίλως κατὰ πόλιν ἑορτάζουσι, Θεσμοφόρια, Σκιρο-
15 P. φόρια, Ἀρρητοφόρια, πολυτρόπως τὴν Φερεφάττης
ἐκτραγῳδοῦσαι ἁρπαγήν.

Τὰ γὰρ Διονύσου μυστήρια τέλεον ἀπάνθρωπα·
ὃν εἰσέτι παῖδα ὄντα ἐνόπλῳ κινήσει περιχο-
ρευόντων Κουρήτων, δόλῳ δὲ ὑποδύντων Τιτάνων,
ἀπατήσαντες παιδαριώδεσιν ἀθύρμασιν, οὗτοι δὴ
οἱ Τιτᾶνες διέσπασαν, ἔτι νηπίαχον ὄντα, ὡς ὁ τῆς
Τελετῆς ποιητὴς Ὀρφεύς φησιν ὁ Θρᾴκιος·

> κῶνος καὶ ῥόμβος καὶ παίγνια καμπεσίγυια,
> μῆλά τε χρύσεα καλὰ παρ᾽ Ἑσπερίδων λιγυ-
> φώνων.

καὶ τῆσδε ὑμῖν τῆς τελετῆς τὰ ἀχρεῖα σύμβολα οὐκ
ἀχρεῖον εἰς κατάγνωσιν παραθέσθαι· ἀστράγαλος,

---

[1] κεντρίον Dindorf. κέντρον MSS.
[2] ἐν . . . οἶμαι] ὃν ὄρεσι κρύφιον βουκολῶ κέντρον φέρων [τὸ—οἶμαι] Tournier.
[3] διηγήσωμαι Dindorf. διηγήσομαι MSS.
[4] χάσμα from Eusebius. σχίσμα MSS.
[5] τοῖν θεοῖν Wilamowitz. τῇ θεᾷ Rohde.

also bears a child, which has the form of a bull.   To be CHAP.
II sure, we are told by a certain mythological poet that

> The bull begets a snake, the snake a bull;
> On hills the herdsman bears his mystic goad,—

the herdsman's goad being, I think, a name for the wand which the Bacchants wreathe.   Would you The rape of
Persephone have me also tell you the story of Persephone gathering flowers, of her basket, and how she was seized by Hades, of the chasm that opened in the earth, and of the swine of Eubouleus that were swallowed up along with the two deities,[a] which is the reason given for the custom of casting swine into the sacred caverns at the festival of the Thesmophoria?   This is the tale which the women celebrate at their various feasts in the city, Thesmophoria, Scirophoria, Arretophoria, where in different ways they work up into tragedy the rape of Persephone.

The mysteries of Dionysus are of a perfectly savage The
mysteries
of Dionysus character.   He was yet a child, and the Curetes were dancing around him with warlike movement, when the Titans stealthily drew near.   First they beguiled him with childish toys, and then,—these very Titans —tore him to pieces, though he was but an infant. Orpheus of Thrace, the poet of the Initiation, speaks of the

> Top, wheel and jointed dolls, with beauteous fruit
> Of gold from the clear-voiced Hesperides.

And it is worth while to quote the worthless [b] symbols of this rite of yours in order to excite condemnation :

[a] The Greek reads, "the two goddesses"; but Clement can hardly have meant this.
[b] For the word-play see p. 28, n. a.

37

CLEMENT OF ALEXANDRIA

CAP.
II
σφαῖρα, στρόβιλος, μῆλα, ῥόμβος, ἔσοπτρον, πόκος.
᾿Αθηνᾶ μὲν οὖν τὴν καρδίαν τοῦ Διονύσου ὑφελο-
μένη Παλλὰς ἐκ τοῦ πάλλειν τὴν καρδίαν προσηγο-
ρεύθη· οἱ δὲ Τιτᾶνες, οἱ καὶ διασπάσαντες αὐτόν,
λέβητά τινα τρίποδι ἐπιθέντες καὶ τοῦ Διονύσου
ἐμβαλόντες τὰ μέλη, καθήψουν πρότερον· ἔπειτα
ὀβελίσκοις περιπείραντες "ὑπείρεχον ῾Ηφαίστοιο."
Ζεὺς δὲ ὕστερον ἐπιφανείς (εἰ θεὸς ἦν, τάχα που
τῆς κνίσης τῶν ὀπτωμένων κρεῶν μεταλαβών, ἧς
δὴ τὸ "γέρας λαχεῖν" ὁμολογοῦσιν ὑμῶν οἱ θεοί)
κεραυνῷ τοὺς Τιτᾶνας αἰκίζεται καὶ τὰ μέλη τοῦ
Διονύσου ᾿Απόλλωνι τῷ παιδὶ παρακατατίθεται
καταθάψαι. ὁ δέ, οὐ γὰρ ἠπείθησε Διί, εἰς τὸν Παρ-
νασσὸν φέρων κατατίθεται διεσπασμένον τὸν νεκρόν.

Εἰ θέλεις δ' ἐποπτεῦσαι καὶ Κορυβάντων ὄργια,
16 P.
τὸν τρίτον | ἀδελφὸν ἀποκτείναντες οὗτοι τὴν κεφα-
λὴν τοῦ νεκροῦ φοινικίδι ἐπεκαλυψάτην καὶ κατα-
στέψαντε ἐθαψάτην, φέροντες ἐπὶ χαλκῆς ἀσπίδος
ὑπὸ τὰς ὑπωρείας τοῦ ᾿Ολύμπου. καὶ ταῦτ' ἔστι
τὰ μυστήρια, συνελόντι φάναι, φόνοι καὶ τάφοι· οἱ
δὲ ἱερεῖς οἱ τῶνδε, οὓς ᾿Ανακτοτελεστὰς οἷς μέλον
καλεῖν καλοῦσι, προσεπιτερατεύονται τῇ συμφορᾷ,
ὁλόριζον ἀπαγορεύοντες σέλινον ἐπὶ τραπέζης τι-
θέναι· οἴονται γὰρ δὴ ἐκ τοῦ αἵματος τοῦ ἀπορ-
ρυέντος τοῦ Κορυβαντικοῦ τὸ σέλινον ἐκπεφυκέναι·
ὥσπερ ἀμέλει καὶ αἱ θεσμοφοριάζουσαι τῆς ῥοιᾶς
τοὺς κόκκους παραφυλάττουσιν ἐσθίειν τοὺς ἀπο-

---

[a] Pallas from *pallein*.
[b] Homer, *Iliad* ii. 426. Over Hephaestus, *i.e.* the fire.
[c] *Iliad* iv. 49.
[d] The "Princes" are the Corybantes or Cabeiri. See
Pausanias x. 38. 7.

the knuckle-bone, the ball, the spinning-top, apples, CHAP.
II
wheel, mirror, fleece! Now Athena made off with
the heart of Dionysus, and received the name
Pallas from its palpitating.[a] But the Titans, they
who tore him to pieces, placed a caldron upon a
tripod, and casting the limbs of Dionysus into it first
boiled them down; then, piercing them with spits,
they "held them over Hephaestus."[b] Later on
Zeus appeared; perhaps, since he was a god, because
he smelt the steam of the flesh that was cooking,
which your gods admit they "receive as their
portion."[c] He plagues the Titans with thunder,
and entrusts the limbs of Dionysus to his son
Apollo for burial. In obedience to Zeus, Apollo
carries the mutilated corpse to Parnassus and lays it
to rest.

If you would like a vision of the Corybantic The
Corybantic
orgies
orgies also, this is the story. Two of the Corybantes
slew a third one, who was their brother, covered the
head of the corpse with a purple cloak, and then
wreathed and buried it, bearing it upon a brazen
shield to the skirts of Mount Olympus. Here we see
what the mysteries are, in one word, murders and
burials! The priests of these mysteries, whom such
as are interested in them call "Presidents of the
Princes' rites,"[d] add a portent to the dismal tale.
They forbid wild celery, root and all, to be placed on
the table, for they actually believe that wild celery
grows out of the blood that flowed from the murdered
brother.[e] It is a similar custom, of course, that is
observed by the women who celebrate the Thesmophoria. They are careful not to eat any pomegranate

[e] For this legend of the Corybantes see A. B. Cook,
Zeus, i. 107–108.

CLEMENT OF ALEXANDRIA

CAP. πεπτωκότας χαμαί, ἐκ τῶν τοῦ Διονύσου αἵματος
II σταγόνων βεβλαστηκέναι νομίζουσαι[1] τὰς ῥοιάς.
Καβείρους δὲ τοὺς Κορύβαντας καλοῦντες καὶ
τελετὴν Καβειρικὴν καταγγέλλουσιν· αὐτὼ γὰρ δὴ
τούτω τὼ ἀδελφοκτόνω τὴν κίστην ἀνελομένω, ἐν ᾗ
τὸ τοῦ Διονύσου αἰδοῖον ἀπέκειτο, εἰς Τυρρηνίαν
κατήγαγον, εὐκλεοῦς ἔμποροι φορτίου· κἀνταῦθα
διετριβέτην, φυγάδε ὄντε, τὴν πολυτίμητον εὐσεβείας
διδασκαλίαν, αἰδοῖα καὶ κίστην, θρησκεύειν παρα-
θεμένω Τυρρηνοῖς. δι' ἣν αἰτίαν οὐκ ἀπεικότως
τὸν Διόνυσόν τινες Ἄττιν προσαγορεύεσθαι θέλουσιν,
αἰδοίων ἐστερημένον.

Καὶ τί θαυμαστὸν εἰ Τυρρηνοὶ οἱ βάρβαροι αἰσχροῖς
οὕτως τελίσκονται παθήμασιν, ὅπου γε Ἀθηναίοις
καὶ τῇ ἄλλῃ Ἑλλάδι, αἰδοῦμαι καὶ λέγειν, αἰσχύνης
ἔμπλεως ἡ περὶ τὴν Δηὼ μυθολογία; ἀλωμένη
γὰρ ἡ Δηὼ κατὰ ζήτησιν τῆς θυγατρὸς τῆς Κόρης
περὶ τὴν Ἐλευσῖνα (τῆς Ἀττικῆς δέ ἐστι τοῦτο τὸ
χωρίον) ἀποκάμνει καὶ φρέατι ἐπικαθίζει λυπουμένη.
τοῦτο τοῖς μυουμένοις ἀπαγορεύεται εἰσέτι νῦν,
ἵνα μὴ δοκοῖεν οἱ τετελεσμένοι μιμεῖσθαι τὴν
17 P ὀδυρομένην. ᾤκουν | δὲ τηνικάδε τὴν Ἐλευσῖνα οἱ
γηγενεῖς· ὀνόματα αὐτοῖς Βαυβὼ καὶ Δυσαύλης
καὶ Τριπτόλεμος, ἔτι δὲ Εὔμολπός τε καὶ Εὐβου-
λεύς· βουκόλος ὁ Τριπτόλεμος ἦν, ποιμὴν δὲ ὁ
Εὔμολπος, συβώτης δὲ ὁ Εὐβουλεύς· ἀφ' ὧν τὸ
Εὐμολπιδῶν καὶ τὸ Κηρύκων τὸ ἱεροφαντικὸν δὴ
τοῦτο Ἀθήνησι γένος ἤνθησεν. καὶ δὴ (οὐ γὰρ
ἀνήσω μὴ οὐχὶ εἰπεῖν) ξενίσασα ἡ Βαυβὼ τὴν Δηὼ

---

[1] νομίζουσαι Wilamowitz.   νομίζουσι mss.

---

[a] i.e. Persephone.
[b] Literally, "the hierophantic clan." The hierophant

40

seeds which fall to the ground, being of opinion that CHAP.
pomegranates spring from the drops of Dionysus' II
blood. The Corybantes are also called by the name The rite
Cabeiri, which proclaims the rite of the Cabeiri. of the
Cabeiri
For this very pair of fratricides got possession of the
chest in which the virilia of Dionysus were deposited,
and brought it to Tuscany, traders in glorious wares!
There they sojourned, being exiles, and communicated
their precious teaching of piety, the virilia and the
chest, to Tuscans for purposes of worship. For this
reason not unnaturally some wish to call Dionysus
Attis, because he was mutilated.

Yet how can we wonder if Tuscans, who are The tale
barbarians, are thus consecrated to base passions, of Demeter
and Baubo
when Athenians and the rest of Greece—I blush
even to speak of it—possess that shameful tale
about Demeter? It tells how Demeter, wandering
through Eleusis, which is a part of Attica, in search
of her daughter the Maiden,[a] becomes exhausted
and sits down at a well in deep distress. This
display of grief is forbidden, up to the present
day, to those who are initiated, lest the worshippers
should seem to imitate the goddess in her sorrow.
At that time Eleusis was inhabited by aborigines,
whose names were Baubo, Dysaules, Triptolemus,
and also Eumolpus and Eubouleus. Triptolemus
was a herdsman, Eumolpus a shepherd, and Eubouleus a swineherd. These were progenitors of
the Eumolpidae and of the Heralds, who form the
priestly clan[b] at Athens. But to continue; for I
will not forbear to tell the rest of the story. Baubo,

(see Appendix on the Mysteries, p. 385) was chosen from
the Eumolpidae, the *dadouchos* or torch-bearer from the
Heralds.

41

CLEMENT OF ALEXANDRIA

CAP.
II
ὀρέγει κυκεῶνα αὐτῇ· τῆς δὲ ἀναινομένης λαβεῖν
καὶ πιεῖν οὐκ ἐθελούσης (πενθήρης γὰρ ἦν) περι-
αλγὴς ἡ Βαυβὼ γενομένη, ὡς ὑπεροραθεῖσα δῆθεν,
ἀναστέλλεται τὰ αἰδοῖα καὶ ἐπιδεικνύει τῇ θεῷ· ἡ
δὲ τέρπεται τῇ ὄψει ἡ Δηὼ καὶ μόλις ποτὲ δέχεται
τὸ ποτόν, ἡσθεῖσα τῷ θεάματι. ταῦτ' ἔστι τὰ
κρύφια τῶν Ἀθηναίων μυστήρια. ταῦτά τοι καὶ
Ὀρφεὺς ἀναγράφει. παραθήσομαι δέ σοι αὐτὰ τοῦ
Ὀρφέως τὰ ἔπη, ἵν' ἔχῃς μάρτυρα τῆς ἀναισχυντίας
τὸν μυσταγωγόν·

ὣς εἰποῦσα πέπλους ἀνεσύρετο, δεῖξε δὲ πάντα |
18 P. σώματος οὐδὲ πρέπονα τύπον· παῖς δ' ἦεν Ἴακχος,
χειρί τέ μιν ῥίπτασκε γελῶν Βαυβοῦς ὑπὸ κόλποις·
ἡ δ' ἐπεὶ οὖν μείδησε θεά, μείδησ' ἐνὶ θυμῷ,
δέξατο δ' αἰόλον ἄγγος, ἐν ᾧ κυκεὼν ἐνέκειτο.

κἄστι τὸ σύνθημα Ἐλευσινίων μυστηρίων· " ἐνή-
στευσα, ἔπιον τὸν κυκεῶνα, ἔλαβον ἐκ κίστης,
ἐργασάμενος[1] ἀπεθέμην εἰς κάλαθον καὶ ἐκ καλάθου
εἰς κίστην." καλά γε τὰ θεάματα καὶ θεᾷ πρέποντα.
ἄξια μὲν οὖν νυκτὸς τὰ τελέσματα καὶ πυρὸς καὶ
τοῦ " μεγαλήτορος," μᾶλλον δὲ ματαιόφρονος
Ἐρεχθειδῶν δήμου, πρὸς δὲ καὶ τῶν ἄλλων
Ἑλλήνων, οὕστινας " μένει τελευτήσαντας ἄσσα

---

[1] ἐγγευσάμενος Lobeck.

[a] The Greek word represents a mixed drink composed of
barley-meal, grated cheese and Pramnian wine. The same
word is used for the draught mentioned in the formula of
the Eleusinian mysteries.

[b] Lobeck suggested "having tasted," which meaning
can be obtained by a slight change in the Greek; see
note on text. This would bring the passage more into
line with the Phrygian formula quoted on p. 35. I have

42

having received Demeter as a guest, offers her a
draught of wine and meal.[a] She declines to take
it, being unwilling to drink on account of her
mourning. Baubo is deeply hurt, thinking she has
been slighted, and thereupon uncovers her secret
parts and exhibits them to the goddess. Demeter is
pleased at the sight, and now at last receives the
draught,—delighted with the spectacle ! These are
the secret mysteries of the Athenians ! These are
also the subjects of Orpheus' poems. I will quote
you the very lines of Orpheus, in order that you may
have the originator of the mysteries as witness of
their shamelessness :

> This said, she drew aside her robes, and showed
> A sight of shame ; child Iacchus was there,
> And laughing, plunged his hand below her breasts.
> Then smiled the goddess, in her heart she smiled,
> And drank the draught from out the glancing cup.

And the formula of the Eleusinian mysteries is as The
Eleusinian
formula
follows : " I fasted ; I drank the draught ; I took
from the chest ; having done my task,[b] I placed in
the basket, and from the basket into the chest."
Beautiful sights indeed, and fit for a goddess ! Yes,
such rites are meet for night and torch fires, and for
the " great-hearted"—I should rather say empty-
headed—people of the Erechtheidae,[c] with the rest
of the Greeks as well, " whom after death there

translated the reading of the MSS., leaving the English as
vague as is the Greek. It seems fairly clear, however, that
some of the worshippers' acts are symbolic imitations of
what the goddess is supposed to have done. See Appendix,
p. 384, n. 3.

[c] The great-hearted people of Erechtheus are mentioned
in Homer, *Iliad* ii. 547. Erechtheus, a legendary king of
Athens, had a temple, the Erechtheum, on the Acropolis.

CAP.
II
19 P.

οὐδὲ ἕλπονται." τίσι δὴ μαντεύεται Ἡράκλειτος
ὁ Ἐφέσιος; "νυκτιπό|λοις, μάγοις, βάκχοις, λήναις,
μύσταις," τούτοις ἀπειλεῖ τὰ μετὰ θάνατον, τούτοις
μαντεύεται τὸ πῦρ· " τὰ γὰρ νομιζόμενα κατὰ ἀνθρώπους μυστήρια ἀνιερωστὶ μυοῦνται."

Νόμος οὖν καὶ ὑπόληψις κενὴ τὰ μυστήρια [1] καὶ
τοῦ δράκοντος ἀπάτη τίς ἐστιν θρησκευομένη, τὰς
ἀμυήτους ὄντως μυήσεις καὶ τὰς ἀνοργιάστους
τελετὰς εὐσεβείᾳ νόθῳ προστρεπομένων. οἶαι δὲ
καὶ αἱ κίσται αἱ μυστικαί· δεῖ γὰρ ἀπογυμνῶσαι
τὰ ἅγια αὐτῶν καὶ τὰ ἄρρητα ἐξειπεῖν. οὐ σησαμαῖ
ταῦτα καὶ πυραμίδες καὶ τολύπαι καὶ πόπανα
πολυόμφαλα χόνδροι τε ἁλῶν καὶ δράκων, ὄργιον
Διονύσου Βασσάρου; οὐχὶ δὲ ῥοιαὶ πρὸς τοῖσδε καὶ
κράδαι [2] νάρθηκές τε καὶ κιττοί, πρὸς δὲ καὶ φθοῖς καὶ
μήκωνες; ταῦτ' ἐστιν αὐτῶν τὰ ἅγια. καὶ προσέτι Γῆς [3] Θέμιδος τὰ ἀπόρρητα σύμβολα ὀρίγανον,
λύχνος, ξίφος, κτεὶς γυναικεῖος, ὅς ἐστιν, εὐφήμως
καὶ μυστικῶς εἰπεῖν, μόριον γυναικεῖον. ὦ τῆς
ἐμφανοῦς ἀναισχυντίας. πάλαι μὲν ἀνθρώποις
σωφρονοῦσιν ἐπικάλυμμα ἡδονῆς νὺξ ἦν σιωπωμένη·
νυνὶ δὲ τοῖς μυουμένοις πεῖρα [4] τῆς ἀκρασίας νὺξ
ἐστι λαλουμένη, καὶ τὸ πῦρ ἐλέγχει τὰ πάθη
δᾳδουχούμενον. ἀπόσβεσον, ὦ ἱεροφάντα, τὸ πῦρ·

---

[1] τὰ μυστήρια after κενὴ Mayor : after δράκοντος mss.
[2] κράδαι Morellus. καρδίαι mss.
[3] Γῆς Wilamowitz. τῆς mss.
[4] πεῖρα Wilamowitz. ἡ ἱερὰ mss.

---

[a] See the mention of the chest in the Cabeiric rite, p.
41, and in the Eleusinian formula, p. 43.

[b] Gē Themis is the result of an emendation of Wilamowitz,
accepted by Stählin. It necessitates only a minute change

CHAP.
II
Heracleitus
bears
witness
against
those who
take part
in the
mysteries

await such things as they little expect." Against whom does Heracleitus of Ephesus utter this prophecy? Against "night-roamers, magicians, Bacchants, Lenaean revellers and devotees of the mysteries." These are the people whom he threatens with the penalties that follow death; for these he prophesies the fire. "For in unholy fashion are they initiated into the mysteries customary among men."

The mysteries, then, are mere custom and vain opinion, and it is a deceit of the serpent that men worship when, with spurious piety, they turn towards these sacred initiations that are really profanities, and solemn rites that are without sanctity. Consider, too, the contents of the mystic chests[a]; for I must strip bare their holy things and utter the unspeakable. Are they not sesame cakes, pyramid and spherical cakes, cakes with many navels, also balls of salt and a serpent, the mystic sign of Dionysus Bassareus? Are they not also pomegranates, fig branches, fennel stalks, ivy leaves, round cakes and poppies? These are their holy things! In addition, there are the unutterable symbols of Gē Themis,[b] marjoram, a lamp, a sword, and a woman's comb, which is a euphemistic expression used in the mysteries for a woman's secret parts. What manifest shamelessness! Formerly night, which drew a veil over the pleasures of temperate men, was a time for silence. But now, when night is for those who are being initiated a temptation to licentiousness, talk abounds, and the torch-fires convict unbridled passions. Quench the fire, thou priest. Shrink from the

in the Greek. The deity referred to is then the earth-goddess, of whom Demeter and Cybele are other forms.

45

CAP.
II

αἰδέσθητι, δᾳδοῦχε, τὰς λαμπάδας· ἐλέγχει σου
τὸν Ἴακχον τὸ φῶς· ἐπίτρεψον ἀποκρύψαι τῇ
νυκτὶ τὰ μυστήρια· σκότει τετιμήσθω τὰ ὄργια.
τὸ πῦρ οὐχ ὑποκρίνεται· ἐλέγχειν καὶ κολάζειν
κελεύεται.[a]

Ταῦτα τῶν ἀθέων τὰ μυστήρια· ἀθέους δὲ
εἰκότως ἀποκαλῶ τούτους, οἳ τὸν μὲν ὄντως ὄντα
θεὸν ἠγνοήκασιν, παιδίον δὲ ὑπὸ Τιτάνων δια-
σπώμενον καὶ γύναιον πενθοῦν καὶ μόρια ἄρρητα ὡς
ἀληθῶς ὑπ' αἰσχύνης ἀναισχύντως σέβουσιν, διττῇ
20 P. ἐνεσχημένοι τῇ | ἀθεότητι,[b] προτέρα μέν, καθ' ἣν
ἀγνοοῦσι τὸν θεόν, τὸν ὄντως ὄντα μὴ γνωρίζοντες
θεόν, ἑτέρα δὲ καὶ δευτέρα δὴ ταύτῃ τῇ πλάνῃ τοὺς
οὐκ ὄντας ὡς ὄντας νομίζοντες καὶ θεοὺς τούτους
ὀνομάζοντες τοὺς οὐκ ὄντως ὄντας, μᾶλλον δὲ οὐδὲ
ὄντας, μόνου δὲ τοῦ ὀνόματος τετυχηκότας. διὰ
τοῦτό τοι καὶ ὁ ἀπόστολος διελέγχει ἡμᾶς " καὶ
ἦτε ξένοι " λέγων " τῶν διαθηκῶν τῆς ἐπαγγελίας,
ἐλπίδα μὴ ἔχοντες καὶ ἄθεοι ἐν τῷ κόσμῳ."

Πολλὰ κἀγαθὰ γένοιτο τῷ τῶν Σκυθῶν βασιλεῖ,
ὅστις ποτὲ ἦν [Ἀνάχαρσις].[1] οὗτος τὸν πολίτην
τὸν ἑαυτοῦ, τὴν παρὰ Κυζικηνοῖς μητρὸς τῶν θεῶν
τελετὴν ἀπομιμούμενον παρὰ Σκύθαις τύμπανόν τε

---

[1] [Ἀνάχαρσις] Casaubon.

---

[a] Clement means that fire is God's instrument for judgment (cp. 1 Corinthians iii. 13) and punishment (St. Matthew
xviii. 8, etc.). The torch-fires of Eleusis are at once a
revelation of misdoings and a premonition of the retribution
to come ; hence they are fulfilling the fire's appointed task,
and not merely playing a spectacular part.

[b] The Greek ἄθεος means something more than " godless,"
and yet less than the positive English word " atheist." It
was applied (see next paragraph) to philosophers who denied

46

flaming brands, torchbearer. The light convicts your Iacchus. Suffer night to hide the mysteries. Let the orgies be honoured by darkness. The fire is not acting a part; to convict and to punish is its duty.[a]

These are the mysteries of the atheists.[b] And I am right in branding as atheists men who are ignorant of the true God, but shamelessly worship a child being torn to pieces by Titans, a poor grief-stricken woman, and parts of the body which, from a sense of shame, are truly too sacred to speak of. It is a twofold atheism in which they are entangled; first, the atheism of being ignorant of God (since they do not recognize the true God); and then this second error, of believing in the existence of beings that have no existence, and calling by the name of gods those who are not really gods,—nay more, who do not even exist, but have only got the name. No doubt this is also the reason why the Apostle convicts us, when he says, " And ye were strangers from the covenants of the promise, being without hope and atheists in the world."[c]

Blessings be upon the Scythian king, whoever he was. When a countryman of his own was imitating among the Scythians the rite of the Mother of the Gods as practised at Cyzicus, by beating a drum and

the existence of the gods; also to Christians, partly on the same ground, partly because they could show no image of their own God. As used here, the word conveys a theological rather than a moral imputation, so that " atheist " is the nearest rendering. Clement continually retorts that his adversaries were the true atheists. See p. 145.

[c] Ephesians ii. 12. " Without God " is the rendering in both the Authorized and the Revised Versions; but " atheist " is necessary here to bring out the point.

Greeks are the real atheists

Noble example of a Scythian king

47

CAP.
II
ἐπικτυποῦντα καὶ κύμβαλον ἐπηχοῦντα καὶ τοῦ
τραχήλου τινὰ μηναγύρτην ἐξηρτημένον, κατετόξευ-
σεν, ὡς ἄνανδρον αὐτόν τε παρ᾽ Ἕλλησι γεγενημέ-
νον καὶ τῆς θηλείας τοῖς ἄλλοις Σκυθῶν διδάσκαλον
νόσου. ὧν δὴ χάριν (οὐ γὰρ οὐδαμῶς ἀποκρυπτέον)
θαυμάζειν ἔπεισί μοι ὅτῳ τρόπῳ Εὐήμερον τὸν
Ἀκραγαντῖνον καὶ Νικάνορα τὸν Κύπριον καὶ
Διαγόραν καὶ Ἵππωνα τὼ Μηλίω[1] τόν τε Κυρηναῖον
ἐπὶ τούτοις ἐκεῖνον ([ὁ][2] Θεόδωρος ὄνομα αὐτῷ)

21 P. καί τινας ἄλλους συχνούς, σωφρόνως βεβιωκότας
καὶ καθεωρακότας ὀξύτερόν που τῶν λοιπῶν
ἀνθρώπων τὴν ἀμφὶ τοὺς θεοὺς τούτους πλάνην,
ἀθέους ἐπικεκλήκασιν, εἰ καὶ τὴν ἀλήθειαν αὐτὴν
μὴ νενοηκότας, ἀλλὰ τὴν πλάνην γε ὑπωπτευκότας,
ὅπερ οὐ σμικρὸν εἰς ἀλήθειαν[3] φρονήσεως ζώπυρον
ἀναφύεται σπέρμα· ὧν ὁ μέν τις παρεγγυᾷ τοῖς
Αἰγυπτίοις, " εἰ θεοὺς νομίζετε, μὴ θρηνεῖτε αὐτοὺς
μηδὲ κόπτεσθε· εἰ δὲ πενθεῖτε αὐτούς, μηκέτι
τούτους ἡγεῖσθε εἶναι θεούς," ὁ δ᾽ Ἡρακλέα ἐκ
ξύλου λαβὼν κατεσκευασμένον (ἔτυχε δὲ ἔψων τι
οἴκοι, οἷα εἰκός) " εἶα δή, ὦ Ἡράκλεις," εἶπεν·
" νῦν σοι ἤδη καιρός, ὥσπερ Εὐρυσθεῖ, ἀτὰρ δὴ καὶ
ἡμῖν ὑπουργῆσαι τὸν τρισκαιδέκατον τοῦτον ἆθλον
καὶ Διαγόρᾳ τοὔψον[4] παρασκευάσαι." κᾆτ᾽ αὐτὸν
εἰς τὸ πῦρ ἐνέθηκεν ὡς ξύλον.

[1] τὼ Μηλίω Münzel. τὸν μήλιον MSS.
[2] [ὁ] Dindorf.
[3] ἀλήθειαν Sylburg. ἀληθείας MSS.
[4] τοὔψον Cobet. τοῦτον MSS.

[a] Literally a " menagyrtes " or " metragyrtes," that is, a
wandering priest of Cybele, the Mother of the Gods. See
p. 168, n. a, for a further description of these priests.
[b] Herodotus iv. 76.

48

clanging a cymbal, and by having images of the CHAP.
goddess suspended from his neck after the manner II
of a priest of Cybele,[a] this king slew him with an
arrow,[b] on the ground that the man, having been
deprived of his own virility in Greece, was now
communicating the effeminate disease to his fellow
Scythians. All this—for I must not in the least The term
conceal what I think—makes me amazed how the "atheist"
term atheist has been applied to Euhemerus of applied
Acragas, Nicanor of Cyprus, Diagoras and Hippo of by Greeks
Melos, with that Cyrenian named Theodorus and a
good many others besides, men who lived sensible
lives and discerned more acutely, I imagine, than
the rest of mankind the error connected with these
gods. Even if they did not perceive the truth itself,
they at least suspected the error; and this suspicion
is a living spark of wisdom, and no small one, which
grows up like a seed into truth. One of them thus
directs the Egyptians: "If you believe they are
gods, do not lament them, nor beat the breast; but
if you mourn for them, no longer consider these
beings to be gods."[c] Another, having taken hold
of a Heracles made from a log of wood—he happened,
likely enough, to be cooking something at home—
said: "Come, Heracles, now is your time to under-
take this thirteenth labour for me, as you did the
twelve for Eurystheus, and prepare Diagoras his
dish!" Then he put him into the fire like a log.

[c] The philosopher referred to is Xenophanes. See
Plutarch, *Amatorius* 763 D and *De Is. et Osir.* 379 B. Mourning for dead gods was a conspicuous feature of some ancient
religions. In Egypt Osiris was mourned for (see the
reference to his funeral rites on pp. 109–11); in Asia Minor,
Attis; and Adonis in Syria. The "weeping for Tammuz"
of Ezekiel viii. 14 is an example of Adonis-worship.

CLEMENT OF ALEXANDRIA

Ἀκρότητες ἄρα ἀμαθίας ἀθεότης καὶ δεισιδαιμονία, ὧν ἐκτὸς μένειν σπουδαστέον. οὐχ ὁρᾷς τὸν
ἱεροφάντην τῆς ἀληθείας Μωσέα προστάττοντα
θλαδίαν καὶ ἀποκεκομμένον μὴ ἐκκλησιάζειν, καὶ
προσέτι τὸν ἐκ πόρνης; αἰνίττεται δὲ διὰ μὲν
τῶν προτέρων τὸν ἄθεον τρόπον τὸν τῆς θείας καὶ
γονίμου δυνάμεως ἐστερημένον, διὰ δὲ τοῦ λοιποῦ
τοῦ τρίτου τὸν πολλοὺς ἐπιγραφόμενον ψευδωνύμους
θεοὺς ἀντὶ τοῦ μόνου ὄντος θεοῦ, ὥσπερ ὁ ἐκ τῆς
πόρνης τοὺς πολλοὺς ἐπιγράφεται πατέρας ἀγνοίᾳ
τοῦ πρὸς ἀλήθειαν πατρός. ἦν δέ τις ἔμφυτος
ἀρχαία πρὸς οὐρανὸν ἀνθρώποις κοινωνία, ἀγνοίᾳ
μὲν ἐσκοτισμένη, ἄφνω δέ που διεκθρώσκουσα τοῦ
σκότους καὶ ἀναλάμπουσα, οἷον δὴ ἐκεῖνο λέλεκταί
τινι τὸ

> ὁρᾷς τὸν ὑψοῦ τόνδ' ἄπειρον αἰθέρα
> καὶ γῆν πέριξ ἔχονθ' ὑγραῖς ἐν ἀγκάλαις;

καὶ τὸ

> ὦ γῆς ὄχημα κἀπὶ γῆς ἔχων ἕδραν,
> ὅστις ποτ' εἶ σύ, δυστόπαστος εἰσιδεῖν, |

22 P. καὶ ὅσα ἄλλα τοιαῦτα ποιητῶν ἄδουσι παῖδες.

Ἔννοιαι δὲ ἡμαρτημέναι καὶ παρηγμέναι τῆς
εὐθείας, ὀλέθριαι ὡς ἀληθῶς, τὸ οὐράνιον φυτόν,
τὸν ἄνθρωπον, οὐρανίου ἐξέτρεψαν διαίτης καὶ
ἐξετάνυσαν ἐπὶ γῆς, γηίνοις προσανέχειν ἀναπεί-
σασαι πλάσμασιν. οἱ μὲν γὰρ εὐθέως ἀμφὶ τὴν

---

[a] " Hierophant " is the literal rendering. For the
hierophant's office see p. 40, n. b, and Appendix p. 385.
[b] See Deuteronomy xxiii. 1, 2.

EXHORTATION TO THE GREEKS

It appears then that atheism and daemon-worship CHAP. are the extreme points of stupidity, from which we II must earnestly endeavour to keep ourselves apart. Atheism Do you not see Moses, the sacred interpreter [a] of the worship truth, ordering that no eunuch or mutilated man due to shall enter the assembly, nor the son of a harlot? [b] By the first two expressions he refers in a figure to the atheistic manner of life, which has been deprived of divine power and fruitfulness; by the third and last, to the man who lays claim to many gods, falsely so called, in place of the only real God; just as the son of a harlot lays claim to many fathers, through ignorance of his true father. But there was of old Man has implanted in man a certain fellowship with heaven, an innate which, though darkened through ignorance, yet at with heaven times leaps suddenly out of the darkness and shines forth. Take for instance the well-known lines in which someone has said,

> Seest thou this boundless firmament on high,
> Whose arms enfold the earth in soft embrace? [c]

and these,

> O stay of earth, that hast thy seat above,
> Whoe'er thou art, by guessing scarce discerned; [d]

and all the other similar things which the sons of the poets sing.

But opinions that are mistaken and deviate from False the right—deadly opinions, in very truth—turned opinion aside man, the heavenly plant, [e] from a heavenly man to manner of life, and stretched him upon earth, by idolatry inducing him to give heed to things formed out of earth. Some men were deceived from the first

---

[c] Euripides, *Frag.* 935.
[d] Euripides, *Trojan Women* 884–5.
[e] Plato, *Timaeus* 90 A; cp. p. 217.

CAP.
II
οὐρανοῦ θέαν ἀπατώμενοι καὶ ὄψει μόνῃ πεπιστευκότες τῶν ἀστέρων τὰς κινήσεις ἐπιθεώμενοι
ἐθαύμασάν τε καὶ ἐξεθείασαν, θεοὺς ἐκ τοῦ θεῖν
ὀνομάσαντες τοὺς ἀστέρας, καὶ προσεκύνησαν ἥλιον,
ὡς Ἰνδοί, καὶ σελήνην, ὡς Φρύγες· οἱ δὲ τῶν ἐκ
γῆς φυομένων τοὺς ἡμέρους δρεπόμενοι καρποὺς
Δηὼ τὸν σῖτον, ὡς Ἀθηναῖοι, καὶ Διόνυσον τὴν
ἄμπελον, ὡς Θηβαῖοι, προσηγόρευσαν. ἄλλοι τὰς
ἀμοιβὰς τῆς κακίας ἐπισκοπήσαντες θεοποιοῦσι τὰς
ἀντιδόσεις προσκυνοῦντες καὶ τὰς συμφοράς. ἐντεῦθεν τὰς Ἐρινύας καὶ τὰς Εὐμενίδας Παλαμναίους
τε καὶ Προστροπαίους, ἔτι δὲ Ἀλάστορας ἀναπε-
πλάκασιν οἱ ἀμφὶ τὴν σκηνὴν ποιηταί. φιλοσόφων
δὲ ἤδη τινὲς καὶ αὐτοὶ μετὰ τοὺς ποιητικοὺς τῶν
ἐν ὑμῖν παθῶν ἀνειδωλοποιοῦσι τύπους τὸν Φόβον
καὶ τὸν Ἔρωτα καὶ τὴν Χαρὰν καὶ τὴν Ἐλπίδα,
ὥσπερ ἀμέλει καὶ Ἐπιμενίδης ὁ παλαιὸς Ὕβρεως
καὶ Ἀναιδείας Ἀθήνησιν ἀναστήσας βωμούς· οἱ
δὲ ἐξ αὐτῶν ὁρμώμενοι τῶν πραγμάτων ἐκθεοῦνται
τοῖς ἀνθρώποις καὶ σωματικῶς ἀναπλάττονται,
Δίκη τις καὶ Κλωθὼ καὶ Λάχεσις καὶ Ἄτροπος
καὶ Εἱμαρμένη, Αὐξώ τε καὶ Θαλλώ, αἱ Ἀττικαί.
ἕκτος ἐστὶν εἰσηγητικὸς τρόπος ἀπάτης θεῶν
περιποιητικός, καθ' ὃν ἀριθμοῦσι θεοὺς τοὺς δώδεκα·
ὧν καὶ θεογονίαν Ἡσίοδος ᾄδει τὴν αὑτοῦ, καὶ
ὅσα θεολογεῖ Ὅμηρος. τελευταῖος δὲ ὑπολείπεται
(ἑπτὰ γὰρ οἱ ἅπαντες οὗτοι τρόποι) ὁ ἀπὸ τῆς

---

[a] This fanciful derivation comes from Plato, *Cratylus*
397 c–d, where Socrates is made to say that the first Greeks
had only the earth and the heavenly bodies for gods. Since
these were in perpetual movement (*thein*, to run) they called

about the spectacle of the heavens. Trusting solely to sight, they gazed at the movements of the heavenly bodies, and in wonder deified them, giving them the name of gods from their running motion.[a] Hence they worshipped the sun, as Indians do, and the moon, as Phrygians do. Others, when gathering the cultivated fruits of plants that spring from the earth, called the corn Demeter, as the Athenians, and the vine Dionysus, as the Thebans. Others, after reflecting upon the punishments of evil-doing, make gods out of their experiences of retribution, worshipping the very calamities. This is the source from which the Erinyes and Eumenides, goddesses of expiation and vengeance, as well as the Alastors,[b] have been fashioned by the poets of the stage. Even certain of the philosophers themselves, following the men of poetry, came to represent as deities the types of your emotions, such as Fear, Love, Joy, Hope; just as, of course, Epimenides did of old, when he set up altars in Athens to Insolence and Shamelessness. Some gods arise from the mere circumstances of life deified in men's eyes and fashioned in bodily form; such are the Athenian deities, Right, the Spinner, the Giver of lots, the Inflexible One, Destiny, Growth and Abundance. There is a sixth way of introducing deception and of procuring gods, according to which men reckon them to be twelve in number, of whose genealogy Hesiod sings his own story, and Homer, too, has much to say about them. Finally (for these ways of error are seven in all), there remains that which arises from the divine

CHAP. II
Causes of idolatry (i.) deification of heavenly bodies
(ii.) deification of the fruits of the earth
(iii.) gods invented to account for calamities
(iv.) gods who are types of human emotions
(v.) gods who arise from human affairs
(vi.) the Homeric pantheon
(vii.) deified heroes

them gods (*theoi*). On learning about other gods they extended the name to them.

[b] *i.e.* avenging deities.

53

CAP.
II
θείας εὐεργεσίας τῆς εἰς τοὺς ἀνθρώπους κατα-
γινομένης ὁρμώμενος. τὸν γὰρ εὐεργετοῦντα μὴ
συνιέντες θεὸν ἀνέπλασάν τινας σωτῆρας Διοσκού-
ρους καὶ Ἡρακλέα ἀλεξίκακον καὶ Ἀσκληπιὸν |
23 P. ἰατρόν.

Αὗται μὲν αἱ ὀλισθηραί τε καὶ ἐπιβλαβεῖς παρεκβάσεις τῆς ἀληθείας, καθέλκουσαι οὐρανόθεν τὸν
ἄνθρωπον καὶ εἰς βάραθρον περιτρέπουσαι. ἐθέλω
δὲ ὑμῖν ἐν χρῷ τοὺς θεοὺς αὐτοὺς ἐπιδεῖξαι ὁποῖοί
τινες καὶ εἴ τινες, ἵν᾿ ἤδη ποτὲ τῆς πλάνης λήξητε,
αὖθις δὲ παλινδρομήσητε εἰς οὐρανόν. "ἦμεν γάρ
που καὶ ἡμεῖς τέκνα ὀργῆς, ὡς καὶ οἱ λοιποί· ὁ δὲ
θεὸς πλούσιος ὢν ἐν ἐλέει, διὰ τὴν πολλὴν ἀγάπην
αὐτοῦ, ἣν ἠγάπησεν ἡμᾶς, ὄντας ἤδη νεκροὺς τοῖς
παραπτώμασιν συνεζωοποίησεν τῷ Χριστῷ." ζῶν
γὰρ ὁ λόγος καὶ ⟨ὁ⟩[1] συνταφεὶς Χριστῷ συνυψοῦται
θεῷ. οἱ δὲ ἔτι ἄπιστοι "τέκνα ὀργῆς" ὀνομάζον-
ται, τρεφόμενα ὀργῇ· ἡμεῖς δὲ οὐκ ὀργῆς θρέμματα
ἔτι, οἱ τῆς πλάνης ἀπεσπασμένοι, ἄσσοντες δὲ ἐπὶ
τὴν ἀλήθειαν. ταύτῃ τοι ἡμεῖς οἱ τῆς ἀνομίας υἱοί
ποτε διὰ τὴν φιλανθρωπίαν τοῦ λόγου νῦν υἱοὶ
γεγόναμεν τοῦ θεοῦ· ὑμῖν δὲ καὶ ὁ ὑμέτερος
ὑποδύεται ποιητὴς ὁ Ἀκραγαντῖνος Ἐμπεδοκλῆς·

τοιγάρτοι χαλεπῇσιν ἀλύοντες κακότησιν
οὔ ποτε δειλαίων ἀχέων λωφήσετε θυμόν.

τὰ μὲν δὴ πλεῖστα μεμύθευται καὶ πέπλασται περὶ
θεῶν ὑμῖν· τὰ δὲ ὅσα καὶ [2] γεγενῆσθαι ὑπείληπται,
ταῦτα δὲ περὶ ἀνθρώπων αἰσχρῶν καὶ ἀσελγῶς
βεβιωκότων ἀναγέγραπται·

---

[1] ⟨ὁ⟩ inserted by Schwartz.
[2] ὅσα καὶ Mayor. [καὶ] ὅσα Stählin. καὶ ὅσα MSS.

beneficence shown towards men ; for, since men did
not understand that it was God who benefited them,
they invented certain saviours, the Twin Brothers,
Heracles averter of evils, and Asclepius the doctor.

These then are the slippery and harmful paths
which lead away from the truth, dragging man down
from heaven and overturning him into the pit. But
I wish to display to you at close quarters the gods
themselves, showing what their characters are, and
whether they really exist; in order that at last
you may cease from error and run back again to
heaven. " For we too were once children of wrath,
as also the rest ; but God being rich in mercy,
through His great love wherewith He loved us, when
we were already dead in trespasses, made us alive
together with Christ." [a]   For the Word is living, and
he who has been buried with Christ is exalted
together with God. They who are still unbelieving
are called " children of wrath," since they are being
reared for wrath. We, on the contrary, are no longer
creatures of wrath, for we have been torn away from
error and are hastening towards the truth. Thus we
who were once sons of lawlessness have now become
sons of God thanks to the love of the Word for man.
But you are they whom even your own poet, Empedocles of Acragas, points to in these lines :

> So then, by grievous miseries distraught,
> Ye ne'er shall rest your mind from woeful pains. [b]

Now the most part of the stories about your gods are
legends and fictions. But as many as are held to
be real events are the records of base men who led
dissolute lives :

[a] Ephesians ii. 3–5.   [b] Empedocles, *Frag.* 145 Diels.

CAP.
II

τύφῳ καὶ μανίῃ δὲ βαδίζετε καὶ τρίβον ὀρθὴν
εὐθεῖαν προλιπόντες ἀπήλθετε τὴν δι' ἀκανθῶν
καὶ σκολόπων. τί πλανᾶσθε, βροτοί; παύσασθε,
μάταιοι,

καλλίπετε σκοτίην νυκτός, φωτὸς δὲ λάβεσθε. |

24 P. ταῦτα ἡμῖν ἡ προφητικὴ παρεγγυᾷ καὶ ποιητικὴ
Σίβυλλα· παρεγγυᾷ δὲ καὶ ἡ ἀλήθεια, γυμνοῦσα
τῶν καταπληκτικῶν τουτωνὶ καὶ ἐκπληκτικῶν
προσωπείων τὸν ὄχλον τῶν θεῶν, συνωνυμίαις τισὶ
τὰς δοξοποιίας διελέγχουσα.

Αὐτίκα γοῦν εἰσὶν οἳ τρεῖς τοὺς Ζῆνας ἀναγρά-
φουσιν, τὸν μὲν Αἰθέρος ἐν Ἀρκαδίᾳ, τὼ δὲ λοιπὼ
τοῦ Κρόνου παῖδε, τούτοιν τὸν μὲν ἐν Κρήτῃ, θάτερον
δὲ ἐν Ἀρκαδίᾳ πάλιν. εἰσὶ δὲ οἳ πέντε Ἀθηνᾶς
ὑποτίθενται, τὴν μὲν Ἡφαίστου, τὴν Ἀθηναίαν·
τὴν δὲ Νείλου, τὴν Αἰγυπτίαν· τρίτην ⟨τὴν⟩[1] τοῦ
Κρόνου, τὴν πολέμου εὑρέτιν· τετάρτην τὴν Διός,
ἣν Μεσσήνιοι Κορυφασίαν ἀπὸ τῆς μητρὸς ἐπι-
κεκλήκασιν· ἐπὶ πᾶσι τὴν Πάλλαντος καὶ Τιτανίδος
τῆς Ὠκεανοῦ, ἣ τὸν πατέρα δυσσεβῶς καταθύσασα
τῷ πατρῴῳ κεκόσμηται δέρματι ὥσπερ κῳδίῳ.

---

[1] ⟨τὴν⟩ inserted by Wilamowitz.

ᵃ Sibylline Oracles, Preface, 23–25, 27.
ᵇ The word Sibyl was applied to prophetesses who
delivered oracles at certain shrines, such as Cumae or
Erythrae. It was appropriated by the authors of that long
series of pseudo-prophetic verses which has come down to
us under the title of the Sibylline Oracles. These date from
various periods between the second century B.C. and the
seventh century A.D. The earliest oracle is a Jewish work,
written in Egypt. Many of the subsequent ones are of
Christian, or Jewish-Christian, authorship. Their chief
object was to denounce the folly of polytheism and image-

> But ye in pride and madness walk ; ye left
> The true, straight path, and chose the way through
>   thorns
> And stakes. Why err, ye mortals? Cease, vain men !
> Forsake dark night, and cleave unto the light.[a]

This is what the prophetic and poetic Sibyl[b] enjoins on us. And truth, too, does the same, when she strips these dreadful and terrifying masks from the crowd of gods, and adduces certain similarities of name to prove the absurdity of your rash opinions.

For example, there are some who record three gods of the name of Zeus[c]: one in Arcadia, the son of Aether, the other two being sons of Cronus, the one in Crete, the other again in Arcadia. Some assume five Athenas: the daughter of Hephaestus, who is the Athenian ; the daughter of Neilus, who is the Egyptian[d]; a third, the daughter of Cronus, who is the discoverer of war; a fourth, the daughter of Zeus, to whom Messenians give the title Coryphasia after her mother. Above all, there is the child of Pallas and Titanis daughter of Oceanus. This is the one who impiously slaughtered her father and is arrayed in the paternal skin, as though it were a

Many
different
gods bear
the same
name

worship, and they are frequently quoted by the early Christian Fathers. Clement would seem to have believed in the antiquity of those known to him, for he asserts (see p. 161) that Xenophon borrowed from them.

[c] With this paragraph compare Cicero, *De natura deorum* iii. 53–59. Both Cicero and Clement are using the work of the "theologians" (*theologoi*), who tried to reduce to some system the mass of Greek legend. On the reasons for this multiplication of gods see Gardner and Jevons, *Manual of Greek Antiquities*, pp. 95–96.

[d] A goddess worshipped at Sais in Egypt, whom the Greeks identified with Athena. See Herodotus ii. 59, etc.

CAP
II
ναὶ μὴν Ἀπόλλωνα ὁ μὲν Ἀριστοτέλης πρῶτον
Ἡφαίστου καὶ Ἀθηνᾶς (ἐνταῦθα δὴ οὐκέτι παρθένος
ἡ Ἀθηνᾶ), δεύτερον ἐν Κρήτῃ τὸν Κύρβαντος,
τρίτον τὸν Διὸς καὶ τέταρτον τὸν Ἀρκάδα τὸν
Σιληνοῦ· Νόμιος οὗτος κέκληται παρὰ Ἀρκάσιν·
ἐπὶ τούτοις τὸν Λίβυν καταλέγει τὸν Ἄμμωνος·
ὁ δὲ Δίδυμος ὁ γραμματικὸς τούτοις ἕκτον ἐπιφέρει
τὸν Μάγνητος. πόσοι δὲ καὶ νῦν Ἀπόλλωνες,
ἀναρίθμητοι θνητοὶ καὶ ἐπίκηροί[1] τινες ἄνθρωποι,
εἰσίν, οἱ παραπλησίως τοῖς προειρημένοις ἐκείνοις
κεκλημένοι; τί δ᾽ εἴ σοι τοὺς πολλοὺς εἴποιμι
Ἀσκληπιοὺς ἢ τοὺς Ἑρμᾶς τοὺς ἀριθμουμένους ἢ
τοὺς Ἡφαίστους τοὺς μυθολογουμένους; μὴ καὶ
περιττὸς εἶναι δόξω τὰς ἀκοὰς ὑμῶν τοῖς πολλοῖς
τούτοις ἐπικλύζων ὀνόμασιν; ἀλλ᾽ αἵ γε πατρίδες
αὐτοὺς καὶ αἱ τέχναι καὶ οἱ βίοι, πρὸς δέ γε καὶ οἱ
τάφοι ἀνθρώπους γεγονότας διελέγχουσιν.

Ἄρης γοῦν ὁ καὶ παρὰ τοῖς ποιηταῖς, ὡς οἷόν τε,
τετιμημένος,

Ἆρες, Ἆρες, βροτολοιγέ, μιαιφόνε, τειχεσιπλῆτα,

25 P. ὁ ἀλλοπρόσαλλος οὗτος καὶ ἀνάρσιος, ὡς μὲν
Ἐπίχαρμός φησι, Σπαρτιάτης ἦν· Σοφοκλῆς δὲ
Θρᾷκα οἶδεν αὐτόν· ἄλλοι δὲ Ἀρκάδα. τοῦτον δὲ
Ὅμηρος δεδέσθαι φησὶν ἐπὶ μῆνας τρισκαίδεκα·

---

[1] ἐπίκηροι Mayor.   ἐπίκουροι MSS.

---

[a] The skin usually worn by Athena is the *aegis*, a goatskin
ornamented with the head of the Gorgon, whom she had
slain. Clement's story is evidently another explanation of
the *aegis*. See Cicero, *De natura deorum* iii. 59.

58

fleece.[a]   Further, with regard to Apollo, Aristotle CHAP.
enumerates, first, the son of Hephaestus and Athena   II
(which puts an end to Athena's virginity); secondly,
the son of Cyrbas in Crete; thirdly, the son of
Zeus; and fourthly, the Arcadian, the son of Silenus,
called among the Arcadians Nomius.[b]   In addition
to these he reckons the Libyan, the son of Ammon;
and Didymus the grammarian adds a sixth, the son
of Magnes.   And how many Apollos are there at
the present time?   A countless host, all mortal and
perishable men, who have been called by similar
names to the deities we have just mentioned.
And what if I were to tell you of the many gods
named Asclepius, or of every Hermes that is
enumerated, or of every Hephaestus that occurs
in your mythology?   Shall I not seem to be
needlessly drowning your ears by the number of
their names?   But the lands they dwelt in, the The gods
arts they practised, the records of their lives, were really
yes, and their very tombs, prove conclusively that lived and
they were men. worked on
    There is for example Ares, who is honoured, so Examples
far as that is possible, in the poets— in proof:
Ares

Ares, thou plague of men, bloodguilty one, stormer of cities ;[c]

this fickle and implacable god was, according to
Epicharmus, a Spartan.   But Sophocles knows him
for a Thracian, others for an Arcadian.   This is the
god of whom Homer says that he was bound in
chains for a space of thirteen months:

[b] *i.e.* the "pastoral" god, from *nomeus* a shepherd.
   [c] Homer, *Iliad* v. 31 and 455.

CAP.
II

τλῆ μὲν Ἄρης, ὅτε μιν Ὦτος κρατερός τ᾽ Ἐφιάλτης,
παῖδες Ἀλωῆος, δῆσαν κρατερῷ ἐνὶ δεσμῷ·
χαλκέῳ δ᾽ ἐν κεράμῳ δέδετο τρισκαίδεκα μῆνας.

πολλὰ κἀγαθὰ Κᾶρες σχοῖεν, οἳ καταθύουσιν αὐτῷ
τοὺς κύνας. Σκύθαι δὲ τοὺς ὄνους ἱερεύοντες μὴ
παυέσθων, ὡς Ἀπολλόδωρός φησι καὶ Καλλίμαχος,

Φοῖβος Ὑπερβορέοισιν ὄνων ἐπιτέλλεται ἱροῖς.

ὁ αὐτὸς δὲ ἀλλαχοῦ

τέρπουσιν λιπαραὶ Φοῖβον ὀνοσφαγίαι.

Ἥφαιστος δέ, ὃν ἔρριψεν ἐξ Ὀλύμπου Ζεὺς " βηλοῦ
ἀπὸ θεσπεσίοιο," ἐν Λήμνῳ καταπεσὼν ἐχάλκευε,
πηρωθεὶς τὼ πόδε, " ὑπὸ δὲ κνῆμαι ῥώοντο
ἀραιαί." ἔχεις καὶ ἰατρόν, οὐχὶ χαλκέα μόνον ἐν
θεοῖς· ὁ δὲ ἰατρὸς φιλάργυρος ἦν, Ἀσκληπιὸς
ὄνομα αὐτῷ. καί σοι τὸν σὸν παραθήσομαι ποιητήν,
τὸν Βοιώτιον Πίνδαρον·

ἔτραπε κἀκεῖνον ἀγάνορι μισθῷ χρυσὸς ἐν χερσὶ
φανείς·

26 P. χερσὶ δ᾽ ἄρα Κρονίων | ῥίψας δι᾽ ἀμφοῖν ἀμπνοὰν[1]
στέρνων καθεῖλεν
ὠκέως, αἴθων δὲ κεραυνὸς ἐνέσκηψε[2] μόρον,
καὶ Εὐριπίδης

Ζεὺς γὰρ κατακτὰς παῖδα τὸν ἐμὸν αἴτιος
Ἀσκληπιόν, στέρνοισιν ἐμβαλὼν φλόγα.

---

[1] ἀμπνοὰν Pindar. ἀμπνοὰς MSS.
[2] ἐνέσκηψε Pindar. ἔσκηψε MSS.

---

[a] Homer, *Iliad* v. 385–387.
[b] Phoebus is of course Apollo. The thought of dogs
being offered to Ares leads Clement on to describe, in a
characteristic digression, an even more absurd sacrifice.
[c] Callimachus, Fragments 187–8 Schneider.

Such was the lot of Ares, when Otus and strong Ephialtes,   CHAP.
Sons of Aloeus, seized him, and chained his limbs in strong   II
    fetters ;
And in a dungeon of brass for thirteen months he lay
    captive.[a]

Blessings be upon the Carians, who sacrifice dogs to
him ! May Scythians never cease offering asses, as
Apollodorus says they do, and Callimachus too, in the
following verse :

> In northern lands ass-sacrifices rise
> When Phoebus first appears.[b]

Elsewhere the same writer says :

> Rich sacrifice of asses Phoebus loves.[c]

Hephaestus, whom Zeus cast out of Olympus, " from
the threshold of heaven," [d] fell to earth in Lemnos
and worked as a smith. He was lame in both feet,
" but his slender legs moved quickly under him." [e]
You have not only a smith among the gods, but a
doctor as well. The doctor was fond of money, and Asclepius
his name was Asclepius. I will quote your own poet,
Pindar the Boeotian :

> Gold was his ruin ; it shone in his hands,
> Splendid reward for a deed of skill ;
> Lo ! from the arm of Zeus on high
> Darted the gleaming bolt for ill ;
> Snatched from the man his new-found breath,
> Whelmed the god in a mortal's death.[f]

And Euripides says :

> 'Twas due to Zeus ; he slew Asclepius,
> My son,—with lightning flame that pierced his heart.[g]

---

[d] Homer, *Iliad* i. 591.   [e] *Iliad* xviii. 411.
[f] Pindar, *Pythian Odes* iii. 97, 100–105.
[g] Euripides, *Alcestis* 3–4.

CLEMENT OF ALEXANDRIA

οὗτος μὲν οὖν κεῖται κεραυνωθεὶς ἐν τοῖς Κυνοσ-
ουρίδος ὁρίοις. Φιλόχορος δὲ ἐν Τήνῳ Ποσειδῶνά
φησι τιμᾶσθαι ἰατρόν, Κρόνῳ δὲ ἐπικεῖσθαι Σικε-
λίαν καὶ ἐνταῦθα αὐτὸν τεθάφθαι. Πατροκλῆς τε
ὁ Θούριος καὶ Σοφοκλῆς ὁ νεώτερος ἔν τισι[1] τραγῳδίαις ἱστορεῖτον[2] τοῖν Διοσκούροιν[3] πέρι· ἀνθρώ-
πω τινὲ τούτω τὼ Διοσκούρω ἐπικήρω ἐγενέσθην,[4]
εἴ τῳ ἱκανὸς πιστώσασθαι Ὅμηρος τὸ λελεγμένον

> τοὺς δ᾽ ἤδη κάτεχεν φυσίζοος αἶα
> ἐν Λακεδαίμονι αὖθι, φίλῃ ἐν πατρίδι γαίῃ.

προσίτω δὲ καὶ ὁ τὰ Κυπριακὰ ποιήματα γράψας

> Κάστωρ μὲν θνητός, θανάτου δέ οἱ αἶσα πέπρωται·
> αὐτὰρ ὅ γ᾽ ἀθάνατος Πολυδεύκης, ὅζος Ἄρηος.

τοῦτο μὲν ποιητικῶς ἐψεύσατο· Ὅμηρος δὲ ἀξιο-
πιστότερος αὐτοῦ εἰπὼν περὶ ἀμφοῖν τοῖν Διοσκούροιν, πρὸς δὲ καὶ τὸν Ἡρακλέα εἴδωλον ἐλέγξας·
" φῶτα " γὰρ " Ἡρακλῆα, μεγάλων ἐπίστορα
ἔργων." Ἡρακλέα οὖν καὶ αὐτὸς Ὅμηρος θνητὸν
οἶδεν ἄνθρωπον, Ἱερώνυμος δὲ ὁ φιλόσοφος καὶ
τὴν σχέσιν αὐτοῦ ὑφηγεῖται τοῦ σώματος, μικρόν,
φριξότριχα, ῥωστικόν· Δικαίαρχος δὲ σχιζίαν,
νευρώδη, μέλανα, γρυπόν, ὑποχαροπόν, τετανό-
τριχα. οὗτος οὖν ὁ Ἡρακλῆς δύο πρὸς τοῖς
πεντήκοντα ἔτη βεβιωκὼς κατέστρεψε τὸν βίον διὰ
27 P. τῆς ἐν Οἴτῃ πυρᾶς | κεκηδευμένος.

---

[1] ἔν τισι Welcker.   ἐν τρισί MSS.
[2] ἱστορεῖτον Sylburg.   ἱστορεῖτων MSS.
[3] τοῖν Διοσκούροιν Sylburg.   τὼ Διοσκούρω MSS.
[4] ἐγενέσθην Dindorf.   γενέσθην MSS.

[a] Homer, *Iliad* iii. 243–244.

This god, then, killed by the thunderbolt, lies on the CHAP.
II frontier of Cynosuris. But Philochorus says that in Poseidon Tenos Poseidon was honoured as a doctor. He adds that Sicily was placed upon Cronus, and there he lies Cronus buried. Both Patrocles of Thurium and the younger Sophocles relate the story of the Twin Brothers in The Twin
Brothers some of their tragedies. These Brothers were simply two men, subject to death, if Homer's authority is sufficient for the statement,

> they ere now by life-giving earth were enfolded,
> There in far Lacedaemon, the well-loved land of their fathers.[a]

Let the author of the Cyprian verses[b] also come forward :

> Castor is mortal man, and death as his fate is appointed ;
> But immortal is great Polydeuces, offspring of Ares.

This last line is a poetic falsehood. But Homer is more worthy of credence than this poet in what he said about both the Brothers. In addition, he has proved Heracles to be a shade. For to him Heracles "Heracles, privy to great deeds," is simply "a man."[c] Heracles, then, is known to be mortal man even by Homer. Hieronymus the philosopher sketches his bodily characteristics also,—small stature, bristling hair, great strength. Dicaearchus adds that he was slim, sinewy, dark, with hooked nose, bright gleaming eyes and long, straight hair. This Heracles, after a life of fifty-two years, ended his days, and his obsequies were celebrated in the pyre on Mount Oeta.

---

[b] *i.e.* an epic poem bearing the name of Cypris, or Aphrodite. The extant fragments are printed at the end of D. B. Monro's *Homeri opera et reliquiae* (Oxford 1891), the above lines being on p. 1015.

[c] Homer, *Odyssey* xxi. 6.

CAP
II

Τὰς δὲ Μούσας, ἃς Ἀλκμὰν[1] Διὸς καὶ Μνημοσύνης
γενεαλογεῖ καὶ οἱ λοιποὶ ποιηταὶ καὶ συγγραφεῖς
ἐκθειάζουσιν καὶ σέβουσιν, ἤδη δὲ καὶ ὅλαι πόλεις
μουσεῖα τεμενίζουσιν[2] αὐταῖς, Μυσὰς[3] οὔσας θεραπαινίδας ταύτας ἐώνηται Μεγακλὼ ἡ θυγάτηρ ἡ
Μάκαρος. ὁ δὲ Μάκαρ Λεσβίων μὲν ἐβασίλευεν, δι-
εφέρετο δὲ ἀεὶ πρὸς τὴν γυναῖκα, ἠγανάκτει δὲ ἡ
Μεγακλὼ ὑπὲρ τῆς μητρός· τί δ᾽ οὐκ ἔμελλε; καὶ
Μυσὰς θεραπαινίδας ταύτας τοσαύτας τὸν ἀριθμὸν
ὠνεῖται καὶ καλεῖ Μοίσας[4] κατὰ τὴν διάλεκτον
τὴν Αἰολέων. ταύτας ἐδιδάξατο ᾄδειν καὶ κιθα-
ρίζειν τὰς πράξεις τὰς παλαιὰς ἐμμελῶς. αἱ δὲ
συνεχῶς κιθαρίζουσαι καὶ καλῶς κατεπάδουσαι τὸν
Μάκαρα ἔθελγον καὶ κατέπαυον τῆς ὀργῆς. οὗ δὴ
χάριν ἡ Μεγακλὼ χαριστήριον αὐτὰς[5] ὑπὲρ τῆς
μητρὸς ἀνέθηκε χαλκᾶς καὶ ἀνὰ πάντα ἐκέλευσε
τιμᾶσθαι τὰ ἱερά. καὶ αἱ μὲν Μοῦσαι τοιαίδε· ἡ
δὲ ἱστορία παρὰ Μυρσίλῳ τῷ Λεσβίῳ.

Ἀκούετε δὴ οὖν τῶν παρ᾽ ὑμῖν θεῶν τοὺς ἔρωτας
καὶ τὰς παραδόξους τῆς ἀκρασίας μυθολογίας καὶ
τραύματα αὐτῶν καὶ δεσμὰ καὶ γέλωτας καὶ
μάχας δουλείας τε ἔτι καὶ συμπόσια συμπλοκάς
τ᾽ αὖ καὶ δάκρυα καὶ πάθη καὶ μαχλώσας ἡδονάς.
κάλει μοι τὸν Ποσειδῶ καὶ τὸν χορὸν τῶν διεφθαρ-
μένων ὑπ᾽ αὐτοῦ, τὴν Ἀμφιτρίτην, τὴν Ἀμυμώνην,
τὴν Ἀλόπην, τὴν Μελανίππην, τὴν Ἀλκυόνην, τὴν
Ἱπποθόην, τὴν Χιόνην, τὰς ἄλλας τὰς μυρίας· ἐν
αἷς δὴ καὶ τοσαύταις οὔσαις ἔτι τοῦ Ποσειδῶνος
ὑμῶν ἐστενοχωρεῖτο τὰ πάθη· κάλει μοι καὶ τὸν

---

[1] Ἀλκμὰν Bergk. ἀλκμανδρος MSS.
[2] τεμενίζουσιν Sylburg. μὲν ἵζουσιν MSS.
[3] Μυσὰς Stählin. μούσας MSS.

64

As for the Muses, Alcman derives their origin from
Zeus and Mnemosyne, and the rest of the poets and
prose-writers deify and worship them; to such an
extent that whole cities dedicate "temples of the
Muses" in their honour.   But these were Mysian
serving-maids purchased by Megaclo, the daughter
of Macar.   Now Macar, who was king over the
Lesbians, was constantly quarrelling with his wife,
and Megaclo was grieved for her mother's sake.
How could she be otherwise ?   So she bought these
Mysian serving-maids, to the correct number, and
pronounced their names Moisai, according to the
Aeolic dialect.   She had them taught to sing of
ancient deeds, and to play the lyre in melodious
accompaniment ; and they, by their continual playing
and the spell of their beautiful singing, were wont to
soothe Macar and rid him of his anger.   As a thank-
offering for these services Megaclo erected, on her
mother's behalf, bronze statues of the maids, and
commanded that they should be honoured in all the
temples.   Such is the origin of the Muses.   The account of them is found in Myrsilus of Lesbos.

Now listen to the loves of these gods of yours ; to
the extraordinary tales of their incontinence ; to
their wounds, imprisonments, fits of laughter, con-
flicts, and periods of servitude.   Listen, too, to their
revels, their embraces, their tears, passions and dissolute pleasures.   Call Poseidon, and the band of
maidens corrupted by him, Amphitrite, Amymone,
Alope, Melanippe, Alcyone, Hippothoë, Chione and
the thousands of others.   Yet in spite of this great
number, the passions of your Poseidon were still un-

---

⁴ Μοίσας Müller.   μύσας MSS.
⁵ αὐτὰς Stählin.   αὐταῖς MSS.

ΟΔΡ. II 'Απόλλω· Φοῖβός ἐστιν οὗτος καὶ μάντις ἁγνὸς
καὶ σύμβουλος ἀγαθός· ἀλλ' οὐ ταῦτα ἡ Στερόπη
λέγει οὐδὲ ἡ Αἴθουσα οὐδὲ ἡ 'Αρσινόη οὐδὲ ἡ
Ζευξίππη οὐδὲ ἡ Προθόη οὐδὲ ἡ Μάρπησσα οὐδὲ
ἡ 'Υψιπύλη· Δάφνη γὰρ ἐξέφυγε μόνη καὶ τὸν
μάντιν καὶ τὴν φθοράν. αὐτός τε ὁ Ζεὺς ἐπὶ πᾶσιν
ἥκέτω, ὁ " πατὴρ " καθ' ὑμᾶς " ἀνδρῶν τε θεῶν
τε." τοσοῦτος περὶ τὰ ἀφροδίσια ἐξεχύθη, ὡς
ἐπιθυμεῖν μὲν πασῶν, ἐκπληροῦν δὲ εἰς πάσας
τὴν ἐπιθυμίαν. ἐνεπίμπλατο γοῦν γυναικῶν οὐχ
ἧττον ἢ αἰγῶν ὁ Θμουιτῶν τράγος. καὶ σοῦ, ὦ
Ὅμηρε, τεθαύμακα τὰ ποιήματα· |

28 P.   ἦ, καὶ κυανέῃσιν ἐπ' ὀφρύσι νεῦσε Κρονίων·
ἀμβρόσιαι δ' ἄρα χαῖται ἐπερρώσαντο ἄνακτος
κρατὸς ἀπ' ἀθανάτοιο· μέγαν δ' ἐλέλιξεν Ὄλυμπον.

σεμνὸν ἀναπλάττεις, Ὅμηρε, τὸν Δία καὶ νεῦμα
περιάπτεις αὐτῷ τετιμημένον. ἀλλ' ἐὰν ἐπιδείξῃς
μόνον, ἄνθρωπε, τὸν κεστόν, ἐξελέγχεται καὶ ὁ
Ζεὺς καὶ ἡ κόμη καταισχύνεται. εἰς ὅσον δ' ἐλήλακεν [1] ἀσελγείας ὁ Ζεὺς ἐκεῖνος ὁ μετ' 'Αλκμήνης
τοσαύτας ἡδυπαθήσας νύκτας· οὐδὲ γὰρ αἱ νύκτες
αἱ ἐννέα τῷ ἀκολάστῳ μακραί (ἅπας δὲ ἔμπαλιν

[1] δ' ἐλήλακεν Dindorf.   διελήλακεν mss.

---

[a] Homer, *Iliad* i. 544 and elsewhere.

[b] This was probably a sacred goat kept at Thmuis, and
treated as the incarnate manifestation of some god. At
the neighbouring town of Mendes such an animal was
worshipped, as we learn from Herodotus ii. 46 ; see also
Clement, on p. 85 of this volume. Thmuis is mentioned in
Herodotus ii. 166 as the name of a town and district in
Egypt. The goat, like the bull, would be chosen for
veneration on account of its procreative force. Clement
regards it (ii. *Stromateis* 118. 5) as a type of the sensual man.

satisfied. Call Apollo, too. He is Phoebus, a holy CHAP.
prophet and good counsellor! But this is not the II
opinion of Sterope, or Aethusa, or Arsinoë, or Apollo
Zeuxippe, or Prothoë, or Marpessa, or Hypsipyle.
For Daphne was the only one who escaped the prophet and his corruption. Above all, let Zeus come Zeus
too, he who is, according to your account, "father of
gods and men." [a] So completely was he given over
to lust, that every woman not only excited his desire,
but became a victim of it. Why, he would take his
fill of women no less than the buck of the Thmuitans [b]
does of she-goats. I am astonished at these verses
of yours, Homer:

Thus spake the son of Cronus, and nodded assent with his
    eyebrows;
Lo! the ambrosial locks of the king flowed waving around
    him
Down from his deathless head; and great Olympus was
    shaken. [c]

It is a majestic Zeus that you portray, Homer; and
you invest him with a nod that is held in honour.
Yet, my good sir, if you but let him catch a glimpse
of a woman's girdle, even Zeus is exposed and his
locks are put to shame. What a pitch of licentiousness did this great Zeus reach when he spent so many
nights in pleasure with Alcmene! Nay, not even the
nine nights [d] were a long period for this debauchee,—

[c] Homer, *Iliad* i. 528–530. Strabo says (354) that Pheidias
had this passage in mind when he carved the famous statue
of Zeus at Olympia.

[d] According to the usual story Heracles was begotten in
three nights (Lucian, *Dialogi deorum* 10), whence he was
called τριέσπερος (Justin Martyr, *Oratio ad Graecos* 3). It
is possible that Clement has confused this with the "nine
nights" of Zeus and Mnemosyne which preceded the birth
of the Muses (Hesiod, *Theogonia* 56).

CLEMENT OF ALEXANDRIA

CAP. ὁ βίος ἀκρασίᾳ βραχὺς ἦν), ἵνα δὴ ἡμῖν τὸν ἀλεξί-
II κακον σπείρῃ θεόν. Διὸς υἱὸς Ἡρακλῆς, Διὸς ὡς
ἀληθῶς, ὁ ἐκ μακρᾶς γεννώμενος νυκτός, τοὺς μὲν
ἄθλους τοὺς δώδεκα πολλῷ ταλαιπωρησάμενος
χρόνῳ, τὰς δὲ πεντήκοντα Θεστίου θυγατέρας
νυκτὶ διαφθείρας μιᾷ, μοιχὸς ὁμοῦ καὶ νυμφίος
τοσούτων γενόμενος παρθένων. οὔκουν ἀπεικότως
οἱ ποιηταὶ " σχέτλιον " τοῦτον καὶ " αἰσυλοεργὸν "
ἀποκαλοῦσιν. μακρὸν δ᾽ ἂν εἴη μοιχείας αὐτοῦ
παντοδαπὰς καὶ παίδων διηγεῖσθαι φθοράς. οὐδὲ
γὰρ οὐδὲ παίδων ἀπέσχοντο οἱ παρ᾽ ὑμῖν θεοί, ὁ
μέν τις Ὕλα, ὁ δὲ Ὑακίνθου, ὁ δὲ Πέλοπος, ὁ δὲ
Χρυσίππου, ὁ δὲ Γανυμήδους ἐρῶντες. τούτους
ὑμῶν αἱ γυναῖκες προσκυνούντων τοὺς θεούς,
τοιούτους δὲ εὐχέσθων εἶναι τοὺς ἄνδρας τοὺς
ἑαυτῶν, οὕτω σώφρονας, ἵν᾽ ὦσιν ὅμοιοι τοῖς θεοῖς
τὰ ἴσα ἐζηλωκότες· τούτους ἐθιζόντων οἱ παῖδες
ὑμῶν σέβειν, ἵνα καὶ ἄνδρες γένωνται εἰκόνα πορ-
νείας ἐναργῆ[1] τοὺς θεοὺς παραλαμβάνοντες.

᾽Αλλ᾽ οἱ μὲν ἄρρενες αὐτοῖς τῶν θεῶν ἴσως μόνοι
ᾄττουσι περὶ τὰ ἀφροδίσια·

> θηλύτεραι δὲ θεαὶ μένον αἰδοῖ οἴκοι ἑκάστη,

φησὶν Ὅμηρος, αἰδούμεναι αἱ θεαὶ[2] διὰ σεμνότητα
Ἀφροδίτην ἰδεῖν μεμοιχευμένην. αἱ δὲ ἀκολα-
σταίνουσιν ἐμπαθέστερον ἐν τῇ μοιχείᾳ δεδεμέναι,
Ἠὼς ἐπὶ Τιθωνῷ, Σελήνη ⟨δ᾽ ἐπὶ⟩[3] Ἐνδυμίωνι,

---

[1] ἐναργῆ Markland. ἐναγῆ mss.
[2] [αἱ θεαὶ] Valckenaer : Stählin.
[3] ⟨δ᾽ ἐπὶ⟩ inserted by Wilamowitz.

indeed, a whole lifetime was short for his incontinence, CHAP.
—especially when the purpose was that he might II
beget for us the god whose work it is to avert evils.
Heracles is the son of Zeus, begotten in this long Heracles
night. And a true son he is; for long and weary as
the time was in which he accomplished his twelve
labours, yet in a single night he corrupted the fifty
daughters of Thestius, becoming at once bridegroom
and adulterer to all these maidens. Not without
reason, then, do the poets dub him "abandoned"
and "doer of evil deeds." [a] It would be a long
story to relate his varied adulteries and his corrup-
tions of boys. For your gods did not abstain even
from boys. One loved Hylas, another Hyacinthus,
another Pelops, another Chrysippus, another Ganymedes. These are the gods your wives are to
worship! Such they must pray for their own
husbands to be, similar models of virtue,—that they
may be like the gods by aspiring after equally high
ideals! Let these be they whom your boys are
trained to reverence, in order that they may grow
to manhood with the gods ever before them as a
manifest pattern of fornication!

But perhaps in the case of the gods, it is the The
males only who rush eagerly after sexual delights, are equally
while   guilty

Each in her home for shame the lady goddesses rested,[b]

as Homer says, because as goddesses they modestly
shrank from the sight of Aphrodite taken in adultery.
Yet these are more passionately given to licentiousness, being fast bound in adultery; as, for instance,
Eos with Tithonus, Selene with Endymion, Nereis

---

[a] Homer, *Iliad* v. 403.   [b] *Odyssey* viii. 324.

CLEMENT OF ALEXANDRIA

CAP.
II
29 P.
Νηρηῒς ἐπὶ Αἰακῷ καὶ ἐπὶ Πηλεῖ Θέτις, ἐπὶ δὲ Ἰασίωνι [1] | Δημήτηρ καὶ ἐπὶ Ἀδώνιδι Φερέφαττα. Ἀφροδίτη δὲ ἐπ᾽ Ἄρει κατῃσχυμμένη μετῆλθεν ἐπὶ Κινύραν καὶ Ἀγχίσην ἔγημεν καὶ Φαέθοντα ἐλόχα καὶ ἤρα Ἀδώνιδος, ἐφιλονείκει δὲ τῇ βοώπιδι καὶ ἀποδυσάμεναι διὰ μῆλον αἱ θεαὶ γυμναὶ προσεῖχον τῷ ποιμένι, εἴ τις αὐτῶν δόξει καλή.

Ἴθι δὴ καὶ τοὺς ἀγῶνας ἐν βραχεῖ περιοδεύσωμεν καὶ τὰς ἐπιτυμβίους ταυτασὶ πανηγύρεις καταλύσωμεν, Ἴσθμιά τε καὶ Νέμεα καὶ Πύθια καὶ τὰ ἐπὶ τούτοις Ὀλύμπια. Πυθοῖ μὲν οὖν ὁ δράκων ὁ Πύθιος θρησκεύεται καὶ τοῦ ὄφεως ἡ πανήγυρις καταγγέλλεται Πύθια· Ἰσθμοῖ δὲ σκύβαλον προσέπτυσεν ἐλεεινὸν ἡ θάλαττα καὶ Μελικέρτην ὀδύρεται τὰ Ἴσθμια· Νεμέασι δὲ ἄλλο παιδίον Ἀρχέμορος κεκήδευται καὶ τοῦ παιδίου ὁ ἐπιτάφιος προσαγορεύεται Νέμεα· Πῖσα δὲ ὑμῖν τάφος ἐστίν, ὦ Πανέλληνες, ἡνιόχου Φρυγός, καὶ τοῦ Πέλοπος τὰς χοάς, τὰ Ὀλύμπια, ὁ Φειδίου σφετερίζεται Ζεύς. μυστήρια ἦσαν ἄρα, ὡς ἔοικεν, οἱ ἀγῶνες ἐπὶ νεκροῖς διαθλούμενοι, ὥσπερ καὶ τὰ λόγια, καὶ δεδήμευνται ἄμφω. ἀλλὰ τὰ μὲν ἐπὶ Ἄγρᾳ [2] μυστήρια καὶ τὰ ἐν Ἁλιμοῦντι τῆς Ἀττικῆς Ἀθήνησι περιώρισται· αἶσχος δὲ ἤδη κοσμικὸν οἵ τε ἀγῶνες

---

[1] Ἰασίωνι Sylburg. ἰάσωνι MSS.
[2] Ἄγρᾳ Meurs. σάγραι MSS.

---

[a] i.e. Hera. The epithet means, literally, "cow-eyed"; but it is frequently applied to Hera in the *Iliad* (e.g. i. 551) in the sense of "with large, bright eyes." For the connexion between Hera and the cow see A. B. Cook, *Zeus*, i. pp. 444–457.

[b] i.e. Paris, son of Priam of Troy. He judged Aphrodite more beautiful than Hera or Athena, and so roused the anger of these two goddesses against Troy.

with Aeacus, Thetis with Peleus, Demeter with CHAP.
Iasion and Persephone with Adonis. Aphrodite, II
after having been put to shame for her love of
Ares, courted Cinyras, married Anchises, entrapped
Phaëthon and loved Adonis. She, too, entered into
a rivalry with the "goddess of the large eyes," [a]
in which, for the sake of an apple, the goddesses
stripped and presented themselves naked to the
shepherd,[b] to see whether he would pronounce one
of them beautiful.

Let us now proceed briefly to review the contests, Review of
and let us put an end to these solemn assemblages the games
at tombs, the Isthmian, Nemean, Pythian, and, above They are
all, the Olympian games. At Pytho worship is paid held in
honour of
to the Pythian serpent,[c] and the assembly held in the dead
honour of this snake is entitled Pythian. At the Pythian
Isthmus the sea cast up a miserable carcass, and the games
Isthmian games are lamentations for Melicertes. At Isthmian
Nemea another, a child Archemorus, lies buried, and
it is the celebrations held at the grave of this child Nemean
that are called by the name Nemean. And Pisa,—
mark it, ye Panhellenic peoples!—your Pisa is the
tomb of a Phrygian charioteer, and the libations
poured out for Pelops, which constitute the Olympian Olympian
festivities, are appropriated by the Zeus of Pheidias.
So it seems that the contests, being held in honour
of the dead, were of the nature of mysteries, just as
also the oracles were; and both have become public
institutions. But the mysteries at Agra and those
in Halimus of Attica[d] have been confined to Athens;
on the other hand, the contests are now a world-

---

[c] See p. 3, n. e.
[d] See Appendix on the Mysteries, p. 382.

CLEMENT OF ALEXANDRIA

CAP. II καὶ οἱ φαλλοὶ οἱ Διονύσῳ ἐπιτελούμενοι, κακῶς ἐπινενεμημένοι τὸν βίον.

Διόνυσος γὰρ κατελθεῖν εἰς Ἅιδου γλιχόμενος ἠγνόει τὴν ὁδόν, ὑπισχνεῖται δ᾿ αὐτῷ φράσειν ⟨τις⟩,[1]
80 P. Πρόσυμνος τοὔνομα, οὐκ | ἀμισθί· ὁ δὲ μισθὸς οὐ καλός, ἀλλὰ Διονύσῳ καλός· καὶ ἀφροδίσιος ἦν ἡ χάρις, ὁ μισθὸς ὃν ᾐτεῖτο Διόνυσος· βουλομένῳ δὲ τῷ θεῷ γέγονεν ἡ αἴτησις, καὶ δὴ ὑπισχνεῖται παρέξειν αὐτῷ, εἰ ἀναζεύξοι, ὅρκῳ πιστωσάμενος τὴν ὑπόσχεσιν. μαθὼν ἀπῆρεν· ἐπανῆλθεν αὖθις· οὐ καταλαμβάνει τὸν Πρόσυμνον (ἐτεθνήκει γάρ)· ἀφοσιούμενος τῷ ἐραστῇ ὁ Διόνυσος ἐπὶ τὸ μνημεῖον ὁρμᾷ καὶ πασχητιᾷ. κλάδον οὖν συκῆς, ὡς ἔτυχεν, ἐκτεμὼν ἀνδρείου μορίου σκευάζεται τρόπον ἐφέζεταί τε τῷ κλάδῳ, τὴν ὑπόσχεσιν ἐκτελῶν τῷ νεκρῷ. ὑπόμνημα τοῦ πάθους τούτου μυστικὸν φαλλοὶ κατὰ πόλεις ἀνίστανται Διονύσῳ. " εἰ μὴ γὰρ Διονύσῳ πομπὴν ἐποιοῦντο καὶ ὕμνεον ᾆσμα[2] αἰδοίοισιν, ἀναιδέστατα εἴργαστ᾿ ἄν,[3] " φησὶν Ἡράκλειτος, " ωὑτὸς δὲ Ἅιδης καὶ Διόνυσος, ὅτεῳ μαίνονται καὶ ληναΐζουσιν," οὐ διὰ τὴν μέθην τοῦ σώματος, ὡς ἐγὼ οἶμαι, τοσοῦτον ὅσον διὰ τὴν ἐπονείδιστον τῆς ἀσελγείας ἱεροφαντίαν.

Εἰκότως ἄρα οἱ τοιοίδε ὑμῶν θεοὶ ⟨δοῦλοι⟩,[4] δοῦλοι παθῶν γεγονότες, ἀλλὰ καὶ πρὸ[5] τῶν Εἱλώτων

---

[1] ⟨τις⟩ inserted by Dindorf.
[2] ᾄσματα Heinsius : Stählin. ᾆσματα, ἃ Dindorf.
[3] εἴργαστ᾿ ἄν Schleiermacher. εἴργασται mss.
[4] ⟨δοῦλοι⟩ inserted by Schwartz.
[5] πρὸ Münzel. πρὸς mss.

---

[a] Heracleitus, *Frag.* 127 Bywater, 15 Diels.   Dionysus

72

wide disgrace, as are also the phalloi consecrated to
Dionysus, from the infection of evil which they have
spread over human life.

This is the origin of these phalloi.   Dionysus was
anxious to descend into Hades, but did not know the
way.   Thereupon a certain man, Prosymnus by name,
promises to tell him ; though not without reward.
The reward was not a seemly one, though to Dionysus
it was seemly enough.   It was a favour of lust, this
reward which Dionysus was asked for.   The god is
willing to grant the request ; and so he promises,
in the event of his return, to fulfil the wish of
Prosymnus, confirming the promise with an oath.
Having learnt the way he set out, and came back
again.   He does not find Prosymnus, for he was
dead.   In fulfilment of the vow to his lover Dionysus
hastens to the tomb and indulges his unnatural lust.
Cutting off a branch from a fig-tree which was at
hand, he shaped it into the likeness of a phallos, and
then made a show of fulfilling his promise to the dead
man.   As a mystic memorial of this passion phalloi
are set up to Dionysus in cities.   " For if it were not
to Dionysus that they held solemn procession and
sang the phallic hymn, they would be acting most
shamefully," says Heracleitus ; "and Hades is the
same as Dionysus, in whose honour they go mad and
keep the Lenaean feast," [a] not so much, I think, for
the sake of bodily intoxication as for the shameful
display of licentiousness.

It would seem natural, therefore, for gods like
these of yours to be slaves, since they have become
slaves of their passions.   What is more, even before

is originally a vegetation god, and is thus but another form
of Hades or Pluto, the " wealth-giver."

CAP.
II

καλουμένων τῶν παρὰ Λακεδαιμονίοις δούλειον
ὑπεισῆλθεν ζυγὸν Ἀπόλλων Ἀδμήτῳ ἐν Φεραῖς,
Ἡρακλῆς ἐν Σάρδεσιν Ὀμφάλῃ, Λαομέδοντι δ' ἐθή-
τευε Ποσειδῶν καὶ Ἀπόλλων, καθάπερ ἀχρεῖος
οἰκέτης, μηδὲ ἐλευθερίας δήπουθεν δυνηθεὶς τυχεῖν
παρὰ τοῦ προτέρου δεσπότου· τότε καὶ τὰ Ἰλίου
τείχη ἀνῳκοδομησάτην τῷ Φρυγί. Ὅμηρος δὲ
τὴν Ἀθηνᾶν οὐκ αἰσχύνεται παραφαίνειν λέγων
τῷ Ὀδυσσεῖ "χρύσεον λύχνον ἔχουσαν" ἐν χεροῖν·
τὴν δὲ Ἀφροδίτην ἀνέγνωμεν, οἷον ἀκόλαστόν τι
θεραπαινίδιον, παραθεῖναι φέρουσαν τῇ Ἑλένῃ τὸν
δίφρον τοῦ μοιχοῦ κατὰ πρόσωπον, ὅπως αὐτὸν εἰς
συνουσίαν ὑπαγάγηται. Πανύασσις γὰρ πρὸς τούτοις καὶ ἄλλους παμπόλλους ἀνθρώποις λατρεῦσαι
θεοὺς ἱστορεῖ ὧδέ πως γράφων·

τλῆ μὲν Δημήτηρ, τλῆ δὲ κλυτὸς Ἀμφιγυήεις,
τλῆ δὲ Ποσειδάων, τλῆ δ' ἀργυρότοξος Ἀπόλλων
ἀνδρὶ παρὰ θνητῷ θητευέμεν[1] εἰς ἐνιαυτόν·
τλῆ δὲ καὶ[2] ὀβριμόθυμος Ἄρης ὑπὸ πατρὸς ἀνάγκης,

καὶ τὰ ἐπὶ τούτοις.

Τούτοις οὖν εἰκότως ἕπεται τοὺς ἐρωτικοὺς ὑμῶν
31 P καὶ παθητικοὺς τούτους θεοὺς ἀνθρω|ποπαθεῖς ἐκ
παντὸς εἰσάγειν τρόπον. "καὶ γὰρ θην κείνοις
θνητὸς χρώς." τεκμηριοῖ δὲ Ὅμηρος, μάλα ἀκρι-
βῶς Ἀφροδίτην ἐπὶ τῷ τραύματι παρεισάγων ὀξὺ
καὶ μέγα ἰάχουσαν αὐτόν τε τὸν πολεμικώτατον
Ἄρη ὑπὸ τοῦ Διομήδους κατὰ τοῦ κενεῶνος οὐτα-
σμένον διηγούμενος. Πολέμων δὲ καὶ τὴν Ἀθηνᾶν

---

[1] θητευέμεν Sylburg. θητευσέμεν MSS.
[2] καὶ inserted by Sylburg.

---

a Homer, *Odyssey* xix. 34.

74

the time of the Helots, as they were called, among
the Lacedaemonians, Apollo bowed beneath the
yoke of slavery to Admetus in Pherae, and Heracles
to Omphale in Sardis.   Poseidon and Apollo were
serfs to Laomedon, Apollo, like a worthless servant,
not having been able, I suppose, to obtain the gift of
freedom from his former master.   It was then that
these two gods built the walls of Ilium for their
Phrygian lord.   Homer is not ashamed to speak of
Athena lighting the way for Odysseus, "holding a
golden lamp" [a] in her hands.   We read of Aphrodite,
how, like a wanton hussy, she brought the stool for
Helen, and placed it in front of her paramour, in
order that Helen might entice him to her arms.[b]
Panyasis, too, relates in addition very many other
instances of gods becoming servants to men.   He
writes in this way :—

> Demeter bore the yoke ; Hephaestus too ;
> Poseidon ; and Apollo, silver-bowed,
> One year endured to serve with mortal man ;
> Likewise strong Ares, by his sire constrained,[c]

—and so on.

As a natural consequence, these amorous and
passionate gods of yours are brought before us as
subject to every sort of human emotion.   "For truly
mortal flesh is theirs." [d]   Homer gives evidence of
this, when in precise terms he introduces Aphrodite
uttering a loud and shrill cry over her wound ;[e] and
when he tells how the arch-warrior himself, Ares, was
pierced in the flank by Diomedes.[f]   Polemon says

---

[b] See *Iliad* iii. 424 and following lines.   The paramour was
Paris, whose abduction of Helen from Sparta brought about
the Trojan war.   [c] Panyasis, *Heracleia*, Frag. 16 Kinkel.
[d] *Iliad* xxi. 568.   [e] *Iliad* v. 343.
[f] *Iliad* v. 855 and following lines.

CAP.
II

ὑπὸ Ὀρνύτου τρωθῆναι λέγει· ναὶ μὴν καὶ τὸν
Ἀιδωνέα ὑπὸ Ἡρακλέους τοξευθῆναι Ὅμηρος
λέγει καὶ τὸν Ἥλιον [Αὐγέαν] [1] Πανύασσις ἱστορεῖ.
ἤδη δὲ καὶ τὴν Ἥραν τὴν ζυγίαν ἱστορεῖ ὑπὸ τοῦ
αὐτοῦ Ἡρακλέους ὁ αὐτὸς οὗτος Πανύασσις '' ἐν
Πύλῳ ἠμαθόεντι.'' Σωσίβιος δὲ καὶ τὸν Ἡρακλέα
πρὸς τῶν Ἱπποκοωντιδῶν κατὰ τῆς χειρὸς οὐτα-
σθῆναι λέγει. εἰ δὲ [2] τραύματα, καὶ αἵματα· οἱ γὰρ
ἰχῶρες οἱ ποιητικοὶ εἰδεχθέστεροι καὶ τῶν αἱμάτων,
σῆψις γὰρ αἵματος ἰχὼρ νοεῖται. ἀνάγκη τοίνυν
θεραπείας καὶ τροφὰς παρεισάγειν αὐτοῖς, ὧν εἰσιν
ἐνδεεῖς. διὸ τράπεζαι καὶ μέθαι καὶ γέλωτες καὶ
συνουσίαι, οὐκ ἂν ἀφροδισίοις χρωμένων ἀνθρωπίνοις [3] οὐδὲ παιδοποιουμένων οὐδὲ μὴν ὑπνωσσόν-
των, εἰ ἀθάνατοι καὶ ἀνενδεεῖς καὶ ἀγήρῳ [4] ὑπῆρχον.
μετέλαβεν δὲ καὶ τραπέζης ἀνθρωπίνης παρὰ τοῖς
Αἰθίοψιν, ἀπανθρώπου δὲ καὶ ἀθέσμου αὐτὸς ὁ
Ζεὺς παρὰ Λυκάονι τῷ Ἀρκάδι ἑστιώμενος·
ἀνθρωπείων γοῦν ἐνεφορεῖτο σαρκῶν οὐχ ἑκών.
ἠγνόει γὰρ ὁ θεὸς ὡς ἄρα Λυκάων ὁ Ἀρκὰς ὁ
ἑστιάτωρ αὐτοῦ τὸν παῖδα κατασφάξας τὸν αὑτοῦ
(Νύκτιμος ὄνομα αὐτῷ) παραθείη ὄψον τῷ Διί.
καλός γε ὁ Ζεὺς ὁ μαντικός, ὁ ξένιος, ὁ ἱκέσιος, ὁ

---

[1] τὸν Ἥλιον [Αὐγέαν] Schwartz.   τὸν ἡλεῖον αὐγέαν MSS.
[2] δὲ Mayor.   δὴ MSS.
[3] ἀνθρωπίνοις Reinkens.   ἀνθρώποις MSS.
[4] ἀγήρῳ Potter.   ἀγήρως MSS.

---

[a] Polemon, Frag. 24 Frag. hist. Graec. iii. p. 122.
[b] Iliad v. 395–397.
[c] Panyasis, Heracleia, Frag. 6. 20 Kinkel.
[d] Sosibius, Frag. 15 Frag. hist. Graec. ii. p. 628.

that Athena too was wounded by Ornytus [a]; yes, and CHAP.
even Hades was struck with an arrow by Heracles, II
according to Homer; [b] and Panyasis relates the Athena
same of Helius. This same Panyasis further relates Helius
that Hera, the goddess of marriage, was wounded by Hera
the same Heracles, "in sandy Pylos." [c] Sosibius Heracles
says that Heracles himself was struck in the hand
by the sons of Hippocoon. [d] If there are wounds
there is also blood; for the "ichor" of the poets
is a more disgusting thing even than blood, the
word ichor meaning putrefaction of the blood. [e] It
is necessary, therefore, to supply the gods with The gods
attendance and nourishment, of which they are in are also
subject to
need; so they have feasts, carousings, bursts of bodily
laughter and acts of sexual intercourse, whereas if needs
they were immortal, and in need of nothing, and
untouched by age, they would not partake of the
pleasures of human love, nor beget children, nor
even go to sleep. Zeus himself shared a human Zeus for
table among the Ethiopians, [f] and an inhuman and example
unlawful table when feasting with Lycaon the
Arcadian; at least, he glutted himself with human
flesh. Not wilfully, however, for the god was
unaware that, as it appears, his host Lycaon the
Arcadian set before him, as a dainty dish, his
own child, Nyctimus by name, whom he had
slaughtered. [g] What a fine Zeus he is, the diviner,
the protector of guests, the hearer of suppliants, the

[e] "Ichor" is the blood that flows in the veins of the
gods; cp. *Iliad* v. 340. But the word is also used of matter,
or corrupt discharges from the body. See references in
Liddell and Scott, *s.v.*

[f] *Iliad* i. 423-424.

[g] See Pausanias viii. 2. 3. The story of Lycaon is dis-
cussed in A. B. Cook, *Zeus*, vol. i. pp. 63-81.

CLEMENT OF ALEXANDRIA

CAP. μειλίχιος, ὁ πανομφαῖος, ὁ προστροπαῖος· μᾶλλον
II δὲ <ὁ>[1] ἄδικος, ὁ ἄθεσμος, ὁ ἄνομος, ὁ ἀνόσιος, ὁ
ἀπάνθρωπος, ὁ βίαιος, ὁ φθορεύς, ὁ μοιχός, ὁ
ἐρωτικός. ἀλλὰ τότε μὲν ἦν, ὅτε τοιοῦτος ἦν, ὅτε
ἄνθρωπος ἦν, νῦν δὲ ἤδη μοι δοκοῦσι καὶ οἱ μῦθοι
ὑμῖν γεγηρακέναι. δράκων ὁ Ζεὺς οὐκέτι, οὐ
κύκνος ἐστίν, οὐκ ἀετός, οὐκ ἄνθρωπος ἐρωτικός·
οὐχ ἵπταται θεός, οὐ παιδεραστεῖ, οὐ φιλεῖ, οὐ
βιάζεται, καίτοι πολλαὶ καὶ καλαὶ καὶ νῦν ἔτι
γυναῖκες καὶ Λήδας εὐπρεπέστεραι καὶ Σεμέλης
ἀκμαιότεραι, μειράκια δὲ ὡραιότερα καὶ πολιτι-
κώτερα τοῦ Φρυγίου βουκόλου. ποῦ νῦν ἐκεῖνος ὁ
32 P. ἀετός; ποῦ δὲ ὁ κύκνος; ποῦ δὲ αὐτὸς | ὁ Ζεύς;
γεγήρακε μετὰ τοῦ πτεροῦ· οὐ γὰρ δήπου μετανοεῖ
τοῖς ἐρωτικοῖς οὐδὲ παιδεύεται σωφρονεῖν. γυμ-
νοῦται δὲ ὑμῖν ὁ μῦθος· ἀπέθανεν ἡ Λήδα, ἀπέθανεν
ὁ κύκνος, ἀπέθανεν ὁ ἀετός. ζήτει σου τὸν Δία·
μὴ τὸν οὐρανόν, ἀλλὰ τὴν γῆν πολυπραγμόνει. ὁ
Κρής σοι διηγήσεται, παρ᾽ ᾧ καὶ τέθαπται, Καλλίμαχος ἐν ὕμνοις

καὶ γὰρ τάφον, ὦ ἄνα, σεῖο
Κρῆτες ἐτεκτήναντο.

τέθνηκε γὰρ ὁ Ζεὺς (μὴ δυσφόρει) ὡς Λήδα, ὡς
κύκνος, ὡς ἀετός, ὡς ἄνθρωπος ἐρωτικός, ὡς
δράκων.

[1] <ὁ> inserted by Sylburg.

[a] i.e. Ganymedes ; see pp. 69 and 111.
[b] Callimachus, *Hymn to Zeus* 8–9. This claim of the
Cretans to possess the tomb of Zeus is said to have earned
for them their traditional reputation as liars. The two lines
of Callimachus, when read in full, distinctly assert this.

78

gracious, the author of all oracles, the avenger of crime! Rather he ought to be called the unjust, the unrestrained, the lawless, the unholy, the inhuman, the violent, the seducer, the adulterer, the wanton lover. Still, there was life about him in those days, when he was all this, when he was a man; but by this time even your legends appear to me to have grown old. Zeus is no longer a snake, nor a swan, nor an eagle, nor an amorous man. He is not a god who flies, or corrupts boys, or kisses, or ravishes; and yet there are still many beautiful women left, fairer even than Leda and nearer their prime than Semele, and lads more blooming and more refined than the Phrygian herdsman.[a] Where is now that famous eagle? Where is the swan? Where is Zeus himself? He has grown old, wings and all. For you may be sure he is not repentant because of his love affairs, nor is he training himself to live a sober life. See, the legend is laid bare. Leda is dead; the swan is dead; the eagle is dead. Search for your Zeus. Scour not heaven, but earth. Callimachus the Cretan, in whose land he lies buried, will tell you in his hymns:

for a tomb, O Prince, did the Cretans
Fashion for thee.[b]

Yes, Zeus is dead (take it not to heart), like Leda, like the swan, like the eagle, like the amorous man, like the snake.

They run as follows:

Cretans ever do lie; for a tomb, O Prince, did they fashion
Even for thee; but thou art not dead, for thy life is unending.

Cp. Titus i. 12, and, for a discussion on the burial-place of Zeus, A. B. Cook, *Zeus*, i. 157-163.

CHAP.
II

These stories prove that Zeus was once alive

But now Zeus is dead

CAP.
II

Ἤδη δὲ καὶ αὐτοὶ φαίνονται οἱ δεισιδαίμονες ἄκοντες μέν, ὅμως δ᾽ οὖν συνιέντες τὴν πλάνην τὴν περὶ τοὺς θεούς·

οὐ γὰρ ἀπὸ δρυός εἰσι παλαιφάτου οὐδ᾽ ἀπὸ πέτρης,

ἀλλ᾽ ἀνδρῶν γένος εἰσί, μικρὸν δὲ ὕστερον καὶ δρύες ὄντες εὑρεθήσονται καὶ πέτραι. Ἀγαμέμνονα γοῦν τινα Δία ἐν Σπάρτῃ τιμᾶσθαι Στάφυλος ἱστορεῖ· Φανοκλῆς δὲ ἐν Ἔρωσιν ἢ ¹ Καλοῖς Ἀγαμέμνονα τὸν Ἑλλήνων βασιλέα Ἀργύννου νεὼν Ἀφροδίτης ἵστασθαι ἐπ᾽ Ἀργύννῳ τῷ ἐρωμένῳ. Ἄρτεμιν δὲ Ἀρκάδες Ἀπαγχομένην καλουμένην προστρέπονται, ὥς φησι Καλλίμαχος ἐν Αἰτίοις. καὶ Κονδυλῖτις ἐν Μηθύμνῃ ἑτέρα τετίμηται Ἄρτεμις. ἔστι δὲ καὶ Ποδάγρας ἄλλης Ἀρτέμιδος ἐν τῇ Λακωνικῇ ἱερόν, ὥς φησι Σωσίβιος. Πολέμων δὲ Κεχηνότος Ἀπόλλωνος οἶδεν ἄγαλμα, καὶ Ὀψο-
33 P. φάγου | πάλιν Ἀπόλλωνος ἄλλο ἐν Ἤλιδι τιμώμενον. ἐνταῦθα Ἀπομυίῳ Διὶ θύουσιν Ἠλεῖοι· Ῥωμαῖοι δὲ Ἀπομυίῳ Ἡρακλεῖ καὶ Πυρετῷ δὲ

---

¹ ἢ Leopardus. τοῖς Sylburg. τῖε MSS.

ᵃ Homer, *Odyssey* xix. 163. The gods were not, according to Clement, primeval beings, but simply men with a human history.

ᵇ Clement seems to allude to his passage about the statues p. 101 and onwards.

ᶜ A local cult of Agamemnon (such as the one which existed at Clazomenae—Pausanias vii. 5. 11) had evidently been combined with the worship of Zeus. See Athenagoras, *Apology* i.

ᵈ Staphylus, Frag. 10 *Frag. hist. Graec.* iv. p. 506.

ᵉ Phanocles, *Frag.* 5 Bach. Cp. Athenaeus, p. 603.

EXHORTATION TO THE GREEKS

But it is clear that even the daemon-worshippers CHAP.
II
The witness
of Greek
writers
against
their own
gods themselves are coming to understand, though against their will, the error about the gods; for

Not from the ancient oak nor rock do they take their beginning.*a*

No; they are of the race of men, though very shortly they will be found to be nothing but oaks and rocks.*b* There is a Zeus Agamemnon *c* honoured at Sparta, according to Staphylus *d* ; and Phanocles, in his book entitled *Loves, or Fair Youths*, says that Agamemnon the king of the Greeks set up a temple to Aphrodite Argynnus, in honour of Argynnus whom he loved.*e* Arcadians worship an Artemis called "the goddess who is hanged," as Callimachus says in his *Causes* *f* ; and at Methymna another, an Artemis Condylitis, is honoured.*g* There is also another, a "gouty" Artemis, with a shrine in Laconia, as Sosibius says.*h* Polemon knows a statue of "yawning" Apollo ; and another, too, of Apollo "the epicure," honoured in Elis.*i* These Eleans sacrifice to Zeus "averter of flies," *k* and the Romans to Heracles of the same title,

f Artemis seems to have been "hanged" annually at Condylea in Arcadia. See Pausanias viii. 23. 6, where the children are probably imitating some ancient ritual. Full discussion in Frazer, *Adonis, Attis, Osiris*, i. pp. 288–297. See also Callimachus, *Frag*. 3 Schneider.

g *Condylitis* may mean "striking," from κονδυλίζειν. But possibly this is another form of "Artemis of Condylea," called *Artemis Condyleatis* in Pausanias viii. 23. 6.

h Sosibius, Frag. 14 *Frag. hist. Graec.* ii. p. 628.

i Polemon, Frag. 71 *Frag. hist. Graec.* iii. p. 135. See Athenaeus, p. 346.

k See Frazer, *Golden Bough*, part 5, vol. ii. p. 282 (3rd ed.).

CAP. καὶ Φόβῳ θύουσιν, οὓς καὶ αὐτοὺς μετὰ τῶν ἀμφὶ
II τὸν Ἡρακλέα ἐγγράφουσιν. ἐῶ δὲ Ἀργείους·
Ἀφροδίτην Τυμβωρύχον θρησκεύουσιν Ἀργεῖοι καὶ
Λάκωνες,[1] καὶ Χελύτιδα δὲ Ἄρτεμιν Σπαρτιᾶται
σέβουσιν· ἐπεὶ τὸ βήττειν χελύττειν καλοῦσιν.

Οἴει ποθὲν παρέγγραπτα[2] ταῦτά σοι κομίζεσθαι
τὰ ὑφ᾽ ἡμῶν παρατιθέμενα; οὐδὲ τοὺς σοὺς γνωρί-
ζειν ἔοικας συγγραφεῖς, οὓς ἐγὼ μάρτυρας ἐπὶ τὴν
σὴν ἀπιστίαν καλῶ, ἀθέου χλεύης, ὦ δείλαιοι, τὸν
πάντα ὑμῶν ἀβίωτον ὄντως βίον ἐμπεπληκότας.[3]
οὐχὶ μέντοι Ζεὺς φαλακρὸς ἐν Ἄργει, τιμωρὸς δὲ
ἄλλος ἐν Κύπρῳ τετίμησθον[4]; οὐχὶ δὲ Ἀφροδίτη
περιβασοῖ[5] μὲν Ἀργεῖοι, ἑταίρᾳ δὲ Ἀθηναῖοι καὶ
καλλιπύγῳ[6] θύουσι Συρακούσσιοι, ἣν Νίκανδρος
ὁ ποιητὴς "καλλίγλουτόν" που κέκληκεν; Διόνυσον δὲ ἤδη σιωπῶ τὸν χοιροψάλαν· Σικυώνιοι
τοῦτον προσκυνοῦσιν ἐπὶ τῶν γυναικείων τάξαντες
τὸν Διόνυσον μορίων, ἔφορον αἴσχους τὸν ὕβρεως
σεβάζοντες ἀρχηγόν. τοιοίδε μὲν αὐτοῖς οἱ θεοί,
τοιοίδε καὶ αὐτοί, παίζοντες ἐν θεοῖς, μᾶλλον δὲ
ἐμπαίζοντες καὶ ἐνυβρίζοντες σφίσιν αὐτοῖς. καὶ
πόσῳ βελτίους Αἰγύπτιοι κωμηδὸν καὶ κατὰ πόλεις
τὰ ἄλογα τῶν ζώων ἐκτετιμηκότες ἤπερ Ἕλληνες
τοιούτους προσκυνοῦντες θεούς; τὰ μὲν γὰρ εἰ
καὶ θηρία, ἀλλ᾽ οὐ μοιχικά, ἀλλ᾽ οὐ μάχλα, παρὰ
φύσιν δὲ θηρεύει ἡδονὴν οὐδὲ ἕν. οἱ δὲ ὁποῖοι,

---

[1] καὶ Λάκωνες placed by Stählin after Ἀργείους (l. 2).
[2] ποθὲν παρέγγραπτα Stählin. πόθεν παραγέγραπται MSS.
[3] ἐμπεπληκότας Stählin. ἐμπεπληκότες MSS.
[4] τετίμησθον Sylburg. τετιμήσθων MSS.
[5] περιβασοῖ Dindorf. περιβασίη MSS.
[6] καλλιπύγῳ Sylburg. καλλιπύργῳ MSS.

[a] Nicander, *Frag.* 23 Schneider.

as well as to "Fever" and "Fear" which they even
enroll among the companions of Heracles. I pass
by the Argives; Aphrodite the "grave-robber" is
worshipped by them, as well as by the Laconians.
Furthermore, Spartans venerate Artemis Chelytis or
the "coughing" Artemis, since the verb corresponding
to Chelytis is their word for "to cough."

Do you think that the examples which I am
adducing are brought to you from some improper
source? Why, it seems as if you do not recognize
your own authors, whom I call as witnesses against
your unbelief. Alas for you! They have filled your
whole life with godless foolery, until life has become
truly intolerable. Tell me, is there not a "bald"
Zeus honoured in Argos, and another, an "avenger,"
in Cyprus? Do not Argives sacrifice to Aphrodite
divaricatrix, Athenians to her as "courtesan," and
Syracusans to her "of the beautiful buttocks," whom
the poet Nicander[a] has somewhere called "of the
beautiful rump"? I will be silent about Dionysus
choiropsalas. The Sicyonians worship this Dionysus
as the god who presides over the woman's secret
parts; thus they reverence the originator of licentiousness, as overseer of what is shameful. Such,
then, is the character of the Greek gods; such,
too, are the worshippers, who make a mockery of
the divine, or rather, who mock and insult themselves. How much better are Egyptians, when in
cities and villages they hold in great honour the
irrational animals, than Greeks who worship such
gods as these? For though the Egyptian gods are
beasts, still they are not adulterous, they are not
lewd, and not one of them seeks for pleasure contrary
to its own nature. But as for the character of the

CAP.
II

τί καὶ χρὴ λέγειν ἔτι, ἀποχρώντως αὐτῶν διελη-
λεγμένων;

'Αλλ' οὖν γε Αἰγύπτιοι, ὧν νῦν δὴ ἐμνήσθην,
84 P. κατὰ τὰς θρησκείας | τὰς σφῶν ἐσκέδανται· σέβουσι
δὲ αὐτῶν Συηνῖται[1] φάγρον τὸν ἰχθύν, μαιώτην δὲ
(ἄλλος[2] οὗτος ἰχθύς) οἱ τὴν Ἐλεφαντίνην οἰκοῦντες,
Ὀξυρυγχῖται τὸν φερώνυμον τῆς χώρας αὐτῶν
ὁμοίως ἰχθύν, ἔτι γε μὴν Ἡρακλεοπολῖται ἰχνεύ-
μονα, Σαῖται δὲ καὶ Θηβαῖοι πρόβατον, Λυκο-
πολῖται δὲ λύκον, Κυνοπολῖται δὲ κύνα, τὸν ⟨Ἆπιν
Μεμφῖται, Μενδήσιοι τὸν τράγον. ὑμεῖς δὲ οἱ
πάντ' ἀμείνους Αἰγυπτίων (ὀκνῶ δὲ εἰπεῖν χείρους),
οἳ τοὺς Αἰγυπτίους ὁσημέραι γελῶντες οὐ παύεσθε,[3]
ποῖοί[4] τινες καὶ περὶ τὰ ἄλογα ζῷα; Θεσσαλοὶ μὲν
ὑμῶν τοὺς πελαργοὺς τετιμήκασι διὰ τὴν συνήθειαν,
Θηβαῖοι δὲ τὰς γαλᾶς διὰ τὴν Ἡρακλέους γένεσιν.
τί δὲ πάλιν Θετταλοί; μύρμηκας ἱστοροῦνται
σέβειν, ἐπεὶ τὸν Δία μεμαθήκασιν ὁμοιωθέντα
μύρμηκι τῇ Κλήτορος θυγατρὶ Εὐρυμεδούσῃ μιγῆναι
καὶ Μυρμιδόνα γεννῆσαι· Πολέμων δὲ τοὺς ἀμφὶ
τὴν Τρωάδα κατοικοῦντας ἱστορεῖ τοὺς ἐπιχωρίους
μῦς ⟨σέβειν⟩,[5] οὓς σμίνθους καλοῦσιν, ὅτι τὰς νευρὰς

---

[1] Συηνῖται Ortelius and Canter (in Sylburg).   εὐηνῖται MSS.
[2] ἄλλος Potter.   ὃς ἄλλος MSS.
[3] παύεσθε Heinsius.   παύσεσθε MSS.
[4] ποῖοί Wilamowitz.   ὁποῖοί MSS.
[5] ⟨σέβειν⟩ inserted by Dindorf.

---

[a] The Apis bull was regarded as an incarnation of the god
Ptah, or Osiris. Certain peculiar bodily marks distinguished
him from other bulls, and when found he was tended with
deep veneration in a shrine at Memphis. At his death
there was great mourning, and a stately funeral. See
Herodotus iii. 27–28.   [b] See Herodotus ii. 46.
[c] The story is given in Antoninus Liberalis, ch. 29. The

Greek gods, what need is there to say more? They Chap. II have been sufficiently exposed.

Egyptians, however, whom I mentioned just now, Examples of Egyptian animal-worship are divided in the matter of their religious cults. The people of Syene worship the fish phagrus; the inhabitants of Elephantine another fish, the maeotes; the people of Oxyrhynchus also worship a fish, that which bears the name of their land. Further, the people of Heracleopolis worship the ichneumon; of Sais and Thebes, the sheep; of Lycopolis, the wolf; of Cynopolis, the dog; of Memphis, the bull Apis [a]; of Mendes, the goat.[b] But as for you, who are in every way better than Egyptians,—I shrink from calling you worse—you who never let a day pass without laughing at the Egyptians, what is your attitude with regard to the irrational animals? The Thessalians among you give honour to storks by But Greeks also worship animals; examples given reason of old custom; Thebans to weasels on account of the birth of Heracles.[c] What else of Thessalians? They are reported to worship ants, because they have been taught that Zeus, in the likeness of an ant, had intercourse with Eurymedusa the daughter of Cletor and begat Myrmidon.[d] Polemon relates that the dwellers in the Troad worship the local mice (which they call *sminthoi*), because these used to gnaw

birth of Heracles was retarded by the Fates to please Hera. But Alcmene's companion Galinthias (cp. *galē*, a weasel) told them that the birth was by the will of Zeus, whereupon they ceased opposing it. They punished Galinthias, however, by turning her into a weasel. When Heracles grew up he remembered her good deed and built her a shrine. The Thebans thereafter used to offer her the first sacrifice at the feast of Heracles.

[d] The legendary ancestor of the Myrmidons, a Thessalian tribe. The name may be connected with *myrmex* an ant.

τῶν πολεμίων διέτρωγον τῶν τόξων· καὶ Σμίνθιον
Ἀπόλλωνα ἀπὸ τῶν μυῶν ἐκείνων ἐπεφήμισαν.
Ἡρακλείδης δὲ ἐν Κτίσεσιν ἱερῶν περὶ τὴν Ἀκαρ-
νανίαν φησίν, ἔνθα τὸ Ἄκτιόν ἐστιν ἀκρωτήριον
καὶ τοῦ Ἀπόλλωνος τοῦ Ἀκτίου τὸ ἱερόν, ταῖς
μυίαις προθύεσθαι βοῦν. οὐδὲ μὴν Σαμίων ἐκλήσομαι (πρόβατον, ὥς φησιν Εὐφορίων, σέβουσι
85 P. Σάμιοι) οὐδέ γε τῶν τὴν Φοινίκην Σύρων | κατ-
οικούντων, ὧν οἱ μὲν τὰς περιστεράς, οἱ δὲ τοὺς
ἰχθῦς οὕτω σέβουσι περιττῶς ὡς Ἡλεῖοι τὸν Δία.

Εἶεν δή· ἐπειδὴ οὐ θεοί, οὓς θρησκεύετε, αὖθις
ἐπισκέψασθαί μοι δοκεῖ εἰ ὄντως εἶεν δαίμονες,
δευτέρᾳ ταύτῃ, ὡς ὑμεῖς φατέ, ἐγκαταλεγόμενοι
τάξει. εἰ γὰρ οὖν δαίμονες, λίχνοι τε καὶ μιαροί.
ἔστι μὲν ἐφευρεῖν καὶ ἀναφανδὸν οὕτω κατὰ πόλεις
δαίμονας ἐπιχωρίους τιμὴν ἐπιδρεπομένους, παρὰ
Κυθνίοις Μενέδημον, παρὰ Τηνίοις Καλλισταγόραν,
παρὰ Δηλίοις Ἄνιον, παρὰ Λάκωσιν Ἀστράβακον.
τιμᾶται δέ τις καὶ Φαληροῖ κατὰ πρύμναν ἥρως·
καὶ ἡ Πυθία συνέταξε θύειν Πλαταιεῦσιν Ἀνδρο-
κράτει καὶ Δημοκράτει καὶ Κυκλαίῳ καὶ Λεύκωνι
τῶν Μηδικῶν ἀκμαζόντων ἀγώνων. ἔστι καὶ

---

[a] Compare the story in Herodotus ii. 141, where Sen-
nacherib's army, invading Egypt, was rendered useless by
the ravages of mice.

[b] Polemon, Frag. 31 *Frag. hist. Graec.* iii. p. 124.

[c] Heracleides Ponticus, *Frag. hist. Graec.* ii. p. 197,
note 2. See also Farnell, *Cults of the Greek States*, i. p. 45.

[d] Euphorion, Frag. 6 *Frag. hist. Graec.* iii. p. 73.

[e] The Syrian goddess Derceto was represented with the
body of a fish, and her daughter Semiramis took the form
of a dove. See Diodorus ii. 4.

[f] See Herodotus vi. 69.

through their enemies' bowstrings *a* ; and they named CHAP.
Apollo 'Smintheus' after these mice.*b* Heracleides, II
in his work on *The Founding of Temples in Acarnania*,
says that on the promontory of Actium, where stands
the temple of Apollo of Actium, a preliminary sacrifice
of an ox is made to the flies.*c* Nor shall I forget the
Samians, who, as Euphorion says, worship the sheep;*d*
no, nor yet the Syrian inhabitants of Phoenicia, some
of whom worship doves, and others fishes,*e* as ex-
travagantly as the Eleans worship Zeus.

Very well! since they whom you serve are not Perhaps
gods, I am resolved to make a fresh examination to the Greek
gods are
see whether it is true that they are daemons, and secondary
should be enrolled, as you say, in this second rank of deities or
daemons
divinities. For if they really are daemons, they are
greedy and foul ones. We can discover perfectly
clear examples of daemons of local origin who glean Examples of
honour in cities, as Menedemus among the Cythnians, such
daemons or
Callistagoras among the Tenians, Anius among heroes
the Delians and Astrabacus among the Laconians.*f*
Honour is paid also at Phalerum to a certain hero " at
the stern," *g* and the Pythian prophetess prescribed
that the Plataeans should sacrifice to Androcrates,
Democrates, Cyclaeus and Leucon when the struggles
with the Medes were at their height.*h* And the man

---

g This hero is Androgeos, on account of whose death at
Athens the annual tribute of seven youths and seven maidens
was imposed by his father Minos upon the Athenians ; from
which they were delivered by Theseus. A scholiast, com-
menting on this passage, says that figures of Androgeos
were set " at the stern of ships." Phalerum was the ancient
port of Attica, whence according to tradition Theseus em-
barked on his journey to Crete. See Pausanias i. 1. 2–4.

h See Plutarch, *Aristeides* xi.

CAP.
II ἄλλους παμπόλλους συνιδεῖν δαίμονας τῷ γε καὶ
σμικρὸν διαθρεῖν δυναμένῳ·

> τρὶς γὰρ μύριοί εἰσιν ἐπὶ χθονὶ πουλυβοτείρῃ
> δαίμονες ἀθάνατοι, φύλακες μερόπων ἀνθρώπων.

τίνες εἰσὶν οἱ φύλακες, ὦ Βοιώτιε, μὴ φθονέσῃς
λέγειν. ἢ δῆλον ὡς οὗτοι καὶ οἱ τούτων ἐπιτιμότε-
ροι, οἱ μεγάλοι δαίμονες, ὁ Ἀπόλλων, ἡ Ἄρτεμις,
ἡ Λητώ, ἡ Δημήτηρ, ἡ Κόρη, ὁ Πλούτων, ὁ
Ἡρακλῆς, αὐτὸς ὁ Ζεύς. ἀλλ' οὐκ ἀποδρᾶναι
ἡμᾶς φυλάττουσιν, Ἀσκραῖε, μὴ ἁμαρτάνειν δὲ
ἴσως, οἱ ἁμαρτιῶν δῆτα οὐ πεπειραμένοι. ἐνταῦθα
δὴ τὸ παροιμιῶδες ἐπιφθέγξασθαι ἁρμόττει

> " πατὴρ ἀνουθέτητα[1] παῖδα νουθετεῖ."

εἰ δ' ἄρα καὶ εἰσὶ φύλακες οὗτοι, οὐκ εὐνοίᾳ τῇ
πρὸς ἡμᾶς περιπαθεῖς, τῆς δὲ ὑμεδαπῆς ἀπωλείας
ἐχόμενοι, κολάκων δίκην, ἐγχρίμπτονται τῷ βίῳ,
δελεαζόμενοι καπνῷ. αὐτοί που ἐξομολογοῦνται οἱ
δαίμονες τὴν γαστριμαργίαν τὴν αὑτῶν,

> λοιβῆς τε κνίσης τε· τὸ γὰρ λάχομεν γέρας ἡμεῖς, |

36 P. λέγοντες. τίνα δ' ἂν φωνὴν ἄλλην, εἰ φωνὴν
λάβοιεν Αἰγυπτίων θεοί, οἷα αἴλουροι καὶ γαλαῖ,
προήσονται ἢ τὴν Ὁμηρικήν τε καὶ ποιητικήν, τῆς
κνίσης τε καὶ ὀψαρτυτικῆς φίλην; τοιοίδε μέντοι
παρ' ὑμῖν οἵ τε δαίμονες καὶ οἱ θεοὶ καὶ εἴ τινες

---

[1] ἀνουθέτητα Wilamowitz. ἀνουθέτητος mss.

[a] Hesiod, *Works and Days* 252–253. Hesiod was a native
of Ascra in Boeotia, which explains the two appellations
that follow this quotation.
[b] Kock, *Comic. Attic. Frag.* pp. 616–7.

88

who is able to make even a slight investigation can get a view of very many other daemons; CHAP.
II

> For thrice ten thousand dwell on mother earth,
> Immortal daemons, guards of mortal men.[a] Witness of
Hesiod

Who are these guardians, thou Boeotian bard? Do not refuse to tell us. Or is it clear that they are these whom I have just mentioned, and others more honoured than they, namely the great daemons, Apollo, Artemis, Leto, Demeter, the Maiden, Pluto, Heracles, and Zeus himself? But it is not to prevent us from running away that they guard us, poet of Ascra! Perhaps it is to prevent us from sinning, seeing that they, to be sure, have had no experience of sins. Here indeed we may fitly utter the proverbial line, Daemons,
great or
small, are
all one

> The father warns his child but not himself.[b]

Yet if, after all, they really are guardians, they are not moved by feelings of good will towards us; but, being intent upon your destruction, they beset human life after the manner of flatterers, allured by the sacrificial smoke. In one place the daemons themselves admit this gluttony of theirs, when they say, They
approach
man not
from love
but for the
sacrifices

Wine and odorous steam; for that we receive as our portion.[c]

If Egyptian gods, such as cats and weasels, were to be endowed with speech, what other cry are they likely to give forth than this from Homer's poems, proclaiming a love for savoury odours and cookery? Be that as it may, such is the character of the Are they
any better
than
Egyptian
animal
gods?

[c] Homer, *Iliad* iv. 49.

CAP.
II
ἡμίθεοι ὥσπερ ἡμίονοι κέκληνται· οὐδὲ γὰρ οὐδὲ ὀνομάτων ὑμῖν πενία πρὸς τὰς τῆς ἀσεβείας συνθέσεις.

III

Φέρε δὴ οὖν καὶ τοῦτο προσθῶμεν, ὡς ἀπάνθρωποι καὶ μισάνθρωποι δαίμονες εἶεν ὑμῶν οἱ θεοὶ καὶ οὐχὶ μόνον ἐπιχαίροντες τῇ φρενοβλαβείᾳ τῶν ἀνθρώπων, πρὸς δὲ καὶ ἀνθρωποκτονίας ἀπολαύοντες· νυνὶ μὲν τὰς ἐν σταδίοις ἐνόπλους φιλονεικίας, νυνὶ δὲ τὰς ἐν πολέμοις ἀναρίθμους φιλοτιμίας ἀφορμὰς σφίσιν ἡδονῆς ποριζόμενοι, ὅπως ὅτι μάλιστα ἔχοιεν ἀνθρωπείων ἀνέδην ἐμφορεῖσθαι φόνων· ἤδη δὲ κατὰ πόλεις καὶ ἔθνη, οἱονεὶ λοιμοὶ ἐπισκήψαντες, σπονδὰς ἀπήτησαν ἀνημέρους. Ἀριστομένης γοῦν ὁ Μεσσήνιος τῷ Ἰθωμήτῃ Διὶ τριακοσίους ἀπέσφαξεν, τοσαύτας ὁμοῦ καὶ τοιαύτας καλλιερεῖν οἰόμενος ἑκατόμβας· ἐν οἷς καὶ Θεόπομπος ἦν ⟨ὁ⟩[1] Λακεδαιμονίων βασιλεύς, ἱερεῖον εὐγενές. Ταῦροι δὲ τὸ ἔθνος, οἱ περὶ τὴν Ταυρικὴν χερρόνησον κατοικοῦντες, οὓς ἂν τῶν

---

[1] ⟨ὁ⟩ inserted from Eusebius, *Praep. Ev.* iv. 16.

---

[a] To understand the point of Clement's onslaught against the "daemons" it must be remembered that the best Greek teachers of his age, such as Plutarch and Maximus of Tyre, used the doctrine of "secondary divinities" as a means of preserving their own monotheism without altogether breaking away from the popular mythology. According to them, the one Supreme God worked through many ministers, to whom worship could rightly be offered. Clement attacks

daemons and gods you worship, and of the demigods CHAP.
too, if you have any called by this name, on the II
analogy of mules, or demi-asses; for you have no
poverty—not even of words to form into the com-
pounds needed for your impiety.ᵃ

III

Come then, let us add this, that your gods are in- The gods
human and man-hating daemons, who not only exult delight in
human
over the insanity of men, but go so far as to enjoy slaughter
human slaughter. They provide for themselves
sources of pleasure, at one time in the armed contests In the
of the stadium, at another in the innumerable contests of
the stadium
rivalries of war, in order to secure every possible In wars
opportunity of glutting themselves to the full with
human blood. Before now, too, they have fallen They
like plagues on whole cities and nations, and have demand
human
demanded drink-offerings of a savage character. For sacrifices
instance, Aristomenes the Messenian slaughtered Examples:
three hundred men to Zeus of Ithome, in the belief Aristomenes
the
that favourable omens are secured by sacrifices of Messenian
such magnitude and quality. Among the victims
was even Theopompus, the Lacedaemonian king, a Human
noble offering. The Taurian race, who dwell sacrifices
among the
along the Taurian peninsula, whenever they capture Taurians

this position from the moral standpoint; the legends and
the animal sacrifices prove that all these divinities, whether
called gods, demigods, or anything else, were evil in character; there was no distinction between Zeus and the
humblest daemon. A clear and valuable account of the
matter will be found in Dill, *Roman Society from Nero, etc.*
pp. 422-434.

91

CAP.
III
ξένων παρ' αὐτοῖς ἕλωσι, τούτων δὴ τῶν κατὰ
θάλατταν ἐπταικότων, αὐτίκα μάλα τῇ Ταυρικῇ
καταθύουσιν Ἀρτέμιδι· ταύτας σου τὰς θυσίας
Εὐριπίδης ἐπὶ σκηνῆς τραγῳδεῖ. Μόνιμος δ' ἱστορεῖ ἐν τῇ τῶν θαυμασίων συναγωγῇ ἐν Πέλλῃ
τῆς Θετταλίας Ἀχαιὸν ἄνθρωπον Πηλεῖ καὶ
Χείρωνι καταθύεσθαι· Λυκτίους[1] γὰρ (Κρητῶν δὲ
ἔθνος εἰσὶν οὗτοι[2]) Ἀντικλείδης ἐν Νόστοις ἀπο-
φαίνεται ἀνθρώπους ἀποσφάττειν τῷ Διί, καὶ
Λεσβίους Διονύσῳ τὴν ὁμοίαν προσάγειν θυσίαν
Δωσίδας λέγει· Φωκαεῖς δέ (οὐδὲ γὰρ αὐτοὺς
παραπέμψομαι)—τούτους Πυθοκλῆς ἐν τρίτῳ Περὶ
87 P. ὁμονοίας τῇ Ταυροπόλῳ Ἀρτέμιδι ἄν|θρωπον ὁλο-
καυτεῖν[3] ἱστορεῖ. Ἐρεχθεὺς δὲ ὁ Ἀττικὸς καὶ
Μάριος ὁ Ῥωμαῖος τὰς αὑτῶν ἐθυσάτην θυγατέρας·
ὧν ὁ μὲν τῇ Φερεφάττῃ, ὡς Δημάρατος ἐν πρώτῃ
Τραγῳδουμένων, ὁ δὲ τοῖς Ἀποτροπαίοις, ὁ
Μάριος, ὡς Δωρόθεος ἐν τῇ τετάρτῃ Ἰταλικῶν
ἱστορεῖ.

Φιλάνθρωποί γε ἐκ τούτων καταφαίνονται οἱ
δαίμονες· πῶς δὲ οὐχ ὅσιοι ἀναλόγως οἱ δεισιδαίμονες; οἱ μὲν σωτῆρες εὐφημούμενοι, οἱ δὲ
σωτηρίαν αἰτούμενοι παρὰ τῶν ἐπιβούλων σωτηρίας. καλλιερεῖν γοῦν τοπάζοντες αὐτοῖς σφᾶς

---

[1] Λυκτίους from Eusebius. λυκίους MSS.
[2] οὗτοι from Eusebius. οὕτως MSS.
[3] ὁλοκαυτεῖν from Eusebius. ὁλοκαεῖν MSS.

---

[a] That is, in his play *Iphigeneia among the Taurians.*
See also Herodotus iv. 103. The Taurian peninsula is the
modern Crimea.

[b] Monimus, Frag. 1 *Frag. hist. Graec.* iv. p. 454.

[c] Anticleides, Frag. 9 Müller, *Script. rerum Alex. Mag.*
p. 149.

strangers in their territory, that is to say, men who CHAP.
III have been shipwrecked, sacrifice them on the spot to Tauric Artemis.   These are your sacrifices which Euripides represents in tragedy upon the stage.[a] Monimus, in his collection of *Wonderful Events*, relates that in Pella of Thessaly human sacrifice is offered to also Peleus and Cheiron, the victim being an Achaean.[b] at Pella Thus too, Anticleides in his *Homecomings*, declares that the Lyctians, a race of Cretans, slaughter men Human to Zeus;[c] and Dosidas says that Lesbians offer a sacrifices
offered by similar sacrifice to Dionysus.[d]   As for Phocaeans,— Lyctians, for I shall not pass them over either—these people are Lesbians,
Phocaeans reported by Pythocles in his third book *On Concord* to offer a burnt sacrifice of a man to Taurian Artemis.[e] Erechtheus the Athenian and Marius the Roman by sacrificed their own daughters, the former to Perse- Erechtheus
and Marius phone, as Demaratus relates in the first book of his *Subjects of Tragedy*;[f] the latter, Marius, to the " Averters of evil," as Dorotheus relates in the fourth book of his *Italian History*.[g]

Kindly beings to be sure the daemons are, as So daemon- these instances plainly show!   And how can the worshippers
become as daemon-worshippers help being holy in a correspond- cruel as the ing way?   The former are hailed as saviours; the daemons latter beg for safety from those who plot to destroy safety.   Certainly while they suppose that they are

[d] Dosidas (or Dosiades), Frag. 5 *Frag. hist. Graec.* iv. p. 400.

[e] Pythocles, Frag. 4 *Frag. hist. Graec.* iv. p. 489.

[f] Demaratus, Frag. 4 *Frag. hist. Graec.* iv. p. 379.

[g] Marius is said to have been warned in a dream to sacrifice his daughter Calpurnia, in order to obtain a victory over the Cimbri by whom he was hard pressed.   Plutarch, *Collect. parall.* 20 ; Dorotheus, Frag. 3 Müller, *Script. rerum Alex. Mag.* p. 156.

CAP
III

αὐτοὺς λελήθασιν ἀποσφάττοντες ἀνθρώπους. οὐ
γὰρ οὖν παρὰ τὸν τόπον ἱερεῖον γίνεται ὁ φόνος,
οὐδ᾽ εἰ ᾿Αρτέμιδί τις καὶ Διὶ ἐν ἱερῷ δῆθεν χωρίῳ
μᾶλλον ἢ ὀργῇ καὶ φιλαργυρίᾳ, ἄλλοις ὁμοίοις
δαίμοσιν, ἐπὶ βωμοῖς ἢ ἐν ὁδοῖς ἀποσφάττοι τὸν
ἄνθρωπον, [ἱερὸν]¹ ἱερεῖον ἐπιφημίσας, ἀλλὰ φόνος
ἐστὶ καὶ ἀνδροκτασία ἡ τοιαύτη θυσία. τί δὴ οὖν,
ὦ σοφώτατοι τῶν ἄλλων ζῴων ἄνθρωποι, τὰ μὲν
θηρία περιφεύγομεν τὰ ἀνήμερα, κἄν που περι-
τύχωμεν ἄρκῳ ἢ λέοντι, ἐκτρεπόμεθα,

> ὡς δ᾽ ὅτε τίς τε δράκοντα ἰδὼν παλίνορσος ἀπέστη
> οὔρεος ἐν βήσσῃς, ὑπό τε τρόμος ἔλλαβε γυῖα,
> ἄψ τ᾽ ἀνεχώρησεν·

δαίμονας δὲ ὀλεθρίους καὶ ἀλιτηρίους ἐπιβούλους τε
καὶ μισανθρώπους καὶ λυμεῶνας ὄντας προαισθό-
88 P. μενοι καὶ συνιέντες οὐκ ἐκ|τρέπεσθε οὐδὲ ἀποστρέ-
φεσθε; τί δ᾽ ἂν καὶ ἀληθεύσαιεν οἱ κακοί, ἢ τίνα
ἂν ὠφελήσαιεν; αὐτίκα γοῦν ἔχω σοι βελτίονα
τῶν ὑμεδαπῶν τούτων θεῶν, τῶν δαιμόνων, ἐπιδεῖξαι τὸν ἄνθρωπον, τοῦ ᾿Απόλλωνος τοῦ μαντικοῦ
τὸν Κῦρον καὶ τὸν Σόλωνα. φιλόδωρος ὑμῶν
ὁ Φοῖβος, ἀλλ᾽ οὐ φιλάνθρωπος. προὔδωκε τὸν
Κροῖσον τὸν φίλον καὶ τοῦ μισθοῦ ἐκλαθόμενος
(οὕτω φιλόδοξος ἦν) ἀνήγαγε τὸν Κροῖσον διὰ τοῦ
῎Αλυος ἐπὶ τὴν πυράν. οὕτω φιλοῦντες οἱ δαίμονες
ὁδηγοῦσιν εἰς τὸ πῦρ. ἀλλ᾽, ὦ φιλανθρωπότερε
καὶ ἀληθέστερε τοῦ ᾿Απόλλωνος ἄνθρωπε, τὸν ἐπὶ
τῆς πυρᾶς οἴκτειρον δεδεμένον, καὶ σὺ μέν, ὦ

---

¹ [ἱερὸν] Wilamowitz. [ἱερεῖον] Potter.

ᵃ Homer, *Iliad* iii. 33–35.

EXHORTATION TO THE GREEKS

offering acceptable sacrifices to the daemons, they

For murder does not become a sacred offering because
of the place in which it is committed, not even if
you solemnly dedicate the man and then slaughter
him in a so-called sacred spot for Artemis or Zeus,
rather than for anger or covetousness, other daemons
of the same sort, or upon altars rather than in roads.
On the contrary, such sacrifice is murder and human
butchery. Why then is it, O men, wisest of all

and turn aside if perchance we meet a bear or a

As in a mountain glade when the wayfarer spieth a serpent,
Swiftly turning his steps, his weak limbs trembling beneath
    him,
Backward he maketh his way ;ᵃ

yet when faced by deadly and accursed daemons,
you do not turn aside nor avoid them, although you
have already perceived and know quite well that
they are plotters and man-haters and destroyers?
What possible truth could evil beings utter, or
whom could they benefit? At any rate, I can at
once prove to you that man is better than these gods

a lover of gifts but not of men. He betrayed his

across the river Halys to his funeral pyre. This is
how the daemons love ; they guide men to the fire !
But do thou, O man of kinder heart and truer speech
than Apollo, pity him who lies bound upon the pyre.

95

CAP.
III
Σόλων, μάντευσαι τὴν ἀλήθειαν, σὺ δέ, ὦ Κῦρε,
κέλευσον ἀποσβεσθῆναι τὴν πυράν. σωφρόνησον
ὕστατον γοῦν, ὦ Κροῖσε, τῷ πάθει μεταμαθών·
ἀχάριστός ἐστιν ὃν προσκυνεῖς, λαμβάνει τὸν
μισθὸν καὶ μετὰ τὸ χρυσίον ψεύδεται πάλιν. τέλος
ἄρα οὐχ ὁ δαίμων, ἀλλὰ ὁ ἄνθρωπός σοι λέγει. οὐ
λοξὰ μαντεύεται Σόλων· τοῦτον εὑρήσεις[1] ἀληθῆ
μόνον, ὦ βάρβαρε, τὸν χρησμόν· τοῦτον ἐπὶ τῆς
πυρᾶς δοκιμάσεις.

Ὅθεν ἔπεισί μοι θαυμάζειν τίσι ποτὲ φαντασίαις
ἀπαχθέντες οἱ πρῶτοι πεπλανημένοι δεισιδαιμονίαν
ἀνθρώποις κατήγγειλαν, δαίμονας ἀλιτηρίους νομοθετοῦντες σέβειν, εἴτε Φορωνεὺς ἐκεῖνος ἦν εἴτε
Μέροψ εἴτε ἄλλος τις, οἳ νεώς καὶ βωμοὺς ἀνέστησαν
αὐτοῖς, πρὸς δὲ καὶ θυσίας παραστῆσαι πρῶτοι
μεμύθευνται. καὶ γὰρ δὴ καὶ κατὰ χρόνους
ὕστερον ἀνέπλαττον θεούς, οἷς προσκυνοῖεν. ἀμέλει
τὸν Ἔρωτα τοῦτον ⟨τὸν⟩[2] ἐν τοῖς πρεσβυτάτοις τῶν
θεῶν εἶναι λεγόμενον ἐτίμα πρότερον οὐδὲ εἷς πρὶν
ἢ Χάρμον μειράκιόν τι ἑλεῖν καὶ βωμὸν ἱδρύσασθαι
ἐν Ἀκαδημίᾳ χαριστήριον[3] ἐπιτελοῦς γενομένης
ἐπιθυμίας· καὶ τῆς νόσου τὴν ἀσέλγειαν Ἔρωτα
κεκλήκασι, θεοποιοῦντες ἀκόλαστον ἐπιθυμίαν.
39 P. Ἀθηναῖοι δὲ οὐδὲ τὸν Πᾶνα ᾔδεσαν ὅστις ἦν, | πρὶν
ἢ Φιλιππίδην εἰπεῖν αὐτοῖς.

---

[1] εὑρήσεις Canter. εὖ θήσεις MSS.

[2] ⟨τὸν⟩ inserted by Markland.

[3] χαριστήριον Valckenaer ; see *Protrepticus* 27 P. (p. 64
above) and 42 P. (p. 106). χαριέστερον MSS.

---

[a] See the whole story in Herodotus i. 30–33 and 85–88.

[b] Cp. Pausanias i. 30. 1, Athenaeus xiii. p. 609 D ; and,
for the antiquity of Eros, Plato, *Symposium* 178 A–C, and
Hesiod, *Theogonia* 120, with Paley's note *ad loc.* The ancient

Do thou, Solon, utter an oracle of truth. Do thou, CHAP. Cyrus, bid the flaming pyre be quenched. Come to III thy senses at the eleventh hour, Croesus, when suffering has taught thee better. Ungrateful is he whom thou dost worship. He takes the reward of gold, and then deceives thee once again. Mark! it is not the daemon, but the man who tells thee the issue of life. Unlike Apollo, Solon utters no double-meaning prophecies. This oracle alone shalt thou find true, O barbarian. This shalt thou prove upon the pyre.[a]

I cannot help wondering, therefore, what delusive How were fancies could have led astray those who were the the first daemon- first to be themselves deceived, and the first also, by worshippers the laws they established for the worship of accursed led astray? daemons, to proclaim their superstition to mankind. I mean such men as the well-known Phoroneus, or Merops, or others like them, who set up temples and altars to the daemons, and are also said in legend to have been the first to offer sacrifices. There can be no doubt that in succeeding ages men used to In later invent gods whom they might worship. This Eros, ages men freely in- for instance, who is said to be amongst the oldest vented gods of the gods,—why, not a single person honoured him before Charmus carried off a young lad and erected an altar in Academia, as a thank-offering for the satisfaction of his lust; and this disease of debauchery is what men call Eros, making unbridled lust into a god![b] Nor did Athenians know who even Pan was, before Philippides told them.[c]

Eros was probably an earth-deity, or god of fertility, and in reality quite different from the winged child who accompanies Aphrodite and is the personification of human love. See Farnell, *Cults of the Greek States*, ii. pp. 625–6.

[c] Herodotus vi. 105.

CAP.
III

Εἰκότως ἄρα ἀρχήν ποθεν ἡ δεισιδαιμονία λαβοῦσα κακίας ἀνοήτου γέγονε πηγή· εἶτα δὲ μὴ ἀνακοπεῖσα, ἀλλ' εἰς ἐπίδοσιν ἐλθοῦσα καὶ πολλὴ δὴ ῥυεῖσα, δημιουργὸς πολλῶν καθίσταται δαιμόνων, ἑκατόμβας θύουσα καὶ πανηγύρεις ἐπιτελοῦσα καὶ ἀγάλματα ἀνιστᾶσα καὶ νεὼς ἀνοικοδομοῦσα, τοὺς[1] δή—οὐδὲ γὰρ οὐδὲ τούτους σιωπήσομαι, πρὸς δὲ καὶ αὐτοὺς ἐξελέγξω—νεὼς μὲν εὐφήμως ὀνομαζομένους, τάφους δὲ γενομένους [τουτέστι τοὺς τάφους νεὼς ἐπικεκλημένους].[2] ὑμεῖς δὲ ἀλλὰ κἂν νῦν δεισιδαιμονίας ἐκλάθεσθε, τοὺς τάφους τιμᾶν αἰσχυνόμενοι. ἐν τῷ νεῷ τῆς Ἀθηνᾶς ἐν Λαρίσῃ ἐν τῇ ἀκροπόλει τάφος ἐστὶν Ἀκρισίου, Ἀθήνησιν δὲ ἐν ἀκροπόλει Κέκροπος, ὥς φησιν Ἀντίοχος ἐν τῷ ἐνάτῳ τῶν Ἱστοριῶν. τί δὲ Ἐριχθόνιος; οὐχὶ ἐν τῷ νεῷ τῆς Πολιάδος κεκήδευται; Ἰμμάραδος[3] δὲ ὁ Εὐμόλπου καὶ Δαείρας οὐχὶ ἐν τῷ περιβόλῳ τοῦ Ἐλευσινίου τοῦ ὑπὸ τῇ ἀκροπόλει; αἱ δὲ Κελεοῦ θυγατέρες οὐχὶ ἐν Ἐλευσῖνι τετάφαται; τί σοι καταλέγω τὰς ⟨ἐξ⟩[4] Ὑπερβορέων γυναῖκας; Ὑπερόχη καὶ Λαοδίκη κέκλησθον, ἐν τῷ Ἀρτεμισίῳ ἐν Δήλῳ κεκήδευσθον, τὸ δὲ ἐν τῷ Ἀπόλλωνος τοῦ Δηλίου ἐστὶν ἱερῷ. Λεάνδριος δὲ Κλέοχον[5] ἐν Μιλήτῳ τεθάφθαι ἐν τῷ Διδυμαίῳ φησίν. ἐνταῦθα τῆς Λευκοφρύνης τὸ μνημεῖον οὐκ ἄξιον παρελθεῖν ἑπομένους Ζήνωνι τῷ Μυνδίῳ, ἢ ἐν τῷ ἱερῷ τῆς
40 P. Ἀρτέμιδος ἐν | Μαγνησίᾳ κεκήδευται, οὐδὲ μὴν

---

[1] τοὺς Schwartz. οὓς mss.
[2] [τουτέστι . . ἐπικεκλημένους] Markland.
[3] Ἰμμάραδος from Pausanias i. 5. 2, etc. ἵμμαρος mss.
[4] ⟨ἐξ⟩ from Eusebius, *Praep. Ev.* ii. 6.
[5] Κλέοχον Müller from Arnobius vi. 6 and Apollodorus iii. 1. 2. κλέαρχον mss.

We must not then be surprised that, once daemon-worship had somewhere taken a beginning, it became a fountain of insensate wickedness. Then, not being checked, but ever increasing and flowing in full stream, it establishes itself as creator of a multitude of daemons. It offers great public sacrifices; it holds solemn festivals; it sets up statues and builds temples. These temples—for I will not keep silence even about them, but will expose them also—are called by a fair-sounding name, but in reality they are tombs. But I appeal to you, even at this late hour forget daemon-worship, feeling ashamed to honour tombs. In the temple of Athena in the Acropolis at Larissa there is the tomb of Acrisius; and in the Acropolis at Athens the tomb of Cecrops, as Antiochus says in his ninth book of *Histories*.[a] And what of Erichthonius? Does not he lie in the temple of Athena Polias? And does not Immaradus, the son of Eumolpus and Daeira, lie in the enclosure of the Eleusinium which is under the Acropolis? Are not the daughters of Celeus buried in Eleusis? Why recount to you the Hyperborean women? They are called Hyperoche and Laodice, and they lie in the Artemisium at Delos; this is in the temple precincts of Delian Apollo. Leandrius says that Cleochus is buried in the Didymaeum at Miletus.[b] Here, following Zeno of Myndus, we must not omit the sepulchre of Leucophryne, who lies in the temple of Artemis in Magnesia; nor yet the altar of Apollo

CHAP. III
Thus daemon-worship grew to its present extent

But the temples are really tombs, as examples prove

---

[a] Antiochus, Frag. 15 *Frag. hist. Graec.* i. p. 184.
[b] Leandrius (or Meandrius), Frag. 5 *Frag. hist. Graec.* ii. p. 336. The Didymaeum is the temple of Zeus and Apollo at Didyma near Miletus.

CAP. τὸν ἐν Τελμησσῷ [1] βωμὸν τοῦ Ἀπόλλωνος· μνῆμα
III εἶναι καὶ τοῦτον Τελμησσοῦ [2] τοῦ μάντεως ἱστοροῦσιν. Πτολεμαῖος δὲ ὁ τοῦ Ἀγησάρχου ἐν τῷ αʹ
τῶν περὶ τὸν Φιλοπάτορα ἐν Πάφῳ λέγει ἐν τῷ
τῆς Ἀφροδίτης ἱερῷ Κινύραν τε καὶ τοὺς Κινύρου
ἀπογόνους κεκηδεῦσθαι. ἀλλὰ γὰρ ἐπιόντι μοι τοὺς
προσκυνουμένους ὑμῖν τάφους

εμοὶ μὲν οὐδ᾽ ὁ πᾶς ἂν ἀρκέσαι [3] χρόνος·

ὑμᾶς δὲ εἰ μὴ ὑπεισέρχεταί τις αἰσχύνη τῶν
τολμωμένων, νεκροὶ ἄρα τέλεον ὄντες νεκροῖς
[ὄντως] [4] πεπιστευκότες περιέρχεσθε·

ἆ δειλοί, τί κακὸν τόδε πάσχετε; νυκτὶ μὲν
ὑμῶν
εἰλύαται κεφαλαί.

IV

Εἰ δ᾽ ἔτι πρὸς τούτοις φέρων ὑμῖν τὰ ἀγάλματα αὐτὰ ἐπισκοπεῖν παραθείην, ἐπιόντες ὡς ἀληθῶς λῆρον εὑρήσετε τὴν συνήθειαν, '' ἔργα χειρῶν
ἀνθρώπων '' ἀναίσθητα προστρεπόμενοι.[5] πάλαι μὲν
οὖν οἱ Σκύθαι τὸν ἀκινάκην, οἱ Ἄραβες τὸν λίθον,
οἱ Πέρσαι τὸν ποταμὸν προσεκύνουν, καὶ τῶν

---

[1] Τελμησσῷ Stählin from Arnobius, and one ms. of
Eusebius. τελμισσῷ mss.
[2] Τελμησσοῦ Stählin. τελμισσοῦ mss.
[3] ἀρκέσαι from Eusebius. ἀρκέσῃ mss.
[4] [ὄντως] Heyse.
[5] προστρεπόμενοι Potter. προτρεπόμενοι mss.

---

[a] Ptolemaeus of Megalopolis, Frag. 1 *Frag. hist. Graec.*
iii. p. 66.

at Telmessus, which is reported to be a monument CHAP. to the prophet Telmessus. Ptolemaeus the son of III Agesarchus in the first volume of his work *About Philopator* says that in the temple of Aphrodite at Paphos both Cinyras and his descendants lie buried.[a] But really, if I were to go through all the tombs held sacred in your eyes,

> The whole of time would not suffice my need.[b]

As for you, unless a touch of shame steals over you for these audacities, then you are going about utterly dead, like the dead in whom you have put your trust.

Oh! most wretched of men, what evil is this that ye suffer? Darkness hath shrouded your heads.[c]

IV

If, in addition to this, I bring the statues them- The images selves and place them by your side for inspection, of the gods you will find on going through them that custom[d] is truly nonsense, when it leads you to adore senseless things, "the works of men's hands."[e] In ancient The first times, then, the Scythians used to worship the dagger, images were the Arabians their sacred stone,[f] the Persians their unwrought river. Other peoples still more ancient erected wood and stone

[b] This verse is not found in Nauck's collection of Tragic Fragments. The sense may be compared with that of St. John xxi. 25.

[c] Homer, *Odyssey* xx. 351-352.

[d] Custom, *i.e.* inherited traditions about the gods and their worship, was pleaded by adherents of the old religions as a defence against Christian attack; see p. 197.

[e] Psalm cxv. 4.

[f] *i.e.* the Kaaba at Mecca.

CAP.
IV

ἄλλων ἀνθρώπων οἱ ἔτι παλαιότεροι ξύλα ἱδρύον-
το περιφανῆ καὶ κίονας ἵστων ἐκ λίθων· ἃ δὴ
καὶ ξόανα προσηγορεύετο διὰ τὸ ἀπεξέσθαι τῆς
ὕλης. ἀμέλει ἐν Ἰκάρῳ τῆς Ἀρτέμιδος τὸ ἄγαλμα
ξύλον ἦν οὐκ εἰργασμένον, καὶ τῆς Κιθαιρωνίας
Ἥρας ἐν Θεσπείᾳ πρέμνον ἐκκεκομμένον· καὶ τὸ
τῆς Σαμίας Ἥρας, ὥς φησιν Ἀέθλιος, πρότερον
μὲν ἦν σανίς, ὕστερον δὲ ἐπὶ Προκλέους ἄρχοντος
41 P. ἀνδριαντοειδὲς ἐγένετο. ἐπεὶ δὲ ἀνθρώποις | ἀπ-
εικονίζεσθαι τὰ ξόανα ἤρξατο, βρέτη τὴν ἐκ
βροτῶν ἐπωνυμίαν ἐκαρπώσατο. ἐν Ῥώμῃ δὲ τὸ
παλαιὸν δόρυ φησὶ γεγονέναι τοῦ Ἄρεως τὸ
ξόανον Οὐάρρων ὁ συγγραφεύς, οὐδέπω τῶν τεχνι-
τῶν ἐπὶ τὴν εὐπρόσωπον ταύτην κακοτεχνίαν
ὡρμηκότων. ἐπειδὴ δὲ ἤνθησεν ἡ τέχνη, ηὔξησεν
ἡ πλάνη.

Ὡς μὲν οὖν τοὺς λίθους καὶ τὰ ξύλα καὶ συνελόντι
φάναι τὴν ὕλην ἀγάλματα ἀνδρείκελα ἐποιήσαντο,
οἷς ἐπιμορφάζετε εὐσέβειαν συκοφαντοῦντες τὴν
ἀλήθειαν, ἤδη μὲν αὐτόθεν δῆλον· οὐ μὴν ἀλλὰ
καὶ ἀποδείξεως ποσῆς ἐπιδεομένου τοῦ τόπου οὐ
παραιτητέον. τὸν μὲν οὖν Ὀλυμπίασι Δία καὶ
τὴν Ἀθήνησι Πολιάδα ἐκ χρυσοῦ καὶ ἐλέφαντος
κατασκευάσαι Φειδίαν παντί που σαφές· τὸ δὲ ἐν
Σάμῳ τῆς Ἥρας ξόανον Σμίλιδι τῷ [1] Εὐκλείδου
πεποιῆσθαι Ὀλύμπιχος ἐν Σαμιακοῖς ἱστορεῖ. μὴ
οὖν ἀμφιβάλλετε, εἰ τῶν Σεμνῶν Ἀθήνησι καλουμέ-

---

[1] Σμίλιδι τῷ Cobet.   σμιλῇ τῇ MSS.

---

[a] Aëthlius of Samos, Fr. 1 Frag. hist. Graec. iv. p. 287.

[b] Varro, Ant. rer. div. xvi. Fr. 34 Agahd (Jahrb. class.
Phil., 1898, Suppl. Bd. p. 210), and cp. S. Augustine, Civ.
Dei iv. 31.

[c] Olympichus, Fr. 1 Frag. hist. Graec. iv. p. 466.

conspicuous wooden poles and set up pillars of
stones, to which they gave the name *xoana,* meaning
scraped objects, because the rough surface of the
material had been scraped off. Certainly the statue
of Artemis in Icarus was a piece of unwrought timber,
and that of Cithaeronian Hera in Thespiae was a
felled tree-trunk. The statue of Samian Hera, as
Aëthlius says, was at first a wooden beam, but afterwards, when Procles was ruler, it was made into
human form.[a] When these rude images began to be *Afterwards
made into
human form*
shaped to the likeness of men, they acquired the
additional name *bretē,* from *brotoi* meaning mortals.
In Rome, of old time, according to Varro the prose-
writer, the object that represented Ares was a spear,[b]
since craftsmen had not yet entered upon the fair-
seeming but mischievous art of sculpture. But the
moment art flourished, error increased.

It is now, therefore, self-evident that out of stones *Proof by
examples
that all
images of
gods are the
work of men*
and blocks of wood, and, in one word, out of matter,
men fashioned statues resembling the human form,
to which you offer a semblance of piety, calumniating
the truth. Still, since the point calls for a certain
amount of argument, we must not decline to furnish
it. Now everyone, I suppose, will admit that the
statues of Zeus at Olympia and Athena Polias at
Athens were wrought of gold and ivory by Pheidias;
and Olympichus in his *Samian History* relates that
the image of Hera in Samos was made by Smilis the
son of Eucleides.[c] Do not doubt, then, that of the
goddesses at Athens called "venerable"[d] two were

[d] These are the same as the Erinyes, goddesses of
vengeance, mentioned on p. 53. They were called
Eumenides, the kindly ones, and at Athens Semnai, the
venerable ones, these titles being euphemistic substitutes
for their real and dreaded name.

CAP.
IV
νων θεῶν τὰς μὲν δύο Σκόπας ἐποίησεν ἐκ τοῦ καλουμένου λυχνέως λίθου, Κάλως δὲ τὴν μέσην αὐταῖν·
ἱστοροῦντα ἔχω σοι[1] Πολέμωνα δεικνύναι ἐν τῇ
τετάρτῃ τῶν πρὸς Τίμαιον· μηδ' εἰ[2] τὰ ἐν Παταροῖς
τῆς Λυκίας ἀγάλματα Διὸς καὶ Ἀπόλλωνος Φειδίας
πάλιν ἐκεῖνος[3] [τὰ ἀγάλματα][4] καθάπερ τοὺς λέοντας τοὺς σὺν αὐτοῖς ἀνακειμένους εἴργασται· εἰ δέ,
ὥς φασί τινες, Βρυάξιος ἡ[5] τέχνη, οὐ διαφέρομαι·
ἔχεις καὶ τοῦτον ἀγαλματουργόν· ὁπότερον αὐτοῖν
βούλει ἐπίγραφε. καὶ μὴν Τελεσίου τοῦ Ἀθηναίου,
ὥς φησι Φιλόχορος, ἔργον εἰσὶν ἀγάλματα ἐννεα-
πήχη Ποσειδῶνος καὶ Ἀμφιτρίτης ἐν Τήνῳ προσ-
κυνούμενα. Δημήτριος γὰρ ἐν δευτέρῳ τῶν Ἀρ-
γολικῶν τοῦ ἐν Τίρυνθι τῆς Ἥρας ξοάνου καὶ τὴν
ὕλην ὄγχνην καὶ τὸν ποιητὴν Ἄργον ἀναγράφει.
πολλοὶ δ' ἂν τάχα που θαυμάσειαν, εἰ μάθοιεν τὸ
42 P. Παλλάδιον τὸ διοπετὲς καλούμενον, | ὃ Διομήδης
καὶ Ὀδυσσεὺς ἱστοροῦνται μὲν ὑφελέσθαι ἀπὸ
Ἰλίου, παρακαταθέσθαι δὲ Δημοφῶντι, ἐκ τῶν
Πέλοπος ὀστῶν κατεσκευάσθαι, καθάπερ τὸν
Ὀλύμπιον ἐξ ἄλλων ὀστῶν Ἰνδικοῦ θηρίου. καὶ
δὴ τὸν ἱστοροῦντα Διονύσιον ἐν τῷ πέμπτῳ μέρει
τοῦ Κύκλου παρίστημι. Ἀπελλᾶς δὲ ἐν τοῖς

---

[1] τὴν μέσην . . σοι Jahn.   ἣν μέσην αὐταῖν ἱστοροῦνται
ἔχουσαι MSS.
[2] μηδ' εἰ Münzel.   μηδὲ MSS.
[3] ἐκεῖνος Wilamowitz.   ἐκεῖνα MSS.
[4] [τὰ ἀγάλματα] Stählin.   [πάλιν . . ἀγάλματα] Heyse.
[5] ἡ Wilamowitz.   ἣν MSS.

---

[a] *Lychneus* is mentioned by Athenaeus (205 F) as a
stone from which images were made. It is probably the
same as *lychnites*, which according to Pliny (*Nat. Hist.*
xxxvi. 14) was a name given to Parian marble, because it

made by Scopas out of the stone called *lychneus*,[a] CHAP.
and the middle one by Calos; I can point out to you IV
the account given by Polemon in the fourth volume
of his work *Against Timaeus*.[b] Neither doubt that
the statues of Zeus and Apollo in Lycian Patara
were also wrought by the great Pheidias, just as
were the lions that are dedicated along with them.
But if, as some say, the art is that of Bryaxis, I do
not contradict. He also is one of your sculptors;
put down which of the two you like. Further,
the nine-cubit statues of Poseidon and Amphitrite
worshipped in Tenos are the work of the Athenian
Telesius, as Philochorus tells us.[c] Demetrius in his
second book of *Argolic History*, speaking of the image
of Hera in Tiryns, records its material, pear-tree
wood, as well as its maker, Argus.[d] Many would
perhaps be astonished to learn that the image of Pallas
called "heaven-sent" (because it fell from heaven),[e]
which Diomedes and Odysseus are related to have
stolen away from Troy, and to have entrusted to the
keeping of Demophon, is made out of the bones of
Pelops, just as the Olympian Zeus is also made out of
bones,—those of an Indian beast.[f] I give you, too,
my authority for this, namely Dionysius, who relates
the story in the fifth section of his *Cycle*.[g] Apellas

[a] was quarried in underground pits by lamplight (*lychnos* =
lamp).

[b] Polemon, Fr. 41 *Frag. hist. Graec.* iii. p. 127.

[c] Philochorus, Fr. 185 *Frag. hist. Graec.* i. pp. 414–15.

[d] Demetrius of Troezen, Fr. 5 Diels (*Frag. hist. Graec.*
iv. p. 383).

[e] Compare this with the image of Artemis at Ephesus,
mentioned in Acts xix. 35, which is also called *diopetes*, or
"fallen from heaven" (R.V. margin).

[f] *i.e.* the tusks of an elephant.

[g] Dionysius, Fr. 5 *Frag. hist. Graec.* ii. pp. 9–10.

CAP.
IV
Δελφικοῖς δύο φησὶ γεγονέναι τὰ Παλλάδια, ἄμφω
δ᾽ ὑπ᾽ ἀνθρώπων δεδημιουργῆσθαι. ἀλλ᾽ ὅπως
μηδεὶς ὑπολάβῃ καὶ ταῦτά με ἀγνοίᾳ παρεικέναι,[1]
παραθήσομαι τοῦ Μορύχου Διονύσου τὸ ἄγαλμα
Ἀθήνησι γεγονέναι μὲν ἐκ τοῦ φελλάτα καλουμένου
λίθου, ἔργον δὲ εἶναι Σίκωνος τοῦ Εὐπαλάμου, ὥς
φησι Πολέμων ἔν τινι ἐπιστολῇ. ἐγενέσθην[2] δὲ καὶ
ἄλλω τινὲ δύω Κρητικὼ οἶμαι ἀνδριαντοποιὼ
(Σκύλλις[3] καὶ Δίποινος ὠνομαζέσθην)· τούτω δὲ
τὰ ἐν Ἄργει τοῖν Διοσκούροιν ἀγάλματα κατ-
εσκευασάτην καὶ τὸν ἐν Τίρυνθι Ἡρακλέους ἀνδριάντα καὶ τὸ τῆς Μουνυχίας Ἀρτέμιδος ξόανον
ἐν Σικυῶνι.

Καὶ τί περὶ ταῦτα διατρίβω, ἐξὸν αὐτὸν τὸν
μεγαλοδαίμονα ὑμῖν ἐπιδεῖξαι ὅστις ἦν, ὃν δὴ
κατ᾽ ἐξοχὴν πρὸς πάντων σεβασμοῦ κατηξιωμένον
ἀκούομεν, τοῦτον ⟨ὃν⟩[4] ἀχειροποίητον εἰπεῖν τε-
τολμήκασιν, τὸν Αἰγύπτιον Σάραπιν; οἱ μὲν γὰρ
αὐτὸν ἱστοροῦσιν χαριστήριον ὑπὸ Σινωπέων Πτο-
λεμαίῳ τῷ Φιλαδέλφῳ τῷ Αἰγυπτίων πεμφθῆναι
βασιλεῖ, ὃς λιμῷ τρυχομένους αὐτοὺς ἀπ᾽ Αἰγύπτου
μεταπεμψαμένους[5] σῖτον [ὁ Πτολεμαῖος][6] ἀνεκτή-
σατο, εἶναι δὲ τὸ ξόανον τοῦτο ἄγαλμα Πλούτωνος·
ὁ δὲ[7] δεξάμενος τὸν ἀνδριάντα καθίδρυσεν ἐπὶ τῆς

---

[1] παρεικέναι Sylburg.   παρηκέναι mss.
[2] ἐγενέσθην Sylburg.   γενέσθην mss.
[3] Σκύλλις Sylburg (from Pausanias ii. 15. 1, etc.).   ἐκύλης
mss.
[4] ⟨ὃν⟩ inserted by Markland.
[5] μεταπεμψαμένους Sylburg.   μεταπεμψάμενος mss.
[6] [ὁ Πτολεμαῖος] Arcerius.
[7] ὁ δὲ Heyse.   ὃς mss.

in his *Delphic History* says that there are two such images of Pallas, and that both are of human workmanship.[a] I will also mention the statue of Morychian Dionysus at Athens,—in order that no one may suppose me to have omitted these facts through ignorance,—that it is made out of the stone called *phellatas*,[b] and is the work of Sicon the son of Eupalamus, as Polemon says in a certain letter.[c] There were also two other sculptors, Cretans I believe, whose names were Scyllis and Dipoenus. This pair made the statues of the Twin Brothers at Argos, the figure of Heracles at Tiryns and the image of Munychian Artemis at Sicyon.[d]

But why do I linger over these, when I can show you the origin of the arch-daemon himself, the one who, we are told, is pre-eminently worthy of veneration by all men, whom they have dared to say is made without hands, the Egyptian Sarapis?[e] Some relate that he was sent by the people of Sinope as a thank-offering to Ptolemy Philadelphus king of Egypt,[f] who had earned their gratitude at a time when they were worn out with hunger and had sent for corn from Egypt; and that this image was a statue of Pluto. On receiving the figure, the king

CHAP.
IV

Even the great Sarapis is man's work

Three versions of its origin

[a] Apellas, Fr. 1 *Frag. hist. Graec.* iv. p. 307.
[b] The scholiast describes this as a rough stone quarried from Phelleus, a rocky district of Attica ; cp. Aristoph. *Clouds* 71.
[c] Polemon, Fr. 73 *Frag. hist. Graec.* iii. p. 136.
[d] For Scyllis and Dipoenus see Pausanias ii. 22. 5, etc.
[e] An account of Sarapis-worship, showing its wide diffusion at this time, will be found in Dill, *Roman Society from Nero*, etc. pp. 560–584.
[f] A different version of this story is to be found in Plutarch, *Isis and Osiris* ch. xxviii.

CLEMENT OF ALEXANDRIA

CAP. IV ἄκρας, ἣν νῦν Ῥακῶτιν καλοῦσιν, ἔνθα καὶ τὸ
ἱερὸν τετίμηται τοῦ Σαράπιδος, γειτνιᾷ δὲ τοῖς
τόποις[1] τὸ χωρίον. Βλιστίχην[2] δὲ τὴν παλλακίδα
τελευτήσασαν ἐν Κανώβῳ μεταγαγὼν ὁ Πτολεμαῖος
ἔθαψεν ὑπὸ τὸν προδεδηλωμένον σηκόν. ἄλλοι δέ
φασι Ποντικὸν εἶναι βρέτας τὸν Σάραπιν, μετῆχθαι
δὲ εἰς Ἀλεξάνδρειαν μετὰ τιμῆς πανηγυρικῆς.
Ἰσίδωρος μόνος παρὰ Σελευκέων τῶν πρὸς Ἀντιοχείᾳ[3] τὸ ἄγαλμα μεταχθῆναι λέγει, ἐν σιτοδείᾳ
καὶ αὐτῶν γενομένων καὶ ὑπὸ Πτολεμαίου διατρα-
48 P. φέντων. ἀλλ᾽ ὅ γε Ἀθηνόδωρος | ὁ τοῦ Σάνδωνος
ἀρχαΐζειν τὸν Σάραπιν βουληθεὶς οὐκ οἶδ᾽ ὅπως[4]
περιέπεσεν, ἐλέγξας αὐτὸν ἄγαλμα εἶναι γενητόν·
Σέσωστριν φησι τὸν Αἰγύπτιον βασιλέα, τὰ πλεῖστα
τῶν παρ᾽ Ἕλλησι παραστησάμενον ἐθνῶν, ἐπανελ-
θόντα εἰς Αἴγυπτον ἐπαγαγέσθαι τεχνίτας ἱκανούς·
τὸν οὖν Ὄσιριν τὸν προπάτορα τὸν αὐτοῦ δαι-
δαλθῆναι ἐκέλευσεν αὐτός[5] πολυτελῶς, κατασκευάζει
δὲ αὐτὸν Βρύαξις ὁ δημιουργός, οὐχ ὁ Ἀθηναῖος,
ἄλλος δέ τις ὁμώνυμος ἐκείνῳ τῷ Βρυάξιδι· ὃς
ὕλῃ κατακέχρηται εἰς δημιουργίαν μικτῇ καὶ
ποικίλῃ. ῥίνημα γὰρ χρυσοῦ ἦν αὐτῷ καὶ ἀργύρου
χαλκοῦ τε καὶ σιδήρου καὶ μολίβδου, πρὸς δὲ καὶ
κασσιτέρου, λίθων δὲ Αἰγυπτίων ἐνέδει οὐδὲ εἷς,
σαπφείρου καὶ αἱματίτου θραύσματα σμαράγδου τε,
ἀλλὰ καὶ τοπαζίου. λεάνας οὖν τὰ πάντα καὶ
ἀναμίξας ἔχρωσε κυάνῳ, οὗ δὴ χάριν μελάντερον

---

[1] τάφοις Mayor. (The map of ancient Alexandria shows the Serapeum to be adjacent to Necropolis.) But τόπος = τάφος in Euripides, *Heracleidae* 1041.
[2] Βλιστίχην Dindorf. βλιστιχιν mss.
[3] Ἀντιοχείᾳ Cobet. ἀντιόχειαν mss.
[4] ὅτῳ Schwartz : Stählin.

set it up upon the promontory which they now call
Rhacotis, where stands the honoured temple of
Sarapis; and the spot is close to the burial-places.
And they say that Ptolemy had his mistress Blistiche,
who had died in Canobus, brought here and buried
under the before mentioned shrine.   Others say that
Sarapis was an image from Pontus, and that it was
conveyed to Alexandria with the honour of a solemn
festival.   Isidorus alone states that the statue was
brought from the people of Seleucia near to Antioch,
when they too had been suffering from dearth of
corn and had been sustained by Ptolemy.   But
Athenodorus [a] the son of Sandon, while intending
to establish the antiquity of Sarapis, stumbled in
some unaccountable way, for he has proved him to
be a statue made by man.   He says that Sesostris
the Egyptian king, having subdued most of the
nations of Greece, brought back on his return to
Egypt a number of skilful craftsmen.   He gave
personal orders, therefore, that a statue of Osiris his
own ancestor should be elaborately wrought at great
expense; and the statue was made by the artist
Bryaxis,—not the famous Athenian, but another of
the same name,—who has used a mixture of various
materials in its construction.   He had filings of gold,
silver, bronze, iron, lead, and even tin; and not a single
Egyptian stone was lacking, there being pieces of
sapphire, hematite, emerald, and topaz also.   Having
reduced them all to powder and mixed them, he
stained the mixture dark blue (on account of which
the colour of the statue is nearly black), and, mingling

---

[a] Athenodorus, Fr. 4 *Frag. hist. Graec.* iii. pp. 487-88.

CAP.
IV

τὸ χρῶμα τοῦ ἀγάλματος, καὶ τῷ ἐκ τῆς Ὀσίριδος
καὶ τοῦ Ἄπιος κηδείας ὑπολελειμμένῳ φαρμάκῳ
φυράσας τὰ πάντα διέπλασεν τὸν Σάραπιν· οὗ καὶ
τοὔνομα αἰνίττεται τὴν κοινωνίαν τῆς κηδείας καὶ
τὴν ἐκ τῆς ταφῆς δημιουργίαν, σύνθετον ἀπό τε
Ὀσίριδος καὶ Ἄπιος γενόμενον Ὀσίραπις.

Καινὸν δὲ ἄλλον ἐν Αἰγύπτῳ, ὀλίγου δεῖν καὶ
παρ᾽ Ἕλλησι, σεβασμίως τεθείακεν θεὸν ὁ βασιλεὺς
ὁ Ῥωμαίων τὸν ἐρώμενον ὡραιότατον[1] σφόδρα γενό-
μενον· Ἀντίνοον [ὂν][2] ἀνιέρωσεν οὕτως ὡς Γανυ-
μήδην ὁ Ζεύς· οὐ γὰρ κωλύεται ῥᾳδίως ἐπιθυμία
φόβον οὐκ ἔχουσα· καὶ νύκτας ἱερὰς τὰς Ἀντινόου
προσκυνοῦσιν ἄνθρωποι νῦν, ἃς αἰσχρὰς ἠπίστατο
ὁ συναγρυπνήσας ἐραστής. τί μοι θεὸν καταλέγεις
τὸν πορνείᾳ τετιμημένον; τί δὲ καὶ ὡς υἱὸν
θρηνεῖσθαι προσέταξας; τί δὲ καὶ τὸ κάλλος
αὐτοῦ διηγῇ; αἰσχρόν ἐστι τὸ κάλλος ὕβρει
μεμαραμμένον. μὴ τυραννήσῃς, ἄνθρωπε, τοῦ κάλλους μηδὲ ἐνυβρίσῃς ἀνθοῦντι τῷ νέῳ· τήρησον
αὐτὸ καθαρόν, ἵνα ᾖ καλόν. βασιλεὺς τοῦ κάλλους
γενοῦ, μὴ τύραννος· ἐλεύθερον[3] μεινάτω· τότε σου
γνωρίσω τὸ κάλλος, ὅτε[4] καθαρὰν τετήρηκας τὴν
εἰκόνα· τότε προσκυνήσω τὸ κάλλος, ὅτε[5] ἀληθινὸν
44 P. ἀρχέτυπόν ἐστι | τῶν καλῶν. ἤδη δὲ τάφος ἐστὶ τοῦ
ἐρωμένου, νεώς ἐστιν Ἀντινόου καὶ πόλις· καθάπερ

---

[1] ὡραιότατον from Eusebius, *Praep. Ev.* ii. 6.   ὡραῖον τῶν
MSS.
[2] [ὂν] Eusebius.
[3] ἐλεύθερον Wilamowitz.   ἐλεύθερος MSS.
[4] ὅτε Wilamowitz.   ὅτι MSS.
[5] ὅτε Stählin.   τὸ MSS.   δ before ἀρχέτυπον in M ; above
the line in P.

110

the whole with the pigment left over from the funeral rites of Osiris and Apis,[a] he moulded Sarapis; whose very name implies this connexion with the funeral rites, and the construction out of material for burial, Osirapis being a compound formed from Osiris and Apis.

Another fresh divinity was created in Egypt,— and very nearly among Greeks too,—when the Roman king[b] solemnly elevated to the rank of god his favourite whose beauty was unequalled. He consecrated Antinous in the same way that Zeus consecrated Ganymedes. For lust is not easily restrained, when it has no fear; and to-day men observe the sacred nights of Antinous, which were really shameful, as the lover who kept them with him well knew. Why, I ask, do you reckon as a god one who is honoured by fornication? Why did you order that he should be mourned for as a son? Why, too, do you tell the story of his beauty? Beauty is a shameful thing when it has been blighted by outrage. Be not a tyrant, O man, over beauty, neither outrage him who is in the flower of his youth. Guard it in purity, that it may remain beautiful. Become a king over beauty, not a tyrant. Let it remain free. When you have kept its image pure, then I will acknowledge your beauty. Then I will worship beauty, when it is the true archetype of things beautiful. But now we have a tomb of the boy who was loved, a temple and a city of Antinous: and it

[a] For the burial of the Apis bull see p. 84, n. *a*, and A. B. Cook, *Zeus*, i. pp. 434–5.

[b] *i.e.* Hadrian. When Antinous was drowned in the Nile, Hadrian gave way to extraordinary grief. He ordered him to be enrolled among the gods, and built Antinoopolis in his memory. See Pausanias viii. 9. 7–8.

CLEMENT OF ALEXANDRIA

CAP.
IV
δέ, οἶμαι, οἱ ναοί, οὕτω δὲ καὶ οἱ τάφοι θαυμάζονται,
πυραμίδες καὶ μαυσώλεια καὶ λαβύρινθοι, ἄλλοι
ναοὶ τῶν νεκρῶν, ὡς ἐκεῖνοι τάφοι τῶν θεῶν.
διδάσκαλον δὲ ὑμῖν παραθήσομαι τὴν προφῆτιν
Σίβυλλαν·

οὐ ψευδοῦς Φοίβου χρησμηγόρον, ὅν τε μάταιοι
ἄνθρωποι θεὸν εἶπον, ἐπεψεύσαντο δὲ μάντιν,
ἀλλὰ θεοῦ μεγάλοιο, τὸν οὐ χέρες ἔπλασαν ἀνδρῶν
εἰδώλοις ἀλάλοισι λιθοξέστοισιν ὅμοιον.

αὕτη μέντοι ἐρείπια τοὺς νεὼς προσαγορεύει, τὸν
μὲν τῆς Ἐφεσίας Ἀρτέμιδος '' χάσμασι καὶ σει-
σμοῖς '' καταποθήσεσθαι προμηνύουσα οὕτως,

ὕπτια δ' οἰμώξει Ἔφεσος κλαίουσα παρ' ὄχθαις
καὶ νηὸν ζητοῦσα τὸν οὐκέτι ναιετάοντα·

τὸν δὲ Ἴσιδος καὶ Σαράπιδος ἐν Αἰγύπτῳ κατ-
ενεχθήσεσθαί φησι καὶ ἐμπρησθήσεσθαι·

Ἴσι, θεὰ τριτάλαινα, μένεις ἐπὶ χεύμασι[1] Νείλου
μούνη, μαινὰς ἄναυδος ἐπὶ ψαμάθοις Ἀχέροντος,

εἶτα ὑποβᾶσα·

καὶ σύ, Σάραπι λίθους ἀργοὺς ἐπικείμενε πολλούς,
κεῖσαι πτῶμα μέγιστον ἐν Αἰγύπτῳ τριταλαίνῃ.

σὺ δὲ ἀλλ' εἰ μὴ προφήτιδος ἐπακούεις, τοῦ γε σοῦ
ἄκουσον φιλοσόφου, τοῦ Ἐφεσίου Ἡρακλείτου,
τὴν ἀναισθησίαν ὀνειδίζοντος τοῖς ἀγάλμασι· '' καὶ
τοῖς ἀγάλμασι τουτέοισιν εὔχονται, ὁκοῖον εἴ τις

---

[1] χεύμασι Sibylline Oracles. χεύματα Stählin : MSS.

112

seems to me that tombs are objects of reverence in just the same way as temples are; in fact, pyramids, mausoleums and labyrinths are as it were temples of dead men, just as temples are tombs of the gods. As your instructor I will quote the prophetic Sibyl, CHAP.
IV

> Whose words divine come not from Phoebus' lips,
> That prophet false, by foolish men called god,
> But from great God, whom no man's hands have made,
> Like speechless idols framed from polished stone.[a]

She, however, calls the temples ruins. That of Ephesian Artemis she predicts will be swallowed up by "yawning gulfs and earthquakes," thus: The Sibyl
predicts the
ruin of
temples

> Prostrate shall Ephesus groan, when, deep in tears,
> She seeks along her banks a vanished shrine.[b]

That of Isis and Sarapis in Egypt she says will be overthrown and burnt up:

> Thrice wretched Isis, by Nile's streams thou stayst
> Lone, dumb with frenzy on dark Acheron's sands.[c]

Then lower down:

> And thou, Sarapis, piled with useless stones,
> In wretched Egypt liest, a ruin great.[d]

If, however, you refuse to listen to the prophetess, hear at least your own philosopher, Heracleitus of Ephesus, when he taunts the statues for their want of feeling: "and they pray to these statues just as Heracleitus
taunts the
Greeks for
praying to
statues

---

[a] *Sibylline Oracles* iv. 4–7.
[b] *Sib. Or.* v. 295–296.
[c] *Sib. Or.* v. 483–484.
[d] *Sib. Or.* v. 486–487.

CAP.
IV

⟨τοῖς⟩[1] δόμοις λεσχηνεύοιτο." ἢ γὰρ οὐχὶ τερατώ-
δεις οἱ λίθους προστρεπόμενοι,[2] εἶτα μέντοι καὶ πρὸ
τῶν πυλῶν ἱστάντες αὐτοὺς ὡς ἐνεργεῖς, Ἑρμῆν
προσκυνοῦντες[3] ὡς θεὸν καὶ τὸν Ἀγυιέα θυρωρὸν
ἱστάντες; εἰ γὰρ ὡς ἀναισθήτους ὑβρίζουσιν, τί
προσκυνοῦσιν ὡς θεούς; εἰ δὲ αἰσθήσεως αὐτοὺς
μετέχειν οἴονται, τί τούτους ἱστᾶσι θυρωρούς;
Ῥωμαῖοι δὲ τὰ μέγιστα κατορθώματα τῇ Τύχῃ
ἀνατιθέντες καὶ ταύτην μεγίστην οἰόμενοι θεόν,
45 P. φέροντες εἰς τὸν κο|πρῶνα ἀνέθηκαν αὐτήν, ἄξιον
νεὼν τὸν ἀφεδρῶνα νείμαντες τῇ θεῷ.

Ἀλλὰ γὰρ ἀναισθήτῳ λίθῳ καὶ ξύλῳ καὶ χρυσίῳ
πλουσίῳ οὐδ᾽ ὁτιοῦν μέλει, οὐ κνίσης, οὐχ αἵματος,
οὐ καπνοῦ, ᾧ δὴ τιμώμενοι καὶ τυφόμενοι ἐκμε-
λαίνονται· ἀλλ᾽ οὐδὲ τιμῆς, οὐχ ὕβρεως· τὰ δὲ καὶ
παντός ἐστιν ἀτιμότερα ζῴου, τὰ ἀγάλματα. καὶ
ὅπως γε τεθείασται τὰ ἀναίσθητα, ἀπορεῖν ἔπεισί
μοι καὶ κατελεεῖν τοὺς πλανωμένους τῆς ἀνοίας
ὡς δειλαίους· εἰ γὰρ καί τινα τῶν ζῴων οὐχὶ
πάσας ἔχει τὰς αἰσθήσεις, ὥσπερ εὐλαὶ καὶ κάμπαι
καὶ ὅσα διὰ τῆς πρώτης γενέσεως εὐθὺς ἀνάπηρα
φαίνεται, καθάπερ οἱ σπάλακες καὶ ἡ μυγαλῆ, ἥν
φησιν ὁ Νίκανδρος "τυφλήν τε σμερδνήν τε"·
ἀλλά γε ἀμείνους εἰσὶ τῶν ξοάνων τούτων καὶ τῶν

---

[1] ⟨τοῖς⟩ inserted from Origen, *Con. Celsum* i. 5, vii. 62.
[2] προστρεπόμενοι Heyse.   προτρεπόμενοι MSS.
[3] προσκυνοῦντες Stählin.   προσκυνοῦσιν MSS.

---

[a] Heracleitus, *Fr.* 126 Bywater, 5 Diels.
[b] Fortuna was originally an earth deity, a goddess of
fertility, and only later became a personification of chance
or luck.   Mr. A. B. Cook (*Zeus*, i. 271–2) cites this passage
as tending to establish her connexion with the earth.

if one were to chatter to his house." [a] Are they
not amazing, these men who make supplication to
stones, and yet set them up before their gates as if
alive and active, worshipping the image of Hermes
as a god, and setting up the "god of the Ways" as
door-keeper? For if they treat them with contumely
as being without feeling, why do they worship them as
gods? But if they believe them to partake of feeling,
why do they set them up as door-keepers? The
Romans, although they ascribe their greatest successes
to Fortuna, and believe her to be the greatest
deity, carry her statue to the privy and erect it
there, thus assigning to her a fit temple. [b]

But indeed the senseless wood and stone and
precious gold pay not the smallest regard to the
steam, the blood, and the smoke. They are blackened
by the cloud of smoke which is meant to honour
them, but they heed neither the honour nor the
insult. There is not a single living creature that is
not more worthy of honour than these statues ; and
how it comes to pass that senseless things have been
deified I am at a loss to know, and I deeply pity for
their lack of understanding the men who are thus
miserably wandering in error. For even though
there are some living creatures which do not possess
all the senses, as worms and caterpillars, and all those
that appear to be imperfect from the first through
the conditions of their birth, such as moles and
the field-mouse, which Nicander calls "blind and
terrible" [c]; yet these are better than those images and

The statues are quite without sense or feeling

Even worms and moles have one sense

---

[c] Nicander calls the field-mouse "terrible" in reference
to its plague-bearing powers. The complete line (*Theriaca*
815) is τυφλήν τε σμερδνήν τε βροτοῖς ἐπὶ λοιγὸν ἄγουσαν
μυγαλέην.

CAP
IV
ἀγαλμάτων τέλεον ὄντων κωφῶν· ἔχουσιν γὰρ
αἴσθησιν μίαν γέ τινα, φέρε εἰπεῖν ἀκουστικὴν ἢ
ἁπτικὴν ἢ τὴν ἀναλογοῦσαν τῇ ὀσφρήσει ἢ τῇ
γεύσει· τὰ δὲ οὐδὲ μιᾶς αἰσθήσεως μετέχει, τὰ
ἀγάλματα. πολλὰ δέ ἐστι τῶν ζῴων, ὅσα οὔτε[1]
ὅρασιν ἔχει οὔτε ἀκοὴν οὐδὲ[2] μὴν φωνήν, οἷον καὶ
τὸ τῶν ὀστρέων γένος, ἀλλὰ ζῇ γε καὶ αὔξεται,
πρὸς δὲ καὶ τῇ σελήνῃ συμπάσχει· τὰ δὲ ἀγάλματα
ἀργά, ἄπρακτα, ἀναίσθητα, προσδεῖται καὶ προσ-
καθηλοῦται καὶ προσπήγνυται, χωνεύεται, ῥινᾶται,
πρίεται, περιξέεται, γλύφεται. κωφὴν μὲν δὴ
γαῖαν ἀεικίζουσιν οἱ ἀγαλματοποιοί, τῆς οἰκείας
ἐξιστάντες φύσεως, ὑπὸ τῆς τέχνης προσκυνεῖν
ἀναπείθοντες· προσκυνοῦσιν δὲ οἱ θεοποιοὶ οὐ
θεοὺς καὶ δαίμονας κατά γε αἴσθησιν τὴν ἐμήν, γῆν
δὲ καὶ τέχνην, τὰ ἀγάλματα ὅπερ ἐστίν. ἔστιν γὰρ
ὡς ἀληθῶς τὸ ἄγαλμα ὕλη νεκρὰ τεχνίτου χειρὶ
μεμορφωμένη· ἡμῖν δὲ οὐχ ὕλης αἰσθητῆς αἰσθητόν,
νοητὸν δὲ τὸ ἄγαλμά ἐστιν. νοητόν, οὐκ αἰσθητόν
ἐστι [τὸ ἄγαλμα][3] ὁ θεός, ὁ μόνος ὄντως θεός.

Καὶ δὴ ἔμπαλιν ἐν αὐταῖς που ταῖς περιστάσεσιν
οἱ δεισιδαίμονες, οἱ τῶν λίθων προσκυνηταί, ἔργῳ
46 P. μαθόντες ἀναίσθητον | ὕλην μὴ σέβειν, αὐτῆς ἡττώ-
μενοι τῆς χρείας ἀπόλλυνται ὑπὸ δεισιδαιμονίας·
καταφρονοῦντες δ᾽ ὅμως τῶν ἀγαλμάτων, φαίνεσθαι
δὲ μὴ βουλόμενοι αὐτῶν ὅλως[4] περιφρονοῦντες,
ἐλέγχονται ὑπ᾽ αὐτῶν τῶν θεῶν, οἷς δὴ τὰ
ἀγάλματα ἐπιπεφήμισται. Διονύσιος μὲν γὰρ ὁ

---

[1] οὔτε Mayor. οὐδὲ MSS.   [2] οὐδὲ Mayor. οὔτε MSS.
[3] [τὸ ἄγαλμα] Wilamowitz.   [4] ὅλως Sylburg. ὅλων MSS.

---

[a] Cicero (*De divinatione* ii. 33) says of oysters and shell-
fish that they "grow bigger and smaller with the moon."

statues which are entirely dumb. For they have at any rate some one sense, that of hearing, let us say, or of touch, or something corresponding to smell or taste; but these statues do not even partake of one sense. There are also many kinds of living creatures, such as the oyster family, which possess neither sight nor hearing nor yet speech; nevertheless they live and grow and are even affected by the moon.[a] But the statues are motionless things incapable of action or sensation; they are bound and nailed and fastened, melted, filed, sawn, polished, carved. The dumb earth is dishonoured[b] when sculptors pervert its peculiar nature and by their art entice men to worship it; while the god-makers, if there is any sense in me, worship not gods and daemons, but earth and art, which is all the statues are. For a statue is really lifeless matter shaped by a craftsman's hand; but in our view the image of God is not an object of sense made from matter perceived by the senses, but a mental object. God, that is, the only true God, is perceived not by the senses but by the mind.

But statues have none at all

The true image of God is a mental image

On the other hand, whenever a crisis arises, the daemon-worshippers, the adorers of stones, learn by experience not to revere senseless matter; for they succumb to the needs of the moment, and this fear of daemons is their ruin.[c] And if while at heart despising the statues they are unwilling to show themselves utterly contemptuous of them, their folly is exposed by the impotence of the very gods to whom the statues are dedicated. For instance, the tyrant Dionysius the younger stripped the statue

The gods can neither help men nor protect their own statues

Dionysius the younger plunders a statue of Zeus

---

[b] A verbal reminiscence of Homer, *Iliad* xxiv. 54.
[c] *i.e.* the gods cannot help them out of their difficulties.

117

CLEMENT OF ALEXANDRIA

τύραννος ὁ νεώτερος θοἰμάτιον τὸ χρύσεον περι
ελόμενος τοῦ Διὸς ἐν Σικελίᾳ προσέταξεν αὐτῷ
ἐρεοῦν περιτεθῆναι, χαριέντως φήσας τοῦτο ἄμεινον
εἶναι τοῦ χρυσέου,[1] καὶ θέρους κουφότερον καὶ
κρύους ἀλεεινότερον. Ἀντίοχος δὲ ὁ Κυζικηνὸς
ἀπορούμενος χρημάτων τοῦ Διὸς τὸ ἄγαλμα τὸ
χρυσοῦν, πεντεκαίδεκα πηχῶν τὸ μέγεθος ὄν,
προσέταξε χωνεῦσαι καὶ τῆς ἄλλης τῆς ἀτιμοτέρας
ὕλης ἄγαλμα παραπλήσιον ἐκείνῳ πετάλοις κε
χρυσωμένον ἀναθεῖναι πάλιν. αἱ δὲ χελιδόνες καὶ
τῶν ὀρνέων τὰ πλεῖστα κατεξερῶσιν[2] αὐτῶν τῶν
ἀγαλμάτων εἰσπετόμενα, οὐδὲν φροντίσαντα οὔτε
Ὀλυμπίου Διὸς οὔτε Ἐπιδαυρίου Ἀσκληπιοῦ οὐδὲ
μὴν Ἀθηνᾶς Πολιάδος ἢ Σαράπιδος Αἰγυπτίου·
παρ' ὧν οὐδὲ αὐτῶν τὴν ἀναισθησίαν τῶν ἀγαλ
μάτων ἐκμανθάνετε. ἀλλ' εἰσὶ μὲν κακοῦργοί τινες
ἢ πολέμιοι ἐπιθέμενοι, οἳ δι' αἰσχροκέρδειαν ἐδῄω
σαν τὰ ἱερὰ καὶ τὰ ἀναθήματα ἐσύλησαν ἢ καὶ
αὐτὰ ἐχώνευσαν τὰ ἀγάλματα. καὶ εἰ Καμβύσης
τις ἢ Δαρεῖος ἢ ἄλλος μαινόμενος τοιαῦτα ἄττα
ἐπεχείρησεν καὶ εἰ τὸν Αἰγύπτιόν τις ἀπέκτεινεν
Ἆπιν, γελῶ μὲν ὅτι τὸν θεὸν ἀπέκτεινεν αὐτῶν,
ἀγανακτῶ δὲ εἰ κέρδους χάριν ἐπλημμέλει. ἑκὼν
οὖν ἐκλήσομαι τῆσδε τῆς κακουργίας, πλεονεξίας
ἔργα, οὐχὶ δὲ ἀδρανείας τῶν εἰδώλων ἔλεγχον
νομίζων. ἀλλ' οὔτι γε τὸ πῦρ καὶ οἱ σεισμοὶ
κερδαλέοι, οὐδὲ μὴν φοβοῦνται ἢ δυσωποῦνται οὐ
τοὺς δαίμονας, οὐ τὰ ἀγάλματα, οὐ μᾶλλον ἢ τὰς
ψηφῖδας τὰς παρὰ τοῖς αἰγιαλοῖς σεσωρευμένας
τὰ κύματα. οἶδα ἐγὼ πῦρ ἐλεγκτικὸν καὶ δεισι

[1] χρυσέου Cobet. χρυσίου MSS.
[2] κατεξερῶσιν Sylburg. κατεξαίρουσιν MSS.

of Zeus in Sicily of its golden cloak and ordered it CHAP.
to be clothed with a woollen one, with the witty IV
remark that this was better than the golden one,
being both lighter in summer and warmer in winter.[a]
Antiochus of Cyzicus, when he was in want of money, Antiochus
ordered the golden statue of Zeus, fifteen cubits high, of Cyzicus
to be melted down, and a similar statue of cheaper down
material covered with gold leaf to be set up in its
place.   Swallows also and most other birds settle on Birds heed
these very statues and defile them, paying no heed to them not
Olympian Zeus or Epidaurian Asclepius, no, nor yet
to Athena Polias or Egyptian Sarapis; and even their
example does not bring home to you how destitute
of feeling the statues are.   But there are certain Thieves and
evil-doers or enemies at war who from base love of warriors
gain ravaged the temples, plundering the votive steal them
offerings and even melting down the statues.   Now
if Cambyses or Darius or some other put his hands
to such deeds in a fit of madness; and if one of
them [b] slew the Egyptian god Apis, while I laugh at
the thought of his slaying their god, I am indignant
when gain is the motive of the offence.   I will
therefore willingly forget these evil deeds, holding
them to be works of covetousness and not an exposure
of the helplessness of the idols.   But fire and earth- Fire and
quakes are in no way intent on gain; yet they are earthquakes
not frightened or awed either by the daemons or by them
their statues, any more than are the waves by the
pebbles strewn in heaps along the seashore.   I know
that fire can expose and cure your fear of daemons;

---

[a] The story is also told by Cicero (*De natura deorum* iii. 83)
who places it in the Peloponnesus instead of in Sicily.

[b] Cambyses.   See Herodotus iii. 29.

CLEMENT OF ALEXANDRIA

CAP. δαιμονίας ἰατικόν· εἰ βούλει παύσασθαι τῆς ἀνοίας,
IV φωταγωγήσει σε τὸ πῦρ. τοῦτο τὸ πῦρ καὶ τὸν ἐν
47 P. Ἄργει νεὼν σὺν καὶ τῇ ἱερείᾳ | κατέφλεξεν Χρυσίδι,
καὶ τὸν ἐν Ἐφέσῳ τῆς Ἀρτέμιδος δεύτερον μετὰ
Ἀμαζόνας καὶ τὸ ἐν Ῥώμῃ Καπιτώλιον ἐπι-
νενέμηται πολλάκις· οὐκ ἀπέσχετο δὲ οὐδὲ τοῦ
ἐν Ἀλεξανδρέων πόλει Σαράπιδος ἱεροῦ. Ἀθήνησι
γὰρ τοῦ Διονύσου τοῦ Ἐλευθερέως κατήρειψε τὸν
νεών, καὶ τὸν ἐν Δελφοῖς τοῦ Ἀπόλλωνος πρότερον
ἥρπασεν θύελλα, ἔπειτα ἠφάνισε πῦρ σωφρονοῦν.
τοῦτό σοι προοίμιον ἐπιδείκνυται ὧν ὑπισχνεῖται
τὸ πῦρ.

Οἱ δὲ τῶν ἀγαλμάτων δημιουργοὶ οὐ δυσωποῦσιν
ὑμῶν τοὺς ἔμφρονας τῆς ὕλης καταφρονεῖν; ὁ μὲν
Ἀθηναῖος Φειδίας ἐπὶ τῷ δακτύλῳ τοῦ Διὸς τοῦ
Ὀλυμπίου ἐπιγράψας " Παντάρκης καλός "· οὐ
γὰρ καλὸς αὐτῷ ὁ Ζεύς, ἀλλ' ὁ ἐρώμενος ἦν· ὁ
Πραξιτέλης δέ, ὡς Ποσείδιππος ἐν τῷ περὶ Κνίδου [1]
διασαφεῖ, τὸ τῆς Ἀφροδίτης ἄγαλμα τῆς Κνιδίας
κατασκευάζων τῷ Κρατίνης τῆς ἐρωμένης εἴδει
παραπλήσιον πεποίηκεν αὐτήν, ἵν' ἔχοιεν οἱ δείλαιοι

---

[1] Κνίδου Sylburg. κνιδίου mss.

---

[a] See Thucydides iv. 133, where the fire is attributed to
the carelessness of Chrysis, who placed a lighted lamp near
the garlands and then fell asleep. According to Thucydides,
however, Chrysis was not burnt with the temple. Fearing
Argive vengeance she fled the same night to Phlius.

[b] i.e. Dionysus of Eleutherae, a town in Attica from
which the worship of Dionysus was introduced into Athens.
See Pausanias i. 2. 5.

[c] According to Stoic teaching, fire was the creative and
sustaining principle diffused throughout the universe. But
this was an ethereal fire, different from common fire (Cicero,

120

if you wish to cease from folly, the fire shall be your CHAP. guiding light. This fire it was that burnt up the IV temple in Argos together with its priestess Chrysis,[a] and also that of Artemis in Ephesus (the second after the time of the Amazons); and it has often devoured the Capitol at Rome, nor did it spare even the temple of Sarapis in the city of Alexandria. The temple of Dionysus Eleuthereus[b] at Athens was brought to ruin in the same way, and that of Apollo at Delphi was first caught by a storm and then utterly destroyed by the "discerning fire."[c] Here you see a kind of prelude to what the fire promises to do hereafter.

Take next the makers of the statues; do not they Sculptors shame the sensible among you into a contempt for make gods mere matter? The Athenian Pheidias inscribed on their the finger of Olympian Zeus, "Pantarces is beautiful," favourites though it was not Zeus Pantarces whom he thought beautiful, but his own favourite of that name.[d] Praxiteles, as Poseidippus shows clearly in his book on Cnidus,[e] when fashioning the statue of Cnidian Aphrodite,[f] made the goddess resemble the form of his mistress Cratina, that the miserable people might

---

De nat. deor. ii. 41), and the Stoics applied to it various epithets, such as τεχνικόν, "skilful," and φρόνιμος, "prudent." In this passage Clement plays with the two meanings. Other references to the "prudent fire" in Clement are iii. *Paed.* 44. 2, vii. *Strom.* 34. 4, *Eclog. Prophet.* 25. 4.

[a] *Pantarces* means "all-powerful," and so could be understood as a title of Zeus.

[e] Poseidippus, Frag. 2 *Frag. hist. Graec.* iv. p. 482.

[f] Marble copies of this celebrated statue are to be seen at Munich and in the Vatican. For a photographic illustration of the latter see *Cambridge Companion to Greek Studies* (1906), p. 258.

CAP.
IV

τὴν Πραξιτέλους ἐρωμένην προσκυνεῖν. Φρύνη δὲ ὁπηνίκα ἤνθει ἡ ἑταίρα ἡ Θεσπιακή, οἱ ζωγράφοι πάντες ‹ τὰς ›[1] τῆς Ἀφροδίτης εἰκόνας πρὸς τὸ κάλλος ἀπεμιμοῦντο Φρύνης, ὥσπερ αὖ καὶ οἱ λιθοξόοι τοὺς Ἑρμᾶς Ἀθήνησι πρὸς Ἀλκιβιάδην ἀπείκαζον. ὑπολείπεται τῆς σῆς κρίσεως τὸ ἔργον ἐπάξαι, εἰ βούλει καὶ τὰς ἑταίρας προσκυνεῖν.

Ἐντεῦθεν, οἶμαι, κινηθέντες οἱ βασιλεῖς οἱ παλαιοί, καταφρονοῦντες τῶν μύθων τούτων, ἀνέδην διὰ τὸ ἐξ ἀνθρώπων ἀκίνδυνον σφᾶς αὐτοὺς θεοὺς ἀνηγόρευον, ταύτῃ κἀκείνους διὰ τὴν δόξαν ἀπηθανατίσθαι[2] διδάσκοντες· Κήϋξ μὲν ὁ Αἰόλου Ζεὺς ὑπὸ τῆς Ἀλκυόνης τῆς γυναικός, Ἀλκυόνη δὲ αὖθις ὑπὸ τοῦ ἀνδρὸς Ἥρα προσαγορευομένη. Πτολεμαῖος δὲ ὁ τέταρτος Διόνυσος ἐκαλεῖτο·

48 P.
καὶ | Μιθριδάτης ὁ Ποντικὸς Διόνυσος καὶ αὐτός· ἐβούλετο δὲ καὶ Ἀλέξανδρος Ἄμμωνος υἱὸς εἶναι δοκεῖν καὶ κερασφόρος ἀναπλάττεσθαι πρὸς τῶν ἀγαλματοποιῶν, τὸ καλὸν ἀνθρώπου πρόσωπον ὑβρίσαι σπεύδων κέρατι. καὶ οὔτι γε βασιλεῖς μόνον, ἀλλὰ καὶ ἰδιῶται θείαις προσηγορίαις σφᾶς αὐτοὺς ἐσέμνυνον, ὡς Μενεκράτης ὁ ἰατρός, Ζεὺς οὗτος ἐπικεκλημένος. τί με δεῖ καταλέγειν Ἀλέξαρχον (γραμματικὸς οὗτος τὴν ἐπιστήμην γεγονώς, ὡς ἱστορεῖ Ἄριστος ὁ Σαλαμίνιος, αὐτὸν κατεσχημάτιζεν εἰς Ἥλιον); τί δεῖ καὶ Νικαγόρου μεμνῆσθαι (Ζελείτης τὸ γένος ἦν κατὰ τοὺς Ἀλεξάνδρου

---

[1] ‹τὰς› inserted by Schäfer.
[2] ἀπηθανατίσθαι Sylburg. ἀπηθανατῆσθαι mss.

---

a Ammon was the Egyptian ram-headed god whom the

EXHORTATION TO THE GREEKS

have the sculptor's mistress to worship. When Phryne the Thespian courtesan was in her flower, the painters
used all to imitate her beauty in their pictures of
Aphrodite, just as the marble-masons copied Alcibiades in the busts of Hermes at Athens. It remains
to bring your own judgment into play, and decide
whether you wish to extend your worship to
courtesans.

Such were the facts, I think, that moved the
kings of old, in their contempt for these legends, to
proclaim themselves gods; which they did without
hesitation, since there was no danger from men. In
this way they teach us that the other gods were also
men, made immortal for their renown. Ceyx the son
of Aeolus was addressed as Zeus by his wife Alcyone,
while she in turn was addressed as Hera by her
husband. Ptolemy the fourth was called Dionysus,
as was also Mithridates of Pontus. Alexander wished
to be thought the son of Ammon, and to be depicted
with horns by the sculptors, so eager was he to
outrage the beautiful face of man by a horn.[a]
Aye,
and not kings only, but private persons too used to
exalt themselves with divine titles, as Menecrates
the doctor, who was styled Zeus.[b] Why need I
reckon Alexarchus? As Aristus of Salamis relates,
he was a scholar in virtue of his knowledge, but he
transformed himself into the Sun-god.[c] And why
mention Nicagoras, a man of Zeleia by race, living in

CHAP.
IV

Kings of old
proclaimed
themselves
gods

And private
persons also

Greeks identified with Zeus. In Greek art the horns are set
on a human head. See illustrations of coins in A. B. Cook,
Zeus, i. pp. 370–2.

[b] Because (Athenaeus 289), through his healing art, he
was the sole cause of life to men! He wrote to Philip:
"You are king in Macedon, I in medicine."

[c] Aristus, Frag. 2 Müller, *Script. rerum Alex. Mag.* p. 154.

123

γεγονὼς χρόνους· Ἑρμῆς προσηγορεύετο ὁ Νικ-
αγόρας καὶ τῇ στολῇ τοῦ Ἑρμοῦ ἐκέχρητο, ὡς
αὐτὸς μαρτυρεῖ); ὅπου γε καὶ ὅλα ἔθνη καὶ
πόλεις αὔτανδροι, κολακείαν ὑποδυόμεναι, ἐξευτε-
λίζουσιν τοὺς μύθους τοὺς περὶ τῶν θεῶν, ἰσοθέους
ἄνθρωποι κατασχηματίζοντες ἑαυτούς, ὑπὸ δόξης
πεφυσημένοι, ἐπιψηφιζόμενοι τιμὰς ἑαυτοῖς ὑπερ-
όγκους· νῦν μὲν τὸν Μακεδόνα τὸν ἐκ Πέλλης τὸν
Ἀμύντου[1] Φίλιππον ἐν Κυνοσάργει νομοθετοῦντες
προσκυνεῖν, τὸν "τὴν κλεῖν κατεαγότα καὶ τὸ
σκέλος πεπηρωμένον," ὃς ἐξεκόπη τὸν ὀφθαλμόν·
αὖθις δὲ τὸν Δημήτριον θεὸν καὶ αὐτὸν ἀναγορεύον-
τες· καὶ ἔνθα μὲν ἀπέβη τοῦ ἵππου Ἀθήναζε
εἰσιών, Καταιβάτου ἱερόν ἐστι Δημητρίου, βωμοὶ
δὲ πανταχοῦ· καὶ γάμος ὑπὸ Ἀθηναίων αὐτῷ ὁ
τῆς Ἀθηνᾶς ηὐτρεπίζετο· ὁ δὲ τὴν μὲν θεὸν ὑπερ-
ηφάνει, τὸ ἄγαλμα γῆμαι μὴ δυνάμενος· Λάμιαν
δὲ τὴν ἑταίραν ἔχων εἰς ἀκρόπολιν ἀνῄει κἂν
τῷ τῆς Ἀθηνᾶς συνεφύρετο παστῷ,[2] τῇ παλαιᾷ
παρθένῳ τὰ τῆς νέας ἐπιδεικνὺς ἑταίρας σχήματα.
οὐ νέμεσις τοίνυν οὐδὲ Ἵππωνι ἀπαθανατίζοντι τὸν
θάνατον τὸν ἑαυτοῦ· ὁ Ἵππων οὗτος ἐπιγραφῆναι
ἐκέλευσεν τῷ μνήματι τῷ ἑαυτοῦ τόδε τὸ ἐλεγεῖον·

Ἵππωνος τόδε σῆμα, τὸν ἀθανάτοισι θεοῖσιν
ἴσον ἐποίησεν Μοῖρα καταφθίμενον.

---

[1] Ἀμύντου Cobet. ἀμύντορος MSS.
[2] κἂν τῷ τῆς Ἀθηνᾶς συνεφύρετο παστῷ Mayor. καὶ τῷ τῆς
ἀθηνᾶς ἐνεφυρᾶτο παστῷ MSS.

[a] See Athenaeus 289 c, where Baton is given as the
authority for this story. Cp. Baton, Frag. 1 *Frag. hist.
Graec.* iv. p. 348.
[b] Demosthenes, *On the Crown* 67.

CHAP.
IV
Cities and
nations
claim the
right to
make gods

the time of Alexander, who was addressed as Hermes
and wore the garb of Hermes, according to his own
evidence?[a] For indeed whole nations and cities with
all their inhabitants, putting on the mask of flattery,
belittle the legends about the gods, mere men, puffed
up with vain-glory, transforming men like themselves into the equals of the gods and voting them
extravagant honours.   At one time they establish by
law at Cynosarges the worship of Philip the son of
Amyntas, the Macedonian from Pella, him of the
"broken collar-bone and lame leg," with one eye
knocked out.[b] At another, they proclaim Demetrius
to be god in his turn; and the spot where he dis-
mounted on entering Athens is now a temple of
Demetrius the Alighter,[c] while his altars are everywhere.   Arrangements were being made by the
Athenians for his marriage with Athena, but he
disdained the goddess, not being able to marry her
statue. He went up to the Acropolis, however, in
company with the courtesan Lamia, and lay with her
in Athena's bridal chamber, exhibiting to the old
virgin the postures of the young courtesan.[d] We
must not be angry, therefore, even with Hippo,[e]
who represented his death as a deification of himself.
This Hippo ordered the following couplet to be inscribed on his monument:

> Behold the tomb of Hippo, whom in death
> Fate made an equal of the immortal gods.

---

[c] A title of Zeus, as descending or alighting in thunder
and lightning; applied in flattery to Demetrius by the
Athenians. See Plutarch, *Demetrius* 10.

[d] Cp. Plutarch, *Demetrius* 26.

[e] Hippo has been mentioned before, among those dubbed
atheists by the Greeks; see p. 49. For the couplet see
Bergk, *Poet. lyr. Graec.* ii. p. 259 (ed. 1915).

CAP εὖ γε, Ἵππων, ἐπιδεικνύεις ἡμῖν τὴν ἀνθρωπίνην
IV πλάνην. εἰ γὰρ καὶ λαλοῦντί σοι μὴ πεπιστεύκασι,
νεκροῦ γενέσθωσαν μαθηταί. χρησμὸς οὗτός ἐστιν
Ἵππωνος· νοήσωμεν αὐτόν. οἱ προσκυνούμενοι
49 P. παρ' ὑμῖν, | ἄνθρωποι γενόμενοί ποτε, εἶτα μέντοι
τεθνᾶσιν· τετίμηκεν δὲ αὐτοὺς ὁ μῦθος καὶ ὁ
χρόνος. φιλεῖ γάρ πως τὰ μὲν παρόντα συνηθείᾳ
καταφρονεῖσθαι, τὰ δὲ παρῳχηκότα τοῦ παραυτίκα
ἐλέγχου κεχωρισμένα χρόνων ἀδηλίᾳ τετιμῆσθαι
τῷ πλάσματι, καὶ τὰ μὲν ἀπιστεῖσθαι, τὰ δὲ καὶ
θαυμάζεσθαι. αὐτίκα γοῦν οἱ παλαιοὶ νεκροὶ τῷ
πολλῷ τῆς πλάνης χρόνῳ σεμνυνόμενοι τοῖς ἔπειτα
νομίζονται θεοί. πίστις ὑμῖν τῶνδε αὐτὰ ὑμῶν τὰ
μυστήρια, αἱ πανηγύρεις, δεσμὰ καὶ τραύματα καὶ
δακρύοντες θεοί·

ὤ μοι ἐγώ, ὅτε μοι Σαρπηδόνα φίλτατον ἀνδρῶν
μοῖρ' ὑπὸ Πατρόκλοιο Μενοιτιάδαο δαμῆναι.

κεκράτηται τὸ θέλημα τοῦ Διὸς καὶ ὁ Ζεὺς ὑμῖν
διὰ Σαρπηδόνα οἰμώζει νενικημένος.
Εἴδωλα γοῦν εἰκότως αὐτοὺς καὶ δαίμονας ὑμεῖς
αὐτοὶ κεκλήκατε, ἐπεὶ καὶ τὴν Ἀθηνᾶν αὐτὴν καὶ
τοὺς ἄλλους θεοὺς κακίᾳ τιμήσας Ὅμηρος δαίμονας
προσηγόρευσεν·

ἡ δ' Οὔλυμπόνδε βεβήκει
δώματ' ἐς αἰγιόχοιο Διὸς μετὰ δαίμονας ἄλλους.

ᵃ Homer, *Iliad* xvi. 433-434.

ᵇ The word is generally translated "idols" or "images,"
but it also means "shades" or "phantoms," which is the
sense wanted here.

ᶜ Or perhaps, "honouring them for their wickedness."
Compare a similar construction, "honoured by reason of

EXHORTATION TO THE GREEKS

Well done, Hippo, you point out for us the error of
men! For though they have not believed you when
you could speak, let them become disciples now you
are a corpse. This is the oracle of Hippo; let us
understand its meaning. Those whom you worship
were once men, who afterwards died. Legend and
the lapse of time have given them their honours.
For somehow the present is wont to be despised
through our familiarity with it, whereas the past,
being cut off from immediate exposure by the
obscurity which time brings, is invested with a
fictitious honour; and while events of the present are
distrusted, those of the past are regarded with
reverent wonder. As an example, the dead men
of old, being exalted by the long period of error,
are believed to be gods by those who come after.
You have proof of all this in your mysteries themselves, in the solemn festivals, in fetters, wounds and
weeping gods:

Woe, yea, woe be to me! that Sarpedon, dearest of mortals,
Doomed is to fall by the spear of Patroclus son of Menoetius.[a]

The will of Zeus has been overcome, and your
supreme god, defeated, is lamenting for Sarpedon's
sake.

You are right then in having yourselves called
the gods "shadows"[b] and "daemons." For Homer
spoke of Athena herself and her fellow-deities as
"daemons," paying them a malicious compliment.[c]

But she was gone to Olympus,
Home of shield-bearing Zeus, to join the rest of the
daemons.[d]

fornication," or "whose honour comes from fornication," on
pp. 110-11.
 [d] Homer, *Iliad* i. 221-222.

CHAP.
IV

This epitaph
points to
the truth
that all gods
were once
men

The gods,
being dead
men, are
rightly
called
"shadows"
and
"daemons"

127

CAP.
IV

πῶς οὖν ἔτι θεοὶ τὰ εἴδωλα καὶ οἱ δαίμονες, βδελυρὰ ὄντως καὶ πνεύματα ἀκάθαρτα, πρὸς πάντων ὁμολογούμενα γήινα καὶ δεισαλέα, κάτω βρίθοντα, "περὶ τοὺς τάφους καὶ τὰ μνημεῖα καλινδούμενα," περὶ ἃ δὴ καὶ ὑποφαίνονται ἀμυδρῶς "σκιοειδῆ φαντάσματα"; ταῦθ' ὑμῶν οἱ θεοὶ τὰ εἴδωλα, αἱ σκιαὶ καὶ πρὸς τούτοις ⟨αἱ⟩[1] "χωλαὶ" ἐκεῖναι καὶ "ῥυσαί, παραβλῶπες ὀφθαλμώ,"[2] αἱ Λιταὶ αἱ Θερσίτου μᾶλλον ἢ Διὸς θυγατέρες, ὥστε μοι δοκεῖν χαριέντως φάναι τὸν Βίωνα, πῶς ἂν ἐνδίκως

50 P. οἱ ἄν|θρωποι παρὰ τοῦ Διὸς αἰτήσονται[3] τὴν εὐτεκνίαν, ἣν οὐδ' αὑτῷ παρασχεῖν ἴσχυσεν; οἴμοι τῆς ἀθεότητος· τὴν ἀκήρατον οὐσίαν, τὸ ὅσον ἐφ' ὑμῖν, κατορύττετε καὶ τὸ ἄχραντον ἐκεῖνο καὶ τὸ ἅγιον τοῖς τάφοις ἐπικεχώκατε, τῆς ἀληθῶς ὄντως οὐσίας συλήσαντες τὸ θεῖον. τί δὴ οὖν τὰ τοῦ θεοῦ τοῖς οὐ θεοῖς προσενείματε γέρα; τί δὲ καταλιπόντες τὸν οὐρανὸν τὴν γῆν τετιμήκατε; τί δ' ἄλλο χρυσὸς ἢ ἄργυρος ἢ ἀδάμας ἢ σίδηρος ἢ χαλκὸς ἢ ἐλέφας ἢ λίθοι τίμιοι; οὐχὶ γῆ τε καὶ ἐκ γῆς; οὐχὶ δὲ μιᾶς μητρὸς ἔκγονα, τῆς γῆς, τὰ πάντα ταῦτα ὅσα ὁρᾷς; τί δὴ οὖν, ὦ μάταιοι καὶ κενόφρονες (πάλιν γὰρ δὴ ἐπαναλήψομαι), τὸν ὑπερουράνιον βλασφημήσαντες τόπον εἰς τοὔδαφος κατεσύρατε τὴν εὐσέβειαν, χθονίους ὑμῖν ἀναπλάττοντες θεοὺς καὶ τὰ γενητὰ ταῦτα πρὸ τοῦ ἀγενήτου μετιόντες θεοῦ βαθυτέρῳ περιπεπτώκατε ζόφῳ;

---

[1] ⟨αἱ⟩ inserted by Kroll.
[2] ὀφθαλμώ Homer. ὀφθαλμῶν MSS.
[3] αἰτήσονται Cobet. αἰτήσωνται MSS.

---

[a] See Plato, *Phaedo* 81 c d.   [b] *Iliad* ix. 502–503.
[c] Thersites is Homer's ridiculous character, hump-backed,

128

How then can the shadows and daemons any longer be gods, when they are in reality unclean and loathsome spirits, admitted by all to be earthy and foul, weighed down to the ground, and "prowling round graves and tombs," [a] where also they dimly appear as "ghostly apparitions [a]"? These are your gods, these shadows and ghosts; and along with them go those "lame and wrinkled cross-eyed deities," the Prayers,[b] daughters of Zeus, though they are more like daughters of Thersites [c]; so that I think Bion made a witty remark when he asked how men could rightly ask Zeus for goodly children, when he had not even been able to provide them for himself.[d] Alas for such atheism! You sink in the earth, so far as you are able, the incorruptible existence, and that which is stainless and holy you have buried in the tombs. Thus you have robbed the divine of its real and true being. Why, I ask, did you assign to those who are no gods the honours due to God alone? Why have you forsaken heaven to pay honour to earth? For what else is gold, or silver, or steel, or iron, or bronze, or ivory, or precious stones? Are they not earth, and made from earth? Are not all these things that you see the offspring of one mother, the earth? Why then, vain and foolish men,—once again I will ask the question,—did you blaspheme highest heaven [e] and drag down piety to the ground by fashioning for yourselves gods of earth? Why have you fallen into deeper darkness by going after these created things instead of the

lame and bandy-legged, with an impudent tongue into the bargain. *Iliad* ii. 211–277.

[d] Bion of Borysthenes, Frag. 44 Mullach, *Frag. phil. Graec.* ii. p. 427.   [e] See Plato, *Phaedrus* 247 c.

CAP. καλὸς ὁ Πάριος λίθος, ἀλλ᾽ οὐδέπω Ποσειδῶν·
IV καλὸς ὁ ἐλέφας, ἀλλ᾽ οὐδέπω Ὀλύμπιος· ἐνδεὴς
ἀεί ποτε ἡ ὕλη τῆς τέχνης, ὁ θεὸς δὲ ἀνενδεής.
προῆλθεν ἡ τέχνη, περιβέβληται τὸ σχῆμα ἡ ὕλη,
καὶ τὸ πλούσιον τῆς οὐσίας πρὸς μὲν τὸ κέρδος
ἀγώγιμον, μόνῳ δὲ τῷ σχήματι γίνεται σεβάσμιον.
χρυσός ἐστι τὸ ἄγαλμά σου, ξύλον ἐστίν, λίθος
ἐστίν, γῆ ἐστιν, ἐὰν ἄνωθεν νοήσῃς, μορφὴν παρὰ
τοῦ τεχνίτου προσλαβοῦσα. γῆν δὲ ἐγὼ πατεῖν,
οὐ προσκυνεῖν μεμελέτηκα· οὐ γάρ μοι θέμις
ἐμπιστεῦσαί ποτε τοῖς ἀψύχοις τὰς τῆς ψυχῆς
ἐλπίδας.

Ἰτέον οὖν ὡς ἔνι μάλιστα ἐγγυτάτω τῶν ἀγαλμάτων, ὡς οἰκεία ἡ πλάνη κἀκ τῆς προσόψεως
ἐλέγχεται·[1] ἐναπομέμακται γὰρ πάνυ δὴ σαφῶς τὰ
εἴδη τῶν ἀγαλμάτων τὴν διάθεσιν τῶν δαιμόνων.
εἰ γοῦν τις τὰς γραφὰς καὶ τὰ ἀγάλματα περινοστῶν
θεῷτο, γνωριεῖ ὑμῶν παραυτίκα τοὺς θεοὺς ἐκ τῶν
ἐπονειδίστων σχημάτων, τὸν Διόνυσον ἀπὸ τῆς
στολῆς, τὸν Ἥφαιστον ἀπὸ τῆς τέχνης, τὴν Δηὼ
ἀπὸ τῆς συμφορᾶς, ἀπὸ τοῦ κρηδέμνου τὴν Ἰνώ,
ἀπὸ τῆς τριαίνης τὸν Ποσειδῶ, ἀπὸ τοῦ κύκνου τὸν
Δία· τὸν δὲ Ἡρακλέα δείκνυσιν ἡ πυρά, κἂν
γυμνὴν ἴδῃ τις ἀνάγραπτον γυναῖκα, τὴν "χρυσῆν"
Ἀφροδίτην νοεῖ. οὕτως ὁ Κύπριος ὁ Πυγμαλίων
51 P. ἐκεῖνος ἐλεφαν|τίνου ἠράσθη ἀγάλματος· τὸ ἄγαλμα
Ἀφροδίτης ἦν καὶ γυμνὴ ἦν· νικᾶται ὁ Κύπριος τῷ
σχήματι καὶ συνέρχεται τῷ ἀγάλματι, καὶ τοῦτο
Φιλοστέφανος ἱστορεῖ. Ἀφροδίτη δὲ ἄλλη ἐν
Κνίδῳ λίθος ἦν καὶ καλὴ ἦν, ἕτερος ἠράσθη ταύτης

---

[1] ἐλέγχηται Potter. ἐλέγχεται MSS.

130

uncreated God? The Parian marble is beautiful, but it is not yet a Poseidon. The ivory is beautiful, but it is not yet an Olympian Zeus. Matter will ever be in need of art, but God has no such need. Art develops, matter is invested with shape; and the costliness of the substance makes it worth carrying off for gain, but it is the shape alone which makes it an object of veneration. Your statue is gold; it is wood; it is stone; or if in thought you trace it to its origin, it is earth, which has received form at the artist's hands. But my practice is to walk upon earth, not to worship it. For I hold it sin ever to entrust the hopes of the soul to soulless things.

We must, then, approach the statues as closely as we possibly can in order to prove from their very appearance that they are inseparably associated with error. For their forms are unmistakably stamped The forms of the statues show whom they represent with the characteristic marks of the daemons. At least, if one were to go round inspecting the paintings and statues, he would immediately recognize your gods from their undignified figures; Dionysus from his dress, Hephaestus from his handicraft, Demeter from her woe, Ino from her veil, Poseidon from his trident, Zeus from his swan. The pyre indicates Heracles, and if one sees a woman represented naked, he understands it is " golden " [a] Aphrodite. So the Men have fallen in love with beautiful statues well-known Pygmalion of Cyprus fell in love with an ivory statue; it was of Aphrodite and was naked. The man of Cyprus is captivated by its shapeliness and embraces the statue. This is related by Philostephanus.[b] There was also an Aphrodite in Cnidus, made of marble and beautiful. Another man fell in

---

[a] Homer, *Odyssey* iv. 14.
[b] Philostephanus, Frag. 13 *Frag. hist. Graec.* iii. p. 31.

CLEMENT OF ALEXANDRIA

καὶ μίγνυται τῇ λίθῳ· Ποσείδιππος ἱστορεῖ, ὁ μὲν
πρότερος ἐν τῷ περὶ Κύπρου, ὁ δὲ ἕτερος ἐν τῷ
περὶ Κνίδου. τοσοῦτον ἴσχυσεν ἀπατῆσαι τέχνη
προαγωγὸς ἀνθρώποις ἐρωτικοῖς εἰς βάραθρον γενομένη. δραστήριος μὲν ἡ δημιουργική, ἀλλ' οὐχ
οἷά τε ἀπατῆσαι λογικὸν οὐδὲ μὴν τοὺς κατὰ λόγον
βεβιωκότας· ζωγραφίας μὲν γὰρ δι' ὁμοιότητα
σκιαγραφήταις περιστεραῖς[1] προσέπτησαν πελειάδες
καὶ ἵπποις καλῶς γεγραμμέναις προσεχρεμέ-
τισαν ἵπποι. ἐρασθῆναι κόρην εἰκόνος λέγουσιν
καὶ νέον καλὸν Κνιδίου ἀγάλματος, ἀλλ' ἦσαν τῶν
θεατῶν αἱ ὄψεις ἠπατημέναι ὑπὸ τῆς τέχνης. οὐδὲ
γὰρ ἂν θεᾷ τις συνεπλάκη, οὐδ' ἂν νεκρᾷ τις συν-
ετάφη, οὐδ' ἂν ἠράσθη δαίμονος καὶ λίθου ἄνθρωπος
σωφρονῶν. ὑμᾶς δὲ ἄλλη γοητείᾳ ἀπατᾷ ἡ τέχνη,
εἰ καὶ μὴ ἐπὶ τὸ ἐρᾶν προσάγουσα, ἀλλ' ἐπὶ τὸ
τιμᾶν καὶ προσκυνεῖν τά τε ἀγάλματα καὶ τὰς
γραφάς. ὁμοία γε ἡ γραφή· ἐπαινείσθω μὲν ἡ
τέχνη, μὴ ἀπατάτω δὲ τὸν ἄνθρωπον ὡς ἀλήθεια.
ἕστηκεν ὁ ἵππος ἡσυχῇ, ἡ πελειὰς ἀτρεμής, ἀργὸν
τὸ πτερόν, ἡ δὲ βοῦς ἡ Δαιδάλου ἡ ἐκ τοῦ ξύλου
πεποιημένη ταῦρον εἷλεν ἄγριον καὶ κατηνάγκασεν
τὸ θηρίον ἡ τέχνη πλανήσασα ἐρώσης ἐπιβῆναι
γυναικός. τοσοῦτον οἶστρον αἱ τέχναι κακοτεχ-

---

[1] σκιαγραφήταις περιστεραῖς Stählin. σκιαγραφίας περιστεραῖ
MSS. ἐσκιαγραφημέναις περιστεραῖς Mayor.

---

[a] Poseidippus, Fr. 1 *Frag. hist. Graec.* iv. p. 482.
[b] Literally, "procuress." Compare Tennyson's "In
Memoriam," 53.

> Hold thou the good : define it well:
> For fear divine Philosophy
> Should push beyond her mark, and be
> Procuress to the Lords of Hell.

love with this and has intercourse with the marble, CHAP.
as Poseidippus relates.[a] The account of the first IV
author is in his book on Cyprus; that of the second
in his book on Cnidus. Such strength had art to
beguile that it became for amorous men a guide[b]
to the pit of destruction. Now craftsmanship is
powerful, but it cannot beguile a rational being, nor
yet those who have lived according to reason. It is
true that, through lifelike portraiture, pigeons have
been known to fly towards painted doves, and horses
to neigh at well-drawn mares. They say that a
maiden once fell in love with an image, and a
beautiful youth with a Cnidian statue[c]; but it was
their sight that was beguiled by the art. For
no man in his senses would have embraced the
statue of a goddess, or have been buried with a
lifeless paramour, or have fallen in love with a daemon
and a stone. But in your case art has another illusion
with which to beguile; for it leads you on, though
not to be in love with the statues and paintings, yet
to honour and worship them. The painting, you
say, is lifelike. Let the art be praised, but let it
not beguile man by pretending to be truth. The
horse stands motionless; the dove flutters not; its
wings are at rest. Yet the cow of Daedalus, made
of wood, infatuated a wild bull; and the beast, led
astray by the art, was constrained to approach a love-
sick woman.[d] Such insane passion did the arts, by

The fascina-
tion of
art for
foolish men

Worship of
statues is
another
form of art's
fascination

Clement had no fear of "divine Philosophy," but only
of art.

[c] Compare Philostratus, *Apollonius of Tyana* vi. 40
(Loeb Classical Library ed. ii. pp. 134–9).

[d] *i.e.* Pasiphaë. Daedalus had put her inside his wooden
cow, that she might satisfy her passion for the bull. Apollodorus iii. 1. 3; Philo Judaeus, *De spec. leg.* 8.

CLEMENT OF ALEXANDRIA

CAP.
IV

νοῦσαι τοῖς ἀνοήτοις ἐνεποίησαν. ἀλλὰ τοὺς μὲν
πιθήκους οἱ τούτων τροφεῖς καὶ μελεδωνοὶ τεθαυ-
μάκασιν, ὅτι τῶν κηρίνων ἢ πηλίνων ὁμοιωμάτων
καὶ κοροκοσμίων ἀπατᾷ τούτους οὐδέν· ὑμεῖς δὲ
ἄρα καὶ πιθήκων χείρους γενήσεσθε λιθίνοις καὶ
ξυλίνοις καὶ χρυσέοις καὶ ἐλεφαντίνοις ἀγαλματίοις
καὶ γραφαῖς προσανέχοντες. τοιούτων ὑμῖν [οἱ] [1]
δημιουργοὶ ἀθυρμάτων ὀλεθρίων οἱ λιθοξόοι καὶ οἱ

52 P.
ἀνδριαντοποιοὶ γραφεῖς τε αὖ καὶ τέκτο|νες καὶ
ποιηταί, πολύν τινα καὶ τοιοῦτον ὄχλον παρ-
εισάγοντες, κατ' ἀγροὺς μὲν Σατύρους καὶ Πᾶνας,
ἀνὰ δὲ τὰς ὕλας Νύμφας τὰς ὀρειάδας καὶ τὰς ἁμα-
δρυάδας, ναὶ μὴν ἀλλὰ καὶ περὶ τὰ ὕδατα καὶ
περὶ τοὺς ποταμοὺς καὶ τὰς πηγὰς τὰς Ναῖδας
καὶ περὶ τὴν θάλατταν τὰς Νηρεῖδας. μάγοι δὲ
ἤδη ἀσεβείας τῆς σφῶν αὐτῶν ὑπηρέτας δαίμονας
αὐχοῦσιν, οἰκέτας αὐτοὺς ἑαυτοῖς καταγράψαντες,
τοὺς κατηναγκασμένους δούλους ταῖς ἐπαοιδαῖς
πεποιηκότες.

Γάμοι τε οὖν ἔτι καὶ παιδοποιίαι καὶ λοχεῖαι
θεῶν μνημονευόμεναι καὶ μοιχεῖαι ᾀδόμεναι καὶ
εὐωχίαι κωμῳδούμεναι καὶ γέλωτες παρὰ πότον
εἰσαγόμενοι προτρέπουσι δή [2] με ἀνακραγεῖν, κἂν
σιωπῆσαι θέλω, οἴμοι τῆς ἀθεότητος· σκηνὴν
πεποιήκατε τὸν οὐρανὸν καὶ τὸ θεῖον ὑμῖν δρᾶμα
γεγένηται καὶ τὸ ἅγιον προσωπείοις δαιμονίων
κεκωμῳδήκατε, τὴν ἀληθῆ θεοσέβειαν δεισιδαι-
μονίᾳ σατυρίσαντες.

αὐτὰρ ὁ φορμίζων ἀνεβάλλετο καλὸν ἀείδειν,

[1] τοιούτων . . [οἱ] Wilamowitz. τοσούτων . . οἱ MSS.
[2] δή Höschel. δέ MSS.

134

their vicious artifices, implant in creatures without
sense. Even monkeys know better than this. They
astonish their rearers and keepers, because no manner
of waxen or clay figures or girls' toys can deceive them.
But you, strange to say, will prove yourselves inferior
even to monkeys through the heed you pay to statues
of stone and wood, gold and ivory, and to paintings.
Such are the pernicious playthings made for you
by marble-masons, sculptors, painters, carpenters and
poets, who introduce this great multitude of gods,
Satyrs and Pans in the fields, mountain and tree
Nymphs in the woods, as well as Naiads about the
lakes, rivers and springs, and Nereids by the sea.
Magicians go so far as to boast that daemons are
assistants in their impious deeds; they have enrolled
them as their own servants, having made them
slaves perforce by means of their incantations.

Further, the marriages of gods, their acts of
child-begetting and child-bearing which are on men's
lips, their adulteries which are sung by bards, their
feastings which are a theme of comedy, and the
bursts of laughter which occur over their cups, these
exhort me to cry aloud, even if I would fain keep
silence,—Alas for such atheism! You have turned
heaven into a stage. You look upon the divine
nature as a subject for drama. Under the masks
of daemons you have made comedy of that which
is holy. For the true worship of God you have
substituted a travesty, the fear of daemons.

Then to the harp's sweet strains a beautiful song he opened;[a]

---

[a] Homer, *Odyssey* viii. 266.

(marginal notes:) CHAP. IV — monkeys are not deceived by lifeless toys — Statues are the toys made for men by craftsmen and poets — The gods are guilty of adultery and drunkenness

^{CAP.} ἆσον ἡμῖν, Ὅμηρε, τὴν φωνὴν τὴν καλήν,
IV

ἀμφ᾿ Ἄρεως φιλότητος ἐϋστεφάνου τ᾿ Ἀφροδίτης
ὡς τὰ πρῶτα μίγησαν ἐν Ἡφαίστοιο δόμοισι
λάθρῃ· πολλὰ δ᾿ ἔδωκε, λέχος δ᾿ ᾔσχυνε καὶ εὐνὴν
Ἡφαίστοιο ἄνακτος.

κατάπαυσον, Ὅμηρε, τὴν ᾠδήν· οὐκ ἔστι καλή,
μοιχείαν διδάσκει· πορνεύειν δὲ ἡμεῖς καὶ τὰ ὦτα
παρῃτήμεθα· ἡμεῖς γάρ, ἡμεῖς ἐσμὲν οἱ τὴν εἰκόνα
τοῦ θεοῦ περιφέροντες ἐν τῷ ζῶντι καὶ κινουμένῳ
τούτῳ ἀγάλματι, τῷ ἀνθρώπῳ, σύνοικον εἰκόνα,
σύμβουλον, συνόμιλον, συνέστιον, συμπαθῆ, ὑπερ-
παθῆ· ἀνάθημα γεγόναμεν τῷ θεῷ ὑπὲρ Χριστοῦ·
"ἡμεῖς τὸ γένος τὸ ἐκλεκτόν, τὸ βασίλειον ἱερά-
τευμα, ἔθνος ἅγιον, λαὸς περιούσιος, οἱ ποτὲ οὐ
λαός, νῦν δὲ λαὸς τοῦ θεοῦ"· οἱ κατὰ τὸν Ἰωάννην
οὐκ ὄντες "ἐκ τῶν κάτω," παρὰ δὲ τοῦ ἄνωθεν
ἐλθόντος τὸ πᾶν μεμαθηκότες, οἱ τὴν οἰκονομίαν
τοῦ θεοῦ κατανενοηκότες, οἱ "ἐν καινότητι ζωῆς
περιπατεῖν" μεμελετηκότες.

Ἀλλ᾿ οὐ ταῦτα φρονοῦσιν οἱ πολλοί· ἀπορρίψαντες δὲ τὴν αἰδὼ καὶ τὸν φόβον οἴκοι τοὺς τῶν
δαιμόνων ἐγγράφονται πασχητιασμούς. πινακίοις
53 P. γοῦν | τισὶ καταγράφοις μετεωρότερον ἀνακειμένοις
προσεσχηκότες ἀσελγείᾳ τοὺς θαλάμους κεκοσμή-
κασι, τὴν ἀκολασίαν εὐσέβειαν νομίζοντες· κἀπὶ
τοῦ σκίμποδος κατακείμενοι παρ᾿ αὐτὰς ἔτι τὰς
περιπλοκὰς ἀφορῶσιν εἰς τὴν Ἀφροδίτην ἐκείνην

---

^a *Odyssey* viii. 267–270.   ^b 1 St. Peter ii. 9–10.
^c St. John viii. 23.   ^d See St. John iii. 31.
^e Romans vi. 4.

EXHORTATION TO THE GREEKS

Sing us that beautiful strain, Homer,

Telling the love of Ares and Aphrodite fair-girdled,
How at the first they met in the halls of Hephaestus in
    secret ;
Many the gifts he gave, and the bed and couch of
    Hephaestus
Sullied with shame.[a]

Cease the song, Homer. There is no beauty in
that ; it teaches adultery. We have declined to
lend even our ears to fornication. For we, yes
we, are they who, in this living and moving statue,
man, bear about the image of God, an image which
dwells with us, is our counsellor, companion, the
sharer of our hearth, which feels with us, feels for
us. We have been made a consecrated offering to
God for Christ's sake. "We are the elect race,
the royal priesthood, a holy nation, a people belonging to God, who in time past were not a people,
but now are the people of God."[b] We are they
who, according to John, are not "from below,"[c]
but have learnt the whole truth from Him who
came from above,[d] who have apprehended the dispensation of God, who have studied "to walk in
newness of life."[e]

But most men are not of this mind. Casting off
shame and fear, they have their homes decorated
with pictures representing the unnatural lust of the
daemons. In the lewdness to which their thoughts
are given, they adorn their chambers with painted
tablets hung on high like votive offerings, regarding
licentiousness as piety ; and, when lying upon the
bed, while still in the midst of their own embraces,
they fix their gaze upon that naked Aphrodite, who

(side notes: CHAP. IV; Homer's witness to the adultery of Ares; Christians must not listen to such stories; Indecent pictures are hung in houses)

137

CAP.
IV

τὴν γυμνήν, τὴν ἐπὶ τῇ συμπλοκῇ δεδεμένην, καὶ τὴ
Λήδᾳ περιποτώμενον τὸν ὄρνιν τὸν ἐρωτικόν, τῆς
θηλύτητος ἀποδεχόμενοι τὴν γραφήν, ἀποτυποῦσι
ταῖς σφενδόναις, σφραγῖδι χρώμενοι καταλλήλῳ
τῇ Διὸς ἀκολασίᾳ. ταῦτα ὑμῶν τῆς ἡδυπαθείας
τὰ ἀρχέτυπα, αὗται τῆς ὕβρεως αἱ θεολογίαι, αὗται
τῶν συμπορνευόντων ὑμῖν θεῶν αἱ διδασκαλίαι·
"ὃ γὰρ βούλεται, τοῦθ' ἕκαστος καὶ οἴεται" κατὰ
τὸν Ἀθηναῖον ῥήτορα. οἷαι δὲ αὖ καὶ ἄλλαι ὑμῶν
εἰκόνες, πανίσκοι τινὲς καὶ γυμναὶ κόραι καὶ
σάτυροι μεθύοντες καὶ μορίων ἐντάσεις, ταῖς
γραφαῖς ἀπογυμνούμεναι, ἀπὸ τῆς ἀκρασίας ἐλεγχό-
μεναι. ἤδη δὲ ἀναφανδὸν τῆς ἀκολασίας ὅλης τὰ
σχήματα ἀνάγραπτα πανδημεὶ θεώμενοι οὐκ αἰσχύνεσθε, φυλάττετε δὲ ἔτι μᾶλλον ἀνακείμενα, ὥσπερ
ἀμέλει τῶν θεῶν ὑμῶν τὰς εἰκόνας, στήλας ἀναισχυντίας καθιερώσαντες οἴκοι, ἐπ' ἴσης ἐγγραφόμενοι τὰ Φιλαινίδος σχήματα ὡς τὰ Ἡρακλέους
ἀθλήματα. τούτων οὐ μόνον τῆς χρήσεως, πρὸς
δὲ καὶ τῆς ὄψεως καὶ τῆς ἀκοῆς αὐτῆς ἀμνηστίαν
καταγγέλλομεν. ἡταίρηκεν ὑμῖν τὰ ὦτα, πεπορ-
νεύκασιν οἱ ὀφθαλμοὶ καὶ τὸ καινότερον πρὸ τῆς
συμπλοκῆς αἱ ὄψεις ὑμῖν μεμοιχεύκασιν. ὦ βιασά-
μενοι τὸν ἄνθρωπον καὶ τὸ ἔνθεον τοῦ πλάσματος
ἐλέγχει ἀπαράξαντες, πάντα ἀπιστεῖτε, ἵνα ἐκπα-
θαίνησθε· καὶ πιστεύετε[1] μὲν τοῖς εἰδώλοις ζηλοῦντες

---

[1] πιστεύετε Arcerius.   πιστεύητε MSS.

ᵃ i.e. bound with the invisible chains which Hephaestus
had made to entrap her. Odyssey viii. 270–299.
ᵇ Demosthenes, Olynthiacs iii. 19.
ᶜ i.e. in houses ; see p. 137.

lies bound in her adultery.[a]   Also, to show they
approve the representation of effeminacy, they
engrave in the hoops of their rings the amorous bird
hovering over Leda, using a seal which reflects the
licentiousness of Zeus. These are the patterns for
your voluptuousness; these are the stories that give
divine sanction for wanton living; these are the
lessons taught by gods who are fornicators like
yourselves. "For what a man desires, that he also
imagines to be true," says the Athenian orator.[b]
Look, too, at other of your images,— little figures
of Pan, naked girls, drunken satyrs; and obscene
emblems, plainly exhibited in pictures, and self-
condemned by their indecency. More than that,
you behold without a blush the postures of the
whole art of licentiousness openly pictured in public.
But when they are hung on high[c] you treasure them
still more, just as if they were actually the images
of your gods; for you dedicate these monuments
of shamelessness in your homes, and are as eager to
procure paintings of the postures of Philaenis as
of the labours of Heracles. We declare that not
only the use, but also the sight and the very
hearing of these things should be forgotten. Your
ears have committed fornication; your eyes have
prostituted themselves;[d] and, stranger still, before
the embrace you have committed adultery by your
looks.[e] You who have done violence to man, and
erased by dishonour the divine image in which
he was created, you are utter unbelievers in order
that you may give way to your passions. You believe
in the idols because you crave after their incontinence;

---

[d] Cp. 2 St. Peter ii. 14.   [e] Cp. St. Matthew v. 28.

CAP. αὐτῶν τὴν ἀκρασίαν, ἀπιστεῖτε δὲ τῷ θεῷ σωφρο-
IV σύνην μὴ φέροντες· καὶ τὰ μὲν κρείττω μεμισήκατε,
τὰ δὲ ἥττω τετιμήκατε, ἀρετῆς μὲν θεαταί, κακίας
δὲ ἀγωνισταὶ γεγενημένοι.

54 P. "Ὄλβιοι" | μόνοι τοίνυν, ὡς ἔπος εἰπεῖν, ὁμο-
θυμαδὸν ἐκεῖνοι πάντες κατὰ τὴν Σίβυλλαν

> οἳ ναοὺς ⟨μὲν⟩[1] πάντας ἀπαρνήσονται ἰδόντες
> καὶ βωμούς, εἰκαῖα λίθων ἱδρύματα κωφῶν,
> καὶ λίθινα ξόανα καὶ ἀγάλματα χειροποίητα,[2]
> αἵματι ἐμψύχῳ μεμιασμένα καὶ θυσίαισι
> τετραπόδων, διπόδων, πτηνῶν θηρῶν τε φόνοισιν.

καὶ γὰρ δὴ καὶ ἀπηγόρευται ἡμῖν ἀναφανδὸν
ἀπατηλὸν ἐργάζεσθαι τέχνην. "οὐ γὰρ ποιήσεις,"
φησὶν ὁ προφήτης, "παντὸς ὁμοίωμα, ὅσα ἐν τῷ
οὐρανῷ ἄνω καὶ ὅσα ἐν τῇ γῇ κάτω." ἢ πού γ᾽ ἂν
ἔτι τὴν Πραξιτέλους Δήμητρα καὶ Κόρην καὶ τὸν
Ἴακχον τὸν μυστικὸν θεοὺς ὑπολάβοιμεν ἢ τὰς
Λυσίππου τέχνας ἢ τὰς χεῖρας τὰς Ἀπελλικάς, αἳ
δὴ τῆς θεοδοξίας τὸ σχῆμα τῇ ὕλῃ περιτεθείκασιν;
ἀλλ᾽ ὑμεῖς μὲν ὅπως ὁ ἀνδριὰς ὅτι μάλιστα
ὡραιότατος τεκταίνηται, προσκαρτερεῖτε, ὅπως δὲ
αὐτοὶ μὴ ὅμοιοι δι᾽ ἀναισθησίαν τοῖς ἀνδριᾶσιν
ἀποτελεσθῆτε, οὐ φροντίζετε· πάνυ γοῦν ἐμφανῶς
καὶ συντόμως ὁ προφητικὸς ἐλέγχει τὴν συνήθειαν
λόγος ὅτι "πάντες οἱ θεοὶ τῶν ἐθνῶν δαιμονίων
εἰσὶν εἴδωλα· ὁ δὲ θεὸς τοὺς οὐρανοὺς ἐποίησεν"

---

[1] ⟨μὲν⟩ inserted from *Sibylline Oracles*.
[2] καὶ λίθινα . . . χειροποίητα not in *Sibylline Oracles*.

---

[a] *Sibylline Oracles* iv. 24, 27–30.

you disbelieve in God because you cannot bear self-control. You have hated the better, and honoured the worse. You have shown yourselves onlookers with regard to virtue, but active champions of vice.

The only men, therefore, who can with one consent, so to speak, be called "blessed," are all those whom the Sibyl describes,

> Who, seeing the temples, will reject them all,
> And altars, useless shrines of senseless stones ;
> Stone idols too, and statues made by hand
> Defiled with blood yet warm, and sacrifice
> Of quadruped and biped, bird and beast.[a]

What is more, we are expressly forbidden to practise a deceitful art. For the prophet says, "Thou shalt not make a likeness of anything that is in heaven above or in the earth beneath."[b] Is it possible that we can still suppose the Demeter and Persephone and the mystic Iacchus of Praxiteles to be gods? Or are we to regard as gods the masterpieces of Lysippus or the works of Apelles, since it is these which have bestowed upon matter the fashion of the divine glory? But as for you, while you take great pains to discover how a statue may be shaped to the highest possible pitch of beauty, you never give a thought to prevent yourselves turning out like statues owing to want of sense. Any way, with the utmost plainness and brevity the prophetic word refutes the custom of idolatry, when it says, "All the gods of the nations are images of daemons; but God made the heavens,"[c] and the things in heaven.

[b] Exodus xx. 4 ; Deuteronomy v. 8.
[c] Psalm xcvi. 5.

CLEMENT OF ALEXANDRIA

καὶ τὰ ἐν τῷ οὐρανῷ. πλανώμενοι γοῦν τινες ἐντεῦθεν οὐκ οἶδ᾽ ὅπως θείαν μὲν τέχνην, πλὴν ἀλλ᾽ οὐ
θεὸν προσκυνοῦσιν ἥλιόν τε καὶ σελήνην καὶ τὸν
ἄλλον τῶν ἀστέρων χορόν, παραλόγως τούτους
θεοὺς ὑπολαμβάνοντες, τὰ ὄργανα τοῦ χρόνου·
"τῷ γὰρ λόγῳ αὐτοῦ ἐστερεώθησαν καὶ τῷ
πνεύματι τοῦ στόματος αὐτοῦ πᾶσα ἡ δύναμις
αὐτῶν." ἀλλ᾽ ἡ μὲν ἀνθρωπεία τέχνη οἰκίας τε καὶ
ναῦς καὶ πόλεις καὶ γραφὰς δημιουργεῖ, θεὸς δὲ
πῶς ἂν εἴποιμι ὅσα ποιεῖ; ὅλον ἴδε τὸν κόσμον,
ἐκείνου ἔργον ἐστίν· καὶ οὐρανὸς καὶ ἥλιος καὶ ἄγ-
55 P. γελοι καὶ ἄνθρωποι "ἔργα τῶν δακτύλων | αὐτοῦ."
ὅση γε ἡ δύναμις τοῦ θεοῦ. μόνον αὐτοῦ τὸ βού-
λημα κοσμοποιία· μόνος γὰρ ὁ θεὸς ἐποίησεν, ἐπεὶ
καὶ μόνος ὄντως ἐστὶ θεός· ψιλῷ τῷ βούλεσθαι
δημιουργεῖ καὶ τῷ μόνον ἐθελῆσαι αὐτὸν ἕπεται
τὸ γεγενῆσθαι. ἐνταῦθα φιλοσόφων παρατρέπεται
χορὸς πρὸς μὲν τὴν οὐρανοῦ θέαν παγκάλως
γεγονέναι τὸν ἄνθρωπον ὁμολογούντων, τὰ δὲ ἐν
οὐρανῷ φαινόμενα καὶ ὄψει καταλαμβανόμενα προσκυνούντων. εἰ γὰρ καὶ μὴ ἀνθρώπινα τὰ ἔργα
τὰ ἐν οὐρανῷ, ἀλλὰ γοῦν ἀνθρώποις δεδημιούργηται. καὶ μή τὸν ἥλιόν τις ὑμῶν προσκυνείτω,
ἀλλὰ τὸν ἡλίου ποιητὴν ἐπιποθείτω, μηδὲ τὸν
κόσμον ἐκθειαζέτω, ἀλλὰ τὸν κόσμου δημιουργὸν
ἐπιζητησάτω. μόνη ἄρα, ὡς ἔοικεν, καταφυγὴ τῷ
μέλλοντι ἐπὶ τὰς σωτηρίους ἀφικνεῖσθαι θύρας
ὑπολείπεται σοφία θεϊκή· ἐντεῦθεν ὥσπερ ἐξ ἱεροῦ
τινος ἀσύλου οὐδενὶ οὐκέτι ἀγώγιμος τῶν δαιμόνων
ὁ ἄνθρωπος γίνεται σπεύδων εἰς σωτηρίαν.

ᵃ See Genesis i. 14.

Some, it is true, starting from this point, go astray,— I know not how,—and worship not God but His handiwork, the sun, moon, and the host of stars besides, absurdly supposing these to be gods, though they are but instruments for measuring time; [a] for "by His word were they firmly established; and all their power by the breath of His mouth." [b] But while human handiwork fashions houses, ships, cities, paintings, how can I speak of all that God creates? See the whole universe; that is His work. Heaven, the sun, angels and men are "the works of His fingers." [c] How great is the power of God! His mere will is creation; for God alone created, since He alone is truly God. By a bare wish His work is done, and the world's existence follows upon a single act of His will. Here the host of philosophers turn aside, when they admit that man is beautifully made for the contemplation of heaven, [d] and yet worship the things which appear in heaven and are apprehended by sight. For although the heavenly bodies are not the works of man, at least they have been created for man. Let none of you worship the sun; rather let him yearn for the maker of the sun. Let no one deify the universe; rather let him seek after the creator of the universe. It seems, then, that but one refuge remains for the man who is to reach the gates of salvation, and that is divine wisdom. From thence, as from a holy inviolate temple, no longer can any daemon carry him off, as he presses onward to salvation.

Marginal notes: CHAP. IV — Some men worship the heavenly bodies instead of God — These are but God's handiwork — Seek after God and not the works of God

---

[b] Psalm xxxiii. 6.   [c] Psalm viii. 3.

[d] Cp. Cicero, *De natura deorum* ii. 140 " Providence . . . made men upright and erect, that by contemplating the heavens they might gain a knowledge of the gods." See also Ovid, *Metamorph.* i. 85–6.

V

Ἐπιδραμωμεν δέ, εἰ βούλει, καὶ τῶν φιλοσόφων
τὰς δόξας, ὅσας αὐχοῦσι περὶ τῶν θεῶν, εἴ πως
καὶ φιλοσοφίαν αὐτὴν κενοδοξίας ἕνεκεν ἀνειδωλο-
ποιοῦσαν τὴν ὕλην ἐφεύρωμεν, ἢ[1] καὶ δαιμόνια
ἄττα ἐκθειάζουσαν κατὰ παραδρομὴν παραστῆσαι
δυνηθῶμεν ὀνειρώττουσαν τὴν ἀλήθειαν. στοιχεῖα
μὲν οὖν ἀρχὰς ἀπέλιπον[2] ἐξυμνήσαντες Θαλῆς
ὁ Μιλήσιος τὸ ὕδωρ καὶ Ἀναξιμένης ὁ καὶ
αὐτὸς Μιλήσιος τὸν ἀέρα, ᾧ Διογένης ὕστερον ὁ
Ἀπολλωνιάτης κατηκολούθησεν. Παρμενίδης δὲ ὁ
Ἐλεάτης θεοὺς εἰσηγήσατο πῦρ καὶ γῆν, θάτερον δὲ
αὐτοῖν μόνον,[3] τὸ πῦρ, θεὸν ὑπειλήφατον Ἵππασός
τε ὁ Μεταποντῖνος καὶ ὁ Ἐφέσιος Ἡράκλειτος·
Ἐμπεδοκλῆς γὰρ ὁ Ἀκραγαντῖνος εἰς πλῆθος
56 P. ἐμπεσὼν πρὸς τοῖς τέτταρσι στοιχείοις τούτοις
νεῖκος καὶ φιλίαν καταριθμεῖται.

Ἄθεοι μὲν δὴ καὶ οὗτοι, σοφίᾳ τινὶ ἀσόφῳ τὴν
ὕλην προσκυνήσαντες καὶ λίθους μὲν ἢ ξύλα οὐ
τιμήσαντες, γῆν δὲ τὴν τούτων μητέρα ἐκθειάσαντες
καὶ Ποσειδῶνα μὲν οὐκ ἀναπλάττοντες, ὕδωρ δὲ
αὐτὸ προστρεπόμενοι. τί γάρ ἐστί ποτε ὁ[4] Ποσειδῶν
ἢ ὑγρά τις οὐσία ἐκ τῆς πόσεως ὀνοματοποιουμένη;
ὥσπερ ἀμέλει ὁ πολέμιος Ἄρης ἀπὸ τῆς ἄρσεως

---

[1] ἢ Diels.   εἰ MSS.
[2] ἀπέλιπον Cobet.   ἀπέλειπον MSS.
[3] μόνον Sylburg.   μόνοιν MSS.
[4] ποτε ὁ Wilamowitz.   πρότερον MSS.   ἕτερον Mayor.

---

[a] i.e. gets a feeble grasp of it.   Cp. Plutarch, De Is. et
Osir. 382 F "The souls of men, while on earth and en-

144

V

Let us now, if you like, run through the opinions which the philosophers, on their part, assert confidently about the gods. Perchance we may find philosophy herself, through vanity, forming her conceptions of the godhead out of matter; or else we may be able to show in passing that, when deifying certain divine powers, she sees the truth in a dream.[a] Some philosophers, then, left us the elements as first principles of all things. Water was selected for praise by Thales of Miletus; air by Anaximenes of the same city, who was followed afterwards by Diogenes of Apollonia. Fire and earth were introduced as gods by Parmenides of Elea; but only one of this pair, namely fire, is god according to the supposition of both Hippasus of Metapontum and Heracleitus of Ephesus. As to Empedocles of Acragas, he chooses plurality, and reckons " love " and " strife " in his list of gods, in addition to these four elements.

The opinions of philosophers

Early philosophers supposed the elements to be first principles

These men also were really atheists,[b] since with a foolish show of wisdom they worshipped matter. They did not, it is true, honour stocks or stones, but they made a god out of earth, which is the mother of these. They do not fashion a Poseidon, but they adore water itself. For what in the world is Poseidon, except a kind of liquid substance named from *posis*, drink? Just as, without a doubt, warlike

They are really atheists who make matter the first cause

cumbered by bodies and passions, can have no companionship with God, except in so far as they get a dim dream of Him through the aid of philosophy."

[b] See p. 47 with note.

CLEMENT OF ALEXANDRIA

καὶ ἀναιρέσεως κεκλημένος, ᾗ καὶ δοκοῦσί μοι
πολλοὶ μάλιστα τὸ ξίφος μόνον πήξαντες ἐπιθύειν
ὡς Ἄρει· ἔστι δὲ Σκυθῶν τὸ τοιοῦτον, καθάπερ
Εὔδοξος ἐν δευτέρᾳ Γῆς[1] περιόδου λέγει, Σκυθῶν δὲ
οἱ Σαυρομάται, ὥς φησιν Ἱκέσιος ἐν τῷ περὶ
μυστηρίων, ἀκινάκην σέβουσιν. τοῦτό τοι καὶ οἱ
ἀμφὶ τὸν Ἡράκλειτον τὸ πῦρ ὡς ἀρχέγονον
σέβοντες πεπόνθασιν·· τὸ γὰρ πῦρ τοῦτο ἕτεροι
Ἥφαιστον ὠνόμασαν. Περσῶν δὲ οἱ μάγοι τὸ
πῦρ τετιμήκασι καὶ τῶν τὴν Ἀσίαν κατοικούντων
πολλοί, πρὸς δὲ καὶ Μακεδόνες, ὥς φησι Διογένης
ἐν α΄ Περσικῶν. τί μοι Σαυρομάτας καταλέγειν,
οὓς Νυμφόδωρος ἐν Νομίμοις βαρβαρικοῖς τὸ πῦρ
σέβειν ἱστορεῖ, ἢ τοὺς Πέρσας καὶ τοὺς Μήδους καὶ
τοὺς μάγους; θύειν ἐν ὑπαίθρῳ τούτους ὁ Δίνων
λέγει, θεῶν ἀγάλματα μόνα τὸ πῦρ καὶ ὕδωρ νομίζον-
τας. οὐκ ἀπεκρυψάμην οὐδὲ τὴν τούτων ἄγνοιαν.
εἰ γὰρ καὶ τὰ μάλιστα ἀποφεύγειν οἴονται τῆς
57 P. πλάνης, ἀλλ' εἰς ἑτέραν κατολισθαίνουσιν | ἀπάτην·
ἀγάλματα μὲν θεῶν οὐ ξύλα καὶ λίθους ὑπειλήφασιν
ὥσπερ Ἕλληνες οὐδὲ μὴν ἴβιδας καὶ ἰχνεύμονας
καθάπερ Αἰγύπτιοι, ἀλλὰ πῦρ τε καὶ ὕδωρ ὡς
φιλόσοφοι. μετὰ πολλὰς μέντοι ὕστερον περιόδους
ἐτῶν ἀνθρωποειδῆ ἀγάλματα σέβειν αὐτοὺς Βήρωσ-

---

[1] Γῆς Diels. τῆς mss. (See p. 44, n. 3.)

---

[a] Cp. Plutarch, *Amatorius* 757 B "Chrysippus says
that Ares is *anairesis*" (so Petersen : mss. have *anairein*=to
destroy). The endeavour to find meanings in the names
of the gods has its literary origin in Plato's *Cratylus* (esp.
pp. 395–412). The Stoics found in this method a support
for their doctrine that the gods of mythology were merely
personified natural forces or processes. See Cicero, *De
natura deorum* ii. 63–72.

146

EXHORTATION TO THE GREEKS

Ares is so called from *arsis* and *anairesis*,[a] abolition CHAP.
and destruction; which is the chief reason, I think, V
why many tribes simply fix their sword in the ground
and then offer sacrifice to it as if to Ares. Such is
the custom of Scythians, as Eudoxus says in his
second book of *Geography*,[b] while the Sauromatians,
a Scythian tribe, worship a dagger, according to
Hicesius in his book on *Mysteries*.[c] This too is the
case with the followers of Heracleitus when they
worship fire as the source of all; for this fire is what
others named Hephaestus. The Persian Magi and Many
many of the inhabitants of Asia have assigned barbarians
honour to fire; so have the Macedonians, as Diogenes worship fire
says in the first volume of his *Persian History*.[d] Why
need I instance Sauromatians, whom Nymphodorus
in *Barbarian Customs*[e] reports as worshipping fire;
or the Persians, Medes and Magi? Dinon says that
these Magi sacrifice under the open sky, believing
that fire and water are the sole emblems of divinity.[f]
Even their ignorance I do not conceal; for although
they are quite convinced that they are escaping the
error of idolatry, yet they slip into another delusion.
They do not suppose, like Greeks, that stocks and
stones are emblems of divinity, nor ibises and ich-
neumons, after the manner of Egyptians; but they Worship of
admit fire and water, as philosophers do. It was the elements
is much
not, however, till many ages had passed that they older than
began to worship statues in human form, as Berosus image-
worship

[b] Eudoxus, Fr. 16 Brandes (*Jahrb. class. Phil.* 1847, Suppl.
13, p. 223).
[c] Hicesius, Fr. 1 *Frag. hist. Graec.* iv. p. 429.
[d] Diogenes of Cyzicus, Fr. 4 *Frag. hist. Graec.* iv. p. 392.
[e] Nymphodorus, Fr. 14 *Frag. hist. Graec.* ii. p. 379.
[f] Dinon, Fr. 9 *Frag. hist. Graec.* ii. p. 91.

CAP.
V

σος ἐν τρίτῃ Χαλδαϊκῶν παρίστησι, τοῦτο Ἀρτα-
ξέρξου τοῦ Δαρείου τοῦ Ὤχου εἰσηγησαμένου, ὃς
πρῶτος τῆς Ἀφροδίτης Ἀναΐτιδος[1] τὸ ἄγαλμα
ἀναστήσας ἐν Βαβυλῶνι καὶ Σούσοις καὶ Ἐκ-
βατάνοις Πέρσαις καὶ Βάκτροις καὶ Δαμασκῷ καὶ
Σάρδεσιν ὑπέδειξε σέβειν. ὁμολογούντων τοίνυν
οἱ φιλόσοφοι τοὺς διδασκάλους τοὺς σφῶν Πέρσας ἢ
Σαυρομάτας ἢ μάγους, παρ᾽ ὧν τὴν ἀθεότητα τῶν
σεβασμίων αὐτοῖς μεμαθήκασιν ἀρχῶν, ἄρχοντα τὸν
πάντων ποιητὴν καὶ τῶν ἀρχῶν αὐτῶν δημιουργὸν ἀγνοοῦντες, τὸν ἄναρχον θεόν, τὰ δὲ "πτωχὰ"
ταῦτα καὶ "ἀσθενῆ," ᾗ φησιν ὁ ἀπόστολος, τὰ εἰς
τὴν ἀνθρώπων ὑπηρεσίαν πεποιημένα "στοιχεῖα"
προστρεπόμενοι.

Τῶν δὲ ἄλλων φιλοσόφων ὅσοι τὰ στοιχεῖα
ὑπερβάντες ἐπολυπραγμόνησάν τι ὑψηλότερον καὶ
περιττότερον, οἱ μὲν αὐτῶν τὸ ἄπειρον καθύμνησαν,
ὡς Ἀναξίμανδρος (Μιλήσιος ἦν) καὶ Ἀναξαγόρας
ὁ Κλαζομένιος καὶ ὁ Ἀθηναῖος Ἀρχέλαος. τούτω
μέν γε ἄμφω τὸν νοῦν ἐπεστησάτην τῇ ἀπειρίᾳ,
ὁ δὲ Μιλήσιος Λεύκιππος καὶ ὁ Χῖος Μητρόδωρος
διττάς, ὡς ἔοικεν, καὶ αὐτὼ ἀρχὰς ἀπελιπέτην, τὸ
πλῆρες καὶ τὸ κενόν· προσέθηκε δὲ λαβὼν τούτοιν
τοῖν δυεῖν τὰ εἴδωλα ὁ Ἀβδηρίτης Δημόκριτος. ὁ
58 P. γάρ τοι Κροτωνιάτης Ἀλκμαίων | θεοὺς ᾤετο τοὺς
ἀστέρας εἶναι ἐμψύχους ὄντας. οὐ σιωπήσομαι τὴν
τούτων ἀναισχυντίαν· Ξενοκράτης (Καλχηδόνιος
οὗτος) ἑπτὰ μὲν θεοὺς τοὺς πλανήτας, ὄγδοον δὲ

[1] Ἀναΐτιδος Bochart.   ταναΐδος MSS.

[a] Berosus, Fr. 16 *Frag. hist. Graec.* ii. p. 508.
[b] Galatians iv. 9.

148

shows in his third book of *Chaldaean History*; [a] for this custom was introduced by Artaxerxes the son of Darius and father of Ochus, who was the first to set up the statue of Aphrodite Anaitis in Babylon, Susa and Ecbatana, and to enjoin this worship upon Persians and Bactrians, upon Damascus and Sardis. Let the philosophers therefore confess that Persians, Sauromatians, and Magi are their teachers, from whom they have learnt the atheistic doctrine of their venerated "first principles." The great original, the maker of all things, and creator of the "first principles" themselves, God without beginning, they know not, but offer adoration to these "weak and beggarly elements," [b] as the apostle calls them, made for the service of men.

Other philosophers went beyond the elements and sought diligently for a more sublime and excellent principle. Some of them celebrated the praises of the Infinite, as Anaximander of Miletus, Anaxagoras of Clazomenae, and Archelaus of Athens. The two latter agreed in placing Mind above the Infinite; while on the other hand Leucippus of Miletus and Metrodorus of Chios left, as it seems, a pair of first principles, "fulness" and "void." Democritus of Abdera took these two and added to them the "images." [c] Nor was this all; Alcmaeon of Croton thought that the stars were endowed with life, and therefore gods. I will not refrain from mentioning the audacity of these others. Xenocrates of Chalcedon intimates that the planets are seven gods and that

CHAP. V

Philosophers therefore get this doctrine from barbarians

Other philosophers sought for a higher principle
The Infinite
Mind
Fulness and Void
The stars and planets as gods

[c] The theory of Democritus was that all natural objects gave off small particles of themselves, which he called "images." These came into contact with the organs of sense and were the cause of perception.

149

CLEMENT OF ALEXANDRIA

CAP.
V
τὸν ἐκ πάντων τῶν ἀπλανῶν[1] συνεστῶτα κόσμον
αἰνίττεται. οὐδὲ μὴν τοὺς ἀπὸ τῆς Στοᾶς παρ-
ελεύσομαι διὰ πάσης ὕλης, καὶ διὰ τῆς ἀτιμοτάτης,
τὸ θεῖον διήκειν λέγοντας, οἳ καταισχύνουσιν
ἀτεχνῶς τὴν φιλοσοφίαν. οὐδὲν δὲ οἶμαι χαλεπὸν
ἐνταῦθα γενόμενος καὶ τῶν ἐκ τοῦ Περιπάτου
μνησθῆναι· καὶ ὅ γε τῆς αἱρέσεως πατήρ, τῶν
ὅλων οὐ νοήσας τὸν πατέρα, τὸν καλούμενον
"ὕπατον" ψυχὴν εἶναι τοῦ παντὸς οἴεται· τουτέστι τοῦ κόσμου τὴν ψυχὴν θεὸν ὑπολαμβάνων
αὐτὸς αὑτῷ περιπείρεται. ὁ γάρ τοι μέχρι τῆς
σελήνης αὐτῆς διορίζων τὴν πρόνοιαν, ἔπειτα τὸν
κόσμον θεὸν ἡγούμενος περιτρέπεται, τὸν ἄμοιρον
τοῦ θεοῦ θεὸν δογματίζων. ὁ δὲ Ἐρέσιος ἐκεῖνος
Θεόφραστος ὁ Ἀριστοτέλους γνώριμος πῆ μὲν
οὐρανόν, πῆ δὲ πνεῦμα τὸν θεὸν ὑπονοεῖ. Ἐπικού-
ρου μὲν γὰρ μόνου καὶ ἑκὼν ἐκλήσομαι, ὃς οὐδὲν[2]
μέλειν οἴεται τῷ θεῷ, διὰ πάντων ἀσεβῶν. τί γὰρ
Ἡρακλείδης ὁ Ποντικός; ἔσθ' ὅπῃ οὐκ ἐπὶ τὰ
Δημοκρίτου καὶ αὐτὸς κατασύρεται εἴδωλα;

VI

Καὶ πολύς μοι ἐπιρρεῖ τοιοῦτος ὄχλος, οἱονεὶ
μορμώ τινα, δαιμονίων παρεισάγων ξένων ἄτοπον

[1] τῶν ἀπλανῶν Davies. αὐτῶν mss. ἄστρων Diels.
[2] οὐδὲν Lowth. οὐδὲ mss.

[a] i.e. Aristotle.
[b] Aristotle sharply divided the celestial spheres, which
were the divine part of the universe, from the sublunary
world, in which alone birth, death, and change take place.
The laws governing the upper world are necessarily different
from those of the lower. Zeller (*Aristotle*, i. 508, n. 3, Eng.

the ordered arrangement of the fixed stars is an eighth. Nor will I omit the Stoics, who say that the divine nature permeates all matter, even in its lowest forms; these men simply cover philosophy with shame. At this point there is, I think, nothing to hinder me from mentioning the Peripatetics also. The father of this sect,[a] because he did not perceive the Father of all things, thinks that he who is called the "Highest" is the soul of the universe; that is to say, he supposes the soul of the world to be God, and so is pierced with his own sword. For he first declares that providence extends only as far as the moon; then by holding the opinion that the universe is God he contradicts himself, asserting that that which has no share in God is God.[b] Aristotle's disciple, the celebrated Theophrastus of Eresus, suspects in one place that God is heaven, and elsewhere that God is spirit. Epicurus alone I will banish from memory, and that willingly, for he, pre-eminent in impiety, thinks that God has no care for the world. What of Heracleides of Pontus? Is there a single place where he too is not drawn away to the "images" of Democritus?

CHAP.
V
The Stoic doctrine: God immanent in all things

The Peripatetic doctrine: God the soul of the universe

Epicurus: God has no care for the world

VI

And a vast crowd of the same description swarms upon me, bringing in their train, like a nightmare, an

Many other absurd doctrines, not worth attention

trans.) says: "Both Christian and heathen opponents have distorted this to mean that the Divine Providence reaches only as far as the moon and does not extend to the earth. How far this representation agrees with the true Aristotelian doctrine may be gathered from what has been already said, at pp. 403, 410, and 421."

151

CAP.
VI

σκιαγραφίαν, μυθολογῶν[1] ὕθλῳ γραϊκῷ· πολλοῦ
γε δεῖ ἀνδράσιν ἐπιτρέπειν ἀκροᾶσθαι τοιούτων
λόγων, οἳ μηδὲ τοὺς παῖδας τοὺς ἑαυτῶν, τοῦτο
δὴ τὸ λεγόμενον, κλαυθμυριζομένους ἐθίζομεν παρ-
ηγορεῖσθαι μυθίζοντες, ὀρρωδοῦντες συνανατρέφειν
αὐτοῖς ἀθεότητα τὴν πρὸς τῶν δοκησισόφων[2]
δὴ τούτων καταγγελλομένην, μηδέν τι νηπίων
μᾶλλον τἀληθὲς εἰδότων. τί γάρ, ὦ πρὸς τῆς
ἀληθείας, τοὺς σοὶ πεπιστευκότας δεικνύεις ῥύσει
καὶ φορᾷ[3] δίναις τε ἀτάκτοις[4] ὑποβεβλημένους; τί
δέ μοι εἰδώλων ἀναπίμπλης τὸν βίον, ἀνέμους τε
ἢ ἀέρα ἢ πῦρ ἢ γῆν ἢ λίθους ἢ ξύλα ἢ σίδηρον,
κόσμον τόνδε, θεοὺς ἀναπλάττουσα, θεοὺς δὲ καὶ
τοὺς ἀστέρας τοὺς πλανήτας, τοῖς ὄντως πεπλα-
νημένοις τῶν ἀνθρώπων διὰ τῆς πολυθρυλήτου
ταύτης ἀστρολογίας, οὐκ ἀστρονομίας, μετεωρο-
59 P λογοῦσα καὶ ἀδολεσχοῦσα; | τὸν κύριον τῶν πνευ-
μάτων ποθῶ, τὸν κύριον τοῦ πυρός, τὸν κόσμου
δημιουργόν, τὸν ἡλίου φωταγωγόν· θεὸν ἐπιζητῶ,
οὐ τὰ ἔργα τοῦ θεοῦ. τίνα δὴ λάβω παρὰ σοῦ
συνεργὸν τῆς ζητήσεως; οὐ γὰρ παντάπασιν
ἀπεγνώκαμέν σε. εἰ βούλει, τὸν Πλάτωνα. πῇ
δὴ οὖν ἐξιχνευτέον τὸν θεόν, ὦ Πλάτων; "τὸν
γὰρ πατέρα καὶ ποιητὴν τοῦδε τοῦ παντὸς εὑρεῖν

---

[1] μυθολογῶν Mayor.   μυθολόγων MSS.
[2] δοκησισόφων Potter.   δοκησεισόφων MSS.
[3] φορᾷ Münzel.   φθορᾷ MSS.
[4] δίναις τε ἀτάκτοις Heyse.   δειναῖς τε καὶ ἀτάκτοις MSS.

---

[a] The doctrine of "flux" was taught by Heracleitus in
his well-known phrase, "All things flow" (πάντα ῥεῖ).
"Motion" and "irregular vortices" refer to Anaxagoras,
who supposed the primitive elements to have been set in

152

absurd picture of strange daemons, and romancing
with all an old wife's extravagance. Far indeed
are we from allowing grown men to listen to such
tales. Even to our own children, when they are
crying their heart out, as the saying goes, we are
not in the habit of telling fabulous stories to soothe
them; for we shrink from fostering in the children
the atheism proclaimed by these men, who, though
wise in their own conceit, have no more knowledge of the truth than infants. Why, in the
name of truth, do you show those who have put their
trust in you that they are under the dominion of
"flux" and "motion" and "fortuitous vortices"?[a]
Why, pray, do you infect life with idols, imagining
winds, air, fire, earth, stocks, stones, iron, this world itself to be gods? Why babble in high-flown language
about the divinity of the wandering stars to those
men who have become real wanderers through this
much-vaunted,—I will not call it astronomy, but
—astrology? I long for the Lord of the winds, the
Lord of fire, the Creator of the world, He who gives
light to the sun. I seek for God Himself, not for
the works of God. Whom am I to take from you
as fellow worker in the search? For we do not
altogether despair of you. "Plato," if you like. Plato is a
better
guide
How, then, Plato, must we trace out God? "It is
a hard task to find the Father and Maker of this

rotatory motion by Mind (νοῦς). This theory is ridiculed by
Aristophanes, *Clouds* 828 "Vortex has ousted Zeus, and
reigns as king." Vortex motion was also a part of the
"atomic theory" of Leucippus. Atoms of various size and
shape constantly impinging upon one another in empty
space would give rise to countless vortices, each of which
might be the beginning of a world.

τε ἔργον καὶ εὑρόντα εἰς ἅπαντας ἐξειπεῖν ἀδύνατον.''
διὰ τί δῆτα, ὦ πρὸς αὐτοῦ; ''ῥητὸν[1] γὰρ οὐδαμῶς
ἐστίν.'' εὖ γε, ὦ Πλάτων, ἐπαφᾶσαι τῆς ἀληθείας·
ἀλλὰ μὴ ἀποκάμῃς· ξύν μοι λαβοῦ τῆς ζητήσεως
τἀγαθοῦ πέρι· πᾶσιν γὰρ ἀπαξαπλῶς ἀνθρώποις,
μάλιστα δὲ τοῖς περὶ λόγους ἐνδιατρίβουσιν ἐνέστακ-
ταί τις ἀπόρροια θεϊκή. οὗ δὴ χάριν καὶ ἄκοντες
μὲν ὁμολογοῦσιν ἕνα γε[2] εἶναι θεόν, ἀνώλεθρον καὶ
ἀγένητον τοῦτον, ἄνω που περὶ τὰ νῶτα τοῦ
οὐρανοῦ ἐν τῇ ἰδίᾳ καὶ οἰκείᾳ περιωπῇ ὄντως
ὄντα ἀεί.

θεὸν δὲ ποῖον, εἰπέ μοι, νοητέον ;
τὸν πάνθ' ὁρῶντα καὐτὸν οὐχ ὁρώμενον,

Εὐριπίδης λέγει. πεπλανῆσθαι γοῦν ὁ Μένανδρός
μοι δοκεῖ, ἔνθα φησίν

ἥλιε, σὲ γὰρ δεῖ προσκυνεῖν πρῶτον θεῶν,
δι' ὃν θεωρεῖν ἔστι τοὺς ἄλλους θεούς·

οὐδὲ γὰρ ἥλιος ἐπιδείξει ποτ' ἂν τὸν θεὸν τὸν
ἀληθῆ, ὁ δὲ λόγος ὁ ὑγιής, ὅς ἐστιν ἥλιος ψυχῆς,
δι' οὗ μόνου ἔνδον ἀνατείλαντος ἐν τῷ βάθει τοῦ
νοῦ[3] αὐτῆς[4] καταυγάζεται τὸ ὄμμα· ὅθεν οὐκ ἀπεικότως ὁ Δημόκριτος ''τῶν λογίων ἀνθρώπων

---

[1] ῥητὸν from Plato.   ῥητέον MSS.
[2] γε Schwartz.   τε MSS.
[3] τοῦ νοῦ Cobet.   τοῦ νοῦ καὶ τοῦ νοός MSS.
[4] αὐτῆς Kroll.   αὐτοῦ MSS.

---

[a] Plato, *Timaeus* 28 c.
[b] Plato, *Epistles* vii. p. 341 c.
[c] Literally "the back" of the heavens. The phrase
comes from Plato, *Phaedrus* 247 c. Both Plato and Clement

universe, and when you have found Him, it is impossible to declare Him to all." [a] Why, pray, in
God's name, why? "Because He can in no way be
described." [b] Well done, Plato, you have hit the
truth. But do not give up. Join me in the search for
the good. For there is a certain divine effluence A divine
effluence
leads
thoughtful
men to
confess to
truth
instilled into all men without exception, but
especially into those who spend their lives in
thought; wherefore they admit, even though against
their will, that God is One, that He is unbegotten
and indestructible, and that somewhere on high in
the outermost spaces [c] of the heavens, in His own
private watch-tower, He truly exists for ever.

> What nature, say, must man ascribe to God?
> He seeth all; yet ne'er Himself is seen,

says Euripides. [d] Certainly Menander seems to me
to be in error where he says,

> O Sun, thee must we worship, first of gods,
> Through whom our eyes can see the other gods. [e]

For not even the sun could ever show us the true
God. The healthful Word or Reason, who is the
Sun of the soul, alone can do that; through Him
alone, when He has risen within in the depth of the
mind, the soul's eye is illuminated. Whence
Democritus not unreasonably says that " a few men

think of the heavens as a series of spheres revolving above
the earth. The dwelling-place of God (or Plato's "real
existence ") is on the outer side of the topmost sphere. See
the whole passage, *Phaedrus* 246 D–249.
    [d] Euripides, Frag. 1129 Nauck.
    [e] Menander, Frag. 609 Kock, *Comic. Attic. Frag.* iii.
p. 184.

CAP.
VI

60 P.

ὀλίγους '' φησίν '' ἀνατείναντας τὰς χεῖρας ἐνταῦθα ὃν νῦν ἠέρα καλέομεν οἱ Ἕλληνες, [πάντα] Δία μυθεῖσθαι[1]· καὶ ⟨γὰρ⟩ πάντα οὗτος οἶδεν καὶ διδοῖ ⟨πάντα⟩[2] καὶ ἀφαιρεῖται, καὶ βασιλεὺς οὗτος τῶν πάντων.'' ταύτῃ πῃ καὶ Πλάτων | διανοούμενος τὸν θεὸν αἰνίττεται '' περὶ τὸν πάντων βασιλέα πάντ' ἐστί, κἀκεῖνο αἴτιον ἁπάντων ⟨τῶν⟩[3] καλῶν.'' τίς οὖν ὁ βασιλεὺς τῶν πάντων; θεὸς τῆς τῶν ὄντων ἀληθείας τὸ μέτρον. ὥσπερ οὖν τῷ μέτρῳ καταληπτὰ τὰ μετρούμενα, οὕτωσὶ δὲ καὶ τῷ νοῆσαι τὸν θεὸν μετρεῖται καὶ καταλαμβάνεται ἡ ἀλήθεια. ὁ δὲ ἱερὸς ὄντως Μωυσῆς '' οὐκ ἔσται,'' φησίν, '' ἐν τῷ μαρσίππῳ σου στάθμιον καὶ στάθμιον μέγα ἢ μικρόν, οὐδὲ ἔσται ἐν τῇ οἰκίᾳ σου μέτρον μέγα ἢ μικρόν, ἀλλ' ἢ στάθμιον ἀληθινὸν καὶ δίκαιον ἔσται σοι,'' στάθμιον καὶ μέτρον καὶ ἀριθμὸν τῶν ὅλων ὑπολαμβάνων τὸν θεόν· τὰ μὲν γὰρ ἄδικα καὶ ἄνισα εἴδωλα οἴκοι ἐν τῷ μαρσίππῳ καὶ ἐν τῇ ὡς ἔπος εἰπεῖν ῥυπώσῃ ψυχῇ κατακέκρυπται· τὸ δὲ μόνον δίκαιον μέτρον, ὁ μόνος ὄντως θεός, ἴσος ἀεὶ κατὰ τὰ αὐτὰ καὶ ὡσαύτως ἔχων, μετρεῖ τε[4] πάντα καὶ σταθμᾶται, οἱονεὶ τρυτάνῃ τῇ δικαιοσύνῃ τὴν τῶν ὅλων ἀρρεπῶς περιλαμβάνων καὶ ἀνέχων φύσιν. '' ὁ μὲν δὴ θεός, ὥσπερ καὶ ὁ παλαιὸς λόγος, ἀρχήν ⟨τε⟩[5] καὶ τελευτὴν καὶ μέσα τῶν ὄντων ἁπάντων ἔχων, εὐθεῖαν περαίνει κατὰ φύσιν περι-

---

[1] Δία μυθεῖσθαι Heinsius. διαμυθεῖσθαι MSS.

[2] καὶ ⟨γὰρ⟩ πάντα . . . καὶ διδοῖ ⟨πάντα⟩ (with omission of πάντα in previous line) Wilamowitz. καὶ πάντα . . . καὶ δ.δοῖ καὶ . . . MSS.

[3] ⟨τῶν⟩ from Plato (but cp. Plotinus i. 8. 2).

[4] μετρεῖ τε Wendland (cp. Plato, Laws 643 c). μετρεῖται MSS.

[5] ⟨τε⟩ from Plato, and Clement, ii. Strom. 132. 2.

of reason[a] stretch out their hands towards that which we Greeks now call air and speak of it in legend as Zeus; for Zeus knows all, he gives and takes away all, and he is king of all things."[b] Plato also has a similar thought, when he says darkly about God: "All things are around the king of all things, and that is the cause of everything good."[c] Who, then, is the king of all things? It is God, the measure of the truth of all existence. As therefore things measured are comprehended by the measure, so also by the perception of God the truth is measured and comprehended. The truly sacred Moses says, "There shall not be in thy bag divers weights, a great and a small, neither shall there be in thy house a great measure and a small, but thou shalt have a weight true and just."[d] Here he is assuming God to be the weight and measure and number of the universe. For the unjust and unfair idols find a home hidden in the depths of the bag, or, as we may say, the polluted soul. But the one true God, who is the only just measure, because He is always uniformly and unchangeably impartial,[e] measures and weighs all things, encircling and sustaining in equilibrium the nature of the universe by His justice as by a balance. "Now God, as the ancient saying has it, holding the beginning and end and middle of all existence, keeps an unswerving

CHAP.
VI

Plato speaks
of the king
of all things,
i.e. God

God is the
measure of
all existence

Moses
speaks
against false
measures,
i.e. false
gods

God, the
true
measure,
is ever
accompanied by
Right, as
Plato says

---

[a] Λόγιος means *learned*, but here it seems to refer back to λόγος.
[b] Democritus, Frag. 30 Diels, *Vorsokratiker* ii. pp. 70-1 (1912).
[c] Plato, *Epistles* ii. p. 312 E.
[d] Deut. xxv. 13–15.
[e] See Plato, *Phaedo* 78 D.

CAP. πορευόμενος· τῷ[1] δ' ἀεὶ ξυνέπεται δίκη τῶν ἀπο-
VI λειπομένων τοῦ θείου νόμου τιμωρός.'' πόθεν, ὦ
Πλάτων, ἀλήθειαν αἰνίττῃ; πόθεν ἡ τῶν λόγων
ἄφθονος χορηγία τὴν θεοσέβειαν μαντεύεται; σοφώ-
τερα, φησίν, τούτων βαρβάρων τὰ γένη. οἶδά σου
τοὺς διδασκάλους, κἂν ἀποκρύπτειν ἐθέλῃς· γεωμε-
τρίαν παρ' Αἰγυπτίων μανθάνεις, ἀστρονομίαν παρὰ
Βαβυλωνίων, ἐπῳδὰς τὰς ὑγιεῖς παρὰ Θρᾳκῶν
λαμβάνεις, πολλά σε καὶ Ἀσσύριοι πεπαιδεύκασι,
νόμους δὲ τοὺς ὅσοι ἀληθεῖς καὶ δόξαν τὴν τοῦ θεοῦ
παρ' αὐτῶν ὠφέλησαι τῶν Ἑβραίων,

οἵτινες οὐκ ἀπάτῃσι κεναῖς, οὐδ' ἔργ' ἀνθρώπων
χρύσεα καὶ χάλκεα καὶ ἀργύρου ἠδ' ἐλέφαντος
καὶ ξυλίνων λιθίνων τε βροτῶν εἴδωλα θανόντων
τιμῶσιν, ὅσα πέρ τε βροτοὶ κενεόφρονι βουλῇ·
ἀλλὰ γὰρ ἀείρουσι[2] πρὸς οὐρανὸν ὠλένας ἁγνάς, |
61 P. ὄρθριοι ἐξ εὐνῆς, ἀεὶ χρόα ἁγνίζοντες
ὕδασι, καὶ τιμῶσι μόνον τὸν ἀεὶ μεδέοντα
ἀθάνατον.

Καί μοι μὴ μόνον, ὦ φιλοσοφία, ἕνα τοῦτον
Πλάτωνα, πολλοὺς δὲ καὶ ἄλλους παραστῆσαι
σπούδασον, τὸν ἕνα ὄντως μόνον θεὸν ἀναφθεγ-
γομένους θεὸν κατ' ἐπίπνοιαν αὐτοῦ, εἴ που τῆς
ἀληθείας ἐπιδράξαιντο. Ἀντισθένης μὲν γὰρ οὐ
Κυνικὸν δὴ τοῦτο ἐνενόησεν, Σωκράτους δὲ ἅτε
γνώριμος "θεὸν οὐδενὶ ἐοικέναι" φησίν· "διόπερ
αὐτὸν οὐδεὶς ἐκμαθεῖν ἐξ εἰκόνος δύναται." Ξενο-

---

[1] τῷ from Plato and Clement, ii. *Strom.* 132. 2. τὴν MSS.
[2] ἀείρουσι *Sibylline Oracles.* αἴρουσι MSS.

path, revolving according to nature ; but ever there
follows along with him Right, to take vengeance
on those who forsake the divine law." [a]   "Whence,
Plato, do you hint at the truth ? Whence comes it
that this abundant supply of words proclaims as in
an oracle the fear of God ?"   "The barbarian races,"
he answers, " are wiser than the Greeks." [b]   I know
your teachers, even if you would fain conceal them.
You learn geometry from the Egyptians, astronomy
from the Babylonians, healing incantations you obtain
from the Thracians, and the Assyrians have taught
you much ; but as to your laws (in so far as they
are true) and your belief about God, you have been
helped by the Hebrews themselves :

> Who honour not with vain deceit man's works
> Of gold and silver, bronze and ivory,
> And dead men's statues carved from wood and stone,
> Which mortals in their foolish hearts revere ;
> But holy hands to heaven each morn they raise
> From sleep arising, and their flesh they cleanse
> With water pure ; and honour Him alone
> Who guards them alway, the immortal God. [c]

And now, O philosophy, hasten to set before me
not only this one man Plato, but many others also,
who declare the one only true God to be God, by
His own inspiration, if so be they have laid hold of
the truth.   Antisthenes, for instance, had perceived
this, not as a Cynic doctrine, but as a result of his
intimacy with Socrates ; for he says, " God is like
none else, wherefore none can know him thoroughly
from a likeness." [d]   And Xenophon the Athenian

---

[a] Plato, *Laws* 715 E, 716 A.   [b] *Phaedo* 78 A.
[c] *Sibylline Oracles* iii. 586–588, 590–594.
[d] Antisthenes, Frag. 24 Mullach, *Frag. phil. Graec.* ii.
p. 277.

CAP.
VI

φῶν δὲ ὁ Ἀθηναῖος διαρρήδην ἂν καὶ αὐτὸς περὶ
τῆς ἀληθείας ἐγεγράφει [1] τι μαρτυρῶν ὡς Σωκράτης,
εἰ μὴ τὸ Σωκράτους ἐδεδίει φάρμακον· οὐδὲν δὲ
ἧττον αἰνίττεται. "ὁ" γοῦν "τὰ πάντα," φησί,
"σείων καὶ ἀτρεμίζων ὡς μὲν μέγας τις καὶ
δυνατός, φανερός· ὁποῖος δὲ τὴν [2] μορφήν, ἀφανής·
οὐδὲ μὴν ὁ παμφαὴς δοκῶν εἶναι ἥλιος οὐδ' αὐτὸς
ἔοικεν ὁρᾶν αὐτὸν ἐπιτρέπειν, ἀλλ' ἤν τις ἀναιδῶς
αὐτὸν θεάσηται, τὴν ὄψιν ἀφαιρεῖται." πόθεν ἄρα
ὁ τοῦ Γρύλλου σοφίζεται ἢ δηλαδὴ παρὰ τῆς
προφήτιδος τῆς Ἑβραίων θεσπιζούσης ὧδέ πως;

τίς γὰρ σὰρξ δύναται τὸν ἐπουράνιον καὶ ἀληθῆ
ὀφθαλμοῖσιν ἰδεῖν θεὸν ἄμβροτον, ὃς πόλον οἰκεῖ;
ἀλλ' οὐδ' ἀκτίνων κατεναντίον ἠελίοιο
ἄνθρωποι στῆναι δυνατοί, θνητοὶ γεγαῶτες.

Κλεάνθης δὲ ὁ Πηδασεύς,[3] ὁ ἀπὸ τῆς Στοᾶς φιλόσοφος, οὐ θεογονίαν ποιητικήν, θεολογίαν δὲ ἀληθινὴν ἐνδείκνυται. οὐκ ἀπεκρύψατο τοῦ θεοῦ πέρι ὅτι
περ εἶχεν φρονῶν·

τἀγαθὸν [4] ἐρωτᾷς μ' οἷόν ἐστ'; ἄκουε δή·
τεταγμένον, δίκαιον, ὅσιον, εὐσεβές,
κρατοῦν ἑαυτοῦ, χρήσιμον, καλόν, δέον,
αὐστηρόν, αὐθέκαστον, ἀεὶ συμφέρον,
ἄφοβον, ἄλυπον, λυσιτελές, ἀνώδυνον,
ὠφέλιμον, εὐάρεστον, ἀσφαλές, φίλον,
ἔντιμον, ὁμολογούμενον * * * * * * * *

62 P

---

[1] ἐγεγράφει Dindorf. ἀναγράφει MSS.
[2] δὲ τὴν Stobaeus (*Eclog.* ii. 1). δέ τις MSS. δ' ἐστὶν
Clement, v. *Strom.* 108. 5.
[3] Πηδασεύς Wilamowitz (see Strabo xiii. p. 611). πισαδεύς
MSS.
[4] τἀγαθὸν Clement, v. *Strom.* 110. 3. εἰ τὸ ἀγαθὸν MSS.

would himself have written explicitly concerning the truth, bearing his share of witness as Socrates did, had he not feared the poison which Socrates received; none the less he hints at it. At least, he says: "He who moves all things and brings them to rest again is plainly some great and mighty One; but what His form is we cannot see. Even the sun, which appears to shine upon all, even he seems not to allow himself to be seen; but if a man impudently gazes at him, he is deprived of sight." [a] From what source, pray, does the son of Gryllus draw his wisdom? Is it not clearly from the Hebrew prophetess, who utters her oracle in the following words?

> What eyes of flesh can see immortal God,
> Who dwells above the heavenly firmament?
> Not e'en against the sun's descending rays
> Can men of mortal birth endure to stand. [b]

Cleanthes of Pedasis, [c] the Stoic philosopher, sets forth no genealogy of the gods, after the manner of poets, but a true theology. He did not conceal what thoughts he had about God.

> Thou ask'st me what the good is like? Then hear!
> The good is ordered, holy, pious, just,
> Self-ruling, useful, beautiful, and right,
> Severe, without pretence, expedient ever,
> Fearless and griefless, helpful, soothing pain,
> Well-pleasing, advantageous, steadfast, loved,
> Esteemed, consistent . . .

---

[a] Xenophon, *Memorabilia* iv. 3. 13–14.

[b] *Sibylline Oracles*, Preface 10–13. These pretended Hebrew prophecies were, of course, much later than the time of Xenophon, though plainly Clement believed in their antiquity. See p. 56, n. *b*.

[c] See note on text. Cleanthes is generally said to be a native of Assos in the Troad. See Strabo xiii. pp. 610–11.

εὐκλεές, ἄτυφον, ἐπιμελές, πρᾶον, σφοδρόν,
χρονιζόμενον, ἄμεμπτον, ἀεὶ διαμένον.

ἀνελεύθερος πᾶς ὅστις εἰς δόξαν βλέπει,
ὡς δὴ παρ᾽ ἐκείνης τευξόμενος καλοῦ τινος.

ἐνταῦθα δὴ σαφῶς, οἶμαι, διδάσκει ὁποῖός ἐστιν ὁ
θεός, καὶ ὡς ἡ δόξα ἡ κοινὴ καὶ ἡ συνήθεια τοὺς
ἑπομένους αὐταῖν, ἀλλὰ μὴ τὸν θεὸν ἐπιζητοῦντας,
ἐξανδραποδιζέσθην. οὐκ ἀποκρυπτέον οὐδὲ τοὺς
ἀμφὶ τὸν Πυθαγόραν, οἵ φασιν "ὁ μὲν θεὸς εἷς,
οὗτος[1] δὲ οὐχ, ὡς τινες ὑπονοοῦσιν, ἐκτὸς τᾶς
διακοσμήσιος, ἀλλ᾽ ἐν αὐτᾷ, ὅλος ἐν ὅλῳ τῷ κύκλῳ,
ἐπίσκοπος πάσας γενέσιος, κρᾶσις τῶν ὅλων αἰώνων[2]
καὶ ἐργάτας τῶν αὐτοῦ δυνάμιων. καὶ ἔργων ἀπάντων
ἐν οὐρανῷ φωστὴρ καὶ πάντων πατήρ, νοῦς καὶ
ψύχωσις τῶ ὅλῳ κύκλῳ,[3] πάντων κίνασις." ἀπόχρη
καὶ τάδε εἰς ἐπίγνωσιν θεοῦ ἐπινοίᾳ θεοῦ πρὸς
αὐτῶν μὲν ἀναγεγραμμένα, πρὸς δὲ ἡμῶν ἐξει-
λεγμένα τῷ γε καὶ σμικρὸν διαθρεῖν ἀλήθειαν
δυναμένῳ.

VII

Ἴτω δὲ ἡμῖν (οὐ γὰρ αὐταρκεῖ μόνον ἡ φιλοσοφία)
ἀλλὰ καὶ αὐτὴ ⟨ἡ⟩[4] ποιητικὴ ἡ περὶ τὸ ψεῦδος τὰ
πάντα ἠσχολημένη, μόλις ποτὲ ἤδη ἀλήθειαν μαρ-
τυρήσουσα, μᾶλλον δὲ ἐξομολογουμένη τῷ θεῷ τὴν
μυθώδη παρέκβασιν· παρίτω δὴ ὅστις καὶ βούλεται

---

[1] οὗτος Wilamowitz. χοῦτος mss. αὐτὸς Justin (Cohor. ad
Graec. 19).
[2] αἰώνων Justin. ἀεὶ ὢν mss.
[3] τῶ ὅλῳ κύκλῳ Stählin. τῷ ὅλῳ κύκλῳ mss.
[4] ⟨ἡ⟩ inserted by Markland.

Renowned, not puffed up, careful, gentle, strong,
Enduring, blameless, lives from age to age.[a]

Slavish the man who vain opinion heeds,
In hope to light on any good from that.[b]

In these passages he teaches clearly, I think, what is the nature of God, and how common opinion and custom make slaves of those who follow them instead of searching after God. Nor must we conceal the doctrine of the Pythagoreans, who say that " God is One ; and He is not, as some suspect, outside the universal order, but within it, being wholly present in the whole circle, the supervisor of all creation, the blending of all the ages, the wielder of His own powers, the light of all His works in heaven and the Father of all things, mind and living principle of the whole circle, movement of all things." These sayings have been recorded by their authors through God's inspiration, and we have selected them. As a guide to the full knowledge of God they are sufficient for every man who is able, even in small measure, to investigate the truth.

The Pytha-goreans

VII

But we will not rest content with philosophy alone. Let poetry also approach,—poetry, which is occupied entirely with what is false,—to bear witness now at last to truth, or rather to confess before God its deviation into legend. Let whichever poet

The witness of poetry

[a] Pearson, *Fragments of Zeno and Cleanthes*, p. 299 (Fr. 75). Pearson remarks : " Clement's mistake in referring these lines to Cleanthes' conception of the Deity, when they really refer to the ethical *summum bonum*, is obvious."

[b] Pearson, p. 320 (Fr. 101).

CAP. ποιητὴς πρῶτος. Ἄρατος μὲν οὖν διὰ πάντων τὴν
VII δύναμιν τοῦ θεοῦ διήκειν νοεῖ,

ὄφρ' ἔμπεδα πάντα φύωνται,
τῷ μιν ἀεὶ πρῶτόν τε καὶ ὕστατον ἱλάσκονται·
χαῖρε, πάτερ, μέγα θαῦμα, μέγ' ἀνθρώποισιν
ὄνειαρ.

ταύτῃ τοι καὶ ὁ Ἀσκραῖος αἰνίττεται Ἡσίοδος τὸν
θεόν· |

63 P.   αὐτὸς γὰρ πάντων βασιλεὺς καὶ κοίρανός ἐστιν,
ἀθανάτων τέο δ'[1] οὔτις ἐρήρισται κράτος ἄλλος.

ἤδη δὲ καὶ ἐπὶ τῆς σκηνῆς παραγυμνοῦσι τὴν
ἀλήθειαν· ὁ μὲν καὶ εἰς τὸν αἰθέρα καὶ εἰς τὸν
οὐρανὸν ἀναβλέψας "τόνδε ἡγοῦ θεόν," φησίν.
Εὐριπίδης· ὁ δὲ τοῦ Σοφίλλου Σοφοκλῆς,

εἷς ταῖς ἀληθείαισιν, εἷς ἐστιν θεός,
ὃς οὐρανόν τ' ἔτευξε καὶ γαῖαν μακρὴν
πόντου τε χαροπὸν οἶδμα κἀνέμων βίας·
θνητοὶ δὲ πολλά[2] καρδίᾳ πλανώμενοι
ἱδρυσάμεσθα πημάτων παραψυχὴν
θεῶν ἀγάλματ' ἐκ λίθων, ἢ χαλκέων
ἢ χρυσοτεύκτων ἢ ἐλεφαντίνων τύπους·
θυσίας τε τούτοις καὶ κενὰς πανηγύρεις
νέμοντες, οὕτως εὐσεβεῖν νομίζομεν.

οὑτοσὶ μὲν ἤδη καὶ παρακεκινδυνευμένως ἐπὶ τῆς
σκηνῆς τὴν ἀλήθειαν τοῖς θεαταῖς παρεισήγαγεν.

---

[1] τέο δ' Stählin.   σέο δ' Clement, v. *Strom.* 112. 3.   τέ
οἱ Buttmann.   τε ὅδ' MSS.

[2] πολλά Heyse.   πολλοὶ MSS.

wishes come forward first. Aratus, then, perceives CHAP.
that the power of God permeates the universe : VII
Aratus

> Wherefore, that all things fresh and firm may grow,
> To Him our vows both first and last shall rise :
> Hail, Father, wonder great, great aid to men.[a]

In the same spirit Hesiod of Ascra also speaks Hesiod
darkly about God :

> For He is king and master over all ;
> No other god hath vied with Thee in strength.[b]

Further, even upon the stage they unveil the truth.
One of them, Euripides, after gazing at the upper Euripides
air and heaven, says, "Consider this to be God." [c]
Another, Sophocles the son of Sophillus, says : Sophocles

> One only, one in very truth is God,
> Who made high heaven and the spreading earth,
> The ocean's gleaming wave, the mighty winds.
> But we, vain mortals, erring much in heart,
> Seek solace for our woes by setting up
> The images of gods made out of stones,
> Or forms of bronze, or gold, or ivory.
> Then sacrifice and empty festival
> To these we pay, and think it piety.[d]

This poet, in a most venturesome manner, introduced
the truth on the stage for his audience to hear.

---

[a] Aratus, *Phaenomena* 13-15.
[b] Hesiod, Frag. 195 Rzach.
[c] Euripides, Frag. 941 Nauck.
[d] [Sophocles] Frag. 1025 Nauck. These lines are also
quoted by Justin Martyr, Athenagoras, Eusebius, and other
Christian writers. They are of Jewish or Christian origin,
as their teaching proves ; certainly not from Sophocles.

CLEMENT OF ALEXANDRIA

ὁ δὲ Θρᾴκιος ἱεροφάντης καὶ ποιητὴς ἅμα, ὁ τοῦ
Οἰάγρου Ὀρφεύς, μετὰ τὴν τῶν ὀργίων ἱεροφαντίαν
καὶ τῶν εἰδώλων τὴν θεολογίαν, παλινῳδίαν ἀληθείας
εἰσάγει, τὸν ἱερὸν ὄντως ὀψέ ποτε, ὅμως δ᾿ οὖν
ᾄδων λόγον·

> φθέγξομαι οἷς θέμις ἐστί· θύρας δ᾿ ἐπίθεσθε
> βέβηλοι
> πάντες ὁμῶς· σὺ δ᾿ ἄκουε, φαεσφόρου ἔκγονε
> Μήνης,
> Μουσαῖ᾿, ἐξερέω γὰρ ἀληθέα, μηδέ σε τὰ πρὶν
> ἐν στήθεσσι φανέντα φίλης αἰῶνος ἀμέρσῃ.
> εἰς δὲ λόγον θεῖον βλέψας τούτῳ προσέδρευε,
> ἰθύνων κραδίης νοερὸν κύτος· εὖ δ᾿ ἐπίβαινε
> ἀτραπιτοῦ, μοῦνον δ᾿ ἐσόρα κόσμοιο ἄνακτα
> ἀθάνατον.

εἶτα ὑποβὰς διαρρήδην ἐπιφέρει· |

> εἷς ἔστ᾿, αὐτογενής, ἑνὸς ἔκγονα πάντα τέτυκται·
> ἐν δ᾿ αὐτοῖς αὐτὸς περινίσσεται, οὐδέ τις αὐτὸν
> εἰσορᾷ θνητῶν, αὐτὸς δέ γε πάντας ὁρᾶται.

οὕτως μὲν δὴ Ὀρφεύς· χρόνῳ γέ[1] ποτε συνῆκεν
πεπλανημένος.

> ἀλλὰ σὺ μὴ μέλλων, βροτὲ ποικιλόμητι, βράδυνε,
> ἀλλὰ παλίμπλαγκτος στρέψας θεὸν ἱλάσκοιο.

εἰ γὰρ καὶ τὰ μάλιστα ἐναύσματά τινα τοῦ λόγου
τοῦ θείου λαβόντες Ἕλληνες ὀλίγα ἄττα τῆς
ἀληθείας ἐφθέγξαντο, προσμαρτυροῦσι μὲν τὴν
δύναμιν αὐτῆς οὐκ ἀποκεκρυμμένην, σφᾶς δὲ αὐτοὺς
ἐλέγχουσιν ἀσθενεῖς, οὐκ ἐφικόμενοι τοῦ τέλους.
ἤδη γὰρ οἶμαι παντὶ τῳ δῆλον γεγονέναι ὡς τῶν

---

[1] γέ Stählin.   τέ MSS.

166

And the Thracian interpreter of the mysteries, who
was a poet too, Orpheus the son of Oeagrus, after
his exposition of the orgies and account of the idols,
brings in a recantation consisting of truth. Now at
the very last he sings of the really sacred Word :

> My words shall reach the pure ; put bars to ears
> All ye profane together.   But hear thou,
> Child of the Moon, Musaeus, words of truth ;
> Nor let past errors rob thee now of life.
> Behold the word divine, to this attend,
> Directing mind and heart aright ; tread well
> The narrow path of life, and gaze on Him,
> The world's great ruler, our immortal king.[a]

Then, lower down, he adds explicitly :

> One, self-begotten, lives ; all things proceed
> From One ; and in His works He ever moves :
> No mortal sees Him, yet Himself sees all.[a]

Thus wrote Orpheus ; in the end, at least, he understood that he had gone astray :

> Inconstant mortal, make no more delay,
> But turn again, and supplicate thy God.[b]

It may be freely granted that the Greeks received
some glimmerings of the divine word, and gave
utterance to a few scraps of truth. Thus they
bear their witness to its power, which has not been
hidden.   On the other hand, they convict themselves of weakness, since they failed to reach the
end.   For by this time, I think, it has become

---

[a] Orpheus, Frag. 5 Abel.
[b] *Sibylline Oracles* iii. 624–625.

χωρὶς τοῦ λόγου τῆς ἀληθείας ἐνεργούντων τι ἢ καὶ
φθεγγομένων ὁμοίων ὄντων τοῖς χωρὶς βάσεως
βαδίζειν βιαζομένοις.

Δυσωπούντων δέ σε εἰς σωτηρίαν καὶ οἱ περὶ
τοὺς θεοὺς ὑμῶν ἔλεγχοι, οὓς διὰ τὴν ἀλήθειαν
ἐκβιαζόμενοι κωμῳδοῦσι ποιηταί. Μένανδρος γοῦν
ὁ κωμικὸς ἐν Ἡνιόχῳ [ἐν Ὑποβολιμαίῳ][1] τῷ
δράματι

> οὐδείς μ᾽ ἀρέσκει (φησὶ) περιπατῶν ἔξω θεὸς
> μετὰ γραός, οὐδ᾽ εἰς οἰκίας παρεισιὼν
> ἐπὶ τοῦ σανιδίου·

[μητραγύρτης][2] τοιοῦτοι γὰρ οἱ μητραγύρται. ὅθεν
εἰκότως ὁ Ἀντισθένης ἔλεγεν αὐτοῖς μεταιτοῦσιν·
" οὐ τρέφω τὴν μητέρα τῶν θεῶν, ἣν οἱ θεοὶ τρέφου-
σιν." πάλιν δὲ ὁ αὐτὸς κωμῳδιοποιὸς ἐν Ἱερείᾳ
τῷ δράματι χαλεπαίνων πρὸς τὴν συνήθειαν δι-
ελέγχειν πειρᾶται τὸν ἄθεον τῆς πλάνης τῦφον,
ἐπιφθεγγόμενος ἐμφρόνως

> εἰ γὰρ ἕλκει τὸν θεὸν
> τοῖς κυμβάλοις ἄνθρωπος εἰς ὃ βούλεται,
> ὁ τοῦτο ποιῶν ἐστι μείζων τοῦ θεοῦ·
> ἀλλ᾽ ἔστι τόλμης καὶ βίου[3] ταῦτ᾽ ὄργανα
> εὑρημέν᾽ ἀνθρώποισιν. |

---

[1] [ἐν Ὑποβολιμαίῳ]Clericus(missing from Justin, *De mon.* 5).
[2] [μητραγύρτης] Dindorf.   [3] βίας Bentley : Stählin.

---

[a] For the fragment see Kock, *Comic. Attic. Frag.* iii.
p. 58.   The priest would seem to have carried on a tray an
image of Attis ; and the "old dame" personated Cybele,
the mother of the gods.   But ἐπὶ may mean "in charge of,"
"presiding over," in which case the priest personates Attis,

plain to everybody that those who do anything or utter anything without the word of truth are like men struggling to walk without a foothold.

The comic poets also, owing to the compelling power of truth, bring into their plays convincing arguments against your gods. Let these shame you into salvation. For instance, the comic poet Menander, in his play *The Charioteer*, says:

> No god for me is he who walks the streets
> With some old dame, and into houses steals
> Upon the sacred tray.[a]

For this is what the priests of Cybele[b] do. It was a proper answer, then, that Antisthenes used to give them when they asked alms of him: "I do not support the mother of the gods; that is the gods' business."[c] Again, the same writer of comedy, in his play *The Priestess*, being angry with prevailing custom, tries to expose the godless folly of idolatry by uttering these words of wisdom:

> For if a man
> By cymbals brings the God where'er he will,
> Then is the man more powerful than God.
> But these are shameless means of livelihood
> Devised by men.[d]

and μητραγύρτης ought perhaps to be retained (see note on text). Grotius observes, however, that "the statement has to do with the god himself, whom the travelling priest carries, and not with the priest." The quotation occurs in Justin Martyr (*De mon.* 5) with this addition: "the god ought to stay at home and take care of his worshippers."

[b] *i.e. Metragyrtae.* See p. 48, n. *a*.
[c] Antisthenes, Frag. 70 Mullach, *Frag. phil. Graec.* ii. p. 287.
[d] Menander, Frag. 245 Kock, *Comic. Attic. Frag.* iii. p. 70.

καὶ οὐχὶ μόνος ὁ Μένανδρος, ἀλλὰ καὶ Ὅμηρος καὶ
Εὐριπίδης καὶ ἄλλοι συχνοὶ ποιηταὶ διελέγχουσιν
ὑμῶν τοὺς θεοὺς καὶ λοιδορεῖσθαι οὐ δεδίασιν οὐδὲ
καθ᾽ ὁπόσον αὐτοῖς. αὐτίκα τὴν Ἀθηνᾶν "κυνά-
μυιαν" καὶ τὸν Ἥφαιστον "ἀμφιγύην" καλοῦσιν,
τῇ δὲ Ἀφροδίτῃ ἡ Ἑλένη φησὶ

μηκέτι σοῖσι πόδεσσιν ὑποστρέψειας Ὄλυμπον.

ἐπὶ δὲ τοῦ Διονύσου ἀναφανδὸν Ὅμηρος γράφει

ὅς ποτε μαινομένοιο Διωνύσοιο τιθήνας
σεῦε κατ᾽ ἠγάθεον Νυσήιον· αἱ δ᾽ ἅμα πᾶσαι
θύσθλα χαμαὶ κατέχευαν ὑπ᾽ ἀνδροφόνοιο Λυκ-
ούργου.

ἄξιος ὡς ἀληθῶς Σωκρατικῆς διατριβῆς ὁ Εὐριπίδης
εἰς τὴν ἀλήθειαν ἀπιδὼν καὶ τοὺς θεατὰς ὑπεριδών,
ποτὲ μὲν τὸν Ἀπόλλωνα,

ὃς μεσομφάλους ἕδρας
ναίει βροτοῖσι στόμα νέμων σαφέστατα,

διελέγχων,

κείνῳ πιθόμενος[1] τὴν τεκοῦσαν ἔκτανον,
ἐκεῖνον ἡγεῖσθ᾽ ἀνόσιον καὶ κτείνετε·[2]
ἐκεῖνος ἥμαρτ᾽, οὐκ ἐγώ,
ἀμαθέστερος γ᾽ ὢν[3] τοῦ καλοῦ καὶ τῆς δίκης,

τοτὲ δ᾽ ἐμμανῆ εἰσάγων Ἡρακλέα καὶ μεθύοντα
ἀλλαχόθι καὶ ἄπληστον· πῶς γὰρ οὐχί; ὃς ἐστιώ-
μενος τοῖς κρέασι

---

[1] τούτῳ πιθόμενος Euripides.   κείνῳ πειθόμενος MSS.
[2] κτείνετε Euripides.   κτείνατε MSS.
[3] γ᾽ ὢν Euripides.   ὢν MSS.

And not only Menander, but also Homer, Euripides CHAP.
and many other poets expose your gods, and do not VII
shrink from abusing them to any extent whatever. Homer
For instance, they call Athena "dog-fly," [a] and
Hephaestus "lame in both feet" [b]; and to Aphrodite
Helen says:

> Never again may thy feet turn back to the halls of
> Olympus.[c]

Of Dionysus Homer writes openly:

> He, on a day, gave chase to the nurses of mad Dionysus
> Over the sacred hill of Nysa ; but they, in a body,
> Flung their torches to earth at the word of the savage
> Lycurgus.[d]

Euripides is indeed a worthy disciple of the Socratic Euripides
school, in that he regarded only the truth and dis-
regarded the audience.   On one occasion, referring
to Apollo,

> Who, dwelling in the central spot of earth,
> Deals out unerring oracles to men,[e]

he thus exposes him:

> His word it was I trusted when I slew
> My mother ; him consider stained with crime,
> Him slay ; the sin was his concern, not mine,
> Since he knew less of good and right than I.[f]

At another time he introduces Heracles in a state
of madness,[g] and elsewhere drunk and gluttonous.[h]
What else could be said of a god who, while being
feasted with flesh,

[a] Homer, *Iliad* xxi. 394, 421.   [b] *Iliad* i. 607 etc.
[c] *Iliad* iii. 407.   [d] *Iliad* vi. 132–134.
[e] Euripides, *Orestes* 591–592.   [f] *Orestes* 594–596, 417.
[g] *i.e.* in the *Hercules Furens*.   [h] *Alcestis* 755–760.

171

χλωρὰ σῦκ᾽ ἐπήσθιεν·
ἄμουσ᾽ ὑλακτῶν ὥστε βαρβάρῳ μαθεῖν.

ἤδη δὲ ἐν Ἴωνι τῷ δράματι γυμνῇ τῇ κεφαλῇ
ἐκκυκλεῖ τῷ θεάτρῳ τοὺς θεούς·

πῶς οὖν δίκαιον τοὺς νόμους ὑμᾶς βροτοῖς
γράψαντας αὐτοὺς ἀδικίας ὀφλισκάνειν;
εἰ δ᾽, οὐ γὰρ ἔσται, τῷ λόγῳ δὲ χρήσομαι,
δίκας βιαίων δώσετ᾽ ἀνθρώποις γάμων,
σὺ καὶ Ποσειδῶν Ζεύς θ᾽, ὃς οὐρανοῦ κρατεῖ,
ναοὺς τίνοντες ἀδικίας κενώσετε.

VIII

Ὥρα τοίνυν τῶν ἄλλων ἡμῖν τῇ τάξει προδιηνυ-
σμένων ἐπὶ τὰς προφητικὰς ἰέναι γραφάς· καὶ γὰρ
66 P. οἱ χρησμοὶ τὰς εἰς τὴν θεοσέ|βειαν ἡμῖν ἀφορμὰς
ἐναργέστατα προτείνοντες θεμελιοῦσι τὴν ἀλήθειαν·
γραφαὶ δὲ αἱ θεῖαι καὶ[1] πολιτεῖαι σώφρονες, σύντομοι
σωτηρίας ὁδοί· γυμναὶ κομμωτικῆς καὶ τῆς ἐκτὸς
καλλιφωνίας καὶ στωμυλίας καὶ κολακείας ὑπάρ-
χουσαι ἀνιστῶσιν ἀγχόμενον ὑπὸ κακίας τὸν ἄνθρωπον, ὑπεριδοῦσαι τὸν ὄλισθον τὸν βιωτικόν, μιᾷ καὶ
τῇ αὐτῇ φωνῇ πολλὰ θεραπεύουσαι,[2] ἀποτρέπουσαι
μὲν ἡμᾶς τῆς ἐπιζημίου ἀπάτης, προτρέπουσαι δὲ
ἐμφανῶς εἰς πρόϋπτον σωτηρίαν. αὐτίκα γοῦν ἡ

---

[1] αἱ θεῖαι, ⟨εἰ⟩ καὶ Schwartz : Stählin.
[2] θεραπεύουσαι Sylburg. θεραπεῦσαι mss.

---

[a] Euripides, Frag. 907 Nauck.
[b] Literally, "with head bare." [c] *Ion* 442–447.
[d] For other references to the "short road" to salvation
see pp. 217, and 240, n. a. Clement means to say that

> Did eat green figs, and howl discordant songs,
> Fit for barbarian ears to understand? [a]

And again, in his play the *Ion*, he displays the gods to the spectators without any reserve [b]:

> How is it right that ye who made men's laws
> Yourselves are authors of unrighteous deeds?
> But if—I say it, though it shall not be—
> Ye pay men penalties for violent rapes,
> Phoebus, Poseidon, Zeus the king of heaven,
> The price of crime shall strip your temples bare. [c]

VIII

Now that we have dealt with the other matters in due order, it is time to turn to the writings of the prophets. For these are the oracles which, by exhibiting to us in the clearest light the grounds of piety, lay a firm foundation for the truth. The sacred writings are also models of virtuous living, and short roads to salvation. [d] They are bare of embellishment, of outward beauty of language, of idle talk and flattery, yet they raise up man when fast bound in the grip of evil. Despising the snare of this life, [e] with one and the same voice they provide a cure for many ills, turning us aside from delusion that works harm, and urging us onward with clear guidance to salvation set before our eyes.

The witness of the prophets

The sacred writings are simple in style, but of great power

Christian teaching puts truth in simple form so that the humblest may at once understand as much of it as is necessary to ensure his salvation. Some aspects of truth are reached through philosophy, but that is a long and difficult process, beyond the efforts of all but a few.

[e] *i.e.* all the dangerous pleasures which this life offers. In the *Paedagogus* Clement uses the same word "snare" in reference to feasting (ii. 9. 4), wine (ii. 23. 1, 28. 2, 29. 2), and laughter (ii. 47. 3).

προφῆτις ἡμῖν ᾀσάτω πρώτη Σίβυλλα τὸ ᾆσμα τὸ
σωτήριον·

οὗτος ἰδοὺ πάντεσσι[1] σαφὴς ἀπλάνητος ὑπάρχει·
ἔλθετε, μὴ σκοτίην δὲ διώκετε καὶ ζόφον αἰεί.
ἠελίου γλυκυδερκές, ἰδού, φάος ἔξοχα λάμπει.
γνῶτε δὲ κατθέμενοι σοφίην ἐν στήθεσιν ὑμῶν.
εἷς θεός ἐστι, βροχάς, ἀνέμους, σεισμούς τ' ἐπι-
πέμπων,
ἀστεροπάς, λιμούς, λοιμοὺς καὶ κήδεα λυγρὰ
καὶ νιφετοὺς καὶ τἆλλα,[2] τί δὴ καθ' ἓν ἐξ-
αγορεύω;
οὐρανοῦ ἡγεῖται, γαίης κρατεῖ αὐτὸς ἀπ' ἀρχῆς.[3]

ἐνθέως σφόδρα τὴν μὲν ἀπάτην ἀπεικάζουσα τῷ
σκότει, τὴν δὲ γνῶσιν ἡλίῳ καὶ φωτὶ τοῦ θεοῦ,
ἄμφω δὲ παραθεμένη τῇ συγκρίσει, τὴν ἐκλογὴν
διδάσκει· τὸ γὰρ ψεῦδος οὐ ψιλῇ τῇ παραθέσει
τἀληθοῦς διασκεδάννυται, τῇ δὲ χρήσει τῆς ἀληθείας
ἐκβιαζόμενον φυγαδεύεται. Ἱερεμίας δὲ ὁ προφήτης
ὁ πάνσοφος, μᾶλλον δὲ ἐν Ἱερεμίᾳ τὸ ἅγιον πνεῦμα
ἐπιδείκνυσι τὸν θεόν. "θεὸς ἐγγίζων ἐγώ εἰμι,"
φησί, "καὶ οὐχὶ θεὸς πόρρωθεν. εἰ ποιήσει τι ἄνθρωπος ἐν κρυφαίοις, καὶ ἐγὼ οὐκ ὄψομαι αὐτόν;
οὐχὶ τοὺς οὐρανοὺς καὶ τὴν γῆν ἐγὼ πληρῶ;
λέγει κύριος." πάλιν δὲ αὖ διὰ Ἡσαΐου "τίς
μετρήσει," φησί, "τὸν οὐρανὸν σπιθαμῇ καὶ πᾶσαν
τὴν γῆν δρακί;" ὅρα τὸ μέγεθος τοῦ θεοῦ καὶ
καταπλάγηθι. τοῦτον προσκυνήσωμεν, ἐφ' οὗ φησιν
ὁ προφήτης "ἀπὸ προσώπου σου ὄρη τακήσονται,

¹ πάντεσσι Sib. Or. and Clement, v. Strom. 115. 6. πάντ'
ἐστι MSS.
² καὶ τἆλλα Cobet. κρύσταλλα MSS.: Stählin.
³ ἀπ' ἀρχῆς Mayor. ὑπάρχει MSS.: Stählin.

EXHORTATION TO THE GREEKS

To begin with, let the prophetess, the Sibyl, first sing to us the song of salvation :

CHAP.
VIII
A prelude
from the
prophetic
Sibyl

> Lo, plain to all, from error free He stands ;
> Come, seek not gloom and darkness evermore ;
> Behold, the sun's sweet light shines brightly forth.
> But mark, and lay up wisdom in your hearts.
> One God there is, from whom come rains and winds,
> Earthquakes and lightnings, dearths, plagues, grievous
>   cares,
> Snowstorms and all besides,—why name each one ?
> He from of old rules heaven, He sways the earth.[a]

With true inspiration she likens delusion to darkness, and the knowledge of God to the sun and light ; and by putting them side by side in her comparison she teaches what our choice should be. For the false is not dissipated by merely placing the true beside it ; it is driven out and banished by the practice of truth. Now Jeremiah, the all-wise prophet, or rather the Holy Spirit in Jeremiah, shows what God is. " I am," he says, " a God who is near, and not a God afar off. Shall a man do anything in secret, and I not see him ? Do not I fill the heavens and the earth, saith the Lord ? "[b] Once again, the same Spirit says through Isaiah : " Who shall measure the heaven with a span, and the whole earth with a hand-breadth ? "[c] See the greatness of God and be amazed ! Him let us worship, about whom the prophet says : " The hills shall melt from before thy face, as wax melteth

---

[a] *Sibylline Oracles*, Preface 28-35.
[b] Jeremiah xxiii. 23-24.
[c] Isaiah xl. 12.

CAP.
VIII ὡς ἀπὸ προσώπου πυρὸς τήκεται κηρός." οὗτος,
φησίν, ἐστὶν ὁ θεός, "οὗ θρόνος μέν ἐστιν ὁ οὐρανός,
ὑποπόδιον δὲ ἡ γῆ," ὃς "ἐὰν ἀνοίξῃ τὸν οὐρανόν,
τρόμος σε λήψεται." βούλει καὶ περὶ τῶν εἰδώλων[1]
ἀκοῦσαι τί φησιν < ὁ >[2] προφήτης οὗτος; "παραδειγ-
ματισθήσονται ἔμπροσθεν τοῦ ἡλίου καὶ ἔσται τὰ

67 P. θνησιμαῖα αὐτῶν βρώματα τοῖς πετεινοῖς τοῦ
οὐρανοῦ καὶ τοῖς θηρίοις τῆς γῆς, καὶ σαπήσεται
ὑπὸ τοῦ ἡλίου καὶ τῆς σελήνης, ἃ αὐτοὶ ἠγάπησαν
καὶ οἷς αὐτοὶ ἐδούλευσαν, καὶ ἐμπρησθήσεται ἡ
πόλις αὐτῶν." φθαρήσεσθαι δὲ καὶ τὰ στοιχεῖα
καὶ τὸν κόσμον σὺν καὶ αὐτοῖς λέγει· "ἡ γῆ,"
φησί, "παλαιωθήσεται καὶ ὁ οὐρανὸς παρελεύσεται," "τὸ δὲ ῥῆμα κυρίου μένει εἰς τὸν αἰῶνα."
τί δὲ ὅταν πάλιν ἑαυτὸν δεικνύναι ὁ θεὸς βουληθῇ
διὰ Μωυσέως; "ἴδετε ἴδετε ὅτι ἐγώ εἰμι καὶ οὐκ
ἔστι θεὸς ἕτερος πλὴν ἐμοῦ. ἐγὼ ἀποκτενῶ καὶ
ζῆν ποιήσω· πατάξω κἀγὼ ἰάσομαι, καὶ οὐκ ἔστιν
ὃς ἐξελεῖται ἐκ τῶν χειρῶν μου."

Ἀλλὰ καὶ ἑτέρου ἐπακοῦσαι θέλεις χρησμῳδοῦ·
ἔχεις τὸν χορὸν πάντα τὸν προφητικόν, τοὺς συνθια-
σώτας τοῦ Μωυσέως. τί φησιν αὐτοῖς τὸ πνεῦμα
τὸ ἅγιον διὰ Ὠσηέ; οὐκ ὀκνήσω λέγειν· "ἰδού,
ἐγὼ στερεῶν βροντὴν καὶ κτίζων πνεῦμα," οὗ αἱ
χεῖρες τὴν στρατιὰν τοῦ οὐρανοῦ ἐθεμελίωσαν. ἔτι

---

[1] εἰδώλων : can this be a scribe's mistake for εἰδωλολατρῶν (cp. p. 178, l. 12)?
[2] <ὁ> inserted by Dindorf.

---

[a] See Isaiah lxiv. 1–3.   [b] Isaiah lxvi. 1.
[c] See Isaiah lxiv. 1 (Septuagint).
[d] The text gives "idols," but the quotation refers to their worshippers. It is possible that there is a slight error in the text. See textual note.

from before the face of the fire." [a] He is God, the prophet says again, "whose throne is heaven, and the earth His footstool" [b]; before whom "if He open heaven, trembling shall seize thee." [c] Would you hear too, what this prophet says about idol-worshippers? [d] "They shall be made a spectacle before the sun; and their dead bodies shall be meat for the fowls of the heaven and the beasts of the earth, and shall be rotted by the sun and the moon, things which they themselves loved and served; and their city shall be burnt up." [e] He says also that the elements and the world shall be destroyed with them. "The earth shall grow old, and the heaven shall pass away;" but "the word of the Lord abideth for ever." [f] What does God say when at another time He wishes to reveal Himself through Moses? "Behold, behold, I am He, and there is no other god beside Me. I will kill and I will make alive; I will smite and I will heal, and there is none that shall deliver out of my hands." [g]

But will you listen to yet another giver of oracles? You have the whole company of the prophets, who are joined with Moses in this sacred fellowship. What says the Holy Spirit to them through Hosea? I will not hesitate to tell you. "Behold, I am He that giveth might to the thunder, and createth the wind," [h] whose hands established the host of heaven. [i]

CHAP. VIII

Isaiah tells of the destruction of idolaters

And also of the whole world

Moses speaks of God's power

The witness of Hosea

---

[e] A collection of passages from Jeremiah, not Isaiah. See viii. 2; xxxiv. 20; iv. 26.

[f] Isaiah li. 6; also compare St. Matthew xxiv. 35 and Isaiah xl. 8.

[g] Deuteronomy xxxii. 39.

[h] Amos iv. 13; not Hosea.

[i] See Jeremiah xix. 13 and Psalm viii. 4 (Septuagint).

177

CAP.
VIII
δὲ καὶ διὰ Ἡσαΐου (καὶ ταύτην ἀπομνημονεύσω σοι τὴν φωνήν) "ἐγώ εἰμι, ἐγώ εἰμι," φησίν, "ὁ κύριος ὁ λαλῶν δικαιοσύνην καὶ ἀναγγέλλων ἀλή-θειαν· συνάχθητε καὶ ἥκετε· βουλεύσασθε ἅμα, οἱ σωζόμενοι ἀπὸ τῶν ἐθνῶν. οὐκ ἔγνωσαν οἱ αἴροντες τὸ ξύλον γλύμμα αὐτῶν, καὶ προσευχόμενοι θεοῖς οἳ οὐ σώσουσιν αὐτούς." εἶθ' ὑποβάς· "ἐγώ," φησίν, "ὁ θεός, καὶ οὐκ ἔστι πλὴν ἐμοῦ δίκαιος, καὶ σωτὴρ οὐκ ἔστι πάρεξ ἐμοῦ· ἐπιστράφητε πρός με καὶ σωθήσεσθε οἱ ἀπ' ἐσχάτου τῆς γῆς. ἐγώ εἰμι ὁ θεὸς καὶ οὐκ ἔστιν ἄλλος· κατ' ἐμαυτοῦ ὀμνύω." τοῖς δὲ εἰδωλολάτραις δυσχεραίνει λέγων "τίνι ὡμοιώσατε κύριον; ἢ τίνι ὁμοιώματι ὡμοιώ-σατε αὐτόν; μὴ εἰκόνα ἐποίησεν τέκτων, ἢ χρυσο-χόος χωνεύσας χρυσίον περιεχρύσωσεν αὐτόν;" καὶ τὰ ἐπὶ τούτοις. μὴ οὖν ἔτι ὑμεῖς εἰδωλολά-τραι· ἀλλὰ κἂν νῦν φυλάξασθε τὰς ἀπειλάς· ὀλολύξει γὰρ τὰ γλυπτὰ καὶ τὰ χειροποίητα, μᾶλ-λον δὲ οἱ ἐπ' αὐτοῖς πεποιθότες, ἀναίσθητος γὰρ ἡ ὕλη. ἔτι φησίν· "ὁ κύριος σείσει πόλεις κατ-οικουμένας καὶ τὴν οἰκουμένην ὅλην καταλήψεται τῇ χειρὶ ὡς νοσσιάν." τί σοι σοφίας ἀναγγέλλω μυστήρια καὶ ῥήσεις ἐκ παιδὸς Ἑβραίου σεσοφισμέ-νου· "κύριος ἔκτισέν με ἀρχὴν ὁδῶν αὐτοῦ εἰς ἔργα αὐτοῦ," καὶ "κύριος δίδωσι σοφίαν καὶ ἀπὸ προσώπου αὐτοῦ γνῶσις καὶ σύνεσις." "ἕως πότε, ὀκνηρέ, κατάκεισαι; πότε δὲ ἐξ ὕπνου ἐγερθήσῃ;

---

[a] Isaiah xlv. 19–20.   [b] Isaiah xlv. 21–23.
[c] Isaiah xl. 18–19.   [d] Isaiah x. 10–11, 14 (Septuagint).
[e] *i.e.* Solomon ; see 1 Kings iii. 7 ; iii. 12.
[f] Proverbs viii. 22.   " Wisdom " is, of course, the speaker.
Clement's quotation, here as everywhere else, is taken from

And again through Isaiah (this utterance too I will remind you of): "I, even I," he says, "am the Lord that speaketh righteousness and declareth truth. Assemble yourselves and come. Take counsel together, ye that are being saved out of the nations. They have no knowledge, who set up their carved image of wood, and pray to gods who shall not save them." [a] Then, lower down, he says: "I am God and there is none righteous except Me, there is no Saviour beside Me. Turn ye unto Me and ye shall be saved, ye who come from the end of the earth. I am God, and there is no other. By Myself do I swear." [b] But He is displeased with idol-worshippers and says: "To whom did ye liken the Lord? Or to what likeness did ye liken Him? Did the carpenter make an image? Did the goldsmith smelt gold and gild it?"—and what follows.[c] Are you then still idol-worshippers? Yet even now beware of God's threats. For the carved images made by hand shall cry out,[d] or rather they who trust in them; for the material is incapable of feeling. Further he says: "The Lord shall shake the inhabited cities, and in His hand shall grasp the whole world as it were a nest." [d] Why tell you of mysteries of wisdom, and of sayings that come from a Hebrew child who was endowed with wisdom? [e] "The Lord created me in the beginning of His ways, for His works"[f]: and, "the Lord giveth wisdom, and from His face are knowledge and understanding." [g] "How long dost thou lie at rest, thou sluggard; when wilt thou awake from

the Septuagint. The Hebrew text of this verse gives a different meaning—"possessed" instead of "created"; but see R.V. margin.   [g] Proverbs ii. 6.

CAP.
VIII
68 P.

ἐὰν δὲ ἄοκνος ᾖς, ἥξει σοι ὥσπερ πηγὴ ὁ ἄμητός σου," ὁ λόγος ὁ πατρικός, | ὁ ἀγαθὸς λύχνος, ὁ κύριος ἐπάγων τὸ φῶς, τὴν πίστιν πᾶσι καὶ σωτηρίαν. "κύριος" γὰρ "ὁ ποιήσας τὴν γῆν ἐν τῇ ἰσχύι αὐτοῦ," ὥς φησιν Ἰερεμίας, "ἀνώρθωσεν τὴν οἰκουμένην ἐν τῇ σοφίᾳ αὐτοῦ." ἀποπεσόντας γὰρ ἡμᾶς ἐπὶ τὰ εἴδωλα ἡ σοφία, ἥ ἐστιν ὁ λόγος αὐτοῦ, ἀνορθοῖ ἐπὶ τὴν ἀλήθειαν. καὶ αὕτη ἡ[1] πρώτη τοῦ παραπτώματος ἀνάστασις· ὅθεν ἀποτρέπων εἰδωλολατρείας ἁπάσης ὁ θεσπέσιος παγκάλως ἀνακέκραγε Μωυσῆς· "ἄκουε Ἰσραήλ· κύριος ὁ θεός σου, κύριος εἷς ἐστι," καὶ "κύριον τὸν θεόν σου προσκυνήσεις καὶ αὐτῷ μόνῳ λατρεύσεις·" νῦν δὴ οὖν σύνετε, ὦ ἄνθρωποι, κατὰ τὸν μακάριον ψαλμῳδὸν ἐκεῖνον τὸν Δαβίδ· "δράξασθε παιδείας, μή ποτε ὀργισθῇ κύριος, καὶ ἀπολεῖσθε ἐξ ὁδοῦ δικαίας, ὅταν ἐκκαυθῇ ἐν τάχει ὁ θυμὸς αὐτοῦ. μακάριοι πάντες οἱ πεποιθότες ἐπ' αὐτῷ." ἤδη δὲ ὑπεροικτείρων ἡμᾶς ὁ κύριος τὸ σωτήριον ἐνδίδωσι μέλος, οἷον ἐμβατήριον ῥυθμόν· "υἱοὶ ἀνθρώπων, ἕως πότε βαρυκάρδιοι; ἵνα τί ἀγαπᾶτε ματαιότητα καὶ ζητεῖτε ψεῦδος;" τίς οὖν ἡ ματαιότης καὶ τί τὸ ψεῦδος; ὁ ἅγιος ἀπόστολος τοῦ κυρίου τοὺς Ἕλληνας αἰτιώμενος ἐξηγήσεται σοι· "ὅτι γνόντες τὸν θεὸν οὐχ ὡς θεὸν ἐδόξασαν ἢ ηὐχαρίστησαν, ἀλλ' ἐματαιώθησαν ἐν τοῖς διαλογισμοῖς αὐτῶν, καὶ ἤλλαξαν τὴν δόξαν τοῦ θεοῦ

[1] αὕτη ἡ Mayor.   αὕτη MSS.

---

[a] Proverbs vi. 9, 11[a]. (The latter verse is found only in the Septuagint.)

[b] Possibly from Proverbs xx. 27 (see the Septuagint reading as quoted by Clement, vii. *Strom.* 37. 6 and by

sleep? If thou art diligent, there shall come to thee
as a fountain thy harvest," [a] that is, the Word of the
Father, the good lamp,[b] the Lord who brings light,
faith and salvation to all. For "the Lord, who made
the earth in His strength," as Jeremiah says, "restored the world in His wisdom," [c] since, when we
have fallen away to idols, wisdom, which is His Word,
restores us to the truth. This is the first resurrection,[d]
the resurrection from transgression; wherefore the
inspired Moses, turning us away from all idolatry,
utters this truly noble cry: "Hear O Israel, the
Lord is thy God; the Lord is one"[e]: and "thou
shalt worship the Lord thy God and Him only shalt
thou serve."[f] Now therefore, learn, ye men, in the
words of that blessed psalmist David: "Lay hold of
instruction, lest at any time the Lord be angry; and
ye shall perish from the right way, if ever His wrath
be hastily kindled. Blessed are all they that trust
in Him."[g] And, in His exceeding great pity for us,
the Lord raises high the strain of salvation, like a
marching song. "Sons of men, how long will ye
be heavy-hearted? Why do ye love vanity and
seek after falsehood?"[h] What, then, is this vanity,
and this falsehood? The holy apostle of the Lord
will explain to you, when he accuses the Greeks:
"because, knowing God, they glorified Him not as
God, neither gave thanks, but became vain in their
reasonings, and changed the glory of God into the

Clement of Rome i. 21. 2). Cp. also Psalm cxix. 105, where,
however, the Septuagint (cxviii. 105) has "Thy law" instead
of "Thy word."   [c] Jeremiah x. 12.
    [d] See Revelation xx. 5.   [e] Deuteronomy vi. 4.
    [f] Deuteronomy vi. 13; x. 20; St. Matthew iv. 10;
St. Luke iv. 8.
    [g] Psalm ii. 12 (Septuagint).   [h] Psalm iv. 2.

CAP.
VIII

ἐν ὁμοιώματι εἰκόνος φθαρτοῦ ἀνθρώπου, καὶ
ἐλάτρευσαν τῇ κτίσει παρὰ τὸν κτίσαντα." καὶ
μὴν ὅ γε θεὸς οὗτος, ὃς "ἐν ἀρχῇ ἐποίησε τὸν
οὐρανὸν καὶ τὴν γῆν"· σὺ δὲ τὸν μὲν θεὸν οὐ νοεῖς,
τὸν δὲ οὐρανὸν προσκυνεῖς, καὶ πῶς οὐκ ἀσεβεῖς;
ἄκουε πάλιν προφήτου λέγοντος "ἐκλείψει μὲν ὁ
ἥλιος καὶ ὁ οὐρανὸς σκοτισθήσεται, λάμψει δὲ ὁ
παντοκράτωρ εἰς τὸν αἰῶνα, καὶ αἱ δυνάμεις τῶν
οὐρανῶν σαλευθήσονται καὶ οἱ οὐρανοὶ εἰλιγήσονται
ὡς δέρρις ἐκτεινόμενοι καὶ συστελλόμενοι" (αὗται
γὰρ αἱ προφητικαὶ φωναί) "καὶ ἡ γῆ φεύξεται
ἀπὸ προσώπου κυρίου."

IX

Καὶ μυρίας ἂν ἔχοιμί σοι γραφὰς παραφέρειν,
ὧν οὐδὲ "κεραία παρελεύσεται μία," μὴ οὐχὶ
ἐπιτελὴς γενομένη· τὸ γὰρ στόμα κυρίου, τὸ
ἅγιον πνεῦμα, ἐλάλησεν ταῦτα. "μὴ τοίνυν μηκέτι," φησίν, "υἱέ μου, ὀλιγώρει παιδείας κυρίου,
μηδ᾿ ἐκλύου ὑπ᾿ αὐτοῦ ἐλεγχόμενος." ὢ τῆς ὑπερ-
βαλλούσης φιλανθρωπίας· οὐδ᾿ ὡς μαθηταῖς ὁ
διδάσκαλος οὐδ᾿ ὡς οἰκέταις ὁ κύριος οὐδ᾿ ὡς

69 P. θεὸς ἀν|θρώποις, "πατὴρ δὲ ὡς ἤπιος" νουθετεῖ
υἱούς. εἶτα Μωυσῆς μὲν ὁμολογεῖ "ἔμφοβος εἶναι
καὶ ἔντρομος," ἀκούων περὶ τοῦ λόγου, σὺ δὲ τοῦ

ᵃ Romans i. 21, 23, 25.
ᵇ Genesis i. 1.
ᶜ A collection of passages from Scripture ; see Isaiah xiii.
10 ; Ezekiel xxxii. 7 ; St. Matthew xxiv. 29 ; Isaiah xxxiv. 4;
Psalm civ. 2 ; Joel ii. 10.   Stählin thinks that the whole may
possibly be taken from the Apocalypse of Peter, with which

likeness of an image of corruptible man, and served CHAP.
the creature rather than the creator." [a] Of a truth VIII
God is He who "in the beginning made the heaven
and the earth." [b] Yet you do not perceive God, but
worship the heaven. How can you escape the
charge of impiety? Hear once more the words of
a prophet: "The sun shall fail and the heaven be Final
darkened, but the Almighty shall shine for ever; warnings
and the powers of the heavens shall be shaken, and of judgment
the heavens shall be folded up, being spread out and
drawn together like a curtain" — these are the
prophetic utterances — "and the earth shall flee
from the face of the Lord." [c]

IX

And I could bring before you ten thousand Many
passages of Scripture, of which not even "one tittle other like
shall pass away" without being fulfilled [d]; for the could be
mouth of the Lord, that is, the Holy Spirit, hath quoted
spoken it. "No longer, then, my son," it says,
"regard lightly the chastening of the Lord, nor faint
when thou art reproved of Him." [e] O surpassing love
for man! He speaks not as a teacher to disciples, nor
as a master to servants, nor as God to men, but as
a "tender father" [f] admonishing his sons. Again, God speaks
Moses confesses that he "exceedingly fears and as a Father
quakes," [g] when hearing about the Word; do you children

we know Clement to have been acquainted (Eusebius, *H.E.*
vi. 14).
   [d] See St. Matthew v. 18; St. Luke xvi. 17.
   [e] Proverbs iii. 11.
   [f] Homer, *Odyssey* ii. 47.
   [g] Hebrews xii. 21.

CAP. λόγου ἀκροώμενος τοῦ θείου οὐ δέδιας; οὐκ ἀγω-
IX
νιᾷς; οὐχὶ ἅμα τε εὐλαβῇ καὶ σπεύδεις ἐκμαθεῖν,
τουτέστι σπεύδεις εἰς σωτηρίαν, φοβούμενος τὴν
ὀργήν, ἀγαπήσας τὴν χάριν, ζηλώσας τὴν ἐλπίδα,
ἵνα ἐκκλίνῃς τὴν κρίσιν; ἥκετε ἥκετε, ὦ νεολαία
ἡ ἐμή· "ἢν γὰρ μὴ αὖθις ὡς τὰ παιδία γένησθε καὶ
ἀναγεννηθῆτε," ὥς φησιν ἡ γραφή, τὸν ὄντως ὄντα
πατέρα οὐ μὴ ἀπολάβητε, "οὐδ' οὐ μὴ εἰσελεύσεσθέ
ποτε εἰς τὴν βασιλείαν τῶν οὐρανῶν." πῶς γὰρ
εἰσελθεῖν ἐπιτέτραπται τῷ ξένῳ; ἀλλ' ὅταν, οἶμαι,
ἐγγραφῇ καὶ πολιτευθῇ καὶ τὸν πατέρα ἀπολάβῃ,
τότε "ἐν τοῖς τοῦ πατρὸς" γενήσεται, τότε
κληρονομῆσαι καταξιωθήσεται, τότε τῆς βασιλείας
τῆς πατρῴας κοινωνήσει τῷ γνησίῳ, τῷ "ἠγα-
πημένῳ"· αὕτη γὰρ ἡ πρωτότοκος ἐκκλησία ἡ ἐκ
πολλῶν ἀγαθῶν συγκειμένη παιδίων· ταῦτ' ἔστι τὰ
"πρωτότοκα τὰ ἐναπογεγραμμένα ἐν οὐρανοῖς"
καὶ τοσαύταις "μυριάσιν ἀγγέλων" συμπανηγυρί-
ζοντα· πρωτότοκοι δὲ παῖδες ἡμεῖς οἱ τρόφιμοι
τοῦ θεοῦ, οἱ τοῦ "πρωτοτόκου" γνήσιοι φίλοι,
οἱ πρῶτοι τῶν ἄλλων ἀνθρώπων τὸν θεὸν νενοηκότες,
οἱ πρῶτοι τῶν ἁμαρτιῶν ἀπεσπασμένοι, οἱ πρῶτοι
τοῦ διαβόλου κεχωρισμένοι.

Νυνὶ δὲ τοσούτῳ τινές εἰσιν ἀθεώτεροι, ὅσῳ
φιλανθρωπότερος ὁ θεός· ὁ μὲν γὰρ ἐκ δούλων
υἱοὺς ἡμᾶς γενέσθαι βούλεται, οἱ δὲ καὶ υἱοὶ γενέσθαι
ὑπερηφανήκασιν. ὦ τῆς ἀπονοίας τῆς πολλῆς· τὸν
κύριον ἐπαισχύνεσθε. ἐλευθερίαν ἐπαγγέλλεται,

ᵃ St. Matthew xviii. 3; St. John iii. 3, 5.
ᵇ St. Luke ii. 49. ᶜ St. Matthew iii. 17 etc.
ᵈ See Hebrews xii. 22, 23.

not fear when you listen to the divine Word Himself?
Are you not troubled? Are you not careful and at
the same time eager to learn; that is to say, are you
not eager for salvation, fearing God's wrath, loving
His grace, striving after the hope, in order that you
may escape the judgment? Come ye, come ye, my
little ones! For "except ye become once more as *Unless we*
little children and be born again," as the Scripture *become children*
says, ye shall not receive the true Father, "nor shall *we cannot*
ye ever enter into the kingdom of heaven." [a] For *enter the Father's*
how is the stranger allowed to enter? Why, in this *kingdom*
way, I think; when he is enrolled, and made a
citizen, and receives the Father, then he will be *Once*
found "in the Father's courts," [b] then he will be *entered we share the*
counted worthy to enter into the inheritance, then *kingdom*
he will share the Father's kingdom with the true Son, *with the*
"the beloved." [c] For this is the "church of the first- *Son*
born," which is composed of many good children.
These are "the first-born that are enrolled in *God's many*
heaven," who join in solemn assembly with all those *children form the*
"innumerable hosts of angels." [d] And we are these *"church of*
first-born sons, we who are God's nurslings, we who *the first-born"*
are the true friends of the "first-born," [e] who have
been the first of all mankind to know God, the
first to be torn away from our sins, the first to be
separated from the devil.

Yet the truth is, that the more God loves them *But many*
the more do some men depart from Him. For He *reject these great*
wishes that we should become sons instead of slaves, *blessings*
but they have disdained even to become sons. What
depth of folly! It is the Lord of whom you are
ashamed. He promises freedom, but you run away

---

[e] Colossians i. 15, 18; Hebrews i. 6.

CAP.
IX

ὑμεῖς δὲ εἰς δουλείαν ἀποδιδράσκετε. σωτηρίαν χαρίζεται, ὑμεῖς δὲ εἰς θάνατον[1] ὑποφέρεσθε. ζωὴν δωρεῖται αἰώνιον, ὑμεῖς δὲ τὴν κόλασιν ἀναμένετε· καὶ "τὸ πῦρ" δὲ προσκοπεῖτε, "ὃ ἡτοίμασεν ὁ κύριος τῷ διαβόλῳ καὶ τοῖς ἀγγέλοις αὐτοῦ." διὰ τοῦτο ὁ μακάριος ἀπόστολος "μαρτύρομαι ἐν κυρίῳ," φησίν, "μηκέτι ὑμᾶς περιπατεῖν, καθὼς καὶ τὰ ἔθνη περιπατεῖ ἐν ματαιότητι τοῦ νοὸς αὐτῶν, ἐσκοτισμένοι τῇ διανοίᾳ ὄντες καὶ ἀπηλλοτριωμένοι τῆς ζωῆς τοῦ θεοῦ, διὰ τὴν ἄγνοιαν τὴν οὖσαν ἐν αὐτοῖς, διὰ τὴν πώρωσιν τῆς καρδίας αὐτῶν· οἵτινες

70 P. ἑαυτοὺς παρέδωκαν | ἀπηλγηκότες τῇ ἀσελγείᾳ εἰς ἐργασίαν ἀκαθαρσίας πάσης καὶ πλεονεξίας." τοιούτου μάρτυρος ἐλέγχοντος τὴν τῶν ἀνθρώπων ἄνοιαν καὶ θεὸν ἐπιβοωμένου, τί δὴ ἕτερον ὑπολείπεται τοῖς ἀπίστοις ἢ κρίσις καὶ καταδίκη; οὐ κάμνει[2] δὲ ὁ κύριος παραινῶν, ἐκφοβῶν, προτρέπων, διεγείρων, νουθετῶν· ἀφυπνίζει γέ τοι καὶ τοῦ σκότους αὐτοῦ τοὺς πεπλανημένους διανίστησιν· "ἔγειρε," φησίν, "ὁ καθεύδων καὶ ἀνάστα ἐκ τῶν νεκρῶν, καὶ ἐπιφαύσει σοι ὁ Χριστὸς κύριος," ὁ τῆς ἀναστάσεως ἥλιος, ὁ "πρὸ ἑωσφόρου" γεννώμενος, ὁ ζωὴν χαρισάμενος ἀκτῖσιν ἰδίαις.

Μὴ οὖν περιφρονείτω τις τοῦ λόγου, μὴ λάθῃ καταφρονῶν ἑαυτοῦ. λέγει γάρ που ἡ γραφή· "σήμερον ἐὰν τῆς φωνῆς αὐτοῦ ἀκούσητε, μὴ σκληρύνητε τὰς καρδίας ὑμῶν ὡς ἐν τῷ παραπικρασμῷ κατὰ τὴν ἡμέραν τοῦ πειρασμοῦ ἐν τῇ ἐρήμῳ, οὗ ἐπείρασαν οἱ πατέρες ὑμῶν ἐν δοκι-

---

[1] θάνατον Stählin.   ἀπώλειαν Sylburg.   ἄνθρωπον MSS.
[2] οὐ κάμνει Münzel.   οὐκ ἀμελεῖ MSS.

186

into—slavery! He bestows salvation, but you sink down into death. He offers eternal life, but you await His punishment; and you prefer "the fire, which the Lord has prepared for the devil and his angels"![a] Wherefore the blessed apostle says: "I testify in the Lord, that ye no longer walk as the Gentiles also walk, in the vanity of their mind, being darkened in their understanding and alienated from the life of God, because of the ignorance that is in them, because of the hardening of their heart, who being past feeling gave themselves up to lasciviousness, to work all uncleanness and greediness."[b] When such a witness reproves the folly of men and calls upon God to hear, what else remains for unbelievers but judgment and condemnation? Yet the Lord does not weary of admonishing, of terrifying, of exhorting, of arousing, of warning; no indeed, He awakes men from sleep, and those that have gone astray He causes to rise from out the darkness itself. "Awake, thou that sleepest," He cries, "and arise from the dead, and there shall shine upon thee Christ the Lord,"[c] the sun of the resurrection, He that is begotten "before the morning star,"[d] He that dispenses life by His own rays.

Let no one then think lightly of the Word, lest he be despising himself unawares. For the Scripture says somewhere,

> To-day if ye shall hear His voice,
> Harden not your hearts as in the provocation,
> Like as in the day of the temptation in the wilderness,
> Where your fathers tempted Me by proving Me.[e]

He exhorts us to hear His voice to-day

---

[a] St. Matthew xxv. 41.   [b] Ephesians iv. 17–19.
[c] Ephesians v. 14.   [d] Psalm cix. 3 (Septuagint).
[e] Hebrews iii. 7–11, from Psalm xcv. 8–11.

CLEMENT OF ALEXANDRIA

μασία.'' ἡ δὲ δοκιμασία τίς ἐστιν εἰ θέλεις μαθεῖν,
τὸ ἅγιόν σοι πνεῦμα ἐξηγήσεται· '' καὶ εἶδον τὰ
ἔργα μου,'' φησί, '' τεσσαράκοντα ἔτη· δι᾿ ὃ προσ-
ώχθισα τῇ γενεᾷ ταύτῃ καὶ εἶπον· ἀεὶ πλανῶνται
τῇ καρδίᾳ· αὐτοὶ δὲ οὐκ ἔγνωσαν τὰς ὁδούς μου·
ὡς ὤμοσα ἐν τῇ ὀργῇ μου, εἰ εἰσελεύσονται εἰς τὴν
κατάπαυσίν μου.'' ὁρᾶτε τὴν ἀπειλήν· ὁρᾶτε τὴν
προτροπήν· ὁρᾶτε τὴν τιμήν· τί δὴ οὖν ἔτι τὴν
χάριν εἰς ὀργὴν μεταλλάσσομεν καὶ οὐχὶ ἀναπεπτα-
μέναις ταῖς ἀκοαῖς καταδεχόμενοι τὸν λόγον ἐν
ἁγναῖς ξενοδοχοῦμεν ταῖς ψυχαῖς τὸν θεόν; μεγάλη
γὰρ τῆς ἐπαγγελίας αὐτοῦ ἡ χάρις, '' ἐὰν σήμερον
τῆς φωνῆς αὐτοῦ ἀκούσωμεν ''· τὸ δὲ σήμερον
καθ᾿ ἑκάστην [αὐτοῦ] [1] αὔξεται τὴν ἡμέραν, ἔστ᾿ ἂν
ἡ σήμερον ὀνομάζηται. μέχρι δὲ συντελείας καὶ ἡ
σήμερον καὶ ἡ μάθησις διαμένει· καὶ τότε ἡ ὄντως
σήμερον ἡ ἀνελλιπὴς τοῦ θεοῦ ἡμέρα τοῖς αἰῶσι
συνεκτείνεται.

Ἀεὶ οὖν τῆς φωνῆς ὑπακούωμεν τοῦ θείου
λόγου· ἡ σήμερον γὰρ ἀιδίου αἰῶνός [2] ἐστιν
εἰκών, σύμβολον δὲ τοῦ φωτὸς ἡ ἡμέρα, φῶς δὲ ὁ
λόγος ἀνθρώποις, δι᾿ οὗ καταυγαζόμεθα τὸν θεόν.
εἰκότως ἄρα πιστεύσασι μὲν καὶ ὑπακούουσιν ἡ
χάρις ὑπερπλεονάσει, ἀπειθήσασι δὲ καὶ πλανω-
μένοις κατὰ καρδίαν ὁδούς τε τὰς κυριακὰς μὴ
ἐγνωκόσιν, ἃς εὐθείας ποιεῖν καὶ εὐτρεπίζειν παρήγ-
γειλεν Ἰωάννης, τούτοις δὲ προσώχθισεν ὁ θεὸς καὶ
ἀπειλεῖ· καὶ δὴ καὶ τὸ τέλος τῆς ἀπειλῆς αἰνιγμα-
71 P. τωδῶς ἀπειλήφασιν οἱ παλαιοὶ τῶν Ἑβραίων

---

[1] [αὐτοῦ] Stählin.
[2] ἀιδίου αἰῶνος Arcerius. ἀίδιος αἰών mss.

If you wish to learn what this "proving" is, the CHAP.
IX
Holy Spirit shall explain to you.

> And they saw My works forty years.
> Wherefore I was displeased with this generation,
> And said, They do always err in their heart :
> But they did not know My ways ;
> As I sware in My wrath,
> They shall not enter into My rest.[a]

See the threat! See the exhortation! See the
penalty! Why then do we still exchange grace for
wrath? Why do we not receive the Word with
open ears and entertain God as guest in souls free
from stain? For great is the grace of His promise, *The meaning*
"if to-day we hear His voice"; and this "to-day" is *of the word*
"to-day"
extended day by day, so long as the word "to-day"
exists.[b] Both the "to-day" and the teaching continue until the consummation of all things; and
then the true "to-day," the unending day of God,
reaches on throughout the ages.

Let us, then, ever listen to the voice of the
divine Word. For "to-day" is an image of the
everlasting age, and the day is a symbol of light,
and the light of men is the Word, through whom
we gaze upon God. Naturally, then, grace will *Grace*
abound exceedingly towards those who have believed *abounds*
towards
and listen; but as for those who have disbelieved *those that*
hear;
and are erring in heart, who know not the ways *others God*
of the Lord, which John commanded us to make *threatens*
with
straight and prepare, with them God is displeased, *punishment*
and them He threatens. Moreover the ancient
Hebrews received in a figure the fulfilment of the
threat when they wandered in the desert. For,

---

[a] Hebrews iii. 7–11, from Psalm xcv. 8–11.
[b] See Hebrews iii. 13.

πλανῆται· οὐ γὰρ " εἰσελθεῖν εἰς τὴν κατάπαυσιν "
λέγονται διὰ τὴν ἀπιστίαν, πρὶν ἢ σφᾶς αὐτοὺς
κατακολουθήσαντας τῷ Μωυσέως διαδόχῳ ὀψέ
ποτε ἔργῳ μαθεῖν οὐκ ἂν ἄλλως σωθῆναι μὴ
οὐχὶ ὡς Ἰησοῦς πεπιστευκότας.

Φιλάνθρωπος δὲ ὢν ὁ κύριος πάντας ἀνθρώπους
" εἰς ἐπίγνωσιν τῆς ἀληθείας " παρακαλεῖ, ὁ τὸν
παράκλητον ἀποστέλλων. τίς οὖν ἡ ἐπίγνωσις;
θεοσέβεια· " θεοσέβεια δὲ πρὸς πάντα ὠφέλιμος "
κατὰ τὸν Παῦλον, " ἐπαγγελίαν ἔχουσα ζωῆς τῆς
νῦν καὶ τῆς μελλούσης." πόσου ὠμολογήσατε, ὦ
ἄνθρωποι, εἰ ἐπιπράσκετο σωτηρία ἀίδιος, ὠνή-
σασθαι ἄν; οὐδὲ εἰ τὸν Πακτωλόν τις ὅλον, τοῦ
χρυσίου τὸ ῥεῦμα τὸ μυθικόν, ἀπομετρήσαι, ἀντ-
άξιον σωτηρίας μισθὸν ἀριθμήσει. μὴ οὖν ἀπο-
κάμητε· ἔξεστιν ὑμῖν, ἢν ἐθέλητε, ἐξωνήσασθαι τὴν
πολυτίμητον σωτηρίαν οἰκείῳ θησαυρῷ, ἀγάπῃ καὶ
πίστει, ζωῆς ὅς ἐστιν ἀξιόλογος μισθός.¹ ταύτην
ἡδέως τὴν τιμὴν ὁ θεὸς λαμβάνει. " ἠλπίκαμεν
γὰρ ἐπὶ θεῷ ζῶντι, ὅς ἐστι σωτὴρ πάντων ἀνθρώπων, μάλιστα πιστῶν." οἱ δὲ ἄλλοι περι-
πεφυκότες τῷ κόσμῳ, οἷα φυκία τινὰ ἐνάλοις
πέτραις, ἀθανασίας ὀλιγωροῦσιν, καθάπερ ὁ Ἰθα-
κήσιος γέρων οὐ τῆς ἀληθείας καὶ τῆς ἐν οὐρανῷ
πατρίδος, πρὸς δὲ καὶ τοῦ ὄντως ὄντος ἱμειρόμενοι ²
φωτός, ἀλλὰ τοῦ καπνοῦ.

---

¹ ἀγάπῃ καὶ πίστει ζωῆς, ὅς . . . μισθός. Stählin. The
punctuation given above is suggested by Mayor.
² ἱμειρόμενοι Markland. ἱμειρόμενος mss.

ᵃ 1 Timothy ii. 4.
ᵇ St. John xv. 26. There is a play on words in the Greek
which it is hard to reproduce in English. The word *para-*

owing to their unbelief, they are said not to have
"entered into the rest," until they followed the
successor of Moses and learnt, though late, by experience, that they could not be saved in any other
way but by believing, as Joshua believed.

But the Lord, being a lover of man, encourages Truth and
all men to come " to a full knowledge of the truth " *a*; salvation come
for to this end He sends the Comforter.*b* What through
then is this full knowledge? It is godliness; and godliness
"godliness," according to Paul, "is profitable for all
things, having promise of the life which now is, and
of that which is to come." *c* If eternal salvation Salvation
were for sale, at what price would you, brother men, could not
have agreed to buy it? Not even if one were to be bought for money
measure out the whole of Pactolus, the legendary
river of gold, would he count a price equivalent to
salvation. But do not despair. It is in your power,
if you will, to buy up this highly precious salvation
with a treasure of your own, namely, love and faith,
which is a fitting payment for eternal life. This But God
price God is pleased to accept. For "we have our accepts
hope set on the living God, who is the Saviour of love as
all men, especially of them that believe." *d* The payment
rest, clinging to the world, as certain sea-weeds
cling to the rocks of the sea,*e* hold immortality of
little account. They are like the old man of Ithaca,
yearning not for truth and their fatherland in
heaven, nor yet for the Light that truly exists, but
for the smoke from the hearth.*f*

kletos, translated Comforter in the New Testament, is
formed from *parakalein*, a verb which combines the meanings
of summon, comfort (*i.e.* strengthen), and encourage; or, to
put it in another way, of invitation coupled with assistance.

  c 1 Timothy iv. 8.   *d* 1 Timothy iv. 10.
  e See Plato, *Republic* 611 D.   *f* Homer, *Odyssey* i. 57–58.

CAP.
IX

Θεοσέβεια δέ, ἐξομοιοῦσα τῷ θεῷ κατὰ τὸ
δυνατὸν τὸν ἄνθρωπον, κατάλληλον ἐπιγράφεται διδάσκαλον θεὸν τὸν καὶ μόνον ἀπεικάσαι κατ' ἀξίαν
δυνάμενον ἄνθρωπον θεῷ. ταύτην ὁ ἀπόστολος
τὴν διδασκαλίαν θείαν ὄντως ἐπιστάμενος " σὺ
δέ, ὦ Τιμόθεε," φησίν, " ἀπὸ βρέφους ἱερὰ
γράμματα οἶδας, τὰ δυνάμενά σε σοφίσαι εἰς
σωτηρίαν διὰ πίστεως ἐν Χριστῷ." ἱερὰ γὰρ ὡς
ἀληθῶς τὰ ἱεροποιοῦντα καὶ θεοποιοῦντα γράμματα,
ἐξ ὧν γραμμάτων καὶ συλλαβῶν τῶν ἱερῶν τὰς
συγκειμένας γραφάς, τὰ συντάγματα, ὁ αὐτὸς
ἀκολούθως ἀπόστολος " θεοπνεύστους " καλεῖ,
" ὠφελίμους οὔσας πρὸς διδασκαλίαν, πρὸς ἔλεγχον,
πρὸς ἐπανόρθωσιν, πρὸς παιδείαν τὴν ἐν δικαιοσύνῃ,
ἵνα ἄρτιος ᾖ ὁ τοῦ θεοῦ ἄνθρωπος πρὸς πᾶν ἔργον
ἀγαθὸν ἐξηρτημένος." οὐκ ἄν τις οὕτως ἐκπλαγείη
τῶν ἄλλων ἁγίων τὰς προτροπὰς ὡς αὐτὸν τὸν
72 P. κύριον τὸν φιλάνθρωπον· οὐδὲν γὰρ | ἀλλ' ἢ τοῦτο
ἔργον μόνον ἐστὶν αὐτῷ σῴζεσθαι τὸν ἄνθρωπον.
βοᾷ γοῦν ἐπείγων εἰς σωτηρίαν αὐτὸς " ἤγγικεν ἡ
βασιλεία τῶν οὐρανῶν "· ἐπιστρέφει τοὺς ἀνθρώπους πλησιάζοντας τῷ φόβῳ. ταύτῃ καὶ ὁ ἀπόστολος τοῦ κυρίου παρακαλῶν τοὺς Μακεδόνας
ἑρμηνεὺς γίνεται τῆς θείας φωνῆς, " ὁ κύριος
ἤγγικεν " λέγων, " εὐλαβεῖσθε μὴ καταληφθῶμεν
κενοί."

Ὑμεῖς δὲ ἐς τοσοῦτον ἀδεεῖς, μᾶλλον δὲ ἄπιστοι,
μήτε αὐτῷ πειθόμενοι τῷ κυρίῳ μήτε τῷ Παύλῳ,
καὶ ταῦτα ὑπὲρ Χριστοῦ δεδεμένῳ.[1] " γεύσασθε

---

[1] δεομένῳ correctiori in P (cp. 2 Corinthians v. 20).

---

[a] 2 Timothy iii. 15.   [b] 2 Timothy iii. 16, 17.

Now when godliness sets out to make man as far as possible resemble God, it claims God as a suitable teacher; for He alone has the power worthily to conform man to His own likeness. This teaching the apostle recognizes as truly divine, when he says, "And thou, Timothy, from a babe hast known the sacred letters, which have power to make thee wise unto salvation, through faith in Christ." [a] For the letters which make us sacred and divine are indeed themselves sacred, and the writings composed from these sacred letters and syllables, namely, the collected Scriptures, are consequently called by the same apostle "inspired of God, being profitable for teaching, for reproof, for correction, for instruction which is in righteousness; that the man of God may be complete, thoroughly furnished unto every good work." [b] No one could be so deeply moved at the exhortations of other holy men as at those of the Lord Himself, the lover of men; for this, and nothing else, is His only work, that man may be saved. In His own person He cries out, urging men on to salvation: "The kingdom of heaven is at hand." [c] He converts men when they draw nigh to Him through fear. On this point the Lord's apostle becomes an interpreter of the divine voice when in appealing to the Macedonians he says, "The Lord is at hand; take care lest we be found empty." [d]

But you have so little fear, or rather faith, that you obey neither the Lord Himself, nor Paul, though Paul was a prisoner for the sake of Christ. "O taste

CHAP.
IX
God
Himself
must be
our teacher

Through the
Scriptures

[c] St. Matthew iv. 17.
[d] Philippians iv. 5; the latter half of the saying is not found in the New Testament.

193

CAP.
IX

καὶ ἴδετε ὅτι χρηστὸς ὁ θεός.ᵃ" ἡ πίστις εἰσάξει,
ἡ πεῖρα διδάξει, ἡ γραφὴ παιδαγωγήσει " δεῦτε,
ὦ τέκνα," λέγουσα, " ἀκούσατέ μου, φόβον κυρίου
διδάξω ὑμᾶς.ᵇ" εἶτα ὡς ἤδη πεπιστευκόσι συντόμως ἐπιλέγει " τίς ἐστιν ἄνθρωπος ὁ θέλων
ζωήν, ἀγαπῶν ἡμέρας ἰδεῖν ἀγαθάς;ᶜ" ἡμεῖς ἐσμεν,
φήσομεν, οἱ τἀγαθοῦ προσκυνηταί, οἱ τῶν ἀγαθῶν
ζηλωταί. ἀκούσατε οὖν " οἱ μακράν," ἀκούσατε
" οἱ ἐγγύς "·ᵈ οὐκ ἀπεκρύβη τινὰς ὁ λόγος· φῶς
ἐστι κοινόν, ἐπιλάμπει πᾶσιν ἀνθρώποις·ᵉ οὐδεὶς
Κιμμέριος ἐν λόγῳ·ᶠ σπεύσωμεν εἰς σωτηρίαν, ἐπὶ
τὴν παλιγγενεσίαν· εἰς μίαν ἀγάπην ¹ συναχθῆναι οἱ
πολλοὶ κατὰ τὴν τῆς μοναδικῆς οὐσίας ἕνωσιν
σπεύσωμεν. ἀγαθοεργούμενοι ἀναλόγως ἑνότητα
διώκωμεν, τὴν ἀγαθὴν ἐκζητοῦντες μονάδα. ἡ δὲ
ἐκ πολλῶν ἕνωσις ἐκ πολυφωνίας καὶ διασπορᾶς
ἁρμονίαν λαβοῦσα θεϊκὴν μία γίνεται συμφωνία,
ἑνὶ χορευτῇ καὶ διδασκάλῳ τῷ λόγῳ ἑπομένη,
ἐπ᾽ αὐτὴν τὴν ἀλήθειαν ἀναπαυομένη, " Ἀββᾶ "
λέγουσα " ὁ πατήρ "· ταύτην ὁ θεὸς τὴν φωνὴν
τὴν ἀληθινὴν ἀσπάζεται παρὰ τῶν αὐτοῦ παίδων
πρώτην καρπούμενος.

¹ Stählin suggests ἀγέλην.

ᵃ Psalm xxxiv. 8.   ᵇ Psalm xxxiv. 11.
ᶜ Psalm xxxiv. 12.
ᵈ Isaiah lvii. 19 ; Ephesians ii. 17.
ᵉ See St. John i. 9.
ᶠ The Cimmerians were a mythical people who dwelt
beyond the Ocean in a land of mist and cloud and total
darkness. See *Odyssey* xi. 13-16.
ᵍ Or, if Stählin's suggestion is accepted (see note on text),
"into one herd," or "flock." The word ἀγέλη is used for
the "flock" of men on p. 247 of this volume, and in i. *Strom.*
156. 3, and 169. 2. Cp. St. John x. 16.

and see that God is good." [a]   Faith shall lead you, CHAP.
IX
experience shall teach you, the Scripture shall train
you. "Come, ye children," it says, "hearken unto
me; I will teach you the fear of the Lord." [b]   Then, All who
desire
as if speaking to those who have already believed, it eternal life
adds briefly, "What man is there that desireth life, may come
and loveth to see good days?" [c]   We are they, we
shall answer, we, the worshippers of the good, we who
are zealous for good things. Hear then, "ye that
are afar off"; hear, "ye that are nigh." [d]   The Word
was not hidden from any; He is a universal light;
He shines upon all men. [e]   No one is a Cimmerian [f]
in respect of the Word. Let us hasten to salvation,
to the new birth. Let us, who are many, hasten to Though
be gathered together into one love [g] corresponding to many, they
are made
the union of the One Being. Similarly, let us follow into a unity
through
after unity by the practice of good works, seeking love and
the good Monad. [h]   And the union of many into one, good works
bringing a divine harmony out of many scattered
sounds, becomes one symphony, following one leader
and teacher, the Word, and never ceasing till it
reaches the truth itself, with the cry, "Abba
Father." [i]   This is the true speech which God
welcomes from His children. This is the first-fruits
of God's harvest.

[h] The Monad, or unit, was a term used by the Pytha-
goreans, who regarded all things as in some way constituted
out of number. Odd numbers were more perfect than even,
and the Monad, from which the rest were derived, was
conceived as the perfect first principle of the universe.
Clement here makes it a name for God, but in another place
(i. *Paedagogus* 71. 1) he says that God is " above the Monad
itself."

[i] See St. Mark xiv. 36 ; Romans viii. 15 and Galatians
iv. 6.

X

’Αλλ’ ἐκ πατέρων, φατέ, παραδεδομένον ἡμῖν
ἔθος ἀνατρέπειν οὐκ εὔλογον. καὶ τί δὴ οὐχὶ τῇ
πρώτῃ τροφῇ, τῷ γάλακτι, χρώμεθα, ᾧ δήπουθεν
συνείθισαν ἡμᾶς ἐκ γενετῆς αἱ τίτθαι; τί δὲ
αὐξάνομεν ἢ μειοῦμεν τὴν πατρῴαν οὐσίαν, | καὶ
οὐχὶ τὴν ἴσην, ὡς παρειλήφαμεν, διαφυλάττομεν; τί
δὲ οὐκέτι τοῖς κόλποις τοῖς πατρῴοις ἐναποβλύ-
ζομεν, ἢ καὶ τὰ ἄλλα, ἃ νηπιάζοντες ὑπὸ μητράσιν
τε ἐκτρεφόμενοι γέλωτα ὤφλομεν, ἐπιτελοῦμεν ἔτι,
ἀλλὰ σφᾶς αὐτούς, καὶ εἰ μὴ παιδαγωγῶν ἐτύχομεν
ἀγαθῶν, ἐπανωρθώσαμεν; εἶτα ἐπὶ τῶν πλόων [1] αἱ
παρεκβάσεις καίτοι ἐπιζήμιοι καὶ ἐπισφαλεῖς οὖσαι,
ὅμως γλυκεῖαί πως προσπίπτουσιν, ἐπὶ δὲ τοῦ βίου
οὐχὶ τὸ ἔθος καταλιπόντες [2] τὸ πονηρὸν καὶ ἐμπαθὲς
καὶ ἄθεον, κἂν οἱ πατέρες χαλεπαίνωσιν, ἐπὶ τὴν
ἀλήθειαν ἐκκλινοῦμεν καὶ τὸν ὄντως ὄντα πατέρα
ἐπιζητήσομεν, [3] οἷον δηλητήριον φάρμακον τὴν συνήθειαν ἀπωσάμενοι; τοῦτ’ αὐτὸ γάρ τοι τὸ κάλλιστον τῶν ἐγχειρουμένων ἐστίν, ὑποδεῖξαι ὑμῖν ὡς
ἀπὸ μανίας καὶ τοῦ τρισαθλίου τούτου ἔθους ἐμισήθη
ἡ θεοσέβεια· οὐ γὰρ ἂν ἐμισήθη ποτὲ ἢ ἀπηγορεύθη
ἀγαθὸν τοσοῦτον, οὗ μεῖζον οὐδὲν ἐκ θεοῦ δεδώ-
ρηταί πω τῇ τῶν ἀνθρώπων γενέσει, εἰ μὴ συν-
αρπαζόμενοι τῷ ἔθει, εἶτα μέντοι ἀποβύσαντες τὰ
ὦτα ἡμῖν, οἷον ἵπποι σκληραύχενες ἀφηνιάζοντες,
τοὺς χαλινοὺς ἐνδακόντες, ἀπεφεύγετε [4] τοὺς λόγους,

---

[1] πλόων Cobet. παίδων Schwartz. παθῶν MSS.
[2] καταλιπόντες Cobet. καταλείποντες MSS.
[3] ἐπιζητήσομεν Sylburg. ἐπιζητήσωμεν MSS.
[4] ἀπεφεύγετε . . . ὑπελαμβάνετε Stählin. ἀποφεύγετε . . .
ὑπολαμβάνετε MSS.

X.

But, you say, it is not reasonable to overthow a way of life handed down to us from our forefathers. *It is objected that men ought not to forsake ancestral customs* Why then do we not continue to use our first food, milk, to which, as you will admit, our nurses accustomed us from birth? Why do we increase or diminish our family property, and not keep it for ever at the same value as when we received it? Why do we no longer sputter into our parents' bosoms, nor still behave in other respects as we did when infants in our mothers' arms, making ourselves objects of laughter? Did we not rather correct ourselves, even if we did not happen to have good attendants for this purpose? Again, in voyages by sea, deviations from the usual course may bring loss and danger, but yet they are attended by a certain charm. *Yet new ways are sometimes good* So, in life itself, shall we not abandon the old way, which is wicked, full of passion, and without God? And shall we not, even at the risk of displeasing our fathers, bend our course towards the truth and seek after Him who is our real Father, thrusting away custom as some deadly drug? This is assuredly the noblest of all the tasks we have in hand, namely, to prove to you that it was from madness and from this thrice miserable custom that hatred of godliness sprang. *Custom is the real obstacle to godliness* For such a boon, the greatest that God has ever bestowed upon the race of men, could never have been hated or rejected, had you not been clean carried away by custom, and so had stopped your ears against us. Like stubborn horses that refuse to obey the reins, and take the bit between their teeth, you fled from our arguments. *Custom refuses all guidance and argument*

CLEMENT OF ALEXANDRIA

CAP. ἀποσείσασθαι μὲν τοὺς ἡνιόχους ὑμῶν τοῦ βίου
X ἡμᾶς ἐπιποθοῦντες, ἐπὶ δὲ τοὺς κρημνοὺς τῆς
ἀπωλείας ὑπὸ τῆς ἀνοίας φερόμενοι ἐναγῆ τὸν
ἅγιον ὑπελαμβάνετε[1] τοῦ θεοῦ λόγον. ἔπεται τοι-
γαροῦν ὑμῖν κατὰ τὸν Σοφοκλέα τὰ ἐπίχειρα τῆς
ἐκλογῆς,

νοῦς φροῦδος, ὦτ' ἀχρεῖα, φροντίδες κεναί,

καὶ οὐκ ἴστε ὡς παντὸς μᾶλλον τοῦτο ἀληθές, ὅτι
ἄρα οἱ μὲν ἀγαθοὶ καὶ θεοσεβεῖς ἀγαθῆς τῆς
ἀμοιβῆς τεύξονται τἀγαθὸν τετιμηκότες, οἱ δὲ ἐκ
τῶν ἐναντίων πονηροὶ τῆς καταλλήλου τιμωρίας,
καὶ τῷ γε ἄρχοντι τῆς κακίας ἐπήρτηται κόλασις.
ἀπειλεῖ γοῦν αὐτῷ ὁ προφήτης Ζαχαρίας "ἐπι-
τιμήσαι ἐν σοὶ ὁ ἐκλεξάμενος τὴν Ἱερουσαλήμ·
οὐκ ἰδοὺ τοῦτο δαλὸς ἐξεσπασμένος ἐκ πυρός;" τίς
οὖν ἔτι τοῖς ἀνθρώποις ὄρεξις ἔγκειται θανάτου
ἑκουσίου; τί δὲ τῷ δαλῷ τῷ θανατηφόρῳ τούτῳ
74 P. προσπεφεύγασιν, μεθ' οὗ κατα|φλεχθήσονται, ἐξὸν
βιῶναι καλῶς κατὰ τὸν θεόν, οὐ κατὰ τὸ ἔθος;
θεὸς μὲν γὰρ ζωὴν χαρίζεται, ἔθος δὲ πονηρὸν μετὰ
τὴν ἐνθένδε ἀπαλλαγὴν μετάνοιαν κενὴν ἅμα τι-
μωρίᾳ προστρίβεται, "παθὼν δέ τε νήπιος ἔγνω,"
ὡς ἀπολλύει δεισιδαιμονία καὶ σῴζει θεοσέβεια.

Ἰδέτω τις ὑμῶν τοὺς παρὰ τοῖς εἰδώλοις λα-
τρεύοντας, κόμῃ ῥυπῶντας, ἐσθῆτι πιναρᾷ καὶ κατ-

---

[1] ἀπεφεύγετε . . . ὑπελαμβάνετε Stählin. ἀποφεύγετε . . .
ὑπολαμβάνετε MSS.

---

[a] Clement plays upon the similarity between *hagios*, holy,
and *enagēs*, accursed.

[b] Sophocles, Frag. 863 Nauck.   [c] Zechariah iii. 2.

198

You yearned to shake yourselves free from us, the CHAP.
charioteers of your life; yet all the while you X
were being carried along by your folly towards the And leads
precipices of destruction, and supposed the holy finally to
Word of God to be accursed.[a] Accordingly the
recompense of your choice attends upon you, in the
words of Sophocles,

Lost senses, useless ears, and fruitless thoughts;[b]

and you do not know that this is true above all else,
that the good and god-fearing, since they have
honoured that which is good, shall meet with a
reward that is good; while the wicked, on the other
hand, shall meet with punishment corresponding to
their deeds: and torment ever hangs over the head
of the prince of evil. At least, the prophet Zechariah
threatens him: "He that hath chosen Jerusalem
take vengeance upon thee! Behold, is not this a
brand plucked out of the fire?"[c] What a strange Why do
longing, then, is this for a self-chosen death which men court
still presses upon men? Why have they fled to this life is pos-
death-bearing brand, with which they shall be burnt sible?
up, when they might live a noble life according to
God, not according to custom[d]? For God grants life;
but wicked custom inflicts unavailing repentance
together with punishment after we depart from this
world. And "by suffering even a fool will learn"[e]
that daemon-worship leads to destruction, and the
fear of God to salvation.

Let any of you look at those who minister in the Description
idol temples. He will find them ruffians with filthy of priests in
the idol
temples

[a] A play upon the words *theos* (God) and *ethos* (custom).
[e] Hesiod, *Works and Days* 218.

199

CAP.
X

ἐρρωγυίᾳ καθυβρισμένους, λουτρῶν μὲν παντάπασιν
ἀπειράτους, ταῖς δὲ τῶν ὀνύχων ἀκμαῖς ἐκτεθηριω-
μένους, πολλοὺς δὲ καὶ τῶν αἰδοίων ἀφηρημένους,
ἔργῳ δεικνύντας τῶν εἰδώλων τὰ τεμένη τάφους
τινὰς ἢ δεσμωτήρια· οὗτοί μοι δοκοῦσι πενθεῖν, οὐ
θρησκεύειν τοὺς θεούς, ἐλέου μᾶλλον ἢ θεοσεβείας
ἄξια πεπονθότες. καὶ ταῦτα ὁρῶντες ἔτι τυφλώτ-
τετε καὶ οὐχὶ πρὸς τὸν δεσπότην τῶν πάντων καὶ
κύριον τῶν ὅλων ἀναβλέψετε; οὐχὶ δὲ καταφεύ-
ξεσθε, ἐκ τῶν ἐνταῦθα δεσμωτηρίων ἐκφεύγοντες,
ἐπὶ τὸν ἔλεον τὸν ἐξ οὐρανῶν; ὁ γὰρ θεὸς ἐκ
πολλῆς τῆς φιλανθρωπίας ἀντέχεται τοῦ ἀνθρώπου,
ὥσπερ ἐκ καλιᾶς ἐκπίπτοντος νεοττοῦ ἡ μήτηρ
ὄρνις ἐφίπταται· εἰ δέ που καὶ θηρίον ἑρπηστικὸν
περιχάνοι τῷ νεοττῷ,

μήτηρ δ' ἀμφιποτᾶται ὀδυρομένη φίλα τέκνα·

ὁ δὲ θεὸς πατὴρ καὶ ζητεῖ τὸ πλάσμα καὶ ἰᾶται τὸ
παράπτωμα καὶ διώκει τὸ θηρίον καὶ τὸν νεοττὸν
αὖθις ἀναλαμβάνει ἐπὶ τὴν καλιὰν ἀναπτῆναι παρ-
ορμῶν. εἶτα κύνες μὲν ἤδη πεπλανημένοι ὀδμαῖς
ῥινηλατοῦντες ἐξίχνευσαν τὸν δεσπότην καὶ ἵπποι
τὸν ἀναβάτην ἀποσεισάμενοι ἑνί που συρίγματι
ὑπήκουσαν τῷ δεσπότῃ. "ἔγνω δέ," φησί, "βοῦς
τὸν κτησάμενον καὶ ὄνος τὴν φάτνην τοῦ κυρίου
αὐτοῦ, Ἰσραὴλ δέ με οὐκ ἔγνω." τί οὖν ὁ κύριος;
οὐ μνησικακεῖ, ἔτι ἐλεεῖ, ἔτι τὴν μετάνοιαν ἀπαιτεῖ.
ἐρέσθαι δὲ ὑμᾶς βούλομαι, εἰ οὐκ ἄτοπον ὑμῖν
δοκεῖ πλάσμα ὑμᾶς τοὺς ἀνθρώπους ἐπιγεγονότας [1]

---

[1] ἐπιγεγονότας MSS. [ἐπι]γεγονότας Stählin.

hair, in squalid and tattered garments, complete strangers to baths, with claws for nails like wild beasts; many are also deprived of their virility. They are an actual proof that the precincts of the idols are so many tombs or prisons. These men seem to me to mourn for the gods, not to worship them, and their condition provokes pity rather than piety. When you see sights like this, do you still remain blind and refuse to look up to the Master of all and Lord of the universe? Will you not fly from the prisons on earth, and escape to the pity which comes from heaven? For God of His great love still keeps hold of man; just as, when a nestling falls from the nest, the mother bird flutters above, and if perchance a serpent gapes for it,

Flitting around with cries, the mother mourns for her offspring.[a]

Now God is a Father, and seeks His creature. He remedies the falling away, drives off the reptile, restores the nestling to strength again, and urges it to fly back to the nest. Once more, dogs who have lost their way discover their master's tracks by the sense of smell, and horses who have thrown their rider obey a single whistle from their own master; "the ox," it is written, "knoweth his owner, and the ass his master's crib, but Israel doth not know Me."[b] What then does the Lord do? He bears no grudge; He still pities, still requires repentance of us. I would ask you, whether you do not think it absurd that you men who are God's last creation,

[a] Homer, *Iliad* ii. 315.
[b] Isaiah i. 3.

CLEMENT OF ALEXANDRIA

CAP.
X τοῦ θεοῦ καὶ παρ' αὐτοῦ τὴν ψυχὴν εἰληφότας καὶ
ὄντας ὅλως τοῦ θεοῦ ἑτέρῳ δουλεύειν δεσπότῃ,
πρὸς δὲ καὶ θεραπεύειν ἀντὶ μὲν τοῦ βασιλέως τὸν
τύραννον, ἀντὶ δὲ τοῦ ἀγαθοῦ τὸν πονηρόν. τίς
γάρ, ὦ πρὸς τῆς ἀληθείας, σωφρονῶν γε τἀγαθὸν
καταλείπων κακίᾳ σύνεστιν; τίς δὲ ὅστις τὸν θεὸν
ἀποφεύγων δαιμονίοις συμβιοῖ; τίς δὲ υἱὸς εἶναι
δυνάμενος τοῦ θεοῦ δουλεύειν ἥδεται; ἢ τίς οὐρανοῦ
75 P. πολίτης εἶναι δυνάμενος ἔρεβος | διώκει, ἐξὸν παρά-
δεισον γεωργεῖν καὶ οὐρανὸν περιπολεῖν καὶ τῆς
ζωτικῆς καὶ ἀκηράτου μεταλαμβάνειν πηγῆς,
κατ' ἴχνος ἐκείνης τῆς φωτεινῆς ἀεροβατοῦντα
νεφέλης, ὥσπερ ὁ Ἡλίας, θεωροῦντα τὸν ὑετὸν
⟨τὸν⟩[1] σωτήριον; οἱ δὲ σκωλήκων δίκην περὶ
τέλματα καὶ βορβόρους, τὰ ἡδονῆς ῥεύματα, καλιν-
δούμενοι ἀνονήτους καὶ ἀνοήτους ἐκβόσκονται
τρυφάς, ὑώδεις τινὲς ἄνθρωποι. ὕες γάρ, φησίν,
"ἥδονται βορβόρῳ" μᾶλλον ἢ καθαρῷ ὕδατι καὶ
"ἐπὶ φορυτῷ μαργαίνουσιν" κατὰ Δημόκριτον. μὴ
δῆτα οὖν, μὴ δῆτα ἐξανδραποδισθῶμεν μηδὲ ὑώδεις γενώμεθα, ἀλλ' "ὡς τέκνα φωτὸς" γνήσια,
ἀναθρήσωμεν καὶ ἀναβλέψωμεν εἰς τὸ φῶς, μὴ
νόθους ἡμᾶς ἐξελέγξῃ ὁ κύριος ὥσπερ ὁ ἥλιος
τοὺς ἀετούς.

Μετανοήσωμεν οὖν καὶ μεταστῶμεν ἐξ ἀμαθίας
εἰς ἐπιστήμην, ἐξ ἀφροσύνης εἰς φρόνησιν, ἐξ
ἀκρασίας εἰς ἐγκράτειαν, ἐξ ἀδικίας εἰς δικαιοσύνην,
ἐξ ἀθεότητος εἰς θεόν. καλὸς ὁ κίνδυνος αὐτομολεῖν

---

[1] ⟨τὸν⟩ inserted by Sylburg.

[a] Clement has drawn together the Elijah of the Trans-
figuration (St. Matthew xvii. 5) and the Elijah of Mount
Carmel (1 Kings xviii. 44).

202

who have received your soul from Him, and are CHAP.
X
entirely His, should serve another master; aye, and
more than that, should pay homage to the tyrant
instead of to the rightful king, to the wicked one
instead of to the good? For, in the name of truth,
what man in his senses forsakes that which is good
to keep company with evil? Who is there that flees
from God to live with daemons? Who is pleased
with slavery, when he might be a son of God? Or
who hastens to a region of darkness, when he might
be a citizen of heaven; when it is in his power to
till the fields of paradise, and traverse the spaces of
heaven, when he can partake of the pure and life-
giving spring, treading the air in the track of that
bright cloud, like Elijah, with his eyes fixed on the
rain that brings salvation?[a] But there are some Yet some
are like
worms and
swine,
loving what
is unclean
who, after the manner of worms, wallow in marshes
and mud, which are the streams of pleasure, and
feed on profitless and senseless delights. These are
swinish men; for swine, says one, "take pleasure in
mud"[b] more than in pure water; and they "are
greedy for offal," according to Democritus.[c] Let us
not then, let us not be made slaves, nor become
swinish, but as true "children of the light,"[d] direct
our gaze steadily upward towards the light, lest the
Lord prove us bastards as the sun does the eagles.

Let us therefore repent, and pass from ignorance Let us
repent, and
come over
to God's
side
to knowledge, from senselessness to sense, from in-
temperance to temperance, from unrighteousness to
righteousness, from godlessness to God. It is a

[b] The words are from Heracleitus: Frag. 54 Bywater,
13 Diels.

[c] Democritus, Frag. 23 Natorp, 147 Diels.

[d] Ephesians v. 8.

CAP.
X

πρὸς θεόν. πολλῶν δὲ καὶ ἄλλων ἔστιν ἀπολαῦσαι ἀγαθῶν τοὺς δικαιοσύνης ἐραστάς, οἳ τὴν ἀίδιον διώκομεν σωτηρίαν, ἀτὰρ δὴ καὶ ὧν αὐτὸς αἰνίττεται ὁ θεὸς διὰ Ἡσαΐου λαλῶν " ἔστι κληρονομία τοῖς θεραπεύουσι κύριον ". καλή γε καὶ ἐράσμιος ἡ κληρονομία, οὐ χρυσίον, οὐκ ἄργυρος, οὐκ ἐσθής, τὰ τῆς γῆς,[1] ἔνθα που σὴς καὶ λῃστής που καταδύεται περὶ τὸν χαμαίζηλον πλοῦτον ὀφθαλμιῶν, ἀλλ' ἐκεῖνος ὁ θησαυρὸς τῆς σωτηρίας, πρὸς ὅν γε ἐπείγεσθαι χρὴ φιλολόγους γενομένους, συναπαίρει δὲ ἡμῖν ἐνθένδε τὰ ἔργα τὰ ἀστεῖα καὶ συνίπταται τῷ τῆς ἀληθείας πτερῷ.

Ταύτην ἡμῖν τὴν κληρονομίαν ἐγχειρίζει ἡ ἀίδιος διαθήκη τοῦ θεοῦ τὴν ἀίδιον δωρεὰν χορηγοῦσα· ὁ δὲ φιλόστοργος οὗτος ἡμῶν πατήρ, ὁ ὄντως πατήρ, οὐ παύεται προτρέπων, νουθετῶν, παιδεύων, φιλῶν· οὐδὲ γὰρ σῴζων παύεται, συμβουλεύει δὲ τὰ ἄριστα· " δίκαιοι γένεσθε, λέγει κύριος· οἱ διψῶντες πορεύεσθε ἐφ' ὕδωρ, καὶ ὅσοι μὴ ἔχετε ἀργύριον, βαδίσατε καὶ ἀγοράσατε καὶ πίετε ἄνευ ἀργυρίου." ἐπὶ τὸ λουτρόν, ἐπὶ τὴν σωτηρίαν, ἐπὶ τὸν φωτισμὸν παρακαλεῖ μονον-

76 P.
ουχὶ | βοῶν καὶ λέγων· γῆν σοι δίδωμι καὶ θάλατταν, παιδίον, οὐρανόν τε καὶ τὰ ἐν αὐτοῖς πάντα ζῷά σοι χαρίζομαι· μόνον, ὦ παιδίον, δίψησον τοῦ πατρός, ἀμισθεί σοι δειχθήσεται ὁ θεός· οὐ καπηλεύεται ἡ ἀλήθεια, δίδωσί σοι καὶ τὰ πτηνὰ καὶ τὰ νηκτὰ καὶ τὰ ἐπὶ τῆς γῆς· ταῦτά σου

---

[1] τὰ τῆς γῆς after ἐσθής Markland : after σὴς καὶ mss. : καὶ [τὰ τῆς γῆς] Stählin.

---

a Isaiah liv. 17 (Septuagint).

204

glorious venture to desert to God's side. Many are CHAP. the good things which we may enjoy who are lovers X of righteousness, who follow after eternal salvation ; but the best of all are those to which God Himself alludes when He says through Isaiah, " there is an We shall inheritance to those who serve the Lord." ^a Aye, then enjoy God's and a glorious and lovely inheritance it is, not of gold, inheritance not of silver, not of raiment, things of earth, into which perchance moth and robber may find a way,^b casting longing eyes at the earthly riches ; but that treasure of salvation, towards which we must press forward by becoming lovers of the Word. Noble deeds set out from hence in our company, and are borne along with us on the wing of truth.

This inheritance is entrusted to us by the eternal covenant of God, which supplies the eternal gift. And this dearly loving Father, our true Father, never ceases to exhort, to warn, to chasten, to love ; for He never ceases to save, but counsels what is best. " Become righteous, saith the Lord. Ye that are thirsty, come to the water ; and as many as have no money, go ye, and buy and drink without money." ^c It is to the font, to salvation, to en- lightenment that He invites us, almost crying out All things and saying : Earth and sea I give thee, my child ; are ours without cost heaven too, and all things living in earth and heaven are freely thine. Only, my child, do thou thirst for the Father ; without cost shall God be revealed to thee. The truth is not sold as merchandise ; He gives thee the fowls of the air and the fishes of the sea and all that is upon the earth. These things

^b See St. Matthew vi. 19, 20.
^c Isaiah liv. 17 (Septuagint) ; lv. 1.

CLEMENT OF ALEXANDRIA

ταῖς εὐχαρίστοις τρυφαῖς δεδημιούργηκεν ὁ πατήρ.
ἀργυρίῳ μὲν ὠνήσεται ὁ νόθος, ὃς ἀπωλείας ἐστὶ
παιδίον, ὃς " μαμωνᾷ δουλεύειν " προῄρηται, σοὶ
δὲ τὰ σὰ ἐπιτρέπει, τῷ γνησίῳ λέγω,[1] τῷ φιλοῦντι
τὸν πατέρα, δι᾽ ὃν ἔτι ἐργάζεται, ᾧ μόνῳ καὶ
ὑπισχνεῖται λέγων· " καὶ ἡ γῆ οὐ πραθήσεται εἰς
βεβαίωσιν "· οὐ γὰρ κυροῦται τῇ φθορᾷ· " ἐμὴ
γάρ ἐστιν πᾶσα ἡ γῆ," ἔστι δὲ καὶ σή, ἐὰν ἀπολάβῃς
τὸν θεόν. ὅθεν ἡ γραφὴ εἰκότως εὐαγγελίζεται τοῖς
πεπιστευκόσιν· " οἱ δὲ ἅγιοι κυρίου κληρονομή-
σουσι τὴν δόξαν τοῦ θεοῦ καὶ τὴν δύναμιν αὐτοῦ."
ποίαν, ὦ μακάριε, δόξαν, εἰπέ μοι· " ἣν ὀφθαλμὸς
οὐκ εἶδεν οὐδὲ οὖς ἤκουσεν, οὐδὲ ἐπὶ καρδίαν ἀνθρώπου ἀνέβη· καὶ χαρήσονται ἐπὶ τῇ βασιλείᾳ
τοῦ κυρίου αὐτῶν εἰς τοὺς αἰῶνας, ἀμήν." ἔχετε,
ὦ ἄνθρωποι, τὴν θείαν τῆς χάριτος ἐπαγγελίαν, ἀκη-
κόατε καὶ τὴν ἄλλην τῆς κολάσεως ἀπειλήν, δι᾽ ὧν
ὁ κύριος σῴζει, φόβῳ καὶ χάριτι παιδαγωγῶν τὸν
ἄνθρωπον· τί μέλλομεν; τί οὐκ ἐκκλίνομεν τὴν
κόλασιν; τί οὐ καταδεχόμεθα τὴν δωρεάν; τί δὲ
οὐχ αἱρούμεθα τὰ βελτίονα, θεὸν ἀντὶ τοῦ πονηροῦ,
καὶ σοφίαν εἰδωλολατρείας προκρίνομεν καὶ ζωὴν
ἀντικαταλλασσόμεθα[2] θανάτου[3]; " ἰδοὺ τέθεικα πρὸ

---

[1] λέγω Stählin. λέγει MSS.
[2] ἀντικαταλλασσόμεθα Heinsius. ἀντικαταλλασσόμενοι MSS.
[3] θανάτου Mayor. θανάτῳ MSS.

---

[a] St. Matthew vi. 24; St. Luke xvi. 13.
[b] See St. John v. 17.
[c] Leviticus xxv. 23.
[d] Clement takes the Old Testament phrase in a spiritual
sense. It is the " inheritance incorruptible . . . reserved
in heaven " (1 St. Peter i. 4) which is not " delivered over
to corruption."

the Father hath created for thy pleasant delights. CHAP.
X
The bastard, who is a child of destruction, who has
chosen to "serve mammon," [a] shall buy them with
money; but to thee, that is, to the true son, He Because we
are God's
children
commits what is thine own,—to the true son, who
loves the Father, for whose sake the Father works
until now,[b] and to whom alone He makes the
promise, "and the land shall not be sold in per-
petuity"[c]; for it is not delivered over to corruption.[d]
"For the whole land is mine," [e] He says; and it
is thine also, if thou receive God. Whence the
Scripture rightly proclaims to believers this good
news: "The saints of the Lord shall inherit God's
glory and His power." What kind of glory, thou
Blessed One? Tell me. A glory "which eye hath
not seen, nor ear heard, nor hath it entered into
the heart of man. And they shall rejoice in the
kingdom of their Lord for ever, Amen." [f] You
have, my fellow-men, the divine promise of grace; Our choice
is between
grace and
punishment
you have heard, on the other hand, the threat of
punishment. Through these the Lord saves, training man by fear and grace. Why do we hesitate?
Why do we not shun the punishment? Why do
we not accept the gift? Why do we not choose
the better things, that is, God instead of the evil
one, and prefer wisdom to idolatry and take life in
exchange for death? "Behold, I have set before

---

[e] Leviticus xxv. 23.

[f] The first part of this passage is from 1 Cor. ii. 9, where
it is introduced by St. Paul as a quotation. Origen tells us,
in his *Commentary on St. Matthew* (see Migne, *Origen* vol. iii.
p. 1769), that St. Paul took it from the Apocalypse of Elijah.
Doubtless the rest of the passage, as given by Clement,
comes from the same source.

CAP.
X

προσώπου ὑμῶν," φησί, "τὸν θάνατον καὶ τὴν ζωήν." πειράζει σε ὁ κύριος ἐκλέξασθαι τὴν ζωήν, συμβουλεύει σοι ὡς πατὴρ πείθεσθαι[1] τῷ θεῷ. "ἐὰν γὰρ ἀκούσητέ μου," φησί, "καὶ θελήσητε, τὰ ἀγαθὰ τῆς γῆς φάγεσθε," ὑπακοῆς ἡ χάρις· "ἐὰν δὲ μὴ ὑπακούσητέ μου μηδὲ θελήσητε, μάχαιρα ὑμᾶς καὶ πῦρ κατέδεται," παρακοῆς ἡ κρίσις. "τὸ γὰρ στόμα κυρίου ἐλάλησεν ταῦτα·" νόμος ἀληθείας λόγος κυρίου. |

π ρ.   Βούλεσθε ὑμῖν ἀγαθὸς γένωμαι σύμβουλος; ἀλλ' ὑμεῖς μὲν ἀκούσατε· ἐγὼ δέ, εἰ δυνατόν, ἐνδείξομαι. ἐχρῆν μὲν ὑμᾶς, ὦ ἄνθρωποι, αὐτοῦ πέρι ἐννοουμένους τοῦ ἀγαθοῦ ἔμφυτον ἐπάγεσθαι πίστιν, μάρτυρα ἀξιόχρεων[2] αὐτόθεν οἴκοθεν, περιφανῶς αἱρουμένην τὸ βέλτιστον, μηδὲ [ζητεῖν][3] εἰ μεταδιωκτέον ἐκπονεῖν. καὶ γὰρ εἴ τῳ μεθυστέον, φέρε εἰπεῖν, ἀμφιβάλλειν χρή· ὑμεῖς δὲ πρὶν ἢ ἐπισκέψασθαι μεθύετε· καὶ εἰ ὑβριστέον, οὐ πολυπραγμονεῖτε, ἀλλ' ἢ[4] τάχος ὑβρίζετε. μόνον δ' ἄρα εἰ θεοσεβητέον, ζητεῖτε, καὶ εἰ τῷ σοφῷ τούτῳ [δὴ][5] τῷ θεῷ καὶ τῷ Χριστῷ κατακολουθητέον, τοῦτο δὴ[6] βουλῆς καὶ σκέψεως ἀξιοῦτε, οὐδ' ὃ πρέπει θεῷ, ὅ τι ποτέ ἐστι, νενοηκότες. πιστεύσατε ἡμῖν κἂν ὡς μέθῃ, ἵνα σωφρονήσητε· πιστεύσατε κἂν ὡς ὕβρει, ἵνα ζήσητε. εἰ δὲ καὶ πείθεσθαι βούλεσθε τὴν ἐναργῆ

---

[1] πείθεσθαι Sylburg.   πείθεσθε MSS.
[2] πίστιν, μάρτυρα ἀξιόχρεων Wilamowitz.   μάρτυρα ἀξιόχρεων, πίστιν MSS.
[3] [ζητεῖν] Mayor.   Stählin retains ζητεῖν, and inserts τὸ δ' ἀγαθὸν (Schwartz) before ἐκπονεῖν.
[4] ἢ Sylburg.   ἡ MSS.
[5] [δὴ] Stählin.
[6] δὴ Stählin.   δὲ MSS.

[a] Deuteronomy xxx. 15.   [b] Isaiah i. 19, 20.

your face," He says, "death and life." [a] The Lord
solicits you to choose life; He counsels you, as a
father, to obey God. "For if ye hearken to Me,"
He says, "and are willing, ye shall eat the good of
the land,"—the grace follows upon obedience. "But
if ye hearken not to Me, and are unwilling, a sword
and fire shall devour you,"—the judgment follows
upon disobedience. "For the mouth of the Lord
hath spoken it;" [b] and a word of the Lord is a law
of truth.

CHAP.
X

Would you have me become a good counsellor to
you? Then do you hearken; and I, if it be possible,
will show myself one. When reflecting upon the
good itself, you ought, my fellow-men, to have
called to your aid faith, implanted in man, which is
a trustworthy witness from within ourselves, with
the utmost clearness choosing what is best. [c] You
ought not to have toiled to discover whether or no
the best is to be followed. Let me give you
an illustration: you ought to doubt whether it is
right for a man to get drunk; but your practice is
to get drunk before considering the question. Or
in the case of riotous indulgence, you do not make
careful examination, but indulge yourselves with all
speed. Only, it would seem, when godliness is in
question, do you first inquire; and when it is a
question of following this wise God and the Christ,
this you think calls for deliberation and reflection,
when you have no idea what it is that befits God.
Put faith in us, even as you do in drunkenness, that
you may become sober. Put faith in us, even as
you do in riotous indulgence, that you may live.
And if, after having contemplated this clear faith

An inborn
faith shows
men what
is good

No long
inquiry is
needed

Men follow
desire, not
judgment,
in most
matters

Only in the
worship of
God do they
inquire
first

[c] Cp. Aristotle, *Eth. Nicom.* 1169 a 17 (p. 192 Bywater).

CLEMENT OF ALEXANDRIA

CAP. τῶν ἀρετῶν ἐποπτεύσαντες[1] πίστιν, φέρε ὑμῖν ἐκ
X περιουσίας τὴν περὶ τοῦ λόγου παραθήσομαι πειθώ.
ὑμεῖς δέ, οὐ γὰρ τὰ πάτρια ὑμᾶς ἔτι τῆς ἀληθείας
ἀπασχολεῖ ἔθη προκατηχημένους, ἀκούοιτ᾽ ἂν ἤδη
τὸ μετὰ τοῦτο ὅπως ἔχει· καὶ δὴ μή τις ὑμᾶς τοῦδε
τοῦ ὀνόματος αἰσχύνη προκαταλαμβανέτω, " ἥτ᾽
ἄνδρας μέγα σίνεται," παρατρέπουσα σωτηρίας.

Ἀποδυσάμενοι δ᾽ οὖν περιφανῶς ἐν τῷ τῆς
ἀληθείας σταδίῳ γνησίως ἀγωνιζώμεθα, βραβεύ-
οντος μὲν τοῦ λόγου τοῦ ἁγίου, ἀγωνοθετοῦντος δὲ
τοῦ δεσπότου τῶν ὅλων. οὐ γὰρ σμικρὸν ἡμῖν τὸ
ἄθλον ἀθανασία πρόκειται. μὴ οὖν ἔτι φροντίζετε
μηδὲ [εἰ][2] ὀλίγον, τί ὑμᾶς ἀγορεύουσι σύρφακές
τινες ἀγοραῖοι, δεισιδαιμονίας ἄθεοι χορευταί, ἀνοίᾳ
καὶ παρανοίᾳ ἐς αὐτὸ ὠθούμενοι τὸ βάραθρον,
εἰδώλων ποιηταὶ καὶ λίθων προσκυνηταί· οἴδε γὰρ
ἀνθρώπους ἀποθεοῦν τετολμήκασι, τρισκαιδέκατον
Ἀλέξανδρον τὸν Μακεδόνα ἀναγράφοντες θεόν, " ὃν
Βαβυλὼν ἤλεγξε νεκρόν." ἄγαμαι τοίνυν τὸν Χῖον[3]
σοφιστήν, Θεόκριτος ὄνομα αὐτῷ· μετὰ τὴν Ἀλεξ-
άνδρου τελευτὴν ἐπισκώπτων ὁ Θεόκριτος τὰς δόξας
τὰς κενὰς τῶν ἀνθρώπων ἃς εἶχον περὶ θεῶν, πρὸς
78 P. τοὺς πολίτας | " ἄνδρες," εἶπεν, " θαρρεῖτε ἄχρις
ἂν ὁρᾶτε τοὺς θεοὺς πρότερον τῶν ἀνθρώπων ἀπο-

---

[1] ἐποπτεύσαντες Potter. ὑποπτεύσαντες MSS.
[2] [εἰ] Kontos.   [3] Χῖον Cobet. θεῖον MSS.

---

[a] This seems to refer to the " implanted faith " mentioned
at the beginning of this paragraph. It may, perhaps, refer
only to the preceding sentence ; in which case we should
translate, " this clear proof of the virtues," *i.e.* the proof
derived from studying the lives of Christians.
  [b] Homer, *Iliad* xxiv. 45 ; Hesiod, *Works and Days* 318.
  [c] *Sibylline Oracles* v. 6. Alexander was called the

210

in the virtues,[a] you desire to be obedient, come then, I will lay before you in abundance persuasive arguments concerning the Word. On your part (for it is no longer the case that the ancestral customs, in which you have formerly been instructed, prevent you from attending to the truth), listen now, I pray you, to the nature of the words that follow. Moreover, let no feeling of shame for the name of Christian deter you; for shame " does great hurt to men," [b] when it turns them aside from salvation.

CHAP. X

But abundant arguments can be provided for him who desires to learn

Having then stripped before the eyes of all, let us join in the real contest in the arena of truth, where the holy Word is umpire, and the Master of the universe is president. For the prize set before us is no small one, immortality. Cease then to pay any further heed, even the slightest, to the speeches made to you by the rabble of the market-place, godless devotees of daemon-worship, men who are on the very verge of the pit through their folly and insanity, makers of idols and worshippers of stones. For these are they who have dared to deify men, describing Alexander of Macedon as the thirteenth god, though " Babylon proved him mortal." [c] Hence I admire the Chian sage, Theocritus by name, who in ridicule of the vain opinions which men held about gods, said to his fellow-citizens after the death of Alexander, " Keep a cheerful heart, comrades, so long as you see gods dying before men." [d] But

The true contest for the prize of immortality

The folly of daemon-worshippers, who called Alexander a god

How Theocritus of Chios ridiculed them

" thirteenth god " because his name was added to the twelve deities of Olympus, to whom Clement alludes on p. 53 of this volume.

[d] For this and other witty remarks attributed to Theocritus of Chios (quite a different person from the poet Theocritus) see *Frag. hist. Graec.* ii. p. 86.

CAP.
X

θνήσκοντας.'' θεοὺς δὲ δὴ τοὺς ὁρατοὺς καὶ τὸν σύγκλυδα τῶν γενητῶν τούτων ὄχλον ὁ προσκυνῶν καὶ προσεταιριζόμενος, αὐτῶν ἐκείνων τῶν δαιμόνων ἀθλιώτερος μακρῷ. θεὸς γὰρ οὐδαμῇ οὐδαμῶς ἄδικος ὥσπερ οἱ δαίμονες, ἀλλ' ὡς οἷόν τε δικαιότατος, καὶ οὐκ ἔστιν αὐτῷ ὁμοιότερον οὐδὲν ἢ ὃς ἂν ἡμῶν γένηται ὅτι δικαιότατος.

βᾶτ' εἰς ὁδὸν δὴ πᾶς ὁ χειρῶναξ λεώς,
οἳ τὴν Διὸς γοργῶπιν Ἐργάνην[1] θεὸν
στατοῖσι λίκνοις προστρέπεσθε,[2]

ἠλίθιοι τῶν λίθων δημιουργοί τε καὶ προσκυνηταί. ὁ Φειδίας ὑμῶν καὶ ὁ Πολύκλειτος ἡκόντων Πραξιτέλης τε αὖ καὶ Ἀπελλῆς καὶ ὅσοι τὰς βαναύσους μετέρχονται τέχνας, γήινοι γῆς ὄντες ἐργάται. τότε γὰρ φησί τις προφητεία δυστυχήσειν τὰ τῇδε πράγματα, ὅταν ἀνδριᾶσι πιστεύσωσιν. ἡκόντων οὖν αὖθις, οὐ γὰρ ἀνήσω καλῶν, οἱ μικροτέχναι. οὐδείς που τούτων ἔμπνουν εἰκόνα δεδημιούργηκεν, οὐδὲ μὴν ἐκ γῆς μαλθακὴν ἐμάλαξε σάρκα. τίς ἔτηξε μυελὸν ἢ τίς ἔπηξεν ὀστέα; τίς νεῦρα διέτεινεν[3]; τίς φλέβας ἐφύσησεν; τίς αἷμα ἐνέχεεν ἐν αὐταῖς ἢ τίς δέρμα περιέτεινεν; ποῦ δ' ἄν τις αὐτῶν ὀφθαλμοὺς ποιῆσαι βλέποντας; τίς ἐνεφύσησε ψυχήν; τίς δικαιοσύνην ἐδωρήσατο; τίς ἀθανασίαν ὑπέσχηται; μόνος ὁ τῶν ὅλων δημιουργός, ὁ '' ἀριστοτέχνας πατήρ,'' τοιοῦτον ἄγαλμα ἔμψυχον [ἡμᾶς][4] τὸν ἄνθρωπον ἔπλασεν· ὁ δὲ

---

[1] Ἐργάνην from Plutarch, *De Fortuna* 99 A. ἐργάπην MSS.
[2] προστρέπεσθε Plutarch. προτρέπεσθε MSS.
[3] διέτεινεν ἢ Wilamowitz.   [4] [ἡμᾶς] Mayor.

ᵃ Cp. Plato, *Theaetetus* 176 B-C.

indeed, as for gods that can be seen, and the motley CHAP.
multitude of these created things, the man who X
worships and consorts with them is far more wretched
than the very daemons themselves. For God is in
no way unrighteous as the daemons are, but righteous A righteous
in the highest possible degree, and there is nothing man is the
nearest
more like Him than any one of us who becomes as approach
to God
righteous as possible.[a]

> Go forth into the way, ye craftsmen all,
> Who supplicate, with winnowing fans aloft,
> The goddess Industry, stern child of Zeus,[b]

—stupid fashioners and worshippers of stones! Let
your Pheidias and Polycleitus come hither, Praxiteles The crafts-
too, and Apelles, and all the others who pursue the men's work
is paltry,
mechanical arts, mere earthly workers in earth. For when com-
a certain prophecy says that misfortune shall over- pared with
God's
take this world of ours, on the day when men put
their trust in statues.[c] Let them come then, I say
again,—for I will not cease to call,—puny artists that
they are. Not one of them has ever fashioned a
breathing image, or made tender flesh out of earth.
Who gave its softness to the marrow? Who fixed
the bones? Who stretched out the sinews? Who
inflated the arteries? Who poured blood into them
and drew the skin around? How could any of these
men make eyes that see? Who breathed life into
man? Who gave him the sense of right? Who
has promised immortality? None but the Creator
of the universe, the " Father, the supreme artist," [d]
formed such a living statue as man; but your

[b] Sophocles, Frag. 760 Nauck. The goddess "Industry,"
whom the craftsmen worshipped in their processions, is
Athena. See Plutarch, *De Fortuna* 99 A.

[c] The source of this quotation is unknown.

[d] See Pindar, Frag. 57 Schroeder.

213

CAP.
X

Ὀλύμπιος ὑμῶν, εἰκόνος εἰκών, πολύ τι τῆς ἀληθείας ἀπᾴδων, ἔργον ἐστὶ κωφὸν χειρῶν Ἀττικῶν. " εἰκὼν " μὲν γὰρ " τοῦ θεοῦ " ὁ λόγος αὐτοῦ (καὶ υἱὸς τοῦ νοῦ γνήσιος ὁ θεῖος λόγος, φωτὸς ἀρχέτυπον φῶς), εἰκὼν δὲ τοῦ λόγου ὁ ἄνθρωπος ‹ὁ›[1] ἀληθινός, ὁ νοῦς ὁ ἐν ἀνθρώπῳ, ὁ " κατ᾽ εἰκόνα " τοῦ θεοῦ καὶ " καθ᾽ ὁμοίωσιν " διὰ τοῦτο γεγενῆσθαι λεγόμενος, τῇ κατὰ καρδίαν φρονήσει τῷ θείῳ παρεικαζόμενος λόγῳ καὶ ταύτῃ λογικός. ἀνθρώπου δὲ τοῦ ὁρωμένου τοῦ γηγενοῦς γήινος εἰκὼν τὰ ἀγάλματα τὰ ἀνδρείκελα ‹καὶ›[2] πόρρω τῆς ἀληθείας ἐπίκαιρον ἐκμαγεῖον καταφαίνεται. οὐδὲν οὖν ἀλλ᾽ ἢ μανίας ἔμπλεως ὁ βίος ἔδοξέ μοι γεγονέναι, τοσαύτῃ σπουδῇ περὶ τὴν ὕλην καταγινόμενος.

Ἐπιτέθραπται[3] δὲ ὑπὸ κενῆς δόξης ἡ συνήθεια δουλείας μὲν γεύσασα ὑμᾶς καὶ ἀλόγου περιεργασίας· νομίμων δὲ ἀνόμων καὶ ἀπατηλῶν ὑποκρίσεων ἄγνοια αἰτία, ἣ δὴ κατασκευὰς εἰσάγουσα εἰς[4] τὸ τῶν ἀνθρώπων γένος κηρῶν ὀλεθρίων καὶ εἰδώλων ἐπιστυγῶν πολλὰς τῶν δαιμόνων ἐπινοήσασα μορφάς, κηλῖδα τοῖς ἑπομένοις αὐτῇ ἐναπεμάξατο θανάτου μακροῦ. λάβετε οὖν ὕδωρ λογικόν, λούσασθε οἱ μεμολυσμένοι, περιρράνατε αὑτοὺς ἀπὸ τῆς συνηθείας ταῖς ἀληθιναῖς σταγόσιν· καθαροὺς εἰς οὐρανοὺς ἀναβῆναι δεῖ. ἄνθρωπος εἶ, τὸ κοινότατον, ἐπιζήτησον τὸν δημιουργήσαντά σε·

---

[1] ‹ὁ› inserted by Mayor.　　[2] ‹καὶ› inserted by Wilamowitz.

[3] ἐπιτέθραπται Mayor. ἐπιτέτριπται MSS.

[4] κατασκευὰς εἰσάγουσα εἰς Schwartz. κατασκευσθεῖσα MSS.
Stählin marks the passage as corrupt.

---

[a] A reminiscence of the Platonic theory of ideas, in which there are three stages of reality : first, the archetypal idea ; secondly, the object, which is a visible expression and a

214

Olympian Zeus, an image of an image, far removed from the truth,[a] is a dumb lifeless work of Attic hands. For "the image of God" is His Word (and the divine Word, the light who is the archetype of light, is a genuine son of Mind[b]); and an image of the Word is the true man, that is, the mind in man, who on this account is said to have been created "in the image" of God, and "in His likeness,"[c] because through his understanding heart he is made like the divine Word or Reason, and so reasonable. But statues in human form, being an earthen image of visible, earthborn man, and far away from the truth, plainly show themselves to be but a temporary impression upon matter. In my opinion, then, nothing else but madness has taken possession of life, when it spends itself with so much earnestness upon matter.

Now custom, in having given you a taste of slavery and of irrational attention to trifles, has been fostered by idle opinion. But lawless rites and deceptive ceremonies have for their cause ignorance; for it is ignorance that brought to mankind the apparatus of fateful destruction and detestable idolatry, when it devised many forms for the daemons, and stamped the mark of a lasting death upon those who followed its guidance. Receive then the water of reason. Be washed, ye that are defiled. Sprinkle yourselves from the stain of custom by the drops that truly cleanse. We must be pure to ascend to heaven. In common with others, thou art a man; seek after Him who created thee. In thine own

(margin notes) CHAP. X — The image of God is his Word — The true man, *i.e.* man's mind, is an image of the Word — Statues are but images of man's body, far from the truth — Ignorance is the cause of idolatrous rites

particular instance of the idea; thirdly, the picture, which is but a representation of the object, nothing more than the image of an image, three stages removed from reality.
[b] *i.e.* the Father. Cp. v. *Strom.* 8. 7.   [c] Genesis i. 26.

CAP.
X

υἱὸς εἶ, τὸ ἰδιαίτατον, ἀναγνώρισον τὸν πατέρα· σὺ δὲ ἔτι ταῖς ἁμαρτίαις παραμένεις, προστετηκὼς ἡδοναῖς; τίνι λαλήσει κύριος "ὑμῶν ἐστιν ἡ βασιλεία τῶν οὐρανῶν"; ὑμῶν ἐστιν, ἐὰν θελήσητε, τῶν πρὸς τὸν θεὸν τὴν προαίρεσιν ἐσχηκότων· ὑμῶν, ἐὰν ἐθελήσητε πιστεῦσαι μόνον καὶ τῇ συντομίᾳ τοῦ κηρύγματος ἔπεσθαι, ἧς ὑπακούσαντες οἱ Νινευῖται τῆς προσδοκηθείσης ἁλώσεως μετανοίᾳ γνησίῳ τὴν καλὴν ἀντικατηλλάξαντο σωτηρίαν.

Πῶς οὖν ἀνέλθω, φησίν, εἰς οὐρανούς; "ὁδός" ἐστιν ὁ κύριος, "στενὴ" μέν, ἀλλ' "ἐξ οὐρανῶν," στενὴ μέν, ἀλλ' εἰς οὐρανοὺς ἀναπέμπουσα· στενὴ ἐπὶ γῆς ὑπερορωμένη, πλατεῖα ἐν οὐρανοῖς προσ-κυνουμένη. εἶθ' ὁ μὲν ἄπυστος τοῦ λόγου συγγνώμην τῆς πλάνης ἔχει τὴν ἄγνοιαν, ὁ δὲ εἰς ὦτα βαλλόμενος καὶ τῇ ψυχῇ παρὰ τῆς γνώμης φέρει τὴν ἀπείθειαν, καὶ ὅσῳ γε φρονιμώτερος εἶναι δόξει, πρὸς κακοῦ ἡ σύνεσις αὐτῷ, ὅτι τῇ φρονήσει κέχρηται κατηγόρῳ
80 P. τὸ βέλτιστον | οὐχ ἑλόμενος· πέφυκε γὰρ ὡς[1] ἄνθρω-πος οἰκείως ἔχειν πρὸς θεόν. ὥσπερ οὖν τὸν ἵππον ἀροῦν οὐ βιαζόμεθα οὐδὲ τὸν ταῦρον κυνηγετεῖν, πρὸς ὃ πέφυκε δὲ ἕκαστον τῶν ζῴων περιέλκομεν, οὕτως ἀμέλει καὶ τὸν ἄνθρωπον ἐπὶ τὴν οὐρανοῦ γενόμενον θέαν, φυτὸν οὐράνιον ὡς ἀληθῶς, ἐπὶ τὴν γνῶσιν παρακαλοῦμεν τοῦ θεοῦ, τὸ οἰκεῖον αὐτοῦ καὶ ἐξαίρετον καὶ ἰδιωματικὸν παρὰ τὰ ἄλλα ζῷα κατειλημμένοι, αὔταρκες ἐφόδιον αἰώνων, θεοσέ-

---

[1] ὡς Schwartz.   ἄλλως MSS.

---

[a] St. Matthew v. 3, 10 ; St. Luke vi. 20.
[b] Compare p. 172, n. *d*.
[c] Jonah iii. 5, 10.   [d] St. John xiv. 6.
[e] St. Matthew vii. 13, 14 ; St. John iii. 13, 31.

self thou art a son; recognize thy Father. But thou, dost thou still abide by thy sins, engrossed in pleasures? To whom shall the Lord say, "Yours is the kingdom of heaven?"[a] It is yours, if you wish, for it belongs to those who have their will set upon God. It is yours, if you are willing simply to trust and to follow the short way of our preaching.[b] This it is which the Ninevites obediently heard; and by sincere repentance they received, in place of the threatened destruction, that glorious salvation.[c]

CHAP. X
God and His kingdom are ours if we will

"How then," you may say, "am I to go up into heaven?" The Lord is "the Way"[d]; a "narrow" way, but coming "from heaven"; a "narrow" way, but leading back to heaven.[e] It is narrow, being despised upon earth; and yet broad, being adored in heaven. Accordingly he who has never heard the Word can plead ignorance as an excuse for his error; whereas he whose ears ring with the message deliberately nurses his disobedience in the soul itself; and, the wiser he may seem to be, his intelligence ever proves a source of evil, because he finds wisdom an accuser, once he has failed to choose what is best. For it is his nature, as man, to be in close fellowship with God. As, then, we do not force the horse to plough, nor the bull to hunt, but lead each animal to its natural work; for the very same reason we call upon man, who was made for the contemplation of heaven, and is in truth a heavenly plant, to come to the knowledge of God. Having laid hold of what is personal, special and peculiar in his nature, that wherein he surpasses the other animals, we counsel him to equip himself with godliness, as a sufficient provision for

The Lord is "the Way"

Ignorance is an excuse only for him who has not heard

Man is made for God

CLEMENT OF ALEXANDRIA

βειαν, παρασκευάζεσθαι συμβουλεύοντες. γεώργει,
φαμέν, εἰ γεωργὸς εἶ, ἀλλὰ γνῶθι τὸν θεὸν γεωρ-
γῶν, καὶ πλεῖθι [1] ὁ τῆς ναυτιλίας ἐρῶν, ἀλλὰ τὸν
οὐράνιον κυβερνήτην παρακαλῶν· στρατευόμενόν
σε κατείληφεν ἡ γνῶσις· τοῦ δίκαια σημαίνοντος
ἄκουε στρατηγοῦ.

Καθάπερ οὖν κάρῳ καὶ μέθῃ βεβαρημένοι ἀνα-
νήψατε καὶ διαβλέψαντες ὀλίγον ἐννοήθητε, τί
θέλουσιν ὑμῖν οἱ προσκυνούμενοι λίθοι καὶ ἃ περὶ
τὴν ὕλην κενοσπούδως δαπανᾶτε· εἰς ἄγνοιαν καὶ
τὰ χρήματα καὶ τὸν βίον ὡς τὸ ζῆν ὑμῶν εἰς
θάνατον καταναλίσκετε, τοῦτο μόνον τῆς ματαίας
ὑμῶν ἐλπίδος εὑρόμενοι τὸ πέρας, οὐδὲ αὑτοὺς οἷοί
τε ὄντες οἰκτεῖραι, ἀλλ' οὐδὲ τοῖς κατελεῶσιν ὑμᾶς
τῆς πλάνης ἐπιτήδειοι πείθεσθαι γίνεσθε, συνηθείᾳ
κακῇ δεδουλωμένοι, ἧς ἀπηρτημένοι αὐθαίρετοι
μέχρι τῆς ἐσχάτης ἀναπνοῆς εἰς ἀπώλειαν ὑπο-
φέρεσθε· " ὅτι τὸ φῶς ἐλήλυθεν εἰς τὸν κόσμον καὶ
ἠγάπησαν οἱ ἄνθρωποι μᾶλλον τὸ σκότος ἢ τὸ
φῶς," [a] ἐξὸν ἀπομάξασθαι τὰ ἐμποδὼν τῇ σωτηρίᾳ
καὶ τὸν τῦφον καὶ τὸν πλοῦτον καὶ τὸν φόβον,
ἐπιφθεγγομένους τὸ ποιητικὸν δὴ τοῦτο

> πῇ δὴ χρήματα πολλὰ φέρω τάδε; πῇ δὲ καὶ αὐτὸς
> πλάζομαι; [b]

οὐ βούλεσθε οὖν τὰς φαντασίας ταύτας τὰς κενὰς
ἀπορρίψαντες τῇ συνηθείᾳ αὐτῇ ἀποτάξασθαι, κενοδοξίᾳ ἐπιλέγοντες·

> ψευδεῖς ὄνειροι χαίρετ', οὐδὲν ἦτ' ἄρα;

---

[1] πλεῖθι Sylburg.   πλῆθι mss.

[a] St. John iii. 19.   [b] Homer, *Odyssey* xiii. 203-4.

his journey through eternity. Till the ground, we say, if you are a husbandman; but recognize God in your husbandry. Sail the sea, you who love sea-faring; but ever call upon the heavenly pilot. Were you a soldier on campaign when the knowledge of God laid hold of you? Then listen to the commander who signals righteousness.

Ye men that are weighed down as with torpor and drink, awake to soberness. Look about you and consider a little what is the meaning of your worship of stones, and of all that you squander with useless zeal upon mere matter. You are wasting both money and livelihood upon ignorance, just as you are wasting your very life upon death. For nothing but death have you gained as the end of your vain hope. You cannot pity yourselves, — nay, you are not even in a fit state to be persuaded by those who have compassion upon you for your error. Enslaved to pernicious custom, you cling to it of your own free will until the latest breath, and sink down into destruction. "For the light has come into the world, and men loved the darkness rather than the light," [a] though they might sweep away the hindrances to salvation, absurd folly and riches and fear, by repeating this verse of the poet:

Whither this wealth do I bear; my journey, where doth it lead me? [b]

Do you not then wish to fling away these vain fancies, and bid good-bye to custom itself, saying these last words to vain opinion?—

Farewell, deceitful dreams; for ye were nought. [c]

---

[c] Euripides, *Iphigeneia among the Taurians* 569.

CAP.
X
81 P.

Τί γὰρ ἡγεῖσθε, ὦ ἄνθρωποι, τὸν Τύχωνα[1] |
Ἑρμῆν καὶ τὸν Ἀνδοκίδου[2] καὶ τὸν Ἀμύητον; ἢ
παντί τῳ δῆλον ὅτι λίθους, ὥσπερ καὶ ⟨αὐτὸν⟩[3] τὸν
Ἑρμῆν. ὡς δὲ οὐκ ἔστι θεὸς ἡ ἅλως καὶ ὡς οὐκ
ἔστι θεὸς ἡ ἶρις, ἀλλὰ πάθη ἀέρος[4] καὶ νεφῶν, καὶ
ὃν τρόπον οὐκ ἔστιν ἡμέρα θεός, οὐδὲ μὴν οὐδὲ
ἐνιαυτὸς οὐδὲ χρόνος ὁ ἐκ τούτων συμπληρού-
μενος, οὕτως οὐδὲ ἥλιος οὐδὲ σελήνη, οἷς ἕκαστον
τῶν προειρημένων διορίζεται. τίς ἂν οὖν τὴν
εὔθυναν καὶ τὴν κόλασιν καὶ τὴν δίκην καὶ τὴν
νέμεσιν εὖ φρονῶν ὑπολάβοι θεούς; οὐδὲ γὰρ
οὐδ' ἐρινῦς οὐδὲ μοῖραι οὐδὲ εἱμαρμένη, ἐπεὶ μηδὲ
πολιτεία μηδὲ δόξα μηδὲ πλοῦτος θεοί, ὃν καὶ
ζωγράφοι τυφλὸν ἐπιδεικνύουσιν· εἰ δὲ αἰδῶ καὶ
ἔρωτα καὶ ἀφροδίτην ἐκθειάζετε, ἀκολουθούντων
αὐτοῖς αἰσχύνη καὶ ὁρμὴ καὶ κάλλος καὶ συνουσία.
οὔκουν ἔτ' ἂν εἰκότως ὕπνος καὶ θάνατος θεὼ
διδυμάονε παρ' ὑμῖν νομίζοιντο, πάθη ταῦτα περὶ
τὰ ζῷα συμβαίνοντα φυσικῶς· οὐδὲ μὴν κῆρα
οὐδὲ εἱμαρμένην οὐδὲ μοίρας θεὰς ἐνδίκως ἐρεῖτε.
εἰ δὲ ἔρις καὶ μάχη οὐ θεοί, οὐδὲ Ἄρης οὐδὲ
Ἐννώ. ἔτι τε ⟨εἰ⟩[5] αἱ ἀστραπαὶ καὶ οἱ κεραυνοὶ
καὶ οἱ ὄμβροι οὐ θεοί, πῶς τὸ πῦρ καὶ τὸ ὕδωρ

---

[1] Τύχωνα Meurs (see Hesychius *s.v.*). τυφῶνα MSS.
[2] Ἀνδοκίδου Heinsius. ἀνδοκίδην MSS.
[3] ⟨αὐτὸν⟩ inserted by Mayor.
[4] ἀέρος Markland. ἀέρων MSS.   [5] ⟨εἰ⟩ inserted by Sylburg.

---

[a] The Hermes was a stone pillar ending in a bust, which
was set up in fields and roads as a landmark, and also before
the doors of Athenian houses. An essential part of the
figure was a phallus, which points to Hermes being originally
a fertility god. He was, therefore, easily identified with
Tycho, an Attic nature divinity of similar character to

EXHORTATION TO THE GREEKS

Why, my fellow-men, do you believe in Hermes

Why, my fellow-men, do you believe in Hermes Tycho and in the Hermes of Andocides and the one called Amyetus?[a] Surely it is plain to everyone that they are stones, just as Hermes himself. And as the halo is not a god, nor the rainbow either, but conditions of the atmosphere and clouds; and precisely as day is not a god, nor month, nor year, nor time which is made up of these; so also neither is the sun or moon, by which each of the before-mentioned periods is marked off. Who then in his right mind would imagine such things as audit, punishment, right and retribution to be gods? No, nor even the Avengers, nor the Fates, nor destiny are gods; for neither is the State, nor glory, nor wealth, the last of which painters represent as blind. If you deify modesty, desire and love, you must add to them shame, impulse, beauty and sexual intercourse. No longer, then, can sleep and death be reasonably held among you to be twin gods, since these are conditions which naturally affect all animals; nor indeed will you rightly say that doom, destiny, or the Fates are goddesses. And if strife and battle are not gods, neither are Ares and Enyo. Further, if flashes of lightning, thunderbolts and showers of rain are not gods, how can fire and water be such?

CHAP. X

Statues are plainly nothing but stones

The absurdity of deifying passions and affections

Priapus (Diodorus iv. 6; Strabo 588). For the identification see Hesychius *s.v.*, and A. B. Cook, *Zeus*, i. pp. 175–6. In 415 B.C., just before the sailing of the expedition to Sicily, all the Hermae in Athens were mutilated except one, which stood in front of the house of Andocides and was called the " Hermes of Andocides " (Plutarch, *Nicias* xiii.). The account of the excitement caused by this outrage, and the accusation made against Andocides, is found in Thucydides vi. 27, and in Andocides, *On the Mysteries*. The Hermes Amyetus was, according to Hesychius, on the Acropolis at Athens.

221

CAP.
X

θεοί; πῶς δὲ καὶ οἱ διάσσοντες καὶ οἱ κομῆται
διὰ πάθος ἀέρος γεγενημένοι; ὁ δὲ τὴν τύχην θεὸν
λέγων καὶ τὴν πρᾶξιν λεγέτω θεόν. εἰ δὴ οὖν
τούτων οὐδὲ ἓν θεὸς εἶναι νομίζεται οὐδὲ μὴν
ἐκείνων τῶν χειροκμήτων καὶ ἀναισθήτων πλασμά-
των, πρόνοια δέ τις περὶ ἡμᾶς καταφαίνεται δυνάμεως θεϊκῆς, λείπεται οὐδὲν ἄλλο ἢ τοῦτο ὁμολογεῖν,
ὅτι ἄρα ὄντως μόνος ἔστι τε καὶ ὑφέστηκεν ὁ μόνος
ὄντως ὑπάρχων θεός.

ʼΑλλὰ γὰρ μανδραγόραν ἤ τι ἄλλο φάρμακον
πεπωκόσιν ἀνθρώποις ἐοίκατε οἱ[1] ἀνόητοι, θεὸς δὲ
ὑμῖν ἀνανῆψαι δοίη ποτὲ τοῦδε τοῦ ὕπνου καὶ
συνιέναι θεὸν μηδὲ χρυσὸν ἢ λίθον ἢ δένδρον ἢ
πρᾶξιν ἢ πάθος ἢ νόσον ἢ φόβον ἰνδάλλεσθαι ὡς
θεόν. "τρὶς γὰρ μύριοί εἰσιν" ὡς ἀληθῶς "ἐπὶ
χθονὶ πουλυβοτείρῃ δαίμονες" οὐκ "ἀθάνατοι"
οὐδὲ μὴν θνητοί (οὐδὲ γὰρ αἰσθήσεως, ἵνα καὶ
θανάτου, μετειλήφασιν), λίθινοι δὲ καὶ ξύλινοι δεσπόται ἀνθρώπων, ὑβρίζοντες καὶ παρασπονδοῦντες
82 P. τὸν βίον διὰ τῆς | συνηθείας. "ἡ γῆ δὲ τοῦ κυρίου,"
φησί, "καὶ τὸ πλήρωμα αὐτῆς·" εἶτα τί τολμᾷς
ἐν τοῖς τοῦ κυρίου τρυφῶν ἀγνοεῖν τὸν δεσπότην;
κατάλειπε τὴν γῆν τὴν ἐμήν, ἐρεῖ σοι ὁ κύριος, μὴ
θίγῃς τοῦ ὕδατος ὃ ἐγὼ ἀναδίδωμι, τῶν καρπῶν
ὧν ἐγὼ γεωργῶ μὴ μεταλάμβανε· ἀπόδος, ἄνθρωπε, τὰ τροφεῖα τῷ θεῷ· ἐπίγνωθί σου τὸν
δεσπότην· ἴδιον εἶ πλάσμα τοῦ θεοῦ· τὸ δὲ οἰκεῖον
αὐτοῦ πῶς ἂν ἐνδίκως ἀλλότριον γένοιτο; τὸ γὰρ

[1] ἐοίκατε οἱ Schwartz. ἐοίκασιν MSS.

a Hesiod: quoted above, p. 89.

222

How, too, can shooting stars and comets, which come about owing to some condition of the atmosphere? Let him who calls fortune a god, call action a god also. If then we do not believe even one of these to be a god, nor yet one of those figures made by hand and devoid of feeling, but there is manifest round about us a certain providence of divine power, then nothing remains save to confess that, after all, the sole truly existing God is the only one who really is and subsists.

We must then confess that there is but one true God

But verily, you who do not understand are like men that have drunk of mandrake or some other drug. God grant that one day you may recover from this slumber and perceive God, and that neither gold nor stone nor tree nor action nor suffering nor disease nor fear may appear to you as God. For it is quite true that "there are thrice ten thousand daemons upon all-nourishing earth," but they are not "immortal" as the poet says.[a] No, nor yet mortal,— for they do not partake of feeling, and therefore cannot partake of death,—but they are stone and wooden masters of mankind, who insult and violate human life through custom. It is written, "The earth is the Lord's, and the fulness thereof."[b] Then how do you dare, while enjoying the delights of the Lord's possessions, to ignore their Master? Leave My earth, the Lord will say to you; touch not the water I send forth; partake not of the fruits My husbandry produces. Give back, O man, to God the recompense for your nurture. Acknowledge your Master. You are God's own handiwork; and how could that which is His peculiar possession rightly become another's? For that which is alienated,

They who think otherwise are in some deep sleep

Daemons are not immortal

They are not even mortal, but lifeless stones

Man belongs to God; how can he become another's?

[b] Psalm xxiv. 1.

223

CLEMENT OF ALEXANDRIA

ἀπηλλοτριωμένον στερόμενον τῆς οἰκειότητος στέρε
ται τῆς ἀληθείας. ἢ γὰρ οὐχ ἡ Νιόβη τρόπον τινά,
μᾶλλον δὲ ἵνα μυστικώτερον πρὸς ὑμᾶς ἀποφθέγ
ξωμαι, γυναικὸς τῆς Ἑβραίας δίκην (Λὼτ ἐκάλουν
αὐτὴν οἱ παλαιοὶ) εἰς ἀναισθησίαν μετατρέπεσθε;
λελιθωμένην ταύτην παρειλήφαμεν τὴν γυναῖκα διὰ
τὸ Σοδόμων ἐρᾶν· Σοδομῖται δὲ οἱ ἄθεοι καὶ οἱ
πρὸς τὴν ἀσέβειαν ἐπιστρεφόμενοι σκληροκάρδιοί
τε καὶ ἠλίθιοι. ταύτας οἵου θεόθεν ἐπιλέγεσθαί
σοι τὰς φωνάς· μὴ γὰρ οἵου λίθους μὲν εἶναι
ἱερὰ καὶ ξύλα καὶ ὄρνεα καὶ ὄφεις, ἀνθρώπους
δὲ μή· πολὺ δὲ τοὐναντίον ἱερούς μὲν ὄντως
τοὺς ἀνθρώπους ὑπολάμβανε,[1] τὰ δὲ θηρία καὶ τοὺς
λίθους ὅπερ εἰσίν. οἱ γάρ τοι δείλαιοι τῶν ἀνθρώ
πων καὶ ἄθλιοι διὰ μὲν κόρακος καὶ κολοιοῦ
νομίζουσι τὸν θεὸν ἐμβοᾶν, διὰ δὲ ἀνθρώπου σιωπᾶν,
καὶ τὸν μὲν κόρακα τετιμήκασιν ὡς ἄγγελον θεοῦ,
τὸν δὲ ἄνθρωπον τοῦ θεοῦ διώκουσιν, οὐ κρώζοντα,
οὐ κλώζοντα, φθεγγόμενον δέ· οἴμοι, λογικῶς καὶ
φιλανθρώπως κατηχοῦντα ἀποσφάττειν ἀπανθρώ
πως ἐπιχειροῦσιν, ἐπὶ τὴν δικαιοσύνην καλοῦντα,
οὔτε τὴν χάριν τὴν ἄνωθεν ἀπεκδεχόμενοι οὔτε τὴν
κόλασιν ἐκτρεπόμενοι. οὐ γὰρ πιστεύουσι τῷ θεῷ
οὐδὲ ἐκμανθάνουσι τὴν δύναμιν αὐτοῦ.

Οὗ δὲ ἄρρητος ἡ φιλανθρωπία, τούτου ἀχώρητος
ἡ μισοπονηρία. τρέφει δὲ ὁ μὲν θυμὸς τὴν κόλασιν
ἐπὶ ἁμαρτίᾳ, εὖ ποιεῖ δὲ ἐπὶ μετανοίᾳ ἡ φιλανθρωπία.
οἰκτρότατον δὲ τὸ στέρεσθαι τῆς παρὰ τοῦ θεοῦ
ἐπικουρίας. ὀμμάτων μὲν οὖν ἡ πήρωσις καὶ τῆς

---

[1] ὑπολάμβανε Markland.   ὑπολαμβάνετε mss.

[a] Genesis xix. 26.   [b] Or, an angel.

being deprived of its connexion with Him, is deprived of the truth. Are you not turned into a state of insensibility after the manner of Niobe, or rather—to address you in more mystical language—like the Hebrew woman whom the ancient people called Lot's wife? This woman, tradition tells us, was turned into stone on account of her love of Sodom; [a] and by Sodomites we understand the atheists and those who are devoted to impiety, who are both hard of heart and without sense. Believe that these utterances are being spoken to you from heaven. Do not believe that stones and stocks and birds and snakes are sacred things, while men are not. Far rather regard men as really sacred, and take beasts and stones for what they are. For indeed the timid and wretched among men believe that God cries out through a raven or a jackdaw, but is silent through man; and they have given honour to the raven as a messenger [b] of God, while they persecute the man of God, who neither caws, nor croaks, but speaks. Yes, alas! they set to work with inhuman hatred to slaughter him when he instructs them with reason and human love, and calls them to righteousness, while they neither look for the grace that comes from above, nor do they seek to avoid the punishment. For they do not trust in God, nor do they fully understand His power.

But He whose love for man is unspeakably great, has also an unbounded hatred for sin. His wrath breeds the punishment to follow upon sin; on the other hand, His love for man brings blessings upon repentance. It is a most pitiable thing to be deprived of the help that comes from God. Now the blinding of the eyes and deafening of the ears are more

CHAP. X
Men who worship stones become like stones

The really sacred things are men

God's messages come through men, not through birds

God hates sin, and will punish it

CAP.
X

ἀκοῆς ἡ κώφωσις ἀλγεινοτέρα παρὰ τὰς λοιπὰς
τοῦ πονηροῦ πλεονεξίας· ἡ μὲν γὰρ αὐτῶν ἀφῄρηται
τῆς οὐρανίου προσόψεως, ἡ δὲ τῆς θείας μαθήσεως
ἐστέρηται. ὑμεῖς δὲ πρὸς τὴν ἀλήθειαν ἀνάπηροι
καὶ τυφλοὶ μὲν τὸν νοῦν, κωφοὶ δὲ τὴν σύνεσιν
ὄντες οὐκ ἀλγεῖτε, οὐκ ἀγανακτεῖτε, οὐ τὸν οὐρανὸν

83 P. ἰδεῖν καὶ τὸν τοῦ οὐρανοῦ ποιητὴν | ἐπεθυμήσατε,
οὐδὲ τὸν τῶν πάντων δημιουργὸν καὶ πατέρα
ἀκοῦσαι καὶ μαθεῖν ἐξεζητήσατε, τὴν προαίρεσιν
τῇ σωτηρίᾳ συνάψαντες; ἐμποδὼν γὰρ ἵσταται
οὐδὲν τῷ σπεύδοντι πρὸς γνῶσιν θεοῦ, οὐκ ἀπαιδευσία,[1] οὐ πενία, οὐκ ἀδοξία, οὐκ ἀκτημοσύνη·
οὐδέ τις τὴν ὄντως ἀληθῆ σοφίαν " χαλκῷ δῃώσας "
μεταλλάξαι εὔχεται οὐδὲ σιδήρῳ· εὖ γάρ τοι παντὸς
μᾶλλον τοῦτο εἴρηται·

ὁ χρηστός[2] ἐστι πανταχοῦ σωτήριος·

ὁ γὰρ τοῦ δικαίου ζηλωτής, ὡς ἂν τοῦ ἀνενδεοῦς
ἐραστής, ὀλιγοδεής, οὐκ ἐν ἄλλῳ τινὶ ἢ ἐν αὐτῷ
[καὶ][3] τῷ θεῷ τὸ μακάριον θησαυρίσας, ἔνθα οὐ σής,
οὐ λῃστής, οὐ πειρατής, ἀλλ' ὁ τῶν ἀγαθῶν ἀίδιος
δοτήρ. ἆρα οὖν εἰκότως ὡμοιώθητε τοῖς ὄφεσιν
ἐκείνοις, οἷς τὰ ὦτα πρὸς τοὺς κατεπάδοντας ἀπο-
κέκλεισται. " θυμὸς γὰρ αὐτοῖς," φησὶν ἡ γραφή,
" κατὰ τὴν ὁμοίωσιν τοῦ ὄφεως, ὡσεὶ ἀσπίδος
κωφῆς καὶ βυούσης τὰ ὦτα αὐτῆς, ἥτις οὐκ εἰσ-

---

[1] ἀπαιδευσία Hopfenmüller. ἀπαιδία MSS.
[2] χρηστός Blass (from Stobaeus, *Flor.* 37. 6). χριστός MSS.
[3] [καὶ] Barnard. ἐν αὐτῷ καὶ Dindorf.

---

[a] Homer, *Iliad* viii. 534. The phrase, well known, no
doubt, to Clement's first readers, is used metaphorically.
Cp. the " sword of the Spirit " in Ephesians vi. 17. The

226

grievous than all the other encroachments of the evil one; for by the first of these we are robbed of the sight of heaven, and by the second we are deprived of the divine teaching. But you, though maimed in respect of the truth, darkened in mind and deaf in understanding, still are not grieved, are not pained, have felt no longing to see heaven and its maker, nor have you sought diligently to hear and to know the Creator and Father of the universe, by fixing your choice on salvation. For nothing stands in the way of him who earnestly desires to come to the knowledge of God, not want of instruction, not penury, not obscurity, not poverty. And when a man has "conquered by brass," [a] or by iron either, the really true wisdom, he does not seek to change it. Indeed no finer word has ever been said than this:

> In every act the good man seeks to save. [b]

For he who is zealous for the right, as one would expect from a lover of Him who is in need of nothing, is himself in need of but little, because he has stored up his blessedness with none other than God Himself, where is no moth, no robber, no pirate, [c] but only the eternal giver of good things. With good reason, therefore, have you been likened to those serpents whose ears are closed to the enchanters. "For their heart," the Scripture says, "is after the likeness of the serpent, even like an adder that is deaf and stoppeth her ears, who will not give heed to the

(marginal notes)
CHAP. X
To be blind and deaf to truth is the worst of all evils

The way to God is open to all

But some are like deaf adders, who listen to no persuasion

earthly warrior is ever bent on fresh conquests and spoils: the spiritual warrior finds "the true wisdom" a sufficient prize, and seeks to save others rather than to destroy.

[b] Menander, Frag. 786 Kock, *Comic. Att. Frag.* iii. p. 217.
[c] See St. Matthew vi. 19, 20.

CAP.
X
ἀκούσεται φωνῆς ἐπᾳδόντων.'' ἀλλ' ὑμεῖς γε κατεπᾴσθητε τὴν ἀγριότητα[1] καὶ παραδέξασθε τὸν ἥμερον καὶ ἡμέτερον λόγον καὶ τὸν ἰὸν ἀποπτύσατε τὸν δηλητήριον, ὅπως ὅτι μάλιστα ὑμῖν τὴν φθοράν, ὡς ἐκείνοις τὸ γῆρας, ἀποδύσασθαι δοθῇ.

Ἀκούσατέ μου καὶ μὴ τὰ ὦτα ἀποβύσητε μηδὲ τὰς ἀκοὰς ἀποφράξητε, ἀλλ' εἰς νοῦν βάλεσθε τὰ λεγόμενα. καλόν ἐστι τὸ φάρμακον τῆς ἀθανασίας· στήσατέ ποτε τοὺς ὁλκοὺς τοὺς ἑρπηστικούς. '' οἱ γὰρ ἐχθροὶ κυρίου χοῦν λείξουσι,'' φησίν [ἡ γραφὴ λέγει][2]· ἀνανεύσατε τῆς γῆς εἰς αἰθέρα, ἀναβλέψατε εἰς οὐρανόν, θαυμάσατε, παύσασθε καραδοκοῦντες τῶν δικαίων τὴν πτέρναν καὶ '' τὴν ὁδὸν τῆς ἀληθείας'' ἐμποδίζοντες· φρόνιμοι γένεσθε καὶ ἀβλαβεῖς· τάχα που ὁ κύριος ἁπλότητος ὑμῖν δωρήσεται πτερόν (πτερῶσαι προῄρηται τοὺς γηγενεῖς), ἵνα δὴ τοὺς χηραμοὺς καταλείποντες οἰκήσητε τοὺς οὐρανούς. μόνον ἐξ ὅλης καρδίας μετανοήσωμεν, ὡς ὅλῃ καρδίᾳ δυνηθῆναι χωρῆσαι τὸν θεόν. '' ἐλπίσατε ἐπ' αὐτόν,'' φησί, '' πᾶσα συναγωγὴ λαοῦ, ἐκχέετε ἐνώπιον αὐτοῦ πάσας τὰς καρδίας ὑμῶν.'' πρὸς τοὺς κενοὺς τῆς πονηρίας λέγει· ἐλεεῖ
84 P. καὶ δικαιοσύνης πληροῖ | πίστευσον, ἄνθρωπε, ἀνθρώπῳ καὶ θεῷ· πίστευσον, ἄνθρωπε, τῷ παθόντι καὶ προσκυνουμένῳ. θεῷ ζῶντι πιστεύσατε οἱ δοῦλοι τῷ νεκρῷ· πάντες ἄνθρωποι πιστεύσατε μόνῳ τῷ πάντων ἀνθρώπων θεῷ· πιστεύσατε καὶ μισθὸν λάβετε σωτηρίαν· '' ἐκζητήσατε τὸν θεόν,

---

[1] ἀγριότητα Heyse. ἀγιότητα mss.
[2] [ἡ γραφὴ λέγει] Mayor.

---

[a] Psalm lviii. 4, 5.   [b] Psalm lxxii. 9.

voice of charmers." [a] But as for you, let your wild- CHAP.
X
ness be charmed away, and receive the gentle Word
we preach, and spit out the deadly poison, in order
that as fully as possible it may be given you to cast
off corruption, as serpents cast their old skin.

Listen to me, and do not stop up your ears or shut Cease to
behave like
serpents
off your hearing, but consider my words. Splendid
is the medicine of immortality ; stay at length your
serpent-like windings. For it is written : "the
enemies of the Lord shall lick the dust." [b] Lift up
your head from earth to the sky, look up to heaven
and wonder, cease watching for the heel [c] of the just
and hindering "the way of truth." [d] Become wise
and yet harmless ; [e] perchance the Lord will grant
you wings of simplicity (for it is His purpose to
supply earth-born creatures with wings) [f] in order
that, forsaking the holes of the earth, you may dwell
in the heavens. Only let us repent with our whole
heart, that with our whole heart we may be able to
receive God. "Hope in Him," the Scripture says,
"all ye congregations of people ; pour out all your
hearts before Him." [g] He speaks to those who Become
empty of
wickedness,
are empty of wickedness ; He pities them and fills
them with righteousness. Trust, O man, in Him and be
filled with
righteous-
ness
who is man and God ; trust, O man, in Him who
suffered and is adored. Trust, ye slaves, in the living
God who was dead. Trust, all men, in Him who
alone is God of all men. Trust, and take salvation Life is the
reward for
finding God
for reward. "Seek after God, and your soul shall

[c] Genesis iii. 15 : Psalm lv. 7 (Septuagint).
[d] 2 St. Peter ii. 2.
[e] See St. Matthew x. 16.
[f] See Plato, *Phaedrus* 248 c, and elsewhere.
[g] Psalm lxii. 8.

CLEMENT OF ALEXANDRIA

CAP.
X

καὶ ζήσεται ἡ ψυχὴ ὑμῶν." ὁ ἐκζητῶν τὸν θεὸν
τὴν ἰδίαν πολυπραγμονεῖ σωτηρίαν· εὗρες τὸν θεόν,
ἔχεις τὴν ζωήν. ζητήσωμεν οὖν, ἵνα καὶ ζήσωμεν.
ὁ μισθὸς τῆς εὑρέσεως ζωὴ παρὰ θεῷ. " ἀγαλ-
λιάσθωσαν καὶ εὐφρανθήτωσαν ἐπὶ σοὶ πάντες οἱ
ζητοῦντές σε καὶ λεγέτωσαν διὰ παντός, μεγαλυν-
θήτω ὁ θεός." καλὸς ὕμνος τοῦ θεοῦ ἀθάνατος
ἄνθρωπος, δικαιοσύνῃ οἰκοδομούμενος, ἐν ᾧ τὰ
λόγια τῆς ἀληθείας ἐγκεχάρακται. ποῦ γὰρ ἀλλαχόθι ἢ ἐν σώφρονι ψυχῇ δικαιοσύνην ἐγγραπτέον;
ποῦ ἀγάπην; αἰδῶ δὲ ποῦ; πραότητα δὲ ποῦ;
ταύτας, οἶμαι, τὰς θείας γραφὰς ἐναποσφραγισαμέ-
νους χρὴ τῇ ψυχῇ καλὸν ἀφετήριον σοφίαν ἡγεῖσθαι
τοῖς ἐφ᾽ ὁτιοῦν τοῦ βίου τραπεῖσι μέρος, ὅρμον
τε τὴν αὐτὴν[1] ἀκύμονα σωτηρίας σοφίαν νομίζειν·
δι᾽ ἣν ἀγαθοὶ μὲν πατέρες τέκνων οἱ τῷ πατρὶ
προσδεδραμηκότες, ἀγαθοὶ δὲ γονεῦσιν υἱοὶ[2] οἱ
τὸν υἱὸν νενοηκότες, ἀγαθοὶ δὲ ἄνδρες γυναικῶν
οἱ μεμνημένοι τοῦ νυμφίου, ἀγαθοὶ δὲ οἰκετῶν
δεσπόται οἱ τῆς ἐσχάτης δουλείας λελυτρωμένοι.

Ὦ μακαριώτερα τῆς ἐν ἀνθρώποις πλάνης τὰ
θηρία· ἐπινέμεται τὴν ἄγνοιαν, ὡς ὑμεῖς, οὐχ
ὑποκρίνεται δὲ τὴν ἀλήθειαν· οὐκ ἔστι παρ᾽ αὐτοῖς
κολάκων γένη, οὐ δεισιδαιμονοῦσιν ἰχθύες, οὐκ
εἰδωλολατρεῖ τὰ ὄρνεα, ἕνα μόνον ἐκπλήττεται τὸν
οὐρανόν, ἐπεὶ θεὸν νοῆσαι μὴ δύναται ἀπηξιωμένα
τοῦ λόγου. εἶτ᾽ οὐκ αἰσχύνεσθε καὶ τῶν ἀλόγων
σφᾶς αὐτοὺς ἀλογωτέρους πεποιηκότες, οἳ διὰ τοσούτων ἡλικιῶν ἐν ἀθεότητι κατατέτριφθε; παῖδες

---

[1] τὴν αὐτὴν Mayor.   τὸν αὐτὸν MSS.
[2] γονεῦσιν υἱοὶ Potter.   γονεῖς υἱάσιν MSS.

---

[a] Psalm lxix. 32.   [b] Psalm lxx. iv.

230

live." [a] He who seeks after God is busy about his own salvation. Have you found God? you have life. Let us seek then, that we may also live. The reward of finding is life with God. "Let all who seek Thee be joyful and glad in Thee, and let them say always, God be exalted." [b] A beautiful hymn to God is an immortal man who is being built up in righteousness, and upon whom the oracles of truth have been engraved. For where else but in a temperate soul should righteousness be inscribed? or love, or modesty, or gentleness? We ought, I think, by having these divine writings stamped deeply into the soul, to regard wisdom as a noble starting-point, to whatever lot in life men turn, and to believe that the same wisdom is a calm haven of salvation. For it is because of wisdom that they whose course has led them to the Father are good fathers of their children; that they who have come to know the Son are good sons to their parents; that they who have been mindful of the Bridegroom are good husbands of their wives; that they who have been ransomed from the deepest slavery are good masters of their servants.

Surely the beasts are happier than men who live in error! They dwell in ignorance, like you, but they do not falsely pretend to truth. Among them are no tribes of flatterers. Fishes do not fear daemons; birds do not worship idols. One heaven alone they marvel at, since God they cannot come to know, having been deemed unworthy of reason. When you think of this, are you not ashamed to have made yourselves less reasonable than even the creatures without reason, you who have wasted so many stages of life in atheism? You have

The best hymn to God is a man who has found Life and Truth

Divine wisdom helps him faithfully to perform all duties

Beasts are in happier state than idolaters

231

CAP. γεγόνατε, εἶτα μειράκια, εἶτα ἔφηβοι, εἶτα ἄνδρες,
X χρηστοὶ δὲ οὐδέποτε. κἂν τὸ γῆρας αἰδέσθητε, ἐπὶ
δυσμαῖς τοῦ βίου γενόμενοι σωφρονήσατε, κἂν ἐπὶ
τέλει τοῦ βίου τὸν θεὸν ἐπίγνωτε, ὡς δὴ τὸ τέλος
ὑμῖν τοῦ βίου ἀρχὴν ἀναλάβοι σωτηρίας. γηράσατε[1]
πρὸς δεισιδαιμονίαν, νέοι ἀφίκεσθε πρὸς θεοσέβειαν·
παῖδας ἀκάκους ἐγκρίνει θεός. ὁ μὲν οὖν Ἀθηναῖος
τοῖς Σόλωνος ἐπέσθω νόμοις καὶ ὁ Ἀργεῖος τοῖς
Φορωνέως καὶ ὁ Σπαρτιάτης τοῖς Δυκούργου, εἰ
85 P. δὲ σεαυτὸν ἀναγράφεις τοῦ θεοῦ, οὐρανὸς | μέν σοι
ἡ πατρίς, ὁ δὲ θεὸς νομοθέτης. τίνες δὲ καὶ οἱ
νόμοι; " οὐ φονεύσεις, οὐ μοιχεύσεις, οὐ παιδο-
φθορήσεις, οὐ κλέψεις, οὐ ψευδομαρτυρήσεις, ἀγαπήσεις κύριον τὸν θεόν σου." εἰσὶ δὲ καὶ τούτων
τὰ παραπληρώματα, λόγιοι νόμοι καὶ ἅγιοι λόγοι ἐν
αὐταῖς ἐγγραφόμενοι ταῖς καρδίαις· " ἀγαπήσεις
τὸν πλησίον σου ὡς σεαυτόν," καὶ " τῷ τύπτοντί
σε εἰς τὴν σιαγόνα πάρεχε καὶ τὴν ἄλλην," καὶ
" οὐκ ἐπιθυμήσεις, ἐπιθυμίᾳ γὰρ μόνῃ μεμοίχευκας."
πόσῳ γοῦν ἄμεινον τοῖς ἀνθρώποις τοῦ τυγχάνειν
τῶν ἐπιθυμιῶν ἀρχὴν μηδὲ ἐπιθυμεῖν ἐθέλειν ὧν
μὴ δεῖ.

Ἀλλ᾽ ὑμεῖς μὲν τὸ αὐστηρὸν τῆς σωτηρίας ὑπο-
μένειν οὐ καρτερεῖτε, καθάπερ δὲ τῶν σιτίων τοῖς
γλυκέσιν ἡδόμεθα διὰ τὴν λειότητα τῆς ἡδονῆς
προτιμῶντες, ἰᾶται δὲ ἡμᾶς καὶ ὑγιάζει τὰ πικρὰ

---

[1] ἐγηράσατε Wilamowitz : Stählin.

---

[a] See Exodus xx. 13–16 ; Deuteronomy vi. 5. For the
added commandment " Thou shalt not corrupt a boy " see
the *Teaching of the Twelve Apostles* ii. 2 ; *Epistle of Barnabas*
xix. 4. The prevalence of this vice in the early centuries of
Christianity doubtless led to the insertion of the precept.

been boys, then lads, then youths, then men, but CHAP.
X good you have never been. Have respect to your old age; become sober now you have reached the sunset of life; even at the end of life acknowledge God, so that the end of your life may regain a beginning of salvation. Grow old to daemon-worship; return as young men to the fear of God; God will enroll you as guileless children. Let the Athenian, then, follow the laws of Solon, the Argive those of Phoroneus, and the Spartan those of Lycurgus, but if you record yourself among God's people, then heaven is your fatherland and God your lawgiver. And what are His laws? "Thou shalt not kill; thou shalt not commit adultery; thou shalt not corrupt a boy; thou shalt not steal; thou shalt not bear false witness; thou shalt love the Lord thy God." [a] There are also the complements of these, wise laws and holy sayings inscribed in the very hearts of men; "Thou shalt love thy neighbour as thyself," [b] and, "to him that smiteth thee on the one cheek, offer also the other," [c] and, "thou shalt not lust, for lust by itself is an act of adultery." [d] How much better is it for men not to have the least wish to lust after forbidden things, rather than to obtain the object of their lusts?

God's children must follow God's laws

But you do not patiently endure the severity of the way of salvation. Nevertheless, just as we take delight in sweet foods, preferring them because they are smooth and pleasant, and yet it is the bitter medicines, rough to the taste, which cure and restore

The way of salvation is severe, but good for us

[b] Leviticus xix. 18, and often in New Testament.
[c] St. Luke vi. 29.
[d] See St. Matthew v. 28.

233

CAP.
X

τραχύνοντα τὴν αἴσθησιν, ἀλλὰ τοὺς ἀσθενεῖς τὸν
στόμαχον ῥώννυσιν ἡ τῶν φαρμάκων αὐστηρία,
οὕτως ἤδει μὲν καὶ γαργαλίζει ἡ συνήθεια, ἀλλ' ἡ
μὲν εἰς τὸ βάραθρον ὠθεῖ, ἡ συνήθεια, ἡ δὲ εἰς
οὐρανὸν ἀνάγει, ἡ ἀλήθεια, "τραχεῖα" μὲν τὸ
πρῶτον, "ἀλλ' ἀγαθὴ κουροτρόφος"· καὶ σεμνὴ μὲν
ἡ γυναικωνῖτις αὕτη, σώφρων δὲ ἡ γερουσία· οὐδέ
ἐστι δυσπρόσιτος οὐδὲ ἀδύνατος λαβεῖν, ἀλλ' ἔστιν
ἐγγυτάτω ἔνοικος[1] ἡμῶν, ᾗ φησιν αἰνιττόμενος
ὁ πάνσοφος Μωυσῆς, τρισὶ τοῖς καθ' ἡμᾶς ἐν-
διαιτωμένη μέρεσι, "χερσὶ καὶ στόματι καὶ
καρδίᾳ." σύμβολον τοῦτο γνήσιον τρισὶ τοῖς πᾶσι
συμπληρουμένης τῆς ἀληθείας, βουλῇ καὶ πράξει
καὶ λόγῳ· μηδὲ γὰρ τόδε δείμαινε, μή σε τὰ
πολλὰ καὶ ἐπιτερπῆ φανταζόμενα[2] ἀφέληται σοφίας·
αὐτὸς ἑκὼν ὑπερβήσῃ τὸν λῆρον τῆς συνηθείας,
καθάπερ καὶ οἱ παῖδες τὰ ἀθύρματα ἄνδρες γενόμενοι
ἀπέρριψαν. τάχει μὲν δὴ ἀνυπερβλήτῳ εὐνοίᾳ τε
εὐπροσίτῳ ἡ δύναμις ἡ θεϊκὴ ἐπιλάμψασα τὴν γῆν

86 P. σωτηρίου σπέρματος ἐνέπλησε | τὸ πᾶν. οὐ γὰρ
ἂν οὕτως ἐν ὀλίγῳ χρόνῳ τοσοῦτον ἔργον ἄνευ θείας
κομιδῆς ἐξήνυσεν ὁ κύριος, ὄψει καταφρονούμενος,
ἔργῳ προσκυνούμενος, ὁ καθάρσιος καὶ σωτήριος
καὶ μειλίχιος, ὁ θεῖος λόγος, ὁ φανερώτατος ὄντως
θεός, ὁ τῷ δεσπότῃ τῶν ὅλων ἐξισωθείς, ὅτι ἦν
υἱὸς αὐτοῦ καὶ "ὁ λόγος ἦν ἐν τῷ θεῷ," οὔθ' ὅτε

---

[1] ἔνοικος Markland.   ἐν οἴκοις MSS.
[2] φανταζόμενα Stählin.   φανταζόμενον MSS.

[a] The epithets are applied by Homer to Ithaca. See
Odyssey ix. 27.
[b] Having compared truth to Ithaca, the home of
Odysseus, Clement goes on to divide it into two parts,
sanctity and prudence, one being represented by the women's

us to health, the severity of the remedies strengthen-
ing those whose stomachs are weak; so custom
pleases and tickles us, but thrusts us into the pit,
whereas truth, which is "rough" at first, but a
"goodly rearer of youth," *a* leads us up to heaven.
And in this home of truth, the chamber of the
women is the abode of sanctity; while the assembly
of the old men is prudent.*b* Nor is truth hard of
approach, nor impossible to grasp, but it is our inner-
most neighbour, dwelling, as the all-wise Moses darkly
says, in the three parts of our being, "hands and
mouth and heart."*c* This is a genuine symbol of truth,
which is made complete by three things in all, by
purpose and action and speech. And be not afraid
of this, that the many delights of the imagination
may draw you away from wisdom; of your own
accord you will willingly pass beyond the childishness
of custom, just as boys throw away their playthings
on reaching manhood. With a swiftness beyond
parallel and a goodwill that is easy of approach, the
divine power has shone forth upon the earth and
filled the whole world with the seed of salvation.
For not without divine care could so great a work
have been accomplished, as it has been in so short
a time by the Lord, who to outward seeming is
despised,*d* but in very deed is adored; who is
the real Purifier, Saviour and Gracious One,*e* the
Divine Word, the truly most manifest God, who is
made equal to the Master of the universe, because
He was His Son and "the Word was in God."*f*

CHAP.
X

Nor is it
far off

Once found
we shall not
forsake it
for custom

The whole
world is
now filled
with this
divine
power

Greatness of
the Word

chamber, the other by the council of old men. Perhaps,
too, there is an allusion to the chastity of Penelope and the
prudence of Odysseus.

c Deuteronomy xxx. 14.　　　*d* See Isaiah liii. 3.
e Titles of Zeus.　　　*f* St. John i. 1.

τὸ πρῶτον προεκηρύχθη, ἀπιστηθείς, οὔθ' ὅτε τὸ
ἀνθρώπου προσωπεῖον ἀναλαβὼν καὶ σαρκὶ ἀνα-
πλασάμενος τὸ σωτήριον δρᾶμα τῆς ἀνθρωπότητος
ὑπεκρίνετο, ἀγνοηθείς· γνήσιος γὰρ ἦν ἀγωνιστὴς
καὶ τοῦ πλάσματος συναγωνιστής, τάχιστα δὲ εἰς
πάντας ἀνθρώπους διαδοθεὶς θᾶττον ἡλίου ἐξ αὐτῆς
ἀνατείλας τῆς πατρικῆς βουλήσεως, ῥᾷστα ἡμῖν
ἐπέλαμψε τὸν θεόν, ὅθεν τε ἦν αὐτὸς καὶ ὃς ἦν,
δι' ὧν ἐδίδαξεν καὶ ἐνεδείξατο, παραστησάμενος,
ὁ σπονδοφόρος καὶ διαλλακτὴς καὶ σωτὴρ ἡμῶν
λόγος, πηγὴ ζωοποιός, εἰρηνική, ἐπὶ πᾶν τὸ
πρόσωπον τῆς γῆς χεόμενος, δι' ὃν ὡς ἔπος
εἰπεῖν τὰ πάντα ἤδη πέλαγος γέγονεν ἀγαθῶν.

XI

Μικρὸν δέ, εἰ βούλει, ἄνωθεν ἄθρει τὴν θείαν
εὐεργεσίαν. ὁ πρῶτος [ὁτὲ][1] ἐν παραδείσῳ ἔπαιζε
λελυμένος, ἐπεὶ παιδίον ἦν τοῦ θεοῦ· ὅτε δὲ
ὑποπίπτων[2] ἡδονῇ (ὄφις ἀλληγορεῖται ἡδονὴ ἐπὶ
γαστέρα ἕρπουσα, κακία γηΐνη, εἰς ὕλας τρε-
φομένη[3]) παρήγετο ἐπιθυμίαις, ὁ παῖς ἀνδριζόμενος
ἀπειθείᾳ καὶ παρακούσας τοῦ πατρὸς ᾐσχύνετο τὸν
θεόν. οἷον ἴσχυσεν ἡδονή· ὁ δι' ἁπλότητα λελυμένος ἄνθρωπος ἁμαρτίαις εὑρέθη δεδεμένος. τῶν
δεσμῶν λῦσαι τοῦτον ὁ κύριος αὖθις ἠθέλησεν, καὶ
σαρκὶ ἐνδεθείς (μυστήριον θεῖον τοῦτο) τὸν ὄφιν
ἐχειρώσατο καὶ τὸν τύραννον ἐδουλώσατο, τὸν

---

[1] [ὁτὲ] Stählin. ὁτὲ μὲν Dindorf. ὅτε ἦν Markland.
[2] ὑποπίπτων Schwartz. ὑπέπιπτεν mss.
[3] στρεφομένη Heyse : Stählin.

When at the first His coming was proclaimed the CHAP.
message was not disbelieved; nor was He unrecog- X
nized when, having assumed the mask of manhood
and received fleshly form, He began to act the drama
of salvation for humanity.   For He was a true He is the
champion, and a fellow-champion with His creatures; true
champion of
and, having been most speedily published abroad to humanity
all men,—for swifter than the sun He rose from the
very will of the Father—He readily lighted up God
for us.   Through His teachings and signs He showed He has
whence He came and who He was, namely, the brought
untold
Word our herald, mediator and Saviour, a spring of blessings
life and peace flooding the whole face of the earth,
thanks to whom the universe has now become, so to
speak, a sea of blessings.

XI

Now consider briefly, if you will, the beneficence Man was
of God from the beginning.   The first man played created
innocent
in Paradise with childlike freedom, since he was a and free
child of God.   But when he fell a victim to pleasure But he fell
(for the serpent, that creeps upon the belly, an through
pleasure
earthy [a] evil, reared to return to matter, is an allegory
for pleasure), and was led astray by lusts, the child,
coming to manhood through disobedience and refusing to listen to the Father, was ashamed to meet
God.   See how pleasure prevailed!   The man who
by reason of innocence had been free was discovered
to be bound by sins.   The Lord purposed once again
to loose him from his bonds.   Clothing Himself The Lord
with bonds of flesh (which is a divine mystery), He took flesh
and died to
subdued the serpent and enslaved the tyrant death; set man free
from sin

[a] Because it feeds on earth; cp. Genesis iii. 14.

237

CAP.
XI

θάνατον, καί, τὸ παραδοξότατον, ἐκεῖνον τὸν ἄνθρωπον τὸν ἡδονῇ πεπλανημένον, τὸν τῇ φθορᾷ δεδεμένον, χερσὶν ἡπλωμέναις ἔδειξε λελυμένον. ὦ θαύμα-
τος μυστικοῦ· κέκλιται μὲν ὁ κύριος, ἀνέστη δὲ
ἄνθρωπος καὶ ὁ ἐκ τοῦ παραδείσου πεσὼν μεῖζον
ὑπακοῆς ἆθλον, οὐρανούς, ἀπολαμβάνει. διό μοι
δοκεῖ, ἐπεὶ αὐτὸς ἧκεν ὡς ἡμᾶς οὐρανόθεν ὁ λόγος,
ἡμᾶς ἐπ᾽ ἀνθρωπίνην ἰέναι μὴ χρῆναι διδασκαλίαν
ἔτι, ᾿Αθήνας καὶ τὴν ἄλλην ῾Ελλάδα, πρὸς δὲ καὶ
᾿Ιωνίαν πολυπραγμονοῦντας. εἰ γὰρ ἡμῖν [ὁ]¹ διδάσκαλος ὁ πληρώσας τὰ πάντα δυνάμεσιν ἁγίαις,

87 P. δημιουργίᾳ σωτηρίᾳ εὐεργεσίᾳ νομο|θεσίᾳ προφη-
τείᾳ διδασκαλίᾳ, πάντα νῦν ὁ διδάσκαλος κατηχεῖ
καὶ τὸ πᾶν ἤδη ᾿Αθῆναι καὶ ῾Ελλὰς γέγονεν τῷ
λόγῳ. οὐ γὰρ δὴ μύθῳ μὲν ἐπιστεύετε ποιητικῷ
τὸν Μίνω τὸν Κρῆτα τοῦ Διὸς ὀαριστὴν ἀναγράφοντι,
ἡμᾶς δὲ ἀπιστήσετε μαθητὰς θεοῦ γεγονότας, τὴν
ὄντως ἀληθῆ σοφίαν ἐπανῃρημένους, ἣν φιλοσοφίας
ἄκροι μόνον ᾐνίξαντο, οἱ δὲ τοῦ Χριστοῦ μαθηταὶ
καὶ κατειλήφασι καὶ ἀνεκήρυξαν. καὶ δὴ καὶ πᾶς,
ὡς ἔπος εἰπεῖν,² ὁ Χριστὸς οὐ μερίζεται· οὔτε
βάρβαρός ἐστιν οὔτε ᾿Ιουδαῖος οὔτε ῞Ελλην, οὐκ
ἄρρεν, οὐ θῆλυ· καινὸς δὲ ἄνθρωπος θεοῦ πνεύματι
ἁγίῳ μεταπεπλασμένος.

Εἶθ᾽ αἱ μὲν ἄλλαι συμβουλαί τε καὶ ὑποθῆκαι

---

¹ [ὁ] Heyse.
² Stählin, following Schwartz, suspects an omission
between εἰπεῖν and ὁ Χριστὸς.

ᵃ It is possible that the Greek means only " with hands
unloosened." But the outstretching of Christ's hands upon
the cross was a familiar thought to the Christian Fathers,

238

and, most wonderful of all, the very man who had CHAP.
erred through pleasure, and was bound by corruption, XI
was shown to be free again, through His outstretched
hands.[a] O amazing mystery! The Lord has sunk Man gains
down, but man rose up; and he who was driven from more than
Paradise gains a greater prize, heaven, on becoming he lost
obedient. Wherefore it seems to me, that since the The Word
Word Himself came to us from heaven, we ought no from heaven
longer to go to human teaching, to Athens and the rest teacher
of Greece, or to Ionia, in our curiosity. If our teacher
is He who has filled the universe with holy powers,
creation, salvation, beneficence, lawgiving, prophecy,
teaching, this teacher now instructs us in all things, and
the whole world has by this time become an Athens
and a Greece through the Word. For surely, after
believing in a poetic legend which records that
Minos the Cretan was "a familiar friend of Zeus,"[b] you
will not disbelieve that we, who have become disciples Christians
of God, have entered into the really true wisdom are His
which leaders of philosophy only hinted at, but which disciples
the disciples of the Christ have both comprehended
and proclaimed abroad. Moreover, the whole Christ,
so to speak, is not divided; there is neither barbarian
nor Jew nor Greek, neither male nor female, but a
new man transformed by the Holy Spirit of God.[c]

Further, all other counsels and precepts, as, for

and is alluded to by Justin (I. *Apol.* 35) and by Irenaeus
(v. 17. 4), though the word used in each of these passages
is ἐκτείνω and not ἀπλόω. Basil uses ἀπλόω in this connexion ;
cp. *In Psalm. xlv.* p. 272, " having his hands outstretched
(ἠπλωμένας) in the manner of the cross." Perhaps Clement
wishes to suggest both meanings.

  [b] Homer, *Odyssey* xix. 179.
  [c] See 1 Corinthians i. 13; Galatians iii. 28; Ephesians
iv. 24; Colossians iii. 9–11.

CAP.
XI
λυπραὶ καὶ περὶ τῶν ἐπὶ μέρους εἰσίν, εἰ γαμητέον,
εἰ πολιτευτέον, εἰ παιδοποιητέον· καθολικὴ δὲ ἄρα
προτροπὴ μόνη καὶ πρὸς ὅλον δηλαδὴ τὸν βίον, ἐν
παντὶ καιρῷ, ἐν πάσῃ περιστάσει πρὸς τὸ κυριώ-
τατον τέλος, τὴν ζωήν, συντείνουσα ἡ θεοσέβεια·
καθ' ὃ καὶ μόνον ἐπάναγκές ἐστι ζῆν, ἵνα ζήσωμεν ἀεί· φιλοσοφία δέ, ᾗ φασιν οἱ πρεσβύτεροι,
πολυχρόνιός ἐστι συμβουλή, σοφίας ἀίδιον μνη-
στευομένη ἔρωτα· "ἐντολὴ δὲ κυρίου τηλαυγής,
φωτίζουσα ὀφθαλμούς." ἀπόλαβε τὸν Χριστόν,
ἀπόλαβε τὸ βλέπειν, ἀπόλαβέ σου τὸ φῶς,

ὄφρ' εὖ γινώσκοις ἠμὲν θεὸν ἠδὲ καὶ ἄνδρα.

"ποθεινὸς"[1] ὁ λόγος ὁ φωτίσας ἡμᾶς "ὑπὲρ
χρυσίον καὶ λίθον τίμιον· γλυκύς[1] ἐστιν ὑπὲρ μέλι
καὶ κηρίον." πῶς γὰρ οὐ ποθεινὸς ὁ τὸν ἐν σκότει
κατορωρυγμένον νοῦν ἐναργῆ ποιησάμενος καὶ τὰ
"φωσφόρα" τῆς ψυχῆς ἀποξύνας "ὄμματα"; καὶ
γὰρ ὥσπερ "ἡλίου μὴ ὄντος ἕνεκα τῶν ἄλλων
ἄστρων νὺξ ἂν ἦν τὰ πάντα," οὕτως εἰ μὴ τὸν λόγον
ἔγνωμεν καὶ τούτῳ κατηυγάσθημεν, οὐδὲν ἂν τῶν
σιτευομένων ὀρνίθων ἐλειπόμεθα, ἐν σκότει πιαινό-
μενοι καὶ θανάτῳ τρεφόμενοι. χωρήσωμεν τὸ φῶς,
88 P. ἵνα χωρή|σωμεν τὸν θεόν· χωρήσωμεν τὸ φῶς καὶ
μαθητεύσωμεν τῷ κυρίῳ. τοῦτό τοι καὶ ἐπήγγελται

---

[1] ποθεινὸς—γλυκύς Mayor (see Psalm xviii. 11 Sept.).
γλυκὺς—ποθεινός mss.

[a] Compare this with what Clement says about the "short
way" of the gospel preaching, pp. 173 and 217.
[b] Psalm xix. 8.   [c] Homer, *Iliad* v. 128.
[d] Psalm xix. 10.
[e] Compare Plato, *Timaeus* 45 B.
[f] Heracleitus, Frag. 31 (Bywater), 99 (Diels).

instance, whether a man should marry, or take part in politics, or beget children, are of small account and of special application. The exhortation that alone would seem to be universal, and concerned plainly with the whole of existence, reaching out in every season and every circumstance towards the supreme end, life, is piety towards God. And it is only necessary to live according to piety, in order to obtain eternal life; whereas philosophy, as the elders say, is a lengthy deliberation, that pursues wisdom with a never-ending love.[a] But "the commandment of the Lord shines afar, giving light to the eyes."[b] Receive the Christ; receive power to see; receive thy light;

Thus shalt thou well discern who is God and who is but mortal.[c]

The Word who has given us light is "to be desired above gold and precious stone; He is sweet above honey and the honeycomb."[d] How can we help desiring Him who has made clear the mind that lay buried in darkness, and sharpened the "light-bearing eyes"[e] of the soul? For just as "if the sun were not, the world would have been in perpetual night, for all the other heavenly bodies could do"[f]; so unless we had come to know the Word, and had been enlightened by His rays, we should have been in no way different from birds who are being crammed with food, fattening in darkness[g] and reared for death. Let us admit the light, that we may admit God. Let us admit the light, and become disciples of the Lord. This is the promise

CHAP. XI

Piety is the only universal precept

A life of piety ensures eternal life

The Word brings us light

Without Him we should have been in darkness

[g] The same simile occurs in Philostratus, *Life of Apollonius* iv. 3.

CAP.
XI

τῷ πατρὶ "διηγήσομαι τὸ ὄνομά σου τοῖς ἀδελφοῖς μου· ἐν μέσῳ ἐκκλησίας ὑμνήσω σε." ὕμνησον καί διήγησαί μοι τὸν πατέρα σου τὸν θεόν· σώσει σου τὰ διηγήματα, παιδεύσει με ἡ ᾠδή. ὡς μέχρι νῦν ἐπλανώμην ζητῶν τὸν θεόν, ἐπεὶ δέ με φωτ-αγωγεῖς, κύριε, καὶ τὸν θεὸν εὑρίσκω διὰ σοῦ καὶ τὸν πατέρα ἀπολαμβάνω παρὰ σοῦ, γίνομαί σου συγκληρονόμος, ἐπεὶ τὸν ἀδελφὸν οὐκ ἐπῃσχύνθης.

Ἀφέλωμεν οὖν, ἀφέλωμεν τὴν λήθην τῆς ἀληθείας· τὴν ἄγνοιαν καί τὸ σκότος τὸ ἐμποδὼν ὡς ἀχλὺν ὄψεως καταγαγόντες τὸν ὄντως ὄντα θεὸν ἐποπτεύ-σωμεν, ταύτην αὐτῷ πρῶτον ἀνυμνήσαντες τὴν φωνήν "χαῖρε φῶς"· φῶς ἡμῖν ἐξ οὐρανοῦ τοῖς ἐν σκότει κατορωρυγμένοις καί ἐν σκιᾷ θανάτου κατακεκλεισμένοις ἐξέλαμψεν ἡλίου καθαρώτερον, ζωῆς τῆς ἐνταῦθα γλυκύτερον. τὸ φῶς ἐκεῖνο ζωή ἐστιν ἀΐδιος, καὶ ὅσα μετείληφεν αὐτοῦ, ζῇ, ἡ νὺξ δὲ εὐλαβεῖται τὸ φῶς καὶ δύνουσα διὰ τὸν φόβον παραχωρεῖ τῇ ἡμέρᾳ κυρίου· τὰ πάντα φῶς ἀκοίμη-τον γέγονεν καὶ ἡ δύσις εἰς ἀνατολὴν περιέστηκεν.[1] τοῦτο ἡ κτίσις ἡ καινὴ βεβούληται· ὁ γὰρ τὰ πάντα καθιππεύων "δικαιοσύνης ἥλιος" ἐπ' ἴσης περιπολεῖ τὴν ἀνθρωπότητα, τὸν πατέρα μιμούμε-νος, ὃς "ἐπὶ πάντας ἀνθρώπους ἀνατέλλει τὸν ἥλιον αὐτοῦ," καὶ καταψεκάζει τὴν δρόσον τῆς ἀληθείας. οὗτος τὴν δύσιν εἰς ἀνατολὴν μετήγαγεν καὶ τὸν θάνατον εἰς ζωὴν ἀνεσταύρωσεν, ἐξαρπάσας δὲ τῆς ἀπωλείας τὸν ἄνθρωπον προσεκρέμασεν αἰθέρι,

[1] εἰς ἀνατολὴν περιέστηκεν Wilamowitz. ἀνατολὴ πεπίστευκεν
MSS.

---

[a] Psalm xxii. 22.   [b] See Romans viii. 17.
[c] See Hebrews ii. 11.

He has made to the Father; "I will declare Thy
name to my brethren; in the midst of the congrega-
tion will I sing praises to Thee." [a]   Sing praises, and
declare unto me God Thy Father.   Thy story shall
save, Thy song shall instruct me.   Until now I was
erring in my search for God, but since Thou, Lord,
dost become my guiding light I find God through
Thee, I receive the Father at Thy hands, I become
joint-heir [b] with Thee, since Thou wert not ashamed
of Thy brother. [c]

Away then, away with our forgetfulness of the
truth !   Let us remove the ignorance and darkness
that spreads like a mist over our sight ; and let us
get a vision of the true God, first raising to Him this
voice of praise, "Hail, O Light."   Upon us who lay
buried in darkness and shut up in the shadow of
death [d] a light shone forth from heaven, purer than
the sun and sweeter than the life of earth.   That
light is life eternal, and whatsoever things partake
of it, live.   But night shrinks back from the light,
and setting through fear, gives place to the day of
the Lord.   The universe has become sleepless light
and the setting has turned into a rising.   This is what
was meant by "the new creation." [e]   For He who
rides over the universe, "the sun of righteousness," [f]
visits mankind impartially, imitating His Father, who
"causes His sun to rise upon all men," [g] and sprinkles
them all with the dew of truth.   He it was who
changed the setting into a rising, and crucified death
into life ; who having snatched man out of the jaws
of destruction raised him to the sky, transplanting

Let us then
banish
ignorance
and dark-
ness

The night of
earth gives
place to the
day of the
Lord

This is the
new creation
coming to
all men
alike

Man is
raised from
earth to
heaven

[d] See Isaiah ix. 2 (St. Matthew iv. 16 and St. Luke i. 79).
  [e] Galatians vi. 15.   (Revised Version margin.)
[f] Malachi iv. 2.   [g] St. Matthew v. 45.

CAP.
XI

μεταφυτεύων τὴν φθορὰν εἰς ἀφθαρσίαν καὶ γῆν
μεταβάλλων εἰς οὐρανούς, ὁ τοῦ θεοῦ γεωργός,
"δεξιὰ σημαίνων, λαοὺς δ' ἐπὶ ἔργον" ἀγαθὸν
"ἐγείρων, μιμνήσκων βιότοιο" ἀληθινοῦ, καὶ τὸν
μέγαν ὄντως καὶ θεῖον καὶ ἀναφαίρετον τοῦ πατρὸς
κλῆρον χαριζόμενος ἡμῖν, οὐρανίῳ διδασκαλίᾳ θεο-

89 P. |ποιῶν τὸν ἄνθρωπον, "διδοὺς νόμους εἰς τὴν
διάνοιαν αὐτῶν καὶ ἐπὶ καρδίαν γράφων αὐτούς."
τίνας ὑπογράφει νόμους; "ὅτι πάντες εἴσονται τὸν
θεὸν ἀπὸ μικροῦ ἕως μεγάλου, καὶ ἵλεως," φησὶν ὁ
θεός, "ἔσομαι αὐτοῖς καὶ τῶν ἁμαρτιῶν αὐτῶν οὐ
μὴ μνησθῶ." δεξώμεθα τοὺς νόμους τῆς ζωῆς,
πεισθῶμεν προτρεπομένῳ θεῷ, μάθωμεν αὐτόν, ἵνα
ἵλεως ᾖ, ἀποδῶμεν καὶ μὴ δεομένῳ μισθὸν εὐ-
χάριστον εὐπαθείας,[1] οἷόν τι ἐνοίκιον [τὴν εὐ-
σέβειαν][2] τῷ θεῷ τῆς ἐνταῦθα ἐνοικήσεως.

χρύσεα χαλκείων, ἑκατόμβοι' ἐννεαβοίων.

ὀλίγης πίστεως γῆν σοι δίδωσι τὴν τοσαύτην
γεωργεῖν, ὕδωρ πίνειν καὶ ἄλλο πλεῖν, ἀέρα ἀναπνεῖν, πῦρ ὑπουργεῖν, κόσμον οἰκεῖν· ἐντεῦθεν εἰς
οὐρανοὺς ἀποικίαν στείλασθαί σοι συγκεχώρηκεν·
τὰ μεγάλα ταῦτα καὶ τοσαῦτά σοι δημιουργήματα
καὶ χαρίσματα ὀλίγης πίστεως μεμίσθωκεν. εἶθ'
οἱ μὲν τοῖς γόησι πεπιστευκότες τὰ περίαπτα καὶ
τὰς ἐπαοιδὰς ὡς σωτηρίους δῆθεν ἀποδέχονται,
ὑμεῖς δὲ οὐ βούλεσθε τὸν οὐράνιον αὐτὸν περιάψα-
σθαι, τὸν σωτῆρα λόγον, καὶ τῇ ἐπῳδῇ τοῦ θεοῦ

---

[1] εὐπαθείας Mayor.   εὐπάθειαν mss.   εὐπείθειαν Heyse.
[2] [τὴν εὐσέβειαν] Heyse.

corruption to the soil of incorruption, and transforming earth into heaven.   He is God's husbandman,
"who gives favourable omens, and rouses the people
to a work" that is good, "reminding us of the true
livelihood," [a] and granting to us the Father's truly
great, divine and inalienable portion, making men
divine by heavenly doctrine, "putting laws into their
minds and writing them upon the heart." [b]   To what
laws does He allude?   "That all shall know God
from the small to the great; and," God says, "I will
be gracious to them and not remember their sins." [b]
Let us receive the laws of life; let us obey God
when He exhorts us; let us learn about Him, that
He may be gracious; let us render Him (though He
is in need of nothing) a recompense of gratitude for
His blessings, as a kind of rent paid to God for our
dwelling here below.

Gold in exchange for brass, a hundred oxen for nine's worth. [c]

At the price of a little faith He gives thee this
great earth to till, water to drink, other water to
sail on, air to breathe, fire to do service, and a world
to dwell in.   From hence He has granted thee power
to send forth a colony into heaven.   All these great
works of creation and gracious gifts He has let out
to thee in return for a little faith.   Again, men who
believe in wizards receive amulets and charms which
are supposed to bring safety.   Do you not rather
desire to put on the heavenly amulet, [d] the Word
who truly saves, and, by trusting to God's enchant-

God's gifts
are ours for
a little faith

The Word
is the only
amulet that
can save
from sin

[a] These words are quoted from Aratus, *Phaenomena*, 6-7.
[b] Jeremiah xxxi. 33, 34 (quoted Hebrews viii. 10-12).
[c] Homer, *Iliad* vi. 236.
[d] See Plato, *Charmides* 157 A.

CLEMENT OF ALEXANDRIA

CAP.
XI

πιστεύσαντες ἀπαλλαγῆναι μὲν παθῶν, ἃ δὴ ψυχῆς
νόσοι, ἀποσπασθῆναι δὲ ἁμαρτίας ; θάνατος γὰρ
ἀΐδιος ἁμαρτία. ἢ τέλεον νωδοὶ καὶ τυφλοὶ καθάπερ
οἱ σπάλακες οὐδὲν ἄλλο ἢ ἐσθίοντες ἐν σκότῳ
διαιτᾶσθε, περικαταρρέοντες τῇ φθορᾷ. ἀλλ᾿ ἔστιν,
ἔστιν ἡ ἀλήθεια ἡ κεκραγυῖα "ἐκ σκότους φῶς
λάμψει." λαμψάτω οὖν ἐν τῷ ἀποκεκρυμμένῳ τοῦ
ἀνθρώπου, ἐν τῇ καρδίᾳ, τὸ φῶς, καὶ τῆς γνώσεως
αἱ ἀκτῖνες ἀνατειλάτωσαν τὸν ἐγκεκρυμμένον ἔνδον
ἐκφαίνουσαι καὶ ἀποστίλβουσαι ἄνθρωπον, τὸν μαθητὴν τοῦ φωτός, τὸν Χριστοῦ γνώριμόν τε καὶ
συγκληρονόμον, μάλιστα ἐπειδὰν τὸ τιμιώτατον καὶ
σεβασμιώτατον εὐσεβεῖ τε καὶ ἀγαθῷ παιδὶ ἀγαθοῦ
πατρὸς ὄνομα εἰς γνῶσιν ἀφίκηται, προστάττοντος
ἤπια καὶ τῷ παιδὶ ἐγκελευομένου τὰ σωτήρια. ὁ
δὲ πειθόμενος αὐτῷ κατὰ πάντα δὴ πλεονεκτεῖ·
ἕπεται τῷ θεῷ, πείθεται τῷ πατρί, ἔγνω πλανώμενος
αὐτόν, ἠγάπησε τὸν θεόν, ἠγάπησε τὸν πλησίον,
ἐπλήρωσε τὴν ἐντολήν, τὸ ἆθλον ἐπιζητεῖ, τὴν
ἐπαγγελίαν ἀπαιτεῖ.

Πρόκειται δὲ ἀεὶ τῷ θεῷ τὴν ἀνθρώπων ἀγέλην
σῴζειν. ταύτῃ καὶ τὸν ἀγαθὸν ποιμένα ὁ ἀγαθὸς
ἀπέστειλεν θεός· ἁπλώσας δὲ ὁ λόγος τὴν ἀλήθειαν
ἔδειξε τοῖς ἀνθρώποις τὸ ὕψος τῆς σωτηρίας, ὅπως
90 P. ἢ | μετανοήσαντες σωθῶσιν ἢ μὴ ὑπακούσαντες
κριθῶσιν. τοῦτο τῆς δικαιοσύνης τὸ κήρυγμα,
ὑπακούσιν εὐαγγέλιον, παρακούσασιν κριτήριον.
ἀλλὰ σάλπιγξ μὲν ἡ μεγαλόκλονος ἠχήσασα
στρατιώτας συνήγαγεν καὶ πόλεμον κατήγγειλεν,

246

ment, to be freed from passions, which are diseases of the soul, and to be torn away from sin?
For sin is eternal death. Surely you are altogether
bereft of sense [a] and sight, spending your lives,
like moles, in darkness, doing nothing but eat, and
falling to pieces through corruption. But it is the
truth, I say, which cries, "Light shall shine out of
darkness." [b] Let the light then shine in the hidden
part of man, in his heart; and let the rays of knowledge rise, revealing and illuminating the hidden
man within, the disciple of the light, friend of Christ
and joint-heir with Him; more especially since there
has come to our knowledge the name, worthy of
all honour and reverence, of one who is a good
Father to a good and dutiful child, whose precepts
are kindly, and whose commands are for His child's
salvation. He who obeys Him gains in all things.
He follows God, he obeys the Father; when erring
he came to know Him; he loved God; he loved
his neighbour; he fulfilled God's commandment; he
seeks after the prize; he claims the promise.

It is ever God's purpose to save the flock of mankind. For this cause also the good God sent the
good Shepherd. [c] And the Word, having spread
abroad the truth, showed to men the grandeur of
salvation, in order that they may either be saved if
they repent, or be judged if they neglect to obey.
This is the preaching of righteousness; to those
who obey, good news; to those who disobey, a
means of judgment. But when the shrilling trumpet
blows, it assembles the soldiers and proclaims war;

---

[a] Νωδοί means literally "toothless," as applied to the aged.
Clement seems to use it metaphorically for senile decay.
[b] 2 Corinthians iv. 6.   [c] See St. John x. 11.

CAP.
XI Χριστὸς δὲ εἰρηνικὸν ἐπὶ τὰ πέρατα τῆς γῆς ἐπι-
πνεύσας μέλος οὐ συνάξει ἄρα τοὺς εἰρηνικοὺς
στρατιώτας τοὺς ἑαυτοῦ; συνήγαγε μὲν οὖν, ὦ
ἄνθρωπε, τὸ στρατιωτικὸν τὸ ἀναίμακτον αἵματι
καὶ λόγῳ, καὶ τὴν βασιλείαν τῶν οὐρανῶν αὐτοῖς
ἐνεχείρισεν. σάλπιγξ ἐστὶ Χριστοῦ τὸ εὐαγγέλιον
αὐτοῦ· ὁ μὲν ἐσάλπισεν, ἡμεῖς δὲ ἠκούσαμεν.
ἐξοπλισώμεθα εἰρηνικῶς, " ἐνδυσάμενοι τὸν θώρακα
τῆς δικαιοσύνης " καὶ τὴν ἀσπίδα τῆς πίστεως
ἀναλαβόντες καὶ τὴν κόρυν τοῦ σωτηρίου περιθέμε-
νοι καὶ " τὴν μάχαιραν τοῦ πνεύματος, ὅ ἐστι ῥῆμα
θεοῦ," ἀκονήσωμεν. οὕτως ἡμᾶς ὁ ἀπόστολος
εἰρηνικῶς ἐκτάττει· ταῦτα ἡμῶν τὰ ὅπλα τὰ
ἄτρωτα· τούτοις ἐξοπλισάμενοι παραταξώμεθα τῷ
πονηρῷ· τὰ πεπυρακτωμένα τοῦ πονηροῦ ἀπο-
σβέσωμεν βέλη ταῖς ὑδατίναις ἀκμαῖς ταῖς ὑπὸ τοῦ
λόγου βεβαμμέναις, εὐχαρίστοις ἀμειβόμενοι τὰς
εὐποιίας εὐλογίαις καὶ τὸν θεὸν τῷ θείῳ γεραίροντες
λόγῳ. " ἔτι γὰρ λαλοῦντός σου ἐρεῖ," φησίν, " ἰδοὺ
πάρειμι."

Ὢ τῆς ἁγίας καὶ μακαρίας ταύτης δυνάμεως,
δι' ἧς ἀνθρώποις συμπολιτεύεται θεός. λῷον οὖν
καὶ ἄμεινον τῆς ἀρίστης τῶν ὄντων οὐσίας μιμητὴν
ὁμοῦ καὶ θεραπευτὴν γενέσθαι· οὐ γὰρ μιμεῖσθαί
τις δυνήσεται τὸν θεὸν ἢ δι' ὧν ὁσίως θεραπεύει[1]
οὐδ' αὖ θεραπεύειν καὶ σέβειν ἢ μιμούμενος. ὅ γέ
τοι οὐράνιος καὶ θεῖος ὄντως ἔρως ταύτῃ προσγίνεται
τοῖς ἀνθρώποις, ὅταν ἐν αὐτῇ που τῇ ψυχῇ τὸ
ὄντως καλὸν ὑπὸ τοῦ θείου λόγου ἀναζωπυρούμενον
ἐκλάμπειν δυνηθῇ· καὶ τὸ μέγιστον, ἅμα τῷ

---

[1] θεραπεύει Schwartz.   θεραπεύσει mss.

and shall not Christ, think you, having breathed to the ends of the earth a song of peace, assemble the soldiers of peace that are His? Yes, and He did assemble, O man, by blood and by word His bloodless army, and to them He entrusted the kingdom of heaven. The trumpet of Christ is His gospel. He sounded it, and we heard. Let us gird ourselves with the armour of peace, "putting on the breast- plate of righteousness," and taking up the shield of faith, and placing on our head the helmet of salva- tion; and let us sharpen "the sword of the spirit, which is the word of God."[a] Thus does the apostle marshal us in the ranks of peace. These are our invulnerable arms; equipped with these let us stand in array against the evil one. Let us quench the fiery darts of the evil one[b] with the moistened sword-points, those that have been dipped in water by the Word,[c] returning thankful praises to God for His benefits and honouring Him through the divine Word. "For while thou art yet speaking," it says, "He will answer, behold, I am with thee."[d]

O sacred and blessed power, through which God becomes a fellow-citizen with men! It is then better and more profitable for man to become at the same time both imitator and servant of the highest of all beings; for he will not be able to imitate God except by serving Him holily, nor yet to serve and worship except by imitating Him. Now the heavenly and truly divine love comes to men in this way, whenever somewhere in the soul itself the spark of true nobility, kindled afresh by the divine Word, is able to shine out; and, greatest thing of all, salva-

---

[a] See Eph. vi. 14–17; 1 Thess. v. 8.   [b] Eph. vi. 16.
[c] The allusion is to Baptism.   [d] Isa. lviii. 9.

CAP.
XI
βουληθῆναι γνησίως τὸ σωθῆναι συντρέχει, ὁμο-
ζυγούντων, ὡς ἔπος εἰπεῖν, προαιρέσεως καὶ ζωῆς.
τοιγάρτοι μόνη αὕτη ἡ τῆς ἀληθείας προτροπὴ τοῖς
πιστοτάτοις ἀπείκασται τῶν φίλων μέχρι τῆς ἐσχάτης ἀναπνοῆς παραμένουσα καὶ παραπομπὸς ἀγαθὴ
ὅλῳ καὶ τελείῳ τῷ τῆς ψυχῆς πνεύματι τοῖς εἰς
οὐρανὸν ἀπαίρουσι γενομένη. τί δή σε προτρέπω;
σωθῆναί σε ἐπείγομαι. τοῦτο Χριστὸς βούλεται·
ἑνὶ λόγῳ ζωήν σοι χαρίζεται. καὶ τίς ἐστιν οὗτος;
μάθε συντόμως· λόγος ἀληθείας, λόγος ἀφθαρσίας,
ὁ ἀναγεννῶν τὸν ἄνθρωπον, εἰς ἀλήθειαν αὐτὸν
ἀναφέρων, τὸ κέντρον τῆς σωτηρίας, ὁ ἐξελαύνων
τὴν φθοράν, ὁ ἐκδιώκων τὸν θάνατον, ὁ ἐν ἀνθρώποις
οἰκοδομήσας νεών, ἵνα ἐν ἀνθρώποις ἱδρύσῃ τὸν
θεόν. ἅγνισον τὸν νεών, καὶ τὰς ἡδονὰς καὶ τὰς
ῥαθυμίας ὥσπερ ἄνθος ἐφήμερον καταλίμπανε ἀνέμῳ
καὶ πυρί, σωφροσύνης δὲ τοὺς καρποὺς γεώργησον
91 P. ἐμφρόνως, καὶ σεαυτὸν ἀκροθίνιον | ἀνάστησον τῷ
θεῷ, ὅπως οὐκ ἔργον μόνον, ἀλλὰ καὶ χάρις ᾖς[1] τοῦ
θεοῦ· πρέπει δὲ ἄμφω τῷ Χριστοῦ[2] γνωρίμῳ, καὶ
βασιλείας ἄξιον φανῆναι καὶ βασιλείας κατηξιῶσθαι.

XII

Φύγωμεν οὖν τὴν συνήθειαν, φύγωμεν οἷον ἄκραν
χαλεπὴν ἢ Χαρύβδεως ἀπειλὴν ἢ Σειρῆνας μυθικάς·
ἄγχει τὸν ἄνθρωπον, τῆς ἀληθείας ἀποτρέπει,
ἀπάγει τῆς ζωῆς, παγίς ἐστιν, βάραθρόν ἐστιν,
βόθρος ἐστί, λίχνον[3] ἐστὶν κακὸν ἡ συνήθεια·

[1] ᾖς Wilamowitz. ᾖ MSS.
[2] Χριστοῦ Mayor. Χριστῷ MSS.
[3] λίχνον Mayor. λίχνος MSS.

250

tion itself runs side by side with the sincere desire for
it, will and life being, as we may say, yoked together.
Wherefore this exhortation to the truth, and this
alone, is like the most faithful of our friends; for
it remains with us until our latest breath, and proves
a good escort for the whole and perfect spirit of
the soul to those who are setting out for heaven.
What then is my exhortation? I urge thee to be
saved. This is the wish of Christ; in one word, He
freely grants thee life. And who is He? Understand
briefly: the Word of truth; the Word of incorruption;
He who regenerates man by bringing him back to
the truth; the goad of salvation; He who banishes
corruption and expels death; He who has built His
temple in men, that in men He may set up the
shrine of God. Purify the temple, and abandon
your pleasures and careless ways, like the flower of
a day, to the wind and fire; but labour in wisdom
for the harvest of self-control, and present yourself
as first-fruits to God, in order that you may be not
only His work, but also His delight. Both things
are necessary for the friend of Christ: he must show
himself worthy of a kingdom, and be counted worthy
of a kingdom.

*CHAP.
XI*

*This ex-
hortation is
a faithful
friend, in
life and at
death*

*Christ
wishes us
to be saved*

*Let us for-
sake sin, and
become
God's de-
light as well
as His work*

XII

Let us then shun custom; let us shun it as some
dangerous headland, or threatening Charybdis, or
the Sirens of legend. Custom strangles man; it turns
him away from truth; it leads him away from life;
it is a snare, an abyss, a pit, a devouring evil.

*Custom is
like the
Sirens;
it allures
only to
destroy*

CLEMENT OF ALEXANDRIA

κείνου μὲν καπνοῦ καὶ κύματος ἐκτὸς ἔεργε
νῆα.

φεύγωμεν, ὦ συνναῦται, φεύγωμεν τὸ κῦμα τοῦτο,
πῦρ ἐρεύγεται, νῆσός ἐστι πονηρὰ ὀστοῖς καὶ
νεκροῖς σεσωρευμένη, ᾄδει δὲ ἐν αὐτῇ πορνίδιον
ὡραῖον, ἡδονή, πανδήμῳ τερπόμενον μουσικῇ·

δεῦρ' ἄγ' ἰών, πολύαιν' Ὀδυσεῦ, μέγα κῦδος
Ἀχαιῶν,
νῆα κατάστησον, ἵνα θειοτέρην ὄπ' ἀκούσῃς.

ἐπαινεῖ σε, ὦ ναῦτα, καὶ πολυύμνητον λέγει, καὶ
τὸ κῦδος τῶν Ἑλλήνων ἡ πόρνη σφετερίζεται·
ἔασον αὐτὴν ἐπινέμεσθαι τοὺς νεκρούς, πνεῦμά σοι[1]
οὐράνιον βοηθεῖ· πάριθι τὴν ἡδονήν, βουκολεῖ·

μηδὲ γυνή σε νόον πυγοστόλος ἐξαπατάτω,
αἱμύλα κωτίλλουσα, τεὴν διφῶσα καλιήν.

παράπλει τὴν ᾠδήν, θάνατον ἐργάζεται· ἐὰν ἐθέλῃς
μόνον, νενίκηκας τὴν ἀπώλειαν καὶ τῷ ξύλῳ προσ-
δεδεμένος ἁπάσης ἔσῃ τῆς φθορᾶς λελυμένος, κυβερ-
νήσει σε ὁ λόγος ὁ τοῦ θεοῦ, κἂν[2] τοῖς λιμέσι
καθορμίσει τῶν οὐρανῶν τὸ πνεῦμα τὸ ἅγιον· τότε
μου κατοπτεύσεις τὸν θεὸν καὶ τοῖς ἁγίοις ἐκείνοις
τελεσθήσῃ μυστηρίοις καὶ τῶν ἐν οὐρανοῖς ἀπο-
λαύσεις ἀποκεκρυμμένων, τῶν ἐμοὶ τετηρημένων,
" ἃ οὔτε οὖς ἤκουσεν οὔτε ἐπὶ καρδίαν ἀνέβη "
τινός.

---

[1] σοι Höschel.   σε MSS.   [2] κἂν Mayor.   καὶ MSS.

---

[a] Homer, *Odyssey* xii. 219-20.
[b] See *Odyssey* xii. 45-46.   [c] *Odyssey* xii. 184-5.
252

Wide of that smoke and wave direct, O helmsman, thy vessel.[a]

Let us flee, comrades, let us flee from this wave. It belches forth fire; it is an island of wickedness heaped with bones and corpses,[b] and she who sings therein is pleasure, a harlot in the bloom of youth, delighting in her vulgar music.

Hither, renowned Odysseus, great glory of all the Achaeans:
Bring thy ship to the land, that a song divine may entrance thee.[c]

She praises thee, sailor, she calls thee renowned in song; the harlot would make the glory of the Greeks her own. Leave her to roam among the corpses; a heavenly wind comes to thine aid. Pass by pleasure; she beguiles.

Let not thy heart be deceived by a woman with trailing garment,
Coaxing with wily words to find the place of thy dwelling.[d]

Sail past the song; it works death. Only resolve, and thou hast vanquished destruction; bound to the wood of the cross[e] thou shalt live freed from all corruption. The Word of God shall be thy pilot and the Holy Spirit shall bring thee to anchor in the harbours of heaven. Then thou shalt have the vision of my God, and shalt be initiated in those holy mysteries, and shalt taste the joys that are hidden away in heaven, preserved for me, "which neither ear hath heard nor have they entered into the heart"[f] of any man.

[d] Hesiod, *Works and Days* 373–4.
[e] An allusion to Odysseus being bound to the mast of his vessel as it passed the land of the Sirens. *Odyssey* xii. 178.
[f] 1 Corinthians ii. 9.

CLEMENT OF ALEXANDRIA

καὶ μὴν ὁρᾶν μοι δύο μὲν ἡλίους δοκῶ,
δισσὰς δὲ Θήβας |

92 P. βακχεύων ἔλεγέν τις εἰδώλοις, ἀγνοίᾳ μεθύων ἀ-
κράτῳ· ἐγὼ δ' < ἂν >[1] αὐτὸν οἰκτείραιμι παροινοῦντα
καὶ τὸν οὕτω παρανοοῦντα ἐπὶ σωτηρίαν παρα-
καλέσαιμι σωφρονοῦσαν, ὅτι καὶ κύριος μετάνοιαν
ἁμαρτωλοῦ καὶ οὐχὶ θάνατον ἀσπάζεται. ἧκε, ὦ
παραπλήξ, μὴ θύρσῳ σκηριπτόμενος, μὴ κιττῷ
ἀναδούμενος, ῥῖψον τὴν μίτραν, ῥῖψον τὴν νεβρίδα,
σωφρόνησον· δείξω σοι τὸν λόγον καὶ τοῦ λόγου
τὰ μυστήρια, κατὰ τὴν σὴν διηγούμενος εἰκόνα.
ὄρος ἐστὶ τοῦτο θεῷ πεφιλημένον, οὐ τραγῳδίαις ὡς
Κιθαιρὼν ὑποκείμενον, ἀλλὰ τοῖς ἀληθείας ἀνα-
κείμενον δράμασιν, ὄρος νηφάλιον, ἀγναῖς ὕλαις
σύσκιον· βακχεύουσι δὲ ἐν αὐτῷ οὐχ αἱ Σεμέλης
" τῆς κεραυνίας " ἀδελφαί, αἱ μαινάδες, αἱ δύσαγνον
κρεανομίαν μυούμεναι, ἀλλ' αἱ τοῦ θεοῦ θυγατέρες,
αἱ ἀμνάδες αἱ καλαί, τὰ σεμνὰ τοῦ λόγου θεσπί-
ζουσαι ὄργια, χορὸν ἀγείρουσαι σώφρονα. ὁ χορὸς οἱ
δίκαιοι, τὸ ᾆσμα ὕμνος ἐστὶ τοῦ πάντων βασιλέως·
ψάλλουσιν αἱ κόραι, δοξάζουσιν ἄγγελοι, προφῆται
λαλοῦσιν, ἦχος στέλλεται μουσικῆς, δρόμῳ τὸν

---

[1] < ἂν > inserted by Stählin.

---

[a] Euripides, *Bacchants* 918-9. The speaker is Pentheus,
king of Thebes, who was stricken with madness for refusing
to worship the god Dionysus. The legend, which tells how
Dionysus took vengeance by visiting the Theban women
with his frenzy and driving them out into the hills, and how
the mad king, in trying to spy out their revels, was torn to
pieces by his own mother and her companions, is the subject
of Euripides' play, the *Bacchants*. In the paragraph following this quotation, Clement has the *Bacchants* constantly in

> And lo! methinks I see a pair of suns
> And a double Thebes,[a]

A warning
from the
mad
Pentheus

said one who was revelling in frenzy through idols,
drunk with sheer ignorance. I would pity him in
his drunkenness, and would appeal to him to return
from this madness to sober salvation, seeing that the
Lord also welcomes the repentance, and not the
death, of a sinner. Come, thou frenzy-stricken one,
not resting on thy wand, not wreathed with ivy!
Cast off thy headdress; cast off thy fawnskin;[b] return
to soberness! I will show thee the Word, and the
Word's mysteries, describing them according to thine
own semblance of them. This is the mountain
beloved of God, not a subject for tragedies, like
Cithaeron, but one devoted to the dramas of truth,
a wineless mountain, shaded by hallowed groves.
Therein revel no Maenads, sisters of "thunder-
smitten"[c] Semele, who are initiated in the loathsome
distribution of raw flesh, but the daughters of God, the
beautiful lambs,[d] who declare the solemn rites of the
Word, assembling a sober company. The righteous
form this company, and their song is a hymn in
praise of the King of all. The maidens play the
harp, angels give glory, prophets speak, a noise of
music rises; swiftly they pursue the sacred band,[e]

Description
of the
Word's sober
mysteries

mind, and his allusions can only be understood by reading
the play.

[b] For the description see Euripides, *Bacchants* 833, 835.

[c] Euripides, *Bacchants* 6, 26.

[d] The Greek *amnades*, lambs, is meant as a play upon
Mainades (Maenads, or women worshippers of Dionysus).

[e] Gr. *thiasos*, or band of Dionysus' followers (cp. *Bacchants*
56). The word is here used of the company of maidens,
angels and prophets, whom the Christian must follow to
reach, not Dionysus, but the Father.

CAP.
XII

θίασον διώκουσιν, σπεύδουσιν οἱ κεκλημένοι πατέρα ποθοῦντες ἀπολαβεῖν. ἧκέ μοι, ὦ πρέσβυ, καὶ σύ, τὰς Θήβας λιπὼν καὶ τὴν μαντικὴν καὶ τὴν βακχείαν[1] ἀπορρίψας πρὸς ἀλήθειαν χειραγωγοῦ· ἰδού σοι τὸ ξύλον ἐπερείδεσθαι δίδωμι· σπεῦσον, Τειρεσία, πίστευσον· ὄψει· Χριστὸς ἐπιλάμπει φαιδρότερον ἡλίου, δι' ὃν ὀφθαλμοὶ τυφλῶν ἀναβλέπουσιν· νύξ σε φεύξεται, πῦρ φοβηθήσεται, θάνατος οἰχήσεται· ὄψει τοὺς οὐρανούς, ὦ γέρον, ὁ Θήβας μὴ βλέπων.

Ὦ τῶν ἁγίων ὡς ἀληθῶς μυστηρίων, ὦ φωτὸς ἀκηράτου. δαδουχοῦμαι τοὺς οὐρανοὺς καὶ τὸν θεὸν ἐποπτεῦσαι,[2] ἅγιος γίνομαι μυούμενος, ἱεροφαντεῖ δὲ ὁ κύριος καὶ τὸν μύστην σφραγίζεται φωταγωγῶν, καὶ παρατίθεται τῷ πατρὶ τὸν πεπιστευκότα αἰῶσι τηρούμενον. ταῦτα τῶν ἐμῶν μυστηρίων τὰ βακχεύματα· εἰ βούλει, καὶ σὺ μυοῦ, καὶ χορεύσεις μετ' ἀγγέλων ἀμφὶ τὸν ἀγένητον καὶ ἀνώλεθρον καὶ μόνον ὄντως θεόν, συνυμνοῦντος 93 P. ἡμῖν τοῦ θεοῦ λόγου. ἀίδιος | οὗτος Ἰησοῦς, εἷς [ὁ][3] μέγας ἀρχιερεὺς θεοῦ τε ἑνὸς τοῦ αὐτοῦ καὶ πατρός, ὑπὲρ ἀνθρώπων εὔχεται καὶ ἀνθρώποις ἐγκελεύεται "κέκλυτε, μυρία φῦλα," μᾶλλον δὲ ὅσοι τῶν ἀνθρώπων λογικοί, καὶ βάρβαροι καὶ Ἕλληνες· τὸ πᾶν ἀνθρώπων γένος καλῶ, ὧν ἐγὼ δημιουργὸς θελήματι πατρός. ἥκετε ὡς ἐμέ, ὑφ' ἕνα ταχθησόμενοι θεὸν καὶ τὸν ἕνα λόγον τοῦ θεοῦ, καὶ μὴ μόνον τῶν ἀλόγων ζώων πλεονεκτεῖτε τῷ λόγῳ, ἐκ δὲ τῶν θνητῶν ἁπάντων ὑμῖν ἀθανασίαν μόνοις καρ-

---

[1] βακχείαν Wilamowitz. βακχικὴν mss.
[2] ἐποπτεῦσαι Schwartz. ἐποπτεύσας mss.
[3] [ὁ] Wilamowitz.

---

[a] i.e. instead of Teiresias' staff; cp. Bacchants 363-4.

256

those who have been called hasting with eager longing to receive the Father. Come to me, old man, come thou too! Quit Thebes; fling away thy prophecy and Bacchic revelry and be led by the hand to truth. Behold, I give thee the wood of the cross to lean upon.[a] Hasten, Teiresias, believe! Thou shalt have sight. Christ, by whom the eyes of the blind see again, shineth upon thee more brightly than the sun. Night shall flee from thee; fire shall fear thee; death shall depart from thee. Thou shalt see heaven, old man, though thou canst not see Thebes.

O truly sacred mysteries! O pure light! In the blaze of the torches I have a vision of heaven and of God. I become holy by initiation. The Lord reveals the mysteries; He marks the worshipper with His seal, gives light to guide his way, and commends him, when he has believed, to the Father's care, where he is guarded for ages to come. These are the revels of my mysteries! If thou wilt, be thyself also initiated, and thou shalt dance with angels around the unbegotten and imperishable and only true God, the Word of God joining with us in our hymn of praise. This Jesus being eternal, one great high priest of one God who is also Father, prays for men and encourages men: "'Give ear, ye myriad peoples,'[b] or rather, so many of mankind as are governed by reason, both barbarians and Greeks; the whole race of men I call, I who was their Creator by the Father's will. Come to me, that ye may be marshalled under one God and the one Word of God; and do not surpass the irrational creatures in reason only, for to you alone of all mortal beings I offer the fruit

Marginal notes:

CHAP.
XII

Even the blind shall see God and heaven

These are the true mysteries

Exhortation to be initiated

The Word Himself calls men to come

He offers immortality

[b] Homer, *Iliad* xvii. 220.

CAP.
XII
πώσασθαι δίδωμι. ἐθέλω γάρ, ἐθέλω καὶ ταύτης ὑμῖν μεταδοῦναι τῆς χάριτος, ὁλόκληρον χορηγῶν τὴν εὐεργεσίαν, ἀφθαρσίαν· καὶ λόγον χαρίζομαι ὑμῖν, τὴν γνῶσιν τοῦ θεοῦ τέλειον ἐμαυτὸν χαρίζομαι. τοῦτό εἰμι ἐγώ, τοῦτο βούλεται ὁ θεός, τοῦτο συμφωνία ἐστί, τοῦτο ἁρμονία πατρός, τοῦτο υἱός, τοῦτο Χριστός, τοῦτο ὁ λόγος τοῦ θεοῦ, βραχίων κυρίου, δύναμις τῶν ὅλων, τὸ θέλημα τοῦ πατρός. ὧ[1] πάλαι μὲν εἰκόνες, οὐ πᾶσαι δὲ ἐμφερεῖς, διορθώσασθαι ὑμᾶς πρὸς τὸ ἀρχέτυπον βούλομαι, ἵνα μοι καὶ ὅμοιοι γένησθε. χρίσω ὑμᾶς τῷ πίστεως ἀλείμματι, δι' οὗ τὴν φθορὰν ἀποβάλλετε, καὶ γυμνὸν δικαιοσύνης ἐπιδείξω τὸ σχῆμα, δι' οὗ πρὸς τὸν θεὸν ἀναβαίνετε. " δεῦτε πρός με πάντες οἱ κοπιῶντες καὶ πεφορτισμένοι, κἀγὼ ἀναπαύσω ὑμᾶς· ἄρατε τὸν ζυγόν μου ἐφ' ὑμᾶς καὶ μάθετε ἀπ' ἐμοῦ, ὅτι πραΰς εἰμι καὶ ταπεινὸς τῇ καρδίᾳ, καὶ εὑρήσετε ἀνάπαυσιν ταῖς ψυχαῖς ὑμῶν· ὁ γὰρ ζυγός μου χρηστὸς καὶ τὸ φορτίον μου ἐλαφρόν ἐστιν." σπεύσωμεν, δράμωμεν, ὦ θεοφιλῆ καὶ θεοείκελα τοῦ λόγου [ἄνθρωποι][2] ἀγάλματα· σπεύσωμεν, δράμωμεν, ἄρωμεν τὸν ζυγὸν αὐτοῦ, ὑπολάβωμεν ἀφθαρσίαν,[3] καλὸν ἡνίοχον ἀνθρώπων τὸν Χριστὸν ἀγαπήσωμεν· τὸν πῶλον ὑποζύγιον ἤγαγε σὺν τῷ παλαιῷ· καὶ τῶν ἀνθρώπων τὴν συνωρίδα καταζεύξας, εἰς ἀθανασίαν κατιθύνει τὸ ἅρμα, σπεύδων πρὸς τὸν θεὸν πληρῶσαι ἐναργῶς ὃ ᾐνίξατο, πρότερον μὲν εἰς Ἱερουσαλήμ, νῦν δὲ εἰσελαύνων

---

[1] ὧ Wilamowitz. ὧν MSS.
[2] [ἄνθρωποι] Heyse.
[3] ὑπολάβωμεν ἀφθαρσίαν Mayor. ὑποβάλωμεν ἀφθαρσίαι MSS. ἐπιβάλωμεν ἀφθαρσίᾳ Wilamowitz (whom Stählin follows).

of immortality. I desire, yea, I desire to impart
to you even this gracious favour, supplying in its
fulness the good gift of incorruption. And I freely
give you divine reason, the knowledge of God; I give
you Myself in perfection. For this is Myself, this is
God's desire, this is the concord, this the harmony
of the Father: this is the Son, this is Christ, this
is the Word of God, the arm of the Lord, the might
of the universe, the Father's will. O ye who of old He will
were images, but do not all resemble your model, I make men true images
desire to conform you to the archetype, that you of Himself
may become even as I am. I will anoint you with
the ointment of faith, whereby you cast away corruption; and I will display unveiled the figure of
righteousness, whereby you ascend to God. ' Come
unto Me, all ye that labour and are heavy laden, He will
and I will give you rest. Take My yoke upon give rest
you and learn of Me; for I am meek and lowly in
heart, and ye shall find rest unto your souls. For
My yoke is easy and My burden is light.' " [a] Let us
hasten, let us run, we who are images of the Word,
beloved of God and made in His likeness. Let us
hasten, let us run; let us take up His yoke; let us
take upon ourselves incorruption; let us love Christ,
the noble charioteer of men. He led the foal and its He drives
parent under the same yoke,[b] and now having yoked the team of mankind
together the team of mankind, He shapes the course into heaven
of His chariot for the goal of immortality. He
hastens to God that He may fulfil clearly what before
He darkly hinted at; for He drove at the first
into Jerusalem, but now into heaven, a most noble

[a] St. Matthew xi. 28-30.
[b] See St. Matthew xxi. 1-7.

CAP.
XII

οὐρανούς, κάλλιστον θέαμα τῷ πατρὶ υἱὸς ἀίδιος νικηφόρος. φιλότιμοι τοίνυν πρὸς τὰ καλὰ καὶ θεοφιλεῖς ἄνθρωποι γενώμεθα, καὶ τῶν ἀγαθῶν[1] τὰ μέγιστα, θεὸν καὶ ζωήν, κτησώμεθα. ἀρωγὸς δὲ ὁ λόγος· θαρρῶμεν αὐτῷ καὶ μή ποτε ἡμᾶς τοσοῦτος

94 P. ἀργύρου καὶ | χρυσοῦ, μὴ δόξῃς ἐπέλθῃ πόθος, ὅσος αὐτοῦ τοῦ τῆς ἀληθείας λόγου. οὐδὲ γὰρ οὐδὲ τῷ θεῷ αὐτῷ ἀρεστόν, εἰ ἡμεῖς τὰ μὲν πλείστου ἄξια περὶ[2] ἐλαχίστου ποιούμεθα, ἀγνοίας[3] δὲ καὶ ἀμαθίας καὶ ῥαθυμίας καὶ εἰδωλολατρείας ὕβρεις περιφανεῖς καὶ τὴν ἐσχάτην δυσσέβειαν περὶ πλείονος αἱρούμεθα.[4]

Οὐ γὰρ ἀπὸ τρόπου φιλοσόφων παῖδες πάντα ὅσα πράττουσιν οἱ ἀνόητοι, ἀνοσιουργεῖν καὶ ἀσεβεῖν νομίζουσιν καὶ αὐτήν γε [ἔτι][5] τὴν ἄγνοιαν μανίας εἶδος ὑπογράφοντες οὐδὲν ἄλλο ἢ μεμηνέναι τοὺς πολλοὺς ὁμολογοῦσιν. οὐ δὴ οὖν ἀμφιβάλλειν αἱρεῖ[6] ὁ λόγος, ὁπότερον αὐτοῖν ἄμεινον, σωφρονεῖν ἢ μεμηνέναι· ἐχομένους δὲ ἀπρὶξ τῆς ἀληθείας παντὶ σθένει ἕπεσθαι χρὴ τῷ θεῷ σωφρονοῦντας καὶ πάντα αὐτοῦ νομίζειν, ὥσπερ ἔστι, πρὸς δὲ καὶ ἡμᾶς τὸ κάλλιστον τῶν κτημάτων μεμαθηκότας ὄντας αὐτοῦ, σφᾶς αὐτοὺς ἐπιτρέπειν τῷ θεῷ, ἀγαπῶντας κύριον τὸν θεὸν καὶ τοῦτο παρ᾽ ὅλον τὸν βίον ἔργον ἡγουμένους. εἰ δὲ "κοινὰ τὰ φίλων," θεοφιλὴς δὲ ὁ ἄνθρωπος (καὶ γὰρ οὖν φίλος τῷ θεῷ,[7] μεσιτεύοντος τοῦ λόγου), γίνεται δὴ οὖν

---

[1] ἀγαθῶν Stählin. ἀπαθῶν mss. [2] περὶ Cobet. ὑπὲρ mss.
[3] ἀγνοίας Markland. ἀνοίας mss.
[4] αἱρούμεθα Stählin. αἱρώμεθα mss.
[5] [ἔτι] Wilamowitz. [6] αἱρεῖ Cobet. ἐρεῖ mss.
[7] τῷ θεῷ after φίλος Wilamowitz, after ἄνθρωπος mss. [τῷ θεῷ] Cobet.

spectacle for the Father, the eternal Son bringing CHAP.
victory! Let us be zealous, therefore, for what is XII
noble, and become men beloved of God; and let us
get possession of the greatest of good things, God
and life. The Word is our helper; let us have confidence in Him, and let no longing after silver and
gold, or after glory, ever come upon us so strongly
as the longing after the Word of truth Himself.
For surely it cannot be pleasing to God Himself
if we hold in least esteem those things which are
of the greatest moment, while we choose as of
higher worth the manifest excesses and the utter
impiety of ignorance, stupidity, indifference and
idolatry.

The sons of the philosophers not inaptly consider Philoso-
that all the works of foolish men are unholy and phers think
impious, and by describing ignorance itself as a form a sort of
of madness they acknowledge that the mass of men are madness
nothing else but mad.[a] Now reason does not allow
us to doubt which of the two is better, to be sane or
to be mad. Holding fast the truth with all our might But we
we must follow God in soundness of mind, and con- must hold
sider all things to be His, as indeed they are; and truth, and
further we must recognize that we are the noblest of not be mad
His possessions and entrust ourselves to Him, loving
the Lord God, and looking upon that as our work
throughout the whole of life. And if " the goods of If we
friends are common," [b] and man is beloved of God become
(for he is indeed dear to God through the mediation God, all
of the Word), then all things become man's, because are ours

[a] The philosophers referred to are the Stoics; cp. Cicero,
Paradoxon iv. and *Tusc. disp.* iii. 5.
[b] Greek proverb. See Plato, *Phaedrus* 279 c.

CAP.
XII

τὰ πάντα τοῦ ἀνθρώπου, ὅτι τὰ πάντα τοῦ θεοῦ,
καὶ κοινὰ ἀμφοῖν τοῖν φίλοιν τὰ πάντα, τοῦ θεοῦ
καὶ ἀνθρώπου. ὥρα οὖν ἡμῖν μόνον τὸν θεοσεβῆ
[Χριστιανόν] [1] εἰπεῖν πλούσιόν τε καὶ σώφρονα καὶ
εὐγενῆ καὶ ταύτῃ εἰκόνα τοῦ θεοῦ μεθ' ὁμοιώσεως,
καὶ λέγειν καὶ πιστεύειν " δίκαιον καὶ ὅσιον μετὰ
φρονήσεως " γενόμενον ὑπὸ Χριστοῦ Ἰησοῦ καὶ εἰς
τοσοῦτον ὅμοιον ἤδη καὶ θεῷ. οὐκ ἀποκρύπτεται
γοῦν ὁ προφήτης τὴν χάριν λέγων, " ἐγὼ εἶπον
ὅτι θεοί ἐστε καὶ υἱοὶ ὑψίστου πάντες." ἡμᾶς γάρ,
ἡμᾶς εἰσπεποίηται καὶ ἡμῶν ἐθέλει μόνους κεκλῆσθαι

95 P. | πατήρ, οὐ τῶν ἀπειθούντων. καὶ γὰρ οὖν ὧδέ
πως ἔχει τὰ ἡμέτερα τῶν Χριστοῦ ὁπαδῶν· οἷαι
μὲν αἱ βουλαί, τοῖοι καὶ οἱ λόγοι, ὁποῖοι δὲ οἱ
λόγοι, τοιαίδε καὶ αἱ πράξεις, καὶ ὁποῖα τὰ ἔργα,
τοιοῦτος ὁ βίος· χρηστὸς ὁ σύμπας ἀνθρώπων βίος
τῶν Χριστὸν ἐγνωκότων.

Ἅλις οἶμαι τῶν λόγων, εἰ καὶ μακροτέρω προ-
ῆλθον ὑπὸ φιλανθρωπίας ὅ τι περ εἶχον ἐκ θεοῦ
ἐκχέων, ὡς ἂν ἐπὶ τὸ μέγιστον τῶν ἀγαθῶν, τὴν
σωτηρίαν, παρακαλῶν· περὶ γάρ τοι τῆς παῦλαν
οὐδαμῇ οὐδαμῶς ἐχούσης ζωῆς οὐκ ἐθέλουσιν
οὐδ' οἱ λόγοι παύσασθαί ποτε ἱεροφαντοῦντες.
ὑμῖν δὲ ἔτι τοῦτο περιλείπεται πέρας τὸ λυσιτε-
λοῦν ἐλέσθαι, ἢ κρίσιν ἢ χάριν· ὡς ἔγωγε οὐδ' ἀμφιβάλλειν ἀξιῶ, πότερον ἄμεινον αὐτοῖν· οὐδὲ μὴν
συγκρίνεσθαι θέμις ζωὴν ἀπωλείᾳ.

---

[1] [Χριστιανόν] Wilamowitz.

---

[a] The Stoics said all this of their " wise man," as Clement
tells us elsewhere (ii. *Strom.* 19. 4): "The Stoic philosophers
hold this doctrine, that kingship, priesthood, prophecy,
legislation, wealth, true beauty, noble birth and freedom

all things belong to God and are common to both friends, God and man. It is time then for us to affirm that only the God-fearing man is rich and of sound mind and well-born,[a] and therefore the image, together with the likeness,[b] of God; and to say and believe that when he has been made by Christ Jesus "just and holy with understanding,"[c] he also becomes in the same degree already like to God. So the prophet openly reveals this gracious favour when he says, "I said, ye are gods, and ye are all sons of the Most High."[d] Now we, I say, we are they whom God has adopted, and of us alone He is willing to be called Father, not of the disobedient. For indeed this is the position of us who are Christ's attendants[e]: as are the counsels, so are the words; as are the words, so are the actions; and as are the deeds, such is the life. The entire life of men who have come to know Christ is good.

Enough, I think, of words. It may be that, moved by love of man, I have run on too long in pouring out what I have received from God, as is natural when one is inviting men to the greatest of good things—salvation. For of a truth, the very words are unwilling ever to cease revealing the mysteries of that life which knows no manner of ending. But with you still rests the final act, namely this, to choose which is the more profitable, judgment or grace. For my own part, I claim that there is no shadow of doubt which of the two is better; nay, it is sinful even to compare life with destruction.

belong to the wise man alone. But even they admit that he is exceedingly hard to find."   [b] See Genesis i. 26.
   [c] Plato, *Theaetetus* 176 B.   [d] Psalm lxxxii. 6.
   [e] This phrase is an allusion to Plato, *Phaedrus* 252 c:
"the attendants of Zeus" (τῶν Διὸς ὀπαδῶν).

THE RICH MAN'S SALVATION

THE Rich Man's Salvation, or, to give the work its literal title, "Who is the rich man that is being saved?" is the only complete example left us of Clement's popular teaching. Although composed in the form of a sermon, it would seem too long to have been delivered orally on any single occasion. Possibly it may be the expansion and elaboration of an actual sermon; but, whether this is so or not, we may be sure that the teaching it contains formed the subject of many a discourse addressed by Clement to the rich Christians of Alexandria. In all probability the Church came into close touch with the cultured and well-to-do classes earlier at Alexandria than elsewhere. Consequently, the problem of reconciling Christianity with the possession of worldly wealth would be likely to have become acute there in the second century. It was not an easy problem to solve. The rich man who was well-disposed towards the new religion had to consider many things which, as Clement in this treatise admits, often drove him to the conclusion that the Church had no place for him. There was

265

the poor and simple life of Christ Himself and of His
apostles; there were the numerous gospel warnings
about the dangers of wealth; there was the severe
command to the rich man to sell all that he had;
there was the communism of the first Christians;
there was the undoubted fact that the Church had
spread among poor people and had always been
chiefly composed of them. All these considerations,
augmented and strengthened by the conviction that
a gospel of the eternal life had but little to do with
comfort in this world, made it difficult both for the
rich to enter the Church and for the poor to receive
them there without jealousy or suspicion. Clement's
extensive learning, for the acquisition of which
money and leisure were certainly necessary, and his
familiarity with the customs of refined society, show
that he was himself a man of at least some wealth
and position. He was therefore personally interested
in the question which he sets out to answer in the
work now before us.

He takes as a basis for his inquiry the passage
about the rich man in St. Mark x. 17-31. Here was
the hardest stumbling-block of all to the rich who
wanted to become Christians, and Clement removes
it in characteristic fashion by denying that Christ's
words mean what they seem to say. Apparently it
never occurred to him that, on the theory of " diver-
sities of gifts," one man might be ordered to give up
his wealth and another to keep it for wise and
generous use. He knew that even in pre-Christian
days some men had felt that their highest work
could only be done at the cost of sacrificing their
possessions; but he was unwilling to allow that
Anaxagoras, Democritus and Crates had, to the

best of their ability, fulfilled the very ideal that Christ had placed before the rich man. It must be something fundamentally different from this that Christ meant, so Clement says. What then was His meaning? The wealth He bade His questioner renounce must be taken in a spiritual sense; it was a wealth of passions, a brood of sins in the soul; not money itself, but the love of money. The rich man might have kept his wealth, and by following Jesus have learned to use it rightly. All that rich men in general have to do, therefore, is to eradicate selfishness and to spend their money liberally for the relief of their poorer brethren, who by interceding with God for such benefactors will return an abundant recompense.

As a result of this exegesis we are robbed of one of the most striking appeals to a man's heroism and contempt of consequences that even the gospels contain. There can be no question that the Christian Church has suffered much, and is still suffering, from that avoidance of the plain meaning of historical records which is characteristic of the Alexandrine system of spiritual or allegorical interpretation. It would, however, be unfair, as well as ungracious, to lay the whole blame of this upon Clement. He was but the exponent of a system for which the age in which he lived was responsible. Nor must we forget the positive advantages that were gained by this interpretation. The mission of Clement and the Alexandrine Church was to give Christianity a firm footing in the world, and to allow it to assimilate all that was good of human thought and culture. In Clement's day the belief in a speedy return of Christ was passing away, and consciously or unconsciously the Church was preparing for its own continuance as a permanent institution in human society ; a citizenship on earth was being claimed alongside of St. Paul's " citizenship in heaven." When once this is admitted, neither philosophy, nor science, nor art, nor even the leisure and refinement that are associated with wealth, can be utterly excluded from the Church. In the *Stromateis* we see Clement boldly claiming for Greek philosophy a place in the life of Christian people ; in the " Rich Man's Salvation " we see him making the same bold claim on behalf of wealth. There is no virtue, he says, in beggary ; there are certain good things which wealth alone can bring ; and if the rich man will but learn to spend his riches in the alleviation of suffering and the brightening and comforting of other lives, he need not despair of a place among the followers of Christ.

The present translation of " The Rich Man," like that of the " Exhortation to the Greeks," has been made from Stählin's edition of Clement, and the text printed here is in the main Stählin's text. Any deviations of importance from the reading of the chief manuscript are noted at the foot of each page. This manuscript is the one in the Escurial library, known as S. A page is missing from the end of S, and also from the Vatican manuscript which was copied from it. This page, however, consisting of the story of St. John and the robber, is almost completely recoverable from Eusebius who quotes it (*H.E.* iii. 23), and from the Scholia of Maximus Confessor on Dionysius the Areopagite. About twenty lines are still lost. A few words that are missing from the first three

THE RICH MAN'S SALVATION

paragraphs have been inserted in the following text according to what seemed the best conjectures available. Before Stählin's edition was issued the text of S had been carefully edited and the manuscript described by P. M. Barnard (*Texts and Studies*, edited by J. Armitage Robinson, D.D., vol. v. No. 2), who has also published a separate translation (S.P.C.K.).

ΤΙΣ Ο ΣΩΙΖΟΜΕΝΟΣ ΠΛΟΥΣΙΟΣ

985 P. 1. Οἱ μὲν τοὺς ἐγκωμιαστικοὺς λόγους τοῖς πλουσίοις δωροφοροῦντες οὐ μόνον κόλακες καὶ ἀνελεύθεροι δικαίως ἂν ἔμοιγε κρίνεσθαι δοκοῖεν, ὡς ἐπὶ πολλῷ προσποιούμενοι χαρίσασθαι τὰ ἀχάριστα, ἀλλὰ καὶ ἀσεβεῖς καὶ ἐπίβουλοι· ἀσεβεῖς μέν, ὅτι παρέντες αἰνεῖν καὶ δοξάζειν τὸν μόνον τέλειον καὶ ἀγαθὸν θεόν, ἐξ οὗ τὰ πάντα καὶ δι᾽ οὗ τὰ πάντα καὶ εἰς ὃν τὰ πάντα, περιάπτουσι το⟨ύτου⟩[1] τὸ γέρας ἀνθρώποις ἐν ἀσ⟨ώτῳ καὶ βορβορώδει⟩[2] βίῳ κυλινδουμένοις ⟨καὶ⟩[3] τὸ κεφάλαιον ὑποκειμένοις[4] τῇ κρίσει τοῦ θεοῦ· ἐπίβουλοι δέ, ὅτι καὶ αὐτῆς τῆς περιουσίας καθ᾽ αὑτὴν ἱκανῆς οὔσης χαυνῶσαι τὰς ψυχὰς τῶν κεκτημένων καὶ διαφθεῖραι καὶ ἀποστῆσαι τῆς ὁδοῦ, δι᾽ ἧς ἐπιτυχεῖν ἔστι σωτηρίας, οἶδε προσεκπλήσσουσι τὰς γνώμας τῶν πλουσίων ταῖς ἡδοναῖς τῶν ἀμέτρων ἐπαίνων ἐπαίροντες καὶ καθάπαξ τῶν ὅλων πραγμάτων πλὴν τοῦ πλούτου,
936 P. δι᾽ ὃν θαυμάζονται, | παρασκευάζοντες ὑπερφρονεῖν, τὸ δὴ τοῦ λόγου πῦρ ἐπὶ πῦρ μετοχετεύοντες, τύφῳ

[1] το⟨ύτου⟩ Lindner : Stählin. (The bracketed words and letters are to fill blank spaces in the MS.)
[2] ἀσ⟨ώτῳ καὶ βορβορώδει⟩ Lindner : Stählin.
[3] ⟨καὶ⟩ Segaar.
[4] ὑποκειμένοις Combefis. ὑποκείμενον MS.

Romans xi. 36.

270

THE RICH MAN'S SALVATION

1. MEN who offer laudatory speeches as presents to the rich may rightly be classed, in my opinion, not
only as flatterers and servile, since in the hope of a
large return they make a show of granting favours
that are really no favours, but also as impious and
insidious.   They are impious, because, while neglect-
ing to praise and glorify the only perfect and good
God, from whom are all things and through whom
are all things and to whom are all things,[a] they invest
with His prerogative men who are wallowing in a
riotous and filthy life and, in short, are lying under
the judgment of God.   They are insidious, because,
although mere abundance is by itself quite enough
to puff up the souls of its possessors, and to corrupt
them, and to turn them aside from the way by which
salvation can be reached, these men bring fresh
delusion to the minds of the rich by exciting them
with the pleasures that come from their immoderate
praises, and by rendering them contemptuous of
absolutely everything in the world except the wealth
which is the cause of their being admired.   In the
words of the proverb, they carry fire to fire,[b] when

The sin of
flattering
rich men

[b] A common Greek proverb, equivalent to our "Carrying
coals to Newcastle." See Plato, *Laws* 666 A. The verb
translated "carry" means literally "to conduct water
through pipes."

τῦφον ἐπαντλοῦντες καὶ ὄγκον πλούτῳ προσανα-
τιθέντες βαρεῖ φύσει φορτίον βαρύτερον, οὗ μᾶλλον
ἐχρῆν ἀφαιρεῖν καὶ περικόπτειν, ὡς σφαλεροῦ νο-
σήματος καὶ θανατηφόρου· τῷ γὰρ ὑψουμένῳ καὶ
μεγαλυνομένῳ παραπέπηγεν[1] ἀντίστροφος ἡ πρὸς τὸ
ταπεινὸν μεταβολὴ καὶ πτῶσις, ὡς ὁ θεῖος διδάσκει
λόγος. ἐμοὶ δὲ φαίνεται μακρῷ φιλανθρωπότερον
εἶναι τοῦ θεραπεύειν ‹ἀνελευθέρως›[2] τοὺς πλου-
τοῦντας ‹καὶ ἐπαινεῖν›[3] ἐπὶ κακῷ τὸ συναίρεσθαι
‹τὴν ζωὴν καὶ›[4] τὴν σωτηρίαν αὐτοῖς ‹κατεργάζεσθαι›[5] ἅπαντα τὸν δυνατὸν τρόπον, τοῦτο μὲν
ἐξαιτουμένους παρὰ θεοῦ τοῦ βεβαίως καὶ ἡδέως
τοῖς ἑαυτοῦ τέκνοις τὰ τοιαῦτα προϊεμένου, τοῦτο
δὲ λόγῳ [6] διὰ τῆς χάριτος τοῦ σωτῆρος ἰωμένους τὰς
ψυχὰς αὐτῶν, φωτίζοντας καὶ προσάγοντας ἐπὶ τὴν
τῆς ἀληθείας κτῆσιν, ἧς ὁ τυχὼν καὶ ἔργοις ἀγαθοῖς
ἐλλαμπρυνόμενος μόνος τὸ [7] βραβεῖον τῆς αἰωνίου
ζωῆς ἀναιρήσεται. δεῖται δὲ καὶ ἡ εὐχὴ ψυχῆς
εὐρώστου καὶ λιπαροῦς ἄχρι τῆς ἐσχάτης ἡμέρας
τοῦ βίου συμμεμετρημένης καὶ ‹ἡ›[8] πολιτεία διαθέσεως χρηστῆς καὶ μονίμου καὶ πάσαις ταῖς
ἐντολαῖς τοῦ σωτῆρος ἐπεκτεινομένης.

2. Κινδυνεύει δὲ οὐχ ἁπλοῦν τι εἶναι τὸ αἴτιον τοῦ
τὴν σωτηρίαν χαλεπωτέραν τοῖς πλουτοῦσι δοκεῖν
ἢ τοῖς ἀχρημάτοις τῶν ἀνθρώπων, ἀλλὰ ποικίλον.
οἱ μὲν γὰρ αὐτόθεν καὶ προχείρως ἀκούσαντες τῆς
τοῦ κυρίου φωνῆς, ὅτι ῥᾷον κάμηλος διὰ τρήματος
ῥαφίδος διεκδύσεται ἢ πλούσιος εἰς τὴν βασιλείαν
τῶν οὐρανῶν, ἀπογνόντες ἑαυτοὺς ὡς οὐ βιωσόμενοι,

---

[1] παραπέπηγεν from *Antonii Melissa*: missing from ms.
[2] ‹ἀνελευθέρως› Fell.   [3] ‹καὶ ἐπαινεῖν› Barnard.
[4] ‹τὴν ζωὴν καὶ› Stählin.   [5] ‹κατεργάζεσθαι› Fell.

they shower pride upon pride, and heap on wealth, heavy by its own nature, the heavier burden of arrogance. Rather they ought to have diminished and curtailed wealth, as a perilous and deadly disease; for the man who exalts and magnifies himself is in danger of a complete reversal of fortune, namely, the change and fall into low estate, as the divine word teaches.[a] It seems to me an act far kinder than servile attention to the rich and praise that does them harm, if we share the burden of their life and work out salvation for them by every possible means; first by begging them from God, who unfailingly and gladly accords such gifts to His own children, and then by healing their souls with reason, through the Saviour's grace, enlightening them and leading them on to the possession of the truth. For only he who has reached the truth and is distinguished in good works shall carry off the prize of eternal life. But prayer requires a soul that runs its course strong and persevering until the last day of life, and the Christian citizenship requires a disposition that is good and steadfast and that strains to fulfil[b] all the Saviour's commandments.

The Christian's duty is rather to pray for the rich

2. Now the reason why salvation seems to be more difficult for the rich than for men without wealth is probably not a simple one, but complex. For some, after merely listening in an off-hand way to the Lord's saying, that a camel shall more easily creep through a needle's eye than a rich man into the kingdom of heaven,[c] despair of themselves,

Reasons why salvation seems difficult for rich men

---

[a] *i.e.* St. Matthew xxiii. 12.
[b] Literally, "stretches out towards." The same word is used by St. Paul in Philippians iii. 13. [c] St. Mark x. 25.

---

[6] λόγῳ Segaar. λέγω MS. [7] τὸ Stählin. οὗτος MS.
[8] ⟨ἡ⟩ inserted by Barnard.

CLEMENT OF ALEXANDRIA

τῷ κόσμῳ πάντα χαριζόμενοι καὶ τῆς ἐνταῦθα ζωῆς
ὡς μόνης ἑαυτοῖς ὑπολειπομένης ἐκκρεμασθέντες
ἀπέστησαν πλέον τῆς ἐκεῖ ὁδοῦ, μηκέτι πολυπραγ-
μονήσαντες μήτε τίνας τοὺς πλουσίους ὁ δεσπότης
καὶ διδάσκαλος προσαγορεύει μήτε ὅπως τὸ ἀδύνατον ἐν ἀνθρώποις[1] δυνατὸν γίνεται. ἄλλοι δὲ τοῦτο
μὲν συνῆκαν ὀρθῶς καὶ προσηκόντως, τῶν δὲ ἔργων
τῶν εἰς τὴν σωτηρίαν ἀναφερόντων ὀλιγωρήσαντες
οὐ παρεσκευάσαντο τὴν δέουσαν παρασκευὴν εἰς τὸ
τῶν ἐλπιζομένων τυχεῖν. λέγω[2] δὲ ταῦτα ἑκάτερα
περὶ[3] τῶν πλουσίων τῶν καὶ τῆς δυνάμεως τοῦ
σωτῆρος καὶ τῆς ἐπιφανοῦς σωτηρίας ᾐσθημένων,
τῶν δὲ ἀμυήτων τῆς ἀληθείας ὀλίγον μοι μέλει.

3. Χρὴ τοίνυν τοὺς φιλαλήθως καὶ φιλαδέλφως
⟨διακειμένους⟩[4] καὶ μήτε καταθρασυνομένους αὐ-
θάδως τῶν πλουσίων κλητῶν μήτε αὖ πάλιν ὑπο-
πίπτοντας αὐτοῖς διὰ οἰκείαν φιλοκέρδειαν, πρῶτον
μὲν αὐτῶν ἐξαιρεῖν τῷ λόγῳ τὴν κενὴν[5] ἀπόγνωσιν
καὶ δηλοῦν μετὰ τῆς δεούσης ἐξηγήσεως τῶν λογίων
937 P. τοῦ κυρίου | διότι οὐκ ἀποκέκοπται τέλεον αὐτοῖς ἡ
κληρονομία τῆς βασιλείας τῶν οὐρανῶν ἐὰν ὑπ-
ακούσωσι ταῖς ἐντολαῖς· εἶθ' ὁπόταν μάθωσιν ὡς
ἀδεὲς δεδίασι δέος καὶ ὅτι βουλομένους αὐτοὺς ὁ
σωτὴρ ἀσμένως δέχεται, τότε καὶ προδεικνύναι καὶ
μυσταγωγεῖν ὅπως ἂν καὶ δι' οἵων ἔργων τε καὶ
διαθέσεων ἐπαύραιντο τῆς ἐλπίδος, ὡς οὔτ' ἀμη-
χάνου καθεστώσης αὐτοῖς οὔτε τοὐναντίον εἰκῇ

---

[1] ἀνθρώποις Barnard. ἀνθρώπῳ ἦ MS.
[2] λέγω Ghisler. λέγων MS.   [3] περὶ Barnard. ἅπερ ἐπὶ MS.
[4] ⟨διακειμένους⟩ Fell.   [5] κενὴν Combefis. καινὴν MS.

---

[a] Literally, " the rich who are called " ; cp. 1 Corinthians
i. 24, and Jude ver. 1.

274

feeling that they are not destined to obtain life. So, complying with the world in everything, and clinging to this present life as the only one left to them, they depart further from the heavenward way, taking no more trouble to ask who are the rich men that the Master and Teacher is addressing nor how that which is impossible with men becomes possible. Others however understand the saying rightly and properly, but, because they make light of the works which bear upon salvation, do not provide the necessary preparation for the satisfaction of their hopes. In both cases I am speaking of the rich who have learnt of the Saviour's power and His splendid salvation; with those who are uninitiated in the truth I have little concern.

3. It is the duty, therefore, of those whose minds are set on love of truth and love of the brethren, and who neither behave with insolent rudeness towards the rich members of the church,[a] nor yet cringe to them through personal love of gain, first, by means of the word of scripture,[b] to banish from them their unfounded despair and to show, with the necessary exposition of the Lord's oracles, that the inheritance of the kingdom of heaven is not completely cut off from them, if they obey the commandments; and afterwards, when they have learnt that their fears are groundless, and that the Saviour gladly receives them if they desire, to point out and instruct them how and through what kind of works and resolves they can enjoy the object of their hope, which is neither beyond their reach nor, on the contrary, to be obtained without settled purpose.

Christians must show them that salvation is not impossible

---

[b] Or perhaps, " by means of reason." See p. 20, n. a.

CLEMENT OF ALEXANDRIA

περιγινομένης. ἀλλ' ὅνπερ τρόπον ἔχει τὸ τῶν
ἀθλητῶν, ἵνα μικρὰ καὶ ἐπίκηρα μεγάλοις καὶ
ἀφθάρτοις παραβάλωμεν, τουτὶ καὶ ἐφ' ἑαυτοῦ[1] ὁ
κατὰ κόσμον πλουτῶν λογιζέσθω. καὶ γὰρ ἐκείνων
ὁ μὲν ὅτι δυνήσεται νικᾶν καὶ στεφάνων τυγχάνειν
ἀπελπίσας οὐδ' ὅλως ἐπὶ τὴν ἄθλησιν ἀπεγράψατο,
ὁ δὲ ταύτην μὲν ἐμβαλόμενος τῇ γνώμῃ τὴν ἐλπίδα,
πόνους δὲ καὶ γυμνάσια καὶ τροφὰς μὴ προσιέμενος
προσφόρους, ἀστεφάνωτος διεγένετο καὶ διήμαρτε
τῶν ἐλπίδων. οὕτως τις καὶ τὴν ἐπίγειον ταύτην
περιβεβλημένος περιβολὴν μήτε τὴν ἀρχὴν ἑαυτὸν
τῶν ἄθλων τοῦ σωτῆρος ἐκκηρυσσέτω, πιστός γε
ὢν καὶ τὸ μεγαλεῖον συνορῶν τῆς τοῦ θεοῦ φιλανθρωπίας, μήτε μὴν αὖθις ἀνάσκητος καὶ ἀν-
αγώνιστος μείνας ἀκονιτὶ κἀνιδρωτὶ[2] τῶν στεφάνων
τῆς ἀφθαρσίας ἐλπιζέτω μεταλαβεῖν· ἀλλ' αὐτὸν
ὑποβαλέτω φέρων γυμναστῇ μὲν τῷ λόγῳ, ἀγωνο-
θέτῃ δὲ τῷ Χριστῷ· τροφὴ δὲ αὐτῷ καὶ ποτὸν
γενέσθω τεταγμένον ἡ καινὴ διαθήκη τοῦ κυρίου,
γυμνάσια δὲ αἱ ἐντολαί, εὐσχημοσύνη δὲ καὶ
κόσμος αἱ καλαὶ διαθέσεις, ἀγάπη, πίστις, ἐλπίς,
γνῶσις ἀληθείας, ⟨ἐπιείκεια,⟩[3] πραότης, εὐσπλαγχ-
νία, σεμνότης, ἵν', ὅταν ⟨ἡ⟩[4] ἐσχάτη σάλπιγξ ὑπο-
σημήνῃ ⟨τὸ τέλος⟩[5] τοῦ δρόμου καὶ τὴν ἐντεῦθεν
ἔξοδον[6] καθάπερ ἐκ σταδίου τοῦ βίου, μετ' ἀγαθοῦ
τοῦ συνειδότος τῷ ἀθλοθέτῃ παραστῇ νικηφόρος,
ὡμολογημένος τῆς ἄνω πατρίδος ἄξιος, εἰς ἣν

---

[1] ἑαυτοῦ Mayor. ἑαυτῷ MS.
[2] ἀκονιτὶ κἀνιδρωτὶ Ghisler. ἀκωνεῖται κἂν ἱδρῶτι MS.
[3] ⟨ἐπιείκεια⟩ Fell (lacuna in MS.).
[4] ⟨ἡ⟩ inserted by Schwartz.
[5] ⟨τὸ τέλος⟩ inserted by Stählin (cp. 2 Timothy iv. 7).
[6] τὴν ... ἔξοδον Stählin. τῆς ... ἐξόδου MS.

276

Well then, as is the case with athletes—if we may compare things small and perishable with things great and incorruptible—so let him who is rich in this world consider it to be with himself. For the athlete who has no hope of being able to win and to obtain crowns does not even enrol himself for the contest; while the one who at heart entertains this hope, but does not submit to hard training and exercises and suitable food, comes out uncrowned and entirely misses the fulfilment of his hopes. In the same way let not one who is clothed with this earthly covering*a* proclaim himself barred at the start from the Saviour's prizes, if, that is, he is faithful and surveys the magnificence of God's love to men; nor, once again, let him hope, by remaining undisciplined and unused to conflict, to partake of the crowns of incorruption without dust and sweat. But let him come and subject himself to reason*b* as trainer and to Christ as master of the contests. Let his appointed food and drink be the Lord's new covenant,*c* his exercise the commandments, his grace and adornment the fair virtues of love, faith, hope,*d* knowledge of the truth, goodness, gentleness, compassion, gravity; in order that, when the last trumpet*e* signals the end of the race and his departure from the present life as from a course, he may with a good conscience stand before the judge a victor, admitted to be worthy of the fatherland above, into

But effort necessary as with athletes

a i.e. riches.

b Again we have the comprehensiveness in the meaning of *logos.* See p. 20, n. *a.* In Clement's thought the different meanings tend to mingle with one another.

c See 1 Corinthians xi. 25.

d See 1 Corinthians xiii. 13.

e See 1 Corinthians xv. 52.

μετὰ στεφάνων καὶ κηρυγμάτων ἀγγελικῶν ἐπανέρχεται.

4. Δοίη τοίνυν ἡμῖν ὁ σωτὴρ ἐντεῦθεν ἀρξαμένοις τοῦ λόγου τἀληθῆ καὶ τὰ πρέποντα καὶ τὰ σωτήρια συμβαλέσθαι τοῖς ἀδελφοῖς πρός τε τὴν ἐλπίδα πρῶτον αὐτὴν καὶ δεύτερον πρὸς τὴν τῆς ἐλπίδος προσαγωγήν. ὁ δὲ χαρίζεται δεομένοις καὶ αἰτοῦντας διδάσκει καὶ λύει τὴν ἄγνοιαν καὶ τὴν ἀπόγνωσιν ἀποσείεται, τοὺς αὐτοὺς πάλιν εἰσάγων λόγους περὶ τῶν πλουσίων, ἑαυτῶν ἑρμηνέας γινομένους καὶ ἐξηγητὰς ἀσφαλεῖς. οὐδὲν γὰρ οἷον αὐτῶν αὖθις ἀκοῦσαι τῶν ῥητῶν, ἅπερ ἡμᾶς ἐν τοῖς εὐαγγελίοις ἄχρι νῦν διετάρασσεν ἀβασανίστως καὶ διημαρτημένως ὑπὸ νηπιότητος ἀκροωμένους.

" Ἐκπορευομένου αὐτοῦ[1] εἰς ὁδὸν προσελθών τις ἐγονυπέτει λέγων· διδάσκαλε ἀγαθέ, τί ποιήσω

938 P. ἵνα | ζωὴν αἰώνιον κληρονομήσω; ὁ δὲ Ἰησοῦς λέγει· τί με ἀγαθὸν λέγεις; οὐδεὶς ἀγαθὸς εἰ μὴ εἷς ὁ θεός. τὰς ἐντολὰς οἶδας· μὴ μοιχεύσῃς, μὴ φονεύσῃς, μὴ κλέψῃς, μὴ ψευδομαρτυρήσῃς, τίμα τὸν πατέρα σου καὶ τὴν μητέρα. ὁ δὲ ἀποκριθεὶς λέγει αὐτῷ· πάντα ταῦτα ἐφύλαξα ⟨ἐκ νεότητός μου⟩[2]. ὁ δὲ Ἰησοῦς ἐμβλέψας ἠγάπησεν αὐτὸν καὶ εἶπεν· ἕν σοι ὑστερεῖ· εἰ θέλεις τέλειος εἶναι, πώλησον ὅσα ἔχεις καὶ διάδος πτωχοῖς, καὶ ἕξεις θησαυρὸν ἐν οὐρανῷ, καὶ δεῦρο ἀκολούθει μοι. ὁ δὲ στυγνάσας ἐπὶ τῷ λόγῳ ἀπῆλθε λυπούμενος· ἦν γὰρ ἔχων χρήματα πολλὰ καὶ ἀγρούς. περιβλεψά

---

[1] αὐτοῦ Barnard. αὐτῷ ms.
[2] ⟨ἐκ νεότητός μου⟩ inserted by Segaar ; see pp. 286, 290.

which with angelic crowns and proclamations he now ascends.[a]

4. May the Saviour grant us power, then, as we begin our address at this point, to impart to the brethren true and fitting and salutary thoughts, first with regard to the hope itself, and secondly with regard to the means of reaching it. He gives freely to those who need, and teaches them when they ask, and disperses their ignorance, and shakes off their despair, by bringing up again the self-same words about the rich and showing them to be their own sure interpreters and expositors. For there is nothing like hearing once more the actual sayings which, because in our childishness we listened to them uncritically and mistakenly, have continued until now to trouble us in the gospels. *A prayer for the Saviour's help*

As He was going forth into the way, one came and kneeled before Him, saying, Good Master, what shall I do that I may inherit eternal life. And Jesus says, Why callest thou me good? None is good save one, even God. Thou knowest the commandments ; do not commit adultery, do not kill, do not steal, do not bear false witness, honour thy father and mother. And he answering says to Him, All these things have I observed from my youth. And Jesus looking upon him loved him, and said, One thing thou lackest. If thou wilt be perfect, sell whatsoever thou hast and distribute to the poor, and thou shalt have treasure in heaven ; and come, follow Me. But his countenance fell at the saying, and he went away sorrowful ; for he was one that had great riches and lands. *The gospel passage about the rich man*

---

[a] The imagery in this fine passage is taken from the Greek games, which St. Paul also had used as an illustration of the spiritual conflict. See 1 Corinthians ix. 25.

μενος δὲ ὁ Ἰησοῦς λέγει τοῖς μαθηταῖς αὐτοῦ·
πῶς δυσκόλως οἱ τὰ χρήματα ἔχοντες εἰσελεύσονται
εἰς τὴν βασιλείαν τοῦ θεοῦ. οἱ δὲ μαθηταὶ ἐθαμ-
βοῦντο ἐπὶ τοῖς λόγοις αὐτοῦ. πάλιν δὲ ὁ Ἰησοῦς
ἀποκριθεὶς λέγει αὐτοῖς· τέκνα, πῶς δύσκολόν ἐστι
τοὺς πεποιθότας ἐπὶ χρήμασιν εἰς τὴν βασιλείαν τοῦ
θεοῦ εἰσελθεῖν· εὐκόλως διὰ τῆς τρυμαλιᾶς τῆς βελόνης κάμηλος εἰσελεύσεται ἢ πλούσιος εἰς τὴν βασιλείαν τοῦ θεοῦ. οἱ δὲ περισσῶς ἐξεπλήσσοντο καὶ
ἔλεγον· τίς οὖν δύναται σωθῆναι; ὁ δὲ ἐμβλέψας
αὐτοῖς εἶπεν· ὅ τι παρὰ ἀνθρώποις ἀδύνατον, παρὰ
θεῷ δυνατόν. ἤρξατο ὁ Πέτρος λέγειν αὐτῷ· ἰδὲ
ἡμεῖς ἀφήκαμεν πάντα καὶ ἠκολουθήσαμέν σοι.
ἀποκριθεὶς δὲ ὁ Ἰησοῦς λέγει· ἀμὴν ὑμῖν λέγω,
ὃς ἂν ἀφῇ τὰ ἴδια καὶ γονεῖς καὶ ἀδελφοὺς καὶ
χρήματα ἕνεκεν ἐμοῦ καὶ ἕνεκεν τοῦ εὐαγγελίου,
ἀπολήψεται ἑκατονταπλασίονα. νῦν ἐν τῷ καιρῷ
τούτῳ ἀγροὺς καὶ χρήματα καὶ οἰκίας καὶ ἀδελφοὺς
ἔχειν μετὰ διωγμῶν εἰς ποῦ;[1] ἐν δὲ τῷ ἐρχομένῳ
ζωή[2] ἐστιν αἰώνιος· [ἐν δὲ][3] ἔσονται οἱ πρῶτοι
ἔσχατοι, καὶ οἱ ἔσχατοι πρῶτοι."

5. Ταῦτα μὲν ἐν τῷ κατὰ Μάρκον εὐαγγελίῳ
γέγραπται· καὶ ἐν τοῖς ἄλλοις δὲ πᾶσιν ⟨τοῖς⟩[4]
ἀνωμολογημένοις ὀλίγον μὲν ἴσως ἑκασταχοῦ τῶν
ῥημάτων ἐναλλάσσει, πάντα δὲ τὴν αὐτὴν τῆς
γνώμης συμφωνίαν ἐπιδείκνυται. δεῖ δὲ σαφῶς
εἰδότας ὡς οὐδὲν ἀνθρωπίνως ὁ σωτήρ, ἀλλὰ πάντα
θείᾳ σοφίᾳ καὶ μυστικῇ διδάσκει τοὺς ἑαυτοῦ, μὴ
σαρκίνως ἀκροᾶσθαι τῶν λεγομένων, ἀλλὰ τὸν ἐν

[1] εἰς ποῦ ; Stählin.   εἰς που MS.   εὕργου Barnard.
[2] ζωή Ghisler.   ζωὴν MS.   [3] [ἐν δὲ] Ghisler.
[4] ⟨τοῖς⟩ inserted by Wilamowitz.

THE RICH MAN'S SALVATION

And Jesus looked round about, and says to His disciples,
How hardly shall they that have riches enter into the
kingdom of God! And the disciples were amazed at His
words. But Jesus answering again says to them,
Children, how hard is it for them that trust in riches to
enter into the kingdom of God! A camel shall more
easily enter through the eye of the needle, than a rich
man into the kingdom of God. And they were exceedingly astonished and said, Who then can be saved? But
He looking upon them said, That which is impossible with
men is possible with God. Peter began to say to him, Lo,
we have left all and followed thee. And Jesus answering says, Verily I say to you, whoever leaves his home
and parents and brothers and riches for My sake and for
the gospel's sake, shall receive back a hundredfold. To
what end is it that in this present time we have lands and
riches and houses and brothers with persecutions? But
in the time to come is life eternal. The first shall be
last and the last first.[a]

5. This is written in the gospel according to Mark,
and in all the other accepted[b] gospels the passage
as a whole shows the same general sense, though
perhaps here and there a little of the wording
changes. And as we are clearly aware that the
Saviour teaches His people nothing in a merely
human way, but everything by a divine and mystical
wisdom, we must not understand His words literally,[c]

The passage must not be interpreted in a merely literal sense

[a] St. Mark x. 17-31. It will be noticed that the text of
St. Mark's gospel used by Clement differed in a number of
small points from that with which we are familiar.
[b] Clement distinguishes the four gospels from others
which he knew, and occasionally uses, but to which he did
not attribute the same authority.
[c] The Greek word is "fleshly" or "carnally"; the
fleshly meaning was the one that lay on the surface, as con-
trasted with the hidden or spiritual meaning. "Literally"
seems the nearest equivalent in modern English.

281

αὐτοῖς κεκρυμμένον νοῦν μετὰ τῆς ἀξίας ζητήσεως καὶ συνέσεως ἐρευνᾶν καὶ καταμανθάνειν. καὶ γὰρ τὰ ὑπ' αὐτοῦ τοῦ κυρίου δοκοῦντα ἡπλῶσθαι πρὸς τοὺς μαθητὰς τῶν ᾐνιγμένων ὑπειρημένων οὐδὲν ἥττονος ἀλλὰ πλείονος ἔτι καὶ νῦν τῆς ἐπιστάσεως εὑρίσκεται δεόμενα διὰ τὴν ὑπερβάλλουσαν τῆς φρονήσεως ἐν αὐτοῖς ὑπερβολήν. ὅπου δὲ καὶ τὰ νομιζόμενα ὑπ' αὐτοῦ διοῖχθαι τοῖς ἔσω καὶ αὐτοῖς τοῖς τῆς βασιλείας τέκνοις ὑπ' αὐτοῦ καλουμένοις ἔτι χρῄζει φροντίδος πλείονος, ἢ πού γε τὰ δόξαντα μὲν ἁπλῶς ἐξενηνέχθαι καὶ διὰ τοῦτο μηδὲ διηρω-
939 P. τημένα πρὸς τῶν ἀκουσάντων, | εἰς ὅλον δὲ τὸ τέλος αὐτὸ τῆς σωτηρίας διαφέροντα, ἐσκεπασμένα[1] δὲ θαυμαστῷ καὶ ὑπερουρανίῳ διανοίας βάθει, οὐκ ἐπιπολαίως δέχεσθαι ταῖς ἀκοαῖς προσῆκεν, ἀλλὰ καθιέντας τὸν νοῦν ἐπ' αὐτὸ τὸ πνεῦμα τοῦ σωτῆρος καὶ τὸ τῆς γνώμης ἀπόρρητον.

6. Ἠρώτηται μὲν γὰρ ἡδέως ὁ κύριος ἡμῶν καὶ σωτὴρ ἐρώτημα καταλληλότατον αὐτῷ, ἡ ζωὴ περὶ ζωῆς, ὁ σωτὴρ περὶ σωτηρίας, ὁ διδάσκαλος περὶ κεφαλαίου τῶν διδασκομένων δογμάτων, ⟨ἡ⟩[2] ἀλήθεια περὶ τῆς ἀληθινῆς ἀθανασίας, ὁ λόγος περὶ τοῦ πατρῴου λόγου, ὁ τέλειος περὶ τῆς τελείας ἀναπαύσεως, ὁ ἄφθαρτος περὶ τῆς βεβαίας ἀφθαρσίας. ἠρώτηται περὶ τούτων ὑπὲρ ὧν καὶ κατελήλυθεν, ἃ παιδεύει, ἃ διδάσκει, ἃ παρέχει, ἵνα δείξῃ τὴν τοῦ εὐαγγελίου ὑπόθεσιν, ὅτι δόσις ἐστὶν αἰωνίου ζωῆς. πρόοιδε δὲ ὡς θεὸς καὶ ἃ μέλλει διερωτηθήσεσθαι καὶ ἃ μέλλει τις αὐτῷ ἀποκρίνεσθαι.

---

[1] διαφέροντα, ἐσκεπασμένα Stählin. διαφερόντων, ἐσκεπασμένων MS.
[2] ⟨ἡ⟩ inserted by Barnard.

but with due inquiry and intelligence we must search out and master their hidden meaning. For the sayings which appear to have been simplified by the Lord Himself to His disciples are found even now, on account of the extraordinary degree of wisdom in them, to need not less but more attention than His dark and suggestive utterances. And when the sayings which are thought to have been fully explained by Him to the inner circle of disciples, to the very men who are called by Him the children of the kingdom,[a] still require further reflexion, surely those that had the appearance of being delivered in simple form and for that reason were not questioned by the hearers, but which are of importance for the whole end of salvation, and are enveloped in a wonderful and super-celestial depth of thought, should not be taken as they strike the careless ear, but with an effort of mind to reach the very spirit of the Saviour and His secret meaning.

6. For our Lord and Saviour is pleased to be asked a question most appropriate to Him; the Life is asked about life, the Saviour about salvation, the Teacher about the chief of the doctrines He was teaching, the Truth about the true immortality, the Word about the Father's word, the perfect one about the perfect rest, the incorruptible about the sure incorruption. He is asked about the things for which He has even come to earth, and which are the objects of His training, His teaching, His bounty; in order that He may reveal the purpose of the gospel, that it is a gift of eternal life. As God He knows beforehand both what questions He will be asked and

The rich man's question was appropriate to our Lord

---

[a] St. Matt. xiii. 38.

τίς γὰρ καὶ μᾶλλον ἢ ὁ προφήτης προφητῶν καὶ
κύριος παντὸς προφητικοῦ πνεύματος; κληθεὶς
δὲ ἀγαθός, ἀπ' αὐτοῦ πρώτου τοῦ ῥήματος τούτου
τὸ ἐνδόσιμον λαβὼν ἐντεῦθεν καὶ τῆς διδασκαλίας
ἄρχεται, ἐπιστρέφων τὸν μαθητὴν ἐπὶ τὸν θεὸν
τὸν ἀγαθὸν καὶ πρῶτον καὶ μόνον ζωῆς αἰωνίου
ταμίαν,[a] ἣν ὁ υἱὸς δίδωσιν ἡμῖν παρ' ἐκείνου
λαβών.[b]

7. Οὐκοῦν τὸ μέγιστον καὶ κορυφαιότατον τῶν
πρὸς τὴν ζωὴν μαθημάτων ἀπὸ τῆς ἀρχῆς εὐθὺς
ἐγκαταθέσθαι τῇ ψυχῇ δεῖ, γνῶναι τὸν θεὸν τὸν
αἰώνιον καὶ δοτῆρα αἰωνίων καὶ πρῶτον καὶ ὑπέρτα-
τον καὶ ἕνα καὶ ἀγαθὸν θεόν. ⟨ὃν⟩[1] ἔστι κτήσασθαι
διὰ γνώσεως καὶ καταλήψεως· αὕτη γὰρ ἄτρεπτος
καὶ ἀσάλευτος ἀρχὴ καὶ κρηπὶς ζωῆς, ἐπιστήμη
θεοῦ τοῦ ὄντος ὄντος καὶ τὰ ὄντα, τουτέστι τὰ
αἰώνια, δωρουμένου, ἐξ οὗ καὶ τὸ εἶναι τοῖς ἄλλοις
ὑπάρχει καὶ τὸ μεῖναι λαβεῖν. ἡ μὲν γὰρ τούτου
ἄγνοια θάνατός ἐστιν, ἡ δὲ ἐπίγνωσις αὐτοῦ καὶ
οἰκείωσις καὶ ἡ πρὸς αὐτὸν ἀγάπη καὶ ἐξομοίωσις
μόνη ζωή.

8. Τοῦτον οὖν πρῶτον ἐπιγνῶναι τῷ ζησομένῳ
τὴν ὄντως ζωὴν παρακελεύεται, ὃν "οὐδεὶς ἐπιγι-
νώσκει εἰ μὴ ὁ υἱὸς καὶ ᾧ ἂν ὁ υἱὸς ἀποκαλύψῃ"·[c]
ἔπειτα τὸ μέγεθος τοῦ σωτῆρος μετ' ἐκεῖνον καὶ
τὴν καινότητα τῆς χάριτος μαθεῖν, ὅτι δὴ κατὰ τὸν

---

[1] ⟨ὃν⟩ inserted by Wilamowitz.

[a] The word used here (*tamias*) is applied in Homer
(*Iliad* iv. 84) and Plato (*Rep.* 379 E) to Zeus, and Clement
is doubtless alluding to these passages.
[b] See St. John v. 26 ; xvii. 2.
[c] See St. John xvii. 3.

what answers will be given Him. For who should know this more than the prophet of prophets and the Lord of every prophetic spirit? And when He is called good, He takes His key-note from this very first word and makes it the starting-point of His teaching, turning the disciple to God who is good, and first of all, and alone dispenser[a] of eternal life, which the Son gives to us after receiving it from Him.[b]

The first of all doctrines—to know God

7. We must therefore store up in the soul right from the beginning the greatest and chiefest of the doctrines that refer to life, namely, to know the eternal God as both giver of eternal gifts and first and supreme and one and a good God.[c] And we can get possession of God through knowledge and apprehension; for this is a firm and unshakable beginning and foundation of life,—the knowledge of God who truly exists and who is the bestower of things that exist, that is, of eternal things, from whom it is that the rest of things take both their existence and their continuance. Ignorance of Him is death, but full knowledge of Him, and close friendship, and love to Him, and growth in His likeness,[d] is alone life.

Then to know the Saviour

8. He therefore that aims at living the true life is bidden first to know Him whom "no man knows except the Son, and he to whomsoever the Son reveals Him"[e]: and then to understand the Saviour's greatness, next to Him, and the newness of His grace; because, according to the apostle, "the law

[d] The thought of "becoming like God" is taken from Plato, *Theaetetus* 176 B, a passage to which Clement often refers.

[e] St. Matthew xi. 27.

ἀπόστολον "ὁ νόμος διὰ Μωσέως ἐδόθη, ἡ χάρις καὶ ἡ ἀλήθεια διὰ Ἰησοῦ Χριστοῦ"· καὶ οὐκ ἴσα τὰ διὰ δούλου πιστοῦ διδόμενα τοῖς ὑπὸ [τοῦ]¹ υἱοῦ γνησίου δωρουμένοις. εἰ γοῦν ἱκανὸς ἦν ὁ Μωσέως νόμος ζωὴν αἰώνιον παρασχεῖν, μάτην μὲν ὁ σωτὴρ αὐτὸς παραγίνεται καὶ πάσχει δι᾽ ἡμᾶς ἀπὸ γενέσεως μέχρι τοῦ σημείου τὴν ἀνθρωπότητα διατρέχων, μάτην δὲ ὁ πάσας πεποιηκὼς "ἐκ νεότητος" τὰς 940 P. νομίμους | ἐντολὰς παρὰ ἄλλου αἰτεῖ² γονυπετῶν ἀθανασίαν. οὐδὲ γὰρ πεπλήρωκε μόνον τὸν νόμον, ἀλλὰ καὶ εὐθὺς ἀπὸ πρώτης ἡλικίας ἀρξάμενος· ἐπεὶ καὶ τί μέγα ἢ ὑπέρλαμπρον γῆρας ἄγονον ἀδικημάτων ὧν ἐπιθυμίαι τίκτουσι νεανικαὶ ἢ ὀργὴ ζέουσα ἢ ἔρως χρημάτων; ἀλλ᾽ εἴ τις ἐν σκιρτήματι νεοτησίῳ καὶ τῷ καύσωνι τῆς ἡλικίας παρέσχηται φρόνημα πέπανον καὶ πρεσβύτερον τοῦ χρόνου, θαυμαστὸς οὗτος ἀγωνιστὴς καὶ διαπρεπὴς καὶ τὴν γνώμην πολιός³. ἀλλ᾽ ὅμως οὗτος ὁ τοιοῦτος ἀκριβῶς πέπεισται, διότι αὐτῷ πρὸς μὲν δικαιοσύνην οὐδὲν ἐνδεῖ, ζωῆς δὲ ὅλως προσδεῖ· διὸ αὐτὴν αἰτεῖ παρὰ τοῦ δοῦναι μόνου δυναμένου· καὶ πρὸς μὲν τὸν νόμον ἄγει παρρησίαν, τοῦ θεοῦ δὲ τὸν υἱὸν ἱκετεύει. "ἐκ πίστεως εἰς πίστιν" μετατάσσεται· ὡς σφαλερῶς ἐν νόμῳ σαλεύων καὶ ἐπικινδύνως ναυλοχῶν εἰς τὸν σωτῆρα μεθορμίζεται.

9. Ὁ γοῦν Ἰησοῦς οὐκ ἐλέγχει μὲν αὐτὸν ὡς πάντα τὰ ἐκ νόμου μὴ πεπληρωκότα, ἀλλὰ καὶ ἀγαπᾷ καὶ

---

¹ [τοῦ] Stählin.
² αἰτεῖ J. A. Robinson. ἔτι MS.
³ πολιός Stählin. πολιώτερος MS.

ª St. John i. 17.

was given through Moses, grace and truth through Jesus Christ," [a] and gifts given through a faithful slave [b] are not equal to those bestowed by a true son. At any rate, if the law of Moses was able to supply eternal life, it is in vain that the Saviour comes Himself to us and suffers on our account,[c] running His human course from birth to the cross [d] ; in vain, too, that he who has kept " from youth " all the commandments of Moses' law kneels and asks immortality from another. For not only has he fulfilled the law, but he began to do so right from his earliest years. For what is there great or especially distinguished about an old age free from the brood of sins that are born of youthful lusts or boiling anger or passion for riches? But if a man in the heyday and heat of youth displays a ripe spirit older than his years, he is a wonderful and illustrious champion and hoary in judgment. Nevertheless the young man in question is positively convinced that while, as regards righteousness, nothing is lacking to him, life is lacking altogether. So he asks it from Him who alone is able to give it. As regards the law, too, he speaks with boldness, but to the Son of God he makes supplication. He passes over " from faith to faith." [e] As he tosses perilously in the dangerous roadstead of the law he is brought to a safe anchorage with the Saviour.

9. Certainly Jesus does not convict him of not having fulfilled all the demands of the law. No, He

(margin note: Moses' law could not give life)

---

[b] The reference is to Moses in Hebrews iii. 5.

[c] See Galatians ii. 21.

[d] Literally, the " sign," a term often used to denote the cross ; cp. *Ep. Barnabas* xii. 5.

[e] Romans i. 17.

ὑπερασπάζεται τῆς ἐν οἷς ἔμαθεν εὐπειθείας, ἀτελῆ
δὲ εἶναί φησιν ὡς πρὸς τὴν αἰώνιον ζωήν, ὡς οὐ
τέλεια πεπληρωκότα, καὶ νόμου μὲν οὖν ἐργάτην,
ἀργὸν δὲ ζωῆς ἀληθινῆς. καλὰ μὲν οὖν κἀκεῖνα
(τίς δ' οὔ φησιν; ἡ γὰρ "ἐντολὴ ἁγία") ἄχρι
παιδαγωγίας τινὸς μετὰ φόβου καὶ προπαιδείας
ἐπὶ τὴν τοῦ Ἰησοῦ νομοθεσίαν τὴν ἄκραν καὶ χάριν
προχωροῦντα, πλήρωμα δὲ "νόμου Χριστὸς εἰς
δικαιοσύνην παντὶ τῷ πιστεύοντι," οὐχὶ δὲ δούλους
ποιῶν ὡς δοῦλος, ἀλλὰ καὶ υἱοὺς καὶ ἀδελφοὺς καὶ
συγκληρονόμους τοὺς ἐπιτελοῦντας τὸ θέλημα τοῦ
πατρός.

10. "Εἰ θέλεις τέλειος γενέσθαι." οὐκ ἄρα πω
τέλειος ἦν· οὐδὲν γὰρ τελείου τελειότερον. καὶ
θείως τὸ "εἰ θέλεις" τὸ αὐτεξούσιον τῆς προσ-
διαλεγομένης αὐτῷ ψυχῆς ἐδήλωσεν. ἐπὶ τῷ
ἀνθρώπῳ γὰρ ἦν ἡ αἵρεσις ὡς ἐλευθέρῳ, ἐπὶ θεῷ
δὲ ἡ δόσις ὡς κυρίῳ. δίδωσι δὲ βουλομένοις καὶ
ὑπερεσπουδακόσι καὶ δεομένοις, ἵν' οὕτως ἴδιον
αὐτῶν ἡ σωτηρία γένηται. οὐ γὰρ ἀναγκάζει ὁ
θεός, βία γὰρ ἐχθρὸν θεῷ, ἀλλὰ τοῖς ζητοῦσι
πορίζει καὶ τοῖς αἰτοῦσι παρέχει καὶ τοῖς κρούουσιν
ἀνοίγει. εἰ θέλεις οὖν, εἰ ὄντως θέλεις καὶ μὴ
ἑαυτὸν ἐξαπατᾷς, κτῆσαι τὸ ἐνδέον. "ἕν σοι
λείπει," τὸ ἕν, τὸ ἐμόν, τὸ ἀγαθόν, τὸ ἤδη ὑπὲρ
νόμον, ὅπερ νόμος οὐ δίδωσιν, ὅπερ νόμος οὐ

---

a Romans vii. 12.   b See Galatians iii. 24.
c Romans x. 4, and xiii. 10.
d i.e. Moses ; cp. Hebrews iii. 5–6.
e See St. Matthew xii. 50, and Romans viii. 14–17.
f St. Matthew xix. 21.
g See St. Matthew vii. 7, and St. Luke xi. 9.

loves him and warmly welcomes him for his ready obedience in what he has learnt. Yet He calls him imperfect as regards eternal life, on the ground that he has fulfilled deeds that are not perfect, and that though he is a worker of the law, he is idle in respect of true life. Now the works of the law are good—who will deny it? for "the commandment is holy," [a] —but only to the extent of being a kind of training, accompanied by fear and preparatory instruction, leading on to the supreme law-giving and grace of Jesus. [b] On the other hand "Christ is the fulfilment of the law unto righteousness to every one that believes," [c] and those who perfectly observe the Father's will He makes not slaves, in the manner of a slave, [d] but sons and brothers and joint-heirs. [e]

The rich man was therefore still imperfect

10. "If thou wilt become perfect." [f] ·So he was not yet perfect; for there are no degrees of perfection. And the "if thou wilt" was a divine declaration of the free-will of the soul that was talking with Him. For the choice lay with the man as a free being, though the gift was with God as Lord. And He gives to those who desire and are in deep earnest and beg, that in this way salvation may become their very own. For God does not compel, since force is hateful to God, but He provides for those who seek, He supplies to those who ask, and He opens to those who knock. [g] If thou wilt, then, if thou really wilt and art not deceiving thyself, get possession of that which is wanting. "One thing thou lackest," [h] the one thing, that which is Mine, the good, that which is already above law, which law does not give, which law does not contain, which

The rich man was free to choose life

[h] St. Mark x. 21 ; St. Luke xviii. 22.

χωρεῖ, ὃ τῶν ζώντων ἴδιόν ἐστιν. ἀμέλει ὁ πάντα
τὰ τοῦ νόμου πληρώσας "ἐκ νεότητος" καὶ τὰ
ὑπέρογκα φρυαξάμενος τὸ ἓν τοῦτο προσθεῖναι τοῖς
ὅλοις οὐ δεδύνηται, τὸ τοῦ σωτῆρος ἐξαίρετον, ἵνα

941 P. λάβῃ ζωὴν αἰώνιον, ἣν ποθεῖ | ἀλλὰ δυσχεράνας
ἀπῆλθεν, ἀχθεσθεὶς τῷ παραγγέλματι τῆς ζωῆς,
ὑπὲρ ἧς ἱκέτευεν. οὐ γὰρ ἀληθῶς ζωὴν ἤθελεν, ὡς
ἔφασκεν, ἀλλὰ δόξαν προαιρέσεως ἀγαθῆς μόνην
περιεβάλλετο, καὶ περὶ πολλὰ μὲν οἷός τε ἦν ἀσχο-
λεῖσθαι, τὸ δὲ ἕν, τὸ τῆς ζωῆς ἔργον, ἀδύνατος καὶ
ἀπρόθυμος καὶ ἀσθενὴς ἐκτελεῖν· ὁποῖόν τι καὶ
πρὸς τὴν Μάρθαν εἶπεν ὁ σωτὴρ ἀσχολουμένην
⟨περὶ⟩¹ πολλὰ καὶ περιελκομένην καὶ ταρασσομέ-
νην² διακονικῶς, τὴν δὲ ἀδελφὴν αἰτιωμένην, ὅτι
τὸ ὑπηρετεῖν ἀπολιποῦσα τοῖς ποσὶν αὐτοῦ παρα-
κάθηται μαθητικὴν ἄγουσα σχολήν· "σὺ περὶ
πολλὰ ταράσσῃ, Μαρία δὲ τὴν ἀγαθὴν μερίδα ἐξ-
ελέξατο, καὶ οὐκ ἀφαιρεθήσεται αὐτῆς." οὕτως
καὶ τοῦτον ἐκέλευε τῆς πολυπραγμοσύνης ἀφέμενον
ἑνὶ προστετηκέναι καὶ προσκαθέζεσθαι, τῇ χάριτι
τοῦ ζωὴν αἰώνιον προστιθέντος.

11. Τί τοίνυν ἦν τὸ προτρεψάμενον αὐτὸν εἰς
φυγὴν καὶ ποιῆσαν ἀπαυτομολῆσαι τοῦ διδασκάλου,
τῆς ἱκετείας, τῆς ἐλπίδος, τῆς ζωῆς, τῶν προ-
πεπονημένων; "πώλησον τὰ ὑπάρχοντά σου." τί
δὲ τοῦτό ἐστιν; οὐχ ὃ προχείρως δέχονταί τινες,
τὴν ὑπάρχουσαν οὐσίαν ἀπορρῖψαι προστάσσει καὶ
ἀποστῆναι τῶν χρημάτων, ἀλλὰ τὰ δόγματα τὰ
περὶ χρημάτων ἐξορίσαι τῆς ψυχῆς, τὴν πρὸς αὐτὰ

¹ ⟨περὶ⟩ inserted by Segaar.
² ταρασσομένην Ghisler. παρατασσομένην MS. παραταρασ-
σομένην Barnard.

is peculiar to those who live. Yet indeed he who has fulfilled every demand of the law "from youth" and has made extravagant boasts, is unable to add to the tale this one thing singled out by the Saviour, in order to obtain the eternal life which he longs for. He went away displeased, being annoyed at the precept concerning the life for which he was making supplication. For he did not truly wish for life, as he said, but aimed solely at a reputation for good intentions. He could be busy about many things, but the one thing, the work that brings life, he was neither able nor eager nor strong enough to accomplish. And just as the Saviour said to Martha when she was busy about many things, distracted and troubled by serving, and chiding her sister because she had left the household work and was seated at His feet spending her time in learning: "Thou art troubled about many things, but Mary hath chosen the good part, and it shall not be taken away from her," [a]—so also He bade this man cease from his manifold activities and cling to and sit beside one thing, the grace of Him who adds eternal life.

But he could not do the one thing needful

11. What then was it that impelled him to flight, and made him desert his teacher, his supplication, his hope, his life, his previous labours? "Sell what belongs to thee." [b] And what is this? It is not what some hastily take it to be, a command to fling away the substance that belongs to him and to part with his riches, but to banish from the soul its opinions about riches, its attachment to them, its

The meaning of the command— "Sell what belongs to thee"

---

[a] See St. Luke x. 38-42.
[b] St. Matthew xix. 21 ; St. Mark x. 21.

συμπάθειαν, τὴν ὑπεράγαν ἐπιθυμίαν, τὴν περὶ
αὐτὰ πτοίαν καὶ νόσον, τὰς μερίμνας, τὰς ἀκάνθας
τοῦ βίου, αἳ τὸ σπέρμα τῆς ζωῆς συμπνίγουσιν.
οὔτε γὰρ μέγα καὶ ζηλωτὸν τὸ τηνάλλως ἀπορεῖν
χρημάτων μὴ οὐκ ἐπὶ λόγῳ ζωῆς (οὕτω μέν γ᾽ ἂν
ἦσαν οἱ μηδὲν ἔχοντες μηδαμῇ, ἀλλὰ ἔρημοι καὶ
μεταῖται τῶν ἐφ᾽ ἡμέραν, οἱ κατὰ τὰς ὁδοὺς
ἐρριμμένοι πτωχοί, "ἀγνοοῦντες" δὲ θεὸν καὶ
"δικαιοσύνην θεοῦ," κατ᾽ αὐτὸ μόνον τὸ ἄκρως
ἀπορεῖν καὶ ἀμηχανεῖν βίου καὶ τῶν ἐλαχίστων
σπανίζειν μακαριώτατοι καὶ θεοφιλέστατοι καὶ
μόνοι ζωὴν ἔχοντες αἰώνιον) οὔτε καινὸν τὸ
ἀπείπασθαι πλοῦτον καὶ χαρίσασθαι πτωχοῖς ἢ
πατρίσιν, ὃ πολλοὶ πρὸ τῆς τοῦ σωτῆρος καθόδου
πεποιήκασιν, οἱ μὲν τῆς εἰς λόγους σχολῆς καὶ
νεκρᾶς σοφίας ἕνεκεν, οἱ δὲ φήμης κενῆς καὶ
κενοδοξίας, Ἀναξαγόραι καὶ Δημόκριτοι καὶ
Κράτητες.

12. Τί οὖν ὡς καινὸν καὶ ἴδιον θεοῦ παραγγέλλει
καὶ μόνον ζωοποιοῦν, ὃ τοὺς προτέρους οὐκ ἔσωσεν;
εἰ δὲ ἐξαίρετόν τι ἡ "καινὴ κτίσις," ὁ υἱὸς τοῦ θεοῦ,
μηνύει καὶ διδάσκει, οὐ τὸ φαινόμενον, ὅπερ ἄλλοι

---

a The allusion is to the parable of the Sower. See St.
Mark iv. 19 and parallel passages.

b Romans x. 3.

c Anaxagoras of Clazomenae, 500–428 B.C., gave up his
property in order to have more leisure for philosophy.
Democritus of Abdera (about 460–361 B.C.) is said to have
spent a large fortune on travels undertaken in search of
knowledge. Crates, the Cynic philosopher (about 320 B.C.)
gave his wealth to his native city Thebes.

d When Clement speaks of the "new creation" (the
phrase comes from Galatians vi. 15 and 2 Corinthians v. 17),
he is thinking in the first place of the great transformation

excessive desire, its morbid excitement over them, its anxious cares, the thorns of our earthly existence which choke the seed of the true life.[a] For it is no great or enviable thing to be simply without riches, apart from the purpose of obtaining life. Why, if this were so, those men who have nothing at all, but are destitute and beg for their daily bread, who lie along the roads in abject poverty, would, though "ignorant" of God and "God's righteousness,"[b] be most blessed and beloved of God and the only possessors of eternal life, by the sole fact of their being utterly without ways and means of livelihood and in want of the smallest necessities. Nor again is it a new thing to renounce wealth and give it freely to the poor, or to one's fatherland, which many have done before the Saviour's coming, some to obtain leisure for letters and for dead wisdom, others for empty fame and vainglory—such men as Anaxagoras, Democritus and Crates.[c]

12. What then is it that He enjoins as new and peculiar to God and alone life-giving, which did not save men of former days? If the "new creation," [d] the Son of God, reveals and teaches something unique, then His command does not refer to the   The command means—to strip the soul of its passions

which has resulted from the presence and work of Jesus Christ on earth: the fear of death has given place to an assurance of union with God and immortality. The life thus opened out to man is eloquently described in the *Exhortation to the Greeks*, 88–89 P. (see pp. 243–7 of this volume). But Clement can also apply the term "new creation" to Christ Himself, the result of Christ's work being gathered up, as it were, into the person of its author. This is what he seems to do here. Yet the main thought is still that the old world has been so entirely left behind that Christ's teaching must in every detail go far beyond anything taught or practised before.

πεποιήκασι, παρεγγυᾷ, ἀλλ' ἕτερόν τι διὰ τούτου
σημαινόμενον μεῖζον καὶ θειότερον καὶ τελεώτερον,
τὸ τὴν ψυχὴν αὐτὴν καὶ τὴν διάθεσιν γυμνῶσαι τῶν
ὑπόντων παθῶν καὶ πρόρριζα τὰ ἀλλότρια τῆς
γνώμης ἐκτεμεῖν καὶ ἐκβαλεῖν. τοῦτο γὰρ ἴδιον
μὲν τοῦ πιστοῦ τὸ μάθημα, ἄξιον δὲ τοῦ σωτῆρος
τὸ δίδαγμα. οἱ γάρ τοι πρότεροι, καταφρονήσαντες
942 P. τῶν ἐκτός, τὰ μὲν κτήματα | ἀφῆκαν καὶ παραπώλε-
σαν, τὰ δὲ πάθη τῶν ψυχῶν οἶμαι ὅτι καὶ προσεπέ-
τειναν· ἐν ὑπεροψίᾳ γὰρ ἐγένοντο καὶ ἀλαζονείᾳ
καὶ κενοδοξίᾳ καὶ περιφρονήσει τῶν ἄλλων ἀνθρώπων, ὡς αὐτοί τι ὑπὲρ ἄνθρωπον ἐργασάμενοι.
πῶς ἂν οὖν ὁ σωτὴρ παρῄνει τοῖς εἰς ἀεὶ βιωσομέ-
νοις τὰ βλάψοντα καὶ λυμανούμενα πρὸς τὴν ζωήν,
ἣν ἐπαγγέλλεται; καὶ γὰρ αὖ κἀκεῖνό ἐστι· δύναταί
τις ἀποφορτισάμενος τὴν κτῆσιν οὐδὲν ἧττον ἔτι
τὴν ἐπιθυμίαν καὶ τὴν ὄρεξιν τῶν χρημάτων ἔχειν
ἐντετηκυῖαν καὶ συζῶσαν καὶ τὴν μὲν χρῆσιν ἀπο-
βεβληκέναι, ἀπορῶν δὲ ἅμα καὶ ποθῶν ἅπερ
ἐσπάθησε διπλῇ λυπεῖσθαι, καὶ τῇ τῆς ὑπηρεσίας
ἀπουσίᾳ καὶ τῇ τῆς μετανοίας συνουσίᾳ. ἀνέφικτον
γὰρ καὶ ἀμήχανον δεόμενον τῶν πρὸς τὸ βιοτεύειν
ἀναγκαίων μὴ οὐ κατακλᾶσθαι τὴν γνώμην καὶ
ἀσχολίαν ἄγειν ἀπὸ τῶν κρειττόνων, ὁπωσοῦν καὶ
ὁθενοῦν ταῦτα πειρώμενον ἐκπορίζειν.

13. Καὶ πόσῳ χρησιμώτερον τὸ ἐναντίον, ἱκανὰ
κεκτημένον αὐτόν τε περὶ τὴν κτῆσιν μὴ κακοπαθεῖν
καὶ οἷς καθῆκεν ἐπικουρεῖν; τίς γὰρ ἂν κοινωνία
καταλείποιτο παρὰ ἀνθρώποις, εἰ μηδεὶς ἔχοι μηδέν;

---

[a] Strictly, service rendered by rowers on a ship, in
relation to the work of sailors and pilot; hence, services
rendered by wealth, etc., for the support and comfort of life.

visible act, the very thing that others have done, but to something else greater, more divine and more perfect, which is signified through this; namely, to strip the soul itself and the will of their lurking passions and utterly to root out and cast away all alien thoughts from the mind. For this is a lesson peculiar to the believer and a doctrine worthy of the Saviour. The men of former days, indeed, in their contempt for outward things, parted with and sacrificed their possessions, but as for the passions of the soul, I think they even intensified them. For they became supercilious, boastful, conceited and disdainful of the rest of mankind, as if they themselves had wrought something superhuman. How then could the Saviour have recommended to those who were to live for ever things that would be harmful and injurious for the life He promises? And there is this other point. It is possible for a man, after having unburdened himself of his property, to be none the less continually absorbed and occupied in the desire and longing for it. He has given up the use of wealth, but now being in difficulties and at the same time yearning after what he threw away, he endures a double annoyance, the absence of means of support [a] and the presence of regret. For when a man lacks the necessities of life he cannot possibly fail to be broken in spirit and to neglect the higher things, as he strives to procure these necessities by any means and from any source.

13. And how much more useful is the opposite condition, when by possessing a sufficiency a man is himself in no distress about money-making and also helps those he ought? For what sharing would be left among men, if nobody had anything? And how

Those only who have money can obey other commands of the Lord

πῶς δ' ἂν τοῦτο τὸ δόγμα πολλοῖς ἄλλοις καὶ καλοῖς
τοῦ κυρίου δόγμασιν οὐχὶ φανερῶς ἐναντιούμενον
εὑρίσκοιτο καὶ μαχόμενον; "ποιήσατε ἑαυτοῖς
φίλους ἐκ τοῦ μαμωνᾶ τῆς ἀδικίας, ἵν' ὅταν ἐκλίπῃ,
δέξωνται ὑμᾶς εἰς τὰς αἰωνίους σκηνάς." "κτήσα-
σθε θησαυροὺς ἐν οὐρανῷ, ὅπου μήτε σὴς μήτε
βρῶσις ἀφανίζει μήτε κλέπται διορύσσουσι." πῶς
ἂν τις πεινῶντα τρέφοι καὶ διψῶντα ποτίζοι καὶ
γυμνὸν σκεπάζοι καὶ ἄστεγον συνάγοι, ἃ τοῖς μὴ
ποιήσασιν ἀπειλεῖ πῦρ καὶ σκότος τὸ ἐξώτερον, εἰ
πάντων αὐτὸς ἕκαστος φθάνοι τούτων ὑστερῶν;
ἀλλὰ μὴν αὐτός τε ἐπιξενοῦται Ζακχαίῳ καὶ Λευεὶ[1]
καὶ Ματθαίῳ τοῖς πλουσίοις καὶ τελώναις, καὶ τὰ
μὲν χρήματα αὐτοὺς οὐ κελεύει μεθεῖναι, τὴν δὲ
δικαίαν χρῆσιν[2] ἐπιθεὶς καὶ τὴν ἄδικον ἀφελὼν
καταγγέλλει· "σήμερον σωτηρία τῷ οἴκῳ τούτῳ."
οὕτω τὴν χρείαν αὐτῶν ἐπαινεῖ, ὥστε καὶ μετὰ τῆς
προσθήκης ταύτης τὴν κοινωνίαν ἐπιτάσσει, ποτίζειν
τὸν διψῶντα, ἄρτον διδόναι τῷ πεινῶντι, ὑποδέχεσθαι τὸν ἄστεγον, ἀμφιεννύναι τὸν γυμνόν. εἰ δὲ
τὰς χρείας οὐχ οἷόν τε ἐκπληροῦν ταύτας μὴ ἀπὸ
χρημάτων, τῶν δὲ χρημάτων ἀφίστασθαι κελεύει, τί
ἂν ἕτερον εἴη ποιῶν ὁ κύριος ⟨ἢ⟩[3] τὰ αὐτὰ διδόναι
τε καὶ μὴ διδόναι παραινῶν, τρέφειν καὶ μὴ τρέφειν,
ὑποδέχεσθαι καὶ ἀποκλείειν, κοινωνεῖν καὶ μὴ
κοινωνεῖν, ὅπερ ἁπάντων ἀλογώτατον;

---

[1] καὶ Λευεὶ J. A. Robinson.　κελεύει MS.
[2] χρῆσιν Olshausen.　κρίσιν MS.
[3] ⟨ἢ⟩ inserted by Ghisler.

---

[a] St. Luke xvi. 9.　　　[b] St. Matthew vi. 20.
[c] See St. Matthew xxv. 41–43.
[d] See St. Luke xix. 5.

could this doctrine be found other than plainly contradictory to and at war with many other noble doctrines of the Lord? "Make to yourselves friends from the mammon of unrighteousness, that when it shall fail they may receive you into the eternal habitations."[a] "Acquire treasures in heaven, where neither moth nor rust doth consume, nor thieves break through."[b] How could we feed the hungry and give drink to the thirsty, cover the naked and entertain the homeless, with regard to which deeds He threatens fire and the outer darkness to those who have not done them,[c] if each of us were himself already in want of all these things? But further, the Lord Himself is a guest with Zacchaeus[d] and Levi and Matthew,[e] wealthy men and tax-gatherers, and He does not bid them give up their riches. On the contrary, having enjoined the just and set aside the unjust employment of them, He proclaims, "To-day is salvation come to this house."[f] It is on this condition that He praises their use, and with this stipulation,—that He commands them to be shared, to give drink to the thirsty and bread to the hungry, to receive the homeless, to clothe the naked. And if it is not possible to satisfy these needs except with riches, and He were bidding us stand aloof from riches, what else would the Lord be doing than exhorting us to give and also not to give the same things, to feed and not to feed, to receive and to shut out, to share and not to share? But this would be the height of unreason.

[e] See St. Mark ii. 15 and parallel passages. The reading "Levi" is obtained by a slight change in the MS. Clement regards Levi and Matthew as two different persons.

[f] St. Luke xix. 9.

14. Οὐκ ἄρα ἀπορριπτέον τὰ καὶ τοὺς πέλας ὠφελοῦντα χρήματα· κτήματα γάρ ἐστι κτητὰ ὄντα,

943 P. καὶ χρήματα χρήσιμα ὄντα καὶ εἰς | χρῆσιν ἀνθρώπων ὑπὸ τοῦ θεοῦ παρεσκευασμένα, ἃ δὴ παράκειται καὶ ὑποβέβληται καθάπερ ὕλη τις καὶ ὄργανα πρὸς χρῆσιν ἀγαθὴν τοῖς εἰδόσι. τὸ ὄργανον, ἐὰν χρῇ τεχνικῶς, τεχνικόν ἐστιν· ἐὰν ὑστερῇς τῆς τέχνης, ἀπολαύει τῆς σῆς ἀμουσίας,[1] ὂν ἀναίτιον. τοιοῦτον καὶ ὁ πλοῦτος ὄργανόν ἐστι. δύνασαι χρῆσθαι δικαίως αὐτῷ· πρὸς δικαιοσύνην καθυπηρετεῖ· ἀδίκως τις αὐτῷ χρῆται· πάλιν ὑπηρέτης ἀδικίας εὑρίσκεται· πέφυκε γὰρ ὑπηρετεῖν, ἀλλ' οὐκ ἄρχειν. οὐ χρὴ τοίνυν τὸ ἐξ ἑαυτοῦ μὴ ἔχον μήτε τὸ ἀγαθὸν μήτε τὸ κακόν, ἀναίτιον ὄν, αἰτιᾶσθαι, ἀλλὰ τὸ δυνάμενον καὶ καλῶς τούτοις χρῆσθαι καὶ κακῶς, ἀφ' ὧν ἂν ἕληται, κατ' αὐτὸ ⟨τοῦτο αἴτιον ὄν⟩[2]. τοῦτο δ' ἐστὶ νοῦς ἀνθρώπου, καὶ κριτήριον ἐλεύθερον ἔχων ἐν ἑαυτῷ καὶ τὸ αὐτεξούσιον τῆς μεταχειρίσεως τῶν δοθέντων· ὥστε μὴ τὰ κτήματά τις ἀφανιζέτω μᾶλλον ἢ τὰ πάθη τῆς ψυχῆς, τὰ μὴ συγχωροῦντα τὴν ἀμείνω χρῆσιν τῶν ὑπαρχόντων, ἵνα καλὸς καὶ ἀγαθὸς γενόμενος καὶ τούτοις τοῖς κτήμασι χρῆσθαι δυνηθῇ καλῶς. τὸ οὖν ἀποτάξασθαι πᾶσι τοῖς ὑπάρχουσι καὶ πωλῆσαι πάντα τὰ ὑπάρχοντα τοῦτον τὸν τρόπον ἐκδεκτέον ὡς ἐπὶ τῶν ψυχικῶν παθῶν διειρημένον.

15. Ἐγὼ γοῦν κἀκεῖνο φήσαιμ' ἄν· ἐπειδὴ τὰ μὲν

---

[1] ἀμουσίας Segaar.   ἀπουσίας MS.
[2] ⟨τοῦτο αἴτιον ὄν⟩ inserted by Stählin.

---

[a] An attempt is here made to reproduce Clement's play upon the words χρήματα . . . χρήσιμα . . . χρῆσιν.

THE RICH MAN'S SALVATION

14. We must not then fling away the riches that Riches are to be used for the good of others are of benefit to our neighbours as well as ourselves. For they are called possessions because they are things possessed, and wealth *a* because they are to be welcomed and because they have been prepared by God for the welfare of men. Indeed, they lie at hand and are put at our disposal as a sort of material and as instruments to be well used by those who know. An instrument, if you use it with artistic skill, is a thing of art; but if you are lacking in skill, it reaps the benefit of your unmusical nature, though not itself responsible. Wealth too is an instrument of the same kind. You can use it rightly; it ministers to righteousness. But if one use it wrongly, it is found to be a minister of wrong. For its nature is to minister, not to rule. We must not therefore put the responsibility on that which, having in itself neither good nor evil, is not responsible, but on that which has the power of using things either well or badly, as a result of choice; for this is responsible just for that reason. And this is the mind of man, which has in itself both free judgment and full liberty to deal with what is given to it. So let a man do away, not with his possessions, but rather with the passions of his soul, which do not consent to the better use of what he has; in order that, by becoming noble and good, he may be able to use these possessions also in a noble manner. "Saying good-bye to all we have," *b* and "selling all we have," *c* must therefore be understood in this way, as spoken with reference to the soul's passions.

15. I for my part would put the matter thus.

b See St. Luke xiv. 33. *c* See St. Matthew xix. 21.

ἐντός ἐστι τῆς ψυχῆς, τὰ δὲ ἐκτός, κἂν μὲν ἡ ψυχὴ
χρῆται καλῶς, καλὰ καὶ ταῦτα δοκεῖ, ἐὰν δὲ
πονηρῶς, πονηρά, ὁ κελεύων ἀπαλλοτριοῦν τὰ
ὑπάρχοντα πότερον ταῦτα παραιτεῖται ὧν ἀναιρεθέντων ἔτι τὰ πάθη μένει, ἢ ἐκεῖνα μᾶλλον ὧν
ἀναιρεθέντων καὶ τὰ κτήματα χρήσιμα γίνεται;
ὁ τοίνυν ἀποβαλὼν τὴν κοσμικὴν περιουσίαν ἔτι
δύναται πλουτεῖν τῶν παθῶν, καὶ τῆς ὕλης μὴ
παρούσης· ἡ γάρ τοι διάθεσις τὸ αὑτῆς ἐνεργεῖ
καὶ τὸν λογισμὸν ἄγχει καὶ πιέζει καὶ φλεγμαίνει
ταῖς συντρόφοις ἐπιθυμίαις· οὐδὲν οὖν προὔργου
γέγονεν αὐτῷ πτωχεύειν χρημάτων πλουτοῦντι τῶν
παθῶν. οὐ γὰρ τὰ ἀπόβλητα ἀπέβαλεν, ἀλλὰ τὰ
ἀδιάφορα, καὶ τῶν μὲν ὑπηρετικῶν ἑαυτὸν περι-
έκοψεν, ἐξέκαυσε δὲ τὴν ὕλην τῆς κακίας τὴν
ἔμφυτον τῇ τῶν ἐκτὸς ἀπορίᾳ. ἀποτακτέον οὖν
τοῖς ὑπάρχουσι τοῖς βλαβεροῖς, οὐχὶ τοῖς ἐὰν
ἐπίστηταί τις τὴν ὀρθὴν χρῆσιν καὶ συνωφελεῖν
δυναμένοις· ὠφελεῖ δὲ τὰ μετὰ φρονήσεως καὶ
σωφροσύνης καὶ εὐσεβείας οἰκονομούμενα. ἀπ-
ωστέα δὲ τὰ ἐπιζήμια, τὰ δὲ ἐκτὸς οὐ βλάπτει.

Οὕτως οὖν ὁ κύριος καὶ τὴν τῶν ἐκτὸς χρείαν
944 P. εἰσάγει, κελεύων ἀποθέσθαι | οὐ τὰ βιωτικά, ἀλλὰ
τὰ τούτοις κακῶς χρώμενα· ταῦτα δὲ ἦν τὰ τῆς
ψυχῆς ἀρρωστήματα καὶ πάθη. 16. ὁ τούτων πλοῦτος παρὼν μὲν ἅπασι θανατηφόρος, ἀπολόμενος
δὲ σωτήριος· οὗ δεῖ[1] καθαρεύουσαν, τουτέστι πτω-
χεύουσαν καὶ γυμνὴν τὴν ψυχὴν παρασχόμενον

---

[1] δεῖ Ghisler.   δὴ ms.

---

[a] A Stoic term denoting things that are in themselves
neither good nor evil. Clement's reasoning in this passage
is strongly influenced by Stoicism.

THE RICH MAN'S SALVATION

Since possessions of one kind are within the soul, Outward things are indifferent and those of another kind outside it, and these latter appear to be good if the soul uses them well, but bad if they are badly used, which of the two is it that He, who orders us to get rid of what we have, asks us to renounce? Is it those after whose removal the passions still remain, or rather those after whose removal even outward possessions become useful? He who has cast away his worldly abundance can still be rich in passions even though his substance is gone. For his disposition continues its own activity, choking and stifling the power of reasoning and inflaming him with its inbred desires. It has proved no great gain then for him to be poor in possessions when he is rich in passions. For he has cast away not the worthless things but the indifferent,[a] and while depriving himself of what is serviceable he has set on fire the innate material of evil by the lack of outward things. A man must say good-bye, then, to the injurious things he has, not to those that can actually contribute to his advantage if he knows the right use of them; and advantage comes from those that are managed with wisdom, moderation and piety. We must reject what is hurtful; but outward things are not injurious.

In this way then the Lord admits the use of out- Poverty of passions is needed ward things, bidding us put away, not the means of living, but the things that use these badly; and these are, as we have seen, the infirmities and passions of the soul. 16. Wealth of these brings death whenever it is present, but salvation when it is destroyed. Of this wealth a man must render his soul pure, that is, poor and bare, and then only must he listen

CLEMENT OF ALEXANDRIA

οὕτως ἤδη τοῦ σωτῆρος ἀκοῦσαι λέγοντος· " δεῦρο
ἀκολούθει μοι." ὁδὸς γὰρ αὐτὸς ἤδη τῷ καθαρῷ
τὴν καρδίαν γίνεται, εἰς δὲ ἀκάθαρτον ψυχὴν θεοῦ
χάρις οὐ παραδύεται· ἀκάθαρτος δὲ ἡ πλουτοῦσα
τῶν ἐπιθυμιῶν καὶ ὠδίνουσα πολλοῖς ἔρωσι καὶ
κοσμικοῖς. ὁ μὲν γὰρ ἔχων κτήματα καὶ χρυσὸν
καὶ ἄργυρον καὶ οἰκίας ὡς θεοῦ δωρεάς, [καὶ]¹ τῷ τε
διδόντι θεῷ λειτουργῶν ἀπ᾽ αὐτῶν εἰς ἀνθρώπων
σωτηρίαν, καὶ εἰδὼς ὅτι ταῦτα κέκτηται διὰ τοὺς
ἀδελφοὺς μᾶλλον ἢ ἑαυτόν, καὶ κρείττων ὑπάρχων
τῆς κτήσεως αὐτῶν, μὴ δοῦλος < ὢν >² ὧν κέκτηται,
μηδὲ ἐν τῇ ψυχῇ ταῦτα περιφέρων, μηδὲ ἐν τούτοις
ὁρίζων καὶ περιγράφων τὴν ἑαυτοῦ ζωήν, ἀλλά τι
καὶ καλὸν ἔργον καὶ θεῖον ἀεὶ διαπονῶν, κἂν ἀπο-
στερηθῆναι δέῃ ποτὲ τούτων, δυνάμενος ἵλεω τῇ
γνώμῃ καὶ τὴν ἀπαλλαγὴν αὐτῶν ἐνεγκεῖν ἐξ ἴσου
καθάπερ καὶ τὴν περιουσίαν, οὗτός ἐστιν ὁ μακαρι-
ζόμενος ὑπὸ τοῦ κυρίου καὶ πτωχὸς τῷ πνεύματι
καλούμενος, κληρονόμος ἕτοιμος οὐρανοῦ βασιλείας,
οὐ πλούσιος ζῆσαι μὴ δυνάμενος· 17. ὁ δὲ ἐν τῇ
ψυχῇ τὸν πλοῦτον φέρων, καὶ ἀντὶ θεοῦ πνεύματος
ἐν τῇ καρδίᾳ χρυσὸν φέρων ἢ ἀγρόν, καὶ τὴν κτῆσιν
ἄμετρον ἀεὶ ποιῶν, καὶ ἑκάστοτε τὸ πλεῖον βλέπων,
κάτω νενευκὼς καὶ τοῖς τοῦ κόσμου θηράτροις
πεπεδημένος, γῆ ὢν καὶ εἰς γῆν ἀπελευσόμενος,
πόθεν δύναται βασιλείας οὐρανῶν ἐπιθυμῆσαι καὶ
φροντίσαι, ἄνθρωπος οὐ καρδίαν ἀλλὰ ἀγρὸν ἢ
μέταλλον φορῶν, ἐν τούτοις εὑρεθησόμενος ἐπ-

---

¹ [καὶ] Schwartz.
² <ὢν> inserted by Mayor.

ᵃ St. Mark x. 21.

302

to the Saviour when He says, " Come, follow Me." [a]
For He Himself now becomes a way to the pure in
heart ;[b] but into an impure soul God's grace does
not steal. An impure soul is that which is rich in
lusts and in travail with many worldly affections.
For he who holds possessions and gold and silver
and houses as gifts of God, and from them ministers
to the salvation of men for God the giver, and knows
that he possesses them for his brothers' sakes rather
than his own, and lives superior to the possession of
them ; who is not the slave of his possessions, and
does not carry them about in his soul, nor limit and
circumscribe his own life in them, but is ever striving
to do some noble and divine deed ; and who, if he is
fated ever to be deprived of them, is able to bear
their loss with a cheerful mind exactly as he bore
their abundance—this is the man who is blessed by
the Lord and called poor in spirit,[c] a ready inheritor
of the kingdom of heaven, not a rich man who cannot
obtain life. 17. But he who carries his wealth in his
soul, and in place of God's spirit carries in his heart
gold or an estate, who is always extending his possession without limit, and is continually on the look-
out for more, whose eyes are turned downwards and
who is fettered by the snares of the world, who is
earth and destined to return to earth [d] — how
can he desire and meditate on the kingdom of
heaven ? A man that bears about not a heart, but
an estate or a mine, will he not perforce be found
among these things on which he fixed his choice ?

Wealth rightly used makes a man blessed

Wealth in the soul shuts out from heaven

---

[b] See St. John xiv. 6 ; St. Matthew v. 8.
[c] St. Matthew v. 3.
[d] See Genesis iii. 19.

CLEMENT OF ALEXANDRIA

ἀνάγκες [1] [ἐν] [2] οἷς εἵλετο· " ὅπου γὰρ ὁ νοῦς
τοῦ ἀνθρώπου, ἐκεῖ καὶ ὁ θησαυρὸς αὐτοῦ."

Θησαυροὺς δέ γε ὁ κύριος οἶδε διττούς, τὸν μὲν
ἀγαθόν, " ὁ " γὰρ " ἀγαθὸς ἄνθρωπος ἐκ τοῦ
ἀγαθοῦ θησαυροῦ τῆς καρδίας προφέρει τὸ ἀγαθόν,"
τὸν δὲ πονηρόν, " ὁ " γὰρ " κακὸς ἐκ τοῦ κακοῦ
θησαυροῦ προφέρει τὸ κακόν, ὅτι ἐκ περισσεύματος
τῆς καρδίας τὸ στόμα λαλεῖ." ὥσπερ οὖν θησαυρὸς
οὐχ εἷς παρ' αὐτῷ καθὸ καὶ παρ' ἡμῖν, ὁ τὸ αἰφνίδιον
μέγα κέρδος ἐν εὑρήσει διδούς, ἀλλὰ καὶ δεύτερος,
ὁ ἀκερδὴς καὶ ἄζηλος καὶ δύσκτητος καὶ ἐπιζήμιος,
οὕτως καὶ πλοῦτος ὁ μέν τις ἀγαθῶν, ὁ δὲ κακῶν,
εἴ γε τὸν πλοῦτον καὶ τὸν θησαυρὸν οὐκ ἀπηρτημέ-
νους ἴσμεν ἀλλήλων τῇ φύσει. καὶ ὁ μέν τις πλοῦτος
κτητὸς ἂν εἴη καὶ περίβλητος, ὁ δὲ ἄκτητος καὶ
945 P. ἀπόβλητος· τὸν αὐτὸν | δὲ τρόπον καὶ πτωχεία
μακαριστὴ μὲν ἡ πνευματική. διὸ καὶ προσέθηκεν
ὁ Ματθαῖος· " μακάριοι οἱ πτωχοί." πῶς; " τῷ
πνεύματι." καὶ πάλιν· " μακάριοι οἱ πεινῶντες καὶ
διψῶντες τὴν δικαιοσύνην τοῦ θεοῦ." οὐκοῦν ἄθλιοι
οἱ ἐναντίοι πτωχοί, θεοῦ μὲν ἄμοιροι, ἀμοιρότεροι
δὲ τῆς ἀνθρωπίνης κτήσεως, ἄγευστοι δὲ δικαιοσύνης θεοῦ.

18. Ὥστε τοὺς πλουσίους μαθηματικῶς ἀκού-

---

[1] ἐπάναγκες Stählin. ἐπ' ἀνάγκαις MS.
[2] [ἐν] Stählin.

---

[a] See St. Matthew vi. 21 ; St. Luke xii. 34. Clement
quotes this saying elsewhere in the same form (vii. *Stromateis*
77. 6).
[b] St. Luke vi. 45.
[c] St. Matthew v. 3. In this and the following quotation,
the qualifying words "in spirit" and "after righteousness"
are omitted from St. Luke's account. St. Matthew's form

THE RICH MAN'S SALVATION

"For where the mind of a man is, there is his treasure also." [a]

Now as for treasures, the Lord knows them to be of two kinds, one good, for "the good man out of the good treasure of the heart brings forth that which is good"; and the other bad, for "the evil man out of his evil treasure brings forth that which is evil, because out of the abundance of the heart the mouth speaks." [b] As therefore treasure is, with Him as with us, not single only, there being that kind which brings great and immediate gain in the finding, but a second kind also that is without gain, unenviable, undesirable and harmful, so also there is one wealth of good things, another of evil ; since we know that wealth and treasure are not by nature separate from each other. And the one kind of wealth would be desirable and worth getting ; the other undesirable and worthless. In the same manner also poverty is blessed, that is, the spiritual kind. Therefore Matthew added to "Blessed are the poor"; how? "in spirit." [c] And again, "Blessed are they that hunger and thirst after God's righteousness." [d] Those then who are poor in the opposite sense [e] are miserable, being destitute of God, more destitute still of human possessions, and unacquainted with God's righteousness.

18. So with regard to the rich, who shall hardly

Christ speaks of two kinds of treasure

Two kinds of wealth and poverty also

---

probably represents the meaning of the original sayings. The word "poor" was applied in an ethical sense among the Jews to those humble souls who waited in patient trust for the coming of the Kingdom.

[d] St. Matthew v. 6.

[e] *i.e.* those who possess no money, and do not hunger after righteousness.

στέον, τοὺς δυσκόλως εἰσελευσομένους εἰς τὴν βασιλείαν, μὴ σκαιῶς μηδὲ ἀγροίκως μηδὲ σαρκίνως· οὐ
γὰρ οὕτως λέλεκται. οὐδὲ ἐπὶ τοῖς ἐκτὸς ἡ σωτηρία,
οὔτε εἰ πολλὰ οὔτε εἰ ὀλίγα ταῦτα ἢ μικρὰ ἢ μεγάλα
ἢ ἔνδοξα ἢ ἄδοξα ἢ εὐδόκιμα ἢ ἀδόκιμα, ἀλλ᾽ ἐπὶ
τῇ τῆς ψυχῆς ἀρετῇ, πίστει καὶ ἐλπίδι καὶ ἀγάπῃ
καὶ φιλαδελφίᾳ καὶ γνώσει καὶ πραότητι καὶ ἀτυφίᾳ
καὶ ἀληθείᾳ, ὧν ἆθλον ἡ σωτηρία. οὐδὲ γὰρ διὰ
κάλλος σώματος ζήσεταί τις ἢ τοὐναντίον ἀπολεῖται·
ἀλλ᾽ ὁ μὲν τῷ δοθέντι σώματι ἀγνῶς καὶ κατὰ θεὸν
χρώμενος ζήσεται, ὁ δὲ φθείρων τὸν ναὸν θεοῦ
φθαρήσεται. δύναται δέ τις καὶ αἰσχρὸς ἀσελ-
γαίνειν καὶ κατὰ κάλλος σωφρονεῖν· οὐδὲ ἰσχὺς
καὶ μέγεθος σώματος ζωοποιεῖ, οὐδὲ τῶν μελῶν
οὐδενία ἀπολλύει, ἀλλ᾽ ἡ τούτοις ψυχὴ χρωμένη τὴν
αἰτίαν ἐφ᾽ ἑκάτερα παρέχεται. ὑπόφερε γοῦν, φησί,
παιόμενος τὸ πρόσωπον, ὅπερ δύναται καὶ ἰσχυρός
τις ὢν καὶ εὐέκτων ὑπακοῦσαι καὶ πάλιν ἀσθενικός
τις ὢν ἀκρασίᾳ γνώμης παραβῆναι. οὕτως καὶ
ἄπορός τις ὢν καὶ ἄβιος εὑρεθείη ποτ᾽ ἂν μεθύων
ταῖς ἐπιθυμίαις, καὶ χρήμασι πλούσιος νήφων καὶ
πτωχεύων ἡδονῶν, πεπεισμένος, συνετός, καθαρός,
κεκολασμένος. εἰ τοίνυν ἐστὶ τὸ ζησόμενον μάλιστα
καὶ πρῶτον ἡ ψυχή, καὶ περὶ ταύτην ἀρετὴ μὲν
φυομένη σῴζει, κακία δὲ θανατοῖ, δῆλον ἤδη σαφῶς
ὅτι αὕτη καὶ πτωχεύουσα ὧν ἄν τις ὑπὸ πλούτου[1]
διαφθείρηται[2] σῴζεται, καὶ πλουτοῦσα τούτων ὧν

---

[1] πλούτου Combefis.   τούτου MS.
[2] διαφθείρηται Segaar.   διαφθείρει MS.

---

enter into the kingdom, we must understand the word in the spirit of disciples, and not clumsily, rudely, or literally;[a] for it is not spoken thus. Salvation does not depend upon outward things, whether they are many or few, small or great, splendid or lowly, glorious or mean, but upon the soul's virtue, upon faith, hope, love, brotherliness, knowledge, gentleness, humility and truth, of which salvation is the prize. For a man will not obtain life on account of bodily beauty, nor perish for want of it; but he who uses holily and according to God's will the body that was given him shall obtain life, and he who destroys the temple of God shall be destroyed.[b] It is possible for a man, though ugly, to be licentious, and in beauty to be chaste. Strength and greatness of body do not give life, nor does insignificance of the limbs destroy, but the soul by its use of these provides the cause that leads to either result. Accordingly the scripture says, "When thou art struck, offer thy face,"[c] which a man can obey even though he is strong and in good health; whereas one who is weakly can transgress through an uncontrolled temper. Thus a man without means of livelihood might perchance be found drunk with lusts, and one rich in possessions sober and poor as regards pleasures, believing, prudent, pure, disciplined. If then it is first and foremost the soul which is destined to live, and virtue growing in the soul saves it while evil kills, it is at once abundantly clear that the soul is being saved when it is poor in those things by wealth of which a man is destroyed, and that it is being killed when it is rich in those things a wealth

[b] See 1 Corinthians iii. 17.
[c] See St. Matthew v. 39 ; St. Luke vi. 29.

ἐπιτρίβει πλοῦτος θανατοῦται[1]· καὶ μηκέτι ζητῶμεν
ἀλλαχοῦ τὴν αἰτίαν τοῦ τέλους πλὴν ἐν τῇ τῆς
ψυχῆς καταστάσει καὶ διαθέσει πρός τε ὑπακοὴν
θεοῦ καὶ καθαρότητα πρός τε παράβασιν ἐντολῶν
καὶ κακίας συλλογήν.

19. Ὁ μὲν ἄρα ἀληθῶς καὶ καλῶς ⟨πλούσιός⟩[2]
ἐστιν ὁ τῶν ἀρετῶν πλούσιος καὶ πάσῃ τύχῃ χρῆσθαι
ὁσίως καὶ πιστῶς δυνάμενος, ὁ δὲ νόθος πλούσιος
ὁ κατὰ σάρκα πλουτῶν καὶ τὴν ζωὴν εἰς ⟨τὴν⟩[3] ἔξω
κτῆσιν μετενηνοχὼς τὴν παρερχομένην καὶ φθειρο-
μένην καὶ ἄλλοτε ἄλλου γινομένην καὶ ἐν τῷ τέλει
946 P. μηδενὸς μηδαμῇ. | πάλιν αὖ κατὰ τὸν αὐτὸν τρόπον
καὶ γνήσιος πτωχὸς καὶ νόθος ἄλλος πτωχὸς καὶ
ψευδώνυμος, ὁ μὲν κατὰ πνεῦμα πτωχός, τὸ ἴδιον,
ὁ δὲ κατὰ κόσμον, τὸ ἀλλότριον. τῷ δὴ κατὰ
κόσμον ⟨οὐ⟩[4] πτωχῷ καὶ πλουσίῳ κατὰ τὰ πάθη ὁ
κατὰ πνεῦμα [οὐ][5] πτωχὸς καὶ κατὰ θεὸν πλούσιος
"ἀπόστηθι," ⟨φησί⟩[6], "τῶν ὑπαρχόντων ἐν τῇ ψυχῇ
σου κτημάτων ἀλλοτρίων, ἵνα καθαρὸς τῇ καρδίᾳ
γενόμενος ἴδῃς τὸν θεόν, ὅπερ καὶ δι' ἑτέρας φωνῆς
ἐστιν εἰσελθεῖν εἰς τὴν βασιλείαν τῶν οὐρανῶν.
καὶ πῶς αὐτῶν ἀποστῇς; πωλήσας. τί οὖν;

---

[1] θανατοῦται Dindorf.   θανοῦται ms.
[2] ⟨πλούσιός⟩ inserted by Wendland.
[3] ⟨τὴν⟩ inserted by Ghisler.
[4] ⟨οὐ⟩ inserted by Jülicher.
[5] [οὐ] Segaar.   Stählin retains this.
[6] ⟨φησί⟩ inserted by Ghisler.

---

[a] Clement's involved antitheses are often difficult to follow,
and this passage has given much trouble to commentators.
I take his meaning to be this : there is a truly rich man and
a truly poor man in the spiritual sense, *independently of
outward possessions*.   On the other hand there is a spurious

308

of which brings ruin. So let us no longer seek
for the cause of our end anywhere else except in
the character and disposition of the soul with regard
to its obedience to God and its purity, to its transgression of commandments and accumulation of evil.

19. The man who is truly and nobly rich, then, is
he who is rich in virtues and able to use every fortune
in a holy and faithful manner; but the spurious rich
man is he who is rich according to the flesh, and has
changed his life into outward possessions which are
passing away and perishing, belonging now to one,
now to another, and in the end to no one at all.
Again, in the same way there is a genuine poor man
and also a spurious and falsely-named poor man, the
one poor in spirit, the inner personal poverty, and
the other poor in worldly goods, the outward alien
poverty. Now to him who is not poor in worldly
goods and is rich in passions the man who is poor in
spirit and is rich towards God says,[a] "Detach yourself from the alien possessions that dwell in your
soul, in order that you may become pure in heart and
may see God,[b] which in other words means to enter
into the kingdom of heaven. And how are you to
detach yourself from them? By selling them. What

rich (*i.e.* a moneyed man), and a spurious poor man (*i.e.* a
beggar). The appeal that follows is addressed by the one
who has the right sort of poverty and the right sort of riches
to him who has neither of these, *i.e.* a rich man who lives for
his riches. These riches which occupy his soul must be
exchanged, not for money, but for the true spiritual wealth.
That the "alien possessions" dwelling in the soul are outward wealth and not mere covetous desires is shown by
iv. *Strom.* 29. 1, where Clement points out that these latter
could hardly be "given to the poor." See notes on text.

[b] St. Matthew v. 8.

CLEMENT OF ALEXANDRIA

χρήματα ἀντὶ κτημάτων λάβῃς; ἀντίδοσιν πλούτου
πρὸς πλοῦτον ποιησάμενος, ἐξαργυρίσας τὴν φανερὰν
οὐσίαν; οὐδαμῶς· ἀλλὰ ἀντὶ τῶν πρότερον ἐνυπαρ-
χόντων τῇ ψυχῇ, ἣν σῶσαι ποθεῖς, ἀντεισαγόμενος
ἕτερον πλοῦτον θεοποιὸν καὶ ζωῆς χορηγὸν αἰωνίου,
τὰς κατὰ τὴν ἐντολὴν τοῦ θεοῦ διαθέσεις, ἀνθ' ὧν σοι
περιέσται μισθὸς καὶ τιμή, διηνεκὴς σωτηρία καὶ
αἰώνιος ἀφθαρσία. οὕτως καλῶς πωλεῖς τὰ ὑπάρχοντα, τὰ πολλὰ καὶ περισσὰ καὶ ἀποκλείοντά σοι
τοὺς οὐρανούς, ἀντικαταλλασσόμενος αὐτῶν τὰ σῶσαι
δυνάμενα. ἐκεῖνα ἐχέτωσαν οἱ σάρκινοι πτωχοὶ
καὶ τούτων δεόμενοι, σὺ δὲ τὸν πνευματικὸν πλοῦτον
ἀντιλαβὼν ἔχοις ἂν ἤδη θησαυρὸν ἐν οὐρανοῖς.''

20. Ταῦτα μὴ συνιεὶς κατὰ τρόπον ὁ πολυχρή-
ματος καὶ ἔννομος ἄνθρωπος, μηδὲ ὅπως ὁ αὐτὸς
καὶ πτωχὸς δύναται εἶναι καὶ πλούσιος καὶ ἔχειν τε
χρήματα καὶ μὴ ἔχειν καὶ χρῆσθαι τῷ κόσμῳ καὶ
μὴ χρῆσθαι, ἀπῆλθε στυγνὸς καὶ κατηφής, λιπὼν
τὴν τάξιν τῆς ζωῆς, ἧς ἐπιθυμεῖν μόνον, ἀλλ' οὐχὶ
καὶ τυχεῖν ἠδύνατο, τὸ δύσκολον ποιήσας ἀδύνατον
αὐτὸς ἑαυτῷ. δύσκολον γὰρ ἦν μὴ περιάγεσθαι
μηδὲ καταστράπτεσθαι τὴν ψυχὴν ὑπὸ τῶν προσ-
όντων ἁβρῶν τῷ προδήλῳ πλούτῳ καὶ ἀνθηρῶν
γοητευμάτων, οὐκ ἀδύνατον δὲ τὸ καὶ ἐν τούτῳ
λαβέσθαι σωτηρίας, εἴ τις ἑαυτὸν ἀπὸ τοῦ αἰσθητοῦ
πλούτου ἐπὶ τὸν νοητὸν καὶ θεοδίδακτον μεταγάγοι
καὶ μάθοι τοῖς ἀδιαφόροις[1] χρῆσθαι καλῶς καὶ ἰδίως
καὶ ὡς ἂν εἰς ζωὴν αἰώνιον ὁρμήσαι[2]. καὶ οἱ
μαθηταὶ δὲ τὸ πρῶτον μὲν καὶ αὐτοὶ περιδεεῖς καὶ

[1] ἀδιαφόροις Ghisler. διαφόρως ms.
[2] ὁρμήσαι Wilamowitz. ὁρμᾶσαι ms.

ᵃ St. Mark x. 21.

310

then? Are you to take riches for possessions, to make
an exchange of one wealth for another by turning
real estate into money? Not at all. But in place of
that which formerly dwelt in the soul you long to
save, bring in another kind of wealth that makes
you divine and provides eternal life, namely, resolves
that are fixed in accord with God's commandment;
and in return for these you shall have abundant
reward and honour, perpetual salvation and eternal
incorruption. In this way you make a good sale of
what you have, of the many things that are superfluous and that shut heaven against you, while you
receive in exchange for them the things that have
power to save. As for the first, let the fleshly poor
who need them have them; but you, having received
in their stead the spiritual wealth, will now have
treasure in heaven." [a]

20. The very rich and law-abiding man, not understanding these things aright, nor how the same man
can be both poor and wealthy, can have riches
and not have them, can use the world and not use it,
went away gloomy and downcast. He abandoned
the rank of that life which he could desire indeed,
but could not attain to; since what was hard he
himself had made impossible. For it was hard to
prevent the soul being led away and dazzled by the
luxuries and splendid allurements that are associated
with visible wealth, yet it was not impossible even
amid this to lay hold of salvation, if one would but
transfer himself from the sensible wealth to that
which belongs to the mind and is taught by God, and
would learn to make good and proper use of things indifferent and how to set out for eternal life. Even
the disciples themselves are at first filled with fear

The rich man mis-understood Christ's command

311

καταπλῆγες γεγόνασιν. ἀκούσαντες τί δήποτε; ἆρά
γε ὅτι χρήματα καὶ αὐτοὶ ἐκέκτηντο πολλά; ἀλλὰ
καὶ αὐτὰ ταῦτα τὰ δικτύφια καὶ ἄγκιστρα καὶ τὰ
ὑπηρετικὰ σκαφίδια ἀφῆκαν πάλαι, ἅπερ ἦν αὐτοῖς
μόνα. τί οὖν φοβηθέντες λέγουσι· "τίς δύναται
σωθῆναι;" καλῶς ἤκουσαν καὶ ὡς μαθηταὶ τοῦ
παραβολικῶς καὶ ἀσαφῶς[1] λεχθέντος ὑπὸ τοῦ
κυρίου καὶ ᾔσθοντο τοῦ βάθους τῶν λόγων. ἕνεκα
947 P. μὲν οὖν χρημάτων ἀκτημοσύνης εὐέλπιδες ἦσαν
πρὸς σωτηρίαν· ἐπειδὴ δὲ συνῄδεσαν ἑαυτοῖς
μήπω τὰ πάθη τέλεον ἀποτεθειμένοις[2] (ἀρτιμαθεῖς
γὰρ ἦσαν καὶ νεωστὶ πρὸς τοῦ σωτῆρος ἠνδρο-
λογημένοι), "περισσῶς ἐξεπλήσσοντο" καὶ ἀπ-
εγίνωσκον ἑαυτοὺς οὐδέν τι ἧττον ἐκείνου τοῦ
πολυχρημάτου καὶ δεινῶς τῆς κτήσεως περιεχο-
μένου, ἥν γε προέκρινεν ζωῆς αἰωνίου. ἄξιον οὖν ἦν
τοῖς μαθηταῖς φόβου πάντως,[3] εἰ καὶ ὁ χρήματα
κεκτημένος καὶ ὁ τῶν παθῶν ἔγκυος, ὧν[4] ἐπλούτουν
καὶ αὐτοί, παραπλησίως ἀπελασθήσονται οὐρανῶν·
ἀπαθῶν γὰρ καὶ καθαρῶν ψυχῶν ἐστιν ἡ σωτηρία.

21. Ὁ δὲ κύριος ἀποκρίνεται διότι "τὸ ἐν ἀνθρώποις ἀδύνατον δυνατὸν θεῷ." πάλιν καὶ τοῦτο μεγάλης σοφίας μεστόν ἐστιν, ὅτι καθ' αὑτὸν μὲν ἀσκῶν
καὶ διαπονούμενος ἀπάθειαν ⟨ὁ⟩[5] ἄνθρωπος οὐδὲν
ἀνύει, ἐὰν δὲ γένηται δῆλος ὑπερεπιθυμῶν τούτου
καὶ διεσπουδακώς, τῇ προσθήκῃ τῆς παρὰ θεοῦ
δυνάμεως περιγίνεται· βουλομέναις μὲν γὰρ ταῖς
ψυχαῖς ὁ θεὸς συνεπιπνεῖ, εἰ δὲ ἀποσταῖεν τῆς προ-

---

[1] ἀσαφῶς Ghisler. σαφῶς ms.
[2] ἀποτεθειμένοις Mayor. ἀποτιθεμένοις ms.
[3] πάντως Wilamowitz. παντὸς ms.
[4] ὧν Stählin. ὧν ms.
[5] ⟨ὁ⟩ inserted by Wilamowitz.

and amazement. For what reason think you? Was it because they too possessed great riches? Why, their very nets and hooks and fishing-boats they had left long ago, and these were all they had. Why then do they say in fear, "Who can be saved?" [a] It was because they understood well and as disciples should that which was spoken in dark parables by the Lord, and perceived the depth of His words. As far as lack of riches and possessions went they had good hopes for salvation, but since they were conscious that they had not yet completely put away their passions—for they were fresh disciples and but lately enlisted by the Saviour—"they were exceedingly amazed," [a] and began to despair of themselves no less than did that very rich man who clung desperately to his possession, which indeed he preferred to eternal life. It was then for the disciples an altogether fit occasion for fear, if both the possessor of outward wealth and also he who carries a brood of passions—in which even they were rich—are equally to be banished from heaven. For salvation belongs to pure and passionless souls.

21. But the Lord answers: "that which is impossible with men is possible for God." [b] This again is full of great wisdom, because when practising and striving after the passionless state by himself man achieves nothing, but if he makes it clear that he is eagerly pursuing this aim and is in deep earnest, he prevails by the addition of the power that comes from God. For God breathes His own power into souls when they desire, but if ever they desist from their

But God helps those who earnestly desire life

[a] St. Mark x. 26.　　　　[b] St. Mark x. 27.

θυμίας, καὶ τὸ δοθὲν ἐκ θεοῦ πνεῦμα συνεστάλη·
τὸ μὲν γὰρ ἄκοντας σῴζειν ἐστὶ βιαζομένου, τὸ
δὲ αἱρουμένους χαριζομένου. οὐδὲ τῶν καθευδόν-
των καὶ βλακευόντων ἐστὶν ἡ βασιλεία τοῦ θεοῦ,
ἀλλ᾽ "οἱ βιασταὶ ἁρπάζουσιν αὐτήν"· αὕτη γὰρ
μόνη [1] βία καλή, θεὸν βιάσασθαι καὶ παρὰ θεοῦ ζωὴν
ἁρπάσαι, ὁ δὲ γνοὺς τοὺς βιαίως, μᾶλλον δὲ βεβαίως [2]
ἀντεχομένους [συνεχώρησεν] [3] εἶξεν· χαίρει γὰρ ὁ
θεὸς τὰ τοιαῦτα ἡττώμενος. τοιγάρτοι τούτων
ἀκούσας ὁ μακάριος Πέτρος, ὁ ἐκλεκτός, ὁ ἐξαίρε-
τος, ὁ πρῶτος τῶν μαθητῶν, ὑπὲρ οὗ μόνου καὶ
ἑαυτοῦ τὸν φόρον ὁ σωτὴρ ἐκτελεῖ, ταχέως ἥρπασε
καὶ συνέβαλε τὸν λόγον. καὶ τί φησιν; "ἰδὲ
ἡμεῖς ἀφήκαμεν πάντα καὶ ἠκολουθήσαμέν σοι."
τὰ δὲ "πάντα" εἰ μὲν τὰ κτήματα τὰ ἑαυτοῦ λέγει,
τέσσαρας ὀβολοὺς ἴσως, ⟨τὸ⟩ [4] τοῦ λόγου, καταλιπὼν
μεγαλύνεται καὶ τούτων ἀνταξίαν ἀποφαίνων ἂν
λάθοι τὴν βασιλείαν τῶν οὐρανῶν. εἰ δέ, ἅπερ
ἄρτι [5] νῦν λέγομεν, τὰ παλαιὰ νοητὰ κτήματα καὶ
ψυχικὰ νοσήματα ἀπορρίψαντες ἕπονται κατ᾽ ἴχνος
τοῦ διδασκάλου, τοῦτ᾽ ἂν ἀνάπτοιτο [6] ἤδη τοῖς ἐν
οὐρανοῖς ἐγγραφησομένοις. τοῦτο [7] γὰρ ἀκολουθεῖν
ὄντως τῷ σωτῆρι, ἀναμαρτησίαν καὶ τελειότητα
τὴν ἐκείνου μετερχόμενον καὶ πρὸς ἐκεῖνον ὥσπερ
κάτοπτρον κοσμοῦντα καὶ ῥυθμίζοντα τὴν ψυχὴν
καὶ πάντα διὰ πάντων ὁμοίως διατιθέντα. |

---

[1] μόνη Stählin (from *Sacra Parallela* of John of Damascus).
μόνον MS.
[2] βιαίως . . . βεβαίως Stählin (from *Sac. Par.*). βεβαίως
. . . βιαίως MS.   [3] [συνεχώρησεν] Stählin.
[4] ⟨τὸ⟩ inserted by Segaar.   [5] ἄρτι Schwartz. ἄχρι MS.
[6] ἀνάπτοιτο Mayor. ἅπτοιτο MS.
[7] τοῦτο Wilamowitz. οὕτως MS.

eagerness, then too the spirit given from God is withdrawn; for to save men against their will is an act of force, but to save them when they choose is an act of grace. Nor does the kingdom of God belong to sleepers and sluggards, but " the men of force seize it." [a] This is the only good force, to force God and to seize life from God; and He, knowing those who forcibly, or rather persistently, cling to Him, yields; for God welcomes being worsted in such contests. Therefore on hearing these things the blessed Peter, the chosen, the pre-eminent, the first of the disciples, on behalf of whom alone and Himself the Saviour pays the tribute, [b] quickly seized upon and understood the saying. And what does he say? " Lo, we have left all and followed Thee." [c] If by " all " he means his own possessions, he is bragging of having forsaken four obols or so, [d] as the saying goes, and he would be unconsciously declaring the kingdom of heaven a suitable equivalent to these. But if, as we are just now saying, it is by flinging away the old possessions of the mind and diseases of the soul that they are following in the track of their teacher, Peter's words would at once apply to those who are to be enrolled in heaven. [e] For this is the true following of the Saviour, when we seek after His sinlessness and perfection, adorning and regulating the soul before Him as before a mirror and arranging it in every detail after His likeness.

What St. Peter had left

---

[a] St. Matthew xi. 12.

[b] See St. Matthew xvii. 27.

[c] St. Mark x. 28.

[d] As we should say, "a few pence." The obol was a small Athenian coin.

[e] See St. Luke x. 20; Hebrews xii. 23.

CLEMENT OF ALEXANDRIA

22. " Ἀποκριθεὶς δὲ Ἰησοῦς· ἀμὴν ὑμῖν λέγω,
ὃς ἂν ἀφῇ τὰ ἴδια καὶ γονεῖς καὶ ἀδελφοὺς καὶ χρήματα ἕνεκεν ἐμοῦ καὶ ἕνεκεν τοῦ εὐαγγελίου, ἀπολήψεται ἑκατονταπλασίονα." ἀλλὰ μηδὲ τοῦθ᾽ ἡμᾶς
ἐπιταρασσέτω, μηδὲ τὸ ἔτι τούτου σκληρότερον
ἀλλαχοῦ ταῖς φωναῖς ἐξενηνεγμένον· " ὃς οὐ μισεῖ
πατέρα καὶ μητέρα καὶ παῖδας, προσέτι δὲ καὶ τὴν
ἑαυτοῦ ψυχήν, ἐμὸς μαθητὴς εἶναι οὐ δύναται."
οὐ γὰρ εἰσηγεῖται μῖσος καὶ διάλυσιν ἀπὸ τῶν
φιλτάτων ὁ τῆς εἰρήνης θεός, ὅ γε καὶ τοὺς ἐχθροὺς
ἀγαπᾶν παραινῶν. εἰ δὲ τοὺς ἐχθροὺς ἀγαπητέον,
ἀνάλογον ἀπ᾽ ἐκείνων ἀνιόντι καὶ τοὺς ἐγγυτάτω
γένους· ἢ εἰ μισητέον τοὺς πρὸς αἵματος, πολὺ
μᾶλλον τοὺς ἐχθροὺς προβάλλεσθαι κατιὼν ὁ λόγος
διδάσκει, ὥστ᾽ ἀλλήλους ἀναιροῦντες ἐλέγχοιντ᾽ ἂν
οἱ λόγοι. ἀλλ᾽ οὐδ᾽ ἀναιροῦσιν οὐδ᾽ ἐγγύς, ἀπὸ γὰρ
τῆς αὐτῆς γνώμης καὶ διαθέσεως καὶ ἐπὶ τῷ αὐτῷ
ὅρῳ πατέρα μισοίη τις ἂν ⟨καὶ⟩ ἐχθρὸν ἀγαπῴη [1] ὁ
μήτε ἐχθρὸν ἀμυνόμενος μήτε πατέρα Χριστοῦ
πλέον αἰδούμενος. ἐν ἐκείνῳ μὲν γὰρ τῷ λόγῳ
μῖσος ἐκκόπτει καὶ κακοποιΐαν, ἐν τούτῳ δὲ τὴν
πρὸς τὰ σύντροφα δυσωπίαν, εἰ βλάπτοι πρὸς
σωτηρίαν. εἰ γοῦν ἄθεος εἴη τινὶ πατὴρ ἢ υἱὸς ἢ
ἀδελφὸς καὶ κώλυμα τῆς πίστεως γένοιτο καὶ
ἐμπόδιον τῆς ἄνω ζωῆς, τούτῳ μὴ συμφερέσθω
μηδὲ ὁμονοείτω, ἀλλὰ τὴν σαρκικὴν οἰκειότητα διὰ
τὴν πνευματικὴν ἔχθραν διαλυσάτω.

23. Νόμισον εἶναι τὸ πρᾶγμα διαδικασίαν. ὁ μὲν
πατήρ σοι δοκείτω παρεστὼς λέγειν " ἐγώ σε
ἔσπειρα καὶ ἔθρεψα, ἀκολούθει μοι καὶ συναδίκει

---

[1] ⟨καὶ⟩ . . . ἀγαπῴη Stählin.   ἀγαπῶν ms.

316

22. And Jesus answered, "Verily I say to you, whoever leaves his home and parents and brothers and riches for My sake and for the gospel's sake shall receive back a hundredfold." [a]   Let not this saying however disturb us, nor yet the still harder one uttered elsewhere in the words, " He that hates not father and mother and children, yes and his own life also, cannot be My disciple." [b]   For the God of peace, who exhorts us to love even our enemies, does not propose that we should hate and part from our dearest ones.   If a man must love his enemies, he must also by the same rule, reasoning upward from them, love his nearest of kin.   Or if he must hate his blood relations, much more does reason, by a downward process, teach him to abhor his enemies ; so that the sayings would be proved to cancel one another.   But they do not cancel one another, nor anything like it ; for from the same mind and disposition, and with the same end in view, a man may hate a father and love an enemy, if he neither takes vengeance on his enemy nor honours his father more than Christ.   For in the one saying Christ cuts at the root of hatred and evil-doing, in the other of false respect for our kindred, if they do us harm as regards salvation.   If, for instance, a man had a godless father or son or brother, who became a hindrance to his faith and an obstacle to the life above, let him not live in fellowship or agreement with him, but let him dissolve the fleshly relationship on account of the spiritual antagonism.

23. Think of the matter as a lawsuit.   Imagine your father standing by you and saying, " I begat you and brought you up, follow me, take part in my

The meaning of Christ's command to leave parents and kinsfolk

The appeal of earthly kindred

[a] St. Mark x. 29.   [b] St. Luke xiv. 26.

CLEMENT OF ALEXANDRIA

καὶ μὴ πείθου τῷ Χριστοῦ νόμῳ'' καὶ ὁπόσα ἂν
εἴποι βλάσφημος ἄνθρωπος καὶ νεκρὸς τῇ φύσει.
ἑτέρωθεν δὲ ἄκουε τοῦ σωτῆρος· ''ἐγώ σε ἀνε-
γέννησα, κακῶς ὑπὸ κόσμου πρὸς θάνατον γεγεν-
νημένον, ἠλευθέρωσα, ἰασάμην, ἐλυτρωσάμην· ἐγώ
σοι παρέξω ζωὴν ἄπαυστον, αἰώνιον, ὑπερκόσμιον·
ἐγώ σοι δείξω θεοῦ πατρὸς ἀγαθοῦ πρόσωπον·
μὴ κάλει σεαυτῷ πατέρα ἐπὶ γῆς· οἱ νεκροὶ τοὺς
νεκροὺς θαπτέτωσαν, σὺ δέ μοι ἀκολούθει· ἀνάξω
γάρ σε εἰς ἀνάπαυσιν ⟨καὶ ἀπόλαυσιν⟩ [1] ἀρρήτων
καὶ ἀλέκτων ἀγαθῶν, ἃ μήτε ὀφθαλμὸς εἶδε μήτε
οὓς ἤκουσε μήτε ἐπὶ καρδίαν ἀνθρώπων ἀνέβη, εἰς
ἃ ἐπιθυμοῦσιν ἄγγελοι παρακύψαι καὶ ἰδεῖν ἅπερ
ἡτοίμασεν ὁ θεὸς τοῖς ἁγίοις ἀγαθὰ καὶ τοῖς
φιλοῦσιν αὐτὸν τέκνοις. ἐγώ σου τροφεὺς ἄρτον
ἐμαυτὸν διδούς, οὗ γευσάμενος οὐδεὶς ἔτι πεῖραν
θανάτου λαμβάνει, καὶ πόμα καθ' ἡμέραν ἐνδιδοὺς
ἀθανασίας· ἐγὼ διδάσκαλος ὑπερουρανίων παιδευ-
μάτων· ὑπὲρ σοῦ πρὸς τὸν θάνατον διηγωνισάμην
καὶ τὸν σὸν ἐξέτισα θάνατον, ὃν ὤφειλες ἐπὶ τοῖς
προημαρτημένοις καὶ τῇ πρὸς θεὸν ἀπιστίᾳ.'' τούτων τῶν λόγων ἑκατέρωθεν διακούσας ὑπὲρ σεαυτοῦ
δίκασον καὶ τὴν ψῆφον ἀνένεγκε τῇ σαυτοῦ σωτηρίᾳ·
κἂν ἀδελφὸς ὅμοια λέγῃ κἂν τέκνον κἂν γυνὴ κἂν
949 P. ὁστισοῦν, πρὸ | πάντων ἐν σοὶ Χριστὸς ὁ νικῶν ἔστω·
ὑπὲρ σοῦ γὰρ ἀγωνίζεται.

24. Δύνασαι καὶ τῶν χρημάτων ἐπίπροσθεν εἶναι;
φράσον καὶ οὐκ ἀπάγει σε Χριστὸς τῆς κτήσεως, ὁ

---

[1] ⟨καὶ ἀπόλαυσιν⟩ Stählin.

[a] See 1 St. Peter i. 3. [b] See St. John xiv. 8–9.
[c] St. Matthew xxiii. 9. [d] St. Matthew viii. 22.

318

wrong-doing and do not obey the law of Christ," and whatever else a man who was a blasphemer and in nature dead might say. But from the other side hear the Saviour; "I gave you new birth,[a] when by the world you were evilly born for death; I set you free, I healed you, I redeemed you. I will provide you with a life unending, eternal, above the world. I will show you the face of God the good Father.[b] 'Call no man your father upon earth.'[c] 'Let the dead bury their dead, but do you follow Me.'[d] For I will lead you up to a rest and to an enjoyment of unspeakable and indescribable good things 'which eye has not seen nor ear heard, nor have they entered into the heart of man, which angels desire to look into and to see what good things God has prepared for His saints and for His children that love Him.'[e] I am your nurse, giving Myself for bread, which none who taste have any longer trial of death,[f] and giving day by day drink of immortality.[g] I am a teacher of heavenly instructions. On your behalf I wrestled with death and paid your penalty of death, which you owed for your former sins and your faithlessness towards God." When you have listened to these appeals from each side pass judgment on your own behalf and cast the vote for your own salvation. Even though a brother says the like, or a child or wife or any one else, before all let it be Christ that conquers in you; since it is on your behalf He struggles.

The appeal of Christ

24. Can you also rise superior to your riches? Say so, and Christ does not draw you away from the

Salvation must come before all else

[e] See 1 Corinthians ii. 9; 1 St. Peter i. 12.
[f] See St. John vi. 50–51; Hebrews xi. 36.
[g] See St. John iv. 14.

CLEMENT OF ALEXANDRIA

κύριος οὐ φθονεῖ. ἀλλ' ὁρᾷς σεαυτὸν ἡττώμενον
ὑπ' αὐτῶν καὶ ἀνατρεπόμενον; ἄφες, ῥῖψον, μίσησον, ἀπόταξαι, φύγε· " κἂν ὁ δεξιός σου ὀφθαλμὸς
σκανδαλίζῃ σε, ταχέως ἔκκοψον αὐτόν." αἱρετώτε-
ρον ἑτεροφθάλμῳ βασιλεία θεοῦ ἢ ὁλοκλήρῳ τὸ πῦρ·
κἂν χεὶρ κἂν ποὺς κἂν ἡ ψυχή, μίσησον αὐτήν· ἂν
γὰρ ἐνταῦθα ἀπόληται ὑπὲρ Χριστοῦ, ⟨ἐκεῖ σωθήσε-
ται⟩[1].

25. Ταύτης δὲ ὁμοίως ἔχεται τῆς γνώμης καὶ τὸ
ἑπόμενον· " νῦν δὲ ἐν τῷ καιρῷ τούτῳ ἀγροὺς καὶ
χρήματα καὶ οἰκίας καὶ ἀδελφοὺς ἔχειν μετὰ διωγμῶν εἰς ποῦ;[2] " οὔτε γὰρ ἀχρημάτους οὔτε ἀν-
εστίους οὔτε ἀναδέλφους ἐπὶ τὴν ζωὴν καλεῖ, ἐπεὶ καὶ
πλουσίους κέκληκεν, ἀλλ' ὃν τρόπον προειρήκαμεν,
καὶ ἀδελφοὺς κατὰ ταὐτὸν[3] ὥσπερ Πέτρον μετὰ
Ἀνδρέου καὶ Ἰάκωβον μετὰ Ἰωάννου, τοὺς Ζεβε-
δαίου παῖδας, ἀλλ' ὁμονοοῦντας ἀλλήλοις τε καὶ
Χριστῷ. τὸ δὲ " μετὰ διωγμῶν " ταῦτα ἕκαστα
ἔχειν ἀποδοκιμάζει· διωγμὸς δὲ ὁ μέν τις ἔξωθεν
περιγίνεται τῶν ἀνθρώπων ἢ δι' ἔχθραν ἢ διὰ
φθόνον ἢ διὰ φιλοκέρδειαν ἢ κατ' ἐνέργειαν δια-
βολικὴν τοὺς πιστοὺς ἐλαυνόντων· ὁ δὲ χαλεπώτατος ἔνδοθέν ἐστι διωγμός, ἐξ αὐτῆς ἑκάστῳ τῆς
ψυχῆς προπεμπόμενος λυμαινομένης ὑπὸ ἐπιθυμιῶν
ἀθέων καὶ ἡδονῶν ποικίλων καὶ φαύλων ἐλπίδων
καὶ φθαρτικῶν[4] ὀνειροπολημάτων, ὅταν, ἀεὶ τῶν
πλειόνων ὀρεγομένη καὶ λυσσῶσα ὑπὸ ἀγρίων
ἐρώτων καὶ φλεγομένη, καθάπερ κέντροις ἢ μύωψι

---

[1] ⟨ἐκεῖ σωθήσεται⟩ Segaar.
[2] εἰς ποῦ; Stählin. εἰς που MS. See p. 280, n. 1.
[3] κατὰ ταὐτὸν Segaar. κατ αὐτὸν MS.
[4] φθαρτικῶν Mayor. φθαρτῶν MS.

possession of them; the Lord does not grudge. But do you see yourself being worsted and overthrown by them? Leave them, cast them off, hate them, say good-bye to them, flee from them. "And if thy right eye cause thee to stumble, quickly cut it out." Better the kingdom of God with one eye, than the fire with both. And if it be a hand or a foot or thy life, hate it. For if here it perishes for Christ's sake, there it shall be saved.[a]

25. This meaning attaches likewise to the passage which follows. "To what end is it that in this present time we have lands and riches and houses and brothers with persecutions?"[b] For it is not simply men without riches or homes or brothers that He calls to life, since He has also called rich men (though in the sense we have before stated); and brothers likewise, as Peter with Andrew, and James with John, the sons of Zebedee, though these were brothers of one mind with each other and with Christ. But He disapproves of our having each of these things "with persecutions." Now one kind of persecution comes from without, when men, whether through hatred, or envy, or love of gain, or by the prompting of the devil,[c] harry the faithful. But the hardest persecution is that from within, proceeding from each man's soul that is defiled by godless lusts and manifold pleasures, by low hopes and corrupting imaginations; when, ever coveting more, and maddened and inflamed by fierce loves,[d] it is stung by

The meaning of "with persecutions"

---

[a] See St. Matthew v. 29-30; xviii. 8; and St. Mark ix. 43-47.   [b] St. Mark x. 30.

[c] Or perhaps, "by slanderous activity."

[d] The phrase comes from Plato, *Phaedrus* 81 A; cp. *Republic* 329 c.

τοῖς προσκειμένοις[1] αὐτῇ πάθεσιν ἐξαιμάσσηται
πρὸς σπουδὰς μανιώδεις καὶ ζωῆς ἀπόγνωσιν καὶ
θεοῦ καταφρόνησιν. οὗτος ὁ διωγμὸς βαρύτερος
καὶ χαλεπώτερος, ἔνδοθεν ὁρμώμενος, ἀεὶ συνών,
ὃν οὐδὲ ἐκφυγεῖν ὁ διωκόμενος δύναται· τὸν γὰρ
ἐχθρὸν ἐν ἑαυτῷ περιάγει πανταχοῦ. οὕτω καὶ
πύρωσις ἡ μὲν ἔξωθεν προσπίπτουσα δοκιμασίαν
κατεργάζεται, ἡ δὲ ἔνδοθεν θάνατον διαπράσσεται[2].
καὶ πόλεμος ὁ μὲν ἐπακτὸς ῥᾳδίως καταλύεται, ὁ
δὲ ἐν τῇ ψυχῇ μέχρι θανάτου παραμετρεῖται. μετὰ
διωγμοῦ τοιούτου πλοῦτον ἐὰν ἔχῃς τὸν αἰσθητὸν
κἂν ἀδελφοὺς τοὺς πρὸς αἵματος καὶ τὰ ἄλλα
ἐνέχυρα, κατάλιπε τὴν τούτων παγκτησίαν τὴν ἐπὶ
κακῷ, εἰρήνην σεαυτῷ παράσχες, ἐλευθερώθητι
διωγμοῦ μακροῦ, ἀποστράφηθι πρὸς τὸ εὐαγγέλιον
ἀπ᾽ ἐκείνων, ἑλοῦ τὸν σωτῆρα πρὸ πάντων, τὸν τῆς
σῆς συνήγορον καὶ παράκλητον ψυχῆς, τὸν τῆς
ἀπείρου πρύτανιν ζωῆς. "τὰ γὰρ βλεπόμενα
πρόσκαιρα, τὰ δὲ μὴ βλεπόμενα αἰώνια·" καὶ
950 P. ἐν μὲν τῷ παρόντι | χρόνῳ ὠκύμορα καὶ ἀβέβαια,
"ἐν δὲ τῷ ἐρχομένῳ ζωή[3] ἐστιν αἰώνιος."

26. "Ἔσονται οἱ πρῶτοι ἔσχατοι καὶ οἱ ἔσχατοι
πρῶτοι." τοῦτο πολύχουν μέν ἐστι κατὰ τὴν
ὑπόνοιαν καὶ τὸν σαφηνισμόν, οὐ μὴν ἔν γε τῷ
παρόντι τὴν ζήτησιν ἀπαιτεῖ· οὐ γὰρ μόνον ῥέπει

---

[1] προσκειμένοις Segaar.   προκειμένοις MS.
[2] διαπράσσεται Barnard.   διαταράσσεται MS.
[3] ζωή Ghisler.   ζωήν MS.

---

[a] Clement seems to have in mind Romans v. 4 ("worketh
probation") and 1 Corinthians iii. 13 ("the fire shall prove
each man's work"). The "inward burning which works
death" may be a reminiscence of 1 Corinthians vii. 9.

322

its attendant passions, as by goads or a gad-fly, into states of frenzied excitement, into despair of life and contempt of God. This persecution is heavier and harder, because it arises from within and is ever with us; nor can the victim escape from it, for he carries his enemy about within himself everywhere. So too with regard to burning; that which falls on us from without effects a testing, but that from within works death.[a]   And war also; that which is brought against us is easily ended, but war in the soul accompanies us till death.   If joined with such persecution you have visible wealth and brothers by blood and all the other separable possessions,[b] abandon your sole enjoyment of these which leads to evil, grant to yourself peace, become free from a persecution that lasts, turn away from them to the gospel, choose before all the Saviour, the advocate and counsel[c] for your soul, the president of the infinite life.   " For the things that are seen are temporal, but the things that are not seen are eternal;"[d] and in the present time things are fleeting and uncertain, but "in the world to come is life eternal."[e]

26. "The first shall be last and the last first."[f] This saying, though fruitful in its deeper meaning and interpretation, does not call for examination at the present time, for it applies not merely to those who

[b] Or "pledges," a term used in Attic law to denote movable property that could be offered as security for debt.   In this passage it may mean "dear ones," like the Latin *pignora*.
[c] Literally, "paraclete."   But the connexion with "advocate" shows that Clement is thinking of the word in its legal meaning.   [d] 2 Corinthians iv. 18.
[e] St. Mark x. 30.   [f] St. Mark x. 31.

πρὸς τοὺς πολυκτήμονας, ἀλλ᾽ ἁπλῶς πρὸς ἅπαντας
ἀνθρώπους τοὺς πίστει καθάπαξ ἑαυτοὺς ἐπιδιδόν-
τας. ὥστε τοῦτο μὲν ἀνακείσθω τὰ νῦν. τὸ δέ
γε προκείμενον ἡμῖν οἶμαι μηδέν τι ἐνδεέστερον [1] τῆς
ἐπαγγελίας δεδεῖχθαι, ὅτι τοὺς πλουσίους οὐδένα
τρόπον ὁ σωτὴρ κατ᾽ αὐτόν γε τὸν πλοῦτον καὶ τὴν
περιβολὴν τῆς κτήσεως ἀποκέκλεικεν οὐδ᾽ αὐτοῖς
ἀποτετάφρευκεν τὴν σωτηρίαν, εἴ γε δύναιντο καὶ
βούλοιντο ὑποκύπτειν τοῦ θεοῦ ταῖς ἐντολαῖς καὶ
τῶν προσκαίρων προτιμῶεν τὴν ἑαυτῶν ζωὴν καὶ
βλέποιεν πρὸς τὸν κύριον ἀτενεῖ τῷ βλέμματι,
καθάπερ εἰς ἀγαθοῦ κυβερνήτου νεῦμα δεδορκότες,
τί βούλεται, τί προστάσσει, τί σημαίνει, τί δίδωσι
τοῖς αὐτοῦ ναύταις [τὸ] [2] σύνθημα, ποῦ καὶ πόθεν
τὸν ὅρμον ἐπαγγέλλεται. τί γὰρ ἀδικεῖ τις, εἰ
προσέχων τὴν γνώμην καὶ φειδόμενος πρὸ τῆς
πίστεως βίον ἱκανὸν συνελέξατο; ἢ καὶ ⟨τὸ⟩[3] τούτου
μᾶλλον ἀνέγκλητον, εἰ εὐθὺς ὑπὸ τοῦ θεοῦ τοῦ τὴν
τύχην [4] νέμοντος εἰς οἶκον τοιούτων ἀνθρώπων εἰσ-
ῳκίσθη καὶ γένος ἀμφιλαφὲς τοῖς χρήμασιν [ἰσχύον] [5]
καὶ τῷ πλούτῳ κρατοῦν; εἰ γὰρ διὰ τὴν ἀκούσιον
ἐν πλούτῳ γένεσιν ἀπελήλαται ζωῆς, ἀδικεῖται
μᾶλλον ὑπὸ τοῦ γειναμένου [6] θεοῦ, προσκαίρου μὲν
ἡδυπαθείας κατηξιωμένος, ἀιδίου δὲ ζωῆς ἀπεστε-
ρημένος. τί δ᾽ ὅλως πλοῦτον ἐχρῆν ἐκ γῆς ἀνα-
τεῖλαί ποτε, εἰ χορηγὸς καὶ πρόξενός ἐστι θανάτου;

---

[1] ἐνδεέστερον Ghisler.   ἀδεέστερον ms.
[2] [τὸ] Stählin.   [3] ⟨τὸ⟩ inserted by Ghisler.
[4] τύχην Segaar.   ψυχὴν ms.   [5] [ἰσχύον] Wilamowitz.
[6] γειναμένου Ghisler.   γινομένου ms.

---

[a] *i.e.* the gospel promise of salvation for all men.

have great possessions, but generally to all men who once devote themselves to faith. So for the time being let it be reserved. But as to the question before us, I think it has been shown that the promise [a] does not fall short in any respect, because the Saviour has by no means shut out the rich, at any rate so far as their actual riches and investments [b] of property are concerned, nor has He trenched off salvation from them, provided they are able and willing to stoop beneath God's commandments and that they value their own life above temporal things and look to the Lord with steadfast gaze, like sailors on the watch for the nod of a good pilot to see what are his wishes, his commands, his signals, what watchword he gives them, where and whence he proclaims the harbour. For what wrong does a man do, if by careful thought and frugality he has before his conversion gathered enough to live on; or, what is still less open to censure, if from the very first he was placed by God, the distributor of fortune, in a household of such men, in a family abounding in riches and powerful in wealth? For if he has been banished from life for being born, through no choice of his own, in wealth, it is rather he who is wronged by God who brought him into existence, seeing that he has been counted worthy of temporal comfort, but deprived of eternal life. Why need wealth ever have arisen at all out of earth, if it is the provider and agent [c] of death? But if a man

Salvation is possible for rich men if they will obey God

It is not wrong to save money

Nor to be born in a rich family

[b] Literally, "clothing" or "covering," as on p. 277, n. *a*.

[c] The word is used in Greek politics of a man who was appointed to represent the citizens of another State than his own, and to act as their friend and protector when they visited his city. Hence it has the meaning of our Consul, or Agent.

ἀλλ' εἰ δύναταί τις ἐνδοτέρω τῶν ὑπαρχόντων
κάμπτειν τῆς ἐξουσίας καὶ μέτρια φρονεῖν καὶ
σωφρονεῖν καὶ θεὸν μόνον ζητεῖν καὶ θεὸν ἀναπνεῖν
καὶ θεῷ συμπολιτεύεσθαι, πτωχὸς οὗτος παρέστηκε
ταῖς ἐντολαῖς, ἐλεύθερος, ἀήττητος, ἄνοσος, ἄτρωτος
ὑπὸ χρημάτων· εἰ δὲ μή, θᾶττον κάμηλος διὰ
βελόνης εἰσελεύσεται ἢ ὁ τοιοῦτος πλούσιος ἐπὶ τὴν
βασιλείαν τοῦ θεοῦ παρελεύσεται. σημαινέτω μὲν
οὖν τι καὶ ὑψηλότερον ἡ κάμηλος διὰ στενῆς ὁδοῦ
καὶ τεθλιμμένης φθάνουσα τὸν πλούσιον, ὅπερ ἐν
τῇ περὶ ἀρχῶν καὶ θεολογίας ἐξηγήσει μυστήριον
τοῦ σωτῆρος ὑπάρχει μαθεῖν· 27. οὐ μὴν ἀλλὰ τό
γε φαινόμενον πρῶτον καὶ δι' ὃ λέλεκται τῆς παρα-
βολῆς παρεχέσθω. διδασκέτω τοὺς εὐποροῦντας
ὡς οὐκ ἀμελητέον τῆς ἑαυτῶν σωτηρίας ὡς ἤδη
προκατεγνωσμένους οὐδὲ καταποντιστέον αὖ πάλιν
951 P. τὸν πλοῦτον οὐδὲ καταδικαστέον ὡς | τῆς ζωῆς ἐπί-
βουλον καὶ πολέμιον, ἀλλὰ μαθητέον τίνα τρόπον
καὶ πῶς πλούτῳ χρηστέον καὶ τὴν ζωὴν κτητέον.
ἐπειδὴ γὰρ οὔτε ἐκ παντὸς ἀπόλλυταί τις, ὅτι
πλουτεῖ δεδιώς, οὔτε ἐκ παντὸς σῴζεται θαρρῶν
καὶ πιστεύων ὡς σωθήσεται, φέρε σκεπτέον ἥντινα
τὴν ἐλπίδα αὐτοῖς ὁ σωτὴρ ὑπογράφει, καὶ πῶς ἂν
τὸ μὲν ἀνέλπιστον ἐχέγγυον γένοιτο, τὸ δὲ ἐλπισθὲν
εἰς κτῆσιν ἀφίκοιτο.

ᵃ Literally, "can bend within the power of his possessions," probably a metaphor from the chariot-race, in which
the driver was required to pass close to the turning-post, yet
not to touch it.   The rich man must not let his wealth run
away with him.   With Clement's remark about the power
of possessions Stählin compares Thucydides i. 38—"the
insolence and power of wealth."

ᵇ St. Mark x. 25.

can keep within bounds the power that possessions bring,[a] and can be modest in thought and self-controlled, seeking God alone, living in an atmosphere of God and as a fellow-citizen with God, here is one who approaches the commandments as a poor man, as free, unconquered, untouched by the diseases or wounds of riches. If not, a camel shall more quickly enter through a needle than shall such a rich man reach the kingdom of God.[b] Now the camel, that passes through a strait and narrow way[c] sooner than the rich man, must be understood to have some higher meaning, which, as a mystery of the Saviour, can be learnt in my *Exposition concerning First Principles and Theology*.[d] 27. Here, however, let me set forth the first and obvious meaning of the illustration,[e] and the reason why it was used. Let it teach the well-to-do that their salvation must not be neglected on the ground that they are already condemned beforehand, nor on the contrary must they throw their wealth overboard or give judgment against it as insidious and inimical to life, but they must learn how and in what manner wealth is to be used and life acquired. For since a man is neither absolutely being lost if he is rich but fearful, nor absolutely being saved because he is bold and confident that he will be saved, let us now go on to inquire what hope it is that the Saviour outlines for the rich, and how the unhoped for may become secure, and the hoped for pass into possession.

The rich must then take pains about their salvation

[c] St. Matthew vii. 14.

[d] In iii. *Stromateis* 13. 1 and 21. 2, Clement mentions a projected work on "First Principles"; but it has not come down to us.

[e] Literally, "parable"; but it is hardly a parable in our sense of the word.

Φησὶν οὖν ὁ διδάσκαλος, τίς ἡ μεγίστη τῶν ἐντολῶν ἠρωτημένος· "ἀγαπήσεις κύριον τὸν θεόν σου
ἐξ ὅλης τῆς ψυχῆς σου καὶ ἐξ ὅλης τῆς δυνάμεώς
σου," ταύτης μείζω μηδεμίαν ἐντολὴν εἶναι, καὶ
μάλα εἰκότως. καὶ γὰρ καὶ περὶ τοῦ πρώτου καὶ
περὶ τοῦ μεγίστου παρήγγελται, αὐτοῦ τοῦ θεοῦ
πατρὸς ἡμῶν, δι' οὗ καὶ γέγονε καὶ ἔστι τὰ πάντα
καὶ εἰς ὃν τὰ σῳζόμενα πάλιν ἐπανέρχεται. ὑπὸ
τούτου τοίνυν προαγαπηθέντας καὶ τοῦ γενέσθαι
τυχόντας οὐχ ὅσιον ἄλλο τι πρεσβύτερον ἄγειν καὶ
τιμιώτερον, ἐκτίνοντας μόνην τὴν χάριν ταύτην
μικρὰν ἐπὶ μεγίστοις, ἄλλο δὲ μηδοτιοῦν ἔχοντας
ἀνενδεεῖ καὶ τελείῳ θεῷ πρὸς ἀμοιβὴν ἐπινοῆσαι,
αὐτῷ δὲ τῷ[1] ἀγαπᾶν τὸν πατέρα εἰς οἰκείαν ἰσχὺν
καὶ δύναμιν ἀφθαρσίαν[2] κομιζομένους. ὅσον γὰρ
ἀγαπᾷ τις θεόν, τοσούτῳ καὶ πλέον ἐνδοτέρω τοῦ
θεοῦ παραδύεται.

28. Δευτέραν δὲ τάξει καὶ οὐδέν τι μικροτέραν
ταύτης εἶναι λέγει τό· "ἀγαπήσεις τὸν πλησίον
σου ὡς σεαυτόν·" οὐκοῦν τὸν θεὸν ὑπὲρ σεαυτόν.
πυνθανομένου δὲ τοῦ προσδιαλεγομένου "τίς ἐστιν
πλησίον;" οὐ τὸν αὐτὸν τρόπον Ἰουδαίοις προ-
ωρίσατο τὸν πρὸς αἵματος οὐδὲ τὸν πολίτην οὐδὲ
τὸν προσήλυτον οὐδὲ τὸν ὁμοίως περιτετμημένον
οὐδὲ τὸν ἑνὶ καὶ ταὐτῷ νόμῳ χρώμενον· ἀλλὰ
ἄνωθεν καταβαίνοντα[3] ἀπὸ Ἰερουσαλὴμ ἄγει τῷ
λόγῳ τινὰ εἰς Ἰεριχὼ καὶ τοῦτον δείκνυσιν ὑπὸ
λῃστῶν συγκεκεντημένον, ἐρριμμένον ἡμιθνῆτα ἐπὶ

[1] αὐτῷ δὲ τῷ Ghisler. αὐτὸ δὲ τὸ MS.
[2] ἀφθαρσίαν Wilamowitz. ἀφθαρσίας MS.
[3] καταβαίνοντα Ghisler. καταβαίνων MS.

[a] St. Mark xii. 30–31.

When asked which is the greatest of the com- The first
and greatest
command-
ment
mandments the Teacher says, "Thou shalt love the
Lord thy God with all thy soul and with all thy
power," and that there is no commandment greater
than this[a]—and quite naturally. For indeed it is
a precept concerning the first and the greatest
existence, God Himself our Father, through whom
all things have come into being and exist, and to
whom the things that are being saved return again.[b]
As therefore we were first loved by Him[c] and took
our beginning from Him, it is not reverent to consider
any other thing as more venerable or more honour-
able. This is the only thanks we pay Him, a small
return for the greatest blessings; and we are not
able to think of the slighest thing else to serve as
recompense for a God who is perfect and in need of
nothing. But by the very act of loving the Father
to the limit of our personal strength and power we
gain incorruption. For in proportion as a man loves
God, he enters more closely into God.

28. Second in order, and in no way less important The second
great com-
mandment
than this, is, He says, the commandment, "Thou
shalt love thy neighbour as thyself"[d]—God therefore
you must love more than yourself. And when His
questioner inquires, "Who is a neighbour?"[e] He
did not point, in the same way as the Jews did, to
their blood-relation, or fellow-citizen, or proselyte,
or to the man who like them was circumcised, or to
a keeper of one and the same law, but He describes
a man going down from Jerusalem to Jericho,[f] showing him stabbed by robbers and flung half dead upon

[b] See Romans xi. 36   [c] See 1 St. John iv. 19.
[d] St. Luke x. 27.   [e] St. Luke x. 29.
[f] See St. Luke x. 30–37.

τῆς ὁδοῦ, ὑπὸ ἱερέως παροδευόμενον, ὑπὸ Λευίτου
παρορώμενον, ὑπὸ δὲ τοῦ Σαμαρείτου τοῦ ἐξωνει-
δισμένου καὶ ἀφωρισμένου κατελεούμενον, ὃς οὐχὶ
κατὰ τύχην ὡς ἐκεῖνοι παρῆλθεν, ἀλλ' ἧκε συνεσ-
κευασμένος ὧν [1] ὁ κινδυνεύων ἐδεῖτο, οἶνον, ἔλαιον,
ἐπιδέσμους, κτῆνος, μισθὸν τῷ πανδοχεῖ, τὸν μὲν
ἤδη διδόμενον, τὸν δὲ προσυπισχνούμενον. "τίς,"
ἔφη, "τούτων γέγονε πλησίον τῷ τὰ δεινὰ παθόντι;"
τοῦ δὲ ἀποκριναμένου ὅτι "ὁ τὸν ἔλεον πρὸς αὐτὸν
ἐπιδειξάμενος· καὶ σὺ τοίνυν πορευθεὶς οὕτω
ποίει," ὡς τῆς ἀγάπης βλαστανούσης εὐποιίαν.

29. Ἐν ἀμφοτέραις μὲν οὖν ταῖς ἐντολαῖς ἀγάπην
εἰσηγεῖται, τάξει δ' αὐτὴν διήρηκε, καὶ ὅπου μὲν τὰ
πρωτεῖα τῆς ἀγάπης ἀνάπτει τῷ θεῷ, ὅπου δὲ τὰ
δευτερεῖα νέμει τῷ πλησίον. τίς δ' ἂν ἄλλος οὗτος
εἴη πλὴν αὐτὸς ὁ σωτήρ; ἢ τίς μᾶλλον ἡμᾶς
952 P. ἐλεήσας | ἐκείνου, τοὺς ὑπὸ τῶν κοσμοκρατόρων
τοῦ σκότους ὀλίγου τεθανατωμένους τοῖς πολλοῖς
τραύμασι, φόβοις, ἐπιθυμίαις, ὀργαῖς, λύπαις, ἀπά-
ταις, ἡδοναῖς; τούτων δὲ τῶν τραυμάτων μόνος
ἰατρὸς Ἰησοῦς, ἐκκόπτων ἄρδην τὰ πάθη πρόρριζα,
οὐχ ὥσπερ ὁ νόμος ψιλὰ τὰ ἀποτελέσματα, τοὺς
καρποὺς τῶν πονηρῶν φυτῶν, ἀλλὰ τὴν ἀξίνην τὴν
ἑαυτοῦ πρὸς τὰς ῥίζας τῆς κακίας προσαγαγών.
οὗτος ⟨ὁ⟩ [2] τὸν οἶνον, τὸ αἷμα τῆς ἀμπέλου τῆς Δαβίδ,
ἐκχέας ἡμῶν ἐπὶ τὰς τετρωμένας ψυχάς, ⟨οὗτος ὁ
τὸ ἔλαιον,⟩ [3] τὸν ἐκ σπλάγχνων πατρὸς ἔλεον,
προσενεγκὼν καὶ ἐπιδαψιλευόμενος, οὗτος ὁ τοὺς

---

[1] ὧν Ghisler. ὦν ms.   [2] ⟨ὁ⟩ inserted by Ghisler.
[3] ⟨οὗτος⟩ inserted by Wilamowitz: ⟨ὁ τὸ ἔλαιον⟩ by Lindner.

---

[a] See St. Luke x. 31.   [b] Ephesians vi. 12.
[c] See St. Matthew iii. 10; St. Luke iii. 9.

the road.   A priest passes him by ; a Levite disregards
him ; but he is pitied by the scorned and outcast
Samaritan, who did not pass along by chance [a] as the
others, but had come fully equipped with what the
man in danger needed, wine, oil, bandages, a beast,
and payment for the innkeeper, some being given
there and then and a further amount promised.
" Which of these," He said, " proved neighbour to
him who endured this outrage ? "   And when he
answered, " He that showed pity towards him," the
Lord added, " Go thou therefore and do likewise."
For love bursts forth into good works.

29. In both commandments therefore He introduces love, but He makes a distinction of order, in
one place attaching to God the highest exercise of
love and in the other allotting its secondary exercise
to our neighbour.   And who else can this be but
the Saviour himself?   Or who more than He has
pitied us, who have been almost done to death by
the world-rulers of the darkness [b] with these many
wounds—with fears, lusts, wraths, griefs, deceits and
pleasures ?   Of these wounds Jesus is the only
healer, by cutting out the passions absolutely and
from the very root.   He does not deal with the
bare results, the fruits of bad plants, as the law
did, but brings His axe to the roots of evil.[c]   This is
He who poured over our wounded souls the wine,
the blood of David's vine ;[d] this is He who has
brought and is lavishing on us the oil, the oil of pity

Jesus Christ is our nearest neighbour

[d] Cp. *Teaching of the Twelve Apostles* ix. 1–2, " with
regard to the giving of thanks (*i.e.* the Eucharist), in this
way give thanks : first with regard to the cup ; ' We give
thanks to Thee, our Father, for the holy vine of David Thy
Son, which Thou hast made known to us through Jesus
Thy Son.' "

τῆς ὑγείας καὶ σωτηρίας δεσμοὺς ἀλύτους ἐπιδείξας,
ἀγάπην, πίστιν, ἐλπίδα, οὗτος ὁ διακονεῖν ἀγγέλους
καὶ ἀρχὰς καὶ ἐξουσίας ἡμῖν ἐπιτάξας ἐπὶ μεγάλῳ
μισθῷ, διότι καὶ αὐτοὶ ἐλευθερωθήσονται ἀπὸ τῆς
ματαιότητος τοῦ κόσμου παρὰ τὴν ἀποκάλυψιν
τῆς δόξης τῶν υἱῶν τοῦ θεοῦ. τοῦτον οὖν ἀγαπᾶν
ἴσα χρὴ τῷ θεῷ. ἀγαπᾷ δὲ Χριστὸν Ἰησοῦν
ὁ τὸ θέλημα αὐτοῦ ποιῶν καὶ φυλάσσων αὐτοῦ
τὰς ἐντολάς. "οὐ γὰρ πᾶς ὁ λέγων μοι κύριε
κύριε εἰσελεύσεται εἰς τὴν βασιλείαν τῶν οὐρανῶν,
ἀλλ' ὁ ποιῶν τὸ θέλημα τοῦ πατρός μου."
καί· "τί με λέγετε κύριε κύριε καὶ οὐ ποιεῖτε ἃ
λέγω;" καί· "ὑμεῖς μακάριοι οἱ ὁρῶντες καὶ
ἀκούοντες ἃ μήτε δίκαιοι μήτε προφῆται," ἐὰν
ποιῆτε ἃ λέγω.

30. Πρῶτος μὲν οὖν οὗτός ἐστιν ὁ Χριστὸν
ἀγαπῶν, δεύτερος δὲ ὁ τοὺς ἐκείνῳ πεπιστευκότας
τιμῶν καὶ περιέπων. ὃ γὰρ ἄν τις εἰς μαθητὴν
ἐργάσηται, τοῦτο εἰς ἑαυτὸν ὁ κύριος ἐκδέχεται καὶ
πᾶν ἑαυτοῦ ποιεῖται. "δεῦτε, οἱ εὐλογημένοι τοῦ
πατρός μου, κληρονομήσατε τὴν ἡτοιμασμένην ὑμῖν
βασιλείαν ἀπὸ καταβολῆς κόσμου. ἐπείνασα γὰρ
καὶ ἐδώκατέ μοι φαγεῖν, καὶ ἐδίψησα καὶ ἐδώκατέ
μοι πιεῖν, καὶ ξένος ἤμην καὶ συνηγάγετέ με, γυμνὸς
ἤμην καὶ ἐνεδύσατέ με, ἠσθένησα καὶ ἐπεσκέψασθέ
με, ἐν φυλακῇ ἤμην καὶ ἤλθετε πρός με. τότε
ἀποκριθήσονται αὐτῷ οἱ δίκαιοι λέγοντες· κύριε,

---

[a] 1 Corinthians xiii. 13.
[b] See Hebrews i. 14 ; Ephesians iii. 10.
[c] See Romans viii. 19-21. St. Paul speaks of "the whole creation" being freed from corruption. The special

from the Father's heart; this is He who has shown us the unbreakable bands of health and salvation, love, faith and hope;[a] this is He who has ordered angels and principalities and powers[b] to serve us for great reward, because they too shall be freed from the vanity of the world at the revelation of the glory of the sons of God.[c] Him therefore we must love equally with God. And he loves Christ Jesus who does His will and keeps His commandments.[d] "For not everyone that saith unto Me, Lord, Lord, shall enter into the kingdom of heaven, but he that doeth the will of My Father."[e] And, "Why call ye Me, Lord, Lord, and do not the things that I say?"[f] And "Blessed are ye that see and hear what neither righteous men nor prophets saw and heard," if ye do what I say.[g]

We must love Him equally with God

30. He then is first who loves Christ, and the second is he who honours and respects those who believe on Christ. For whatever service a man does for a disciple the Lord accepts for Himself, and reckons it all His own. "Come, ye blessed of My Father, inherit the kingdom prepared for you from the foundation of the world. For I was hungry and ye gave Me to eat, and I was thirsty and ye gave Me to drink, and I was a stranger and ye took Me in, I was naked and ye clothed Me, I was sick and ye visited Me, I was in prison and ye came unto Me. Then shall the righteous answer Him saying, Lord,

Next we must love Christ's brethren

thought of the angelic powers as destined to share in this deliverance seems to be Clement's own, though possibly it was in St. Paul's mind when he wrote.

[d] See St. John xiv. 15.
[e] St. Matthew vii. 21.
[f] St. Luke vi. 46.
[g] See St. Matthew xiii. 16–17; St. John xiii. 17.

πότε σε εἴδομεν πεινῶντα καὶ ἐθρέψαμεν, ἢ διψῶντα
καὶ ἐποτίσαμεν; πότε δὲ εἴδομέν σε ξένον καὶ συν-
ηγάγομεν, ἢ γυμνὸν καὶ περιεβάλομεν; ἢ πότε σε
εἴδομεν ἀσθενοῦντα καὶ ἐπεσκεψάμεθα; ἢ ἐν φυλακῇ
καὶ ἤλθομεν πρὸς σέ; ἀποκριθεὶς ὁ βασιλεὺς ἐρεῖ
αὐτοῖς· ἀμὴν λέγω ὑμῖν, ἐφ' ὅσον ἐποιήσατε ἑνὶ
τούτων τῶν ἀδελφῶν μου τῶν ἐλαχίστων, ἐμοὶ
ἐποιήσατε." πάλιν ἐκ τῶν ἐναντίων τοὺς ταῦτα
μὴ παρασχόντας αὐτοῖς εἰς τὸ πῦρ ἐμβάλλει τὸ
αἰώνιον, ὡς αὐτῷ μὴ παρεσχηκότας. καὶ ἀλλαχοῦ·
"ὁ ὑμᾶς δεχόμενος ἐμὲ δέχεται, ὁ ὑμᾶς μὴ δεχόμενος ἐμὲ ἀθετεῖ."

31. Τούτους καὶ τέκνα καὶ παιδία καὶ νήπια καὶ
φίλους ὀνομάζει καὶ μικροὺς ἐνθάδε ὡς πρὸς τὸ
μέλλον ἄνω μέγεθος αὐτῶν, "μὴ καταφρονήσητε,"
953 P. λέγων, "ἑνὸς | τῶν μικρῶν τούτων· τούτων γὰρ οἱ
ἄγγελοι διὰ παντὸς βλέπουσι τὸ πρόσωπον τοῦ
πατρός μου τοῦ ἐν οὐρανοῖς." καὶ ἑτέρωθι· "μὴ
φοβεῖσθε, τὸ μικρὸν ποίμνιον· ὑμῖν γὰρ ηὐδόκησεν ὁ
πατὴρ παραδοῦναι τὴν βασιλείαν" τῶν οὐρανῶν.
κατὰ τὰ αὐτὰ καὶ τοῦ μεγίστου ἐν γεννητοῖς
γυναικῶν Ἰωάννου τὸν ἐλάχιστον ἐν τῇ βασιλείᾳ
τῶν οὐρανῶν, τουτέστι τὸν ἑαυτοῦ μαθητήν, εἶναι
μείζω λέγει. καὶ πάλιν· "ὁ δεχόμενος δίκαιον
ἢ προφήτην εἰς ὄνομα δικαίου ἢ προφήτου τὸν
ἐκείνων μισθὸν λήψεται, ὁ δὲ μαθητὴν ποτίσας εἰς
ὄνομα μαθητοῦ ποτήριον ψυχροῦ ὕδατος τὸν μισθὸν
οὐκ ἀπολέσει." οὐκοῦν οὗτος μόνος ὁ μισθὸς οὐκ

ᵃ St. Matthew xxv. 34–40.
ᵇ See St. Matthew x. 40 ; St. Luke x. 16.
ᶜ See St. Mark x. 24 ; St. John xxi. 5 ; St. Matthew xi.
25 ; St. John xv. 15 ; St. Luke xii. 4.

when saw we Thee hungry and fed Thee, or thirsty and gave Thee drink? When saw we Thee a stranger and took Thee in, or naked and clothed Thee? Or when saw we Thee sick and visited Thee? Or in prison and came unto Thee? The King shall answer and say unto them; Verily I say unto you, inasmuch as ye did it unto one of these My brethren, even these least, ye did it unto Me." [a] Again, on the other hand, those who did not provide these things for them He casts into the eternal fire, on the ground that they have not provided them for Him. And in another place: "He that receiveth you receiveth Me; he that receiveth you not rejecteth Me." [b]

31. These who believe on Him He calls children and young children and babes and friends; [c] also little ones here, [d] in comparison with their future greatness above. "Despise not," He says, "one of these little ones, for their angels always behold the face of My Father who is in heaven." [e] And elsewhere; "Fear not, little flock, for it is the Father's good pleasure to give you the kingdom" [f] of heaven. After the same manner He says that the least in the kingdom of heaven, that is, His own disciple, is greater than the greatest among them that are born of women, namely John. [g] And again, "He that receiveth a righteous man or a prophet shall obtain the reward meet for these, and he that hath given a cup of cold water to a disciple in the name of a disciple shall not lose his reward." [h] This then is

Names of love and honour for Christ's disciples

[d] See St. Matthew x. 42.
[e] St. Matthew xviii. 10.
[f] St. Luke xii. 32.
[g] See St. Matthew xi. 11; St. Luke vii. 28.
[h] St. Matthew x. 41–42.

335

ἀπολλύμενός ἐστι. καὶ αὖθις· "ποιήσατε ἑαυτοῖς
φίλους ἐκ τοῦ μαμωνᾶ τῆς ἀδικίας, ἵνα ὅταν ἐκλίπῃ,[1]
δέξωνται ὑμᾶς εἰς τὰς αἰωνίους σκηνάς." φύσει
μὲν ἅπασαν κτῆσιν, ἣν αὐτός τις ἐφ᾽ ἑαυτοῦ κέκτηται
ὡς ἰδίαν οὖσαν καὶ οὐκ εἰς κοινὸν τοῖς δεομένοις
κατατίθησιν, ἄδικον οὖσαν ἀποφαίνων, ἐκ δὲ ταύτης
τῆς ἀδικίας ἐνὸν καὶ πρᾶγμα δίκαιον ἐργάσασθαι
καὶ σωτήριον, ἀναπαῦσαί τινα τῶν ἐχόντων αἰώνιον
σκηνὴν παρὰ τῷ πατρί.

Ὅρα πρῶτον μὲν ὡς οὐκ ἀπαιτεῖσθαί σε κεκέλευ-
κεν οὐδὲ ἐνοχλεῖσθαι περιμένειν, ἀλλὰ αὐτὸν ζητεῖν
τοὺς εὖ πεισομένους ἀξίους τε ὄντας τοῦ σωτῆρος
μαθητάς. καλὸς μὲν οὖν καὶ ὁ τοῦ ἀποστόλου
λόγος· "ἱλαρὸν γὰρ δότην ἀγαπᾷ ὁ θεός," χαίροντα
τῷ διδόναι καὶ μὴ φειδομένως[2] σπείροντα, ἵνα μὴ
οὕτως καὶ θερίσῃ, δίχα γογγυσμῶν καὶ διακρίσεως
καὶ λύπης [καὶ][3] κοινωνοῦντα, ὅπερ ἐστὶν εὐεργεσία
καθαρά.[4] κρείττων δ᾽ ἐστὶ τούτου ὁ τοῦ κυρίου
λελεγμένος ἐν ἄλλῳ χωρίῳ· "παντὶ τῷ αἰτοῦντί
σε δίδου·" θεοῦ γὰρ ὄντως ἡ τοιαύτη φιλοδωρία.
οὑτοσὶ δὲ ὁ λόγος ὑπὲρ ἅπασάν ἐστι θεότητα, μηδὲ
αἰτεῖσθαι περιμένειν, ἀλλ᾽ αὐτὸν ἀναζητεῖν ὅστις
ἄξιος εὖ παθεῖν, ἔπειτα τηλικοῦτον μισθὸν ὁρίσαι τῆς
κοινωνίας, αἰώνιον σκηνήν. 32. ὦ καλῆς ἐμπορίας,
ὦ θείας ἀγορᾶς· ὠνεῖται χρημάτων τις ἀφθαρσίαν,

---

[1] ἐκλίπῃ Stählin. ἐκλίπητε MS.
[2] φειδομένως (from 2 Cor. ix. 6) Segaar. φειδόμενον MS.
[3] [καὶ] Segaar.
[4] καθαρά Segaar. καθά MS.

---

[a] St. Luke xvi. 9.
[b] The phrase comes from Acts iv. 32.
[c] 2 Corinthians ix. 7.

the only reward that cannot be lost.   And once
more : " Make to yourselves friends from the
mammon of unrighteousness, that when it shall fail,
they may receive you into the eternal habitations." [a]
Thus He declares that all possessions are by nature
unrighteous, when a man possesses them for personal
advantage as being entirely his own,[b] and does not
bring them into the common stock for those in need ;
but that from this unrighteousness it is possible to
perform a deed that is righteous and saving, namely,
to give relief to one of those who have an eternal
habitation with the Father.

See, first, how His command is not that you should
yield to a request or wait to be pestered, but that
you should personally seek out men whom you may
benefit, men who are worthy disciples of the Saviour.
Now the Apostle's saying also is good, " God loveth
a cheerful giver," [c] one who takes pleasure in giving
and sows not sparingly, for fear he should reap
sparingly,[d] but shares his goods without murmurings
or dispute or annoyance.   This is sincere kindness.
Better than this is that which is said by the Lord
in another place ; " Give to everyone that asketh
thee ; " [e] for such generosity is truly of God.   But
more divine than all is this saying, that we should
not even wait to be asked,[f] but should personally
seek after whoever is worthy of help, and then fix
the exceedingly great reward of our sharing, an
eternal habitation.   32. What splendid trading !
What divine business !   You buy incorruption with

*The great
reward of
service to
Christ's
disciples*

---

[a] See 2 Corinthians ix. 6.   [e] St. Luke vi. 30.
[f] Clement interprets the saying, " Make to yourselves
friends . . . ," as a command to the rich man to give without
being asked.

καὶ δοὺς τὰ διολλύμενα τοῦ κόσμου μονὴν τούτων
αἰώνιον ἐν οὐρανοῖς ἀντιλαμβάνει. πλεῦσον ἐπὶ
ταύτην, ἂν σωφρονῇς, τὴν πανήγυριν, ὦ πλούσιε,
κἂν δέῃ, περίελθε γῆν[1] ὅλην, μὴ φείσῃ κινδύνων καὶ
πόνων, ἵν᾽ ἐνταῦθα βασιλείαν οὐράνιον ἀγοράσῃς.
τί σε λίθοι διαφανεῖς καὶ σμάραγδοι τοσοῦτον εὐφραί-
νουσι καὶ οἰκία,[2] τροφὴ πυρὸς ἢ χρόνου παίγνιον
ἢ σεισμοῦ πάρεργον ἢ ὕβρισμα τυράννου; ἐπι-
θύμησον ἐν οὐρανοῖς οἰκῆσαι καὶ βασιλεῦσαι μετὰ
θεοῦ· ταύτην σοι τὴν βασιλείαν ἄνθρωπος δώσει
θεὸν ἀπομιμούμενος· ἐνταῦθα μικρὰ λαβὼν ἐκεῖ
δι᾽ ὅλων αἰώνων σύνοικόν σε ποιήσεται. ἱκέτευσον
954 P. ἵνα λάβῃ· σπεῦσον, ἀγω|νίασον, φοβήθητι μή
σε ἀτιμάσῃ· οὐ γὰρ κεκέλευσται λαβεῖν, ἀλλὰ
σὺ παρασχεῖν. οὐ μὴν οὐδ᾽ εἶπεν ὁ κύριος δός,
ἢ παράσχες, ἢ εὐεργέτησον, ἢ βοήθησον, φίλον
δὲ ποίησαι· ὁ δὲ φίλος οὐκ ἐκ μιᾶς δόσεως
γίνεται, ἀλλ᾽ ἐξ ὅλης ἀναπαύσεως καὶ συνουσίας
μακρᾶς· οὔτε γὰρ ἡ πίστις οὔτε ἡ ἀγάπη οὔτε[3] ἡ
καρτερία μιᾶς ἡμέρας, ἀλλ᾽ "ὁ ὑπομείνας εἰς τέλος,
οὗτος σωθήσεται."

33. Πῶς οὖν ὁ ἄνθρωπος ταῦτα δίδωσιν; ὅτι διὰ
τὴν ἐκείνου τιμὴν καὶ εὔνοιαν καὶ οἰκείωσιν ὁ κύριος
δίδωσι· "δώσω γὰρ οὐ μόνον τοῖς φίλοις, ἀλλὰ καὶ
τοῖς φίλοις τῶν φίλων." καὶ τίς οὗτός ἐστιν ὁ
φίλος τοῦ θεοῦ; σὺ μὲν μὴ κρῖνε, τίς ἄξιος καὶ τίς

---

[1] γῆν Combefis. τὴν MS.
[2] οἰκία Combefis. οἰκεία MS.
[3] οὔτε . . . οὔτε . . . οὔτε Stählin. οὐδὲ . . . οὔτε . . .
οὔτε MS.

---

[a] The word means "assembly" and was applied to the
great national and religious festivals of the Greeks at

money. You give the perishing things of the world
and receive in exchange for them an eternal abode
in heaven. Set sail, rich man, for this market,[a] if
you are wise. Compass the whole earth if need be.
Spare not dangers or toils, that here you may buy
a heavenly kingdom. Why so delighted with
glittering stones and emeralds, with a house that
is fuel for fire or a plaything for time or sport for an
earthquake or the object of a tyrant's insolence?
Desire to live and reign in heaven with God. This
kingdom a man, imitating God, shall give you.
Having taken little from you here, he will make you
through all the ages a fellow-inhabitant there. Beg
him to take it. Hasten, strive earnestly, fear lest
he reject you. For he has not been commanded
to take, but you to provide. Furthermore, the Lord
did not say, "give," or "provide," or "benefit," or
"help," but "make a friend"[b]; and a friend is
made not from one gift, but from complete relief
and long companionship. For neither faith nor love
nor patience is the work of one day, but "he that
endureth to the end, the same shall be saved."[c]

33. How then does a man give these things?
Why, the Lord gives them, on account of your
esteem and favour and relationship with this man.
"For I will give not only to my friends, but also to
the friends of my friends."[d] And who is this friend
of God? Do not yourself decide who is worthy and

Olympia and elsewhere. It is used of the Christian church
in Hebrews xii. 23. As we should expect, these gatherings
were made the occasion of fairs and markets (Strabo 486).
It is this aspect of them which Clement seems to have most
in mind here.

[b] St. Luke xvi. 9.   [c] St. Matthew x. 22.

[d] This saying is not found in the gospels.

ἀνάξιος· ἐνδέχεται γάρ σε διαμαρτεῖν περὶ τὴν
δόξαν· ὡς ἐν ἀμφιβόλῳ δὲ τῆς ἀγνοίας ἄμεινον καὶ
τοὺς ἀναξίους εὖ ποιεῖν διὰ τοὺς ἀξίους ἢ φυλασ-
σόμενον τοὺς ἧσσον ἀγαθοὺς μηδὲ τοῖς σπουδαίοις
περιπεσεῖν. ἐκ μὲν γὰρ τοῦ φείδεσθαι καὶ προσ-
ποιεῖσθαι δοκιμάζειν τοὺς εὐλόγως ἢ μὴ τευξο-
μένους ἐνδέχεταί σε καὶ θεοφιλῶν ἀμελῆσαί τινων,
οὗ τὸ ἐπιτίμιον κόλασις ἔμπυρος αἰώνιος· ἐκ δὲ
τοῦ προῖεσθαι πᾶσιν ἑξῆς τοῖς χρῄζουσιν ἀνάγκη
πάντως εὑρεῖν τινα καὶ τῶν σῶσαι παρὰ θεῷ
δυναμένων. "μὴ κρῖνε" τοίνυν, "ἵνα μὴ κριθῇς·
ᾧ μέτρῳ μετρεῖς, τούτῳ καὶ ἀντιμετρηθήσεταί
σοι· μέτρον καλόν, πεπιεσμένον καὶ σεσαλευμένον,
ὑπερεκχυνόμενον, ἀποδοθήσεταί σοι." πᾶσιν ἄν-
οιξον τὰ σπλάγχνα τοῖς τοῦ θεοῦ μαθηταῖς ἀπο-
γεγραμμένοις, μὴ πρὸς σῶμα ἀπιδὼν ὑπερόπτης,
μὴ πρὸς ἡλικίαν ἀμελῶς διατεθείς, μηδ᾽ εἴ τις ἀκτή-
μων ἢ δυσείμων ἢ δυσειδὴς ἢ ἀσθενὴς φαίνεται,
πρὸς τοῦτο τῇ ψυχῇ δυσχεράνῃς καὶ ἀποστραφῇς.
σχῆμα τοῦτ᾽ ἔστιν ἔξωθεν ἡμῖν περιβεβλημένον τῆς
εἰς κόσμον παρόδου προφάσει,[1] ἵν᾽ εἰς τὸ κοινὸν
τοῦτο παιδευτήριον εἰσελθεῖν δυνηθῶμεν· ἀλλ᾽ ἔνδον
κρυπτὸς ἐνοικεῖ ὁ[2] πατὴρ καὶ ὁ τούτου παῖς ὁ ὑπὲρ
ἡμῶν ἀποθανὼν καὶ μεθ᾽ ἡμῶν ἀναστάς.

34. Τοῦτο τὸ σχῆμα τὸ βλεπόμενον ἐξαπατᾷ τὸν
θάνατον καὶ τὸν διάβολον· ὁ γὰρ ἐντὸς πλοῦτος
καὶ τὸ κάλλος αὐτοῖς ἀθέατός ἐστι· καὶ μαίνονται
περὶ τὸ σαρκίον, οὗ καταφρονοῦσιν ὡς ἀσθενοῦς,
τῶν ἔνδον ὄντες τυφλοὶ κτημάτων, οὐκ ἐπιστάμενοι

---

[1] προφάσει Wilamowitz. πρόφασις ms.
[2] ὁ before πατὴρ Stählin : before κρυπτὸς ms.

who unworthy, for you may happen to be quite mis- Do not distinguish between the "worthy" and the "un-worthy" taken in your opinion; so that when in doubt through ignorance it is better to do good even to the unworthy for the sake of the worthy than by being on your guard against the less good not to light upon the virtuous at all. For by being niggardly and by pretending to test who will deserve the benefit and who will not, you may possibly neglect some who are beloved of God, the penalty for which is eternal punishment by fire. But by giving freely to all in turn who need, you are absolutely certain to find one of those men who have power to save you with God. Therefore, "judge not, that you may not be judged; with what measure you mete, it shall be measured to you again. Good measure, pressed down and shaken together, running over, shall be given back to you." [a] Open your heart to all who are enrolled as God's disciples, not gazing scornfully on their body, nor being led to indifference by their age. And if one appear needy or ill-clad Outward appearance is unimportant or ungainly or weak, do not in your soul take offence at this and turn away. This is a form thrown round us from without for the purpose of our entrance into the world, that we may be able to take our place in this universal school; but hidden within dwells the Father, and His Son [b] who died for us and rose with us.

34. This form that is seen deceives death and the The real wealth and beauty are within devil; for the inward wealth and beauty are invisible to them. And they rage round the bit of flesh, which they despise as weak, while they are blind to the inner possessions, not knowing how great a

[a] See St. Matthew vii. 1; St. Luke vi. 38.
[b] See St. John xiv. 23.

πηλίκον τινὰ "θησαυρὸν ἐν ὀστρακίνῳ σκεύει"
βαστάζομεν, δυνάμει θεοῦ πατρὸς καὶ αἵματι θεοῦ
παιδὸς καὶ δρόσῳ πνεύματος ἁγίου περιτετειχισ-
μένον. ἀλλὰ σύ γε μὴ ἐξαπατηθῇς, ὁ γεγευμένος
ἀληθείας καὶ κατηξιωμένος τῆς μεγάλης λυτρώσεως,
ἀλλὰ τὸ ἐναντίον τοῖς ἄλλοις ἀνθρώποις σεαυτῷ
955 P. κατάλεξον στρατὸν ἄοπλον, ἀπόλεμον, ἀναίμακτον,
ἀόργητον, ἀμίαντον, γέροντας | θεοσεβεῖς, ὀρφανοὺς
θεοφιλεῖς, χήρας πραότητι ὡπλισμένας, ἄνδρας
ἀγάπῃ κεκοσμημένους. τοιούτους κτῆσαι τῷ σῷ
πλούτῳ καὶ τῷ σώματι καὶ τῇ ψυχῇ δορυφόρους,
ὧν στρατηγεῖ θεός, δι᾽ οὓς καὶ ναῦς βαπτιζομένη
κουφίζεται μόναις ἁγίων εὐχαῖς κυβερνωμένη, καὶ
νόσος ἀκμάζουσα δαμάζεται χειρῶν ἐπιβολαῖς
διωκομένη, καὶ προσβολὴ λῃστῶν ἀφοπλίζεται
εὐχαῖς εὐσεβέσι σκυλευομένη, καὶ δαιμόνων βία
θραύεται προστάγμασι συντόνοις ἐλεγχομένη.

35. Ἐνεργοὶ[1] οὗτοι πάντες [οἱ][2] στρατιῶται καὶ
φύλακες βέβαιοι, οὐδεὶς ἀργός, οὐδεὶς ἀχρεῖος. ὁ
μὲν ἐξαιτήσασθαί σε δύναται παρὰ θεοῦ, ὁ δὲ παρα-
μυθήσασθαι κάμνοντα, ὁ δὲ δακρῦσαι καὶ στενάξαι
συμπαθῶς ὑπὲρ σοῦ πρὸς τὸν κύριον τῶν ὅλων, ὁ
δὲ διδάξαι τι τῶν πρὸς τὴν σωτηρίαν χρησίμων, ὁ
δὲ νουθετῆσαι μετὰ παρρησίας, ὁ δὲ συμβουλεῦσαι
μετ᾽ εὐνοίας, πάντες δὲ φιλεῖν ἀληθῶς, ἀδόλως,
ἀφόβως, ἀνυποκρίτως, ἀκολακεύτως, ἀπλάστως. ὦ
γλυκεῖαι θεραπεῖαι φιλούντων, ὦ μακάριοι δια-
κονίαι θαρρούντων, ὦ πίστις εἰλικρινὴς θεὸν μόνον
δεδιότων, ὦ λόγων ἀλήθεια παρὰ τοῖς ψεύσασθαι
μὴ δυναμένοις, ὦ κάλλος ἔργων παρὰ τοῖς θεῷ

[1] ἐνεργοὶ Stählin.   ἐν ἔργοις MS.
[2] [οἱ] Schwartz.

342

" treasure " we carry " in an earthen vessel," [a] fortified
by the power of God the Father and the blood of
God the Son and the dew of the Holy Spirit. Do
not you be deceived, however, who have tasted of
truth, and have been deemed worthy of the great
redemption ; but, contrary to the rest of men, enlist
on your behalf an army without weapons, without The great
war, without bloodshed, without anger, without stain, army of Christian
an army of God-fearing old men, of God-beloved saints
orphans, of widows armed with gentleness, of men
adorned with love. Obtain with your wealth, as
guards for your body and your soul, such men as
these, whose commander is God. Through them
the sinking ship rises, steered by the prayers of saints
alone ; and sickness at its height is subdued, put to
flight by the laying on of hands ; the attack of
robbers is made harmless, being stripped of its
weapons by pious prayers ; and the violence of
daemons is shattered, reduced to impotence by
confident commands.

35. Effective soldiers are all these, and steadfast The many
guardians, not one idle, not one useless. One is able services they can
to beg your life from God, another to hearten you render
when sick, another to weep and lament in sympathy
on your behalf before the Lord of all, another to
teach some part of what is useful for salvation, another
to give outspoken warning, another friendly counsel,
and all to love you truly, without guile, fear, hypocrisy,
flattery or pretence. What sweet services of loving
friends ! What blessed ministries of men of good
cheer ! What pure faith of those who fear God alone !
What truth of speech among those who cannot lie !
What beauty of deeds among those who are resolved

[a] 2 Corinthians iv. 7.

343

διακονεῖν πεπεισμένοις, πείθειν θεόν, ἀρέσκειν θεῷ·
οὐ σαρκὸς τῆς σῆς ἅπτεσθαι δοκοῦσιν, ἀλλὰ τῆς
ἑαυτοῦ ψυχῆς ἕκαστος, οὐκ ἀδελφῷ λαλεῖν, ἀλλὰ
τῷ βασιλεῖ τῶν αἰώνων ἐν σοὶ κατοικοῦντι.[a]

36. Πάντες οὖν οἱ πιστοὶ καλοὶ καὶ θεοπρεπεῖς
καὶ τῆς προσηγορίας ἄξιοι, ἣν ὥσπερ διάδημα
περίκεινται. οὐ μὴν ἀλλ' εἰσὶν ἤδη τινὲς καὶ
τῶν ἐκλεκτῶν ἐκλεκτότεροι, καὶ τοσούτῳ μᾶλλον
⟨ἢ⟩[1] ἧττον ἐπίσημοι, τρόπον τινὰ ἐκ τοῦ κλύδωνος
τοῦ κόσμου νεωλκοῦντες ἑαυτοὺς καὶ ἐπανάγοντες
ἐπ' ἀσφαλές, οὐ βουλόμενοι δοκεῖν ἅγιοι, κἂν εἴπῃ
τις, αἰσχυνόμενοι, ἐν βάθει γνώμης ἀποκρύπτοντες
τὰ ἀνεκλάλητα μυστήρια, καὶ τὴν αὐτῶν εὐγένειαν
ὑπερηφανοῦντες ἐν κόσμῳ βλέπεσθαι, οὓς ὁ λόγος
"φῶς τοῦ κόσμου" καὶ "ἅλας τῆς γῆς"[b] καλεῖ.
τοῦτ' ἔστι τὸ σπέρμα,[d] εἰκὼν καὶ ὁμοίωσις θεοῦ, καὶ
τέκνον αὐτοῦ γνήσιον καὶ κληρονόμον,[c] ὥσπερ ἐπί
τινα ξενιτείαν ἐνταῦθα πεμπόμενον ὑπὸ μεγάλης
οἰκονομίας καὶ ἀναλογίας τοῦ πατρός· δι' ὃ[2] καὶ τὰ
φανερὰ καὶ τὰ ἀφανῆ τοῦ κόσμου δεδημιούργηται,
τὰ μὲν εἰς δουλείαν, τὰ δὲ εἰς ἄσκησιν, τὰ δὲ εἰς
μάθησιν αὐτῷ, καὶ πάντα, μέχρις ἂν ἐνταῦθα τὸ
σπέρμα μένῃ, συνέχεται, καὶ συναχθέντος αὐτοῦ
πάντα[3] τάχιστα λυθήσεται. |

---

[1] ⟨ἢ⟩ inserted by Segaar.
[2] δι' ὃ Schwartz. δι' οὗ ms.
[3] πάντα Schwartz. ταῦτα ms.

---

[a] 1 Timothy i. 17.   [b] St. Matthew v. 13–14.

[c] See Genesis i. 26; Romans viii. 17; 1 Timothy i. 2;
Titus i. 4.

[d] The "seed" is a gnostic term for those higher souls
who contain within themselves in a special degree the spark
of divine life. They walk by knowledge, or direct intuition,

to minister to God, to persuade God, to please God! They seem to touch not your flesh but each his own soul, not to be talking with a brother but with the King of the ages [a] who dwells in you.

36. All the faithful then are noble and godlike, and worthy of their title, which they wear as a diadem. Not but that there are already some who are even more elect than the elect, and more elect in proportion as they are less conspicuous. These are they who in a manner haul themselves up out of the surf of the world and retire to a place of safety, who do not wish to appear holy, and are ashamed if one calls them so, who hide in the depth of their mind the unutterable mysteries, and scorn to let their nobility of nature be seen in the world. These the Word calls "light of the world" and "salt of the earth." [b] This is the seed, God's image and likeness, and His true child and heir,[c] sent here, as it were, on a kind of foreign service by the Father's high dispensation and suitable choice. For his sake both the visible and invisible things of the world have been created, some for his service, others for his training, others for his instruction; and all are held together so long as the seed remains on earth, and when it has been gathered in all will speedily be dissolved.[d]

The highest grade of the elect

rather than by faith. Justin Martyr (2 *Apology* ch. 7) makes the same statement as Clement, viz. that the world is preserved solely on account of the "seed"; but he means by this term the whole body of Christians. Clement however seems plainly to restrict it to those who are "more elect than the elect." For the "gathering in" of the elect see St. Matthew iii. 12 and xxiv. 31; *Teaching of the Twelve Apostles* ix. 4 and x. 5; Clement's *Extracts from Theodotus* xxvi. 3.

37. Τί γὰρ ἔτι δεῖ; θεῷ τὰ τῆς ἀγάπης μυστήρια,
καὶ τότε ἐποπτεύσεις τὸν κόλπον τοῦ πατρός, ὃν
ὁ μονογενὴς θεὸς μόνος ἐξηγήσατο. ἔστι δὲ καὶ
αὐτὸς ὁ θεὸς ἀγάπη καὶ δι' ἀγάπην ἡμῖν ἐθεάθη.[1]
καὶ τὸ μὲν ἄρρητον αὐτοῦ πατήρ, τὸ δὲ εἰς ἡμᾶς
συμπαθὲς γέγονε μήτηρ. ἀγαπήσας ὁ πατὴρ
ἐθηλύνθη, καὶ τούτου μέγα σημεῖον ὃν αὐτὸς
ἐγέννησεν ἐξ αὐτοῦ· καὶ ὁ τεχθεὶς ἐξ ἀγάπης
καρπὸς ἀγάπη. διὰ τοῦτο καὶ αὐτὸς κατῆλθε, διὰ
τοῦτο ἄνθρωπον ἐνέδυ, διὰ τοῦτο τὰ ἀνθρώπων
ἑκὼν ἔπαθεν, ἵνα πρὸς τὴν ἡμετέραν ἀσθένειαν οὓς
ἠγάπησε μετρηθεὶς ἡμᾶς πρὸς τὴν ἑαυτοῦ δύναμιν
ἀντιμετρήσῃ. καὶ μέλλων σπένδεσθαι καὶ λύτρον
ἑαυτὸν ἐπιδιδοὺς καινὴν ἡμῖν διαθήκην καταλιμ-
πάνει· "ἀγάπην ὑμῖν δίδωμι τὴν ἐμήν." τίς δέ
ἐστιν αὕτη καὶ πόση; ὑπὲρ ἡμῶν ἑκάστου κατέθηκε[2] τὴν ψυχὴν τὴν ἀνταξίαν τῶν ὅλων· ταύτην
ἡμᾶς ὑπὲρ ἀλλήλων ἀνταπαιτεῖ. εἰ δὲ τὰς ψυχὰς
ὀφείλομεν τοῖς ἀδελφοῖς, καὶ τοιαύτην τὴν συνθήκην
πρὸς τὸν σωτῆρα ἀνθωμολογήμεθα, ἔτι τὰ τοῦ
κόσμου, τὰ πτωχὰ καὶ ἀλλότρια καὶ παρρέοντα,
καθείρξομεν ταμιευόμενοι; ἀλλήλων ἀποκλείσομεν,
ἃ μετὰ μικρὸν ἕξει τὸ πῦρ; θείως γε καὶ ἐπιπνόως[3]

---

[1] ἐθεάθη (cp. v. *Stromateis* 16. 5) Lindner. ἐθηράθη ms.

[2] κατέθηκε Segaar. καθῆκε ms.

[3] ἐπιπνόως Lindner. ἐπιπόνως ms.

---

[a] St. John i. 18. This passage strongly supports the
reading noted in the margin of the Revised Version.

[b] See 1 St. John iv. 8, 16.

[c] This thought of the Motherhood of God has a parallel
in Synesius (Bishop of Ptolemais in Libya early in the fifth
century), *Hymn II.* 63–4:

> Thou art Father, thou art Mother,
> Thou art male, and thou art female.

87. What else is necessary? Behold the mysteries God is love
of love, and then you will have a vision of the bosom
of the Father, whom the only-begotten God alone
declared.[a] God in His very self is love,[b] and for
love's sake He became visible to us. And while the
unspeakable part of Him is Father, the part that has
sympathy with us is Mother.[c] By His loving the
Father became of woman's nature, a great proof of
which is He whom He begat from Himself; and the
fruit that is born of love is love. This is why the
Son Himself came to earth, this is why He put on
manhood, this is why He willingly endured man's
lot, that, having been measured to the weakness of us
whom He loved, He might in return measure us to
His own power. And when He is about to be
offered [d] and is giving Himself up as a ransom He
leaves us a new testament: "I give you my love."[e]
What love is this, and how great? On behalf of
each of us He laid down the life that is equal in
value to the whole world. In return He demands
this sacrifice from us on behalf of one another. But God expects
if we owe our lives to the brethren, and admit such us to show
a reciprocal compact with the Saviour, shall we still to another
husband and hoard up the things of the world, which
are beggarly and alien to us and ever slipping away?
Shall we shut out from one another that which in a
short time the fire will have? Divine indeed and

Gnostic speculation introduced a Mother as the cause of
Creation (cp. Irenaeus i. 4), but the present passage would
seem to have no connexion at all with this. Clement is
simply trying to account, in a mystical way, for the love of
God as shown in the Incarnation.

[d] i.e. as a drink-offering—the same word that St. Paul
uses of himself in 2 Timothy iv. 6.

[e] See St. John xiii. 34; xiv. 27.

ὁ Ἰωάννης "ὁ μὴ φιλῶν" φησὶ "τὸν ἀδελφὸν
ἀνθρωποκτόνος ἐστί," σπέρμα τοῦ Κάιν, θρέμμα
τοῦ διαβόλου· θεοῦ σπλάγχνον οὐκ ἔχει, ἐλπίδα
κρειττόνων οὐκ ἔχει, ἄσπορός ἐστιν, ἄγονός ἐστιν,
οὐκ ἔστι κλῆμα τῆς ἀεὶ ζώσης ὑπερουρανίας ἀμπέλου, ἐκκόπτεται, τὸ πῦρ ἄθρουν ἀναμένει.

38. Σὺ δὲ μάθε τὴν "<καθ'>[1] ὑπερβολὴν ὁδόν,"
ἣν δείκνυσι Παῦλος, ἐπὶ σωτηρίαν· "ἡ ἀγάπη τὰ
ἑαυτῆς οὐ ζητεῖ, ἀλλ' ἐπὶ τὸν ἀδελφὸν ἐκκέχυται·
περὶ τοῦτον ἐπτόηται, περὶ τοῦτον σωφρόνως
μαίνεται. "ἀγάπη καλύπτει πλῆθος ἁμαρτιῶν· ἡ
τελεία ἀγάπη ἐκβάλλει τὸν φόβον· οὐ περπερεύεται,
οὐ φυσιοῦται, οὐκ ἐπιχαίρει τῇ ἀδικίᾳ, συγχαίρει
δὲ τῇ ἀληθείᾳ· πάντα στέγει, πάντα πιστεύει,
πάντα ἐλπίζει, πάντα ὑπομένει. ἡ ἀγάπη οὐδέποτε ἐκπίπτει. προφητεῖαι καταργοῦνται, γλῶσσαι
παύονται, ἰάσεις ἐπὶ γῆς καταλείπονται. μένει δὲ
τὰ τρία ταῦτα, πίστις, ἐλπίς, ἀγάπη· μείζων δὲ ἐν
τούτοις ἡ ἀγάπη." καὶ δικαίως. πίστις μὲν γὰρ
ἀπέρχεται, ὅταν αὐτοψίᾳ πεισθῶμεν ἰδόντες θεόν,
καὶ ἐλπὶς ἀφανίζεται τῶν ἐλπισθέντων ἀποδοθέντων,
ἀγάπη δὲ εἰς πλήρωμα συνέρχεται καὶ μᾶλλον
αὔξεται τῶν τελείων παραδοθέντων. ἐὰν ταύτην
ἐμβάληταί τις τῇ ψυχῇ, δύναται, κἂν ἐν ἁμαρτήμασιν
ᾖ γεγεννημένος, κἂν πολλὰ τῶν κεκωλυμένων
εἰργασμένος, αὐξήσας τὴν ἀγάπην καὶ μετάνοιαν
καθαρὰν λαβὼν ἀναμαχέσασθαι τὰ ἐπταισμένα. |

---

[1] <καθ'> inserted by Combefis from 1 Corinthians xii. 31.

---

[a] 1 St. John iii. 15.
[b] See St. John xv. 5-6.

inspired is the saying of John: "He that loveth not his brother is a murderer," [a] a seed of Cain, a nursling of the devil. He has no tender heart of God, no hope of better things. He is without seed and without offspring. He is no branch of the ever-living heavenly vine. He is cut off; he awaits the fire at once.[b]

38. But do you learn the "more excellent way" [c] to salvation, which Paul shows. "Love seeketh not its own," [d] but is lavished upon the brother. For him love flutters with excitement, for him it is chastely wild. "Love covereth a multitude of sins. Perfect love casteth out fear. Love vaunteth not itself, is not puffed up, rejoiceth not in unrighteousness, but rejoiceth with the truth; beareth all things, believeth all things, hopeth all things, endureth all things. Love never faileth; prophecies are done away, tongues cease, healings are left behind on earth; but these three remain, faith, hope, love; and the greatest among these is love." [e] And rightly; for faith departs, when we believe through having seen God with our own eyes; and hope vanishes away when what we hoped for has been granted; but love goes with us into the fulness of God's presence and increases the more when that which is perfect has been bestowed. Even though a man be born in sins, and have done many of the deeds that are forbidden, if he but implant love in his soul he is able, by increasing the love and by accepting pure repentance, to retrieve his failures.

The greatness of love

Love with true repentance gains God's forgiveness

[c] 1 Corinthians xii. 31.

[d] 1 Corinthians xiii. 5.

[e] See 1 St. Peter iv. 8; 1 St. John iv. 18; 1 Corinthians xiii. 4–13.

957 P. μηδὲ[1] γὰρ τοῦτο εἰς ἀπόγνωσίν σοι καὶ ἀπόνοιαν
καταλελείφθω, εἰ καὶ τὸν πλούσιον μάθοις ὅστις
ἐστὶν ὁ χώραν ἐν οὐρανοῖς οὐκ ἔχων καὶ τίνα τρόπον
τοῖς οὖσι χρώμενος (39) ἄν τις τό τε ἐπίρρητον[2] τοῦ
πλούτου καὶ χαλεπὸν εἰς ζωὴν διαφύγοι καὶ δύναιτο
τῶν αἰωνίων [τῶν][3] ἀγαθῶν ἐπαύρασθαι, εἴη δὲ
τετυχηκὼς ἢ δι' ἄγνοιαν ἢ δι' ἀσθένειαν ἢ περίστασιν
ἀκούσιον μετὰ τὴν σφραγῖδα καὶ τὴν λύτρωσιν
περιπετὴς τισιν ἁμαρτήμασιν ἢ παραπτώμασιν, ὡς
ὑπενηνέχθαι τέλεον, < ὅτι >[4] οὗτος κατεψήφισται παντάπασιν ὑπὸ τοῦ θεοῦ. παντὶ γὰρ τῷ μετ' ἀληθείας
ἐξ ὅλης τῆς καρδίας ἐπιστρέψαντι πρὸς τὸν θεὸν
ἀνεῴγασιν αἱ θύραι καὶ δέχεται τρισάσμενος πατὴρ
υἱὸν ἀληθῶς μετανοοῦντα· ἡ δ' ἀληθινὴ μετάνοια
τὸ μηκέτι τοῖς αὐτοῖς ἔνοχον εἶναι, ἀλλὰ ἄρδην
ἐκριζῶσαι τῆς ψυχῆς ἐφ' οἷς ἑαυτοῦ κατέγνω
θάνατον ἁμαρτήμασιν· τούτων γὰρ ἀναιρεθέντων
αὖθις εἰς σὲ θεὸς εἰσοικισθήσεται. μεγάλην γάρ
φησι καὶ ἀνυπέρβλητον εἶναι χαρὰν καὶ ἑορτὴν ἐν
οὐρανοῖς τῷ πατρὶ καὶ τοῖς ἀγγέλοις ἑνὸς ἁμαρτωλοῦ
ἐπιστρέψαντος καὶ μετανοήσαντος. διὸ καὶ κέκρα-
γεν· ''ἔλεον θέλω καὶ οὐ θυσίαν· οὐ βούλομαι τὸν
θάνατον τοῦ ἁμαρτωλοῦ, ἀλλὰ τὴν μετάνοιαν· κἂν
ὦσιν αἱ ἁμαρτίαι ὑμῶν ὡς φοινικοῦν ἔριον, ὡς
χιόνα λευκανῶ, κἂν μελάντερον τοῦ σκότους, ὡς
ἔριον λευκὸν ἐκνίψας ποιήσω.'' θεῷ γὰρ μόνῳ
δυνατὸν ἄφεσιν ἁμαρτιῶν παρασχέσθαι καὶ μὴ
λογίσασθαι παραπτώματα, ὅπου γε καὶ ἡμῖν παρα-

---

[1] μηδὲ Dindorf. μήτε MS.   [2] ἐπίρρητον Segaar. ἐπίρρεῖ τὸν MS.
[3] αἰωνίων [τῶν] Ghisler. αἰώνων τῶν MS.
[4] <ὅτι> inserted by Stählin.

---

[a] See St. Luke xv. 7, 10.

THE RICH MAN'S SALVATION

For if you understand who is the rich man that has
no place in heaven, and also in what manner a man
may so use his substance (39) as to win his way
to life through the censure and difficulties caused
by wealth, and to be able to enjoy the eternal good
things,—yes, even though he has happened either
because of ignorance or of weakness or of circumstances not of his own choice to fall after the
baptismal seal and redemption into certain sins or
transgressions so as to have become completely subject to them,—let not this thought remain with you
to lead to despair and despondency, namely, that
such an one has been condemned outright by God.
For to every one who turns to God in truth with his
whole heart the doors are opened and a thrice-glad
Father receives a truly penitent son.   And genuine
repentance is to be no longer guilty of the same
offences, but utterly to root out of the soul the
sins for which a man condemned himself to death ;
because when these have been destroyed God will
once again enter in and dwell with you.   For He
says that there is great and unsurpassable joy and
feasting in heaven for the Father and the angels
when one sinner has turned and repented.[a]   Accordingly He cries, " I wish for mercy and not sacrifice,
I desire not the death of the sinner, but his repentance.   Though your sins be as scarlet wool, I will
whiten them as snow ; though blacker than the
darkness, I will wash them and make them as white
wool." [b]   For God alone can grant remission of
sins and not reckon trespasses,[c] though even we

[b] See St. Matthew ix. 13 ; xii. 7 (from Hosea vi. 6) ;
Ezekiel xviii. 23 ; Isaiah i. 18.
[c] See St. Mark ii. 7 ; St. Luke v. 21 ; 2 Corinthians v. 19.

κελεύεται τῆς ἡμέρας ἑκάστης ὁ κύριος ἀφιέναι
τοῖς ἀδελφοῖς μετανοοῦσιν. εἰ δὲ ἡμεῖς πονηροὶ
ὄντες ἴσμεν ἀγαθὰ δόματα διδόναι, πόσῳ μᾶλλον
"ὁ πατὴρ τῶν οἰκτιρμῶν." ὁ ἀγαθὸς πατὴρ "πάσης
παρακλήσεως," ὁ πολύσπλαγχνος καὶ πολυέλεος
πέφυκε μακροθυμεῖν· τοὺς ἐπιστρέψαντας περι-
μένει. ἐπιστρέψαι δέ ἐστιν ὄντως ἀπὸ τῶν ἁμαρ-
τημάτων τὸ παύσασθαι καὶ μηκέτι βλέπειν εἰς
τὰ ὀπίσω.

40. Τῶν μὲν οὖν προγεγενημένων θεὸς δίδωσιν
ἄφεσιν, τῶν δὲ ἐπιόντων αὐτὸς ἕκαστος ἑαυτῷ.
καὶ τοῦτ' ἔστι μετανῶναι, τὸ καταγνῶναι τῶν
παρῳχημένων καὶ αἰτήσασθαι τούτων ἀμνηστίαν
παρὰ πατρός, ὃς μόνος τῶν ἁπάντων οἷός τέ ἐστιν
ἄπρακτα ποιῆσαι τὰ πεπραγμένα ἐλέῳ τῷ παρ' αὑτοῦ
καὶ δρόσῳ πνεύματος ἀπαλείψας τὰ προημαρτημένα.
"ἐφ' οἷς γὰρ ἂν εὕρω ὑμᾶς," φησίν, "ἐπὶ τούτοις
καὶ κρινῶ·" καὶ παρ' ἕκαστα βοᾷ τὸ τέλος πάντων·
ὥστε καὶ τῷ τὰ μέγιστα εὖ πεποιηκότι ⟨κατὰ⟩[1] τὸν
βίον, ἐπὶ δὲ τοῦ τέλους ἐξοκείλαντι πρὸς κακίαν,
ἀνόνητοι[2] πάντες οἱ πρόσθεν πόνοι, ἐπὶ τῆς κατα-
στροφῆς τοῦ δράματος ἐξάθλῳ γενομένῳ, τῷ τε
958 P. χεῖρον | καὶ ἐπισεσυρμένως βιώσαντι πρότερον ἔστιν
ὕστερον μετανοήσαντι πολλοῦ χρόνου πολιτείαν

---

[1] ⟨κατὰ⟩ inserted by Segaar (from Sac. Par.).
[2] ἀνόνητοι Ghisler (from Sac. Par.). ἀνόητοι MS.

---

[a] See St. Luke xvii. 3-4.
[b] St. Matthew vii. 11 ; St. Luke xi. 13.
[c] 2 Corinthians i. 3.   [d] St. James v. 11.
[e] St. Luke ix. 62.
[f] This saying, not found in our gospels, is mentioned in
slightly different form by Justin Martyr (Dialogue with Trypho
47) who expressly attributes it to our Lord. It has some

are exhorted by the Lord each day to forgive our brothers when they repent.[a] And if we, being evil, know how to give good gifts,[b] how much more does "the Father of mercies."[c] The good Father "of all comfort,"[c] full of pity[d] and full of mercy, is by nature long-suffering. He waits for those who turn to Him. And to turn to Him truly is to cease from sins and no more to look back.[e]

40. Of sins already committed, then, God gives remission, but of those that are to come each man procures his own remission. And this is repentance, to condemn the deeds that are past and to ask forgetfulness of them from the Father, who alone of all is able to make undone what has been done, by wiping out former sins with the mercy that comes from Him and with the dew of the Spirit. "For in whatever things I find you," He says, "in these will I also judge you;"[f] and at each step He proclaims the end of all things.[g] So that even when a man has done the greatest works faithfully through life, but at the end has run on the rocks of evil, all his former labours bring him no profit, since at the turning-point[h] of the drama he has retired from the contest; whereas he who has at first led an indifferent and slipshod life may, if afterwards he repents, utterly wipe out a wicked course of long continuance with the time

Repentance means a complete change of life

resemblance to Ezekiel xxxiii. 20 (Sept.)—"I will judge you each one in his ways"—and in both Clement and Justin it occurs in connexion with teaching drawn from Ezekiel xxxiii. 10-20.　　　　　[g] See 1 St. Peter iv. 7.

[h] The "catastrophe" or turning-point towards the end of a play when the issue stands definitely revealed. Used here, as elsewhere in Greek literature, for the conclusion of life, when a man might be expected to have settled down to a course either good or evil.

CLEMENT OF ALEXANDRIA

πονηρὰν ἐκνικῆσαι τῷ μετὰ τὴν μετάνοιαν χρόνῳ·
ἀκριβείας δὲ δεῖ πολλῆς, ὥσπερ τοῖς μακρᾷ νόσῳ
πεπονηκόσι σώμασι διαίτης χρεία καὶ προσοχῆς
πλείονος. ὁ κλέπτης, ἄφεσιν βούλει λαβεῖν; μηκέτι
κλέπτε· ὁ μοιχεύσας, μηκέτι πυρούσθω· ὁ πορ-
νεύσας, λοιπὸν ἁγνευέτω· ὁ ἁρπάσας, ἀποδίδου καὶ
προσαποδίδου· ὁ ψευδομάρτυς, ἀλήθειαν ἄσκησον·
ὁ ἐπίορκος, μηκέτι ὄμνυε· καὶ τὰ ἄλλα πάθη σύν-
τεμε, ὀργήν, ἐπιθυμίαν, λύπην, φόβον, ἵνα εὑρεθῇς
ἐπὶ τῆς ἐξόδου πρὸς τὸν ἀντίδικον ἐνταῦθα
διαλελύσθαι φθάνων. ἔστιν μὲν οὖν ἀδύνατον ἴσως
ἀθρόως ἀποκόψαι πάθη σύντροφα, ἀλλὰ μετὰ θεοῦ
δυνάμεως καὶ ἀνθρωπείας ἱκεσίας καὶ ἀδελφῶν
βοηθείας καὶ εἰλικρινοῦς μετανοίας καὶ συνεχοῦς
μελέτης κατορθοῦται.

41. Διὸ δεῖ πάντως σε τὸν σοβαρὸν καὶ δυνατὸ
καὶ πλούσιον ἐπιστήσασθαι ἑαυτῷ τινα ἄνθρωπον
θεοῦ καθάπερ ἀλείπτην καὶ κυβερνήτην. αἰδοῦ κἂν
ἕνα, φοβοῦ κἂν ἕνα, μελέτησον ἀκούειν κἂν ἑνὸς παρ-
ρησιαζομένου καὶ στύφοντος ἅμα καὶ θεραπεύοντος.
οὐδὲ γὰρ τοῖς ὀφθαλμοῖς συμφέρει τὸν ἀεὶ χρόνον
ἀκολάστοις μένειν, ἀλλὰ καὶ δακρῦσαι καὶ δηχθῆναί
ποτε ὑπὲρ τῆς ὑγείας τῆς πλείονος. οὕτω καὶ ψυχῇ
διηνεκοῦς ἡδονῆς οὐδὲν ὀλεθριώτερον· ἀποτυφλοῦ-
ται γὰρ ἀπὸ τῆς τήξεως, ἐὰν ἀκίνητος τῷ παρρη-
σιαζομένῳ διαμείνῃ λόγῳ. τοῦτον καὶ ὀργισθέντα
φοβήθητι, καὶ στενάξαντα λυπήθητι,[1] καὶ ὀργὴν
παύοντα αἰδέσθητι, καὶ κόλασιν παραιτούμενον[2]

---

[1] στενάξαντος λυπήθητι Mayor.   στενάξαντα εὐλαβήθητι
Segaar.   δυσωπήθητι Schwartz.   Stählin and Barnard mark
the passage as corrupt.
[2] παραιτούμενον Segaar.   παραιτουμένῳ MS.

left after his repentance. But great care is needed, just as bodies that are labouring under a long disease require treatment and special attention. Thief, do you wish to receive forgiveness? steal no more.[a] Adulterer, no longer burn.[b] Fornicator, keep pure in future. Extortioner, repay with interest. False witness, practise truth. Oath-breaker, swear no more. And repress the rest of the passions, anger, lust, grief, fear, in order that at your departure you may be found to have already become reconciled here on earth with your adversary.[c] Now it is perhaps impossible all at once to cut away passions that have grown with us, but with God's power, human supplication, the help of brethren, sincere repentance and constant practice success is achieved.

41. It is therefore an absolute necessity that you who are haughty and powerful and rich should appoint for yourself some man of God as trainer and pilot. Let there be at all events one whom you respect, one whom you fear, one whom you accustom yourself to listen to when he is outspoken and severe, though all the while at your service. Why, it is not good for the eyes to remain all our life-time undisciplined; they should sometimes weep and smart for the sake of better health. So, too, nothing is more destructive to the soul than incessant pleasure, the softening influence of which blinds it, if it continues obstinate against the outspoken word. Fear this man when he is angry, and be grieved when he groans; respect him when he stays his anger, and be before him in begging release from punishment.

The rich need outspoken advice and warning

---

[a] See Ephesians iv. 28.
[b] See 1 Corinthians vii. 9.
[c] See St. Matthew v. 25; St. Luke xii. 58.

φθάσον. οὗτος ὑπὲρ σοῦ πολλὰς νύκτας ἀγρυπνη-
σάτω, πρεσβεύων ὑπὲρ σοῦ πρὸς θεὸν καὶ λιτανείαις
συνήθεσι μαγεύων τὸν πατέρα· οὐ γὰρ ἀντέχει
τοῖς τέκνοις αὐτοῦ τὰ σπλάγχνα δεομένοις. δεήσεται
δὲ καθαρῶς ὑπὸ σοῦ προτιμώμενος ὡς ἄγγελος τοῦ
θεοῦ καὶ μηδὲν ὑπὸ σοῦ λυπούμενος, ἀλλ᾽ ὑπὲρ σοῦ·
τοῦτό ἐστι μετάνοια ἀνυπόκριτος. "θεὸς οὐ μυκτη-
ρίζεται" οὐδὲ προσέχει κενοῖς ῥήμασι· μόνος γὰρ
ἀνακρίνει μυελοὺς καὶ νεφροὺς καρδίας καὶ τῶν ἐν
πυρὶ κατακούει καὶ τῶν ἐν κοιλίᾳ κήτους ἱκετευόν-
των ἐξακούει καὶ πᾶσιν ἐγγύς ἐστι τοῖς πιστεύουσι
καὶ πόρρω τοῖς ἀθέοις, ἂν μὴ μετανοήσωσιν.

42. Ἵνα δὲ ἐπιθαρρήσῃς,[1] οὕτω μετανοήσας
ἀληθῶς, ὅτι σοὶ μένει σωτηρίας ἐλπὶς ἀξιόχρεως,
ἄκουσον μῦθον οὐ μῦθον, ἀλλὰ ὄντα λόγον περὶ
Ἰωάννου τοῦ ἀπο|στόλου παραδεδομένον καὶ μνήμῃ
πεφυλαγμένον. ἐπειδὴ γὰρ τοῦ τυράννου τελευτή-
σαντος ἀπὸ τῆς Πάτμου τῆς νήσου μετῆλθεν ἐπὶ
τὴν Ἔφεσον, ἀπῄει παρακαλούμενος καὶ ἐπὶ τὰ
πλησιόχωρα τῶν ἐθνῶν, ὅπου μὲν ἐπισκόπους κατα-
στήσων, ὅπου δὲ ὅλας ἐκκλησίας ἁρμόσων, ὅπου
δὲ κλῆρον ἕνα γέ[2] τινα κληρώσων τῶν ὑπὸ τοῦ
πνεύματος σημαινομένων. ἐλθὼν οὖν καὶ ἐπί τινα

959 P.

---

[1] ἐπιθαρρήσῃς Barnard and Stählin (from Maximus Confessor). ἔτι θαρρῇς MS.

[2] γέ Stählin (from Eusebius and Maximus Confessor).
τε MS.

---

[a] Galatians vi. 7.

[b] For this sentence see Hebrews iv. 12 ; Jeremiah xvii. 10;
Psalm vii. 9 ; Daniel iii. ; Jonah ii. ; Revelation ii. 23.

[c] Domitian, by whom St. John is said to have been exiled,
is generally thought to be referred to here. But he died in
A.D. 96, and it is practically certain that St. John the
apostle's active ministry must have ended before this date.

Let him spend many wakeful nights on your behalf,
acting as your ambassador with God and moving the
Father by the spell of constant supplications; for
He does not withstand His children when they beg
His mercies. And this man will beg them, if he is
sincerely honoured by you as an angel of God and is
in nothing grieved by you, but only for you. This
is unfeigned repentance. "God is not mocked," [a]
nor does He attend to empty phrases. For He alone
discerns the marrow and reins of the heart; and
hears those who are in the fire; and listens to those
who in the whale's belly entreat Him; and is near to all
believers and far from the godless unless they repent. [b]

42. And to give you confidence, when you have
thus truly repented, that there remains for you a
trustworthy hope of salvation, hear a story that is no
mere story, but a true account of John the apostle
that has been handed down and preserved in memory.
When after the death of the tyrant [c] he removed
from the island of Patmos to Ephesus, he used to
journey by request to the neighbouring districts of the
Gentiles, in some places to appoint bishops, in others
to regulate whole churches, in others to set among
the clergy some one man, it may be, of those indicated
by the Spirit. [d] He came then to one of the cities

Story of
St. John
and the
robber

Either his exile was earlier, *i.e.* in Nero's reign, or else there
has been a confusion between the apostle and John the
presbyter of Ephesus.

[d] The phrase κληρώσων κλῆρον means literally " to allot a
lot." Κλῆρος was used to designate a " lot " or " share " in
the Christian ministry (cp. Acts i. 17) and its use was afterwards extended to the ministers themselves or " clergy."
In this passage both meanings are suggested. Those " indicated by the Spirit " would be men whose spiritual gifts,
such for instance as pastoral authority or teaching, marked
them out as fit candidates for office in the Church.

357

τῶν οὐ μακρὰν πόλεων, ἧς καὶ τοὔνομα λέγουσιν
ἔνιοι, καὶ τὰ ἄλλα ἀναπαύσας τοὺς ἀδελφούς, ἐπὶ
πᾶσι τῷ καθεστῶτι προσβλέψας ἐπισκόπῳ, νεανίσκον ἱκανὸν τῷ σώματι καὶ τὴν ὄψιν ἀστεῖον καὶ
θερμὸν τὴν ψυχὴν ἰδών, "τοῦτον" ἔφη "σοὶ
παρακατατίθεμαι¹ μετὰ πάσης σπουδῆς ἐπὶ τῆς
ἐκκλησίας καὶ τοῦ Χριστοῦ μάρτυρος." τοῦ δὲ
δεχομένου καὶ πάνθ' ὑπισχνουμένου καὶ πάλιν τὰ
αὐτὰ διετείνατο καὶ διεμαρτύρατο. εἶτα ὁ μὲν
ἀπῆρεν ἐπὶ τὴν Ἔφεσον, ὁ δὲ πρεσβύτερος ἀναλαβὼν οἴκαδε τὸν παραδοθέντα νεανίσκον ἔτρεφε,
συνεῖχεν, ἔθαλπε, τὸ τελευταῖον ἐφώτισε· καὶ μετὰ
τοῦτο ὑφῆκε τῆς πλείονος ἐπιμελείας καὶ παρα-
φυλακῆς, ὡς τὸ τέλειον αὐτῷ φυλακτήριον ἐπι-
στήσας τὴν σφραγῖδα τοῦ κυρίου. τῷ δὲ ἀνέσεως
πρὸ ὥρας λαβομένῳ προσφθείρονταί τινες ἥλικες
ἀργοὶ καὶ ἀπερρωγότες, ἐθάδες κακῶν· καὶ πρῶτον
μὲν δι' ἑστιάσεων πολυτελῶν αὐτὸν ὑπάγονται, εἶτά
που καὶ νύκτωρ ἐπὶ λωποδυσίαν ἐξιόντες συνεπάγον-
ται, εἶτά τι καὶ μεῖζον συμπράττειν ἠξίουν. ὁ δὲ
κατ' ὀλίγον προσειθίζετο καὶ διὰ μέγεθος φύσεως
ἐκστὰς ὥσπερ ἄστομος καὶ εὔρωστος ἵππος ὀρθῆς

---

¹ παρακατατίθεμαι Stählin (from Eus. and Max. Conf.).
παρατίθεμαι MS.

ª It will be noticed that Clement here applies the terms
"bishop" and "presbyter" to the same person. This may
be due to the fact that in this story he followed a written
authority coming down from a time when the two terms
were synonymous, as they are in the New Testament. On
the other hand, it is possible that the sharp distinction
between "bishop" and "presbyter," though well-known
elsewhere, was not yet recognized at Alexandria. Jerome

not far distant, the very name of which is told by some. After he had set the brethren at rest on other matters, last of all he looked at him who held the office of bishop, and, having noticed a strongly built youth of refined appearance and ardent spirit, he said: "This man I entrust to your care with all earnestness in the presence of the church and of Christ as witness." When the bishop accepted the trust and made every promise, the apostle once again solemnly charged and adjured him in the same words. After that he departed to Ephesus; but the presbyter[a] took home the youth who had been handed over to him, and brought him up, made a companion of him, cherished him, and finally enlightened him by baptism. After this he relaxed his special care and guardianship, thinking that he had set over him the perfect guard, the seal of the Lord. But the youth had obtained liberty too soon. Certain idle and dissolute fellows, accustomed to evil deeds, form a ruinous companionship with him. At first they lead him on by means of costly banquets; then perhaps on their nightly expeditions for robbery they take him with them; then they urge him to join in some even greater deed. He on his part gradually became used to their life; and, like a restive and powerful horse which starts aside from the right path and takes the bit between its teeth, he rushed all the

(*Epistle* cxlvi.) says that until the times of Heraclas and Dionysius (A.D. 233) the presbyters at Alexandria always elected a bishop from among their own number. Clement in other places sometimes mentions two orders of the ministry, sometimes three; and it is not easy to discover his actual belief. For a short summary of Clement's references to this subject see Tollinton, *Clement of Alexandria*, ii. 111–114.

ὁδοῦ καὶ τὸν χαλινὸν ἐνδακὼν μειζόνως κατὰ τῶν
βαράθρων ἐφέρετο. ἀπογνοὺς δὲ τελέως τὴν ἐν θεῷ
σωτηρίαν οὐδὲν ἔτι μικρὸν διενοεῖτο, ἀλλὰ μέγα τι
πράξας, ἐπειδήπερ ἅπαξ ἀπολώλει, ἴσα τοῖς ἄλλοις
παθεῖν ἠξίου. αὐτοὺς δὴ τούτους ἀναλαβὼν καὶ
λῃστήριον συγκροτήσας, ἕτοιμος λήσταρχος ἦν,
βιαιότατος, μιαιφονώτατος, χαλεπώτατος. χρόνος
ἐν μέσῳ, καί τινος ἐπιπεσούσης χρείας ἀνακαλοῦσι
τὸν Ἰωάννην. ὁ δέ, ἐπεὶ τὰ ἄλλα ὧν χάριν ἧκεν
κατεστήσατο, "ἄγε δή," ἔφη, "ὦ ἐπίσκοπε, τὴν
παραθήκην ἀπόδος ἡμῖν, ἣν ἐγώ τε καὶ ὁ
Χριστός [1] σοι παρακατεθέμεθα ἐπὶ τῆς ἐκκλησίας,
ἧς προκαθέζῃ, μάρτυρος." ὁ δὲ τὸ μὲν πρῶτον
ἐξεπλάγη, χρήματα οἰόμενος, ἅπερ οὐκ ἔλαβε,
συκοφαντεῖσθαι, καὶ οὔτε πιστεύειν εἶχεν ὑπὲρ ὧν
960 P. οὐκ εἶχεν οὔτε ἀπιστεῖν Ἰωάννῃ· ὡς δὲ "τὸν
νεανίσκον" εἶπεν "ἀπαιτῶ καὶ τὴν ψυχὴν τοῦ
ἀδελφοῦ," στενάξας κάτωθεν ὁ πρεσβύτης καί τι
καὶ ἐπιδακρύσας, "ἐκεῖνος" ἔφη "τέθνηκε."
"πῶς καὶ τίνα θάνατον;" "θεῷ τέθνηκεν" εἶπεν·
"ἀπέβη γὰρ πονηρὸς καὶ ἐξώλης καὶ τὸ κεφάλαιον
λῃστής, καὶ νῦν ἀντὶ τῆς ἐκκλησίας τὸ ὄρος κατ-
είληφε μεθ' ὁμοίου στρατιωτικοῦ. καταρρηξάμενος
τὴν ἐσθῆτα ὁ ἀπόστολος καὶ μετὰ μεγάλης οἰ-
μωγῆς πληξάμενος τὴν κεφαλήν, "καλόν γε" ἔφη
"φύλακα τῆς τἀδελφοῦ ψυχῆς κατέλιπον· ἀλλ' ἵππος
ἤδη μοι παρέστω καὶ ἡγεμὼν γενέσθω μοί τις
τῆς ὁδοῦ." ἤλαυνεν, ὥσπερ εἶχεν, αὐτόθεν ἀπὸ
τῆς ἐκκλησίας. ἐλθὼν δὲ εἰς τὸ χωρίον ὑπὸ τῆς

[1] Χριστός Eusebius. σωτήρ ms.

360

more violently because of his great nature down towards the pit. Having quite given up hope of salvation in God he no longer meditated any slight offence, but, seeing he was lost once and for all, decided to do something great and to suffer the same penalty as the rest. So he took these very men, and organized a robber band, of which he was a ready chieftain, the most violent, the most blood-thirsty, the most cruel. Time went by, and some need having arisen the church again appeals to John, who, when he had set in order the matters for the sake of which he had come, said: "Now, bishop, return us the deposit which Christ and I together entrusted to your care in the presence and with the witness of the church over which you preside." The bishop was at first amazed, thinking he was being falsely accused about money which he had not received; and he could neither believe a charge that concerned what he did not possess nor could he disbelieve John. But when he said, "It is the youth and the soul of our brother that I demand back," the old man groaned deeply and even shed tears. "That man," he said "is dead." "How and by what manner of death?" "He is dead to God" he replied; "for he turned out a wicked and depraved man, in short a robber, and now deserting the church he has taken to the hills in company with a troop of men like himself." The apostle, rending his clothes and with a loud groan striking his head, said: "A fine guardian of our brother's soul it was that I left! But let a horse be brought me at once, and let me have someone as a guide for the way." Just as he was he rode right from the very church; and when he came to the

προφυλακῆς τῶν λῃστῶν ἁλίσκεται, μήτε φεύγων
μήτε παραιτούμενος, ἀλλὰ βοῶν· "ἐπὶ τοῦτ' ἐλή-
λυθα, ἐπὶ τὸν ἄρχοντα ὑμῶν ἀγάγετέ με." ὃς
τέως, ὥσπερ ὥπλιστο, ἀνέμενεν· ὡς δὲ προσιόντα
ἐγνώρισε τὸν Ἰωάννην, εἰς φυγὴν αἰδεσθεὶς ἐτρά-
πετο. ὁ δὲ ἐδίωκεν ἀνὰ κράτος, ἐπιλαθόμενος τῆς
ἡλικίας τῆς ἑαυτοῦ, κεκραγώς· "τί με φεύγεις,
τέκνον, τὸν σαυτοῦ πατέρα, τὸν γυμνόν, τὸν
γέροντα; ἐλέησόν με, τέκνον, μὴ φοβοῦ· ἔχεις ἔτι
ζωῆς ἐλπίδας· ἐγὼ Χριστῷ λόγον δώσω ὑπὲρ σοῦ·
ἂν δέῃ, τὸν σὸν θάνατον ἑκὼν ὑπομενῶ, ὡς ὁ κύριος
τὸν ὑπὲρ ἡμῶν· ὑπὲρ σοῦ τὴν ψυχὴν ἀντιδώσω τὴν
ἐμήν. στῆθι, πίστευσον, Χριστός με ἀπέστειλεν."
ὁ δὲ ἀκούσας πρῶτον ἔστη μὲν κάτω βλέπων, εἶτα
ἔρριψε τὰ ὅπλα, εἶτα τρέμων ἔκλαιε πικρῶς· προσ-
ελθόντα δὲ τὸν γέροντα περιέλαβεν, ἀπολογούμενος
ταῖς οἰμωγαῖς ὡς ἐδύνατο καὶ τοῖς δάκρυσι
βαπτιζόμενος ἐκ δευτέρου, μόνην ἀποκρύπτων
τὴν δεξιάν. ὁ δὲ ἐγγυώμενος, ἐπομνύμενος ὡς
ἄφεσιν αὐτῷ παρὰ τοῦ σωτῆρος εὕρηται, δεόμενος,
γονυπετῶν, αὐτὴν τὴν δεξιὰν ὡς ὑπὸ τῆς μετανοίας κεκαθαρμένην καταφιλῶν, ἐπὶ τὴν ἐκκλησίαν
ἐπανήγαγε, καὶ δαψιλέσι μὲν εὐχαῖς ἐξαιτούμε-
νος, συνεχέσι δὲ νηστείαις συναγωνιζόμενος, ποικίλαις δὲ σειρῇσι λόγων κατεπᾴδων αὐτοῦ τὴν
γνώμην, οὐ πρότερον ἀπῆλθεν, ὥς φασι, πρὶν αὐτὸν

---

[a] See Hebrews xiii. 17.
[b] See St. Matthew xxvi. 75 ; St. Luke xxii. 62.
[c] If we read ἀποκατέστησε (with Barnard) or some
similar word, the translation will be "restored him to the
church." But ἐπιστῆσαι is almost certainly right. See
note on text, p. 364.

place he is captured by the robbers' sentry, not attempting to fly or to expostulate, but shouting, "I have come for this purpose; bring me to your leader." For a time the leader, armed as he was, awaited them; but when he recognized John approaching he turned to flight, smitten with shame. Forgetful of his years John followed after him with all his strength, crying out: "Why do you fly from me, child, from your own father, from this old, unarmed man? Have pity on me, child, do not fear. You have still hopes of life, I myself will give account [a] to Christ for you. If need be, I will willingly undergo your penalty of death, as the Lord did for us. I will give my own life in payment for yours. Stand; believe; Christ has sent me." On hearing this he at first stood still, looking down; then threw away his weapons; then trembling began to weep bitterly.[b] When the old man had come near the robber embraced him, making excuse as best he could by his groans, and being baptized a second time with his tears, hiding his right hand alone. But the apostle gave his pledge and solemn assurance that he had found pardon for him from the Saviour. Kneeling down and praying, and tenderly kissing the right hand itself as having been purified by his repentance, he then brought him back to the church. There he interceded for him with abundant prayers, helped his struggles by continual fasting, and by manifold siren-like words laid a soothing spell upon his mind. Nor did he depart, as they say, before he had set him over [c] the church,

ἐπιστῆσαι¹ τῇ ἐκκλησίᾳ, διδοὺς μέγα παράδειγμα μετανοίας ἀληθινῆς καὶ μέγα γνώρισμα παλιγγενεσίας, τρόπαιον ἀναστάσεως βλεπομένης.

. . . φαιδροῖς γεγηθότες, ὑμνοῦντες, ἀνοιγνύντες τοὺς οὐρανούς. πρὸ δὲ πάντων αὐτὸς ὁ σωτὴρ 961 P. προαπαντᾷ δεξιούμενος, φῶς ὀρέγων ἄσκιον, ἄπαυστον, ὁδηγῶν εἰς τοὺς κόλπους τοῦ πατρός, εἰς τὴν αἰώνιον ζωήν, εἰς τὴν βασιλείαν τῶν οὐρανῶν. πιστευέτω ταῦτά τις καὶ θεοῦ μαθηταῖς καὶ ἐγγυητῇ θεῷ, προφητείαις, εὐαγγελίοις, λόγοις ἀποστολικοῖς· τούτοις συζῶν καὶ τὰ ὦτα ὑπέχων καὶ τὰ ἔργα ἀσκῶν ἐπ᾽ αὐτῆς τῆς ἐξόδου τὸ τέλος καὶ τὴν ἐπίδειξιν τῶν δογμάτων ὄψεται. ὁ γὰρ ἐνταῦθα τὸν ἄγγελον τῆς μετανοίας προσιέμενος οὐ μετανοήσει τότε, ἡνίκα ἂν καταλίπῃ τὸ σῶμα, οὐδὲ καταισχυνθήσεται, τὸν σωτῆρα προσιόντα μετὰ τῆς αὑτοῦ δόξης καὶ στρατιᾶς ἰδών· οὐ δέδιε τὸ πῦρ· εἰ δέ τις αἱρεῖται μένειν ἐπεξαμαρτάνων ἑκάστοτε ἐπὶ ταῖς ἡδοναῖς καὶ τὴν ἐνταῦθα τρυφὴν τῆς αἰωνίου ζωῆς προτιμᾷ καὶ διδόντος τοῦ σωτῆρος ἄφεσιν ἀποστρέφεται, μήτε τὸν θεὸν ἔτι μήτε τὸν πλοῦτον μήτε τὸ προπεσεῖν αἰτιάσθω, τὴν δὲ ἑαυτοῦ ψυχὴν ἑκουσίως ἀπολουμένην. τῷ δὲ ἐπιβλέποντι τὴν σωτηρίαν καὶ ποθοῦντι καὶ μετὰ ἀναιδείας καὶ βίας αἰτοῦντι παρέξει τὴν ἀληθινὴν κάθαρσιν καὶ τὴν ἄτρεπτον ζωὴν ὁ πατὴρ ὁ ἀγαθὸς ὁ ἐν τοῖς οὐρανοῖς. ᾧ διὰ τοῦ παιδὸς Ἰησοῦ

---

¹ ἐπιστῆσαι Stählin, from some MSS. of Eusebius. Other MSS. give ἀπεστήριξεν, κατέστησε, ἀποκατέστησεν, etc. Rufinus translates: "Nec prius abstitit, quam eum in omnibus emendatum etiam ecclesiae praeficeret."

thus affording a great example of sincere repentance and a great token of regeneration, a trophy of a resurrection that can be seen.[a]

. . . with bright faces rejoicing, singing praises, opening the heavens. And before them all the Saviour Himself comes to meet him, greeting him with His right hand, offering shadowless, unceasing light, leading the way to the Father's bosom, to the eternal life, to the kingdom of heaven. In this let a man trust to the authority of God's disciples and of God their surety, to the authority of the prophecies, gospels and words of the apostles. If he dwells with these, giving ear to them and practising their works, he will see at the very moment of his departure hence the end and proof of the doctrines. For he who here on earth admits the angel of repentance will not then repent when he leaves the body; nor will he be put to shame when he sees the Saviour approaching with His own glory and heavenly host. He does not dread the fire. If, however, a man chooses to remain in his pleasures, sinning time after time, and values earthly luxury above eternal life, and turns away from the Saviour when He offers forgiveness, let him no longer blame either God or wealth or his previous fall, but his own soul that will perish voluntarily. But he who looks for salvation and earnestly desires it and asks for it with importunity and violence [b] shall receive the true purification and the unchanging life from the good Father who is in heaven, to whom through His Son Jesus

[a] About twenty lines here are lost. See Introduction, p. 268.

[b] See St. Luke xi. 8; St. Matthew xi. 12.

Χριστοῦ, τοῦ κυρίου ζώντων καὶ νεκρῶν, καὶ διὰ
τοῦ ἁγίου πνεύματος εἴη δόξα, τιμή, κράτος,
αἰώνιος μεγαλειότης καὶ νῦν καὶ εἰς γενεὰς γενεῶν
καὶ εἰς τοὺς αἰῶνας τῶν αἰώνων. ἀμήν.

---

^a See Romans xiv. 9.

Christ, the Lord of living and dead,[a] and through the Holy Spirit be glory, honour, might, and eternal majesty both now and for all generations and ages to come. Amen.[b]

[b] With this doxology compare 1 Clement of Rome lxi. and lxv. (Loeb Classical Library, *Apostolic Fathers*, vol. i. pp. 117 and 121).

EXHORTATION TO ENDURANCE

OR

TO THE NEWLY BAPTIZED

INTRODUCTION

THE following fragment was discovered by Barnard in the Escurial Library with the heading "Precepts of Clement," and was issued by him as an appendix to his edition of "The Rich Man" (*Texts and Studies,* edited by J. Armitage Robinson D.D., vol. v. No. 2). He conjectured that it might be part of a work mentioned by Eusebius (*H.E.* vi. 13) as being written by Clement of Alexandria and entitled "Exhortation to Endurance, or, To the Newly Baptized." Stählin has accordingly printed it in his edition of Clement under this title. There can be little doubt but that Barnard's conjecture was right, as the style and thoughts are quite suitable both to Clement and to the subject. If this is so, we have a notable addition to our knowledge of Clement as teacher. Small though the fragment is, it is enough to present a clear and beautiful picture of the ideal of Christian conduct as he understood it; indeed, it would be hard to find another work which, in the same short compass, could give advice that so perfectly described the good manners, the self-control, the purity of heart, the strenuous activity, the hopeful courage and the wide sympathy of the true Christian gentleman.

The fragment has been translated in full by J. Patrick in his *Clement of Alexandria*, pp. 183–185.

Ο ΠΡΟΤΡΕΠΤΙΚΟΣ ΕΙΣ ΥΠΟΜΟΝΗΝ

Η

ΠΡΟΣ ΤΟΥΣ ΝΕΩΣΤΙ ΒΕΒΑΠΤΙΣΜΕΝΟΥΣ

ΚΛΗΜΕΝΤΟΣ ΠΑΡΑΓΓΕΛΜΑΤΑ

Stählin
vol. iii.
p. 221

Ἡσυχίαν μὲν λόγοις ἐπιτήδευε, ἡσυχίαν δὲ ἔργοις,
ὡσαύτως δὲ ἐν γλώττῃ καὶ βαδίσματι· σφοδρότητα
δὲ ἀπόφευγε προπετῆ· οὕτως γὰρ ὁ νοῦς διαμενεῖ
βέβαιος, καὶ οὐχ ὑπὸ τῆς σφοδρότητος ταραχώδης
γενόμενος ἀσθενὴς ἔσται καὶ βραχὺς περὶ φρόνησιν
καὶ σκοτεινὸν ὁρῶν[1]· οὐδὲ ἡττηθήσεται μὲν γαστρι-
μαργίας, ἡττηθήσεται δὲ ἐπιζέοντος θυμοῦ, ἡττηθήσεται δὲ τῶν ἄλλων παθῶν, ἕτοιμον αὐτοῖς
ἅρπαγμα προκείμενος. τὸν γὰρ νοῦν δεῖ τῶν
παθῶν ἐπικρατεῖν ὑψηλὸν ἐπὶ ἡσύχου θρόνου[2]
καθήμενον ἀφορῶντα πρὸς θεόν. μηδὲν ὀξυχολίας
ἀνάπλεως ἔσο περὶ ὀργάς, μηδὲ νωθρὸς[3] ἐν λόγοις,
μηδὲ ἐν βαδίσμασιν ὄκνου πεπληρωμένος, ἵνα σοι
ῥυθμὸς ἀγαθὸς τὴν ἡσυχίαν κοσμῇ καὶ θειῶδές τι

---

[1] σκοτεινὸν ὁρῶν J. A. Robinson.   σκοτεινῶν ὁρῶν ms.
[2] θρόνου Barnard.   θρόνον ms.
[3] μηδὲ νωθρὸς Barnard.   μὴ δὲν ωθὸς ms.

EXHORTATION TO ENDURANCE

OR

TO THE NEWLY BAPTIZED

PRECEPTS OF CLEMENT

CULTIVATE quietness in word, quietness in deed, likewise in speech and gait; and avoid impetuous eagerness. For then the mind will remain steady, and will not be agitated by your eagerness and so become weak and of narrow discernment and see darkly; nor will it be worsted by gluttony, worsted by boiling rage, worsted by the other passions, lying a ready prey to them. For the mind, seated on high on a quiet throne looking intently towards God, must control the passions. By no means be swept away by temper in bursts of anger, nor be sluggish in speaking, nor all nervousness in movement; so that your quietness may be adorned by good proportion and your bearing may appear something divine

371

καὶ ἱερὸν τὸ σχῆμα φαίνηται. φυλάττου δὲ καὶ τῆς
ὑπερηφανίας τὰ σύμβολα, σχῆμα ὑψαυχενοῦν καὶ
κεφαλὴν ἐξηρμένην καὶ βῆμα ποδῶν ἁβρὸν καὶ
μετέωρον.

Ἤπιά σοι πρὸς τοὺς ἀπαντῶντας ἔστω τὰ ῥήματα,
καὶ προσηγορίαι γλυκεῖαι· αἰδὼς δὲ πρὸς γυναῖκας
καὶ βλέμμα τετραμμένον εἰς γῆν. λάλει δὲ περι-
εσκεμμένως ἅπαντα, καὶ τῇ φωνῇ τὸ χρήσιμον
ἀποδίδου, τῇ χρείᾳ τῶν ἀκουόντων τὸ φθέγμα
μετρῶν,[1] ἄχρι ἂν[2] καὶ ἐξάκουστον ᾖ,[3] καὶ μήτε
διαφεῦγον[4] τὴν ἀκοὴν τῶν παρόντων ὑπὸ σμικρό-
τητος, μήτε ὑπερβάλλον[5] μείζονι τῇ κραυγῇ.
φυλάττου δὲ ὅπως μηδέν ποτε λαλήσῃς ὃ μὴ
προεσκέψω καὶ προενόησας· μηδὲ προχείρως καὶ
μεταξὺ <τῶν>[6] τοῦ ἑτέρου λόγων ὑπόβαλλε τοὺς
σαυτοῦ[7]. δεῖ γὰρ ἀνὰ[8] μέρος ἀκούειν καὶ δια-
λέγεσθαι, χρόνῳ μερίζοντα λόγον καὶ σιωπήν·
μάνθανε δὲ ἀσμένως, καὶ ἀφθόνως δίδασκε, μηδὲ
ὑπὸ φθόνου ποτὲ σοφίαν ἀποκρύπτου πρὸς τοὺς
ἑτέρους, μηδὲ μαθήσεως ἀφίστασο δι' αἰδώ. ὕπεικε
πρεσβυτέροις ἴσα πατράσιν· τίμα θεράποντας θεοῦ·
κάταρχε σοφίας καὶ ἀρετῆς. μηδὲ ἐριστικὸς ἔσο
πρὸς τοὺς φίλους, μηδὲ χλευαστὴς κατ' αὐτῶν καὶ
γελωτοποιός· ψεῦδος δὲ καὶ δόλον καὶ ὕβριν
ἰσχυρῶς παραιτοῦ· σὺν εὐφημίᾳ δὲ φέρε καὶ τὸν
ὑπερήφανον καὶ ὑβριστὴν <ὡς>[9] πρᾷός τε καὶ
μεγαλόψυχος ἀνήρ.

Κείσθω δέ σοι πάντα εἰς θεὸν καὶ ἔργα καὶ λόγοι,

p. 222

---

[1] μετρῶν J. A. Robinson. μέτρον MS.
[2] ἂν Wilamowitz. δὴ MS.   [3] ᾖ Wilamowitz. εἴη MS.
[4] διαφεῦγον Wilamowitz. διαφεύγων MS.
[5] ὑπερβάλλον Wilamowitz. ὑποβάλλων MS.

TO THE NEWLY BAPTIZED

and sacred. Guard also against the signs of arrogance, a haughty bearing, a lofty head, a dainty and high-treading footstep.

Let your speech be gentle towards those you meet, and your greetings kind; be modest towards women, and let your glance be turned to the ground. Be thoughtful in all your talk, and give back a useful answer, adapting the utterance to the hearers' need, just so loud that it may be distinctly audible, neither escaping the ears of the company by reason of feeble-ness nor going to excess with too much noise. Take care never to speak what you have not weighed and pondered beforehand; nor interject your own words on the spur of the moment and in the midst of another's; for you must listen and converse in turn, with set times for speech and for silence. Learn gladly, and teach ungrudgingly;[a] never hide wisdom from others by reason of a grudging spirit, nor through false modesty stand aloof from instruction. Submit to elders just as to fathers.[b] Honour God's servants. Be first to practise wisdom and virtue. Do not wrangle with your friends, nor mock at them and play the buffoon. Firmly renounce falsehood, guile and insolence. Endure in silence, as a gentle and high-minded man, the arrogant and insolent.

Let everything you do be done for God, both deeds

---

[a] This generous precept finds an echo in Chaucer's

> And gladly wolde he lerne, and gladly teche.

(*Canterbury Tales*, Prologue l. 308.)

[b] Cp. 1 Timothy v. 1. In several places this fragment reminds us of the *Pastoral Epistles*.

⟨τῶν⟩ inserted by Barnard.
ἀνὰ Barnard. ἕνα MS. ⟨ὡς⟩ inserted by Schwartz.

καὶ πάντα ἀνάφερε Χριστῷ τὰ σαυτοῦ, καὶ πυκνῶς
ἐπὶ θεὸν τρέπε τὴν ψυχήν, καὶ τὸ νόημα ἐπέρειδε
τῇ Χριστοῦ δυνάμει ὥσπερ ἐν λιμένι τινὶ τῷ θείῳ
φωτὶ τοῦ σωτῆρος ἀναπαυόμενον ἀπὸ πάσης
λαλιᾶς τε καὶ πράξεως. καὶ μεθ᾽ ἡμέραν πολλάκις
[μὲν][1] μὲν ἀνθρώποις κοίνου τὴν σεαυτοῦ φρόνησιν,
θεῷ δὲ ἐπὶ πλεῖστον ἐν νυκτὶ ὁμοίως καὶ ἐν ἡμέρᾳ·
μὴ γὰρ ὕπνος σε ἐπικρατείτω πολὺς τῶν πρὸς θεὸν
εὐχῶν τε καὶ ὕμνων· θανάτῳ γὰρ ὁ μακρὸς ὕπνος
ἐφάμιλλος. μέτοχος Χριστοῦ ἀεὶ καθίστασο ‹τοῦ›[2]
τὴν θείαν αὐγὴν καταλάμποντος ἐξ οὐρανοῦ· εὐ-
φροσύνη γὰρ ἔστω σοι διηνεκὴς καὶ ἄπαυστος ὁ
Χριστός.

Μηδὲ λῦε τὸν τῆς ψυχῆς τόνον ἐν εὐωχίᾳ καὶ
ποτῶν ἀνέσει, ἱκανὸν δὲ ἡγοῦ τῷ σώματι τὸ
χρειῶδες. καὶ μὴ πρόσθεν ἐπείγου πρὸς τροφὰς
πρὶν ἢ καὶ δείπνου παρῇ καιρός· ἄρτος δὲ ἔστω
σοι τὸ δεῖπνον, καὶ πόαι γῆς προσέστωσαν καὶ τὰ
ἐκ δένδρων ὡραῖα· ἴθι[3] δὲ ἐπὶ τὴν τροφὴν εὐσταθῶς[4]
καὶ μὴ λυσσώδη γαστριμαργίαν ἐπιφαίνων· μηδὲ
σαρκοβόρος μηδὲ φίλοινος ἔσο, ὁπότε μὴ νόσος[5] τις
ἴασιν ἐπὶ ταύτην ἄγοι. ἀλλ᾽ ἀντὶ τῶν ἐν τούτοις
ἡδονῶν τὰς ἐν λόγοις θείοις καὶ ὕμνοις εὐφροσύνας
αἱροῦ τῇ παρὰ θεοῦ σοι χορηγουμένας[6] σοφίᾳ,
οὐράνιός τε ἀεί σε φροντὶς ἀναγέτω πρὸς οὐρανόν.

Καὶ τὰς πολλὰς περὶ σώματος ἀνίει μερίμνας
τεθαρσηκὼς ἐλπίσι ταῖς πρὸς θεόν, ὅτι σοί γε τὰ |

---

[1] πολλάκις [μὲν] after ἡμέραν Stählin : after θεῷ δὲ MS.
[2] ‹τοῦ› inserted by Barnard. [3] ἴθι Mayor. ἴσθι MS.
[4] εὐσταθῶς Wilamowitz. ἀσταθῶς MS.
[5] νόσος Barnard. νόσου MS.
[6] χορηγουμένας Stählin. χορηγουμένῃ MS.

and words; and refer all that is yours to Christ; and constantly turn your soul to God; and lean your thought on the power of Christ, as if in some harbour by the divine light of the Saviour it were resting from all talk and action. And often by day communicate your thoughts to men, but most of all to God at night as well as by day;[a] for let not much sleep prevail to keep you from your prayers and hymns to God, since long sleep is a rival of death. Show yourself always a partner of Christ who makes the divine ray shine from heaven;[b] let Christ be to you continual and unceasing joy.

Relax not the tension of your soul with feasting and indulgence in drink, but consider what is needful to be enough for the body. And do not hasten early to meals before the time for dinner comes; but let your dinner be bread, and let earth's grasses and the ripe fruits of trees be set before you; and go to your meal with composure, showing no sign of raging gluttony. Be not a flesh-eater nor a lover of wine, when no sickness leads you to this as a cure.[c] But in place of the pleasures that are in these, choose the joys that are in divine words and hymns,[d] joys supplied to you by wisdom from God; and let heavenly meditation ever lead you upward to heaven.

And give up the many anxious cares about the body by taking comfort in hopes towards God; because for you He will provide all necessary things

---

[a] Cp. 1 Timothy v. 5.

[b] This and the previous sentence may allude to Ephesians v. 14.

[c] Is there an allusion to 1 Timothy v. 23?

[d] Cp. Ephesians v. 18, 19.

p. 223 ἀναγκαῖα παρέξει διαρκῆ τροφήν τε τὴν εἰς ζωὴν
καὶ κάλυμμα σώματος καὶ χειμερινοῦ ψύχους
ἀλεξητήρια. τοῦ γὰρ δὴ σοῦ βασιλέως γῆ τε
ἅπασα καὶ ὅσα ἐκφύεται· ὡς μέλη δὲ αὐτοῦ[1] τῶν
αὐτοῦ θεραπόντων ὑπερβαλλόντως περιέπει καθάπερ
ἱερὰ καὶ ναοὺς αὐτοῦ. διὰ δὴ τοῦτο μηδὲ νόσους
ὑπερβαλλούσας δέδιθι μηδὲ γήρως ἔφοδον χρόνῳ
προσδοκωμένου· παύσεται γὰρ καὶ νόσος, ὅταν
ὁλοψύχῳ προθέσει ποιῶμεν τὰς αὐτοῦ ἐντολάς.

Ταῦτα εἰδὼς καὶ πρὸς νόσους ἰσχυρὰν κατα-
σκεύαζε τὴν ψυχήν, εὐθάρσησον ὥσπερ τις ἀνὴρ ἐν
σταδίοις ἄριστος ἀτρέπτῳ τῇ δυνάμει τοὺς πόνους
ὑφίστασθαι. μηδὲ ὑπὸ λύπης πάνυ πιέζου τὴν
ψυχήν, εἴτε νόσος ἐπικειμένη βαρύνει εἴτε ἄλλο τι
συμπίπτει δυσχερές, ἀλλὰ γενναίως ἀνθίστα τοῖς
πόνοις τὸ νόημα, χάριτας ἀνάγων θεῷ καὶ ἐν μέσοις
τοῖς ἐπιπόνοις πράγμασι ἅτε δὴ σοφώτερά τε ἀνθρώπων φρονοῦντι καὶ ἅπερ οὐ δυνατὸν οὐδὲ ῥᾴδιον
ἀνθρώποις εὑρεῖν. ἐλέει δὲ κακουμένους,[2] καὶ τὴν
παρὰ τοῦ θεοῦ βοήθειαν ἐπ᾽ ἀνθρώποις αἰτοῦ·
ἐπινεύσει γὰρ αἰτοῦντι τῷ φίλῳ τὴν χάριν, καὶ τοῖς
κακουμένοις[3] ἐπικουρίαν παρέξει, τὴν αὐτοῦ δύναμιν
γνώριμον ἀνθρώποις καθιστάναι βουλόμενος, ὡς ἂν
εἰς ἐπίγνωσιν ἐλθόντες ἐπὶ θεὸν ἀνίωσιν καὶ τῆς
αἰωνίου μακαριότητος ἀπολαύσωσιν, ἐπειδὰν ὁ
τοῦ θεοῦ υἱὸς παραγένηται ἀγαθὰ τοῖς ἰδίοις ἀπο-
καθιστῶν.

---

[1] Barnard and Stählin insert τὰ σώματα after αὐτοῦ.
[2] κακουμένους Stählin.   καλουμένοις MS.
[3] κακουμένοις Stählin.   καλουμένοις MS.

in sufficiency, food to support life, covering for the body, and protection against winter cold. For to your King belongs the whole earth and all that is produced from it;[a] and God treats the bodily parts of His servants with exceeding care, as if they were His, like His own shrines and temples.[b] On this account do not dread severe diseases, nor the approach of old age, which must be expected in time; for even disease will come to an end, when with whole-hearted purpose we do His commandments.

Knowing this, make your soul strong even in face of diseases; be of good courage, like a man in the arena, bravest to submit to his toils with strength unmoved. Be not utterly crushed in soul by grief, whether disease lies heavily upon you, or any other hardship befalls, but nobly confront toils with your understanding, even in the midst of your struggles rendering thanks to God; since His thoughts are wiser than men's, and such as it is not easy nor possible for men to find out. Pity those who are in distress, and ask for men the help that comes from God; for God will grant grace to His friend when he asks, and will provide succour for those in distress, wishing to make His power known to men,[c] in the hope that, when they have come to full knowledge, they may return to God, and may enjoy eternal blessedness when the Son of God shall appear and restore good things to His own.

[a] Cp. Psalm xxiv. 1.
[b] Cp. 1 Corinthians vi. 15 and 19.
[c] Cp. Romans ix. 22.

APPENDIX ON THE GREEK MYSTERIES

Meaning of the Term " Mysteries."—The term is applied to certain religious rites, the details and meaning of which are kept secret from all except those who have been formally initiated. Μυστήριον is derived from μύειν, to close the lips (cp. mute, mutter), and thus the idea of secrecy·is contained in the·word itself. Clement suggests three derivations different from this,[1] but they are plainly no more than random guesses. Rites analogous to the Greek Mysteries are found among primitive peoples all over the world. In Greece, however, the Mysteries reached a high degree of development, and proved themselves able for many centuries to provide some satisfaction to the cravings of men for communion with the divine.

Origin of the Mysteries.—The Mysteries are generally connected with the gods called *chthonic, i.e.* earth divinities, whose worship goes back to a time before the arrival of the anthropomorphic gods of Greece. M. Foucart holds that the Eleusinian Mysteries were

[1] See p. 31.

imported from Egypt,[1] and that Demeter is the same as the Egyptian Isis. But while it is possible, we may even say probable, that the intercourse which existed between Egypt and Greece from the earliest times helped to shape the ideas of the Mysteries, most authorities believe that at Eleusis, as elsewhere, an ancient nature-worship, with magical rites designed to secure the fertility of the soil, was the source from which later developments sprang. When Greece was overrun by warlike tribes from the north, the inhabitants of the plain of Eleusis kept secret, we may suppose, these rites upon which so much depended, entrusting the performance of them to certain priestly families[2] who were careful to preserve the old ceremonies unaltered. By degrees, as the prestige of these Mysteries grew, other ceremonies were added, and legends, symbolic explanations, and religious teaching about the future life gradually gathered round the primitive institution.

The Mysteries in Classical Times.—The Mysteries of Eleusis overshadowed all others in importance during the classical period, a fact partly due, no

---

[1] P. Foucart, *Les Mystères d'Éleusis*, chs. i.–v. Clement mentions the tradition that Melampus brought the Mysteries of Demeter from Egypt (p. 33).

[2] These families, the Eumolpidae and the Heralds, are mentioned on p. 41. It is sometimes thought that the Heralds were an Athenian family who were given a share in the management of the Mysteries when Eleusis became part of the Athenian state. On the other hand, they are often closely coupled with the Eumolpidae, and Clement (p. 40) seems to include both when he speaks of τὸ ἱεροφαν-τικὸν . . . γένος. This use of the singular noun also occurs in a phrase (τὸ γένος τὸ Κηρύκων καὶ Εὐμολπιδῶν) quoted from an inscription by Farnell, *Cults of the Greek States*, vol. iii. p. 163.

doubt, to the connexion of Eleusis with Athens. The chief deities concerned in them were Demeter, her daughter Core (*i.e.* the Maiden) or Persephone, and Pluto or Hades. The first two are an older and a younger form of the earth-mother, the great goddess who under various names and titles (Rhea, Cybele, etc.) was worshipped from very early days in all the lands bordering on the eastern Mediterranean.[1] Pluto is the god of the underworld, the giver of wealth (in the form of fruits of the earth), as his name, connected with *ploutos*, wealth, implies. By the seventh century B.C. the ancient ritual had given rise, under the influence of the Greek spirit, to the legend embodied in the *Homeric Hymn to Demeter*. Persephone, while gathering flowers, is seized by Pluto and carried down to the underworld. Demeter is in deep distress at the loss of her daughter, and wanders everywhere to seek her.[2] Failing to find her, she refuses to help the corn to grow, and mankind is in danger of perishing, when Zeus prevails upon Pluto to restore the maiden to the upper world for eight months of each year. The growth of the corn, so plainly pictured here, seems to have been the chief original concern of the rites, though there were doubtless other elements in them with which the poet did not deal.

About the sixth century B.C. another deity was introduced into the Mysteries, viz. Iacchus,[3] who is a form of Dionysus. Under yet another form, that

---

[1] Thus Demeter is the mother of Zeus (p. 35 ; cp. Arnobius, *Adv. Nationes* v. 20), instead of his sister as in the later Greek mythology.

[2] The legend is alluded to by Clement ; see pp. 31 and 37.

[3] See p. 47.

of Zagreus, Dionysus was worshipped by the Orphics, whose teaching dealt with the soul's destiny in the future life. Though we know little of the actual course of events, it is likely that the deepening of religious thought in Greece in the sixth century, of which Orphism was one sign, had its effect at Eleusis. The legend of the rending of Dionysus is told by Clement,[1] who omits, however, to say that from the head, preserved by Athena, a fresh Dionysus was born. The story is, in fact, one of death and resurrection, akin to those of Osiris in Egypt and Attis in Phrygia;[2] and in spite of its details, repulsive as they are to us, it probably served as a basis for teaching on the subject of human immortality.

The events of the Eleusinian festivals were briefly as follows :—

A ceremony called the *Lesser Mysteries* was celebrated at Agra[3] on the Ilissus, close to Athens, in February each year. This was regarded as a preparation for the more important rites of Eleusis. A late author says that the Agra festival consisted of "a representation of the things that happened to Dionysus."[4]

The *Greater Mysteries* began on the 13th day of the month Boedromion (corresponding to our September), when Athenian youths went in procession to Eleusis and brought back the "sacred objects" (τὰ ἱερά). These ἱερά were perhaps the

---

[1] See pp. 37–39.
[2] Clement mentions (p. 41) that some identified Dionysus with Attis.   [3] See p. 71.
[4] Stephanus Byz., quoted in A. B. Cook, *Zeus*, i. 692, and in Farnell, *op. cit.* vol. iii. p. 352. The Mysteries held at Halimus in Attica (p. 71) were also concerned with Dionysus ; see Arnobius, *Adv. Nationes* v. 28.

APPENDIX

playthings of Dionysus mentioned by Clement.[1]
They were enclosed in chests [2] and carefully guarded
from sight. Their resting-place while in Athens
was the temple of Demeter and Core, called the
Eleusinium.[3] On the 15th a gathering was held of
candidates for initiation, at which a herald proclaimed
the conditions—that no criminal or barbarian could
be admitted. Certain instruction was then given by
officials called *mystagogues* (*i.e.* introducers or guides)
as to the various acts and formulas,[4] a knowledge of
which was necessary in the course of the initiation;
and to this may have been added a symbolic explanation of the ἱερά and of the dramatic scenes
represented in the Mysteries. There were also some
fasts and abstinences to be observed. Strict secrecy
was enjoined on all. On the following day the cry
"To the sea, *mystae*" (ἅλαδε μύσται) was raised, and
the candidates underwent a ceremonial purification
by bathing in the sea at Phalerum, and by offering
a pig to the goddesses.

The return journey to Eleusis took place on the
19th. Besides the ἱερά there was carried a statue
of Iacchus, to whom hymns were sung along the
road.[5] The next four days were occupied with the
Mysteries proper. The site of the Hall of Initiation
(τελεστήριον) has been found and examined. The

---

[1] Pp. 37-39. Foucart (*op. cit.* pp. 408-12) denies that
Clement is here speaking of the Eleusinian Mysteries. He
thinks that the most important of the ἱερά was an archaic
wooden image of Demeter.

[2] These "mystic chests" are mentioned on pp. 41, 43
and 45.

[3] Clement (p. 99) describes this temple as being "under
the Acropolis."   [4] See p. 43.

[5] Aristophanes, *Frogs* 325 ff.

Hall was large and capable of seating about three thousand people. There is no trace of secret passages, or of any arrangement for producing startling scenic effects. The roof, or perhaps a second story,[1] was supported by many columns; and there was a lantern (ὀπαῖον) above the shrine (ἀνάκτορον) of Demeter.

There are many references to the Mysteries in ancient writers, but they are for the most part vague and general. Only the Christian Fathers profess to give details, and even they do not attempt a complete description, but select those parts which will help their attack on the old religion. The following list will give some idea of the ceremonies, though we cannot be sure of the order in which they took place.

(i.) Solemn sacrifice to Demeter and Core.

(ii.) Ritual acts to be performed and a formula to be said.[2] Included in the acts was the drinking of a draught similar to that which Demeter had drunk when wandering in search of Core.[3]

(iii.) A journey representing the progress of the soul after death through the lower regions to the abode of the blessed. After much wandering in darkness amid scenes of terror

[1] Plutarch (*Pericles* 13) speaks of the "upper columns" as distinct from those on the ground.

[2] See p. 43.

[3] There may also have been the sacramental eating of a cake from the chest, if the emendation ἐγγευσάμενος (p. 42, n. *b*) is right. But this is by no means certain. Arnobius (*Adv. Nationes* v. 26), who seems to follow Clement in this passage, leaves out the expression, which may mean that he read ἐργασάμενος and could not understand it. Probably some ritual action with the contents, whatever they were, of the chest is purposely concealed under a vague word.

the initiate was suddenly introduced into brilliant light.[1]

(iv.) An exposition of the ἱερά, or sacred objects, by the hierophant, who derives his name (ὁ ἱερὰ φαίνων) from this office.

(v.) Dramatic representations of the Rape of Core, the sorrowful wandering of Demeter, and the finding of Core.[2]

(vi.) The exposition of an ear of corn, a symbol of Demeter.[3]

(vii.) Representation of a marriage between Zeus and Demeter,[4] and the announcement that Demeter (under her name Brimo) has borne a son Brimos.[5]

(viii.) Magical cries uttered by the initiates, e.g. ὕε, κύε (rain! conceive!),[6] and a ceremony consisting of the pouring of water from two jars on to the earth.[7] This was evidently an ancient fertility charm.

It is probable that a pilgrimage was also made to the sacred places round Eleusis visited by Demeter in her wanderings. It may have been on this journey, when the well called *Callichorus* [8] was reached, that

---

[1] Clement's language on p. 257 alludes to this.

[2] See p. 31. There seems also to have been a torchlight search for Core, in which the initiates joined.

[3] Hippolytus, *Ref. om. haer.* v. 8.

[4] The complete evidence for this can be found in Foucart, *op. cit.* pp. 475 ff. Not all authorities admit, however, that this ceremony formed part of the Eleusinian Mysteries. But there must have been something to account for the language of Clement on pp. 45–47, and the sacred marriage, of which other Christian writers speak in definite terms, would account for it.

[5] Hippolytus, *op. cit.* v. 8.   [6] *Ib.* v. 7.

[7] Athenaeus, p. 496 A.   [8] Pausanias i. 38. 6.

the initiates were forbidden to make any signs of grief.[1] As a rule they were required to imitate the goddess, and this prohibition is singular.

There were two grades of initiates at Eleusis. The story of Zeus and Demeter, together with the exposition of the ear of corn, seems to have been revealed only to the highest grade, the *epoptae* (*i.e.* those admitted to a *vision* of the sacred things; from ἐποπτεύειν).

The Eleusinian Mysteries were held in high repute for many centuries, and ancient writers (if we exclude the Christian Fathers) speak frequently of the good effect they produced on those who were initiated.[2] The annual death and rebirth of nature, expressed in various mythological forms such as the rape of Core and the rending and rebirth of Dionysus, was made to point to a future life for man. By the actual initiation, a bond was created between the two goddesses and their worshippers, which assured the latter of divine protection on earth and beyond the grave. If the child of the sacred marriage was Plutus (wealth),[3] then the union of the deities would symbolize the blessings they together brought to mankind. But we need not suppose that the ancients inquired so curiously as we do into the exact meaning of their holy rites. They were for the most part content to observe in all simplicity old customs that came to them with divine sanction, and upon the due performance of which they believed so much depended, both of social well-being and of the soul's future destiny.

It should be noticed that, so far as Eleusis is con-

[1] See p. 41. [2] *e.g.* Cicero, *De legibus* ii. 36.
[3] Foucart, *op. cit.* p. 479.

cerned, Clement, in spite of his vehement language, makes no charge of immoral practices. He considers the legends to be absurd and repulsive; while the sacred objects and the marriage of Zeus and Demeter seem to him indecent. But what he attacks is chiefly the interpretation he puts upon these things, an interpretation, we must admit, that is not altogether unreasonable. The worst item in his indictment—the story of Baubo—comes, as he frankly says, from the Orphic poems.[1] The *Hymn to Demeter* gives a different account of Demeter drinking the draught—she is persuaded to do so by the harmless pleasantry of a servant maid.[2] This was no doubt the official account at Eleusis.

Many other mysteries existed in classical times, notably the Phrygian, the Samothracian, and those that were celebrated at Andania in Messenia. None of them enjoyed such widespread fame as those of Eleusis. There was, of course, a certain broad resemblance between all mysteries, and the Eleusinian may be taken as the highest instance of this type of religious worship.

Mysteries in the Hellenistic Age.—After the conquests of Alexander, the popularity of mystery cults increased, reaching its height towards the end of the second century A.D. Thus Clement was making his attack upon them at a critical time, when they were in full vigour and serious rivals of Christianity. Most, if not all, of those he mentions were doubtless of ancient origin, but there had been much cross influence at work. Clement speaks of mysteries associated with Aphrodite, Deo or Demeter, Attis

[1] See p. 43.
[2] *Hymn to Demeter* 202 ff.

387

and Cybele, the Corybantes, the Cabeiri, Dionysus, Zeus Sabazius and Ge Themis. He also tells us that the mysteries of Attis and Cybele were similar to those of Zeus Sabazius and Demeter.[1] Both of these had their home in Phrygia. The legend of Zeus consorting with Demeter under the form of a bull, and then again with Persephone under the form of a snake, is common to Phrygia and Eleusis.[2] But the cult seems to have been differently worked out, if we may judge by the two formulas that Clement has left us. In Phrygia the worshipper underwent a mystical marriage with the god, who was represented by his proper symbol, a serpent.[3] At Eleusis the marriage was between the two deities. We may suspect that the omission of repulsive elements, and the general refinement and idealization of the legends, was carried further at Eleusis than elsewhere.

The Mysteries and Christianity. — Two questions may be asked, and briefly answered, here. (i.) Was Clement's attack on the Mysteries justified? (ii.) What influence did the Mysteries have on Christianity?

(i.) Rites which were held in respect by men like Sophocles and Cicero cannot have been merely the mass of stupidity and immorality that Clement might at first sight lead us to suppose. He makes no

---

[1] See p. 35.

[2] This seems to be Clement's meaning; see pp. 35–37.

[3] See the sign on p. 35, "the god over the breast." According to this, the worshipper must have assumed the character of a feminine consort of the god. But the formula "I stole into the bridal chamber" suggests a mystical union with the goddess, in which the worshipper must have been considered as masculine. The difficulty is dealt with by A. B. Cook, *Zeus,* i. 392 ff.

APPENDIX

attempt to describe the Mysteries fully, nor does he give them credit for any good they contained. Yet it can hardly be doubted that he was on the whole right. What angers him is not so much the general ideas and teaching of the Mysteries (with much of which he certainly must have been in sympathy) as the symbols displayed in them—the childish playthings, the *phalloi*, the representation of sacred marriages, etc. These things had their origin in a rude society, where they were natural enough. But a time comes when a civilized people ought no longer to be content with the relics, however venerable, of a past age, when in fact such relics suggest quite different thoughts from those associated with them in the beginning, and when they have as a consequence to be continually explained afresh in order to meet moral or intellectual objections. The Greeks of the second century A.D. were no longer an unsophisticated people, and the ritual of the Mysteries was not an adequate expression of their highest religious ideas.

(ii.) Much has been written on this question and widely different views are held. Christianity was preached by St. Paul to people who were well acquainted with the terminology of the Mysteries, and probably in many cases with the rites themselves. St. Paul uses words like τέλειος and μυστήριον,[1] adapting them without difficulty to Christian teaching. Clement goes so far as to describe the whole Christian scheme of salvation in mystery language.[2] The bitter hostility of the Church towards the Mysteries would forbid any direct or conscious borrowing; but

---

[1] *e.g.* 1 Corinthians ii. 6, 7 ; xv. 51.
[2] See pp. 255-57.

when words are taken, ideas are apt to come with them. It is not without significance that the word "mysteries" was afterwards used to describe the Christian sacraments, and above all the rite of Holy Communion. Moreover, both Christianity and the mystery religions were aiming at the same end: both promised "salvation" to their adherents. Christianity had a far truer idea than the Mysteries of what salvation meant, and this is one reason why it survived while the Mysteries died. But since both had to deal with the same human hopes and fears, the same problems of sin, purification, death and immortality, it would be surprising if the one owed nothing at all to the other. A comparison of the Synoptic Gospels with the developed theology of the fourth and fifth centuries will make it plain that, while Christianity had from the first its own distinctive character, which it never lost, it did not refuse the help of any elements in current thought and practice by means of which its message could be presented in a clearer or more acceptable form.

INDEX OF PROPER NAMES

References in italics are to be found in the notes or the Appendix.

References marked with an asterisk (*) are commented on in the notes

INDEX OF PROPER NAMES

INDEX OF PROPER NAMES

INDEX OF PROPER NAMES

INDEX OF PROPER NAMES

395

INDEX OF PROPER NAMES

397

INDEX OF PROPER NAMES

INDEX OF PROPER NAMES

INDEX OF PROPER NAMES

INDEX OF PROPER NAMES

INDEX OF SCRIPTURAL PASSAGES

References in italics are to allusions only, or to passages mentioned in notes or Appendix.

For references marked with a † see the Septuagint.

INDEX OF SCRIPTURAL PASSAGES

INDEX OF SCRIPTURAL PASSAGES

INDEX OF SCRIPTURAL PASSAGES

INDEX OF SCRIPTURAL PASSAGES

INDEX OF SCRIPTURAL PASSAGES